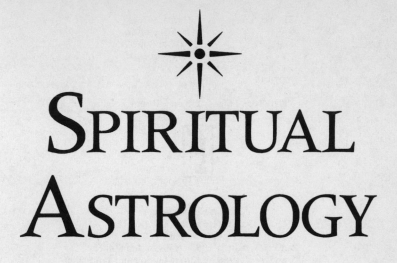

SPIRITUAL ASTROLOGY

By
Jan Spiller
and
Karen McCoy

A FIRESIDE BOOK
Published by Simon & Schuster
New York London Toronto Sydney Tokyo Singapore

Thanks to editors: Barbara Gess
Judith Horton
Arlene Robertson
Ray Merriman

Artwork:
The Glyphs of the
Planets and Signs: Kerry Tinney

Rockefeller Center
1230 Avenue of the Americas
New York, New York 10020
Part I copyright © 1985, 1988 by Jan Spiller
Part II copyright © 1988 by Karen McCoy and Jan Spiller
Part III copyright © 1988 by Jan Spiller and Karen McCoy

Portions of this work were previously published by Seek-It Publications.

FIRESIDE and colophon are registered trademarks
of Simon & Schuster Inc.

Designed by Irving Perkins and Assoc.
Manufactured in the United States of America

11 12 13 14 15 16 17 18 19 20

Library of Congress Cataloging-in-Publication Data
Spiller, Jan.
  Spiritual astrology / by Jan Spiller and Karen McCoy. p. cm.
  "A Fireside book."
  ISBN 0-671-66041-1
  1. Astrology. 2. Spiritual life. I. McCoy, Karen. II. Title.
BF1711.S67 1988   88-25007
133.5—dc19   CIP

*THE Moon tables were provided through the courtesy of the
Astrological Bureau of Ideas and are used with their permission.*

*All other tables (except for the eclipse tables) copyright © 1965
by Sydney Omarr. Printed with permission of the publisher,
Fleet Press Corporation, New York, N.Y.*

DEDICATIONS

My work on this book is dedicated to those spiritual forces available in the world today that gave us the insights we needed, and to the people everywhere whose inner beauty inspired our love and created the space for this book to be written.

Jan Spiller

I want to dedicate my work on Part II of this book to my son, John McCoy, for all the nights he fixed himself soup and tuna fish, screened telephone calls, and ran interference for Jan and me while we used our time together to work on the book. Thanks, John, for all your support, encouragement, and patience. You are truly my greatest blessing. I love you.

Mom
(Karen McCoy)

THIS volume has been divided into three parts, designed to offer the layperson a complete introductory text on how to use astrology as a tool for gaining in-depth self-understanding and self-mastery.

Each part has a separate introduction and section on how to use it. Using this volume is easy. The only astrological knowledge needed is your birth date.

Simply use the tables in Part III to locate the *signs* in which your planets and prenatal eclipses are located. To interpret the meaning of your planets, see Part I. To interpret the meaning of your prenatal eclipses, see Part II.

CONTENTS

PART III:

Mathematical Tables: Finding the Signs in Which Your Planets and Eclipses Are Located

FOREWORD

THIS book is designed as a guide to self-unfoldment through basic astrological analyses. The form of analyses utilized is in-depth interpretation of the signs and houses for each of the natal planets. Though the determination of these placements is a relatively easy process (that is, simply look them up in the back of this volume), the power and significance behind them cannot be underscored. These placements are, in a sense, the crux of an individual's personality, the "map" of a person's potential strengths and weaknesses. In this respect it is hoped that this work will be a truly valuable guide to both beginning astrologers as well as individuals seeking greater self-understanding on their own.

As the beginning student advances in his or her studies of astrology, much more complex and detailed modifications of these analyses will be seen. For instance, the student will discover the mathematical relationships existing between planets, known as aspects. Another area of important study will be the comparison of planetary positions today to those present at birth, known as "transits" (which describe the "transitory" dynamics in effect at any given point in a person's life).

The beauty about astrology is that it can accurately describe psychological dynamics, or qualities, in effect at any given time (for instance, at one's birth) and in any given situation (for example, one's life). If one knows the basic principles of the planets, signs, and houses, then the rest of astrology is simply a matter of art: applying the manifold possibility of combinations involving these principles into meaningful expression. In this regard *Spiritual Astrology* represents one of the best primers available to starting one's journey toward astrological mastery.

RAYMOND A. MERRIMAN

ACKNOWLEDGMENTS

PART I of this volume would have been impossible without the loving support and encouragement of my ex-husband, Steven Spiller. I would also like to acknowledge the late Kerry Tinney for his participation in the early formation of Part I. As the initial coauthor he helped to supply the traditional information regarding the planets and their effects. Kerry was also the creator of the planetary artwork contained in this volume.

My heartfelt thanks go to Ray and Debby Merriman of Seek-It Publications in Birmingham, Michigan, for believing in me and for being willing to release publication rights on Part I so that it could reach a wider public with a larger publishing company. I would also like to acknowledge Debra Burrell and Henry Weingarten of the New York School of Astrology in Manhattan for prodding me to reach greater horizons.

Much appreciation to editor Judith Horton for her painstaking work on Part II and her ability to clarify the meaning while keeping the integrity of the material intact. The difference a talented editor can make in bridging the gap between writer and reader is enormous.

I want especially to recognize my coauthor on Part II, Karen McCoy. Her pioneering research into the effect of the eclipses on individual destiny has given an added dimension to the field of astrology.

JAN SPILLER

There are some very special people I want to thank whose influence and assistance have been instrumental to the success of this project.

My original astrology teacher, Suzie Carrson, taught me more than astrology; she taught me to listen to my inner voice first and *then* to investigate.

I want to acknowledge my indebtedness to one of the finest astrologers and metaphysicians I've had the pleasure to know, Mr. Robert (Buz) Myers, who introduced me to the theory of the eclipses. When I shared my research findings with Buz and thanked him for the spark, he said to pass the thanks on to the spark's originator, the late Robert Jansky.

I would also like to thank Julia Wright, Mimi Donner Levine, and Diane and Jerry Church, special friends without whose love, support, and time this book could never have been written.

Finally, a very special thanks to my partner and friend Jan Spiller for her faith and determination.

KAREN P. MCCOY

PART

I

✦

The
PLANETS,
SIGNS,
and
HOUSES

—

by Jan Spiller

CHAPTER ONE

Introduction

YOU are totally unique.

A birthchart cannot be duplicated within a period of less than twenty-five thousand years. All the planets are traveling at different speeds around the Sun, and it takes more than twenty-five thousand years for all of them to line up the same way twice. Consequently, in terms of the astrology chart, each individual is totally unique. Astrology is not a study of general truth but rather a key to specific knowledge that can unlock the power of one's inner self.

A common denominator of all astrologers is the use of the basic mathematical tools of the planets, signs, and houses. There are as many different approaches to interpreting the astrology chart as there are astrologers. This is because each of us is unique, and the astrologer brings the dimension of himself or herself to the science and to the interpretation of the basic symbols. The meaning of the birthchart is filtered through the biases and basic outlook on life of the astrologer who is interpreting. For this reason the validation of your inner self is the ultimate judge of the accuracy and completeness of the insights offered you, as is the case with psychiatry, psychology, and any of the other social science approaches dealing with the uniqueness of a human being.

Different astrologers see different things when they look at a birthchart. Consequently, I wish to share some basic premises I hold about life as a whole, my biases, so that you will know consciously the filter through which this information is being presented. I also want to share my goals in coauthoring this book and the practical benefit that I feel it can be to the reader.

Many people believe that everything in astrology is predestined, that free will is precluded. In fact, quite the opposite is true. The astrology chart is simply a picture of the inner person just as the physical body is a picture of the outer person.

Without boundaries there is no free will or choice; there is nothing to choose between. In that sense your astrology chart, which shows a picture of your inner self, is set/predestined in the same way that your body is set/predestined at the moment of your birth. Your physical body, though it grows and matures, remains essentially the same. It is still your body, unique from others on Earth and the only body you have. In the same way, the astrology chart pictures your intangible body. It is a picture of your inner being, unique from everyone else on Earth and the only inner being that you have. The tangible aspects of a person, the body, can be seen physically. The intangible aspects of a person, the being within the body, can be seen mathematically through the astrology chart.

It is how we *use* what we have that the area of free will, or choice, enters in. Physically, we are aware of choice. We know what actions lead inevitably to pain, and if we do not want pain, we do not do those actions. On the intangible level the guideposts are just as inevitable, yet not as obvious except through mathematical tools that can display the energies graphically, such as astrology.

For example, if you were to start your automobile, "rev it up" to forty miles per hour, and drive into a brick wall, you know that would inevitably lead to pain. There is no way of getting around it, pain would be an unavoidable consequence of taking that action.

On the other hand, on the intangible level, each of us is continually putting into motion factors that inevitably lead to experiencing pain emotionally, mentally, and/or psychically. The only difference is that we are not as aware of the connection between cause and consequence when it is not on the strictly physical level. Astrology is a means of becoming aware of that connection on the intangible levels of experiencing oneself. Psychologically, we are doing things just as foolish as driving a car into a brick wall and then wondering, What went wrong? Why isn't life supporting me? I use astrology as a means for objectively getting in touch with brick walls for myself and others.

I'd like to share with you what I'm actually "up to" with astrology. I'm interested in experiencing happiness while on planet Earth, so for me astrology is a tool, not an end in itself.

The first thing I notice about personal happiness is that most of the people on this planet don't believe in it. Most of us are operating (consciously or unconsciously) out of a belief structure that says life is about suffering. We therefore go along with major compromises in our lives: we give away bits and pieces of ourselves; we stay in self-destructive situations; we give up our heart's dreams until one day we cash in all our chips and out we go. I have no intention of being on this planet (or any other) if I'm not going to enjoy myself and feel all the love of the universe flowing through me in a way that works for me and for everyone around me. The challenge is creating personal happiness on a planet that doesn't believe in it.

In order to do this realistically, the first thing we need to do is get in touch with the laws of happiness operating here and begin to cooperate with them rather than resist them. The most important thing to notice about happiness is that all the joy we have ever experienced on this planet has been felt in one place and one place only: inside our own hearts. That's where we have experienced happiness, and that's where the source of it is. Personal happiness is a by-product of the times when our minds are centered inside the heart. When the mind is inside the heart, it's happy because it's home.

There are certain materialistic experiences, common to most of us, that can temporarily produce that state of happiness. One of these experiences is falling in love. If you have never fallen in love, the experience of infatuation is an effective facsimile. Before you fall in love your mind runs around telling you, "If only I get *this*, then I'll be happy"; "If only I get *that*, then I'll be happy"; "If only that person will go along with me, *then* I'll be happy." And the time comes when you fall in love. Well, since the mind is not programmed to handle love, as soon as you feel it, it "pops" the mind from its attachment to the world back into the heart center (where it is naturally attached), and for a while you're happy because for a while you're "home."

And it feels *great* when you're in love. There is a feeling that everything is "right," regardless of what seems to be happening in the external environment. When shopping at the supermarket, if somebody bumps into your cart, you don't mind. You just flow with it. If you happen to pass people arguing with each other, you still feel love. You may stop to help, but you don't stop feeling the joy inside yourself to do it. And you don't become less effective. You still work and play and wash your hair, and do all the things you normally do, but everything has a feeling of *magic* about it, a feeling of joy.

This is your birthright. Living in this state of consciousness is how it's supposed to be for all of us, all the time. It's natural.

Now we all know that the happiness you experienced when you were in love had nothing to do with the other person because if the other person stays around long enough, the mind goes out and tries to *change* the other person. The moment it does that, it leaves the heart center, and the restlessness, the sense that something is "missing," comes back.

There are other materialistic experiences that can temporarily produce happiness. Reaching a goal is a good example. Let's say you want to make a million dollars. It's easy to reach goals here— you simply put all your life energy into it to the exclusion of everything else, and sooner or later you'll get there. So one day you wake up, look at your checkbook, and it says "plus one million dollars." Well, the mind is not programmed to handle success (like love, the feeling of success is spiritual), so as soon as the goal is reached, it pops the mind from its attachment to the world, and back the mind flies into the heart center.

And for a while you are happy. That happiness lasts until the mind becomes restless and begins to say, "Well, if a million made us *this* happy, think how happy *two* million will make us. Probably *twice* as happy!" And out the mind goes into the world to make that second million. When it does that, it leaves the heart center, and the unhappiness comes back, the incompleteness, the feeling that "something has to happen" in order for you to be happy again.

Other things can temporarily produce happiness, such as a moment of beauty in nature. Seeing someone do something nice for someone else, with no motive for personal gain, can produce joy as the mind flies back into the heart again. But then you walk a little farther down the street and see a neighbor kicking a dog, and the mind goes out to make a judgment. The moment it does that, it leaves the heart center, and the unhappiness, the vague dissatisfaction, returns.

So obtaining personal happiness has to do with getting the mind to go into the heart center and remain there. Then we can do whatever we like—experience romantic love, make lots of money, do all the things that are happy and fun. But everything is approached from a feeling of lightness, of "play," because we already have what we need: that feeling of internal happiness.

Two basic approaches can bring this state of consciousness about on a permanent basis. One is some form of meditation. Meditation works because on a daily basis it takes the mind away from its habit of attachment to the world, turns it inward to the heart, and gently says: "Here's where the happiness is; it's *inside*, not outside." And little by little the mind, which is a slow learner, begins to get the idea. With *proper* meditation, the power of contacting reality within yourself for even twenty minutes a day can grow so strong that you can spend the remaining twenty three hours and forty minutes of the day out in the world without losing the feeling of assurance and inner joy.

In the second approach to claiming personal happiness on a permanent basis (and there's no reason not to use both approaches simultaneously), we have to ask ourselves: Why does the mind go outward to begin with? When you were in love, why did the mind go out and try to change the other person? When you reached a goal, why did the mind go out and immediately try to reach another one? When you had a high meditation and felt joyous, why could somebody "push your buttons" and send you out again? This has to do with basic imbalances inside the mind itself that are karmic, stemming from past life patternings and tendencies.

Astrology is the fastest, most precise technique I know for getting in touch with those imbalances on an individual basis and making the corrections. That's why I use astrology.

Because each of us is so totally unique, an individual astrological reading is required in order to see the overall pattern in your life, (stemming from past lives) that is seeking to be corrected so bliss can be obtained permanently. Knowledge of the pattern is obtained through a synthesis of the factors that need purification in each of your planets, signs, and houses. As each of these factors is purified individually, your entire inner structure becomes harmonized and resolved.

It is for this reason that I have divided each of the planets into the "static" and "dynamic" categories as they travel through each of the signs. The "static" category is a picture of past life tendencies, habitual karmic responses that result in personal defeat and isolation from inner joy. The "dynamic" category suggests the purification process that can provide the antidote for the specific past life self-defeating tendency.

It's an experiment. As you begin actively practicing in your daily life one or more of the approaches outlined in the "dynamic" category (with the appropriate planet and sign placement in your individual birthchart), you will find yourself less affected by environmental stimuli throwing you off the center of inner joy.

I do not view your astrology chart as an accident. The moment of your birth, which is what your chart is based on, is perfect and very carefully *chosen* on the spiritual level of your own soul. Our soul chose its moment for manifestation, how it wanted things to be, only we forgot and lost the authority of our own energies. The curtain dropped, and we forgot that we chose it all. In this way the birthchart is a means of getting back in touch with the way we wanted it to be, our life or soul's direction. The astrology chart defines precisely the path we need to follow in order to fulfill personal potential and gain the satisfaction of self-completion. It is, in terms of individual completeness, the map back home.

When I look at an astrology chart, what I see is the soul's direction, the specific direction that one's life wants to go. Your life is going in the direction it's going whether you or I approve of it or not. When you are cooperating with your own direction of energy, everything on the physical plane works (love, sex, money, friendship, business, and so forth). When you are resisting the natural flow of your own energy, everything on the physical plane stops working in those areas where resistance is occurring. The idea is to have it all on a physical level by aligning and cooperating with the direction of one's own internal energies.

The purpose of this book is simply exposure—to show the choices for action in planets located in specific signs. It is then possible to exercise free will within the framework of what is going on. This book addresses the specific challenge of each of the planets in each of the signs. Essentially, it says: "If you do this . . . you experience these things . . ." (that is, happiness); on the other hand, "If you do this . . . you experience . . ." (that is, unhappiness).

The astrology chart is a means for *objectively viewing* the intangible (nonphysical) dimension of oneself. When the intangible aspects of oneself are seen in a tangible way, it is at last possible to create realistically the unique conditions that will lead to individual satisfaction and happiness in life. To attempt to deal with the nonphysical aspects of oneself without scientifically knowing the dimensions and form of that self is to seek satisfaction from life on the levels of blind belief, happenstance, and superstition. It is neither scientific nor realistic and thus does not produce results that are consistently satisfying.

The astrology chart shows the inner person and where the individual needs to manifest potential outwardly in order to experience satisfaction inwardly. We all want to be happy, yet there are no magic rules that lead to happiness for everyone. For example, a person whose Moon is in Cancer can find emotional security through establishing a deep, intimate connection with another; a person whose Moon is in Libra finds emotional security through establishing a sense of harmonious cooperation in relationships. What works for one person does not work for another. The idea is to get in touch with what works for you. It is in recognizing and respecting the differences between us that individual happiness and satisfaction can be established in a realistic way.

A belief in reincarnation is not necessary to receive practical value from the reading of this book. Again, so that you may know my biases, I accept the idea of reincarnation and know that the moment of your birth was not an accident. You are not a victim of your birthchart, and it is not a matter beyond your control. I view the planets and signs in the birthchart as totally perfect and appropriate for the individual involved; it is exactly what the individual needs for completion and happiness. The chart is a scientific picture of the life that one's soul has chosen as a process for its own growth and completion.

Each chart is perfect. In terms of reincarnation, before you were born your soul said something like this:

"Okay, now *this* time I'm going to handle (this) . . . and (this) . . . and . . . (this). . . . I want to complete this one, so I'll set it up *this* way. . . . That should complete it. I'll also handle this and this . . . and as long as I'm at it, I'll take care of this one in the process. Okay. That's it."

And then turning to the angelic beings:

"See ya!"

And in you came as a baby on planet Earth and took your first breath. So the birthchart is a picture of how *you* wanted it to be. It's the role you promised yourself you would play, the individual you said you would be (in the wisdom of your soul) in order to make your completions. In making your own completions, you simultaneously contribute to the rest of life. The birthchart shows the role you promised you would play, and when you are who you said you would be, life works. Happiness, joy, fulfillment are realistically available for everyone in the process of keeping your promises and being who you are. There are no victims.

Frankly, I'm a Leo, and I love victory. I see life as a very clear process of winning and losing. Winning is what works—what produces happiness, joy, an increased level of clear energy for the individual. Losing is what does not work—what produces unhappiness and a lowering of energy for the individual.

Consequently, this book is written in the context of "static" and "dynamic," how to lose and how to win. When I refer to victory, I do not mean at somebody's expense but rather as against the self-negating ways of one's own patterns. When you defeat self-negating patterns and emerge victorious over those fears and aspects that keep you miserable, not only do you win but through your upliftment everyone around you also wins.

If you were in bliss all the time, I would love it. What I see is that, as a process, bliss is obtained through alignment with one's inner self. Basically, there is you and there is your soul. If you were at one with your soul, everything you touched would turn to gold, to joy, to love, to peace.

Between you and being at one with your soul is a pile of unconsciousness, and each of us has a personal, unique pile of unconsciousness. The astrology chart is a key to seeing the unconsciousness on an *objective* and *specific* level that is capable of dissolving it. This book exposes that unconsciousness so that it can rise to a conscious level and be released, and then it offers alternative methods for handling the individual energies.

The unconsciousness (or static condition, as it is referred to in this book) is like a dark room. Turn the light on, and the darkness is dissolved with no contest. It is the same with the unconsciousness. There is nothing to figure out or do with it. It is not psychological. Simply expose it, and the light from your inner self will dissolve it. Expose it, and then it can be released and a new choice can be made.

As you determine the location of each of your planets in the signs, either through an already prepared astrology chart or through the tables from Part III, you are ready to read the static and dynamic descriptions for that planet in the sign that you have. As you read the static category, the corresponding unconsciousness is stimulated and rises to the surface to be released. It's okay to feel totally devastated after reading the static condition. In fact, it is appropriate. The degree to which you allow yourself to feel totally hopeless when reading the static condition is the depth to which the unconsciousness can be cleared out and released, being replaced with a sense of inner freedom and ease as you read the dynamic description.

None of us breaks ancient patterns of unconsciousness all at once. It's a process, a game of choosing to do things a little differently, with a little more awareness of what's going on, step by step. It's gradual. Take one aspect and experiment with expressing that area of yourself differently in daily situations of your life. See what happens. It's an experiment. The idea is to use what works, what produces an increase of happiness and ease in your relationship with life.

Your own soul is the only entity with your total records, and you are the only one who knows what things are so for you. For this reason the validation of your inner self is the ultimate judge of the completeness and accuracy of the insights offered you. On some planets you may feel an inner sense of "Yes, that's exactly how I experience it," and on some planets there may be no immediate recognition. You are the authority. Your practical experience of what is leading to productive and nonproductive results for you is the best measurement.

JAN SPILLER

CHAPTER TWO

How to Use Part I

THE astrology chart is a mathematical graph depicting the exact location of each of the planets at the moment of your birth.

Although systems for interpreting the astrology chart vary, all astrologers deal within the boundaries of three basic components of the astrology chart: the planets, the signs, and the houses.

THE PLANETS

There are ten planets used in astrology. Each of us is identical in that all ten of these planets are located in one's birthchart. The sign containing each planet and the house in which that planet is located varies with each individiual, yet each of us is working with the same planets.

The planets represent and define the ten basic and distinct urges found in each of us. An *urge* refers to the desire to express and experience a unique and specific energy. We each have different kingdoms, and each planet is the king of its own realm of experience. The path to fulfillment of our urges is different for each of us, as denoted by the sign, yet the urge or the basic game is the same for all.

For example, you and I have the planet Mars located somewhere in our birthcharts. Regardless of the sign or the house, Mars always represents the urge within each of us to initiate action and move toward a goal. For a more specific description of the ten basic urges within each of us, as represented and defined by the planets, it is recommended that you read the planet descriptions at the beginning of each chapter.

Each of the ten planets is represented in astrology by a symbol, or glyph. If you have a copy of your birthchart, you will notice that there are ten glyphs drawn in the inner circle of the chart (or see the sample chart at the end of this chapter). The following is a list of the symbol or glyph for each of the ten planets.

PLANET		SYMBOL or GLYPH
Sun	=	☉
Moon	=	☽
Mercury	=	☿
Venus	=	♀
Mars	=	♂
Jupiter	=	♃
Saturn	=	♄
Uranus	=	♅
Neptune	=	♆
Pluto	=	♇

THE SIGNS

Although the basic games or human urges are the same, the path to fulfilling these urges is different for everyone.

The sign containing each of your planets denotes the specific challenge through which you experience the urge of the planet. The signs characterize the mood through which you experience the planet in question. It is as though the signs were the costumes available for the planet to masquerade in, through which to present its basic energies. The sign modifies the planet it contains, filtering the basic energy through its own tones and coloring.

The sign shows the specific desire for individual expression and need for fulfillment. It is only by expressing the planetary urge according to the specific boundaries of the sign that fulfillment and completion are possible in that aspect of yourself.

For example, the planet Venus represents the urge within each of us to experience a sense of our own individual worth. Yet if your Venus is located in the sign of Taurus, the process that leads to self-worth is very different than if Venus is in the sign of Gemini at the moment of your birth. In Taurus, self-worth (Venus) is directly built and established through a material and sensual process; in Gemini, self-worth (Venus) is strengthened and produced through a social communication process. We will discuss the specific process for fulfillment of each planet in each of the signs.

There are twelve signs in astrology, corresponding to the twelve constellations in our galaxy. As the planets travel around the Sun, they move through the constellation or the signs of the zodiac. Both astrology and astronomy define the mathematical location of the planets in the heavens, relative to time and space.

To determine in which sign each of your planets was located at the moment of your birth, consult the Tables in Part III (located in the back of this book).

Once you have located your planet in the appropriate sign for your moment of birth, you can interpret its meaning through consulting the chapters interpreting the significance of planets in signs. Please note that if your birth time is either very early in the morning or late at night and is close to the date of a planet moving from one sign into the next, it is possible that mathematically for you the planet may be in the next sign. If you are in doubt, it is recommended that you read both possible sign descriptions for the planet in question. If one of your planets is on the borderline between two signs, it is also recommended that you send for a full copy of your computerized birthchart. This will assure with full accuracy the exact mathematical sign location for each of your planets (see Full Computer Service on page 451).

The following is a list of the twelve signs of the heavenly constellations and the equivalent astrological symbol or glyph for each sign:

	SIGN		SYMBOL or GLYPH
	Aries	=	♈
	Taurus	=	♉
	Gemini	=	♊
	Cancer	=	♋
	Leo	=	♌
	Virgo	=	♍
	Libra	=	♎
	Scorpio	=	♏

Sagittarius	=	♐
Capricorn	=	♑
Aquarius	=	♒
Pisces	=	♓

THE HOUSES

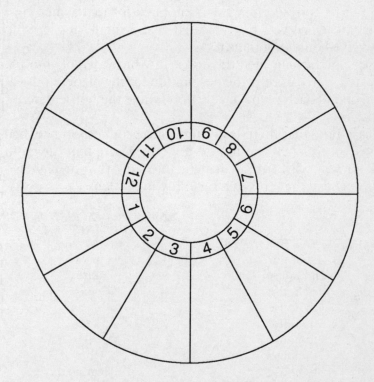

Basically, the houses denote the arena of life in which you tangibly experience the specific energy of the planet in the sign. For example, if Venus is located in the 3rd House of your birthchart, the issue of self-worth (Venus) can be most directly noticed during the process of communication (3rd House); if Venus is located in your 6th House, the issue of self-worth (Venus) is felt when interacting with your coworkers or on the job (6th House). Each house shows the material area of your life in which you will most vividly experience the urge indicated by the planet(s) located there. The houses are the arena in the material world where we experience the consequences of the way we are handling the basic game depicted by the planet.

There are twelve houses in the astrology chart. Each of your planets is located in one of the twelve houses. The houses are mathematically calculated according to your individual time, date, and place of birth. If you have a complete birthchart that includes your planets in the houses, you may wish to locate the houses for each of your planets in the following manner. Using the list of planets and their symbols found earlier in this section, look for the Sun and its corresponding symbol. Look for that symbol in your birthchart. Once you have located that symbol, notice which of the twelve houses contains it.

Once you have located the house in which each of your planets is located, you can read the description for the planet in the house at the end of each planetary section where the house descriptions are listed.

Please note that there is an interesting connection between the houses your planets are in and the sign descriptions given in the book. If you wish further insight into any of your planets, it is recommended that you use the following system:

PLANETS LOCATED IN YOUR	READ THE DESCRIPTION FOR THAT PLANET IN THE SIGN OF
1st house	Aries
2nd house	Taurus
3rd house	Gemini
4th house	Cancer
5th house	Leo
6th house	Virgo
7th house	Libra
8th house	Scorpio
9th house	Sagittarius
10th house	Capricorn
11th house	Aquarius
12th house	Pisces

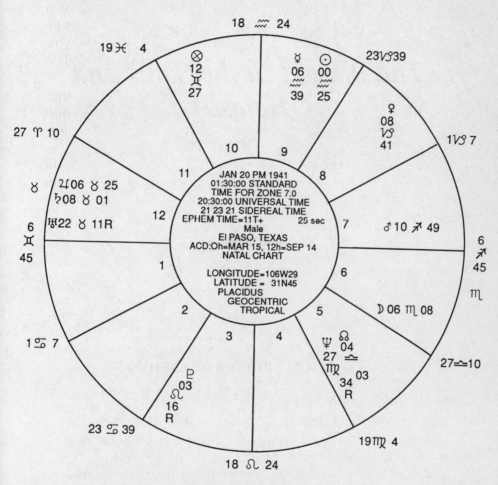

18 ♒ 24

19 ♓ 4

⊗ 12 ♊ 27

☿ 06 ♒ 39   ☉ 00 ♒ 25

23♑39

27 ♈ 10

♀ 08 ♑ 41

1♑7

10   9

8

11

♂ 10 ♐ 49

♉ ♃06 ♉ 25
♄08 ♉ 01

12

7

JAN 20 PM 1941
01:30:00 STANDARD
TIME FOR ZONE 7.0
20:30:00 UNIVERSAL TIME
21 23 21 SIDEREAL TIME
EPHEM TIME=11T+   25 sec
Male
El PASO, TEXAS
ACD:0h=MAR 15, 12h=SEP 14
NATAL CHART

LONGITUDE=106W29
LATITUDE = 31N45
PLACIDUS
GEOCENTRIC
TROPICAL

♅22 ♉ 11R

6 ♉ 45

1

6

6 ♐ 45

2

5

♏

1 ♋ 7

3   4

☽ 06 ♏ 08

♇ 03 ♌ 16 R

☊ 04 ♍ 27

♆ 34 ♎ 03 R

27♎10

23 ♋ 39

19♍4

18 ♌ 24

Sample of a Birthchart

CHAPTER THREE

The Planets in the Signs and Houses

Sun

SUN: KEY TO FULL SELF-EXPRESSION

The Sun in the Birthchart:

· Signifies power and talent in individual, creative self-expression.

· Defines the key for manifesting personal power and talent in ways that inspire others to express their creativity and unites your leadership abilities with theirs, thus promoting feelings of fellowship and love for all concerned.

· Reveals that process by which you may unconsciously express personal power in a way that leads to resentment from others.

· Conveys self-expression by divine right, showing that area of life where your talents can be spontaneously expressed.

· Denotes how you can increase physical and emotional vitality through the instinctive expression of the warmth and enthusiasm of your nature.

· Indicates in what area you need to express yourself spontaneously in order to attain and maintain personal vitality.

· Discloses the area of radiance, creativity, and greatest childlike joy where your talents for contributing to the well-being of others reflect your natural ability for benevolent expression.

The static and dynamic descriptions are not *intended* to denote absolute states. When you are in the *static* state, you are encountering resistance, lacking new movement and feeling nonproductive; while you are in the *dynamic* state, you are feeling powerful, energetic, and productive.

None of us is in the dynamic mode all the time. The dynamic state describes a means of experimentation, making different choices in expression that lead to a more satisfying result. The degree to which you can accept the static description in a nonjudgmental way is the degree to which you are open to receive the dynamic energies as a transformative agent.

The Sun signs have received by far the most attention and coverage by modern-day astrology writers. Many fine in-depth studies of the behavior of the Sun in the various signs are already available, so we have purposely kept our discussion of the Sun brief. We deal with the primary choice that the Sun offers, regardless of sign: to use your vital energies to demand center stage and attention from others; or to use your vital energies to give *others* center stage, empowering them by radiating your own Sun power according to the nature of the sign.

SUN IN ARIES
Sun in Aries individuals feel they have the right to do as they please; to display independent action and thought; to act on a whim without regard for protocol, timing, or the wishes or opinions of others.

Static
When your attention focuses on gaining recognition for your independence from others, you may unknowingly act in ways that result in disruption and alienation. Wanting to be recognized as your own person, you can resist cooperating in team efforts. When you behave with rashness and lack of consideration, you experience other people blocking your path of action. Thus, using your natural independence in a way that dominates by insisting that

others put you first can result in a lack of confidence when they fail to respond.

Dynamic
When your attention is on sharing your talents and abilities with others, you notice how your independent action can be an inspiration to them. By being aware of this natural leadership you can encourage those around you to express *their* independence and thus eliminate the need for constant battle. Recognizing your own talents in contributing a quick, courageous assertion of your positive spirit enables you to inspire others. This leaves you free to exit on the desired positive note. Awareness of this impact allows you to express your exuberance in ways that endear you to others. Then you will find others responding with love and appreciation for your dynamic energy.

SUN IN TAURUS
Sun in Taurus individuals feel they have the right to actualize their material and sensual values; to never change those values; to accumulate a level of comfortable material security. Also, they may feel the right to establish rigid, fixed *nonmaterialistic* values, and to opt for a stubborn passivity in using their talents.

Static
When you focus on gaining agreement from others on the validity of your tangible and material values, you can appear as stubborn and intractable. You may give into the Taurean tendency to want to be recognized as worthwhile and important. This tendency can cause you to resist the efforts of others to expand your position by adding their input. You can be totally dedicated to establishing your merit by accumulating money and goods. When this happens and you fail to consider the values of others, you cheat yourself of the opportunity to enhance and expand your levels of material security and comfort.

Dynamic
You can direct your attention to uplifting others through expressing your talents and abilities. This allows other people to respond by sharing their own values. Thus, you give others center stage in establishing their own worth, and give yourself an opportunity to become more objective about your values. From this objectivity

you can create an even deeper sense of security in relationships. You revitalize your worth in the process of recognizing the worth of others. Being conscious of other people's values results in an expansion of your material security in the world.

SUN IN GEMINI
Sun in Gemini individuals feel they have the right to experience the superficial variety in life; to change their minds frequently; and to dance over the surface of existence.

Static
When your attention is directed toward gaining a quick, superficial interaction with others through stimulating conversation, you tend to give the impression of being unable to maintain deep friendships. Indulging in the Gemini tendency toward superficiality can create a shallow experience of life without realizing it. If you want to be recognized as quick-witted and congenial, you may tend to talk in a manner others don't trust. You may become a gadfly, refusing to discuss personal feelings or matters of any depth, impatient with profound thinking, and looking for fast, logical insights. This quick and superficial approach can cause loved ones to mistrust your spontaneity and yearn to impose restrictions on you.

Dynamic
When your attention is directed toward uplifting others, you have the knack of expressing a lighthearted, friendly approach. This ability can create a feeling of ease in tense or serious circumstances. By giving others the opportunity to communicate you allow them to share the depth of their feelings, knowledge, and goals. Then you are able to respond in an open-minded way that enhances the congeniality of the moment. By listening you can expand your viewpoints and opportunities to connect with others on a broader range of ideas. When you become conscious of their ideas, you inspire them to enjoy and realize the value of a variety of experiences. This leads to mutual love and appreciation. The acceptance of others' ideas increases your vitality.

SUN IN CANCER
Sun in Cancer individuals feel they have the right to be emotionally self-centered; to be pampered by others; to be motherly to a fault; and to demand that others respect their sensitivity.

Static

When your attention is on yourself, you might expect others to react in such a way that your sensitivities are never injured. This leads you to appear as hypersensitive, moody, and self-protective. When you yearn to be recognized for your sensitivity, you may demand that others respond by being constantly perceptive to every mood. You may require that any intimacy center around your feelings. This leads to others feeling alienated since they cannot share themselves for fear of a potential defensive reaction. You might be so dedicated to protecting your sense of vulnerability that the slightest input can cause you to withdraw into your shell.

Dynamic

When your attention is directed toward sharing your talents for emotional perception with others, you can care for and assist them. This results in your becoming more objective and contented with your feelings. You can use your natural sensitivity to recognize the hidden emotional pains of others. This recognition enables you to inspire them and also yourself through your sympathetic understanding of their distress. You can give others center stage in the expression of their feelings and vulnerabilities. As you empathize with their suffering, your vitality increases, and others can appreciate you for your intuitive and loving nature. In the process of expressing your gifts for emotional perception in a way that serves others, you come to realize that your best security rests in caring for those *outside* yourself.

SUN IN LEO

Sun in Leo individuals feel they have the right to express themselves gloriously; to be noticed and admired for simply being themselves.

Static

When you focus on yourself and on gaining the admiration and attention of others, you may act in ways that are needlessly dramatic, understated, or overstated. In the Leonine desire to be admired, you may subdue true emotional expression. This desire can lead you to respond to situations with empty displays of drama. You may fall into Leo traps: demanding attention whether it is earned or not; being hypersensitive, taking criticism as a personal affront; and refusing to accept the input from others that could actually lead to a more powerful expression of your creative gifts. By trying to obtain the attention and approval of others you might compromise your own identity. This process leads to defeating the natural and healthy expression of your spontaneous, childlike ego.

Dynamic
When your attention is directed toward encouraging others, you have the ability to create warmth and sunshine. You can experience your vitality and power in the process of recognizing and uplifting those around you. Your natural enthusiasm inspires the life in others by drawing them onto the stage. This dramatic ability can motivate them to become excited about themselves. When you consider yourself part of the team and truly seek to enrich and enhance those around you, you can experience not only their magnificence but yours as well. When you acknowledge others' uniqueness, you allow them to occupy the center of the stage. This gives you the objectivity needed for confidence to express yourself. As an example of childlike innocence and spontaneous vitality, you can inspire others to express the radiance within themselves.

SUN IN VIRGO
Sun in Virgo individuals may feel they have the right to be right; to discriminate, to criticize and analyze themselves and others; and to be acknowledged for their righteousness.

Static
When you focus on wanting others to recognize your righteousness and purity, you may unconsciously behave in Virgo ways that are stuffy, prudish, puritanical, compulsively ordered, and haughty. To be acknowledged you might elicit judgment on right and wrong, and use your analytical ability to appear important and set apart from others. In proving your ultimate rightness you may use your finely honed critical talents to point out your own flaws. This backfires by resulting in a basic lack of confidence in your own spontaneity. Additionally, you may attempt to appear more righteous by pointing out the flaws in others, in accordance with your value system of rigid rules and regulations for perfect behavior. When others don't appreciate or understand your good intentions, you are surprised. Indulging in the Virgo tendency to compulsive self-righteousness can scatter and deplete your ener-

gies. This indulgence may disrupt the focus and self-confidence that are needed to act.

Dynamic
You can focus your attention on *uplifting* others through your talents and abilities for creating order. Then you notice the ways in which you can truly serve others without having to feel right about it. Recognizing the inherent worth of others gives you trust in your vision of their perfection. This frees you to contribute in a way that effectively supports them. Your desire to serve is appreciated when you expose to others your perception of their inherent value. This reinforces mutual self-worth. By being aware of others' personal desires you can motivate them successfully through assisting them in reaching what they want. The resultant success increases their vitality and sense of well-being. When you place serving others above your judgment about whether or not it is the right thing to do, you can abandon rules and regulations. This results in self-trust, allowing you to act spontaneously in a way that automatically works to facilitate any situation. If you are aware that your intentions are truly pure, your sense of acting rightly is fulfilled.

SUN IN LIBRA
Sun in Libra individuals feel they have the right to develop harmonious relationships; the right to know what others want; and the right to be treated fairly.

Static
When you focus on wanting to be recognized as a fair and harmonious person, you may behave in ways that are compromising and manipulative. You may act like "Mr. or Ms. Nice Person" and naively expect others to respond in the same way. When you use good manners to get your way, your manipulations create only an artificial harmony. If your attention is on achieving a positive image of yourself, you may indulge in the Libran tendency to play tit-for-tat games. This puts you in situations where your integrity can be manipulated merely by being convinced that you are being treated fairly and are getting an equal portion. When you allow yourself to become lost in the realm of cooperatively sharing ideas, you may not realize that whatever you do to control others, others can also do to you.

Dynamic

When your attention focuses on uplifting others through sharing of talents, you can enliven social situations by contributing to the inherent harmony. You can do this by adding the missing ingredient of your independent point of view. By trusting the overall picture you intuitively perceive you are able to interject your ideas of justice and fair play into situations. This occurs in a spontaneous way that brings about a higher level of cooperation but does not offend. Recognition of your abilities to bring a larger truth into a situation enables you to contribute your ideas of justice, fairness, and harmony. This sharing increases your level of vitality and well-being.

You can create true harmony in relationships through your willingness to communicate the full truth of what you're experiencing. Through this integrity a higher harmony may establish itself. Thus, rather than trying to manipulate others into a state of false harmony, you learn to establish good relationships by facing the existing harmonies and disharmonics with acceptance and objectivity. This frees you to share your intuitive sense of fair play with others.

SUN IN SCORPIO

Sun in Scorpio individuals feel they have the right to possess, investigate, control; to search out the secrets of people's desires and needs.

Static

When your attention is directed toward getting a reaction from others that reflects your power, you may instigate conflicts. In doing so, merely as a cheap thrill and test of your dominance, you may alienate those closest to you. If you covertly insist that others recognize your ultimate strength, you may become impatient and insecure when they do not offer you the deference expected. When your potency is not acknowledged, you may become angry and demand attention through an inappropriate provocation.

The unpredictability of the Scorpio's sharp responses may be emotional and destructive in nature. Indulging in agitating others may lead to their mistrust and wariness in including you on the core levels most wanted. You might rely on inciting others as a means of validating and measuring your power and control by their responses. This can lead to a type of self-expression that defeats your independence.

Dynamic
When you focus on uplifting other people, you can express your abilities for manifesting power in a way that is constructive and vital for both parties. Revealing your perceptions of another's inner thoughts and feelings allows you to feel the aliveness of significant participation. You can inspire others when you validate your self-control by exposing those factors that enable them to achieve the same self-mastery.

You can be aware of the ambitions and goals that others are seeking. This awareness allows you to contribute your perceptions effectively in a way that others can accept. This results in your increased vitality and well-being. You give others an opportunity to know you and to appreciate the power of your discernment when you reveal the psychological insights that further them. Seeing the foibles and hidden motivations of others can inspire you to help them become aware of their own deepest desires. In this way you can experience the satisfaction and acknowledgment of the Scorpion power to transform the lives of others constructively.

SUN IN SAGITTARIUS
Sun in Sagittarius individuals feel they have the right to be free; to be the intellectual authority; to be acknowledged and appreciated as noble and deserving.

Static
If your attention focuses on wanting others to acknowledge your intellectual superiority continually, your intellect may inadvertently become pompous and self-serving. When this occurs, your communication might become directed only toward proving your moral righteousness. Indulging in the Sagittarius need to be recognized for a broad mental perspective may bring a focus on one area of perception. Then you might demand to be at center stage, whether you deserve it or not, "spouting off" ideas in that area. Thus, you may unknowingly alienate others by insisting that they agree with you. As a consequence, the base you could effectively expand on is lost when you refuse to add their factual input into your calculations.

When others do not agree with your conclusions, your vitality diminishes, and you may lose contact with the Sagittarius ideals and sense of humanity. If you need others to acknowledge you as noble and deserving, you may inflate your words of action. This may distract you from putting the energy into accomplishing the action itself.

Dynamic
When you focus on inspiring *others*, you can effectively listen for the areas in which they are asking questions. This enables you to share relevant insights that can be appreciated by the other person. You have the ability to use your intellect to help other people by demonstrating your capacity to see their lives from a broader, more optimistic viewpoint. When you share those beliefs that enhance other people's levels of self-trust, you can effectively expand their faith in themselves. This automatically brings about acknowledgment and appreciation of your intellect.

The awareness of yourself as part of a larger brotherhood can enable you to express your perceptions spontaneously in a loving way. This enhances the situation for everyone and increases your vitality and well-being. Consequently, you experience pride and a sense of responsibility as your reward when you use enthusiasm to recognize the significance of others and to bring out their importance.

SUN IN CAPRICORN
Sun in Capricorn individuals feel they have the right to authority, to govern and control others in terms of establishing order; to be respected for their achievements and position.

Static
When you focus on wanting recognition and respect from others for your being in control, you may use your authority to dominate those around you. If you become totally dedicated to appearing authoritative and earning approval for your achievements, you may neglect using your talents to get the job done. This comes about when being in control and getting respect have become more important than actually accomplishing the task. You also may expect others to be as *sensitive* to your ambitions as you are *insensitive* to theirs, and when they do not offer the deference expected, you may become defensive and critical.

Tension with co-workers can be aroused if you want your behavior to be sanctioned as perfect in their eyes. You might not use your organizational talents to benefit others but solely to manipulate them into improving your social image. Thus, you may create, through self-interest, the necessity of having to manage them constantly in order to stay in control of the situation. This might limit success and put a tremendous drain on your energy and vitality, which may leave you in a state of tense watchfulness.

Dynamic
You can direct your attention to encouraging others with your organizational talents and abilities. This allows your sensitivity to expand into areas in which others are disorganized and could use the benefits of your natural sense of order. In the process of effectively assisting them, with an awareness of their feelings, you automatically acquire their respect without having to justify it. Recognizing the intangible order and perfection of things can allow you to plan on a material level with less tension.

Awareness of your emotional connection with the whole allows you to organize coworkers effectively. You can do this in a way that improves the situation and increases your vitality and well-being. In managing others to more effectively produce results that are in *their* best interests, you automatically gain their esteem and admiration for your executive abilities. This eliminates the need for further supervision. Increased self-respect can come through your process of organizing and delegating authority in order to get the job done most effectively for all concerned.

When your integrity comes to the fore, you cease to justify your position through the regard of other people, allowing you to forcefully channel your energy into accomplishing the task at hand. In so doing you can produce results that earn you lasting respect.

SUN IN AQUARIUS
Sun in Aquarius individuals feel they have the right to be different and unique; to be impersonal and objective in their search for individuality; to intellectualize the sensitivities of others.

Static
Your attention might focus on wanting others to reflect a public acknowledgment of the Aquarius uniqueness. This focus may lead to behaving in ways that do not actually contribute to the group

or to individuals but merely serve as ego enhancement. You might want to be recognized as cooperative and fair, yet feel defensive about losing your identity in relationships. This may lead to responding in ways that are erratic and disruptive to others, and can result in alienating them.

If, under the pretense of objectivity, you try to impress others with the Aquarius certainty of knowledge, you may develop detachment and insensitivity to individuals as well as the group. This might result in a lowering of vitality if you become uncertain of your own wisdom in interplay with others.

Dynamic

When you focus on inspiring others, you may realize that your knowledge is less important than the individuality of other people. By allowing others to express *their* point of view you can expand the facets of your intelligence. Then you can share appropriate knowledge that contributes to the situation for mutual inspiration. When you use your objectivity within the framework of other people's sensitivity, your unique talents are enhanced.

Awareness of the power of your identity and natural independence allows you to share insights in a balanced way. This revitalizes you and the relationship. You can recognize the power and the willfulness of the free child within yourself. This gives you the clarity to handle relationships with a sense of humor and perspective to relate peacefully.

You possess the ability to view any situation objectively. Thus, you can inspire, enhance, and lead group activities without giving an impression of dominance. You have a soothing ability to take the vote or get the data effortlessly. This automatically leads to the cooperation of others since they feel included in the government of the group.

SUN IN PISCES

Sun in Pisces individuals feel they have the right to live in a dream world of ideals; to express their artistic or other-worldly talents; to disregard having a worldly ambition.

Static

When you focus on seeking an indulgent, sympathetic ear for your ideals, you may behave in ways that appear impractical, untested, and irresponsible. If you want others to recognize the inherent Pisces goodness and compassion, you might try unconsciously to live up to their expectations. This may result in a loss of your own values and a process of self-defeat.

You might appear indecisive, hesitant, ambivalent, and lacking commitment to a particular goal or direction. Consequently, you may experience the role of the destitute victim. Instead of pursuing your ideals, your Pisces sensitivity may respond to the hidden psychological pulls of others by trying to be all things to all people. This eventually sabotages your self-worth and vitality.

You might not be aware of the difference between grandoise desires and realistic aspirations. If so, you may experience the personal lack of fulfillment of your ideals.

Dynamic

When you focus on using your sensitivity to uplift others, you can become the mystic, the artist, the poet, the voice of humankind's spiritual and emotional ideals. Recognizing the necessity for practical step-by-step methods in enacting your ideals empowers you to commit yourself to express compassion for humanity tangibly. You can do this through realistic channels that will be of inspirational benefit to others.

By being aware of your resources for systematic implementation, you can express your visions in a solid or artistic form. Thus, you can assist, soothe, and heal other people. This results in a feeling of universal belonging for both.

You can commit yourself to establishing with others those standards and values that *you* consider to be worthwhile. Then you can use your Pisces sensitivity to reveal others' hidden desires and motivations for the purpose of combining with them those ideals that could heal. By being aware of your own values you are able to relate compassionately to others' desires without losing integrity. This can increase your vitality and well-being as well as your worth to both yourself and the other person.

SUN IN THE HOUSES

1st: Expresses the right to be acknowledged as a leader and the ability to bring this about by asserting one's independence.
2nd: Pinpoints the right to establish personal values and the ability to attract monetary success.

3rd: Represents the right to communicate at one's will and the talent to create circumstances for sharing knowledge.

4th: Expresses the right to be accepted on a personal level and the talent to dominate the immediate (domestic) environment.

5th: Denotes the right to enjoy pleasure, to be a child forever, and the ability to share pleasure with others.

6th: Describes the right to enjoy one's daily work and the ability to express a sense of duty effectively.

7th: Represents the right to be acknowledged by others as an equal and the talent to create that circumstance.

8th: Imparts the right to use other people's resources and the ability to do this in ways that increase mutual power.

9th: Expresses the right to be a perpetual teacher and the ability to contact all the answers.

10th: Describes the right to social achievement and public recognition, and the ability to create it.

11th: Denotes the right and the ability to lead through the expression of one's unique individuality in group situations (the "no leader" leader).

12th: Represents the right and the ability to express one's divinity, intangible identity, or private dream.

Moon

MOON: KEY TO EMOTIONAL SECURITY

The Moon in the Birthchart:

· Defines your deepest personal, emotional needs.

· Indicates the process through which you may separate yourself emotionally from other people, thereby depriving yourself of the closeness and intimacy you need for a sense of personal security.

· Discloses the unconscious process by which you attempt to manipulate people through dependencies and sensitivities, and by expressing emotional needs in a way that repels others.

· Shows the path to gaining inner fulfillment and illuminates your ability to integrate change without being disrupted.

· Pinpoints where the lessons of emotional dependency and personal insecurity arise that need to be made conscious and be purified in order for you to pass through the changing situations of life with a stable emotional foundation.

· Reveals that area of life in which you need to nourish others and to be nourished in a way that produces a sense of intimacy, acceptance, and nonverbal caring.

· Describes your ability to adjust emotionally to the changing situations of life.

· Represents habits of survival dependency from childhood that result in insecurity and a perpetual lack of true inner satisfaction when carried into adult life.

· Shows where the need for emotional nurturing and deep personal caring can be met in a way that satisfies your sense of emotional survival.

MOON IN ARIES

Static

When you habitually seek to be in control of situations relating to personal independence, you can be competitive to the point of "winning" by withdrawing from interaction with others. You may avoid asserting your needs and then working it out with the other person, due to not wanting to risk the Aries independence. This nonassertion leads to repressing your independent impulses and creating situations where others dominate you. If you unconsciously need others' permission before leading and initiating, you may experience insecurity and loss of personal power. This leads to a resentment of others because you feel they are responsible for your inability to act. You may react to their outbursts by withdrawing and feeling violated when they are insensitive to your repressed emotions. This situation adds to your own state of angry, unexpressed, and tightly controlled feelings.

When you hide your emotional needs in order to maintain distance and control the circumstances, you lose touch with the power of your own independent, inner core. If you are unwilling to assert your needs and feelings and work it out with others, you may find you are not able to work it out at all. As a result you may withdraw from participation. Such an action leads to frustration and anger, of feeling unable to express and accept recognition for your natural executive abilities.

Dynamic

When you take responsibility for creating the independence you need, you may notice that repressing your feelings and letting others have their way does not lead to your feeling in control. The truth is that others cannot provide sensitivity to your emotional states. *You* are the one with the gift of sensitivity to underlying foundational feelings. Your lesson is to acknowledge the need to feel close by initiating a mutual awareness of basic human feelings and needs. You can accomplish this by moving your attention away from yourself and toward perceiving the human insecurities and feelings of others.

Avoiding judgmental thoughts about another's lack of sensitivity enables you to recognize the true nature of one's feelings behind the outward expression. This knowledge leads the Arian to become sensitive to others as individuals rather than taking their expression personally. Thus, the basic insecurities of others can put you in touch with your own underlying feelings in an objective, balanced way. You then possess the clarity you need to work constructively in relationships.

You can show your sensitivity and vulnerability to others' insecurities. When you reveal your feelings and needs, your innate power is acknowledged, and you win the emotional support of others. You can then express feelings successfully since you are sharing yourself with diplomacy born of awareness of another's sensitivities. Consquently, you are able to feel close by having your true feelings accepted and shared. Then you work out situations with others.

In this process you gain security of independence and courage in relating to others. When you support the authority of other people to handle situations, you reinforce their self-confidence. Thus, your own independence and initiative are spontaneously recognized, respected, and appreciated.

Past Lives

Unconscious past life memories of battlegrounds, direct physical combat, and competition for the attainment of your personal needs have made issues of personal survival strong in this lifetime. You are always on the alert but camouflaged so that you can spot the enemy without showing your own strength. In order to maintain this disguise you must suppress your strength, which actually invites provocations and attacks from the outside. By suppressing your spirit you invite others to walk all over you.

Due to these past life experiences and the tendency to view everything in terms of personal survival, you interpret any opposition in this lifetime as a direct threat to your own goals. Thus, you may respond with either vehement resistance or by "cutting off" the other person entirely and going your own, independent way.

The lesson you are learning is to incorporate the resistance of others into your plan, to see it as a means of actualizing your goals more efficiently. You are learning to be objective enough to welcome the input of others. By taking into consideration their objections, needs, and feelings relative to your own plans, you can expand your objectives to ensure genuine partnership and harmony in working together toward a mutual goal.

As you learn to stop projecting your identity (either positive or negative) onto other people, you can begin to see them objectively and take them into account. Then you can "be first" in a way that allows other persons' needs to be met as well. Many past lifetimes have been spent developing your own identity, and you are not accustomed to easy cooperation with others in the context of joint projects and team efforts. Rather than feeling that you need to compete with others to get your own way, you are learning to include others' desires and fears in working out solutions that are fair to both parties.

Past lives spent in high-speed activity, without time for tact and diplomacy, have led to a certain naiveté and directness in fulfilling your personal needs. This makes your intentions clear for all to see; thus, those who feel threatened by your goals may try to block or manipulate you in some way. When this happens you feel you have to fight to survive and get what you want, in direct opposition to the other person. The only other alternative you see is allowing the other person to be the conqueror and to totally suppress your own needs. You don't realize that your impatience and carelessness are creating the very opposition you fear.

As you learn to be less naive and direct in your speech and more diplomatic in communicating your wants and needs, others will not feel threatened and so will have no need to oppose you. Through this new tactfulness you will encourage others to feel that they are also winning by going along with your plan. You are learning to enlist the support of others in going toward the goals that fulfill your own personal needs.

MOON IN TAURUS

Static

You might habitually seek others to provide the Taurean need for attention, pampering, and love by supplying material and sensual comforts. This dependency may create an impression of personal inadequacy in order to induce others into giving you their tangible resources. By projecting a helplessness in obtaining material goods they may furnish you with comforts. When this happens you tend to feel loved, secure, and worthwhile. But in displaying an image of helplessness to others, you also begin to believe it.

Your self-worth can be undermined when others respond by contributing to your sustenance. Their aid reinforces the belief that you lack the energy or abilities to provide your support. When your security is dependent upon the material aid of others, you cannot be creative or capable for fear that these comforts may be taken away. This results in feeling helpless and unable to actively establish your material sense of worth in the world.

Dynamic

You may notice that relying on others for creating your self-worth has not worked. Others cannot provide this sense because you possess a supply of personal resources that are not being used. The lesson is to contribute your resources to the world, thus earning the Taurean comforts and establishing self-esteem. You can accomplish this by recognizing other people's emotions coming into expression. This recognition can inspire you to get in touch with your creativity.

You can gain a deeper sense of inner stability and self-worth by supporting and contributing to the material stability of the environment. In choosing to sacrifice the role of pampered child, you create goals and objectives that motivate you to establish a set of values. When you notice that the people who feel good about themselves are those who are contributing their talents and resources in a tangible way, you are inspired to manifest and establish your creativity. When you appreciate your ideals enough to manifest them, you find the confirmation of self-worth that you need.

Past Lives

Past lives spent in positions of affluence, material security, and comfort have caused you to come into this lifetime seeking material security above all else. You associate having a strong financial base with emotional stability and ease.

Because you are accustomed to accumulation, you can have a difficult time letting go of anything, even things that are holding you back. This can impede the flow of money coming into your life. The first things you need to let go of are your ideas: the idea that you have a difficult time with money; the idea that you have to earn every penny on your own and that it's going to be a tough process; and the idea that you have to do everything yourself, in exactly your way, for your needs to be met.

You can have such a strong fear of losing your material security that you actually create a "poverty consciousness" in your life, feeling that resources are limited and that you must be very careful as to how you spend every penny. Your lesson is to learn to trust the universe and be open to the flow of money coming in and out of your life. You can do this by not focusing so intensely on your financial restrictions (that is, exactly how much this month's bills are) and by simply being open to the universe blessing you with prosperity! You need to focus your creative mind less on financial worry and more on visualizing the universe's just pouring money on you and your joyful response. In this way you can open yourself at last to the abundance you seek.

You are also learning to accept the gift of money by allowing the resources of others to enrich your life without feeling you have to "pay back every penny." You need to be open to the joy of freely accepting money from other people and releasing the ego identification, not feeling that you have to do something in return.

Due to past lives of physical sensitivity and indulgence, you have strong physical desires for sensuality, touching, and physical contact in this incarnation. Once again you are learning to accept the natural healthiness of your needs and be open to having them fulfilled by others. In this area as well as in the area of finances, you are learning to focus less on your needs and to be more aware of the enrichment that the universe is offering you through other people.

You are also learning to accept the idea of "bargaining" and "discounts," and not assume that you have to pay the "full dollar amount" for everything you want. Through being aware of others' motives to "sell," your capacity to "buy" what you want at discount is enhanced.

MOON IN GEMINI

Static

When you seek others to provide an emotional escape from the isolation of your mental gymnastics, you embark on a search for the perfect person. This may lead to the frustration of never finding a single relationship that can satisfy and provide release from idealistic mental visions.

If you lack confidence in your instincts, you may fear losing one option by choosing another. Such behavior does not bring stability in relationships. Constant disillusionment can result in an endless series of relationships, a scattering of energies, and loss of identity.

It can be difficult to see inspiring influences that you can trust and aim toward. This results in a loss of confidence in your ability to be spontaneous. You may hold back in communicating due to fearing that others will judge you; thus, you lose the benefit of others' abilities to put your ideas in a practical perspective. You may deprive yourself of the very solutions you seek by withholding the truth.

Dynamic

You can create an atmosphere in which you get your point across by noticing that logical methods have not worked. The truth is that others cannot accept ideas that are not relevant to the practical solutions they are seeking. The lesson is to allow the needs of others to direct your mental talents so that you can share ideas they can accept. This is accomplished by focusing beyond the threat of others' motives. Then you can see the disorder in their lives and their attempts to organize themselves.

Sacrificing the assumption that you know what is right in the long run enables you to accept the needs of others. This acceptance allows their goals to guide your intuitive talents for mutually beneficial and practical results. When you realize that in order to achieve happiness it must be given to others, you experience what you are giving in the process. This interaction brings about wholehearted participation in assisting others to find their answers.

While you pay attention to problems others are having in their daily lives, you can make a commitment to serve on a practical level. Thus, you discover the very solutions that are next on your own path. You gain the spontaneous faith you need by encouraging others to believe in themselves. The power to direct your life is finally realized as a by-product of inspiring others, and your own role as a mentor is appropriately exercised. The realization that your excitement comes from serving and inspiring others develops unshakable self-confidence and a sense of variety in all relationships.

Past Lives
Past lifetimes spent as gatherers and dispensers of information, such as travelers, teachers, wandering bards and minstrels, have left you with a feeling of incessant restlessness. You feel the urge to move on, thinking that there is always something new and exciting over the next hill or that the grass is greener in the next location. What actually lures you on is the past life memory that the next piece of information to be gained and shared with others is to be found in the next town. Thus, the urge for continual movement from person to person continues into this lifetime.

In past lives you were not accustomed to having a family, you were accustomed to being a traveler. Therefore, you are constantly seeking new mental stimulation and may have a difficult time settling down with one person in a family relationship. An internal restlessness drives you on with the lure: The best relationship is just over the next hill. This idea served you well in past lives, but in this one it can lead to a feeling of dissatisfaction in whatever relationship you are in, no matter how idyllic or healthy it may be for you.

You are learning to relax, to deepen your mental connection with those in your immediate environment so that the stimulation you seek can be satisfied at deeper, more profound levels. You are learning to exchange a *quantity* of ideas for the *quality* of a deep rapport by integrating the dimension of feeling into your arena of mental exchange. In this way your desires for constant communication take on a new dimension of satisfaction and fulfillment.

In order to develop deep mental connections with others you are learning that you must first develop a connection with your own spiritual, intuitive processes. Once in touch with your intuition you will have access to the information you need, when you need it, without the restless feeling that you continually need more information in order to feel secure. Then you can share ideas with others with a feeling of ease based on the joy of exchanging those energies that release both people into truth.

MOON IN CANCER

Static
You may have an impulsive tendency to trample on or ignore the feelings of others when you habitually seek to fill your emotional needs first. If you indulge in the Cancerian world of self-centered emotion, it may be difficult to see beyond your own needs to the solutions offered by others for emotional balance. Wanting others to pay attention to you can lead to feeling crushed if you are rebuffed. This can result in a negative self-image, of feeling unable to create positive and nourishing emotional situations in your life.

Dynamic
When you take responsibility for creating the emotional closeness you need, you may notice that the methods you have been using do not work. The truth is that others cannot provide your fulfillment because you already have a surplus of emotional fullness. Your lesson is to empty your own cup first so that it can be refilled. You can do this by discovering the other people who exist in your universe.

After first choosing to sacrifice your emotional demands, you can fill the cups of others by discerning their needs for self-confidence and by encouraging them to assert their feelings. When you give your attention to others and fill their needs for personal closeness and empathy, you find yourself experiencing the tender intimacy and security you want.

Past Lives
Past lives spent in situations of enforced dependency on family members have resulted in a basic insecurity and fear of needing to be taken care of by others. You fear needing someone else's sympathy to survive. There are active subconscious past life memories of having sustained a physical injury or handicap that prevented you from being able to take care of yourself (for example, a coal mine accident); or you fear becoming too old to take care of yourself or having to rely on family members to do things for you.

Such memories lend urgency to your need for an emotional "parent" figure to rely on for protection and care. Thus, family is extremely important in this incarnation and is subconsciously related to basic survival. This insecurity results in unhealthy patterns of manipulation through dependencies, clinging, and controlling family members by being overprotective.

The lesson here is to enjoy the nourishment of intimacy and empathy without accompanying debilitating bondage. To do this you must learn to rely on authority within yourself. Past tendencies to cling need to be redirected to "clinging" to goals and ideals that are larger than your personal life. Then the sense of dependency will shift to depending on yourself to hold true to your goals and ideals.

Since you are learning that there is a "higher authority" you can rely on to take care of your needs, you are able to release family members from these debilitating dependencies. In this way you open yourself to experiencing true intimacy and loving closeness because the clinging attachment has been replaced by an atmosphere of freedom, support, and confidence in your family member's ability to achieve great heights and to take care of themselves.

MOON IN LEO

Static

If you subconsciously seek to confirm your worth by superiority, you may expect others to come to you, like the king waiting to receive his audience. You may use the pretense of objectivity to ensure that others will admire you on your pedestal. If you unconsciously select associates on the basis of their ability to increase the Leo material status, you can experience the discomfort of relating without inner affinity. Thus, in needing others as tools to further your *own* values and goals, the door is closed to receiving rewards that are beyond your expectations or defined objectives.

Needing to be entertained, you can go on "automatic" and unconsciously use your charm to increase your material position. This is born of an inner attitude of "what can *you* do for *me?*" and costs you your self-confidence in expressing truly spontaneous feelings. You may hoard resources, begrudgingly sharing them with those who are close. Concealing assets causes you to lose status in their eyes and, consequently, in your own. Confidence in others is eroded when you seek to take advantage to enhance your material position and feel superior in comparison.

Dynamic
You can create the self-worth you need as you notice that old methods for achieving admiration from others do not result in success. The values projected may not be what others want or need. You must first relinquish the position of director, producer, and main character in your life drama. This enables you to get in touch with the audience and find out which of your many talents and resources are appropriate to the situation.

When you approach relationships thinking, "It's not what you can do for me, it's what *I* can do for *you*," you experience an unshakable sense of your own worth. When you open yourself to the desires and needs of others, you gain insight into the role you can play. By inspiring others you are not only entertained but gain a sense of self-worth in the process.

Choosing to focus on others' needs frees you to express the flamboyant, generous Leo nature in a way that supports the worth of others. In the process your worth is validated. As a by-product of contributing your talents to uplift others, you find enjoyment and happiness. The loyalty and love of your family are earned when you support their values and needs in establishing their worth. Stepping out of your drama and realizing how much fun you're having in your dramatics lightens your whole outlook on life.

Past Lives
You were celebrated royalty in other lives: actors, actresses, musicians, kings, queens, and "stars" in one form or another. Consequently, you came into this lifetime with a need for recognition, approval, and praise. You are accustomed to applause, and insecurity results when you feel ignored or not treated as someone special.

This insecurity can result in feeling that you must perform according to other people's standards and to further other people's goals in order to gain applause. You can be almost childlike in your need for approval, totally dependent on being with people who will flatter you and pamper your ego. Your need for constant reassurance can tax the energies of those who love you, and rob you of your freedom and self-confidence.

During this lifetime you are learning to dedicate yourself to more universal causes that allow you to do your part in furthering the evolution of the race. When you focus on the larger drama and allow yourself to be a vehicle for an energy that furthers the goals of humankind, your powerful ego assumes a lovely balanced role. Seeing yourself as a channel for helping your brothers and sisters allows you to accept your childlike qualities and be more tolerant of your mistakes because you know your motive was of the highest.

Regarding those you are close to as friends rather than subjects or your private audience, allows you to support their special life force, which will naturally result in their freely acknowledging you.

Clarity about the ideals of humanity that you support allows you to offer approval and vital support to others without expectations of loyalty. This opens the gateway to a flood of unexpected appreciation of your generosity of spirit when you least expect it.

MOON IN VIRGO

Static
If you want to be perfect in the eyes of others, you may use the Virgo analytical powers to defend your behavior when others question you. When others do not behave according to your expectations, you may feel affronted and react with sarcasm or cold silence. You might withhold helpful opinions and valuable perceptions because you fear criticism from others.

Often, you may refuse to share your internal reactions with a loved one and unwittingly create a secret barrier. As a result you sacrifice integrity in order to be accepted, at least momentarily. You may then feel guilty and not know why. Relating superficially deprives others of the value of the Virgo perception and deprives you of the opportunity to feel useful. In violating your code you undergo severe self-criticism which, in turn, takes away the security needed.

Dynamic
You can communicate the Virgo standards in a way that confirms your goodness and perfection. When you let go of your own standards and notions of what perfect behavior ought to look like (yours or the other person's), you rid yourself of ideas that prevent closeness.

As you empty your mind of the judgments that cause separations, you experience the joy and closeness in the communication you want. You can do this by casting aside the need to have others think of you as perfect. This frees you to have faith in your intuition. Then you can tell what, for you, is the truth in the situation expressed as your own point of view.

In releasing scattered pictures of what you think service to others ought to look like, you are able to speak with integrity and transcend superficiality. You first need to sacrifice judgments of your "rightness" and others' "wrongness," then you can discover that what you formerly judged as imperfect behavior in others was only their lack of information needed to put their lives in order. You can satisfy your own need to feel useful in relationships by looking beyond fears of personal rejection and sharing what you see.

When you use the Virgo practical ability for analysis to share your reactions and assist others in dealing with their emotional systems, you experience a sense of your true ability to serve. This gives you the self-acceptance you need to feel close.

Past Lives
Past lives spent in positions of ministering to others, healing them, taking care of their needs, and helping to put them "back together" have resulted in a gentle humility and the desire to serve. From lifetimes spent as artisans, craftspeople, and physical healers, you have become concerned with the details of perfection in your work. Thus, in this life you have a tendency to feel that all aspects of your behavior and performance must be perfect before they can be allowed expression. This attitude can interfere with the flow of your charitable deeds in the world.

You are learning to express whatever piece of the puzzle you have at the moment, without having to see the "whole, complete picture." When your piece of the puzzle has been added, the larger vision becomes clearer for all concerned, and others can cooperate more easily with you in attaining mutually beneficial results.

Lifetimes spent as doctors, nurses, and nuns have left you feeling that your behavior has to be exemplary—an example of perfection above the behavioral standards of the rest of mankind. You may feel separate from others due to this inflated sense of "rightness" that is actually part of a past life egotism.

In this life you are learning to relax, to dissolve past life rigidities, to trust the perfection of the universal unfoldment of events, and to be responsible for simply doing your part. By freely adding your piece of the puzzle—whether it be a feeling, thought, perception, or momentary desire—without needing it to be perfect before expression, you are cooperating with the people and events that flow through your life. And you become an example of perfection to others by operating from the integrity of expressing yourself fully and innocently, piece by piece, along the way.

MOON IN LIBRA

Static
When you habitually expect others to notice your sensitivity to discord and aggression, you respond with emotional touchiness if confronted in any way. You may compromise your own direction and sense of fairness in order to appease others, expecting them to reciprocate by providing the rapport needed for your stability. When your manipulations don't work, you can revert to an abrasive attitude of independence and carelessness, or give vent to wounded feelings to gain their attention.

If you depend on others to be compatible with you, you are easily thrown off the center of harmony when unpleasantness occurs. Thus, you swallow your own feelings and appease everyone for fear that otherwise you may offend them or they may consider you unfair. This action may invite them to take the advantage until finally all unacknowledged previous difficulties burst forth from you in a disastrous tirade. Such frantic emotional smoke screens may repel others who do not know how to penetrate your defenses. The result is that you are unable to understand when these actions keep others from trusting you.

If you are afraid of creating scenes, you may withhold sharing your internal reactions to others' emotional demands. Then later you wonder why they are not more considerate. As a result you may lose confidence in their trustworthiness and your own ability to discriminate. Indulging in the Libra tendency to internalize and identify with the disharmony from others may also result in sudden emotional outbursts.

Dynamic
When you take responsibility for creating the internal balance you need to feel close in relationships, you may notice that your methods of compromising and expecting others to create peacefulness and fairness have simply not worked. The truth is that you may be

unable to experience harmony because you are waiting for others to initiate it. Those who are not attuned to your sense of fair play may be unable to treat you fairly until you state the injustices you perceive (that is, ''I don't feel good about this . . . ''). This gives you strength and completeness in your *own direction.*

Pledging yourself to a goal external to the relationship can supply confidence to state your needs for support of that goal in a direct, objective, and organized way. This gives others the opportunity to cooperate with you in attaining the goal. You can commit yourself to the integrity of your own direction in relationships by trusting that the outcome will be for your highest good. The result brings you the self-respect you need to put yourself forward and declare the truth of your feelings regardless of the consequences. When you thus assert yourself, the situations around you automatically come into balance according to their higher plan, regardless of outer appearance. When you realize that the supply of people is absolutely unlimited, it encourages you to express your own identity and display who you are. This acts as an automatic means of attracting people who are akin to you.

If you give voice to the reality of your independent point of view, you will attract appreciation and love for the person you truly are. Thus, in surrounding yourself with people of true affinity, you experience the joy of knowing that you are valued simply for being there in the present moment with them. When you trust your own perceptions and act from them to create an inner equilibrium, you add the peacefulness of your presence to the situation.

When you go to your deep self and then express the balance and stability that is there, you silently invite others to go to that place within themselves. The power of your harmony impels others to go to their depths also if they wish to relate to you; in this way, through claiming your center, you create harmony.

Past Lives
Past lives have been spent in positions of support, as mediators, diplomats, concubines, or traditional female supportive roles. These lives have resulted in an identity based on sharing; your survival has depended on a sense of inner emotional accord with your partner. In this lifetime you may find yourself compromising your true identity in order to maintain the feeling of internal accord with your mate or partner.

Your lesson now is to learn to express yourself—to *be* yourself

—in the context of a relationship. To do this you must become aware of your own needs, realizing that if your needs aren't met, the relationship as a whole will suffer. You are learning to put yourself back into the picture so that a fairness of exchange can take place. This requires that you let your partner know verbally what you would like to have occur in the relationship in a way that invites a response about what your partner would like. Once both persons' needs are out in the open, you are naturally able to suggest a solution or plan that is mutually satisfactory.

However, you need to learn not to overassert for fear of not getting your way. You have a defensiveness based on resentment from past lives, and a present life assumption that others are going to object to your having your own way. Thus, when you do assert your needs (which is rare), you have a tendency to do it in a rather harsh and defensive way that cuts off the honest response of your partner.

Through fear of compromising your own needs, you sometimes overcompensate with unnecessary forcefulness. Unknown to you, this actually provokes the other person's resistance to cooperating with you. This leads to a reinforcement of the sense of separation in the relationship, the feeling that you can't relax and be yourself but have to be always on the alert to either resist or accommodate the nonverbal needs of your partner.

You can be so afraid of losing the relationship altogether by not keeping the other person's emotional state harmonized at all times that you subvert your own identity in order to keep the partner pleased and content. The self-suppression that was necessary in past lives to support and flatter the person in power can harden into a resentment that can erupt in the future with rather violent consequences.

This lifetime you can learn to share your needs with others as an equal, with the confident expectation that they will want to please and accommodate you in the relationship. You need to realize that others *want* your harmonious, pleasant, happy disposition around them, and to keep you, they will go out of their way to make you happy.

You are also learning to assume the role of manager in relationships by objectively equalizing the injustices that are the cause of social discontent. You do this best only after your own needs and goals are verbally expressed and the other person's corresponding needs have been solicited on the verbal level. In this way a fair

and balanced plan that fills the needs of both partners can be
realized.

MOON IN SCORPIO

Static
When you habitually require others to give you their unconditional loyalty and allegiance, you may become crushed, insecure,
and angered when they don't. You may unconsciously respond
with defiance, exercising the instinctive power you have over others, and subtly attempt to enforce loyalty and control. Therefore,
in your eyes, they lose power. In this process you lose your capacity to feel the joys of equal interaction and consequently create
emotional stagnation for yourself.

If you feel insecure about losing control, you could attempt to
have all the answers for everyone in a way that creates a dependency in them and assures you of one-upman-ship. In diminishing
another's power, you unknowingly lessen the potency of the relationship. Thus, it cannot provide you with the emotional intensity, change, and new levels of depth that you may need for
personal fulfillment. When you sense another's vulnerabilities and
provoke that person's response, you get to be powerful but may
feel isolated. There is a basic Scorpio tendency to feel insecure in
financial and sexual relationships. This can lead to a need to manipulate everyone to prove potency.

Dynamic
When you take responsibility for creating situations in which you
can experience the deep feelings of joy, vitality, and intensity that
the Scorpio energy needs in relationships, you may notice that
relying on others to recognize your worth does not work. The
truth is that others cannot renew you. You are the one withholding the depths of perception that would bring this about.

Your lesson is first to release manipulative control of others, and
then you can experience the combining of resources that results in
the regeneration of your own energy and creativity. You accomplish this renewal by pledging your loyalties to those ideals and
potentials for growth that cause you to feel good about yourself.
By releasing your vision of being in command, you are able to find
out what others are really made of. As you enter onto uncharted
ground and are willing to take risks by letting go of power, you

can combine with another in a manner that is exhilarating for you. When you choose the stimulation of change over a stagnant status quo, you are able to go forward. Then you can gain knowledge of what enhances self-worth through an exciting process of risk and the unpredictable mystery you need for fulfillment.

You may realize that you can gain more knowledge and strength only by first releasing what you already have. This encourages you to contribute your inspiring insights generously, exposing perceptions that awaken others to their hidden resources. As you communicate your recognition of others' hidden abilities, it empowers them to reach their own objectives. This creates deeper, more satisfying camaraderie. You can then allow yourself to participate spontaneously in the direction others want to go rather than resisting the current. This enables you to interact with them on deeper, previously unknown levels.

Committed to freedom through renewal, you can realize that the way to win the most is to share the power. Thus, you reach deeper levels by releasing the Scorpio tendency to control. Finally, in the process of expressing loyalty to your ideals, you contribute potency by exposing your hidden perceptions to others. You can then experience your inner worth and the fun of your transformative process coming into expression.

Past Lives
Past lifetimes have carried extremes of emotional intensity and battles for power. You have been severely wounded, which has resulted in an overdevelopment of the survival instinct in this lifetime. Past lives filled with crisis and betrayal have resulted in an attitude of distrust, and you are attuned to the possibility of others having evil motives. This is so strong that the power of your belief (and resulting unconscious provocations) can actually bring out the worst in other people, which only heightens your feelings of emotional isolation.

To compensate for severe loneliness you seek that one other person you can trust, your soul mate, sensing that this will somehow bring you peace. But because of past life experiences, your approach to relationships is so obsessive and demanding that it often becomes mutually destructive. Instead of finding the peace you seek, you again experience being wounded.

You are learning to balance these intense past life experiences with a feeling of peacefulness and serenity in this incarnation. To do this you need to discover what it is you want to build with another person in this lifetime. Then you can bond with a trustworthy person who is interested in building the same kind of solid, mutually nourishing relationship. With the focus on what you want to create, in terms of a spiritual goal, you can use the power and intensity gained in past lives to build the life that will bring you peace.

For successful fulfillment of the long-sought soul mate relationship, you must build step by step and not skip any stages in laying the foundation. And by taking the other person's desires into account, the foundation will receive the benefit of both people's creative energies. Since past lives were spent in destruction, you need to remember that it may take only three weeks to demolish a skyscraper but three years to build one. By going slowly and keeping your mind on the goal you can enjoy the process of mutually creating a solid relationship.

MOON IN SAGITTARIUS

Static
If you feel the need to strive perpetually to confirm your intellectual superiority, you may become obsessed with feeling you have to obtain a tangible result. You may seek the ultimate "grand vision" that will empower you to put your physical universe in order. You might believe that by demonstrating perfection in all aspects of your life, others will bow to your moral knowledge and bestow the faith that you need.

You may unconsciously search for the elusive ideal of the perfect solution that gives you proof of your righteousness. In the absence of an ultimate ideal you may feel unable to act and can become lost and confused, lacking confidence in your perspective.

Dynamic
When you take responsibility for creating closeness with others, you may find that spreading your theoretical conclusions does not result in effective communication. You can become so preoccupied with imperfection that you fail to see your perfect image in the eyes of others. The truth is that others already see the nobility of your striving. Work on ridding yourself of judgments and evaluations so that you can accept your own perfection. You accomplish this by concentrating on the deeper messages of others, thus ex-

periencing their perfection which puts you in touch with your own.

By sacrificing the Sagittarius need to prove superior knowledge, you can hear what others are asking. Responding with spontaneous intuitive answers enables others to find the truth and source of their own perfection. In this way you also find security and the closeness with others that you want. By putting others in touch with their completeness, you experience your own.

You can communicate innocently by sharing your Sagittarius vision and allowing others to apply it in their own lives. This technique allows you to contribute to them in a way they can accept, and this acceptance is the acknowledgment you need. When you discover that you are able to communicate truth, you experience your own security along with the idealistic closeness with others that you desire.

Past Lives
Past lives have been spent gaining and being an example of spiritual truth as philosophers, spiritual leaders, and naturalists. In some cases misuse of positions of spiritual authority in past lives (putting oneself above the law) has resulted in a blind spot regarding social mores in this lifetime. Until this is understood there may be blundering in this life accompanied by (seemingly unfair) social punishment and retribution. If this is the case, you are learning not to put yourself above social laws and ethics of appropriate conduct. Once you decide to cooperate with prevailing social mores, the blind spot is removed and you will no longer experience society as unexpectedly inhibiting your desire for freedom.

You have a long history of going your own way, unfettered by the demands of society—a law unto yourself. Consequently, you have been socially isolated from others and come into this lifetime with a sense of loneliness and wanting to be understood and accepted by others. You want to be able to share the truth and inspiration gained in past lives with others in this lifetime, hoping that the vitality of this exchange will reconnect you with your own source.

When you come off your philosophical mountaintop and learn to relate, you will realize that to be understood you must first seek to understand others. You are learning to drop isolating self-righteous attitudes and to use your mind to discover the unspoken rules of personality interactions that others take for granted. When you accept these boundaries of socially accepted behavior, you will be able to share your philosophical awarenesses with others in a way they can accept and appreciate.

MOON IN CAPRICORN

Static

When you unconsciously need others' reassurance that you are the most important part of their interpersonal situations, you may unknowingly manipulate them emotionally to gain respect. This can lead to needless dramas of personal suffering that force them to acknowledge and admire your ability to survive. You may instinctively guard your image and try to appease others by becoming, for that moment, what they respect.

In sacrificing your "self" for the respect of another, you may lose your own identity. Indulging in the Capricorn tendency to control the relationship can rob others of their authority and ability to give you the admiration you want. Simultaneously, in order to feel loved you may need constant reassurance. This tendency gives your power to others and may leave you insecure and bewildered.

Dynamic

When you recognize the Capricorn need for establishing control in relationships, you notice that past methods of having others validate your identity have not lead to self-respect. The truth is that others cannot give respect when you are so busy cloaking yourself with their personalities. This process leaves you with no identity available to receive recognition!

The lesson is to relinquish control over others in order to see to whom you are relating. This is achieved by acknowledging the uniqueness of the person with whom you are dealing. As a result this action can give you insight into your own unique being and appreciation of yourself as different from others.

When you give others confidence in developing their ability to take charge of their lives, you become aware of your power. Your sensitivity can nurture others and reflect back to them your assurance of their ability to succeed and get on top of their emotions. Then you find that their self-esteem enables them to rise to the occasion. This technique of support allows you to experience your ability to organize others to reach a goal.

When you encourage authority and leadership abilities in others, you recognize those qualities in yourself. In respecting the needs of others to establish their identity, you can honor your wants. This gives you a sense of self. As you pursue the personal needs of your identity, you can choose independent action. When you make a commitment to your direction and follow through on it, you gain confidence in your authority as well as the respect of others.

Past Lives
Past lives spent in positions of control and authority have left you feeling that you must have absolute control in order to be emotionally secure. Past lives as figureheads and political leaders, and in positions of social prestige, have accustomed you to receiving respect, deference, and automatic cooperation from those around you. When this isn't forthcoming in the present incarnation, you feel that something is missing, and you experience insecurity in your relationships. You seek to "plug up the hole" in order to feel that the foundation is firm and so you can enter into relationships with the confidence of knowing you can handle any situation.

Unconscious past life tendencies to close down emotionally and be invulnerable by virtue of noninvolvement will not bring the emotional satisfaction you want in this lifetime. You are seeking emotional control, but the first step in gaining control is to be open to experiencing and expressing your feelings in the moment. Even though you don't have all the pieces under control at the onset, you must be willing to walk through the process of experiencing and integrating the male and female parts of yourself (emotions and control). You must be willing to "walk the path" to obtain the desired result of emotional involvement in relationships balanced with a calm sense of self-authority.

As you learn not to judge or invalidate your feelings, you can simply express them to others in the spirit of sharing self-identity. This allows the other person to share his or her feelings, leading to a positive, alchemical change in the relationship. Then you can identify your desires and the desires of the other person, which gives you a sense of clarity and allows you to view the relationship from an entirely new perspective.

Once you gain this new perspective you can see a vision of yourself in the future—a new sense of self that is emerging through the relationship. This is the important thing for you to work on. Through expressing your feelings you come into a new sense of balance and adjustment between yourself and your circumstances. You also gain the confidence of knowing that no matter what comes to you, you will know where each particle belongs in the overall scheme of things. From this you will derive a solid sense of your own authority in relating to the world.

MOON IN AQUARIUS

Static
When you habitually seek the feedback of others to supply your need for feelings of self-worth in your personal and emotional situations, you can inadvertently relinquish power and self-control. You are attuned to the hidden motives and desires of other people. If you use this knowledge to manipulate your worth and value in their eyes, you may find yourself unable to maintain your integrity and identity. Consequently, your self-worth can be at the precarious mercy of the outside world and the success of your manipulations of it.

When you look to others for feedback, you may be left feeling uncertain about what action to take. Needing validation leaves you uneasy about your material and sexual connections with other people. Thus, you may feel afraid that any intimate relationship might put you in a vulnerable position where unexpected emotional rejection could be experienced.

To avoid this you may create emotional drama that ensures others will stay at a distance. This game results in a negative self-image and emotional isolation.

Dynamic
When you take responsibility for creating loving relationships, you may notice that past methods have brought about a consistent feeling of being worthwhile to others. Others cannot provide you with idealism in relationships because in seeking their approval you may not be aware of what they offer to bring about your ideal. Your lesson is to release the need for others' approval in order to determine what is valuable to you in other people.

Having a sense of your own worth puts you in touch with your value systems. At the same time, doing what *you* feel is worthwhile and needs to be done automatically enhances self-worth. Then you have something to offer other people, and the relationship with them automatically begins to meet the idealism you want. As a by-product, others give unexpected approval without your consciously seeking it.

Getting in touch with the spontaneity of your own inner child enables you to express yourself in ways that invite others to play with you. Performing those values that keep you feeling a sense of fun about life keeps you in touch with your own vitality and worth.

As you inspire confidence in others and encourage them to express their talents and abilities, you see them furthering your ideals of brotherhood whether or not they are aware of it. In this process you can create the many loving friendships you want, and experience the fulfillment of seeing your own humanitarian ideals and values being actualized.

Past Lives
Past lives spent in communal living situations (harems, monasteries, orphanages, etc.) have given you self-awareness in the context of group situations, so your emotional stability tends to be dependent upon maintaining mental accord and harmony with those around you. You may compromise your own individuality in order to keep the peace with others since you fear you may need to count on these friendships at a later date for survival. Past life group involvement has made you too dependent on your peers for support, to the extent that you may concentrate on friendships to the exclusion of more intimate involvements.

One lesson you are learning in this incarnation is to make yourself strong. By becoming more aware of what it is that you want and then exercising your creative power to bring about the fulfillment of these wants, you revitalize your past life attachment to disassociation and get reinvolved in life in a healthy way. You are learning to take hold and enjoy the creative process by using the tools of excitement, romance, and playfulness to enlist others to follow your lead in creating mutual goals that are for the common good.

Since there has been a lack of wholehearted personal love and a sense of impersonalness from past incarnations, you naturally feel insecure about entering into a deeply personal relatedness. You are learning to infuse your more personal, intense relationships with humane treatment of the other person to create closeness while working for the common good.

From your past life experiences you have an inborn sense of what is for the good of the whole and a natural predisposition for doing what is best for others. Yours can be the highest form of friendship. You are learning to combine this awareness with a realization of what *you* want to create in the relationship, and then to joyously go about creating a structure that encompasses the needs of both people.

You are learning to create what you want, giving attention to those relationships that are important to you and carefully monitoring the situation to see that it is still headed in the direction of your goals. Having a goal in your relationships is important; its creation and attainment validates your effective participation. You need to learn that giving attention to a relationship makes it thrive, while withdrawing attention allows it to wither. Then the other person will go somewhere else, looking for involvement that is more constant.

Your natural humor allows you to take the more selfish foibles and perspectives of others in stride, and this serves as a safety valve in the event that your experimentation with close personal involvement occasionally goes awry.

MOON IN PISCES

Static
When you habitually seek the behavior of others to automatically validate your concept of universal perfection, you may refuse to see life as it exists. Living in your vision of universal perfection on Earth, you can unknowingly lose yourself in ivory tower beliefs. These beliefs prevent you from *listening* to people and seeing them in a realistic and unpredictable way.

When others fail to live up to your Pisces vision of their perfection, you might feel personally betrayed. By seeking a higher perspective to make them or yourself wrong, you may create self-isolation in the process. This constant disappointment brought on by others violating your expectations results in self-invalidation, confusion, and an inability to cope in relationships.

Dynamic
When you take responsibility for imparting your vision of other people's perfection, you may notice that past methods of theoretical communications have simply not worked. The truth is that

others cannot provide the perfection you seek. They are preoccupied with thinking about their own imperfection. Your lesson is to heal the negative thoughts of others so that there is room for the positive solutions within them to come forth. Then they are able to alter their behavior and align themselves with their inward perfection.

You can heal negative beliefs by noticing the *reality* of other points of view. You need to realize that a person's perspective in a given situation automatically dictates behavior. When you first choose to sacrifice the idea of expecting others to be perfect and spontaneously accept your answers, you are able to truly listen to their logic about their problems and reasons for lack of perfection. When you recognize that individuals want only to share their disturbances with you so that they can be healed, you might feel encouraged to listen to what they are saying.

You can heal others instantly when you listen to their opinions and negativity from a silent perspective of: "Yes, now you are telling me what it is that makes you suffer."

Misunderstandings are cleared up when you question the other person and compassionately seek to understand that person's point of view. You can relate on an equal and sharing level when you encompass the point of view and thoughts behind the other person's action. By opening this door you experience the unconditional love you seek.

As you create a positive atmosphere you reassure individuals with your trust in the perfection of things as they are. You can supply a larger picture of the appropriateness of their specific process. When your perceptive powers are used to discern where another is feeling a lack of self-perfection, you can contribute the communication that promotes the faith and self-acceptance. In this process you validate your vision and are also healed.

Past Lives
Past lives spent in monasteries or convents, or otherwise shut away from society, have left you with an idealistic and naive approach to life. You seem to float through the harsh realities of daily routine, smelling only the flowers along the way. Deep disappointments can result when the world does not live up to your idealistic standards of humane behavior, but before too long you pick yourself up and put on your rose-colored glasses again.

These past life monastic experiences have lead to certain material dependencies that you feel are necessary to maintain your healing spiritual consciousness. You are used to having others take care of you, cook for you, and set your daily routine. In the monastery, for example, someone rang the gong, signaling when you should get up, when you should go to church or temple, when you should eat, and so forth. Consequently, you have never developed self-discipline, which is a task for this lifetime; you are learning to accept these responsibilities and to "ring your own gong."

You are accustomed to living in a timeless reality, but in this lifetime you need to learn the practical value of infusing celestial reality into daily life by sticking to a routine and by paying attention to being on time. These factors can make your life strong and give you confidence in relating your spiritual consciousness effectively to daily living.

You are also learning to pay attention to diet and health. In other lifetimes you were not responsible for your own nutritional well-being. In this life you are learning to discriminate and to ingest those foods that give the body a feeling of balanced strength, which allows your spiritual consciousness to flow without interruption.

In past lives the reaching of material goals was discouraged because you were learning to trust the universe completely and to merge yourself with total reliance on the universal flow. This patterning was overdone, however, and has led to a certain stagnation in the current incarnation. It is only by learning to apply your sense of faith and unconditional love in daily life that your bliss feelings can be regenerated. Again, focusing on your clearly defined goals and applying the necessary discipline are necessary.

In this incarnation you will be paying society back for the many lifetimes where its institutions have supported your enlightenment by taking care of your material needs. It is time for you to use the fruits of your spiritual practices—unconditional love, the ability to heal, your vision of loveliness—to freely and effectively work for the good of those in your circle of influence.

This is a serve-or-suffer lifetime. You can choose either to actively and constructively serve society or to suffer behind the private walls of feeling misunderstood and walked on by the world. When you have taken responsibility for setting up the necessary structures in your life, this will act as a support system through which universal emotional energies can flow in a balanced way.

Then you will be on the path to emotional fulfillment in this lifetime.

MOON IN THE HOUSES

1st: Emotional security can be gained by the honest, forthright expression of feelings and through the willingness to express emotions on the surface.

2nd: Emotional security can be gained through the establishment of concrete material values and through acquiring and building a secure material structure.

3rd: Emotional security can be gained by communicating changeable conscious thought processes and through teaching and writing.

4th: Emotional security can be gained by nourishing others with your sensitive, personal feelings and through a secure family environment.

5th: Emotional security can be gained by using your dramatic expression of personal feelings in ways that inspire others and by being able to dramatize the self through creative efforts.

6th: Emotional security can be gained by becoming involved in serving others in practical ways that express your sense of obligation and duty, and by being of service to others on a material level.

7th: Emotional security can be gained through uniting with another in partnership situations (including marriage), and through involving yourself in a social interaction with other people and establishing partnerships out of those situations.

8th: Emotional security can be gained by establishing a psychological, material, or emotional bond with someone else and by experiencing others on deep emotional levels that lead to psychological realignment of the self-image.

9th: Emotional security can be gained through sharing lofty, philosophical thoughts with other people and through teaching, traveling, and involving yourself in experiences that expand the self to new horizons.

10th: Emotional security can be gained by involving yourself in public activity that will bring personal recognition and a position of authority, and by acquiring positions of authority where you can organize others.

11th: Emotional security can be gained through involving yourself in group or friendship activities that allow for the expression of personal feelings and ideals, and through participating in a wide range of impersonal interactions and group activities that are geared toward humanitarian goals.

12th: Emotional security can be gained through identifying with ideals and esoteric visions that are beyond the realm of material existence and through interacting in a way that you feel is being of spiritual service to others through universal compassion and healing vision.

Mercury

MERCURY: KEY TO REWARDING COMMUNICATION

Mercury in the Birthchart:

· Signifies your talent for verbal communication with others.

· Indicates the fear may unconsciously keep you from being yourself and telling the truth.

· Illuminates the motives that cause you to withhold yourself verbally, which inevitably causes misunderstandings with others.

· Displays the process by which you may create endless mental worries and negative expectations that lead to isolating and withholding yourself from true contact with others out of fear.

· Shows the way to communicate in a manner that inspires a sense of affinity and mutual sharing with other people.

· Reveals the type of mental connection with others that can bring about a true sharing of information resulting in mutual understanding and expansion.

· Defines the nature of your mental talents and intellectual approach.

· Signifies the area upon which you can focus mental attention so that communcation becomes a vehicle leading to the satisfaction of being completely understood by others.

MERCURY IN ARIES

Static
When you fear losing the visible impact of direct and authoritative communication, you cease to communicate successfully with others. You may have a tendency to speak in ways that appear aggressive, overbearing, and almost militant in expression. This challenging, intimidating attitude toward the audience can result in alienation and misunderstanding.

Dynamic
When your attention is on communicating in a way that inspires others to act, your natural sense of combat is turned into a creative, stimulating interaction. By focusing on inspiring others you are able to express yourself in ways that awaken them to new perceptions of their immediate circumstances. By becoming aware of their reactions you can know in advance the impact your communication will have. This awareness of the other person leads to gaining the Aries sense of freedom for assertive expression.

MERCURY IN TAURUS

Static
If you indulge in the Taurus fear of losing tangible support, from a rational point of view this may lead into your repeating ideas and plans. The result can be an overstructured mind that gets tied up in a material or literal level of thought and stifles your creativity. Indulging in the tendency to resist ideas that are not your own can result in excluding others from assisting you in bringing your values into material manifestation.

Dynamic
When you are willing to communicate openly and to acknowledge that the ideas of others can be as valuable as yours, you can discover that these ideas may actually transform and enhance your own. You can decide to use other people's ideas as resources; thus, your own concepts gain acceptance through the resultant transfor-

mation. When you listen to others and communicate those Taurus perceptions of how their ideas can produce tangible results, your sense of self-worth can be increased.

MERCURY IN GEMINI

Static
If you are afraid of losing the ability to connect on a surface level with a variety of people and ideas, your rational mind might become submerged in superficial thinking. This master of trivia can collect bits and pieces of information that may or may not be of any practical value. Indulging in the Gemini tendency to flit from thought to thought may result in a great deal of talking and no true communication.

Dynamic
When your attention is concentrated on any *one* of your many interests, your quick mind, adaptability, and pure logic can bring about clear communication with a variety of people. By focusing, communicating clearly, and reaching a conclusion before moving on, you can cease to be the perpetual student and are able to teach and direct others to various sources of knowledge.

MERCURY IN CANCER

Static
If you are afraid of losing your emotional connections with other people, your rational mind can become dominated almost entirely by Cancerian feelings and emotions. This might result in your communicating with other people in a way that inadvertently forces them to respond with either sympathetic indulgence or overt rejection. Indulging in communications that demand the sympathy of others may expose you to unnecessary rejection.

Dynamic
When your attention focuses on perceiving the sensitivities of others as well as your own, your ability to communicate goes beyond words. You are then able to reach out emotionally, sensitively, and empathetically in ways that are a true reflection of your caring for others.

MERCURY IN LEO

Static

If you are afraid of losing your dramatic impact and the loyalty of others, you might express yourself in ways that appear dictatorial, arrogant, and egotistical. This can result in one-sided communication that inadvertently implies everything you have to say is more important than what anyone else has to say. This unbalanced communication can unintentionally alienate those closest.

Dynamic

By being conscious of the effects you have on others, you may notice that the Leo dramatic ability to communicate can enhance or destroy what you are saying. This talent for communicating with a theatrical impact leaves a lasting impression, for good or ill. When the focus is on conversing with an awareness of shared humanity, you are able to energize the ideas of others with creativity and inspiration. By being aware of your love for others you can instinctively express yourself in a way that inspires loyalty.

MERCURY IN VIRGO

Static

If you indulge in the Virgo tendency to analyze and judge what is right and wrong in yourself and others, you could create endless categories in your mind. Thus, it may become difficult to communicate in an orderly or confident way. This compartmental analysis of right or wrong might appear harsh and inadvertently alienate those close to you. Concurrently, in judging others you can pave the way for heavy self-criticism if you distort perfectionism in any way.

Dynamic.

When you put trust in the universal, unseen order of things, you can cease to be so defensive about the way actions reflect imperfection. Through developing self-tolerance you can accomplish a job with a sense of perfection but without applying the same high standards of performance to your personal life. By detaching from perfectionism, relationships and communications with others can be transformed to a new level. You will not have to be defensive with others since you no longer need to justify your humanness to yourself.

MERCURY IN LIBRA

Static
When you indulge in fears of not saying the right thing and look to others for a reflection of immediate acceptance, communications can stop. By withholding honest interchange for fear of rejection, your mind may bog down in a swamp of considerations that brings indecision. If you withhold disclosing what is actually on your mind, you may lose your perspective, integrity, and perceptual balance.

Dynamic
By focusing attention on your point of view and sharing your independent opinion, you can discover the spontaneous awareness of your impact when communicating with others. Concentrating on what needs to be said rather than on what you think other people want to hear can contribute the justice, truth, and balance required by the situation. You then may discover that you have a natural talent for diplomacy and communication that spontaneously restores harmony without compromising any sense of personal integrity.

MERCURY IN SCORPIO

Static
When you indulge in Scorpio fears of losing power over others by exposing your motives and desires, your communication can become defensive, secretive, and vindictive. Constant inner turmoil may result if you withhold expressing your thoughts, fearing that hidden emotions will be exposed and you might become vulnerable. As a consequence, either anger, impatience, and intimidation can be brought forth or all communication may be withheld, thus alienating other and isolating yourself.

Dynamic
When you focus on manifesting what is valuable to you, your keen perception can penetrate and reveal to others the deeper meaning of their communication. You are able to unveil those powerful

secrets that can transform all concerned. By sharing the Scorpio incisive ability to perceive the heart behind the words, hidden motivations are exposed within their communications. This awareness can make a positive contribution to others and actually increase your insight and sense of self-possession.

MERCURY IN SAGITTARIUS

Static
When you indulge in fears of losing the appearance of intellectual superiority, you may jump to hasty conclusions. The rational mind can become lost in empty theories with no logic or facts for a foundation. These theories may then be unwittingly presented to others in a moralizing manner, from a platform of inflated expressions of pompous self-righteousness.

Dynamic
When your attention is on clearly distinguishing emotionally biased thoughts from factual and logically based thoughts, you can relinquish the Sagittarius tendency of self-righteous mental isolation. You then can communicate your inspired perceptions without any need to prove intellectual superiority. Your ability to uplift others is through opening a *two-way* sharing and communication.

MERCURY IN CAPRICORN

Static
When you indulge in Capricorn fears of losing status by not knowing the answers to everything, you can develop a pretense of being the final intellectual authority in all fields. You may use every opportunity to gather knowledge and impress others, always assuming an authoritarian attitude. This can result in alienation and a breakdown of your credibility with other people. A pretentious manner when speaking may disenchant others, provoking them to withhold information. This can lead to a constant disruption of any attempted communication.

Dynamic
When you focus on the informational needs of others, you can effortlessly share ideas relevant to the situation. When your motive in giving information is to support others, you automatically com-

municate true knowledge and eliminate pretense. Relinquishing the Capricorn need to maintain authority allows others to share the information necessary for further mutual advancement.

You can cease to take yourself so seriously by paying attention to the sensitivities of others. Then you can organize the situation effectively and share authority. This opens the door for others to show appreciation and respect for your abilities.

MERCURY IN AQUARIUS

Static
By indulging in fears of losing mental objectivity, the Aquarius rational mind can become cold and detached from feeling or empathetic intuition. Thus, sensitivity to others in communication may be lost. By immersing yourself in nonjudgmental objectivity, you can inadvertently alienate others with a brittle manner. Fear of losing a detached concept of universal love can bring on abstract and thoughtless retorts to the personal communcations of others. This may keep people at a distance.

Dynamic
When your attention focuses on making personal connection with others, you can become aware of their sensitivities. Recognizing the individuality in others enables you to apply the ideal of universal love. You are able to establish a connection for communication that allows others to share these unique ways of perceiving life. This is done by opening yourself to experience mental empathy with others. You experience ease in getting your point across when your ability for objective communication is tempered by both an awareness of the point of view of others and their emotional sensitivities.

MERCURY IN PISCES

Static
When you indulge in Pisces fears of losing a vision of how perfect the ideal could be, you may sacrifice reality for a private world of fantasy. You may withhold intuitive perceptions for fear of being invalidated by others. Then the ability to communicate clearly becomes muddled and lost in the distractions of your emotional world. When you retreat into your private reality and exclude

interaction with others, you may lose those relevant perceptions that can help to make your thought manifest.

Dynamic
You can focus your attention on the reality of spiritual poverty and confusion that is seen in daily life. This vision inspires you to rise above fears and make a real contribution to others. Communicating your creative and intuitive abilities allows others to enter through into your psychic perceptions. Ideals can become a healing reality in the world when you make a tangible contribution by communicating your intuitive vision.

MERCURY IN THE HOUSES

1st: Conveys a strong ability for verbal expression and a tendency toward flexibility or, in the extreme, to superficiality.

2nd: Discloses the ability to use a natural sense of practical perception and to communicate in ways that bring about tangible results.

3rd: Represents the ability to perceive the thought processes of others and to manipulate their thinking for good or ill.

4th: Reveals the ability to perceive the deepest sensitivities of others and to communicate in a way that acknowledges those sensitivities.

5th: Expresses the ability to perceive the opportunity to dramatically enhance one's communication.

6th: Signifies the ability to analyze separate facts and weave them into a cohesive whole and communicate one's perceptions, either through insensitive petty criticism or through objective analysis.

7th: Describes the ability to perceive the positions of other people and then communicate in a way that reaches them. The choice must be made between communicating the truth about what one is experiencing or telling others what they want to hear.

8th: Illuminates the ability to perceive the motives of others that are hidden in their communication and to communicate in ways that transform other people, for good or ill.

9th: Conveys the ability to perceive and speak from the philosophical, intuitive mind. The choice here is between intim-

idating others through judging them as intellectually inferior or causing the intuition to teach and communicate to
others in a way they can learn.

10th: Denotes the ability to perceive those things that will lead to
control for good or ill and to communicate with authority
before a public audience.

11th: Indicates the ability for objective perception and to communicate in a friendly, impersonal manner that does not
alienate or put others on the defensive.

12th: Reveals the ability to perceive the intangible truth behind
physical occurrences and to communicate that truth to others.

Venus

VENUS: KEY TO PERSONAL SELF-WORTH

Venus in the Birthchart:

· Points out the way that social harmony can enter your personal life.

· Indicates the process by which you may lose confidence and self-
esteem in social situations.

· Reveals the area in which withholding yourself socially results in
feelings of personal inadequacy, while sharing your personal sense of
social expression results in feelings of satisfaction and self-worth.

· Illuminates the process through which you unconsciously prevent
self-esteem by not sharing fully in social situations, and the area in
which you may suppress natural gifts for fear of being rejected or of
receiving negative reactions from others.

· Signifies the area where you may relinquish inner pleasure in order to
live up to the values of others.

- Shows your natural talent for experiencing and expressing pleasure that can be shared with others in the spirit of harmonious interaction.
- Defines your natural gift for putting other people at ease in social situations, contributing to an atmosphere of open sharing through contributing your own brand of warmth.
- Denotes the specific key to building a sense of personal self-worth and establishing a firm sense of your value to others and to social situations.
- Expresses the receiving, rather than initiating, sexual principle and reveals those personal values that give you pleasure.

VENUS IN ARIES

Static

If you value aggressive independence in relationships, you might without knowing it relate to others thoughtlessly and forcefully. Thus, you may experience an endless series of temporary alliances. In attempting to prove the Aries self-worth by disregarding the values of others, you may ultimately win the conquest yet end up alone.

Consequently, a reluctance to sustain closeness often results in a lack of confidence in your worth and ability to relate to others. When you withhold your ability for positive leadership in social situations, it may lead to a competitive viewpoint that is destructive for all concerned.

Dynamic

You possess the ability to take the initiative in social situations. You can be a spontaneous leader. With the natural Aries gifts of enthusiasm and courage you inspire others to contribute to the group.

You can realize your inherent value when you share your independence in a manner that helps others to help themselves. This encourages others to actualize their potential for self-sufficiency. You can become aware that others feel insecure about their sense of self-reliance. This awareness enables you to motivate them to believe in themselves and assert their individuality. As you help others to build their own independence, you simultaneously come to a realization of your true worth.

Combining your talent for seizing leadership with the recognition of other people's feelings can lead to a sense of confidence in your ability to stimulate others to interact socially. This situation maintains your independence and validates the worth of all concerned.

VENUS IN TAURUS

Static
If you place an obsessive value on comfort in social situations, it may result in withholding possessions from others. This deprives you both of the benefits of sharing your Taurus talents for accumulating material things. Repressing the obligation to share your belongings leads to a lack of confidence in your ability to acquire more material goods for yourself.

At certain times you might hold back your special sensitivities to the tactile sensual part of life due to feeling unable to share them. This may result in a lack of enjoyment in relations with others.

Dynamic
You can take the initiative to share both your material possessions and your ability for the organization and accumulation of goods. Initiative well taken leads to the stabilizing effect of reflected merit. Additionally, you gain a feeling of social worth and material security in your life by verbally sharing value systems that have brought you stability.

As you become aware of other people's psychological insecurities concerning their own importance, you are able to validate them. Consequently, the realization of your true benefit to others can emerge. When you share your gift of sensual sensitivity to life through a form of sensual contact with others, you experience the pleasure and satisfaction of physically extending yourself to add comfort to the social environment.

VENUS IN GEMINI

Static
By placing an obsessive value on quick wit in social situations, you may unknowingly withhold from others your special ability for adding lightness and open communication. When you neglect listening to others' ideas, you might feel a distinct lack of confidence in communicating with them at all. Indulging in flightiness in

social relationships may result in a feeling of lack of worth in yourself or others.

When you use your talent for communication to manipulate, to deceive, or to create a superficial excitement with glib wit, you may experience a lack of your own sense of value. In trying to look good to others, you might get caught up in superficiality. This type of communication leads to feelings of insecurity and to being at the mercy of how others see you.

Dynamic

When you are willing to share the Gemini natural gift of light-heartedness, you cheer others. The ability to listen to other points of view strengthens your capacity to contribute an appropriate optimistic insight to any social situation. Your talent for stimulating, elevating conversation can result in your experiencing a deep sense of your social self-worth.

When you see the larger picture of others' viewpoints, you can communicate in such a way that their burdens are lightened. This leads to feeling a reaction of zest and satisfaction. You establish a firm sense of self-worth and confidence in social situations by expressing cheerfulness and lightness to uplift others.

VENUS IN CANCER

Static

If you place an obsessive value on your sensitivity and self-protection in social situations, you may unwittingly indulge your feelings of isolation. Through self-absorption you might withhold the Cancerian ability to empathize with others on deep, personal levels for fear that such caring may be rejected. Feelings of inadequacy and withdrawal in relationships may result.

You may tend to cling to private pictures of how people should respond so that your feelings won't be hurt and you'll feel worthwhile. This process may lead to experiencing others as being abrasive and unsympathetic to your subjective personal needs.

If you seek to manipulate others' emotions to gain attention and caring, you may unknowingly hold back the Cancerian ability to care for and nourish others. This behavior results in social isolation and deep feelings of inadequacy.

Dynamic

Through the willingness to share your gift of sensitivity you can develop a sense of other people's situations. You can assist them by sharing the wealth of your Cancerian loving emotional nature. In the process of extending empathy to help others overcome their emotional hurt, you can realize a deep sense of social worth. When this ability to put people in touch with their sensitivities is brought forth, you are appreciated for your value in the world.

You experience an unshakable sense of self-worth when you encourage others to communicate their feelings and respond to those feelings with your usual sensitivity. When you give others confidence in their capabilities to achieve what they want, you confirm your usefulness and value. Emotional nourishment and security in all social relations become yours when love is freely given to others and nothing is expected in return.

VENUS IN LEO

Static

If you obsessively seek the approval of others in social situations, the fear of disapproval may result in holding back your ability to spread sunshine and light. You might feel trapped in self-absorption when you withhold your ability to inspire others with your warm and gregarious nature.

You may censor yourself by expressing a type of spontaneity you feel will be "approved of." If you indulge in the Leo fear that others may hold back their love, ignore you, or judge you harshly, you experience a lack of social ease.

Inadvertently, you might manipulate others by moderating your expressiveness in order to gain recognition. Social isolation and powerlessness ensue when you interpret others' reactions as a personal rejection.

Dynamic

When you are willing to share your natural gift for drama with others, you can pay attention to their needs for acceptance and respond by supporting them with your warmth. You may find that in taking the initiative to include others you are automatically included as part of the group. You can use your charismatic dramatic flair to share the center of the stage. By recognizing others' individuality you can provide emotional upliftment, enabling them to overcome disabling emotions and the monotony of daily life.

You are sensitive to the inner reactions of others, and by using this knowledge objectively you lift the audience to new heights of inspired experience. You can bring about ease of communication through your inclusive "open arms" policy in which each person is able to relate comfortably with others.

When you use your generosity and sensitivity to help others reach positive emotional states, you can experience, without fear, your own social worth. You have a dramatic talent for inspiring others and an inbred confidence, warmth, and enthusiasm that bring about self-worth. Security with others comes from knowing that you have acted according to your humanitarian ideals.

VENUS IN VIRGO

Static
If you obsessively value being right in social interactions, you may unknowingly use relationships in a way that is self-serving rather than serving others. Thus, you might become frustrated in having relationships fall short of your high standards. You may engage in the Virgo tendency to discriminate against and criticize others, and then try to hide your biases in order to prevent alienation. This indulgence might result in feelings of isolation that come from silent separative judgments.

If you give into fears that your service may not be accepted by others, that you are unworthy to serve others, or that you might be criticized, the result is a disintegration of the Virgo ability to make practical use of relationships. You may withhold your gift for unselfish service and instead seek to serve in a way that you think will elicit a particular response. This withholding may result in feelings of inadequacy and lack of self-worth.

Dynamic
You have a natural gift for serving others in practical ways that are compatible with your ideals. When you serve others according to these high standards, you experience the satisfaction of relating in a way that is consistent with your integrity.

By sharing your understanding of order and discrimination, adjusting relationships in such a way that the whole is served, you can experience a heightened sense of self-worth.

When you overcome the Virgo fear that your service to others may not be accepted, you can trust your inner feelings and the higher order that you see. Then you can experience the perfection inherent in being and sharing yourself. In knowing that you have been useful to others, you feel a deep sense of enduring personal worth.

VENUS IN LIBRA

Static
If you value harmony in social situations, regardless of the cost, you may withhold your opinions and sense of justice. You may gain a false sense of harmony with others when in effect you are constantly at the mercy of their approval.

When you withhold the Libra qualities for creating harmony and instead seek to appease others by telling them what you think they want to hear (according to *their* sense of fair play), your manipulations may inadvertently create chaos. Inevitably, such chaos leads to feelings of self-doubt and worthlessness.

In situations of conflict, if you fear that the solution you envision may not be followed or accepted, then you may withhold an honest sharing of yourself for the sake of harmony. This can lead to confusion and helplessness in your relationships.

Dynamic
When you are willing to risk losing your role of Mr. or Ms. Nice Person in social situations, you can choose to share the injustices that you feel as well as the fair solution that you see. In so doing, your courage can pave the way for a higher, fairer order to take place. By asserting integrity and openly sharing your insights you can come to appreciate and value yourself in your relationships.

When you state your independent value system, your sense of balance and harmony is acknowledged. This can give you a feeling of self-worth. Declaring your innate perception of fair play to others (and risking the threat of possible disharmony in order to reach a greater harmony) results in experiencing inner satisfaction from sharing your fine Libra gifts of social organization.

By taking the initiative to create harmony that is in *alignment* with the integrity of your inner sense of justice and fair play, you can experience a firm, consistent sense of self-worth.

VENUS IN SCORPIO

Static
By placing an obsessive value on controlling your power in social situations you might withhold sharing your abilities to perceive

the hidden talents and resources of other people. You may have a tendency to use others as a means of fulfilling your desires. As a result you may experience tension from constantly trying to maintain secret control of those around you, thus being the one who is actually controlled by your fear that others may withdraw their resources.

When you ignore bringing others to an awareness of their talents and abilities, stagnation and rigidity may result from your incomplete interaction with the material world.

When rigid personal values are formed, the result might be lost opportunity for interacting with others. In neglecting to stimulate self-worth in other people, you may lose your own feeling of worth.

Dynamic

You have the aptitude and awareness to perceive and encourage the undiscovered abilities of others. You can inspire them to use their assets and potentials. When you bring out other people's talents in such a way that you both benefit, you can experience a transformation of your values and material opportunities.

You experience a continual dynamic transformation of your feelings of self-worth when you take the initiative to draw others into awakening their latent talents, thus showing them their hidden worth. The more you arouse and enhance the power of others in social situations, the more valuable you become to them and the more worthwhile you feel about yourself.

VENUS IN SAGITTARIUS

Static

You might obsessively value the personal freedom you gain from the power of your philosophical perspectives in relationships. This may lead to withholding your special ability for providing inspiration to other people. When you indulge in the fear of being limited by relating to others on deep, personal levels, you may become the person who's always "out of town"—never really there for anybody, including yourself.

If you allow tension and fear of commitment to block you from any relationship, you might experience a haunting sense of rootlessness. This results in a curiously empty feeling when you are thrust into unexpected situations. If you are content with fickle infatuations and careless involvements, you may eventually sink into low self-esteem. Your sense of values can be eroded if you neglect to establish worthwhile goals in partnerships.

Dynamic
You have a special gift for being able to teach others true freedom in relationships. You can do this by allowing the dynamics of the relationship to guide it to its own goals. Imparting your trust and optimism to others allows you to share with them a larger perspective of the situation. Thus, you can experience a constant expansion and excitement in your alliances.

This process of conveying trust can enable you to focus on a few deeper yet more rewarding partnerships. When you are in touch with the psychological processes of other people, you can experience a continual sense of self-worth by inspiring and encouraging them to lofty goals that free them from the limitation of old beliefs.

VENUS IN CAPRICORN

Static
You might place too much value on your projection to others of being absolutely on top of everything. This may stifle your special ability to exemplify and share awareness of social appropriateness. If you neglect demonstrating such knowledge, you may feel self-doubt and lack of control when others reflect your ineptitude.

When relationships are used for the purpose of ensuring your social position, people can become mere objects on the way toward your prestigious or sensual ends. Thus, the spirit of true relationships may be lost in pursuit of materialism that eventually leaves you alone with only your tangible assets for company.

You might deny your special ability to achieve material success in every area of your life because of giving in to fears of social rejection if you fail. This may lead to feeling sorry for yourself. You might lose your sense of self-worth if your values are not accepted and praised by others and are not reflected through material success.

Dynamic
You possess the ability to demonstrate social appropriateness as a means toward attaining a desired social position. You can express your unique gifts by sharing your perception and encouraging oth-

ers to execute their intentions in a practical way. This produces a result that brings you a solid sense of your own worth.

You have the ability to use the social and material values of others for your own goals. Thus, in attaining material success you set an example and demonstrate your awareness of social values. This assists others in tangibly expressing their talents and intentions at the highest level of public acceptance.

You are able to establish a firm, reliable sense of self-worth when you share with others your understanding of how to manipulate the material world toward one's intended ends. Above all, you become an inspirational example when you demonstrate your natural knowledge of social suitability, utilizing those standards in a creative way to produce the desired results.

VENUS IN AQUARIUS

Static
You might withhold your gift of objective understanding and loving acceptance because of a desire to create more excitement. If so, you may experience a series of shallow, chaotic, and scattered encounters. You might use the pretext of universal love for mankind as an excuse for neglecting to establish personal relationships. Eventually, you may undergo the haunting realization that this detachment is simply feeling an inability and unwillingness to relate to anyone on a personal level.

Dynamic
You experience the joy and exhilaration of coming into contact with others when you are willing to share openly your unique gift of loving in an impartial way. No matter how intimate or personal a relationship may be, you have the ability to retain your sense of individual freedom.

If you do not abuse your freedom through eccentric behavior in an attempt to guarantee your independence, you can attract people who are willing to be your equal. In doing so you eliminate the possibility of your dependency through their independence. A firm sense of your self-worth can be established when you allow a deep personal pledge to develop within your intimate relationship.

VENUS IN PISCES

Static
You might lose your sense of self-worth if you withhold sharing your compassion with others. Fears of inadequacy may suppress potential psychic healing ability. The result may be a feeling of helplessness to alleviate the discomforts that affect others.

When you allow other people to take advantage of your gentle, sympathetic manner and you absorb their ills, you might experience a depletion of energy. Indiscriminately indulging in the Pisces romantic ideal of serving and helping others may diminish your self-worth.

Dynamic
You have a natural gift for relating to others on the level of unconditional love. Your compassion can overcome any social disharmony that arises.

When you see beyond the rules and regulations to the spiritual *purpose* of relationships, your compassionate understanding and willingness to fully participate can automatically heal the situation. You are able to establish a firm sense of self-worth through sharing with others your ability to respond with compassion to both the seen and unseen sources of disharmony.

VENUS IN THE HOUSES

1st: Self-worth can be found by using one's personality as a vehicle for expressing love to others. This position indicates a *need* to be liked by all or the special *ability* to personally express love of others.

2nd: Self-worth can be obtained by using one's personal resources in the world; by utilizing the ability to organize the material world in such a way that optimum comfort along with an awareness of artistic value is created.

3rd: Self-worth can be obtained by communicating, learning, and teaching a variety of people in ways that add lightness to all; by utilizing one's ability for diplomatic communication with an awareness of opposing points of view.

4th: Self-worth can be obtained by using personal resources to build a firm foundation for those closest; by integrating one's social life with the home environment.

5th: Self-worth can be obtained through using one's creative talents as a vehicle for self-expression; through initiating and utilizing the special ability to enjoy and enhance any social situation.

6th: Self-worth can be obtained through being of practical service to others; through enjoying one's duties and facilitating a harmonious working environment.

7th: Self-worth can be obtained through the generous sharing of one's personal resources and affections with a partner; through exercising the abiliy to be tolerant and tactful with people, always giving them the benefit of the doubt.

8th: Self-worth can be obtained through merging resources with other people on deep sexual or material levels; through utilizing one's ability to connect harmoniously with other people on psychic levels.

9th: Self-worth can be obtained by inspiring others through sharing philosophical insights; through exercising the ability to teach others, assisting them to undestand philosophical or theoretical ideas.

10th: Self-worth can be obtained through using personal resources to achieve public goals in the world to produce a result; through utilizing one's ability to move toward goals while maintaining a sensitivity to social circumstances and social values.

11th: Self-worth can be obtained by sharing personal resources in group situations; through exercising the ability to initiate and bring harmony into one's friendships and groups.

12th: Self-worth can be obtained by sharing the experience of spiritual love and order. The gift of tolerance allows people to be where they are. This position reveals the *need* to be understood by all or the *ability* to be understanding of the actions of others.

Mars

MARS: KEY TO PERSONAL ASSERTIVENESS

Mars in the Birthchart:

· Depicts the nature of your unique skill in taking the initiative; shows the key to successful and effective personal assertion and leadership.

· Reveals the process by which you may unintentionally separate yourself and alienate others.

· Displays a specific method for constructive self-assertion that can be accepted by others and encourages a creative and satisfying interaction with them.

· Defines the power of a specific individual commitment that can inspire productive self-assertion.

· Indicates the initiating, rather than receiving, sexual principle and reveals the desire that motivates you to act.

· Denotes the area in which self-assertion leads to joyous independence and renewed physical energy.

MARS IN ARIES

Static
You may have a tendency to alienate others by aggressively refusing to accept demands placed upon you. By acting on the Aries premise that "everyone looks out for himself," your behavior may appear rash, abrasive in exaggerated independence, and inconsiderate to others. You can lose energy and acceptance by fiercely maintaining your right to absolute independence.

Dynamic
You can constructively interact by using independence in ways that inspire others to take the initiative. As you view your impact

on them objectively, you can naturally assert your courage and initiative in ways that lead to freedom for all concerned. You can gain physical energy by considering the other person and giving that person confidence in his or her ability to follow destiny.

MARS IN TAURUS

Static
You may have a tendency to alienate others by judging or ignoring their values in order to confirm your own sense of self-worth. This mental competitiveness may bring about defeat by cutting off others on a material or sensual level. You can lose the energy needed to establish your worth if you refuse to allow the experience of others to be incorporated into a rigid Taurean value system.

Dynamic
You can constructively interact with others by allowing them to contribute their ideas and values in a way that is supportive in manifesting material results. When you commit yourself to participating actively in the world, a solid foundation for material security can be established. Your values can be transformed and translated into greater material and sensual results by viewing others as *your* resources.

MARS IN GEMINI

Static
You may have a tendency to alienate others by aggressively using sharp logic to prove that you have the fastest mind. This is often done in a competitive manner at the expense of others. If you confront and provoke in a verbal, combative way, you may create shallow and meaningless mental skirmishes. You can lose energy by inflicting incisive, passionate logic, proving personal points that win the battle but lose the war.

Dynamic
You can be constructively assertive with others by directing mental energies to a wider perspective than yourself. As you accept the larger outlook of others' views, you are able to brilliantly translate information intuitively received. Your communication can become a sharing experience rather than a pointless battle of wits when

you welcome and adjust your thinking to include the knowledge of others. Your energy increases in direct proportion to responsible communication.

MARS IN CANCER

Static
You have a tendency to alienate others by competing with them for fulfillment of emotional needs. You may aggressively demand attention and assume that the needs of others are a threat to your security. When others don't give you the support and attention you think you need, you can lose energy by using the Cancerian emotional touchiness to reject them.

Dynamic
You can be constructively assertive with others by using sensitivity to become aware of other's needs as well as your own. When you are willing to set aside self-centeredness and adopt a position of responsibility, you can acknowledge the feelings of others as well as express your own needs positively. You can gain energy when you commit yourself to initiating closeness and objectively organizing situations in which everyone's needs can be met.

MARS IN LEO

Static
You may have a tendency to alienate others by asserting in ways that make you appear larger than life. If you compete for center stage in order to ensure that you will be acknowledged, you may, as a consequence, sacrifice leadership. You can lose energy by indulging in the Leo dramatic demonstrations of authority over others and by pressing to get your way regardless of their feelings.

Dynamic
You can constructively assert leadership by using the power of dramatic emotional expression to inspire and encourage others in their self-expression. Acting on a commitment to inspire others through your enthusiasm can reinforce your sense of independence. Your energies increase in direct proportion to your willingness to unite with others.

MARS IN VIRGO

Static
You may have a tendency to alienate others by taking what they do or say too personally and then aggressively demanding to be acknowledged as right all the time. Consequently, you may seek to prove the Virgo rightness by making others wrong. When your own or the actions of others fall short of your standards, you can be quick to criticize and judge. By focusing on errors you may lose your momentum.

Dynamic
You can constructively assert yourself by taking the initiative in assisting others to straighten out their lives. Acting on your commitment to serve effectively, you might allow yourself to share responsibility and overcome the need to be right about everything, as well as the feeling that you have to do others' work for them. You can develop practical methods that aid others in achieving their ideals of perfection. Through humanely applying your passionate sense of order to chaotic situations in a tolerant way, you can experience satisfaction and a new sense of system. Your energy is increased in the process of initiating these changes.

MARS IN LIBRA

Static
You may have a tendency to alienate others by manipulating their responses in an aggressive way that produces false harmony. You may demand the Libra version of harmony by behaving as you think others want you to and expecting them to act as you want them to in exchange. You may subtly compete with others to see who can be the most harmonious person and thus victimize yourself by continually demanding that others act fairly. You can lose energy by holding others responsible for creating justice and co-operation in your world, and when disruption occurs, blaming them for the disharmony.

Dynamic
You can assert yourself constructively by actively, responsibly, and directly initiating social interaction on the basis of personal integrity. When you ask others what it is they want from the relation-

ship and honestly share what it is you want, you are then able to create harmony based on truth. Thus, you can gain energy by experiencing yourself as the source of harmony or disharmony in your interactions.

MARS IN SCORPIO

Static
You may have a tendency to alienate others by competing for power over your environment. Consequently, you can lose energy if you suppress your desires and motives in order to maintain control. The Scorpio secretiveness in taking action may cause others to mistrust you and thus set the stage for explosive confrontations.

Dynamic
You can assert leadership constructively by committing yourself to responsible expression of motives and intentions. When you reveal your desires, others will know and trust your leadership and ability to use existing circumstances to transform a stagnant situation. You can gain energy in exposing your motives to others and thus free yourself to act.

MARS IN SAGITTARIUS

Static
You may have a tendency to alienate others by competitively pitting your philosophical understanding against another's intelligence. You can inadvertently imply that the beliefs of others are based on inferior understanding and intellectual ability. You may lose energy for expanded insights by using the power of the Sagittarius intellect to intimidate others with demonstrations of self-righteousness.

Dynamic
You can assert a powerful intellect by inspiring others to attain their intellectual heights. When you are willing to learn as well as teach, you can accept the views of others and incorporate their ideas with yours. Taking the time to understand another's point of view first allows you to establish a line of communication. You can gain energy by acknowledging the intellectual contributions

of others and actively inspiring them to reach out and expand their
goals and ideals.

MARS IN CAPRICORN

Static
You may have a tendency to alienate others by competitively pitting the Capricorn need for maintaining a social image against the
well-being of others. When you regard social prestige as a means
of self-justification, you can treat yourself and others as objects to
be used in fulfilling your ambitions. In adopting austerity to
achieve your aims, you may lose energy by cutting off your feelings
and emotions.

Dynamic
You can assert leadership by sharing a sense of organization and
social protocol. By encouraging others to accomplish their ambitions you can relieve the tension brought on by the need to justify
yourself. When you share the natural Capricorn ability for organizational leadership, you can experience the more personal rewards of career accomplishment. Your energy can be increased by
establishing social prestige for an organization that is bigger than
yourself.

MARS IN AQUARIUS

Static
You may tend to alienate others by asserting that the Aquarian
ability to expres and achieve humanitarian ideals is exclusive. As
a result you may think you need to become coldly dispassionate
toward others in order to act freely on these ideals. Thus, you can
inadvertently estrange yourself from those who might participate
in group effort. You may lose energy by cutting yourself off from
the dynamics of the group consciousness.

Dynamic
You can assert for the group ideals rather than using the group to
support personal plans or models. When you are able to identify
yourself as part of the group rather than separate, you can implement the Aquarian humanitarian ideals for human beings. You

can gain energy by inspiring yourself and others in the group to grow toward and manifest these ideals.

MARS IN PISCES

Static
You may alienate others by assuming that you are the only one who sees the true spiritual vision. Consequently, by operating from a belief in the Piscean spiritual superiority, you can camouflage your motives and desires and negate the input of others. In withholding yourself from direct involvement you can lose the vitality of your direction and become confused. This may result in a scattering of your personal energies.

Dynamic
You can assert yourself by communicating openly about problems that exist in the personal life. As you share spiritual solutions to practical problems and allow others to share their insights also, everyone benefits from an expanded spiritual awareness. You can gain energy from practical service and a revitalizing sense of faith in your vision when you allow open and direct interaction with others.

MARS IN THE HOUSES

1st: Denotes that the egocentric ability for assertion is connected to an expressive and impulsive personality.

2nd: Reveals that the egocentric drive to accomplish is connected to a need for material things and the ability to attain them.

3rd: Indicates that the egocentric ability for assertion is connected to logic and the talent for clear communication.

4th: Discloses that ego assertiveness is connected to one's sensitivity and the ability to express personal feelings.

5th: Pinpoints that the egocentric drive to accomplish is connected to the ability for artistic, dramatic, and creative expression.

6th: Indicates that ego assertiveness is connected with a sense of duty and self-perfection. It is the ability to attain a sense of self-perfection by taking the initiative in actively serving others.

7th: Expresses that ego assertion is connected to the reactions of others. It is the ability to initiate activity with other people.

8th: Signifies that the egocentric drive to accomplish is activated by one's material connections with others in the areas of sex, money, and shared resources.

9th: Expresses that ego assertiveness is connected to the theoretical mind and intellectual accomplishments as recognized by society.

10th: Pinpoints that the egocentric drive to accomplish is connected to positions of authority and how those positions enhance one's personal position.

11th: Denotes that the egocentric ability for assertion is connected to humanitarian goals or ideals, and impersonal or group relationships.

12th: Illuminates that the egocentric drive to accomplish is connected to one's private dream and to manifesting universal urges and visions.

Jupiter

JUPITER: KEY TO SOCIAL OPPORTUNITY AND REWARD

Jupiter in the Birthchart:

· Defines the means of building trust and faith in yourself and, consequently, in others.

· Represents that key of understanding by which you can independently and actively create value and personal growth out of any circumstances that life presents.

- Reveals where you naturally see the larger perspective, which leads to a sense of faith in life and confidence in yourself.
- Shows how trust can be cultivated—faith in yourself and in your ability to handle any unfamiliar or unexpected circumstance that may occur—by taking a more philosophical view of life.
- Pinpoints the perspective that can free you to act in a way that automatically leads to joy through utilizing social opportunity for personal expansion.
- Denotes an area of natural good fortune that, when activated, overcomes feelings of limitation and fear.
- Illuminates that area of life where your perspective teaches faith in an ordered universe behind chaotic appearances and locates the source of trust that can be tapped and developed within each individual.

JUPITER IN ARIES

Static
Whenever you delay taking the initiative to go your own way, fears of inadequacy arise that may block your actions. If you succumb to a lack of faith in your independence, you may unwittingly neglect the social opportunity for leadership and, as a result, feel a deep sense of frustration. By indulging in distrust and not following the Aries sense of immediate and personal expression, you may fail to reach beyond the state of survival and into creativity.

Dynamic
If you take the leap of faith and wholeheartedly express confidence, vision, and a sense of opportunity, you can feel the joy of uncompromised self-expression. You can build trust in others by taking the initiative to pioneer activities that naturally attract and enlist other people. By trusting yourself you can appreciate the value of independence and thus expand your field of leadership and opportunity for initiating new enterprises.

JUPITER IN TAURUS

Static
Failure to use current and nearby resources to their greatest potential can result in a lack of confidence in one's ability to ensure a stable financial base. Such rigid values may bring about the disap-

pointment of achieving less materially than what you knew were potentially able to achieve.

Dynamic
When you take the leap of faith and invest yourself in the potential of what you consider materially valuable, you increase your opportunities to satisfy those values and desires. In trusting yourself to actualize these Taurus ideals, you are supported by many opportunities to accomplish your ends and to fulfill yourself in practical ways.

JUPITER IN GEMINI

Static
If you postpone communicating insights to others, you may experience an endless accumulation of trivial information. When you use your buoyant expressions carelessly as a defense mechanism against other people's unfamiliar points of view, you may undergo a transitory trust in yourself. But this may unwittingly lead to shallow conversations and a frivolous attitude, lessening your chances to better yourself in the world.

Dynamic
When you actively expand your curiosity into dealing with information creatively, you might find answers instead of being stuck in a perpetual question machine. As you take the leap of faith and seek information from others and yourself, trusting that there is an answer and listening for that answer, you can experience truly meaningful communication with others. You can build inner faith by sincerely listening for the right answers to your questions.

JUPITER IN CANCER

Static
If you postpone sharing personal feelings and emotions with other people and fear that they may not empathize with you, you may then lose the opportunity to relate deeply with others. You may unknowingly use the Cancerian emotionally subjective beliefs as a defense mechanism against unfamiliar situations, and you may do so in such a way that the result is self-righteous alienation and a loss of your faith in others as well as yourself.

Dynamic

When you expand your Cancerian ability to make other people feel that they belong to a given social situation, your skill in building a feeling of family in any circumstance can create faith in your basic security instincts. By actively using your talent to bring about a realization in others of their belonging and acceptance, you can build faith and confidence in yourself and everyone around you.

JUPITER IN LEO

Static

If you do not participate joyfully with others because you fear that they might not be loyal to your leadership, you may experience frustration over your eventual failure to obtain this desired position. You can have so much faith in your Leo ego that you may unknowingly act in ways that discount the value of others. As a result you can become bewildered by others' lack of allegiance to your guidance. In the end you may inadvertently alienate others by your dramatic demonstrations of belief in yourself.

Dynamic

You may find that others welcome your generosity when your aim is to be morally or intellectually equal. By taking the leap of faith and acting in the best interests of the situation, you can concentrate on producing beneficial results for all and gain the opportunity for natural leadership. When you trust your ability to give to others, you can actively initiate situations in which you attract those social rewards you most value.

JUPITER IN VIRGO

Static

If you fear never being "perfect enough" to serve, you may postpone and thus lose the opportunity to serve others. This can result in a general lack of self-trust in your abilities. Using analytical talents to find fault with your service may leave you lacking confidence and afraid to contribute. Withholding actual assistance and instead substituting righteous beliefs about service may submerge you in unncessary behavorial details. An exaggerated self-critical attitude can lead to feelings of insufficiency, necessitating constant preparation that is never complete enough to contribute.

Dynamic
If you trust the purity of your motives and are willing to make some mistakes in your desire to serve other people, you can experience the freedom of finding social situations in which you serve and develop yourself. Thus, by taking the leap of faith and consciously putting your desire to assist before your personal concept of how you think you should serve, you can expand your arena and attract many vocational and social opportunities. Self-trust increases as you use your finely honed analytical abilities to actively support others.

JUPITER IN LIBRA

Static
If you postpone dealing with other people on a one-to-one level, fearing inability to maintain harmony in your relationships, you may experience many shallow, unsatisfying associations throughout life. If you avoid a deep, intimate alliance and instead adopt an insensitive attitude of expectation toward your friends and partners, you may inadvertently create isolation from others.

Dynamic
When you decide to take the leap of faith and put yourself in situations where you will experience intimate contacts with people, you can undergo a sense of expansion and joy. As you accept and trust deep relationships and get close to people on more than superficial levels, you may find a continuous inspiration to self-growth. Self-trust increases as you use your natural abilities for creating ease in social situations to unite others into a harmonic whole.

JUPITER IN SCORPIO

Static
If you postpone participating with others on business, sexual, and deep psychological levels, fearing the loss of personal control, you may create deadlocked situations in which no one is able to use mutual resources. When you avoid transformative connections with others, you can experience a frustrating sense of losing power while being obsessed with the need to control others.

Dynamic

When you decide to take the leap of faith and risk exposing your hidden motivations by sharing intimately with another, you can experience expansion, opportunities, and trust that emerge from allowing yourself to become a part of another's life. It is no longer necessary to control or be controlled by them. By trusting the occult vision of the transformative energy of relationships to manifest in mutually beneficial ways, you can surrender to its power. You may then discover that you possess intuitive perception to use these resources in such a way that each person is benefited. Through this process you can expand your own power and opportunity on all levels of close relationships.

JUPITER IN SAGITTARIUS

Static

If you postpone participating with others in deep philosophical pursuits, you may instead fritter away the time as a perpetual traveler, both in mind and body. If you are content to be motivated by superficial reasons and internal reflections, you can inadvertently create a situation of intellectual isolation by presuming you know the answers to everything.

Dynamic

When you decide to involve yourself seriously with deep philosophical study and communication with other people, trusting your knowledge to flow spontaneously, you can experience the joy and personal expansion in learning and teaching. Consequently, when you take the leap in faith and let yourself share new ideas (rather than using knowledge to establish intellectual authority), you can truly become a teacher. Self-trust increases as you take the initiative in sharing your positive outlook and philosophical insights with others.

JUPITER IN CAPRICORN

Static

In delaying or postponing the use of the Capricorn natural talents to fulfill your desires, formulate plans, or manipulate business dealings, you may experience insecurity about your inner integrity that is aimed toward achievement. Thus, you can be at a loss to manifest those talents within you. If you give in to righteous ideas about controlling others or repress your fine managerial abilities, you may undergo frustration and doubts about yourself.

Dynamic

When you trust your integrity and utilize your natural managerial talents to organize what you truly believe in, you may discover that your abilities to manage others bring joy to everyone as well as yourself. By taking a leap of faith and putting yourself in situations where you can delegate authority and manage resources, you can experience an expansion of faith in yourself to use your talents with integrity.

JUPITER IN AQUARIUS

Static

If you postpone openly expressing knowledge out of the fear that you may not have enough to share or that the information you have is not important, you can unwittingly repress communication of your learning. Personal frustration can result. You may inadvertently allow righteous judgments about the *un*importance of all knowledge, including your own, to prevent you from sharing with others. The result is likely to be intense internal frustration.

Dynamic

When you take the leap of faith and allow your knowledge to flow freely into group situations, you can experience the joy and expansion that inevitably comes as a natural result of your generous sharing. By not trying to prove uniqueness or superiority and instead seeking to share in a way that actually contributes to situations at hand, you can begin to experience the joy and freedom of speaking from higher levels of intuitive knowing in a way that expands the circumstances for everyone. Self-trust increases as you use your innate connectedness with groups to promote a natural sharing of objective knowledge.

JUPITER IN PISCES

Static

If you postpone using the Pisces visionary abilities to see through and beyond the limiting, insensitive social, intellectual, and moralistic values of society, it can result in a widespread state of perpetual confusion. You may inadvertently allow righteous ideas about how circumstances should be, but are not, to alienate you from trusting yourself and from life in general. The lack of faith that ensues can create a state of helpless stagnation and confusion about how to improve your present circumstances.

Dynamic

In deciding to take a leap of faith and greet the many facets of life with a basic trust in the universe, you can experience the joy of having your vision fulfilled at every moment. When you accept circumstances as they are, with your vision on the perfection behind the appearance—on the Divinity behind the clay—you can undergo the joy and personal expansion of being able to assist people in realizing their potential. Self-trust is increased as you use your natural trust in the unseen workings behind the appearances of life as a personal foundation.

JUPITER IN THE HOUSES

1st: Social opportunities and rewards can be forthcoming when you concentrate on expanding your self-expression and the impact of your personality.

2nd: Social opportunities and rewards can be forthcoming when you actively expand your material values and act on your ability to earn money.

3rd: Social opportunities and rewards can be forthcoming when you expand your intellect by following your thirst for knowlege and sharing that knowledge with others. The arena of formal education brings many rewards.

4th: Social opportunities and rewards can be forthcoming when you expand your understanding of the past to include the whole world as your home. Increasing your security may give rise to latent talents in business, finance, and real estate.

5th: Social opportunities and rewards can be forthcoming through working with children, theater, and arts, and expanding your abilities to express creative talents.

6th: Social opportunities can be forthcoming when you expand your ability to serve in the world. The areas of health and helping professions bring social rewards.

7th: Social opportunities can be forthcoming when you align yourself with a partner. The establishment of a primary relationship can lead to personal rewards.

8th: Social opportunities and rewards can be forthcoming through the areas of deep psychological or sexual involvement, or business partnerships.

9th: Social opportunities and rewards can be forthcoming through the areas of publishing, philosophy, higher consciousness, education, and foreign travel.

10th: Social opportunities can be forthcoming through expanding your public expression in the world. Positions of management and authority bring social rewards.

11th: Social opportunities and rewards can be forthcoming through aligning yourself in group activities with scientific or humanitarian aims.

12th: Social opportunities can be forthcoming by becoming aware of the most spiritual and esoteric part of the self. By expanding your understanding of your role in the universe and allowing the universal mind to flow through you in the form of poetry, music, acting, or other spiritual or artistic forms of self-expression, you can attract social rewards.

Saturn

SATURN: KEY TO PUBLIC ACHIEVEMENT

Saturn in the Birthchart:

· Shows the process of fulfilling your sense of social obligation in a public way that results in a sense of personal chievement.

· Indicates the process by which fears may deflect you from fulfilling your ambitions.

- Pinpoints the areas of your greatest desire and greatest fear.
- Represents the factor of self-discipline and physical responsibility; your endurance and ability to see things through.
- Illuminates the area of purpose, direction, and social responsibility in your life, showing those factors that can lead to a life direction that brings the respect of others for your natural authority in the world.
- Reveals the area where the power of personal commitment to contribute to society gives you the courage to rise above inhibition and fear, making those personal corrections that are necessary to contribute in a way that is supported and respected by the rest of the world.
- Pinpoints where you do not yet "have it straight," that area where you must apply repeated effort to gain mastery on a non-ego level. Only through accepting and meeting the tests of Saturn can the bliss and freedom of transpersonal states of consciousness (represented by Uranus, Neptune, and Pluto) be obtained.

SATURN IN ARIES

Static
You might strive to stand out as a leader by ignoring established protocol and being impatient. This form of assertion may lead the material world to exercise harsh discipline over your energies by severe limitations. When you endeavor to lead for self-serving motivations only, your Arian manner might become restless and narrow. This may alienate others and result in frustration of your productive efforts.

Dynamic
You possess the skills and social ability to be a leader. You can acknowledge yourself as creator of your sense of independence and of situations in which you lead or follow. This self-recognition allows you to feel secure enough to act independently. As you use your leadership capacity, more and more you become aware of others' wishes. Fostering new ideals and ideas into a form that answers a collective need, your innovative ambitions have the potential for reaching and affecting society at large.

Past Lives
Karmically, your destiny is to formulate a new identity. An entire cycle of ego expression through an old sense of self has ended, and

that ego has dissolved. This is why you feel so vulnerable in this lifetime: You have no instinctive ego to serve as a buffer against environmental stimuli. Thus, there is a tendency either to over-react or to underreact when asserting yourself because you don't yet have a solid sense of self to assert from. Your job is to rise above the limitations of past life personality expressions and for-mulate a new, more powerful sense of identity.

SATURN IN TAURUS

Static
You might try to accumulate money or possessions for the purpose of standing out as a separate identity and justifying your worth to others. This motive results in poverty consciousness and a feeling of being victimized by the material world in relation to your per-sonal security and self-esteem. The upshot is feeling continually thwarted from accumulating the money, comfort, and status you seek. If you struggle to avoid pursuing practical Taurean ambi-tions, frustration with material status might ensue.

Dynamic
You possess the social skills to manifest material abundance, com-fort, and security in the world. You can recognize yourself as cre-ating the limitations stemming from your values, which brings about circumstances that render you unable to regenerate your financial situation. Then your self-worth can be expanded to in-clude new methods for making money.

Once you are willing to use your abilities to build tangible re-sources in a way that also helps others build their tangible re-sources, you can experience the worldly abundance and sensual satisfaction that you seek.

Past Lives
You have formulated a new sense of self in recent past lifetimes and now must build a foundation that will give strength, stability, and support to the fresh identity that has emerged. Material re-sources can be scanty in this lifetime until you gain a clear sense of what is really important; what has meaning and value in your life; what principles that, when manifested, will give you an inter-nal sense of stability, comfort, and self-worth. Then material re-

sources know no limitation, and you can become wealthy through your own efforts.

SATURN IN GEMINI

Static
You might try to build barriers against intimate relationships in order to ensure the Gemini option to mingle with many people and to pursue goals and friendships in a superficial, social manner. This form of relating to life may lead to the jack-of-all-trades, master-of-none syndrome. The upshot can be frustration due to a failure to complete long-range goals because of your need to detach from everything. You may experience defeat by always creating an option and by refusing to commit yourself.

Dynamic
You possess the skill and social responsibility in the world for bringing many ideas into manifestation. When you acknowledge your need for a variety of ambitious outlets, you can notice that a flitting-about, social frame of reference does not encourage a consistent, conscious center from which you can handle your divergent ambitions.

   You can dedicate yourself to building an inner focus point, which gives you security in the ability to complete your ideas one at a time or give them to someone who can bring them to completion. If you follow a consistent philosophical identity within yourself, you can use your many talents and abilities to communicate information that organizes and supports others in a solid way. Thus, you will attract a variety of people and experiences. The result will be the positive stimulus and the variety of challenges needed for fulfillment.

Past Lives
Learning to communicate clearly, honestly, and openly is your challenge. Recent past lives have yielded a strong internal sense of self, and you are now recognizing your own strength through interrelating, connecting, and communicating with others. This lifetime you are learning how to be open to a clear and mutually beneficial exchange of information through eliminating a tendency to self-censorship. Your job is to live in the moment and to verbalize clearly the ideas that come into consciousness as they arise.

Through cultivating this innocent, spontaneous honesty with others you find that the people around you take their rightful positions in your life without any need for conscious manipulation on your part.

SATURN IN CANCER

Static
If you feel that other people should respect your feelings because you are a sensitive person, you may experience rejection. The resulting self-protection might lead to a neurotic Cancerian need to create emotional limitations in your life that appear to be security. When you are afraid of dealing directly and objectively with others about your sensitivities, you may experience a severe limitation and repression of your emotional nature. This eventually cuts off your ability to experience feeling anything at all.

Dynamic
You possess the skill and social responsibility to experience your subjective feelings deeply and then to bring those feelings into manifestation. You can do this in a way that benefits others as well as yourself. When you acknowledge yourself as the creator of the personal feelings experienced, you can begin to feel secure enough to delve into your private sensitivities.

Once you are in touch with your true feelings you have the ability to bring those feelings to the surface in an objective way that clears the air and benefits everyone. You possess the ability and the responsibility in the world for creating an environment in which everyone, including yourself, is nurtured and secure.

Past Lives
You have reached a stage in your evolutionary path where it is necessary to bring past life talents into an organized format for public expression. This process emerges from the subconscious levels, and suddenly you may find yourself excited and involved in activities that have the potential to lead to a profession or career. As you begin to use and express these instictive past life talents, you gain a sense of the career that can be truly fulfilling to your basic inner needs. You are learning to take responsibility for the expression of past life identities, desires, and talents in the context of the current lifetime environment.

You feel insecure about really belonging in the home and family environment, and so you feel needy and overly dependent on others for emotional support. Karmically, you are bringing in new ideas that are not yet familiar to society or understood by your family. It is as though you are from another planet and do not find affinity with the consciousness of your family structure. Your job is to find a sense of belonging and comfort within yourself, and to make new families based on inner connection with others.

SATURN IN LEO

Static
You might try to impose your Leonine right for self-expression by creating situations that are larger than life. If you dramatize your ups and downs in order to gain respect and awe, your experiences might resemble those of the heroes in Shakespeare's tragedies. The dramas produced may be self-destructive and unfulfilling. You may find the outer world unsympathetic and limiting to your dramatic behavior.

Dynamic
You possess the skill and social responsibility to bring your capacity for moving dramatic expression into manifestation. When you are willing to acknowledge yourself as the originator of the melodramas in your life, you can feel secure in your ability to be responsible for the intense scenes you attract. You gain confidence in your skill to handle emotional display when you are in touch with the love center within yourself. Then the potential to align your dramatic sense with the knowledge that you can serve a larger community comes forth.

You can contribute to others by giving expression to your *true* inner feelings, inspiring them through your own courageous example in dramatically revealing your innermost sentiments. You can commit yourself to your ability to use drama as a means of consciously inspiring constructive goals in the world. Then you experience the excitement and security of designing extravaganzas that you know will not undermine your most profound creative abilities.

Past Lives
You have reached a stage of needing to be responsible for creating what you really want. To do this you must first have a vision of

the goal or ideal you want to manifest. From this dream your energies can begin to flow in a constructive, consistent direction that is supportive to your childlike spirit.

Past lives spent as entertainers or kings have left you feeling that you have to perform within a rigid structure that keeps you on top and in control of the audience. Your job is to allow to dissolve all the feelings of having to play an approved role so that your child-like spirit of excitement and fun can begin to emerge and lead you home, into the fulfillment of your dreams.

SATURN IN VIRGO

Static
You might try to fit spontaneous expression into structures that block it, fearing imperfection in expressing yourself or in your ability to be of service. This form of perfectionism leads to the painful self-imposed restriction of failing to live up to your own standards.

Your power to perform may be undermined by feeling the painful, abrasive Virgo self-criticism and might result in health or work imbalances. Feeling unable to use your strong sense of duty can lead to withdrawal from participation on almost every level of life.

Dynamic
You possess the skill and social responsibility to manifest your talents for creating order in the world. By acknowledging yourself as the creator of any debilitating, Virgoian thoughts used against yourself or others, you can cease to take yourself so seriously. This gives you more security in actualizing yourself in ways that serve other people. You can then offer your precise analytical talents to give aid to the community; by seeing its imperfections, you can use your power of discrimination to bring about order where there is chaos.

When you are able to see yourself as the servant of life, a form of nonjudgmental perfectionism can enter into your affairs. Then you can offer in a balanced, sharing, spontaneous way your vision of helping others. You experience the confidence to be of practical service to other people by creating appropriate outlets for your strong sense of duty.

Past Lives
You are learning to be responsible for an effective integration between your body and mind. When any aspect within becomes too

extreme or out of balance, the result is a breakdown in the areas of health or work. You are learning to allow health to be a barometer of the degree of balance in your life. In this incarnation you want to work on yourself, to perfect yourself, so that you can manifest your spirituality and visionary ideals in a practical, tangible way.

Past lives have been spent in service to others on a menial level that resulted in your ego being attached to a sense of perfection about how you did your job and carried through your duties. This lifetime you want to relinquish a sense of superiority about being perfect, above the rest of society, and allow your vision to manifest in a flowing way through your work. You are learning to release the tension of preplanning and to focus on the abstract vision you want to manifest. By handling the details of your life spontaneously as they arise, you do your part and fulfill your role as a disciple of life.

SATURN IN LIBRA

Static
You might try to maintain the Libra emotional security by clinging to certain social ideals and always being pleasant. This form of harmony may result in difficulty with being yourself since it cuts off personal expression with others. When you place a limit on your actions with expectations of how others should respond, severe limitations may be felt. The result may be that all of your relationships become burdensome and disappointing.

Dynamic
You have the skill and social responsibility to create relationships that actually work by bringing into manifestation their natural inherent harmony. Acknowledging yourself as creator of the harmony and disharmony that you experience gives you security in your ability to experience what is created. Once you are willing to undergo the possibility of disharmony in relationships, you have the capacity to actualize yourself by sharing your honest, individual point of view. A natural, authentic balance can manifest in response.

You can commit yourself to your integrity, sharing your independent point of view honestly, and then objectively notice how others respond. This process allows you to use your diplomatic abilities on an impersonal level that serve a collective need. The result can bring about the necessary structure to produce an alliance that answers both your needs and the needs of the other person, with no limiting justifications of how you think the relationship should appear.

Past Lives
You have come to manifest a marriage or partnership in the truest sense in this lifetime. You have reached a point in your evolution where your own sense of separate identity has been completed and perfected as an effective, self-integrated entity.

In past lives you were counselors, advisors, and diplomats, playing the role of the supportive other to the exclusion of involving your own identity in creating a partnership. This lifetime you are looking for another person with whom to share, recognizing your own independence and seeing a partnership with another who is also a fully self-integrated, independent being.

SATURN IN SCORPIO

Static
If you think you are all-powerful and must take responsibility for everybody else's physical or material situation, your power might be limited by the Scorpio compulsion for control and dominance. Through the need to create roles of control and dependency, you may inadvertently block your energies from others. This form of using power may lead to giving your partner and yourself the experience of frustrating isolation. Due to a paralyzing fear of losing command, you may deny yourself and others the deep, powerful connection with the very intimacy and energy you seek.

Dynamic
You possess the skill and social responsibility for powerfully manifesting the latent forces of mutual transformation and regeneration of values in your intimate relationships. You can acknowledge yourself as the creator of drives for power and control that you experience with others, which gives you security in your ability to undergo the challenges created. You can gain even more personal security from realizing that the power you release is strong enough to allow you to easily experience an intimate contact with another.

You can accept and work with the responsibility of dependence on others or having others depend on you, or both simultaneously.

Then you can realize that past secretive, selfish values served only to undermine and rob yourself and others. Risking your role of power enables you to relate to another on a truly intimate, equal, trusting level where you both can experience the sensual enjoyment of deep emotional transformation and regeneration.

Through using and sharing the power to release yourself to higher levels of worth and value, you can experience increased power and vitality.

Past Lives
In this stage of your evolutionary pattern it's time to deal with your fear of bonding with another on a psychic level. You are learning that you will not be dissolved by the power released in the process of achieving oneness with another. By not getting stuck in your awareness of the desires of others, you can hold to the realization of your own value system and build what you consider important into the context of merging with another. You are learning to use power consciously, to validate your worth, and to bond with another on levels that are mutually constructive.

Past lives have been spent in the military and on battlegrounds of power where survival depended on playing a role of absolute and invulnerable power. This lifetime you are learning to discard your psychic defenses against oneness with another, allowing yourself to build the ideals you value into the power of the relationship. In this way the relationship becomes a source of energy that works to the mutual, lasting benefit of both parties involved.

SATURN IN SAGITTARIUS

Static
You might seek to justify your superiority or inferiority by exhibiting the Sagittarius knowledge in a way that makes you right through the established reputation and credibility of others (for example: "I'm smarter than you or superior to you because I have a degree" or "I'm not smart because I don't have a degree"). This may lead to the tension of thinking that you never have enough justification for the righteousness of your knowledge or lack of knowledge.

Dynamic
You possess the skill and social responsibility for manifesting the inspiring energies of philosophy and higher thought in the world.

You can acknowledge yourself as the creator of the responsibility of being or wanting to be intellectually superior. Then you can feel more secure in your ability to learn as well as to teach.

In committing yourself to increase your knowledge in order to serve a larger community more effectively, you are able to use your abilities to organize inspiring, expansive thoughts. This process also frees you to employ knowledge in a way that fosters your social identity without threatening your intellectual ambitions.

Past Lives

You are in a stage of evolution where you are learning to release and surrender old, outworn belief structures regarding the nature of right conduct and truth based on outer authority. Past lifetimes have been spent as religious figures and authorities of spiritual truth, accepting church doctrines and holding to the letter of dogmatic law. There is a fear of disobeying a higher spiritual authority that accompanies this pattern, and this lifetime you are learning to release a sense of punitive subservience to the fear of breaking spiritual law. As you begin to get in touch with you own ideas and opinions, you can integrate your values into the constructs of society's righteous beliefs.

Once you accept the responsibility of connecting directly with spiritual truth yourself rather than being subservient to any outer spiritual or religious dogma, you can allow the universal energy of spiritual truth to flow through you into the constructs of society.

SATURN IN CAPRICORN

Static

If you try to justify your current actions on the basis of the false authority of time, ambition, material accomplishment, or some other highly structured or traditional reason that you think justifies your actions, you might experience accomplishment without fulfillment. You may also experience the resentment of others against your position of authority, which is the price of always having to be in control.

Dynamic

You possess the skill and the social responsibility for manifesting your authority in the world. You can acknowledge yourself as the creator of the authority or lack of authority and respect that you have in the world, which gives you security in your abilities to climb above self-imposed limitations. By committing yourself to use the Capricorn natural abilities to organize, manage, and systematize, without crushing the spirit of those involved, you gain respect for your natural authority and executive leadership.

Past Lives

This is the lifetime of fruition and accomplishment. Past lifetimes have gone along a path of steady preparation for the accomplishment that is desinted to manifest in this incarnation. There is a feeling of having a "public destiny," something that one is supposed to accomplish for the good of all. Frustration arises when you hold back from assuming an active role in the affairs of the world.

It is a leadership lifetime in the sense of your being willing to act as a figurehead in guiding others along a partiuclar path. It is time to stand up and be counted. When you accept the responsibility and authority for manifesting the goals that you determine to be for the public good, you are fulfilling your destiny.

SATURN IN AQUARIUS

Static

You might contradict yourself, accentuating your behavior by being commonplace. This may lead to social limitations because of the compulsive Aquarius need always to be the all-around ordinary person. You may secretly seek to separate from others by being what you picture an ordinary person is. This separation might result in repression and frustration from continually trying to justify that picture to others.

Dynamic

You have the skill and social responsibility for manifesting your individuality and the Aquarian principles of social progress, brotherhood, and humanitarian ideals. When you are willing to acknowledge yourself as the creator of your uniqueness, or lack of it, you can feel secure in bringing forth your personality in ways that serve others. By being committed to expressing nonconformity in humanitarian or political roles, you can experience a new security in your social identity.

Past Lives

This is a lifetime pledged to breaking away from old conventions and turning to innovative ways of serving others that extend beyond the boundaries of what is usually considered to be publicly acceptable. In recent past lives, conventional ways of behaving led to public acclaim, prestige, and the attainment of positions of authority and respect. It is no longer necessary, however, for you to receive public approval in order to thrive. It is time to look within to find values that extend beyond what is currently acceptable and that can lead humanity to new levels of freedom and universal love.

Frustration arises from trying to behave appropriately and do things in the old ways that led to social acclaim. Instead, you need to turn your attention to formulating new goals and ideals for humankind that extend beyond current social structures. You see the next step for humanity, and when you begin to manifest this in your own life, your destiny is fulfilled.

SATURN IN PISCES

Static

You might seek to justify your lack of alignment with any worldly purpose because nothing measures up to your ideals of service. This may result in frustration from failing to undertake action that contributes to bringing these Pisces ideals into manifestation. When you feel helpless in bringing about your visions and ideals, you may lose a sense of having a constructive purpose in society.

Dynamic

You possess the skill and social responsibility for bringing your private dream and ideals into the world. By acknowledging yourself as creator of your private visions and dreams, you can gain confidence in the ability to bring about a true manifestation of what has already been created in your imagination.

You have the power to demonstrate your private dreams. By committing yourself unconditionally to manifesting those dreams that serve humanity, you can accept the opportunities that are currently available. Through consistent, daily demonstration of your spiritual ideals, no matter how seemingly insignificant, you can gain a sense of achievement. This leaves you with the knowledge that you have contributed to the manifestation of society's ideals in a realistic way.

Past Lives
In this lifetime it's time to dissolve ego identification with all past accomplishments. You can become immersed in feelings of vague frustration and helplessness that keep you from manifesting your dreams. This is because the vision is changing: The old cycle of identity is dissolving, and the new is not yet on the threshold. But visions of a new identity and what the new cycle of manifestation will be like do occur.

It can be frustrating when you try to implement the new vision. This is because your destiny is to allow the vision of the new to give you enough confidence to release old forms of ego expression that are not working in the current incarnation. In this way you can become identified with the source, rather than activity, and your destiny is fulfilled.

SATURN IN THE HOUSES

1st: Shows the need to acknowledge the desire to appear in control and to be committed to developing those attitudes of personal responsibility that lead to control without domination.

2nd: Shows the need to acknowledge the desire to find security in your values and material possessions. Saturn offers the responsibility of changing your fixed value systems to include the potentials inherent in your current circumstances.

3rd: Indicates the need to acknowledge the desire to have your communication taken seriously. Saturn offers the responsibility of gaining the education and the learning that others will respect.

4th: Depicts the need to acknowledge a desire to feel strong emotional bonds with others. Saturn offers the responsibility of establishing your personal security through open, honest communication of your real feelings.

5th: Shows the need to acknowledge the desire to feel secure by playing a leading role in life. Saturn offers the responsibility of expressing your creative talents in constructive ways that bring closeness to loved ones rather than isolation.

6th: Shows the need to acknowledge the desire to express a strong sense of duty. Saturn offers the responsibility of doing a good job without disrupting your life through over-work.

7th: Indicates the need to acknowledge the desire for a partner you can lean on to gain social balance. Saturn offers the responsibility and talent for creating a partnership that will support you and the other person constructively.

8th: Depicts the need to acknowledge the desire to have power over others. Saturn offers the responsibility of control by expressing a level of integrity that will constructively transform you as well as those closest to you.

9th: Shows the need to acknowledge the desire to inspire others through your knowledge. Saturn offers the responsibility of having faith in your philosophical belief system, allowing it to expand to incllude the information that comes from new ideas and experiences.

10th: Depicts the need to acknowledge the desire to be taken seriously as an authority in the world. Saturn offers the responsibility of expressing yourself on a public level in the area of your expertise.

11th: Shows the need to acknowledge the desire to distinguish yourself among your peers. Saturn offers the responsibility of gaining the knowledge that will make you an authority among equals.

12th: Indicates the need to acknowledge your desire to manifest your private dream. Saturn offers the responsibility of continuing to manifest your spiritual ideal with a commitment to what goes beyond the visible and tangible.

Uranus

URANUS: KEY TO INDEPENDENCE AND FREEDOM

Uranus in the Birthchart:

· Illuminates the circumstances in which an intuitive perception of life can be received, enabling you to rise above the confusion of interfering ideas.

· Indicates the process by which your unpredictable behavior leads others to feel that you are too untrustworthy, disruptive, and eccentric to be taken seriously.

· Shows that area of life where you must experience a sense of personal independence and assume responsibility to safeguard and express your need for freedom in a way that does not alienate others.

· Pinpoints that area in which you need to experience, in a responsible, conscious way, the excitement of independence and personal freedom in order to maintain clear perceptions.

· Reveals the manner in which your unconscious expression of careless, eccentric indifference to other people can lead to unexpected situations of emotional disruption, separation, and alienation.

· Denotes the area in which you have the potential to express innovative ideas that can alter antiquated situations that no longer meet people's needs.

Uranus spends approximately seven years in each sign before moving on. It is one of the three outer planets, along with Neptune and Pluto, that depict the nature of a *generation* in addition to defining personal qualities. As such, the sign containing Uranus shows the need for change and progress within an entire peer group, as well as being an indicator of the need for personal change and progress. In many ways the personal and generational effect is the same. As the necessary intuitive connections are made by the individual, the entire generation is elevated, and the influence of that generation, in turn, introduces that element of change and progress into the world.

On a strictly personal level, it is in the house location of your chart that the influence of Uranus is felt and worked with. The term "planetary mind," as used in the following descriptions of Uranus, refers to the mind of God. It is omniscience—the place where creative ideas originate, where problems are solved, and from which all inventions come. When you tap into Uranus you tap into a higher frequency of mental energy.

URANUS IN ARIES: Those born in the generation having Uranus in Aries have the ability to intuitively receive from the planetary mind a new direction for mankind. They will have individualistic ideas of how to pioneer new ways. Disruption occurs only when a path of leadership is sought that is not in accord with the good of society as a whole.

URANUS IN TAURUS: Those born in the generation having Uranus in Taurus have the ability to receive intuitively from the planetary mind timely ideas for materially implementing the new directions that are being taken on the planet. They will receive insights about ways to structure the new directions, to establish innovative energies in a practical, essential way. Disruption occurs only through holding on to old value systems that are not in harmony with the new direction of society as a whole.

URANUS IN GEMINI: Those born in the generation having Uranus in Gemini have the ability to receive from the planetary mind new forms of communication to reach people with the message of the times. They will have fresh insights into how to verbalize and promote the new directions that have been estabilshed. Disruption occurs only when attempts are made to stay on a logical, rational level with their messages instead of expanding the mind to a more intuitive form of communication.

URANUS IN CANCER: Those born in the generation having Uranus in Cancer have the ability to receive intuitively from the planetary mind new emotional states that cause trauma or transformation on a very personal level. The insights received about the potential of these new emotional states can be upsetting to the home life and traditional roots of personal security. Disruption occurs through being attached to or relying upon the traditional forms of security, such as home and family on a private, noncollective level.

URANUS IN LEO: Those born in the generation having Uranus in Leo have the ability to receive intuitively from the planetary mind new ways of creatively expressing their emotions and talents. The ego can experience intense disruption by taking one's creativity too personally. Confusion occurs through demanding personal recognition for creative or artistic expression.

URANUS IN VIRGO: Those born in the generation having Uranus in Virgo will have the ability to receive intuitively from the planetary mind new ways of cleaning up the social environment on both physical and mental levels. Disruption occurs when new ways of serving society are misunderstood and taken too literally.

URANUS IN LIBRA: Those born in the generation having Uranus in Libra have the ability to receive intuitively from the planetary mind innovative ways of relating to people and handling the area of personal relationships from a new level of understanding. Disruption occurs from outmoded ideals about the marriage relationship, and in the arena of partnership agreements in general.

URANUS IN SCORPIO: Those born in the generation having Uranus in Scorpio have the ability to receive intuitively from the planetary mind new ways to substantially transform the society as it is presently operating, especially on a worldly and sexual level. Disruption occurs by holding on to outworn sexual standards and outmoded ideas about material partnerships.

URANUS IN SAGITTARIUS: Those born in the generation having Uranus in Sagittarius have the ability to receive intuitively from the planetary mind new philosophical directions and new horizons for society's moral behavior. Disruption occurs in hanging on to belief systems and moral attitudes that justify old social behaviors.

URANUS IN CAPRICORN: Those born in the generation having Uranus in Capricorn have the ability to receive intuitively from the planetary mind ways to plan and establish a new social order. Experiences include insights of innovative ways to organize society in a collective whole. Disruption occurs by hanging on to old forms of society's governmental structures.

URANUS IN AQUARIUS: Those born in the generation having Uranus in Aquarius have the ability to receive intuitively from the planetary mind new ideas to link humanity beyond the level of traditional social order into an integrated whole that is in alignment with humanitarian ideals and standards for relating. A creative form of disorder occurs when Uranus in Aquarius operates on its highest, most inventive and original level. A form of disruption occurs through the awareness of obsolete social systems.

URANUS IN PISCES: Those born in the generation having Uranus in Pisces have the ability to receive intuitively from the planetary mind new pinnacles of understanding that have the effect of dissolving all previous knowledge. The way will be cleared for change and revolution, to make way for renewed ideals for humanity. Disruption occurs by holding on to old belief systems and old perceptions of reality.

URANUS IN THE 1ST HOUSE

Static
You might have a tendency to demand independence in such a way that your freedom becomes a limitation or a burden to others. The result may be constant personal disruption, a scattering of your energy, and a loss of independence. This occurs when you unwittingly react with eccentric behavior that is more destructive than creative.

Dynamic
You can uniquely express individuality through your willingness to be an example of responsible independence. As a result of your ability to see everyone including yourself as an equal, you can be respected as an innovative leader of your group or community. By knowing no class boundaries you become the people's choice.

URANUS IN THE 2ND HOUSE

Static
You might have a tendency to demand independence in a way that results in a scattering of personl talents and resources. If you seek to impose the Uranian's unusual and eccentric sense of material values on others, the result may be dependence on others for support and well-being. If you have no regard for practical responsibility, the result may be dependence on others for support and well-being.

Dynamic
You can uniquely express individuality by implementing your unusual ideas on a practical, material level. In doing this your innovative vision can develop into operative ideas and structures through which a unique means for accumulating money can be established.

URANUS IN THE 3RD HOUSE

Static
You might have a tendency to demand independence through carelessly using your communication in a way that is disruptive. If you choose to be so erratic and abstract that you purposely confuse others, the result may be a scattering of mental energies, misunderstanding, and a loss of any true communication.

Dynamic
You can uniquely express individuality through using your mind to innovate new ways by which you can more effectively and clearly communicate with others. The result can be a sensation of excitement through stimulation from true mind-to-mind communication.

URANUS IN THE 4TH HOUSE

Static
You might have a tendency to demand independence by rebelling against close relationships. You may rebel for the sake of asserting a false sense of emotional freedom and self-centered indepen-

dence, resulting in feeling instability about your roots and constant disruption from loved ones.

Dynamic
You can express your individuality through your unique talent to be sensitive to people's needs. You have the ability to be impersonally loving enough to allow those who are emotionally close to be free from any debilitating dependency. If you choose this road, the result can be a sense of personal emotional freedom that allows you to be truly yourself, even in close relationships.

URANUS IN THE 5TH HOUSE

Static
You might have a tendency to be demanding by carelessly using your own expression to disrupt the expression of other people. There is a temptation to dramatize and flaunt your independence for the purpose of drawing attention to yourself. When this road is chosen, the result may be a reputation as an eccentric rebel and a person whom others do not trust.

Dynamic
You can express your distinctive individuality by asserting your independence in ways that are constructively creative. When you use innovative abilities to allow for and enhance the free expression of those close by, you can experience a feeling of loyalty that supports your uniqueness.

URANUS IN THE 6TH HOUSE

Static
You might have a tendency to demand independence by distorting your sense of duty to justify the refusal to assist others in a practical way. This may result in a constant change of jobs and dissatisfaction with your pragmatic ability to serve.

Dynamic
You can creatively express a sense of personal duty through your unique ability to serve others by disclosing to them the knowledge of freedom. When you follow a personal sense of duty to serve by

imparting your universal knowledge, you can attract and success-fully fill unusual job opportunities.

URANUS IN THE 7TH HOUSE

Static
You might have a tendency to demand independence by dealing with others on the basis of how much stimulation and excitement they can provide. By indulging in such behavior you may attract sporadic, disruptive relationships that scatter and deplete your energy. You may also experience boredom in close involvements, expecting too much from too few.

Dynamic
You can creatively express the ability for variety and exciting stimulation in your responses to others by recognizing this need and enlarging your shpere to include impersonal alliances as well as a primary personal one. When you understand that having many deep, intimate relationships scatters and depletes your energy, you can expand to a natural interaction of impersonal connections. This results in having all the associations you need for stimulus without a disruption of your energy.

URANUS IN THE 8TH HOUSE

Static
You might have a tendency to be demanding by bringing eccentric, bizarre, independent attitudes into a sexual relationship with no regard for the other person's needs. The result of this approach may be sexual encounters that are intense, explosive, erratic, energy-draining, and transitory.

Dynamic
You can express individuality by connecting deeply with other people on sexual levels with the intention of creating freedom for them as well as for yourself. By bringing out the uniqueness in your partner you may discover an expansion in your sexuality. This approach can also increase your power to break through archaic beliefs and inhibitions surrounding your sexuality.

URANUS IN THE 9TH HOUSE

Static

You might have a tendency to be demanding by thoughtlessly destroying the belief systems of others without taking the responsibility of replacing them with appropriate knowledge. This frequently may disrupt and divide the group. There is also a temptation to make erratic, theoretical statements simply for shock effect or to try to prove that you possess superior knowledge that invalidates all perspectives, even yours. When you yield to this temptation, the result may be that no one listens or takes you seriously.

Dynamic

You can express perceptive, philosophical talents by expanding the beliefs of others with objective, factual knowledge. This connection can inspire others to go beyond believing in you, to knowing for themselves. By becoming an example of an individual's quest for objective, workable knowledge, you can inspire others to tap into their abilities to acquire intuitive, impersonal learning. Thus, you experience a truly stimulating meeting with the minds of others.

URANUS IN THE 10TH HOUSE

Static

You might have a tendency to be demanding by believing that you can alter things in the world through careless, rash behavior. You may attain worldly positions that are made in your image without being aware of the social responsibilities of what you seek to accomplish in the world. There is a temptation to destroy for destruction's sake, which may result in disrupting instead of freeing the status quo, a revolution with no social purpose.

Dynamic

You can use your unique abilities by responsibly taking on the role of world reformer. When you act with awareness of the social structure of which you are a part and with awareness of how much can be creatively changed for the good of all, the result is executive or political genius.

URANUS IN THE 11TH HOUSE

Static
You might have a tendency to demand your independence by assuming that you know everything. You may unwittingly use a permanently impersonal position to justify avoiding responsibility for using knowledge in a creative and constructive way. This position can result in attracting disruptive circumstances through groups and peers, and experiencing limited freedom to be yourself.

Dynamic
You have the unique ability to use ideas in such a way that others are encouraged to express their original insights and individuality without judgments of themselves or others. The result of this approach can be an expanded sense of freedom and personal independence in situations that involve groups and peers.

URANUS IN THE 12TH HOUSE

Static
You might have a tendency to demand independence by pretending to others that you are not a unique and free individual with dreams and ideas of your own. The result may be disruption through inner pressure building until you express your eccentric tendencies in ways that are unconsciously and inadvertnetly destructive.

Dynamic
You can take the responsibility to use your unique intuitive vision and impulses by creatively expressing them to other people. When you choose to follow your unusual insights constructively, the result is public acknowledgment of that ideal and a perception of the inner knowledge that will sustain the spirit.

Neptune

NEPTUNE: KEY TO EMOTIONAL ECSTASY

Neptune in the Birthchart:

· Removes the illusion and reveals the truth, thereby showing the way to actualize ideals in a way that works and produces rewards in the material world.

· Depicts the self-defeating and confusing patterns where your expectations are the highest and disappointments are the most intense.

· Defines why your personal pictures of how the ideal would manifest must be sacrificed in order for the reality of the ideal to appear.

· Shows those patterns through which your perpetuate the self-deception and emotional illusions that prevent you from experiencing the ecstasy inherent in the true ideal.

· Indicates the area where you can begin the process of trusting the universe in order to fulfill an idealistic desire; or where you allow the universe to manifest, according to its standards of perfection, by releasing your preconceived pictures, personal standards, and ideals.

· Signifies that area of life offering the strength, serenity, and ecstasy of a Divine contact, and a vision and trust in the workings of the universe.

Since Neptune spends approximately fourteen years in each sign, in many ways the sign containing Neptune is an earmark of a generation. As such, Neptune shows the idealistic desires of an entire group of people, as well as being an indicator of personal idealism. Thus, the personal and generational effects of Neptune are the same. As the energies of the planet are purified on a personal level, the entire generation is uplifted, and the influence of that generation, in turn, raises the ideals of the world. On a strictly personal level, it is in the house location of your chart that Neptune's influences are felt and worked with.

(For the purpose of this book, Neptune is covered in the signs of those who are living now. In the houses, Neptune's influence is shown through all twelve positions.)

NEPTUNE IN CANCER: Those born in the generation of Neptune in Cancer have the potential for realizing the higher levels of personal and family security on a planetary basis. They are infused with the vision of initiating an awareness of the "world family." The League of Nations was formed naturally from the efforts of those born in this age. On a personal level it indicates the dilemma of dealing with idealistic expectations of an automatic emotional fulfillment coming out of one's position in a family. It offers the choice of accepting or denying the responsibility to develop the personal security necessary to experience the realization of one's highest family ideals.

NEPTUNE IN LEO: Those born in the generation of Neptune in Leo have the potential for realizing the higher aspects of sharing art and playacting that inspire others on a planetary level. This is the generation infused with the vision of performing in a way that has inspired and uplifted countless numbers through dramatic performances in motion pictures, on the stage, and in television. On a personal level, Neptune in Leo indicates the dilemma of dealing with the idealistic expectations of automatic joyous emotional states coming through the experience of parenthood, the expression of creative and artistic talents, or romantic affairs. It offers the choice of accepting or denying the responsibility to appreciate the inherent perfection that already exists in one's children, creative expression, and romantic involvements. It is the opportunity to manifest one's creative ideals, seeing the existing perfection in things as they are.

NEPTUNE IN VIRGO: Those born in the generation of Neptune in Virgo have the potential for realizing the higher aspects of health and service on a planetary level. They are infused with the vision of plans to make perfect health available to everyone. Growing world concern over the effects of pollution, environmental hazards, and devitalized foods has increased through the efforts of this generation. On a personal level it indicates the dilemma of dealing with idealistic expectations of automatic emotional fulfillment coming from one's job in life. If offers the choice of accepting or denying the responsibility of serving one's fellow man in whatever capacity one may find oneself. A sense of true inner joy is possible through the conscious dedication of manifesting one's ideals of service in one's line of work.

NEPTUNE IN LIBRA: Those born in the generation of Neptune in Libra have the potential for realizing the higher aspects of relating to people on the level of planetary awareness. They are infused with the vision of creating lasting peace and the abolition of war on this planet. It is also the generation following an ideal of spiritual union and oneness among people. They initiated new ethics of living together that replaced old forms of marriage. On a personal level it indicates the dilemma of dealing with idealistic expectations in relationships. If offers the choice of accepting or denying the commitment to personal integrity that is necessary to realize one's highest ideals in relationships.

NEPTUNE IN SCORPIO: Those born in the generation of Neptune in Scorpio have the potential for realizing the higher levels of shared material ownership on a planetary level. They are infused with the vision of the spiritual responsibility for the Earth's resources as a whole. They are aware of the current human material values and the potential for transformation of those values that will lead humanity to a higher level of relating to the physical world. On a personal level it indicates the dilemma of dealing with establishing one's value with other people. It is the choice between idealistically expecting the automatic support of other people's resources or responsibly defining material values with them. It also deals with the choice between expecting automatic emotional fulfillment through sex or commiting oneself to the self-purification that will actually bring about the realization of those ideals.

NEPTUNE IN SAGITTARIUS: Those born in the generation of Neptune in Sagittarius have the potential for realizing the higher levels of communicating in the areas of intellect, philosophy, and religion on a planetary basis. They are infused with the vision of the rise of enlightenment in the realms of religion and philosophy, and the struggle to find a worldwide media for positive communication. On a personal level it indicates the dilemma of expecting automatic emotional fulfillment to come from following a philosophy. It offers the choice of accepting or denying the commitment to rise above blind philosophical belief and reliance on others. Their opportunity for fulfillment lies in allowing personal experience in the real world to transform and expand their philosophical ideals.

NEPTUNE IN THE 1ST HOUSE

Static
When you try to express yourself on the basis of a preconceived ideal of personal behavior, you might unwittingly deceive yourself and others. Consequently, you may feel confused and misunderstood when others do not understand your good intentions and react with mistrust. This results in the frustrating feeling that you have never expressed yourself perfectly enough or lived up to your ideal of being a positive influence in the world.

Dynamic
You can relinquish pictures of perfect self-expression and simply tell the truth about your feelings at the time. This example inspires others to be more in touch with their immediate feelings. As you look to the universe for support, you can purge yourself by objectively exposing that inner core that is not yet the ideal. Thus, you heal those close by with truth. You can then experience the ecstasy of emotional purity by being an inspiring example of personal integrity, expressing your feelings and perceptions, and being unconcerned about others' reaction.

NEPTUNE IN THE 2ND HOUSE

Static
When you try to create a show of self-value, you may lose contact with your inner sense of self-esteem. While desiring to prove your individual worth by making money (or not making money), you might undergo disillusionment because others do not accept your worth as you think they should. This may also result in frustration when you are unable to buy the feeling of self-esteem that is sought.

Dynamic

You can release your pictures of how you should establish your worth. This enables you to use your assets for building something of worthwhile emotional and spiritual service. Allowing the universe to support you gives you confidence to trust and look to life for material rewards. These will come to you because your goal performs a true service to others. When you realize that money or lack of it is not the way to acquire self-esteem, you can pledge yourself to establishing universal values. Consequently, you experience emotional ecstasy by knowing that the universe always supports you and gives you its material possessions when you use these resources to heal others. This in turn provides the realization of your worth to the universe.

NEPTUNE IN THE 3RD HOUSE

Static

You might try to communicate from a preconceived idea of what to say in order to appear a certain way. This shuts down true communication. The motive may be fearing that others will take your words in the wrong way. Yet in failing to verbalize your spontaneous perceptions, you lost touch with your ideas. Thus, if you project the illusion of well-being when it is not really there, and communicate from that state, you may experience the isolation of feeling that no one understands you. The result is frustration and disappointment because you are unable to communicate in a way that lives up to your ideals.

Dynamic

When you let go of your pictures of what to say in social interactions, you can allow the universe to communicate through you. By focusing attention on how to verbalize what your intuition is showing you rather than on the impression you want to make, you experience the ecstasy of sharing true communication. As you learn to trust the universe to offer you appropriate words to communicate the truth of your feelings your speech automatically heals the exchange. You experience the emotional satisfaction of serving yourself and others by allowing the truth to be spoken through you, with a lack of concern for the results.

NEPTUNE IN THE 4TH HOUSE

Static
If you expect your immediate family to be the perfect kin that you always wanted and never had, you may continue to be dissatisfied and disappointed with them. In addition, the family group around you might take you feelings of dissatisfaction personally. This may cause them to lose confidence in their ability to meet their own ideals, and they may feel increasingly unable to relate to you.

Dynamic
When you realize that your family is not here to live up to your personal ideals, you can give yourself the opportunity to experience true, unconditional, emotional communion with them. In trusting the universe to provide you with perfection in your own kindred as they are, you can experience the ecstasy of emotional satisfaction and security. From there you can come to realize that all humanity is your family, while you let go of your expectations and trust the universe.

NEPTUNE IN THE 5TH HOUSE

Static
You might try to create a dramatic love life based on preconceived ideas of glamour. This process may result in no lasting satisfaction from your sexual relationships. If you play the role of the ideal lover rather than yourself, you may lose touch with the joy and spontaneity of the inner child. By projecting and playing our romantic Neptunian ideals, you may unwittingly create continuous frustration when these fantasies unexpectedly turn into tragic disillusionments.

Dynamic
You can choose to play your true self, acknowledging and expressing your feelings and needs for loyalty. Then you can become the lover that you actually are, creating mutual trust. You inspire enthusiasm in others and release creative healing energy when you innocently display the exuberance and joy of your childlike nature. By being yourself, spontaneously expressing your playful inner nature, you can attract the right person. When you relinquish your fantasies, you can gain confidence in trusting the uni-

verse to provide the satisfaction you seek. Then you attract that one person who can lead you toward experiencing the inner emotional ecstasy of your ideal.

NEPTUNE IN THE 6TH HOUSE

Static
You might try sacrificing on the altar of duty. If you seek to measure up to some perfected ideal in your work, you may fail to be recognized as the willing servant that you aim to be. In an effort to be acknowledged as a self-sacrificing spiritual person, you may create severe health conditions, tensions with coworkers, and a tremendous sense of frustration and paranoia in the job.

Dynamic
When you let go of your pictures of how you should look as the worker, you can focus on serving others rather than your image. You can create the opportunity to serve others in a positive way by releasing your need for reflected perfection. In this way you free yourself to experience joy and union with coworkers in getting the job done together. When you relax and trust that the universe is supporting you in your work, you can experience the ecstasy of consciously participating in being of service in your career.

NEPTUNE IN THE 7TH HOUSE

Static
You might try, through the power of your expectations, to have partners live up to the Neptunian ideals of perfection. This leads to experiencing harsh disappointment in people as human beings. Through continuous disenchantment in relationships and disappointment when people do not behave as stock characters in your protected fantasies, you may unknowingly cause feelings of inadequacy in others. Also, in a close relationship you may find the other person falling constantly short of your ideal. This leaves you feeling unable to relate without fearing disappointment. An unwillingness to experience the way the other person really is, not how you may want that person to be, might lead to the isolation and unfulfillment of relating to a fantasy that never quite comes true.

Dynamic
You can cease relating to your partner as a fantasy and trust that life will be fulfilling if you experience others as they are. Then you can inspire the best in them. You are able to dismiss petty standards by accepting your partner as human. This leads to discovering the ecstasy in truly relating to another person the way he or she is. As you share in the idealistic goals of others, encouraging them to follow their highest ideals, you are freed to experience the ecstasy that comes through participating in their natural unfoldment.

NEPTUNE IN THE 8TH HOUSE

Static
You might try to relate intimately to others on the basis of a preconceived ideal of personal power in the relationship. This may lead to experiencing the surprise and disappointment of their constantly acting in opposition to your ideals. You can create an obsession with material ideals and erotic fantasies when you allow your imagnation to combine with your sexual power. This automatically leaves you unfulfilled and alienated from the sexual bonding that you seek to experience.

Dynamic
When you release your pictures of how you should be powerful in order to manifest the ideal of sexual fulfillment, you open up to the experience of relating on an intimate level with another human being. Eliminating your stance of personal strength can enable you to perceive the potential force in the relationship itself. You can experience a sense of ecstasy and fulfillment in both sexual and financial contacts with others when you trust the universe to bring forth mutual power through relationships.

NEPTUNE IN THE 9TH HOUSE

Static
If you try to create an illusion of appearing intelligent, you may act on the basis of how you think intellectual superiority should be manifested. In displaying an attitude of intellectual superiority over other people, you may unwittingly invite the disappointment of being unable to substantiate your authority. You might be con-

cerned with projecting the image that you exclusively possess spiritual knowledge. This may lead to making false assumptions and giving too much importance to those things not yet checked for validity. As a result you experience confusion and disappointment when others become alienated and suspicious of your perceptions.

Dynamic

When you let go of trying to live up to your ideal of being the spiritual teacher, you are able to relax pretensions and open to receive new and higher ideas. You can gain the base on which you may philosophize and expand when you are willing to work with the new perceptions and acquaint yourself with the facts relevant to your subject matter. Then you can spontaneously communicate the spiritual ideals shown you through your intuition. You are able to do this in a way that inspires others as well as yourself to reach new intellectual heights and spiritual insights.

NEPTUNE IN THE 10TH HOUSE

Static

You might try to create the impression of being the greatest authority according to your pictures of how you should appear to others. This leads to experiencing the disappointment and isolation that results from never being able to abandon your role. If your ego identifies with the feeling of having a destiny ordained by the gods, you might seek to act it out according to your nearsighted, limited ideals. This inadvertently cuts you off from the true sense of inspiration. You may then feel like the abandoned victim or puppet of the gods when people contest or contradict your authority. This process may leave you confused, helpless, and feeling unable to live up to your idealized potential.

Dynamic

You can release your preconceived pictures of being a spiritual authority and role model in the world. This frees you to commit yourself to participating in the world as it really is, according to its own ideals, and gives you a feeling of confidence. Not demanding that a personal ideal be met before you commit yourself enables you to actively join in within the framework of the world's established standards and models of success, honor, respect, and credibility. This then allows you to enact the best of those traditions.

Confidence comes from releasing your vision of what it looks like to be on top and, instead, trusting that the universe is manifesting its authority in the world through you, without your involvement with the results. As you continue to focus on making a solid contribution in the world by channeling spontaneous participation and overlooking any acknowledgment, you experience the ecstasy that comes from your inner sense of accomplishment.

NEPTUNE IN THE 11TH HOUSE

Static
When you try to relate in groups according to your ideal of what this interaction ought to be, you may experience an endless search for the perfect group. This might lead to the disappointment of failing to find friends with whom you can accomplish humanitarian visions and goals. You may actually contribute to the dissension and confusion existing in the group situation when you project your pictures of perfection onto them. This results in deep personal feelings of being misunderstood and isolated from your peers.

Dynamic
When you let go of your personal pictures of the ideal group, you can open yourself to honestly and transpersonally relating your experience in the closed circle as it currently exists. Thus, you can create the stage for a new perfection to occur. As you allow fresh visions to present themselves in the framework of your peers, the inspiration that comes from your ideals can inspire them to attain new heights beyond your vision. You experience ecstasy when you openly trust the universe to flow through you in situations involving friends and acquaintances.

NEPTUNE IN THE 12TH HOUSE

Static
You might try to commune with the universe on the basis of preconceived ideas of how the universe ought to be treating you. The result may be experiencing the frustration that God Himself is not living up to your ideals. Indulging in the belief that you are above the material world may lead to idealizing universal reality according to your picture of what that source should be. Inevitably, this

results in the confusion and disappointment of being unable to depend on or trust either the tangible or intangible realms of existence.

Dynamic
When you stop inflicting your visions of perfection upon the universe, you can acknowledge and appreciate the perfection of things as they already are. This unlocks the key to understanding why things happen the way they do. Releasing personal expectations of how things ought to be gives you the confidence to trust that the universe is unfolding according to its own truly perfect nature. Then you are open to inspiring new revelations of the universal purpose behind specific material situations.

In the process of accepting the premise that people and events are perfect the way they are, you can be shown a higher meaning resulting from an all-encompassing view of the universe. As you trust in the intangible perfection, you experience the ecstasy of being in constant communion and harmony with the unseen mechanisms of life.

Pluto

PLUTO: KEY TO TOTAL SELF-MASTERY

Pluto in the Birthchart:

· Reveals where you most covertly resist change; where a willingness to change will have the biggest impact on your life and will result in a realization of fearlessness.

· Depicts the part of yourself that is the most difficult to face and to expose to others.

- Shows the way to release the area of greatest internal repression and, in the process, experience a new sense of personal power and self-mastery.
- Represents the area where you are constantly challenged to use your power to alter stagnant situations drastically.
- Illuminates that area of life in which you can obtain the rewards of true self-mastery if you are willing to risk it all, exposing personal perceptions and values on the deepest levels.
- Exposes the temptation to use divine power as a tool of the personal ego and self-will, which can have explosive repercussions that lead to self-suppression.
- Indicates the area in which you need to be willing to die *psychologically* in order to be reborn into an experience of life on a whole new level.
- Signifies where you can claim the high consciousness of clear right action and alignment with the self, which is also the area where your fear is recognizing that you already have the power and completeness of the high consciousness because you feel it would make you different from everyone else.

Pluto takes approximately 256 years to orbit one time around the zodiac and remains in one sign for up to thirty years. The influences of the sign bearing Pluto mark an entire generation, in addition to having an individual impact. Thus Pluto signifies the transformation of an entire group of people as well as being an indicator of personal challenge for transformation and mastery.

In many ways the personal and generational effects are the same. As the challenge is accepted and the necessary risks are dealt with on an individual basis, the entire generation is activated and its energy, in turn, is released to transform the world. On a strictly personal level, it is in the house location of your chart that Pluto's most intense emotional influences are felt and worked with.

(For the purposes of this book, Pluto is covered in the signs of those who are living now. In the houses, Pluto's influence is shown through all twelve positions.)

PLUTO IN GEMINI: Those born in the generation having Pluto in Gemini experience the call to participate in world transformation through a greater sense of global contact. As a generation they are handed the challenge of transforming the existing methods of communication and transportation to a position that puts them in contact with the rest of the world.

On a personal level those born with Pluto in Gemini experience their greatest fears in the area of openly communicating their thoughts and ideas with other people. Their challenge is to risk the honest expression of their perceptions and ideas and to accept the response of others.

PLUTO IN CANCER: Those born in the generation having Pluto in Cancer experience the call to participate in world transformation by creating a new security based on cooperation with other nations. During the depression their sense of isolation as a key to their basic survival was transformed.

On a personal level those born with Pluto in Cancer experience their greatest fears in the area of maintaining control over their personal safety. Their challenge is to risk their self-protective instincts for a larger security in cooperation with others.

PLUTO IN LEO: Those born in the generation having Pluto in Leo experience the call to participate in world transformation by altering their creative self-expression and communicating with other nations on the level of art, music, and the new consciousness. They are also handed the challenge of dealing with each nation asserting itself as a power in the world.

On a personal level, those born with Pluto in Leo experience their greatest fears in the area of expressing their emotions honestly through their sense of drama and creative talents. Their challenge is to risk the disapproval of others for a larger sense of self-approval through open and powerful self-expression.

PLUTO IN VIRGO: Those born in the generation having Pluto in Virgo experience the call to participate in world transformation on the levels of health and service to those less fortunate. They are also given the challenge of transforming the ecology of planet Earth.

On a personal level those born with Pluto in Virgo experience their greatest fears by risking the criticism of others through a commitment to their sense of duty. Their challenge is to serve others on practical levels even though they may not have attained the perception of self-perfection they seek.

PLUTO IN LIBRA: Those born in the generation having Pluto in Libra experience the call to participate in world transformation by introducing new forms of cooperation between nations. They are also given the challenge of transforming traditional ideas of partnership relationships on planet Earth.

On a personal level those born with Pluto in Libra experience their greatest fears in risking disharmony through disclosure of what they feel to be unjust. Their challenge is to be willing to discard personal illusions of balance and objectively express their power in relationships in order that a new and greater harmony can be established.

PLUTO IN THE 1ST HOUSE

Static
You might withhold your ability to stimulate others toward deeper awareness because you fear their violent response. If you hide under the pretense of being harmless, you may attract people who are basically incompatible. Withholding honest responses may rob you and others of the opportunity to transform the situation to a higher level.

Conversely, you might express your perceptions but with an ego motive of wanting to intimidate or manipulate others to live up to your expectations. If you try to force others to change their self-expression, you may find yourself entangled in intense resistance from them. This impasse results in personal stagnation and a frustrating repression of involvement in your relationships.

Dynamic
When you are willing to go beyond your greatest fears, you can surrender to the power of your personality. By asserting yourself fully and honestly even though it may provoke others, you are likely to experience a momentary disruption in your environment. This leads to a process of purification, eliminating those factors that inhibit self-expression. By taking the risk of expressing your deep perceptions as they arise, you can rise above stagnant levels of unspoken conflicts.

When your motive is a commitment to your integrity, you are able to graciously reveal your perceptions of other's expressions. This allows them to accept or reject your insights as they choose. Others may temporarily invalidate your discernment because they feel deeply exposed and publicly unmasked. If you can allow their quick denials of your truth to pass by and move on to other areas of interaction, you leave them free to consider what you have said.

As you appreciate the gift of power in your personality, you can be willing to go through the risks of declaring yourself regardless of the consequences. When you become committed to independent self-assertion, you are led past your greatest fears and into self-mastery.

PLUTO IN THE 2ND HOUSE

Static
You might withhold your power to use personal resources to transform your financial situation. Such withholding defeats all opportunity for an expansion of material security. You may neglect to take your ideas and talents out into the world for fear of being victimized. Thus, your values are not given a chance to produce material results for anyone.

In seeking to maintain total control over your personal resources, you may perpetuate a pattern of repressed and stagnant values. The result might be frustrated mediocrity.

Dynamic
You can be willing to go beyond your greatest fears and surrender to the will of manifesting your usefulness. By taking the risk of using the power of high consciousness, you can experience a transformation of your assets. This leads to greater alignment with yourself. Committing yourself to working with those resources that are available leads to a temporary disruption of your old value systems. This process opens to a new, unanticipated freedom and ease in accepting the inflowing bounty of life.

When you open to expand your resources into the world, you can receive the will that brings about results. Appreciating life makes you willing to go through the suffering to obtain the values of life, and hence its worth.

In revealing your values you can establish what you feel is tangibly important. You can sacrifice the desire to enforce your values on others. This frees you to accept temporary invalidation for what you consider important, understanding that people may need time to align with their power. Commitment to manifesting what you feel in life gives you the confidence to use the power of your will. This leads you past your greatest fears and into self-mastery.

PLUTO IN THE 3RD HOUSE

Static
When you withhold communicating penetrating perceptions to others, you might suppress your desire to ask questions that arouse them to a deeper awareness of themselves. Thus, you may unknowingly defeat all opportunity of bringing new insights to yourself and others. If you seek to control others by not revealing information due to fear of rejection, you may experience the confusion of being unable to trust your perceptions. As a result you might resent them, feeling unable to communicate in a powerful way.

If you use your mind for the purpose of forcing your perceptions on others, expecting them to agree with your ideas through mental intimidation, you may experience resistance.

Dynamic
You can be willing to go beyond your greatest fears, surrendering to the power of your communicative ability. The fear that you may be misunderstood can cause a momentary disruption in your thought processes when you expose your perceptions. By continuing to communicate, this disruption is followed by a purification of your ability to divulge insights without personally identifying the ideas.

You can overcome conflict and attain self-mastery by sharing your perceptions, insights, and honest reactions. Sacrificing the desire to control or invalidate the thought processes, ideas, or statements of another frees you to offer your own points of view. By realizing that your perceptions can occasionally shake others to their core, you can give them room to invalidate ideas temporarily until they have had a chance to review your teaching and make their own choice.

PLUTO IN THE 4TH HOUSE

Static
You might withhold using your sensitivities to people's feelings in ways that provoke them them into confronting a deeper awareness

of themselves. This repression may rob them of the opportunity to experience new feelings, and also rob yourself.

You may give in to fears of being rejected and thus withhold your deepest responses to your family. This repression of openness might lead to a resentment of others' insensitivities. The result may be overcontrol and emotional stagnation.

Dynamic

You can be willing to go beyond your greatest fears, surrendering to your sensitivity. When you reveal what you are feeling, in spite of fearing the consequences, you undergo a transformation of feelings. This allows for a truer alignment with your deepest sensitivities. By sharing your responses and deep perceptions of others' feelings, you may experience a temporary invalidation from those who are closest. A purge of both your insecurities and theirs can follow.

When you cease trying to control others' feelings to protect your vulnerability, you free yourself to operate from a stable position. This vantage empowers you to express and share from the integrity of your deepest sensitivities. Selfless commitment to recognizing and exposing your awareness of the realm of feelings leads past your greatest fears and into self-mastery.

PLUTO IN THE 5TH HOUSE

Static

You might withhold using your talents in ways that arouse a creative, spontaneous reaction in others. Failing to tune them into a deeper awareness of their emotional and sexual expression can rob you and them of being in touch with truly creative energies.

You might repress responding dramatically and spontaneously to situations because you fear awakening energies that you or others might not be able to handle. Thus, you may undergo emotional stagnation. When you use ego to repress creativity, it might lead to resenting others for the loss of your spontaneity of self-expression.

Dynamic

You can be willing to go beyond your greatest fears and use your power of dramatic expression. You can provoke others into a deeper contact with their inhibitions about expressing themselves completely. Giving voice to your inner child tunes you in to a deeper meaning of loyalty. You can commit to fully expressing dynamic spontaneity when you realize that the creative power that flows through you is not from your ego. As a consequence you may encounter at first a temporary disruption and invalidation in your relationship with others, followed by emotional purification.

When you sacrifice the unconscious motive of wanting to control others' opinions through your ego power, you are able to operate from a clear motive. Then you can express yourself with a buoyant sense of drama for the purpose of contributing inspiration. Taking the risk of recognizing and exposing your sense of creative spontaneity leads you past your greatest fears and into self-mastery.

PLUTO IN THE 6TH HOUSE

Static
You might withhold using your intense perception of order to provoke others into a deeper awareness of their abilities to organize their lives effectively. This repression can invoke the frustration of feeling powerless to create precision in your world. You may likewise resent others for failing to do their part.

If you give in to fears of being criticized and thought petty, you might not communicate your awareness of environmental inefficiencies. This may unknowingly rob you and others of the opportunity to discover a higher order. The result may be a stagnant situation in which you are unable to clean up the disorder on the most personal and impersonal levels.

Dynamic
You can be willing to go beyond your greatest fears, surrendering to the power of your sense of order. By divulging perceptions of disorder you may experience a temporary disruption and invalidation of your internal ordering. This disruption is followed by an emotional purging and the emergence of a new sense of duty. You can provoke others into a deeper experience of their perfection as you express your concept of the imperfection you see around you.

You have the option to sacrifice the motive of wanting others to change their behavior and become nearer to perfection according to your standards. This frees you to reveal perceptions of disorder from a clear, stable motive: simply wanting to express service by sharing your awareness of life.

You can reveal these observations, not defending them or taking them personally. This opens the way for a clearer sense of organization to occur in your relationships. Thus, by recognizing and offering your concept of order regardless of the consequences, you can be led past your greatest fears and into self-mastery.

PLUTO IN THE 7TH HOUSE

Static

You might withhold using your awareness of others, especially your mate, in a way that provokes them into deeper self-awareness. Suppressing this insight may rob you and them of the chance to reach new levels of intimacy and depth in the relationship. You might fear disrupting the interaction with your mate or losing control of the relationship. Thus, you may not share your perceptions and true reactions. This withholding leads to frustration and feeling powerless to have the kind of relationship you really want.

In order to control and hold on to the alliance, you might repress yourself and secretly resent your mate for your own reluctance to risk sharing yourself fully. This may result in being in control of stagnant relationships that you do not want.

Dynamic

You can be willing to overcome your greatest fears by surrendering to the power in a relationship. Then you can allow your partner to be powerful by sharing your perceptions and reactions with him or her. As a consequence, you may experience a momentary disruption and invalidation in the confrontation that leads to a process of purification. This process eliminates those factors that block a mutual sense of power in the alliance.

Self-mastery can be attained by allowing the high consciousness to emerge through a relationship. Revealing your deepest experiences and perceptions of the other person and the relationship itself, regardless of the consequences, maintains the integrity of the alliance. This leads to the unfolding of mutual power. By giving high consciousness to the other person, you empower yourself.

You have the option to sacrifice the desire to control your partner or deceive your partner into thinking he or she is in control. This frees you to operate from a clear and stable motive, expressing a desire for a complete sharing and enhancement of power. By revealing the perceptions you really see, you can be led past your greatest fears and into self-mastery.

PLUTO IN THE 8TH HOUSE

Static
You might withhold your perceptions of people's motives, not provoking them into a deeper self-awareness. This suppression robs you and them of the opportunity to experience the potency of mutual impact. You may fail to reveal awareness of the desires and deeper yearnings of others because you fear losing control or becoming vulnerable by exposing yourself. This withdrawl leaves you unaffected by your most intimate connections with them. It also brings about stagnation in close relationships.

You might experience frustration in anticipating an intensity in close relationships. This occurs when you neglect sharing the depth of your perceptions and when you don't allow yourself to become too involved. You might also experience intense dissatisfaction as well as the resentment of others from needing many relationships because you allow none of your unions to go deeply enough to find satisfaction.

Dynamic
You can be willing to go beyond your greatest fears by surrendering to the power of yielding. This frees you to enter into deep psychic and material commitments with others and thus experience personal transformation. Through surrendering your individual force and merging it fully into the strength of the relationship, you may experience a momentary disruption and invalidation in your sense of power. This can lead to a process of purification. It eliminates those unconscious values that have blocked you from experiencing the deepest meaning of potency in your life.

Self-mastery is attained in the process of experiencing the real strength emerging from the bond of your deep psychic and material commitment to another. When you sacrifice the desire for exclusive control, you can operate from a clear motive of wanting to increase the potency of the mutual bond.

By being committed to being powerful enough to risk giving up your self-control, you can wholly combine with another. This leads past your greatest fears and into self-mastery.

PLUTO IN THE 9TH HOUSE

Static

You might withhold revealing spontaneous intuitions, thus not provoking other people into a deeper awareness of their truths and intellectual values in life. This holding back robs others and you of the chance to see newer, even higher knowledge. You may not communicate your awareness due to not wanting others to see your intellectual independence. Also, you may fear losing control of possessing superior knowledge by sharing it.

Repressing the share of your current understanding with others may result in the frustration of failing to reach new levels of awareness. Additionally, because of your belief in personal and intellectual superiority, you may resent others' levels of perception. Thus, you may unknowingly limit your own awareness. This can lead to a stagnation in the breadth of your intellectual ideals.

Dynamic

You can be willing to go beyond your greatest fears by surrendering to the true power of insights. You do this by sharing your spontaneous perceptions with others in spite of fears of provoking or being misunderstood. You may then experience a momentary disruption and invalidation of your sense of intellectual pride.

This leads to a process of purification and eliminates those factors of misunderstanding that caused you to be aloof. By not identifying with the power of the intuitive insights you receive, you can commit yourself to sharing those insights without judgment. This allows others' ideas to combine with your thought processes. Thus, you open up to an expansion of your intellectual values.

You have the option to operate from the clear and stable motive of simply wanting to express yourself by sharing the answers you see with others. You can sacrifice the motives of wanting to prove you have superior knowledge or wanting to use your intellect to force others' alignment with your beliefs. By being selflessly committed to taking the risk and exposing your spontaneous perceptions, you are led past your greatest fears and into self-mastery.

PLUTO IN THE 10TH HOUSE

Static

You might not use your perceptive abilities to establish true authority in the world. This leads to inviting others to victimize you.

By being afraid to risk your public image, you might repress yourself and fail to attempt the ultimate goal. If you shun the risk of public failure, you may pretend to be successful while suppressing desires to attain specific goals.

By settling for mediocrity you find a sense of control that you may fear losing if you become powerful in the world. And so, by withholding your power, you may unknowingly rob yourself and others of the consequence of your impact. If you do not risk using all your power and perceptive resources to attain what you seek professionally, you might deny your own destiny. Thus, you may experience the frustrating powerlessness that comes from being unwilling to venture the use of your authority on a public level.

Dynamic
When you are willing to go beyond your greatest fears, you can surrender to the true power of your ambitions. You can take the risk of recognizing and fully establishing your authority with integrity in a public arena. Taking this risk leads to experiencing a positive alteration in your sense of power. In the process of going forth to establish goals, you can allow your highest goals for achievement to be combined with the power of your will. This results in experiencing a momentary disruption and invalidation of control over your public image.

A process of purification follows, eliminating those feelings of inadequacy that kept you from a sense of destiny and expression of authority. Self-mastery can be attained by exposing your power on a public level. Allowing the integrity of your perceptions to provoke the public into transforming expands your authority into appropriate leadership.

You can experience the emergence of your true mastery as you cease to identify with the power and the authority that is released through you into the world. You also have the option to sacrifice the motive of wanting to force ego control over the direction of others. This frees you to operate from a clear and stable motive of simply wanting to express a sense of destiny. By being committed to recognizing and publicly establishing the power and authority within yourself, regardless of the consequences, you can be led past your greatest fears and into self-mastery.

PLUTO IN THE 11TH HOUSE

Static

You might withhold the power to expose factors in group situations that are not in alignment with the universal goals you see. Fearing the loss of acceptance if you express unconventional ideas, you can unknowingly rob yourself and others of a chance to actualize the potential of a collective ideal. You may fail to share your knowledge and then resent your peers for not being of higher intent.

If you separate your ideals from those of your peers, you can repress insights that, if revealed, would contribute to a higher sense of group unity. When you indulge in egotistical motives, such as forcing on others the certainty of your knowledge or desiring to be accepted and validated by the group, you may experience resistance.

By failing to release the power, you can lose the opportunity of allowing the power of the group or friends to combine with you and effect a mutual change. When you fail to risk personal power, you stay in total control of a stagnant sense of collective ideals and values. As a result you may feel intimidated, powerless, and isolated.

Dynamic

You can be willing to go beyond your greatest fears aligning with your ideals by revealing unconventional knowledge. By sharing objective perceptions during interaction with peers, regardless of the consequences, you can experience a transformation into power. When you risk exposing those hidden factors that you perceive do not support the ideal, you may experience a temporary disruption and invalidation of your knowledge.

This can lead to a process of purification, eliminating unconscious factors that blocked you and your peers from experiencing combined and expanded powers. Self-mastery can be attained through the objective sharing of information, increasing the potency of the group as an entity unto itself. Thus, you experience your own mastery emerging through your impersonal commitment to increasing the power of the ideal. You access the high consciousness as you cease to identify with the power that is released through you when you express knowledge. This allows you to reveal with integrity your most threatening insights.

In exposing unusual awareness you may release an intense power that stuns others. Realizing this enables you to accept the fact that they may temporarily invalidate the revelations until they have had a chance to reevaluate and accept them on their own. You can sacrifice wanting to enforce ideals through maintaining power over group ideals or wanting to prove the power of your information through peer validation. Then you are free to operate from a clear and stable motive, simply wanting to contribute your insights.

You can accept the commitment to establish the ideal by participating in groups and with friends. In those arenas you can expose the truth of your desires and the ideals you see, allowing your peers to transform and support or not support you. Thus, you are led past your greatest fears and into the high consciousness of self-mastery.

PLUTO IN THE 12TH HOUSE

Static
You might withhold the power to use contact with larger, unseen spiritual forces of life in ways that provoke you and others into deeper awareness of the spiritual dimension of self. This holding back robs everyone of the chance to experience life by personally contacting the deepest source of power and identity. You might deny the power of your ideals and fail to express your vision.

You might repress responding to circumstances on the basis of a vision you see if you fear the loss of control or the disruption of the rest of your life. This may lead to frustration, a feeling of being misunderstood by the world, and a resentment of others for their lack of vision and understanding.

Fearing you may lose your spiritual security by sharing it may lead to not exposing the power of intangible causes to others. This leaves you with only a stagnant sense of the power of the real self.

Dynamic
You can be willing and determined to go beyond your greatest fears by surrendering to the power of your vision. When you take the risk of trusting life to support you, knowing you are acting in accord with right action, you may express your spiritual vision. This can result in a temporary disruption and invalidation of your private sense of security. It leads to the purging of repressive un-

conscious fears and the purification of a new contact with the unseen forces of life.

You can claim high consciousness by revealing the perceptions of hidden causes and profound inner meanings of others' lives. You can expose the truth of the visions that you see regardless of the consequences. Taking the risk of fully expressing your vision releases power. This allows you to both experience and perceive a deeper relationship with self.

Exposing your discernment can release an intense power that stuns others. This allows you to understand with compassion that others may temporarily invalidate the insight until they have had a chance to accept and incorporate it. You can sacrifice the motive of wanting your observations validated by others or wanting to force them to align with their real self as you envision it. This frees you to operate from a clear motive of accepting and sharing the private insights you receive.

As you cease to identify with the power of the intangible insights that flow through you, you experience true spiritual security. This allows you to share your perceptions without taking the reactions of others personally. By being selflessly committed to taking the risk and revealing the spiritual visions you receive, you can be led past your greatest fears and into self-mastery.

CHAPTER FOUR

Conclusion

THE astrology chart is an objective picture, a graph of one's personality structure or individuality. It depicts the ego, the personal self, the structure within us that makes us different (and separate) from everyone else on the planet.

Ultimately, happiness does not come from a sense of being separate from one another. Happiness is a by-product of being in touch with the source of happiness within ourselves. This happiness unites us with others.

It has been our purpose to illustrate that there are choices we can make about the quality of our life. Our choices determine the effects that we experience in life.

Nobody does anything *to* us. We create what we experience. That is why an astrologer knows from your birthchart what your parents were like (or the way you saw them).

We create what we experience. Because we have the power to create it, we also have the power to change it. The key is in accepting personal responsibility, which leads directly to personal power.

Again, a professional astrologer can look at your birthchart and tell you exactly what your mother was like (as you saw her) and the kind of relationship you had with your father. This information would be based on the moment of your birth. So, did your parents do it *to* you?

For example, in my birthchart I have Saturn (the planetary symbol representing my father) in the 10th house, squared by my

Neptune opposing Moon in the 1st and 7th houses. This indicates that my father was a harsh authority figure who ruled me with an iron hand. (And it's true!)

On the other hand, my brother's astrology chart has Saturn in a grand trine with Venus and his ascendent. And sure enough, his relationship with our father was harmonious and peaceful—quite different from mine. And yet we both had the same father, the same environment, the same circumstances. My brother brought out one facet of him and I brought out another. It had little to do with my father. We just drew from him what we needed to fulfill our own individual personality structures.

Now I can look at my birthchart and say, "Aha! Because of father I'll have a problem with authority figures my whole life." Or every time I start feeling shy or repressed because I've attracted someone who is insensitively telling me what to do, I can say, "Wait a minute here! That's *my* Saturn square Neptune opposing Moon. Nobody's doing it *to* me! I'm attracting it! So what can I do to become my own authority in this situation?"

Once I have asked that question I have given myself the power to deal creatively with the situation in a way that will work for me.

The mass thought form idea of having to endure pain and suffering on this planet is archaic. We have reached a point of choice. The biblical idea of experiencing the kingdom of heaven on earth is a realistic option. This is a garden, and we can play and be free if we want to.

You are in control of the way you use the energies depicted in your birthchart. When you use these energies positively, considering the good of all concerned, life magically shifts to your personal advantage. If you give the responsibility of your happiness to others, you subjugate yourself to the ups and downs of the material world. When you accept sole responsibility for actualizing the energies in your birthchart, you gain power to mold your life in a way that is realistically fulfilling and happy.

PART

II

PRENATAL ECLIPSES:
Key to
LIFE PATH
and
DESTINY

by Karen McCoy and Jan Spiller

CHAPTER FIVE

Introduction

WITHIN the eclipses of the sun and moon lies one of the keys to the question, "Why me?" The new information presented in Part II concerning the meaning of the solar and lunar eclipses in our lives is the result of many hours of meditation and study. A lecture by astrologer Robert (Buz) Myers in 1982 gave me the initial idea, and for the next four years I researched over four thousand charts, watching carefully for the effect of the eclipses on personality and behavior. What I found was that, for the vast majority of people, the sign of their solar eclipse indicated lessons they had come to teach their fellow beings, while the sign of the lunar eclipse guided them to the lessons they needed to learn in order to continue their own soul growth.

Another aspect of eclipses that became clear in my research is that the energy pattern of a particular solar eclipse is similar to the energy a birth brings to that child's parents. When a child is born, look closely at the parents' relationship. Notice that the life force represented by the Sun sign of the child is the energy that this particular union needs in order to be revitalized. For example, when a Gemini is born into a relationship, those parents need to communicate more. This little Gemini child is ruled by the planet of communications. At the time of conception the signal sent out by these parents was: We need help learning to communicate more clearly. In a similar manner, at the time of a solar eclipse the inhabitants of the earth are asking for what is needed for the greatest good of the planet and the continued evolution of our own collective consciousness.

At the time of an eclipse the sheath of the Earth is broken, and a surge of energy from the collective higher consciousness enters the atmosphere of the planet. This energy is sent as a helping hand. The sign in which the eclipse occurs determines the type of help that is sent through the souls who enter at that time and the gift or ability the universe has bestowed on them. How aware and evolved these souls are will determine how well they utilize their gifts. Remember when looking at these eclipse patterns that a gift received is not necessarily a gift used. Dealing with karma, or soul growth patterns as I prefer to call them, I find that the more talents or spiritual assets are used to help your fellow beings, the more personal spiritual growth you gain.

The solar eclipse represents the aspect of the collective higher consciousness that you have to offer your fellow beings. The sign and house of the eclipse will tell you in what area of your life and in what mode of expression the abilities are most accessible to you. The lunar eclipse pattern will show you what is needed to continue the growth of your soul, and the house and sign will show how and where these lessons can best be acquired. It is at these points that growth is stimulated and character is built. The level of awareness the soul has when entering this plane will determine whether it will seek the lessons of its lunar eclipse with compassion and understanding or with resentment.

The body represents the vehicle for the energies of these two eclipses to merge in order to aid in their joint venture of sharing and learning, giving and receiving. And the body also brings with it the genetic memory of all ancestors that have shared and blended together in the past.

I believe that everything in this universe can be perceived as having been created in trinities, including body, mind, and soul. The basic principle of this work is to show us how to function as the complete trinity we are. Body represents the physical form and the Earth we temporarily make our home; soul, the evolving essence that is constantly striving for perfection; mind, the instrument we use to reach the spark of the collective higher consciousness, to reach out to one another, and to discover our group responsibility. For in each of us there resides a part of everyone else. There are no throwaways; the puzzle needs all its pieces, so Godspeed in letting your spark shine through.

KAREN McCOY

In my experience with astrology over the past two decades I have noticed that many people tend to discount its validity, thereby depriving themselves of a unique opportunity for self-growth and fulfillment. The primary argument against astrology is usually that it is based on superstition, but nothing could be further from the truth. This is an ancient science, and the astrology chart itself is based on a series of most exacting and precise mathematical formulas.

There are many other nonmaterial realities that have very definite physical effects. Gravity is not visible, yet its existence is self-evident. While radio waves are not perceivable by the physical senses and one hundred years ago it was fashionable to be a skeptic about the validity of these waves, today no one doubts their existence. In the same way the final "proof" of astrology's validity is whether or not it can be of practical use in your own life. The value of the insights gained through astrology can be enormous, enabling us to see ourselves differently. This allows us to change the way we express ourselves and to alter the effects of what we are manifesting in our lives.

I would like to acknowledge the tremendous contribution to humankind that astrologers, past and present, have made by dedicating their lives to investigating the cause-and-effect relationship between planetary energies and human behavior. Their research has given us all a tool with which we can consciously assume power and control over our destinies. If, as well-known astrologer Noel Tyl has said, "character is destiny," then the type of objective self-knowledge that astrology can provide is truly a valid prerequisite for self-mastery and thus control over the direction of our lives.

Part II is designed to facilitate your understanding of the lessons you have come to learn in order to continue your evolutionary progress and the natural gifts you have promised to share with others while you are here. The purpose is to expand self-awareness. The final authority as to the accuracy of the text is that sense of rightness you experience while reading it. Ultimately, truth works, and if experimenting with the suggestions in this book leads to more clarity and ease in your relationships and greater happiness within yourself, then you know you are on the right track.

JAN SPILLER

CHAPTER SIX

How to Use Part II

REINCARNATION

A belief in reincarnation (having previously experienced life in a physical body other than the current one) is not necessary in order to obtain full value from this book. However, an openness to the possibility of permanently transcending old, limiting mental states and conditions is necessary for receiving the full impact of change.

Phrases such as "past incarnations" and "previous lifetimes" are used. Such phrases may be interpreted to mean prior experiences in other bodies or prior realities experienced in the current body (such as experiences of early childhood with parents or siblings, or the subconscious memories of adolescence in dealing with peers, relationships in puberty, and so forth). A third interpretation is that the experiences of early childhood are merely a re-creation of individual patternings and habitual responses active in past lives, brought into the current incarnation for further growth and resolution.

Any of these viewpoints will work. It depends on your individual belief system. The main idea is to be willing to take responsibility for manifesting and mastering the lessons you currently need to work through and resolve.

ECLIPSES

DETERMINING THE SIGNS OF YOUR ECLIPSES

Check the eclipse tables at the back of the book (page 439). In the Solar Eclipse table, locate the date closest to your birthdate. Note the *sign* of the solar eclipse that occurs directly prior to the date of your birth. That is the sign position of your prenatal solar eclipse. For example, if you were born on March 31, 1953, your prenatal solar eclipse would be in the sign of Aquarius, and you would look up the meaning of your eclipse under the section on Aquarius. If born on December 13, 1941, your prenatal solar eclipse would be located in the sign of Virgo, and you would look up the corresponding meaning under the section on Virgo.

Follow the same procedure for determining the sign in which your prenatal lunar eclipse is located, using the Lunar Eclipse tables beginning on page 445. For example, with the March 31, 1953, birthdate, the lunar eclipse would be located in the sign of Leo; with the December 13, 1941, birthdate, the lunar eclipse would be located in the sign of Pisces.

HOW THE ECLIPSES WORK

When the Moon passes between the Sun and the Earth, a solar eclipse occurs; a lunar eclipse occurs when the Earth passes between the Sun and the Moon. Prior to your birth (sometime between conception and the first breath of life) there were at least two eclipses—one solar and one lunar. These prenatal eclipses have a profound influence on the unborn child, and the energy pattern dispensed during these eclipses follows you the rest of your life.

The magnetic pull of the Sun and the Moon eclipsing the Earth is strong enough to open the Earth's sheath temporarily so that these energies can be received. At the time of the solar eclipse the planet is seeded with the energy pattern that correlates to the psychodynamics of the constellation the Sun is in at the time.

One way to think about this is that when the Earth's "window" opens to receive this "cosmic dusting," the "view" (energy, information, and knowledge) that is in front of the window is what is perceived. So if the Sun is in Sagittarius when the eclipse occurs, the knowledge and information available through Sagittarius is visible. When the window is open, not only is that knowledge visible but the Earth's magnetic field pulls in the energy of that constellation. When the Moon is eclipsed, a similar process takes place.

At birth, both of these energies enter the body. By knowing the sign of the solar eclipse preceding your birth, you can identify the convenant you made with the universe in exchange for the privilege of having a body and being on the planet.

The sign of the solar eclipse shows a *universal* destiny: It is the energy of the collective unconscious that needs to be actively expressed on the Earth at that given point in time for its own balance. The souls that are born into each solar eclipse have been dusted with that energy and have promised to spread that energy on the Earth to help with the growth and evolution of the planet.

Thus, whatever solar eclipse preceded your birth is the energy the universe has invested in you and that you have promised to share during your travels on Earth. The solar eclipse energy is what you are here to clarify for the collective whole. Where your solar eclipse is concerned, you must share as you have promised in your covenant with the universe. Your only choice lies in whether to share your gift in a positive or in a negative way. You can go about your life willingly sharing this gift with your fellow beings, or you can teach the lesson by having such negative traits that those around you learn what not to do from your behavior and personality. If you do choose to teach these lessons in a negative manner, you are creating an imbalance within your life that causes your own lessons to be learned with more difficulty than is necessary.

You promised that you would share the energy of the *solar* eclipse in order to earn the right to come onto this plane and learn the lessons represented by your *lunar* eclipse. The universe operates in perfect balance—if you give something, you open yourself to receiving something. So when you accepted the gift represented by your solar eclipse and promised to share it with others, you earned the right to learn the lessons you need in order to evolve, as shown by your lunar eclipse. The lunar eclipse is what you need for your own soul growth pattern: what you have come to learn, where you hurt, where you need completion. And as you master these lessons, the entire planet learns them, and part of the universal balance is attained.

Evolved souls cooperate with this universal plan, spreading their solar eclipse teachings and mastering their lunar eclipse lessons, thus fulfilling their contracts with the universe. At that point they are freed to enjoy being on the planet without obstructions, free to attract and experience the beauty, fun, and bounty available on planet Earth.

IMPACT OF THE ECLIPSES

The immense impact of the eclipses on individual destiny seems to be tied in with the workings of the planet Pluto. Our research has shown that those born prior to the discovery of Pluto in January 1930 may not be as subject to the effect of their prenatal eclipses. However, those born before 1930 who are particularly evolved and aware beings are just as sensitive to these influences as those born after January 1930.

This can be explained, in part, by the fact that even though the planet Pluto was in existence prior to 1930, humankind's consciousness had not yet evolved to the point where Pluto's energies could be received. Once that point was reached (in 1930), Pluto was "discovered" on the physical plane.

SOLAR ECLIPSE

The sign of your solar eclipse determines what your responsibility is to the collective whole, the energy you have promised to share with your fellow beings. It's a gift that the universe gave you so you could teach others, thus raising and balancing the consciousness of the collective whole. Use it wisely, for by freely sharing your gift you ease the burden of your own lessons. The section on your solar eclipse will tell you what it is you have come to share with your fellow beings in this lifetime.

LUNAR ECLIPSE

The sign of your lunar eclipse indicates those qualities you need to integrate for personal balance, the lessons you have chosen to learn in this lifetime. You are not judged by how you undertake this journey, for it is you who decided to begin the quest. This is a personal destiny: It is the lesson that the soul wants to integrate into its evolutionary pattern.

UNCONSCIOUS EXPRESSION (SOLAR AND LUNAR)

By unconscious expression we mean the type of behavior that manifests when you are bucking the tides of growth and choosing not to integrate your lessons. It is the result of swimming upstream and taking yourself out of the natural flow. This is a picture of what life looks like when you have become willful and are not listening to your inner voice. When you are not paying attention to your life lesson, you set yourself up to learn things the hard way, as depicted by the eclipse energies shown under this category. Many of us begin our process of personal growth at this level, until life becomes too painful and we decide to move on to the conscious level.

CONSCIOUS EXPRESSION (SOLAR AND LUNAR)
By conscious expression we mean the type of experiences and inner reactions that occur when you choose to approach life consciously. At this stage of evolution you have decided to listen to your inner voice and follow the flow of life, seeking your lessons in a gentler way. By learning to read the signs of the times and taking into account the responses of those around you, you become more fluid and allow yourself to bend like a willow. By being aware and conscious, growth comes more easily.

TRANSPERSONAL EXPRESSION (SOLAR AND LUNAR)
By transpersonal expression we mean the attitudes and types of experiences that become active when you have elected to transcend the ego and function in a way that serves the highest good. Personal growth and maturity lead to a sense of greater ease in life. Many people begin the process of personal growth on the unconscious level. As you grow you become less resistant to life, and you naturally learn to operate more from the conscious level. With further experience on the planet another option becomes evident, that of living your life transpersonally, viewing life in a larger context than that of personal survival.

In this stage you are aware of the support and good intent of the universal forces, including Mother Nature, and you become open to receiving the natural bounty of life. You realize that in the process of cooperating for the good of the whole, individual happiness is a natural by-product and your needs are easily and naturally provided. This is the stage in which you decide to give up the separative functions of ego and open yourself as a channel for receiving and sharing light and love with your fellow beings on the planet.

PHYSICAL INTEGRATION (SOLAR AND LUNAR)
In the area of physical integration, the body assists you in fine-tuning your lessons and provides you with a way to gauge your

behavior. Your physical state can be a very personal barometer to soul growth. The body can make your journey easier through the advice it can render. Listen carefully, for it knows you very well.

The section on physical integration has been added to provide a physical checkpoint for determining when the psychological energies of the solar or lunar eclipse life lessons are out of balance. It is based on the premise that mental or emotional imbalance, when ignored on the psychological level, can manifest on the physical level in order to gain your attention and muster your resolve to remedy the situation. *In no way are the suggestions made in these sections to be interpreted as a substitute for taking physical precautions and appropriate remedies in handling physical illnesses.*

THE DOUBLE SOLAR EFFECT

The double solar effect occurs when two solar eclipses occur between your birthdate and the most recent lunar eclipse. For example, referring to the table in the back of the book, if you were born on December 12, 1964, your prenatal lunar eclipse would be located in Capricorn. This lunar eclipse occurred on June 25, 1964. Note that two solar eclipses occur between this lunar eclipse and your birthdate—one on December 4, 1964, in Sagittarius and one on July 9, 1964, in Cancer. If you were born on this date, you have a double solar eclipse.

Those born with a double solar eclipse can have a more active path than the rest of us. You have two special gifts, two things you have promised to share. You have accepted the responsibility of sharing two separate sets of lessons with your fellow human beings. You will draw people to you who are in need of both lessons, and you have promised to handle the responsibility of both. If you could not handle such a responsibility, it would not have been given to you.

THE DOUBLE LUNAR EFFECT

The double lunar effect occurs when two lunar eclipses occur between your birthdate and the most recent solar eclipse (refer to the tables in the back of the book). For example, if you were born on February 18, 1952, your prenatal solar eclipse would be located in Virgo, occurring on September 1, 1951. Note that two lunar eclipses occur between this solar eclipse and your birthdate—one in Leo on February 11, 1952, and one in Pisces on September 15, 1951. If you were born on this date, you have a double lunar eclipse.

There is a distinctive psychological effect for those having a double lunar eclipse. You may feel as if you have two strong drawing influences, two roads in life you must travel. Truly, there are two sets of lessons that you have chosen to integrate into your life experience during this incarnation.

Sometimes you feel that you are two distinctively different people with two different directions pulling at you. People close to you may even suggest that you have a split personality, as your two parts surface at different times. What actually occurs is that two main issues need to be addressed and two parts of you need fulfillment in this lifetime.

The soul has chosen to walk two paths simultaneously. When you have learned to work on both lessons simultaneously, you can allow these lessons to travel a parallel course in your life. A positive use of this energy would be to allow yourself the freedom to explore more than one avenue. You could have two careers, two different social environments, or two main areas of interest.

Operating unconsciously, the double lunar eclipse can sometimes give the appearance of having a split personality. This occurs when you have not learned to master and understand the necessity of learning both lessons. Then you flounder back and forth from one to the other instead of taking control and guiding your own life.

Having a double lunar eclipse does not mean you have a split personality, however. As long as you are consciously striving to learn your lessons, there will be a bond of unity in your internal diversity. Problems with split personality occur only if you try to avoid responsibility for either of your lessons.

HOUSES

The houses tell you in which area of your life you are learning to share and teach (the house in which your solar eclipse is found) and in which area of your life you are learning to integrate your lessons (the house in which your lunar eclipse is found).

The houses containing your prenatal solar and lunar eclipses cannot be ascertained from the logs in this book. If you do not yet have a copy of your full birthchart containing this information, we have made a computer service available at a nominal fee. See page 451 for information.

However, if you already know your rising sign (sometimes referred to as the ascendant), refer to the wheel below. It will enable you to figure out which houses your eclipses are in.

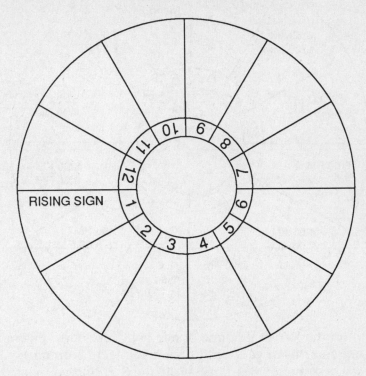

NATURAL ORDER OF ZODIAC

Aries	Libra
Taurus	Scorpio
Gemini	Sagittarius
Cancer	Capricorn
Leo	Aquarius
Virgo	Pisces

Place your rising sign in the slice of the pie labeled 1. Then fill in the other slices, following the natural order of the zodiac in a *counterclockwise* direction, according to where your rising sign begins. Know that the zodiac is a circle that has no beginning or ending, so your rising sign becomes your personal beginning and the other signs follow in their natural chronological order.

If you do not know your rising sign, you can find an approximation of it by using the wheel below.

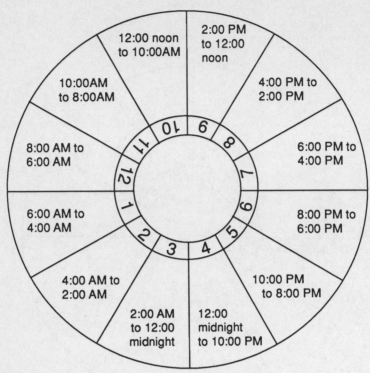

Find on the wheel the time of day you were born. Please sub--tract one hour from your birth time if you were born during daylight savings time or war time. Write the Sun sign you were born under in the slice of the pie corresponding to that time. Then continue filling in the rest of the zodiac wheel counterclockwise from the place your Sun sign begins. For example, if you were born at 9 A.M. and your Sun is in the sign of Leo, you would write Leo in slice 11. Because Virgo comes after Leo in the zodiac, you would write Virgo in slice 12. Then you would continue around the wheel, following the natural order of the zodiac.

The sign you write in slice 1 will be your approximate rising sign. Your actual rising sign could be the one before or the one after, so when using this approximated method, read all three house placements. After finding your approximated eclipse houses, decide for yourself which ones fit.

CHAPTER SEVEN

Solar and Lunar Eclipses

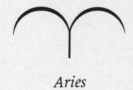

Aries

ARIES

SOLAR ECLIPSE: (In order to fully activate your solar eclipse energy in Aries, you first must integrate the lessons of the Aries *lunar* eclipse with your emotional body. For a full explanation see "How to Use Part II," page 166.)

You are teaching your fellow beings the lessons of assertiveness, independence, courage of convictions, and overcoming fear of new beginnings. Through this process you will draw people to you who have a tendency to be clingy and overly dependent. You must assist these persons in becoming more self-reliant, but you must also avoid falling into the trap they set for you so that you don't begin to take over the lives of those around you.

In teaching self-reliance through example, you must remain independent and hold firm to the idea that all positive relationships are glyphs for infinity—separate yet connected. In a relationship both parties must go out and experience the world, then return and share. Through their experiences in the world each gains something to share, thereby remaining of value to the other.

You intuitively understand the value of being independent, the value of being self-sufficient and self-supported. You have a tendency to draw people to you who are overly dependent on doing things with others. Through your ability to be independent and assertive you can teach the value of getting out there and doing what needs to get done, no matter what obstacles are in the way. Or you can teach this lesson through procrastination, always looking for more data, never thinking you have enough information, and remaining too fearful to move on. Either way, the lesson gets taught. And if you teach voluntarily, it can be an accelerating process with your particular pattern, for life can renew itself almost minute by minute.

To teach your fellow beings to have the courage of their convictions, you use your innate sense of fair play. You will always come to the defense of those who cannot defend themselves, but you will leave them to fight their own battles if you find they are not gaining courage with your support. You intuitively understand it is wrong for you to fight for those who will not stand up for themselves. This would only make your own muscles stronger and not benefit them in a lasting way.

Assisting the weak without allowing the weak to lean on you can sometimes appear heartless to an outsider who does not see that you are teaching others true inner courage and strength by allowing them to stand alone. But you see the option of allowing others to become dependent on you as so much more cruel in the long run. This is why you fight for your independence as well as theirs.

You are also teaching fellow beings proper leadership through your example. In positive leadership you must pass the seed to those who are responsible for nurturing it and move on. You understand that leaders must never remain behind, or they are not truly leaders, just manipulators.

As a true leader you begin the process, head it in the proper direction, and set a positive example of courage, assertiveness, and strength of convictions. You go forward with your project without sending another to find the way first. Like Daniel Boone, you are right out there clearing the path for others to follow. You teach others not to be afraid of something new or of new beginnings, that it is all right to move forward, and that everything must change. Nothing can survive in a static environment.

LUNAR ECLIPSE: In this incarnation you are learning to stand on your own two feet and have the courage of your convictions.

During previous lifetimes you have been overly dependent on the opinions of those around you. Somehow you developed a belief that others were more intelligent and you were less capable. There is also a fear of not being liked, a fear of rejection, and a fear of creating disharmony through conflict.

To compensate for these fears you have allowed others to dominate your life. You need to learn that you are entitled to your own thought processes and that there is a definite reason for all of humankind to be thinking differently about different areas of life. It is very important that you learn to share your convictions, even if it creates conflicts.

The very process of standing up for your beliefs creates change. With change there is growth. Without growth nothing can exist. Even the universe is constantly expanding and contracting. If you never defend your convictions, how will you ever know to change when you are wrong? How can you help those around you who need to change if you continue backing down whenever you feel someone else is a stronger personality?

You are also learning to become independent. Coming from a history of overdependency on others, you are not accustomed to functioning as a separate being. But if you are to be happy in any relationship, you must first gain your independence, for if you marry before you define yourself, you will surrender before the battle of identity is won. Then you could fall back into past life patterns of becoming too dependent on those around you, and postpone finding your own strength and courage until your mate (or friend, parent, employer, and so forth) decides that she or he is tired of holding you up. If you wait to be shoved out the door, you are making your lesson more difficult than the universe intends it to be.

What you need to learn is to function independently, within society and relationships, simultaneously contributing to the whole and benefiting from the whole. If you cannot do this within a relationship, you will fiind it necessary to separate yourself to learn this lesson before you can live harmoniously with another.

You are learning to find factors of individual identity that allow you to have a sense of self within the context of a relationship. For instance, when you have your own profession, creative project, or separate area of interest in which you maintain a sense of separate identity, it give you confidence in being yourself and holding to your own views in the relationship. The idea is to do those things that assist you in establishing your own identity and still be able to have a nurturing relationship.

Another lesson is that of assertiveness. Because of a fear of not being right, you allow mates and associates to make all the decisions. You have learned in the past to value the decisions of others over your own. You also have a tendency to attract strong-willed people who are very assertive.

We always draw to us what we need to learn, and if the energy from your mannerisms tells the universe that you are lacking in assertiveness, the universe will send people and situations to you that will force you to incorporate this quality into your being. It is up to you whether you learn from this or allow yourself to be suppressed by it. In order to survive, you will either learn to assert yourself or "buckle under" to the will of the other person. Either way, the issue of self-assertion will be uppermost in your mind.

You are extremely uncomfortable around raised voices and any form of anger, but you've come to practice asserting yourself when you are right and breaking the habit of backing away from what you want when another raises his or her voice. You are learning that might is not always right and that it is okay to go after what you want. It is not healthy to step aside because someone else wants the same thing that you want, and you need to learn this assertiveness so you can compete successfully in the world. So strong is your fear of rejection and defeat that when any kind of competition arises, your inclination is to concede. It's important for you to realize that you may have to compete for some of the things you want. A cause, game, or object cannot say, "I belong to you, come and take me"; you first have to recognize it as a goal and then have the assertiveness to go after it.

You are learning to overcome the obstacle of having such a fear of losing that you don't get in the running. Once you understand that the only humiliation connected to competing is in not even trying, you can overcome your fear of competition and learn to enjoy it.

Another important lesson you are learning is not to be afraid to start over. The Aries energy is an energy of new beginnings. This ability to begin anew must be incorporated into your soul growth pattern.

Accustomed to operating from a need to know all the facts and figures before any decision is made, new beginnings can be extremely difficult for you. In any new beginning there is an element of the unknown. You must learn to trust that you can handle what is ahead. Until you learn to trust the self, life will be a series of forced new beginnings.

These forced new beginnings probably seem to occur without rhyme or reason. You may find yourself continually going down dead-end streets, as in going to work for a company that soon afterward goes into bankruptcy; taking a job that is in the process of being phased out; getting involved in relationships that can't possibly work; forming friendships with people who are about to move.

You only go down dead-end streets, however, when you follow what other people offer rather than getting in touch with the spark within and following those options that make you feel energized inside. When you learn to do what you want—finding those projects and relationships that "charge your battery"—you will find you are instinctively attracted to those situations that will not let you down.

There will be no relief to the pattern of dead-end streets until you learn that on a subconscious level you already know what you need to do and you have enough faith in yourself to go out in the world without fear of competition and rejection. You must have the courage of your convictions and enough trust in yourself to be able to stand up and try again if something doesn't work out. Self-trust is the most important lesson for you to learn. Once this attitude has been developed, there is very little that you cannot achieve.

UNCONSCIOUS EXPRESSION: Operating unconsciously, through your fear of rejection you can manifest a false state of independence, thereby pushing those people away who could be most valuable to you. You may feel that if you push them away first, you won't have to deal with them walking out on you later. Once you learn not to fear your ability to handle whatever life offers, you can allow yourself to be vulnerable enough to receive life's pleasures.

You have come to learn the value of independence in this lifetime. A previous existence of overdependency on others causes you to try to connect in unhealthy ways with those around you, not setting your path in motion toward independence. If you indulge this tendency, you will always feel held down by the desires, wants, and needs of others. If you operate at this unconscious level, you will find very little personal freedom in this lifetime—restrictions and repressions will arise all around you. When this occurs you may externalize intense anger, which can be seen by the trained eye as a volcano on the verge of erupting. In this mode you can develop tremendous amounts of aggression and are capable of a great deal of violence.

At the same time you fear anger and external displays of hostility. You may fear standing up for yourself yet harbor this anger that tends to surface in the wrong places. It often manifests around people who are less powerful than you, as with children, or in restaurants with waiters or waitresses in response to slow service or bad food.

This anger will surface everywhere except where it should surface: in the relationship in which you have allowed yourself to become dependent. This may be at work or in your marriage—any area of your life where you are allowing others to do for you what you should be doing for yourself. You suppress this anger, for it is caused by fear of losing that particular situation or person. But the anger comes out in those situations where you feel in control and have no fear of loss.

You need to learn to confront and handle anger and resentment at the source. In so doing you will harmonize the other areas of your life. One of the better ways to learn how to do this is by recognizing that you have a great need to master the energy of assertiveness and that the anger is undirected, unharnessed assertiveness. Once you learn self-confidence, you can use your assertive energy to pursue your own direction. Until then you may find yourself allowing others to take what they want while you feel resentful.

You are coming from a previous existence in which your mate gave you everything you wanted. In this existence you now find that there's only the self to rely on, but if you are to have any of your heart's desires, you must be self-sufficient. This means that you must learn to be assertive enough and have enough faith in yourself to compete in life's arena for what brings you happiness.

The negative expression of your lunar eclipse is that you have no faith or trust in yourself. From this lack of self-trust can spring a tendency to lie to yourself and to others. This occurs when you have allowed others to dominate your life and make decisions for you. You then program yourself not to have the confidence, faith, and trust to make your own decisions. Unconsciously, you have taught yourself that you are not capable of seeing truth. The problem compounds itself when the subconscious does not allow this negative thought to enter, but counteracts it by lying to the self, so that when you twist it around, a false idea becomes your truth. You may twist truths in a self-defeating way, project fears, or act from a base of unwarranted insecurities. You therefore experience mixed signals within because you are not in touch with what is truth and what is not.

One of the pitfalls of the unconscious Aries lunar eclipse can be the way you form relationships. You have a tendency to put others on pedestals, whether it be your boss, your lover, a friend, an employee, or your child. And when that "other" does not function the way you feel he or she should, the pedestal comes tumbling down. Unfortunately, you are usually standing underneath and get hurt. Then, in a burst of anger that can reach extremes of violence, you chastise the person for not living up to your expectations. This pushes people further and further away from you, thereby forcing you to take the negative path to your ulimate goal of independence.

A more positive approach would be to recognize that you need to function independently—not necessarily solo but as a leader. It is not your role to push people out ahead but to lead the way. Your expectations have to be of yourself, not of others.

It is imperative that you learn to discern between truth and nontruth by following the inner voice and learning to trust the self, thereby reprogramming the subconscious to tell the truth always. In the beginning this process can be difficult because the subconscious is programmed to do the opposite. As the subconscious learns that you are ready to accept the truth, it starts projecting with more honesty. But when you first begin to "turn things around," there are some gray areas, and you must have the courage to come through these unknown spaces.

Once those with this eclipse pattern pass through the gray and into the light, very few ever return to darkness.

CONSCIOUS EXPRESSION: Operating consciously, you recognize your need to become independent in this lifetime. You realize that it is easier for you to become dependent on others than it is to become self-sufficient. To overcome this you have a tendency to push yourself to be self-sufficient and sometimes reject honest assistance. You must learn that you can accept assistance along the way without falling back into past patterns of dependency.

You are usually more comfortable working for yourself than working for another because you are still overcoming a fear of being overly influenced by others. When you learn to trust yourself and to relate with others from a place of strength, you can become very successful in business, as your need to achieve can be a driving force.

There is a tendency to push out into the world and away from the shelter of home and family since you recognize this as a potential weakness for you and deliberately aspire to overcome it. You are probably a very driven, success-oriented, achievement-oriented person. You need to be careful not to push yourself into being an overachiever and/or workaholic. In your desire to prove your self-worth and become independent, you can suffer from periods of physical burnout. While it is good to push yourself in the direction of achievement, it is not necessary for all the achievement to happen immediately!

You have an ability to recognize truth within yourself and within those around you. Once you have pushed yourself from the nest, you tend to move too quickly and be intolerant of those who learn more slowly. It is important not to lose your sensitivities as you push outward.

As you make your way through life and find your place in the world, you almost always take a stand for the oppressed and truly want to aid all those who are struggling for survival. You work extremely well in areas that call for devotion to principles and in assisting those who need help; you are a friend to those who need to be shown the light or the way to find a new beginning.

You are learning to stand up for yourself in all life situations, breaking a past pattern of being so fearful of rejection and being proven wrong that you were afraid to speak up when your opinion was different from others. Now you are looking to become the best you possibly can be and to feel pride in yourself, and you find it necessary to speak up when you are in disagreement with others. Operating consciously, you recognize the value of developing inner strength and find that it is easier to express your feelings than to live with yourself when you don't. Though it is important that you express yourself, it is also important that you learn to think before you talk. To be truly able to express yourself with the courage of your convictions, you must be firm within your own belief.

Your opposite polarity, Libra, needs to have all the facts before expressing, and as a newly emerging Aries, you must learn from your counterpart to look before you leap. If you can retain the qualities of both—the assertiveness of the Aries and the tact of the Libra—you will be well suited on your journey.

As you progress you find yourself exhilarated by the thought of a new beginning but also fearful of being able to handle it. Yet so strong is the desire to learn to trust the self that you will go through a series of new beginnings until the qualities of strength and inner trust are mastered. Then the urge to push yourself into new beginnings dissipates since you are secure no matter where you are and know that you can move on at any time if you become uncomfortable.

TRANSPERSONAL EXPRESSION: You have incarnated with the group consciousness of raising the vibration of the planet. You have a sense that many of your fellow beings have lost sight of their origins, and you teach renewed faith and trust through your childlike naiveté that all is working according to universal plan.

In this existence you share faith with all your fellow beings, trusting each and every one as if all are members of the same family, for you understand that we truly are.

You recognize the weakness in all of us yet do not judge us since you look upon us as children not yet grown, children still learning the rules and regulations and social amenities of the universe. Yours is a lifetime of teaching us, through the way you live, that ours is a family whose members must have as much faith in one another as we have in the God of our consciousness. You teach that unless we support and assist one another, there will always be someone missing at family reunion time. As a joyful, playful soul you teach us to love our brothers and sisters, for you have incarnated as the original life source (fresh from the Father) still able to see good and innocence in all. You can show us all the spark of light from within.

PHYSICAL INTEGRATION: On a physical level you need to listen to your body in the areas of the head, face, and left eye. When you are not consciously learning your lessons or teaching what you promised to teach, there can be a tendency toward weakness in the muscle of the left eye. There may be twitching in the left eye, banging your head when you are not paying attention, and refusing to listen to your own inner voice. This is all part of your lesson of learning to pay attention and trust the inner self.

If you go for extended periods of time without listening, you can suffer from headaches, from a dull throb to a migraine, depending on how neglectful you have become. When you devaluate your own ideals and put too much energy into the ideas and concepts of those around you, thereby neglecting the self, you may find yourself urinating frequently or suffering from lower back pains. This is a warning system you have devised to force yourself to pay more attention to your own needs.

Taurus

TAURUS

SOLAR ECLIPSE:　(In order to fully activate your solar eclipse energy in Taurus, you first must integrate the lessons of the Taurus *lunar* eclipse with your emotional body. For a full explanation see "How to Use Part II," page 166).

Through you, your fellow beings can learn a proper prosperity consciousness. You have incarnated with a very solid sense of moral, financial, and spiritual values, and have a tendency to draw to you people who need to have their value systems realigned. Attracted to you are those having financial difficulties who need to learn to handle their resources properly and to build solid financial foundations. You understand intuitively that you can climb high only if you have a firm foundation to support you. This is why you can teach those around you how to make sure that every brick has been laid securely and mortared in before they take the next step.

If you choose not to share your knowledge and refuse to teach the basic economic structure that you understand so well, you may experience the negative repercussions within your own family. You may be exposed to a wife, husband, son, daughter, father, or mother who has severe financial difficulties. Or you or someone close to you may have to experience personal bankruptcy. You are only responsible to teach this lesson through your own example. If you choose to take it a step further, however, and actually assist others with your financial understanding, you are sharing yourself beyond the call of duty, which will lead to your own lessons being eased in other areas.

What is important is for you to keep your sense of value amid the financial havoc that you find all around you. Through this alone you teach people a stronger sense of security and financial patience. Very often you tend to draw to you people who are very impatient with finances, and through your example of slowly and securely accomplishing your financial goals, you help to teach them patience. As everything falls apart, those around you recognize that you are still standing on solid ground. Thus, you help others to recognize the value of building on solid ground, and you can assist them in adding security to their lives.

You would do well to choose a profession as a loan officer, financial advisor, accountant, bookkeeper, office controller, or a position in the building or financial industries. With your natural ability to understand financial resources, choosing one of these avenues affords you a place to offer your services where you can be of maximum benefit to your fellow beings. But any field that requires building a solid foundation can benefit from your talents. If you choose not to help others professionally in these areas, you will still be teaching those around you the value of having a strong foundation. You understand in your home life as well as in your business life what it means to say, "The buck stops here."

If you are teaching the lesson of finances in a negative way, you will create havoc in the financial lives of those close to you. If you choose to teach the value of finances on a positive level, you can be of great assistance to your family and associates. You can be extremely intuitive in knowing which investments will reap a profit. Others can benefit greatly if you help them plan for their future in a very practical manner that allows room for growth while retaining a strong foundation. You do not take risks with anyone's resources. You are not one of the gamblers of the zodiac —you are a builder.

If you choose to teach the lesson of moral values negatively, you will be viewed as a person of low moral character. You may cause disappointment and pain to those around you through lack of a proper value system. But even if you choose this path, you still teach the most negative expression of all by setting yourself up as an example of self-destruction. If you teach moral values in a positive way, you will set a personal example with an impeccable reputation. In this mode you are extremely monogamous, loyal, family-oriented, and concerned with family security and home stability. Due to your strong moral fiber and your stability within your family and community, you are usually found in a position of responsibility and high esteem.

You are also here to teach the importance of having strong spiritual values. If you choose to teach spiritual responsibility in a negative way, you will show yourself as a person having no regard for the collective consciousness or the God-consciousness within yourself. Thus, you will not respect yourself or those around you, and will work only for what you want, not for the good of all concerned. If you teach this lesson positively, you can show that the thread of universal consciousness and the need to work for the most good for the most people must begin within your own family unit and extend out to the rest of humanity. You teach that the respect you use in dealing with your fellow beings directly correlates to your own personal sense of self-respect and your respect for the universe. You truly can be of spiritual value to those whose lives you touch.

The negative expressions are rare cases in this eclipse pattern since the majority have been born with a very advanced consciousness. You usually choose to teach your lessons by your own good example, by strengthening the values of others, and by being a valuable asset to the world.

You have the ability to validate the good you see in others, thereby strengthening their positive direction. You naturally recognize the value in everything. Most important, you intuitively understand the value of the human spirit, the human heart, and the human desire that prods us all to achievement. Through understanding this value and appreciating your fellow beings, you teach others to value themselves. If you do not value yourself, you cannot achieve anything because you think you are not worthy of the achievement.

Quite often in your lifetime you will meet people who are down on their luck and have very little feeling of self-worth. You have the ability to assist them in finding their sense of value from the core of their own being. With sensitivity and patience you can put them in contact with their own inner beauty, the essence of the God-consciousness within. Then, through logic and perseverance, you can aid them in removing the debris that has hidden their true value.

Your innate appreciation for the natural beauty of the Earth allows you to walk on its surface and experience its peaceful nourishment. You are very much in touch with all the senses of the body, and through your enjoyment you teach and inspire others to enjoy their senses as well. You would be an excellent artist, for you can physically manifest your appreciation of beauty, art, and nature, thus enabling others to appreciate the beauty you see in all that surrounds us. You are a sculptor, builder, engineer, or architect—if only with sand on the beach. You were born to mold.

LUNAR ECLIPSE: Your lesson is to develop a proper prosperity consciousness in this lifetime. You are coming from a previous existence that was extremely spiritual but materially poverty-stricken. Some of you took vows of poverty in past incarnations in order to focus your energy fully on your spiritual development. Thus, you come into this incarnation with the false idea that money and spirituality are never to blend. You are here to learn that, on the contrary, when you allow your spirituality to manifest through good works that support your fellow beings, money is a natural by-product of that service. Part of your lesson is to learn that money is not a "negative"; money is simply another aspect of life that needs to be mastered.

You have mastered how to have nothing and still keep a proper spiritual consciousness. In this existence it is your turn to learn how to have. During this process you are acquiring the knowledge that it is not *having* money that matters, it is what you *do* with the money and the ways in which you obtain it. During prior existences you studied a great deal on the spiritual level, and exposure to those who misused resources taught you to distrust anyone who had money. Consequently, during this existence you have a tendency to self-destruct where finances are concerned.

Many of you recognize that your quest is to learn how to handle money, and you have a strong desire and need for it. Yet, due to this self-destruct mechanism, when you reach a state of comfort you may do something on a subconscious level to destroy your financial position so you can feel good about yourself spiritually. You are learning to recognize that it is all right to have; the universe is concerned only with how you acquire what you have and what you do with it. Your job is to learn to manifest the abundance of the universe and feel free to have and enjoy the comforts of life.

As part of this lesson you need to learn not to measure your self-worth or the worth of those around you by their wealth or material possessions. This would be a negative pattern for you since any judgment you pass on others limits your own sense of freedom and self-worth. You are learning how to have without judging those around you. You still want to keep your spiritual values, yet you recognize that everyone is walking a different path and that this time your path leads to material prosperity. Now it is time for you to learn to accept money and allow it to validate your efforts and the spiritual energy that you are giving to your fellow beings. You are learning that it is natural for the universe to reward you with money when you give service to others.

Some of you come from a prior existence where you misused other people's resources and did not give adequate service for what you charged. In order to overcome a feeling of guilt and a fear of overcharging for your services, you have a tendency to undercharge for your services in this existence. You need to understand that in undercharging you are overcompensating and actually stealing from yourself. To bring this into balance you need to realize that the appropriate fee to charge is the equivalent value of the services rendered.

In learning to relate morally with those you come in contact, you may draw to you those who have very poor morals, and you may be used sexually by others. Or, in the reverse, you can regress into past life patterns and become sexually abusive yourself, having no regard for the other's feelings before entering into a sexual encounter. You are learning the value of appropriate sexual behavior. Learning to appreciate the wants, needs, and desires of another helps you to eliminate patterns where you think only of self-gratification. Through this process you also become more in touch with your own sexual needs and desires. By learning to interpret correctly the responses of your partner, you can become an extremely sensual person in this existence, mastering the ability to bring pleasure to yourself and the other person.

As you learn and grow and accept moral responsibility for your interactions with others, you learn to feel better about yourself and your physical body. If you choose to learn these lessons negatively, it brings discord into your existence, including the financial aspect of your life, thus creating financial stress. Moral, financial, and spiritual values are all interconnected parts of your life process and your lesson.

On a spiritual level you are learning to overcome a previous pattern of misusing your spiritual energies. You may have indulged in a direct misuse of power, such as misinforming others about spiritual awarenesses or psychic insights for the sake of material gain. In this existence you are learning the value of being honest in your spiritual communications to others. You are holding yourself accountable and working off the debt of using others inappropriately, either by taking what did not belong to you or by encouraging others to form a dependency on you for financial rewards.

In this learning process you are seeking a point of equilibrium from which you do not misuse others and yet do not cheat yourself by giving everything away. You are learning to develop a proper spiritual prosperity consciousness by recognizing the value in everything and everyone, including yourself. You can balance the guilt for prior lifetimes of misusing money and people by consciously using your power in this lifetime to validate your own self-worth and that of others.

You have entered into this existence with an extremely low sense of self-esteem. One of the lessons you are learning is to build up your feelings of self-worth and to feel better about yourself. It is very important for you to validate yourself and to accept recognition from others. Your challenge is to give yourself an opportunity to receive the positive reinforcement that benefits you so greatly. You need to know that you are a valuable asset to humankind; that there is a reason for you to be living other than to eat, sleep, and work; and that your fellow human beings care about you. You can learn to feel better about yourself by helping others and by accepting the verbal and financial gratitude of those you aid. And the more self-esteem you feel, the more valuable you become to those around you.

Part of your lesson is to get in touch with the physical body and the pleasures of physically living in a body on the Earth plane. Through this process you learn to understand about the Earth and the soil. As you learn all about Mother Earth, you discover that just by putting your hands into the ground you feel a sense of belonging. You can smell and appreciate the sweetness of the air you breathe. You are learning to be aware of the air entering your nostrils and feeding your body. You are learning to feel the earth beneath your feet and to appreciate the consistency of the ground you walk on, the soil that brings forth the life that sustains you.

You are learning to appreciate the fruits of the Earth—even, on a sensual level, the taste of the foods the Earth offers. When you look upon the world, you are learning to appreciate the vastness of its beauty, and you are beginning to hear the sounds and harmony of nature. Through this learning process you will be able to recognize how much the Earth plane offers you in terms of your soul growth. In return you will pay homage to the Earth by learning to use its resources and enhance its beauty, especially in your own surroundings. By being in touch with nature you find an awareness that is very personally gratifying. Through getting in touch with all your physical senses, you learn what gives you pleasure, and this enables you to teach others the value of taking pleasure from the Earth plane. You are helping those around you to develop a deep, healthy connection with the physicality of the Earth.

UNCONSCIOUS EXPRESSION: On an unconscious level you can defeat the purpose of your life lesson by blocking the flow of prosperity. You have come to learn a positive prosperity consciousness, but if you do not allow yourself to develop a secure base for your resources, you will find that you constantly have to reestablish yourself financially. You are driven to succeed financially, yet you find yourself losing touch with your original plan, failing to build a secure enough foundation, and rushing off to fill your financial desires too quickly.

Those with this eclipse are prone to experiences of bankruptcy. There is also a tendency not to value the self enough to feel deserving of achievement. Some of you have come from previous existences of a spiritual nature. You are aware of wanting to be of great value to your fellow beings in this lifetime, but when unconscious you forget to allow yourself the financial reimbursement due for your services.

Those of you who have chosen to learn your financial lessons the hard way may go through life thinking that money is the answer to all your problems. As you feed this negative thought process, you begin to judge those around you by their material possessions. Some of you have an ability to accumulate abundant resources, but due to this judgmental thought process you may find that the money and material possessions you acquire do not bring internal happiness.

If you continue judging yourself and those around you by these standards, it can put you in a negative frame of mind and expose you to very ruthless people. You can attract people who use others at their weakest point. If you avoid developing the proper prosperity consciousness, you rob yourself of experiencing the pleasures of life no matter how much wealth you accumulate. It is necessary for you not only to accumulate resources but also to develop moral and spiritual values.

While you may be aware that it is necessary for you to accumulate material resources in this lifetime, you still may feel that this makes you unscrupulous in some way. Because of this misconception you may set limitations on yourself, and when you reach a certain point, you unconsciously undermine your success. You may make poor investments or through poor judgment walk away from everything you have accumulated. Then you must start all over. Though you are capable of starting over, as time goes on this becomes a tiring process, and with each new beginning you have less motivation and experience less success. This may continue until you finally recognize what a proper prosperity consciousness is all about. Then you can also reevaluate your moral and spiritual values and develop a more sharing attitude toward others. This approach, in turn, opens you to receiving more material abundance.

On an unconscious level some of you have a tendency to be manipulative, scheming con artists when it comes to dealing with other people's resources. This can occur if you neglect your lesson of learning to develop your own resources. These are the souls who have lost confidence to the extent that their basic morality has been affected. This particular group can stoop to the most socially unacceptable levels when it comes to financial, moral, or spiritual values. Some of you can be complete social outcasts. Fearing that you can't do it on your own, you become parasites, feeding off others for your very survival. Your manipulative tactics degrade both yourself and other people, and undermine the very lessons you came to learn. In these cases a total reevaluation is necessary since you must begin to form proper behavior patterns that allow you to respect yourself again. Once you have reversed the negative process and begin to value yourself, you can find your way back to social acceptability.

CONSCIOUS EXPRESSION: On a conscious level you recognize that this is the lifetime to reevaluate and reestablish yourself in the spiritual, financial, and physical realms. You are coming from previous existences in which there was an overabundance of spiritual teachings and a nonattachment to material and physical reality. To balance your growth, in this incarnation you have come to learn how to acquire material things that bring physical comfort and serenity, and to realize that it is not negative to enjoy being in your body. You are learning that it is not wrong to acquire what you want and enjoy having it.

You are developing the understanding that the universe does not care if you go the River of Life with a teaspoon or a bucket. The universe will fill whatever size container you bring as long as you fulfill your needs while still respecting the self and those around you. There is no negativity in abundance if the resources are honorably gained and honorably used.

As you walk through life there may be financial problems, and you will have the opportunity to learn that with each new problem there is a new solution. As you remain open to the guidance that surrounds you, you will gain an understanding of how to build the foundations necessary to achieve financial stability in this lifetime. You can then begin to build this foundation and acquire great wealth. Not all of you have a need for great amounts of money, but all have a need to understand the place that money has in the universal scheme. You must come to understand that you govern money—it does not rule you. Those who are conscious accept this reality and free themselves from the misconceptions of the past. Your previous belief system was that having wealth left a person attached to the physical plane and therefore unable to connect with the God presence within.

You are also learning about your sexual values and sensuality in relation to your moral values. Past lifetimes of overindulgence on a physical level or a total abstinence of sexual participation have left you with a need to feel, sense, and become comfortable with physical pleasure. By learning to appreciate the senses of the physical body you can bring into balance your tendency to extreme physical behavior. You are learning about the senses themselves and how to be comfortable and appropriate within a physical body.

Many incarnations have been spent in either abusing yourself physically or totally ignoring that you had a physical body so that now you must learn to find a happy medium. There is a need for physical gratification, and at the same time there is a need for moral responsibility. When you consciously recognize that both of these needs must be satisfied, you will work on developing your sensuality while staying aware of the social and moral repercussions of your behavior.

TRANSPERSONAL EXPRESSION: You are here to develop the group consciousness of your fellow beings on the moral and financial levels. You teach us that we all are jointly responsible— morally, financially, and physically—for one another, and you show us how to interact and depend on one another in appropriate ways. You are also teaching us how to appreciate the Earth and her value—not only as the mother that sustains our lives but also as a valuable and integral part of the universe.

Through your natural ability to appreciate the value in all things and all persons, you help others to appreciate the value in themselves. You are extremely logical and have an innate sense of appreciation for all that is valuable in both the physical and spiritual realms. You can share these insights in simple ways that enable even children to expand their awareness.

You are acutely aware of the body, mind, and soul principles as they are activated by walking through a physical existence. You understand your relationship to the Earth plane and gladly accept the stability the Earth offers. When you feel the need to rebalance yourself, you can be found with your hands in the soil, for you have an intuitive awareness that this will put you back in touch with physical reality and with your internal balance. You understand that until we accept our physical reality we cannot truly set ourselves free from it. The Earth dimension will continue to pull us back until we have learned to appreciate and enjoy it.

You are teaching that until we totally understand and respect this plane that gives us life—until we totally understand and respect the physical body—we cannot free ourselves from coming back to experience another lifetime on the physical plane. You are teaching us the value of the physical plane in relation to the value of the spiritual plane, and you are helping us to understand their interdependency. Ultimately, you are teaching us the value of *appreciation* and its ability to free us from physical attachment.

PHYSICAL INTEGRATION: When you resist the lessons you have chosen to learn in this lifetime, you will find that the body communicates to you through the areas of the senses. You may find that the ear, neck, and throat areas become extremely sensitive when you are allowing your prosperity consciousness to slip. The skin may produce rashes when you do not allow yourself to experience physical comfort since the skin is connected to the sense of feeling. The ears may be prone to infections or other irritations when you are not listening to others. The throat may become sore and/or there may be a tendency toward sores in the mouth when you fail to appreciate the sense of taste. The eyes may become swollen and irritated if you resist the foresight you need for success. The nose may become overly sensitive and prone to allergic reactions when you do not remember to value the self. If you choose to ignore the lessons you have come to learn in this lifetime, one of the five physical senses will react in order to get your attention.

During your process of growth it would be wise to pay attention to these areas of the body, for through watching the body you can learn things you are not able to perceive intellectually. The senses are most easily set off-balance in this eclipse pattern while you are learning about the senses.

You also need to be mindful of the thyroid—it can become either over- or underactive, depending on how intensely you pursue the lessons of becoming comfortable within your physical body. The ears, neck, and throat areas should be watched most closely when your prosperity consciousness is out of balance since these are the areas of the body that communicate when the value system is in need of alignment. By watching these areas for early symptoms you can avoid many obstacles in your life.

Gemini

GEMINI

SOLAR ECLIPSE: (In order to fully activate the solar eclipse energy in Gemini, you first must integrate the lessons of the Gemini *lunar* eclipse with your emotional body. For a full explanation see "How to use Part II," page 166.)

In this incarnation you are teaching your fellow beings the value of communication. You have the ability to understand the importance of the spoken and written word, and one of your responsibilities in this incarnation is to keep information circulating. You have the natural ability to say the right thing at the right time, and you can talk to anyone about anything.

You have a knack for being in the right place at the right time to hear specific information that is needed by someone else. And the information that you share with others has the ability to change the direction of their lives. Through you they come to understand that they are in total control of their ability to communicate and that they must take responsibility for the frame of mind they allow themselves to have. As a natural teacher you have the ability to stimulate mental growth processes in others. Through your command of your native language, you awaken in those around you a desire to develop their mental abilities. During this process those you touch come to understand their fellow beings better and to broaden their consciousness. Thus, you bring the lesson of brotherhood to your social environment and teach us all to deal with one another in a more caring way.

On some levels you are teaching freedom of movement. You find confinement difficult since you are the storyteller, the jester, the town crier. Part of the uniqueness that you are here to offer is levity and a clear direction of consciousness through teaching others to see the humor within their own being. You have an ability to laugh and to create a change in an atmosphere that could otherwise block communication and understanding between people because of too much severity.

Yours is the eclipse pattern responsible for humankind's moving about the Earth and interacting with one another in larger numbers than ever before in history. This broadening of the circle comes from your insatiable need for more information that keeps you searching further afield and constantly expanding your environment. You are like the child whose first environment is limited to the home and then broadens to the school and to the neighborhood. Eventually the child grows up and goes away to college, then moves out into the business world, into a relationship, and to another city. Everything is continually expanding so that more experience can be assimilated, and you teach the value of this process to others.

This lesson may be taught either positively or negatively; the choice is yours, but the lesson must be taught. You may teach the value of extended horizons, increased communications, alert awareness, and flexible mental abilities by setting an example and taking an expansive approach to how you live your life. Or you may teach these lessons by being an example of what *not* to do through negative personality traits such as rigidity, improper social behavior, belittling others by making fun of them, and burying yourself in activities without sharing what you are learning.

You understand intuitively that life is too short for you to become a master in any of the many areas you want to experience. You have chosen in this incarnation not to master any one but to experience and taste a bit of everything. You are teaching those around you the value of having a vast number of experiences, and at the same time you are introducing others to these experiences. This allows the people you come into contact with to choose the directions in which they want to broaden their minds. You help people realize that there are more horizons and perspectives than they might originally have been able to see. Actually, you are teaching others to stop, look, listen, and investigate what the options are before setting themselves too firmly in any one place. You are helping people to recognize their options and to make educated decisions, and not fix themselves in such rigid mind-sets that they can't change course.

You are opening your fellow beings to the perception that they can experience more than one lesson or one set of lessons in a lifetime. You help them to realize that there is no end to the learning experience, just as there is no end to the universe—it is constantly expanding. You help to set us free and teach us that there are more places to go, more knowledge to gain, more information to pass on. It is a never-ending cycle, and you open up our consciousness to the awareness of this concept of infinity.

LUNAR ECLIPSE: Your lesson is in how to communicate. You are learning about the correct use of language and appropriate social behavior. You are learning not to take things for granted or assume that others perceive things the same way you do. In the process of honoring this lesson you must depart from your past life "hermit consciousness" and embark on a path of social awareness. In order to integrate your lessons you must align your consciousness with that of your fellow beings so that you can be of use on this planet by sharing the knowledge you have gained in previous existences.

In your journey through life you come to recognize that others seem to misunderstand your communications. The reason for these misunderstandings is that, accustomed to living within your own mind, you often do not realize that your internal thought processes have not been expressed verbally. Having thought about something, you sometimes think you have said it when you haven't. Then you get frustrated because someone didn't act on it. You are learning to ask for feedback to see if what you said—or thought you said—was clearly understood by the other person. You are learning that communication is more than verbalization; it has to do with the clear, effective giving and receiving of information.

To eliminate the frustration of being misunderstood it is important for you to ask for feedback. When the people you communicate with are able to tell you what they have heard, this will ease your frustration and teach you how to be more articulate in your communications. As you learn to communicate more effectively you will be able to reduce the number of times you solicit feedback.

Although you know intuitively that in this lifetime you must learn to relate with society, you still feel fearful. This is because you do not yet trust your own mental abilities and the soundness of your belief systems. You think that if you interact too much with others, their views and opinions may rub off on you. You fear that you can be too easily swayed from your own mental process and ideas by the communications of others. You arc so easily distracted that, as a defense mechanism, you sometimes block out others and don't hear what they have to say at all.

You also have a tendency to verbalize what you *want* to have happen instead of what is actually going on. This is because you want to program only positive information. You need to learn that sometimes the "negative" information is what you need to put yourself on a positive path! You are learning to accept the awareness of what *is* transpiring and the reason for being in an existence in which you need social interaction. The purpose is to accelerate your own growth process while on the physical plane. And if you refuse to integrate the so-called negative side of things, then you won't have the information you need for your own future growth.

During the process of learning to be sociable, you need to be able to understand how people are seeing you so that you can adjust your behavior and learn to participate more appropriately in social situations. This isn't something that we are born knowing how to do, but it is particularly important for you to integrate this information into your personality. You often think that being gracious means saying everything nice, while sometimes gracious means "thank you, but no." It is truly more gracious to decline an invitation politely than to accept out of a fear that if you say no, the person will never invite you again. Out of fear you may reflect too much sweetness and not enough honesty. It is not your intent to be dishonest; you just don't want to close any doors because you are aware of needing to learn how to interact socially in this lifetime.

As you become more open to learning from others how to socialize with mutually clear communication, you learn that there is a time to say no. This allows you to socialize in a more balanced way and also ensures that you have the time alone that you need. By not overcommitting, your lessons become easier and you avoid social blunders. By learning to say no you can actually begin to enjoy socializing, for it is no longer a strain: You do it when you want to instead of out of fear.

It is also important for you to recognize that you do need time alone. This is very important for you because when you feel that you have given too much of yourself to others and given away too much of your time—which you value so highly—you may find yourself trapped in a pattern of not showing up, not keeping your appointments and being unreliable. When you learn to respect your need for time alone and simultaneously integrate the social awareness you are here to learn, you can balance both inner needs. Another manifestation of this process can be seen in those of you who promise too much of your time, keep all your agreements, and then find yourselves feeling stressed, put upon, and exploited. In this pattern you may even become ill temporarily in order to gain the time alone that you need.

When you have learned to respect your needs, you can integrate your lesson of sociability with your desire to escape from the crowd. By facing both desires openly and honestly communicating your needs to others, you will be able to master the art of communication. This reflects that you have learned to communicate with the self, and this is what you have come to learn.

Your desire to be alone and spend time going within is very important to respect in this lifetime. It is through allowing yourself this time that you get in touch with the essence of your own being. You are coming from a previous existence in which you embodied a very monastic frame of mind. You walked a spiritual path, meditated in the mountains, or integrated a myriad of psychological and philosophical studies. Society has supported your personal spiritual growth in past lifetimes. In return you are bringing the value of all you have learned to your current existence. You have been allowed the gift of spending many existences studying and going within to understand humankind's role on the universal level. For those who are given the opportunity to study long enough to reach this depth of learning and perception, the gift must come full circle. Now you must find ways to share your knowledge for the good of all.

The importance of this for your particular time on the planet is that you have learned the common denominator, the common thread, that runs through all philosophy and all religion. You thereby have the ability to impart a nonprejudiced attitude in your interactions with others. Your challenge is to find a way to share this information in the course of your everyday life. This does not mean that you must stand on a soapbox and preach, but through your mannerisms, your lack of prejudice, and your understanding of theology, you can impart this information to those around you. This will only be possible, however, if you have learned your lessons regarding appropriate social interactions. And because of the importance of what you have to share, including your soul awareness and your ability to understand a more universal consciousness, you must take the time to be sure that you are perceived properly and are not misunderstood.

UNCONSCIOUS EXPRESSION: In this incarnation it would be possible for you to become a pathological liar. You want good so badly in your life and you want so much to please everyone that you can't bring yourself to deal with harsh realities. Everything you say tends to be "flowered" to tell the other person exactly what he or she wants to hear. If you lie, you please the other person, if only for a short while. Even if you don't like the way someone looks, you say: "My, don't you look lovely." Then you feel the gratification of communicating something nice, seeing a smile, and getting pleasure back from the other person. You don't want to hear or communicate any negative thoughts.

You are learning to integrate your communication skills with society in this incarnation. Yet, due to fear of rejection, you sometimes lack confidence in your ability to integrate any negative feedback from the outside. You need to communicate with yourself on a rational level in order to understand that negative response is not a personal rejection. You need to accept the spoken word for what it is—information about how the speaker is perceiving something. Then you can see that in every communication there is the potential for growth and learning. Through being objectively receptive to the other person's communication, you can gain the factual information you need in order to continue in your own growth. If you limit your communications only to positive information, there cannot be any growth, only "frosting." This "pseudo-communication" lacks the depth and honest interchange that leads to mutual growth.

At times you may feel like the world is "ripping you off," and in defense you have a tendency to take the initiative and do the "ripping off" first. Sometimes you feel that because you work so hard you have the right to take what you want, even if it doesn't belong to you. The basis of this self-defeating pattern goes back to an unconscious belief that you must not rise above your father's station in life. Thus, you may unconsciously circumvent your own success, causing your own downfall and putting yourself in situations where you have to do hard physical labor or work very hard to build your reputation. No sooner do you gain a reputation, however, than you do something to destroy it, and then you have to work very hard to get back on top again. Or else you change occupations often, starting new businesses and always having to build things up from the ground level.

You do this unconsciously because your abilities are so great that if you stayed in one profession you would eventually pass your father's level of success. In your belief system the "father" is the pinnacle, and your subconscious will not allow you to outshine him. This is due to former existences when you studied theology and gained a tremendous respect for the God-Father. Now there is confusion between that ideal and your earthly father. This misconception on the subconscious level disallows you from seeing yourself on any level as better than your creator. Through appropriate social interaction and growth in personal awareness, however, you can reestablish your spiritual path and recognize the proper place of love for the Father/father in your life. This frees you to become as successful as you desire in this existence. Then you will no longer feel as though you are being "ripped off" as a result of unrewarded efforts, for you can at last allow yourself to succeed.

It is most important for you to learn to deal honestly on all levels of awareness and social interaction. If you choose to be dishonest, you separate yourself from the realm of responsible conscious awareness. This means that you would no longer be of any use to the spiritual planes for imparting the information and the consciousness you are to give to others during the later years of this existence.

During the first fifty-six years of life you are allowing the growth process to manifest and build your reputation and sense of social honor and reliability. If you have established a reputation for being untrustworthy up to this point, you have obligated yourself to learn your lessons with more difficulty than was necessary—possibly through social disgrace. If this occurs it is because you have betrayed your own spirituality. It is of the utmost importance that you maintain a reputation for honesty and good character. The integration of appropriate social skills must have been accomplished by this point, including the development of gentle yet persuasive mannerisms, for it is through these abilities that you can share your spiritual consciousness effectively with your fellow beings.

CONSCIOUS EXPRESSION: Operating consciously, you recognize when you are misunderstood and go about making sure that you are being clear. Education is extremely important to you, for this is the avenue through which you learn to articulate your thoughts and ideas effectively to others. You can also learn the art of communication by developing your writing skills. The physical nature of using pen and paper allows you to bring out your thought processes more clearly. This avenue of expression is less threatening for you at first then direct communication with others. Writing will help you gain confidence in your communication skills, at which point you will be better able to communicate in the context of social relationships.

You might find yourself working in a sales-oriented profession, possibly in customer service or a position in which you afford yourself an opportunity to communicate with people from all walks of life. You may spend a great deal of time reading all forms of printed material and literature, perhaps watching television and simultaneously reading the newspaper. You are constantly busy and ask many questions. You recognize that your lesson is to learn the art of communication, and so you pursue it by going directly to the source: the classroom, television, books, newspapers. You try to expose yourself simultaneously to all the worlds you did not have access to in the past. It is not uncommon for you to watch two, three, even four television programs at the same time, or to read four and five books, since this intensified communication process activates your mind.

Physical movement is also very important to you. It seems that due to confinement in previous existences, movement and the motion of the body accelerates your communicative skills and your whole developmental process in this lifetime.

You are a gentle, aware soul with such a strong connection with the God-Father consciousness that at times you feel humbled in the presence of this awareness. This can lead to some blockages that prevent you from sharing your knowledge and awareness; on some level you don't think you have the right to rise above your earthly father's role in life. This is an extreme reverence to the Father-consciousness and may be a point of resentment for you. In facing these issues revolving around the physical father and the spiritual God-Father consciousness, you can learn to separate the reality of the physical plane from your spiritual awareness. Once you have these realms clearly separated in your thinking, you can integrate them more appropriately and to your great benefit in many areas of your life.

TRANSPERSONAL EXPRESSION: The reason you are here is to teach your fellow beings to communicate with one another because the consciousness of humankind is in need of realignment. You are working to restore the clarity of communication that existed among all people before the biblical time of Babylon. At that time there was a rift in the consciousness of humankind: The various tribes were split into different tongues (languages) and could no longer communicate with one another. Your consciousness contains the necessary ingredients to reunite all languages, thought processes, and belief systems. In a way your job is to heal Babylon.

With your communication skills you have the ability to convey to others an understanding of the common thread running through all things in the universe. Operating transpersonally, you can combine the discipline of communication with your sensitivity, manifesting the inspiration that allows others to recognize that they are one, yet separate. This awareness will lead to an interdependency based upon trust and faith in humankind that allows us to see the spiritual consciousness within all.

PHYSICAL INTEGRATION: If you choose not to learn the lessons of communications, you may experience some difficulty with the lungs, the nervous system, and the hands, arms, and shoulders. The body will begin to communicate with you in basically the same way you are supposed to be learning to communicate—by dealing with issues that create or are created by blocks in communication. The nervous system communicates to the different areas of the body. The lungs "process" oxygen for the entire body, and the hands, arms, and shoulders reach out to communicate to others literally and through body language. Your body communicates with you by drawing your attention to these areas, reminding you that the lesson of communication is being blocked.

The way to understand and alleviate these symptomatic physical responses is to reevaluate the way you have been communicating in daily life. When these symptoms occur, ask youself: Am I communicating everything—or am I holding back? Am I allowing my communications to flow forward, or am I blocking myself due to fear of rejection? Am I dealing with life honestly, or am I manipulating and making excuses so that I will not have to deal with the other person's response to an area I feel has not yet been integrated properly in my own consciousness?

Psychological health and physical balance can be restored by recognizing that during this process you must keep the communication flowing. It is necessary to remain honest and verbal, remembering to include the other person's insights into your perspective at all times. By learning to see the world through the eyes of others, you become free inside yourself. By integrating the information others give to you on the psychological level, you set your body free, opening the channels of communication to your lungs and nervous system. When all channels of communication are kept open, energy can flow freely through the body, maintaining perfect balance and health within your being.

You are learning how to communicate effectively with all aspects of yourself: body, mind, and soul. If in this process you tell yourself that the opinions of others are not useful, then you are unconsciously telling yourself that we are not interconnected but are all separate beings. The body receives the message that it is separate from the mind and the mind is separate from the soul, and so forth. Instead of functioning as a trinity you begin to function as three separate people, which causes confusion and disorder within the body. Then the body is unable to communicate clearly within itself and send the proper messages to its different parts. Thus, your physical problems manifest mainly in the nervous system, which circulates energy and messages throughout the body. When you learn to value the opinions of others and integrate what is appropriate, you are teaching your body to function as an integrated unit.

Cancer

CANCER

SOLAR ECLIPSE: (In order to fully activate the solar eclipse energy in Cancer, you first must integrate the lessons of the Cancer *lunar* eclipse with your emotional body. For a full explanation see "How to Use Part II," page 166.)

You are teaching people to understand, deal with, and express emotions, and how to feel. You are a healer who affects the emotional body of those around you. This helps those you aid to feel more stable and secure in dealing with their feelings.

You tend to draw to you those who don't understand their emotional problems because they are too connected to the external world. When confronted with problems on the emotional level, these people don't know how to react. Often you unknowingly heal others by taking on the negativity of their emotional upsets. You have the ability to heal their emotions through absorbing the negativity into yourself, dissipating it, and then releasing the healed energy back into the universe.

As a natural healer you heal the emotions and the soul. You lighten people's hearts; giving them a shoulder to cry on relieves their emotional block, allowing the natural balance of their emotional body to emerge.

The convenant that you have made with the universe is to relieve your fellow beings of their emotional burdens and upsets. To facilitate this process the universe has granted you the gift of being able to release this negativity back into the universe. The universe has promised to relieve your emotional burdens in return. You don't need anyone else to process them for you because as you take on and release the emotional burdens of others your own emotional burdens are released too.

You tend naturally to attract status quo, business-oriented, reputation-minded, "stiff upper lip" people since these individuals are unable to "throw away" anything, even their own negativity, and thus need a "receptacle" in which to deposit their emotional hurts. Due to their business orientation they naturally need everything to have a usefulness to it, and consequently they want even their emotional wounds transformed into something positive. You can facilitate this process.

It is important for you to recognize and respect the pattern with which those you help are resonating. These are people with an accumulation consciousness, and they have difficulty realizing that the accumulation of emotional debris is a negative process. They must deposit their negative emotions somewhere, so they gravitate to you. It is your job to accept with maternal understanding the negativity of others and then to allow that negativity to be dispersed into the universe.

You must avoid falling into the trap of self-pity by not appropriately understanding the importance of your role in the universe. You are not supposed to become overly involved in the emotional lessons of those you help but rather allow yourself to receive their burdens, share your empathy, and get on with your own life. If you focus on people "dumping" on you instead of on the gift they are sharing, you can become an actual garbage pail instead of an emotional recycling plant. The universe gave you the job of listening to the emotional ills of others because you have the capacity to release emotional pain—both your own and that of other people. As you serve your universal function you are rewarded by being allowed to experienced an incredible depth of closeness with many other people.

The emotional support you provide is extremely important. If others do not find a way to release their emotional debris, they walk through life emotionally constipated and entirely shut off their feelings. There is no room for their emotions to flow because they have created blockages, so they become cold, calculating, and very unemotional. You relieve these blocks in others, thereby restoring their capacity to feel. You can heal the emotional imbalance in others and simultaneously keep your own emotional flow active by reaching out to share.

There is a nurturing energy surrounding you that automatically relaxes other people and makes them feel comfortable. You project the serenity of a calm lake as you become accustomed to your path and willingly take on the role of assisting others in emotional purification. On a spiritual level you are known as Earth Mothers and Earth Fathers.

You were born with a high degree of emotional sensitivity and need to form behavior patterns that keep your sensitivity in a positive mode. If you are unwilling to share the gift of your sensitivity with others, you may close down and become overly sensitive on a personal level. This can lead to defensive, emotionally exaggerated responses that keep you from the closeness with others that is your birthright.

Learning how to channel your own emotionally sensitivity is very important. When you are helping those who are emotionally out of balance, you can usually process their emotional negativity properly. But you sometimes have a tendency to take others' upsets personally. This happens when you absorb the negativity into your body before the other person asks for emotional assistance. Sometimes you do not give people a chance to become comfortable and sort out their own emotions before you intervene and try to resolve their upsets for them. They feel this to be an invasion of emotional privacy. You must learn to be more aware of whether those close to you are truly in need of and are seeking your assistance.

When you violate the freedom of others to process their emotions, it leads to situations where you feel defensive and your feelings get hurt. Because you are an emotional healer, you will attract people who are not in touch with their emotions. They need time to process their emotional entanglements. If you try to pull out their negative emotions before they have finished processing and are ready to release the feelings, you pull to yourself more pain than is necessary. You need to allow others the privacy of their emotions before you go in and try to yank them out; you are a receptacle, not an emotional surgeon. Other people may "deposit" their negativity, but you don't have the right to "withdraw" it from them.

You must also be wary of allowing your feelings for others to interfere with your own process—your personal integrity in knowing what is right and wrong action. When you allow yourself to feed or overlook wrong action in those you are trying to help because you have no emotional bond with them, you end up retaining their negativity within your own being. On a physical level you may have a tendency to retain water if you restrict your activity and/or opinions due to your dependency on others or their dependency on you. Other people will simply dump their negativity. You must absorb the impact and then respond with your own *true* feelings about the situation.

It is your responsibilty to be yourself, to express your feelings and natural responses regardless of what you anticipate the negative or hurtful reaction of other people will be. You need to absorb their negativity without feeling responsible for the distresses that people go through in their lives. Keeping this perspective allows you to maintain your own ethics, truly helping others to heal their emotions. It also helps you to prevent your own emotional attachments from getting in the way of the healing process. You need to remember that when other people are going through personal suffering, it is simply the universe's way of waking them up and putting them back into alignment with their true purpose.

LUNAR ECLIPSE: You are learning to interact with others on an emotional level and to stabilize the emotions.

Your temperament contains an accumulated past life residue of feeling that you have to perform, to be "on top and in control" of the people and situations in your life in order to be accepted by others on an emotional level. In your youth you may have problems relating to your family unit because you don't understand your usefulness within the unit. You feel you must earn your way in order to achieve a feeling of belonging with others. In later years this can lead to difficulty in emotional situations if you don't learn to separate your ability to provide from your ability to experience emotional nourishment.

On an unconscious level you have incarnated into a family group you have never been with before, and you therefore feel uncomfortable within your own family. You have many lessons to learn about the emotions and the emotional responsibility family members have toward one another.

Your discomfort forces you to learn to deal with your emotions. You can either learn to be responsible for your moods and attitudes, choosing not to create friction for those around you because of your extreme emotional sensitivity, or be at odds with everyone in the family and have to learn through constant emotional irritation.

One of the ways you can learn to deal with your emotions is to become more aware of the effects your emotional outbursts have on those around you. You need to understand that everyone deals with emotions differently and has the right to emote in his or her own way. Being overly sensitive you should refrain from making emotional judgments prior to digesting everything that has occurred in any given situation. You are learning not to take on feelings that don't belong to you, not to project that others are in a bad mood because of you, and not to feel that you have to defend your own existence because someone in your family is in a bad mood.

If you respond defensively to the moods of others, you become an annoyance to the very people with whom you are trying to learn your lessons. As the agitation gets stronger you feel even less wanted, for you are so sensitive that you feel the annoyance of others and know when they don't want to be around you. But usually you are not in touch with the fact that your own defensive attitude is separating you from your family, not the true essence of who you really are. You need to allow other family members emotional freedom and to recognize their right to feel differently from you about any given thing. As you become less defensive, others will enjoy being around you, and the learning process can take a positive course that is less painful for everyone involved.

Prior soul memories of tremendous success in the realms of business, management, and worldly success simultaneously accompanied a neglect of family interaction and warmth in past lifetimes. Overemphasis on business and neglect of the family have created an imbalance that necessitates your making emotions a top priority in this lifetime. Although you are loved by your family, quite often you don't recognize it because you do not know what emotions feel like. You are here to break the pattern of walking away from emotional situations and hiding in the outside world.

You tend to feel isolated even when with others because you don't have a sense of belonging within yourself. One of your first lessons is to learn to be comfortable and centered within your own body so that you can feel emotionally secure when in the company of others. Once you feel that sense of belonging you will begin to sense your own value in relationships with others. Then you will feel secure enough to confront issues and situations instead of sidestepping everything. When you reach the point of allowing yourself to be cared for, you are well on the road to learning your lessons.

All the fears you have about coming out of your emotional shell are the result of not knowing this inner sense of security. Consequently, when others approach you to share and exchange nurturing on an intimate level, you feel uncomfortable unless you know exactly what they expect of you. Before you can allow yourself to feel, you need the security of knowing you can fulfill the other's expectations. At times this can cause you to appear cold and calculating when actually you're a marshmallow.

On the emotional level you are a child of the universe. You have natural abilities with business and function very comfortably in the business world. Yet back in your home environment many of you have a tendency to be emotionally immature. The male expects to be mothered by his wife, and the female expects to be coddled by her husband. Through your mate and those in your intimate circle you are seeking to replace the emotional nurturing you did not allow yourself to feel as a child. This is why it is important for you to learn to feel secure within your own being; you do not have to go through life seeking approval from those you love. Feeling every adjustment and criticism as a personal rejection can lead to your withdrawing into your inner shell.

You are learning to accept yourself as a being who is going through different phases of life and has ups and downs and makes mistakes just like everyone else. You are beginning to realize that mistakes do not mean you are not worthy of love or are not a useful human being. It just means "whoops, I guess I need to try that again."

UNCONSCIOUS EXPRESSION: The main way you defeat your own happiness is by wallowing in self-pity. You say to yourself, "Nobody loves me and everybody is criticizing me and everyone wants something from me and nobody appreciates me or accepts me the way I am." Actually, you are unconsciously projecting these fears from inside yourself. These are not facts of objective reality, but your fears can become self-fulfilling prophecies. Your negative outlook may actually draw into your life people who *are* like that, or you can bring out these qualities in the people close to you. There is also a tendency to draw takers and users because you are feeling so sorry for yourself that the universe responds to that energy by supporting your expectations. Since your expectations are that you are going to be taken advantage of, life sends you a person or situation to rape you emotionally.

When you get too involved in self-pity, you can go into long periods of "brooding" that make it difficult to let go of past hurts. This indulgence is your main stumbling block. The reason you have this tendency is that self-pity evokes the semblance of "self-nurturing" feelings. But indulging in this process actually prevents you from future growth since it is by learning from your unpleasant experiences that you grow beyond the need to repeat them.

A second self-defeating mechanism is your difficulty in "letting go" of what is familiar (a job, a situation, a person, and so on). Holding on to the old, even if it has become stagnating and emotionally unsatisfying, offers a semblance of security. But this can actually prevent the present and future emotional satisfaction that you long for. By letting go of situations that are no longer conducive to your personal growth and vitality you become open to receiving the bounty of fulfilling emotional situations into your life.

Another way you inadvertently defeat yourself is by overcompensating for your emotional insecurities. You may be unwilling to leave a familiar home environment even though it is no longer productive for you to be there. In severe cases some persons with this eclipse pattern suffer from agoraphobia (fear of open spaces). Your insecurity and fear of being rejected by the outside world can leave you with a sense of being unfulfilled. You may also tend to indulge in compensatory activities such as overeating, substituting food as a source of emotional nurturing and comfort.

Overcompensation can also result in a tendency to retain water for emotional support. There may be a strong desire for dairy products due to their subconscious relationship with mother's milk. These compensating tendencies will continue until you become a truly self-nurturing individual.

CONSCIOUS EXPRESSION: One of your first steps should be to learn how to nurture yourself. Self-love will build the confidence you need to take the emotional risks necessary for emotional triumphs.

One psychological technique that can increase self-love is the practice of creative visualization. Try to remember a particular time in your childhood when you felt unloved by one or both parents. In your mind rewrite the script, "seeing" your parent(s) giving you exactly the kind of nurturing you needed at the time. Repeat this exercise until you can do it easily and comfortably. Next, practice visualizing yourself as an adult walking up to your "child self" and hugging that child. These exercises can free you from feeling the need to be accepted by others, which totally frees you to be yourself!

Another way for you to nurture yourself is to take responsibility for building emotional safety into your relationships by honestly sharing your emotional responses, fears, and tender feelings. Such verbalizations validate the existence of your feelings, and through this process you gain a sense of inner centeredness and strength. If rejection and disappointment do arise, this enables you to handle them without the sense of woundedness that would ordinarily drive you back into your shell.

By taking chances in expanding your emotional horizons, you open yourself to the types of relationships that can bring real emotional satisfaction. On a subconscious level you are teaching yourself to manifest emotional satisfaction through believing that you deserve it and can handle it.

Through difficult emotional experiences you learn to develop a sense of "grit" that serves to keep you above the dangers of an endless pit of emotional quicksand. A willingness to grow beyond these hurts is a prerequisite for climbing out of the emotional muck that you were born to transcend. It is, in fact, the difficult emotional experiences that actually earmark the path you must walk and master, one step at a time, in order to obtain the full emotional satisfaction that is your birthright.

TRANSPERSONAL EXPRESSION: You sense that your emotional fiber is actually not personal at all but rather your link with the universe. As you listen to your emotional body and allow it to be expressed honestly and naturally, without censorship, in whatever environment you find yourself, you restore a healthy emotional balance for those around you. Thus, giving your own feelings a voice, expressing the subtle emotional undercurrents you sense going on around you, clears the emotional atmosphere for everyone involved.

You do not take the emotions you feel personally by reacting to them or holding on to them. You understand that you are working out the group karma of emotions on the planet and thus process emotional upsets readily and willingly, realizing that you are simultaneously helping to cleanse the emotional body of the planet. You have the capacity to link with the most intimate part of other people—their personal feelings, hurts, longings, and disappointments—and to establish this link from an objective, transpersonal level. Operating at this level you can allow the unconditional love and acceptance of the universe to channel through you to heal the emotional wounds of the people who cross your path.

Born under this eclipse pattern, you entered onto the Earth with an etheric "coating" of emotional hypersensitivity. When this sensitivity is directed *inward,* from a motive of self-protection, the result is emotional starvation and isolation from others. When directed *outward* on the transpersonal level, if your gift of sensitivity is used to be aware of others' emotional essences, your inner serenity becomes your strongest support system. This sensitivity comes from a motive of healing the emotions of others. The result is an internal experience of calm self-nurturing, total satisfaction, and fulfillment from within.

PHYSICAL INTEGRATION: Resistence to learning your lessons can lead to physical symptoms of ulcers and other stomach disturbances such as gastritis, indigestion, hearburn, belching, or water retention. Other symptoms of imbalance with the Cancerian energies can be abscesses, malignant and nonmalignant growths, disturbances in the pancreas, and afflictions of the uterus. Occasionally, the breast area may also be affected. Problems with calcium levels can lead to deterioration of the bone marrow, knee problems, or soft teeth. Of all the eclipse patterns yours is most positively affected on a physical level by periodic visits to the ocean or other large bodies of water.

On a holistic level the body is physically integrating the pattern of learning to nurture and be nurtured. Every cell in the body is relating to this nurturing process, so the body is constantly absorbing—either someone's negative emotions or food or water. That is why you have a tendency to retain water. Your body will continue to do this until you have integrated your process and no longer have to exaggerate "absorption" to draw attention to your need to nurture others or to be nurtured. Conversely, you may be a very thin person and have difficulty keeping anything in your system. In this case the exaggeration is in refusing to accept nurturing.

On a deep psychological level, water retention is actually the cells saying to the inner organs of the body, "We'll love you, we'll coddle you. Feel it, sense it. We'll hold you." As you begin to practice self-nurturing on the psychological level, the need to overnurture on the cellular level will begin to dissipate.

Leo

LEO

SOLAR ECLIPSE: (In order to fully activate the solar eclipse energy in Leo, you first must integrate the lessons of the Leo *lunar* eclipse with your emotional body. For a full explanation see "How to Use Part II," page 166.)

As the solar eclipse in the sign of Leo, you have come to teach your fellow beings how to accept love.

People drawn to you are extremely aloof and have difficulty accepting too much affection or what they would view as too much affection. They tend to feel that love is limiting, that love would hold them down. They find themselves continually detaching instead of learning that they can accept love and retain freedom simultaneously.

You can help others learn this lesson in different ways. One way is to persevere, not taking "no" for an answer, and continuing to love and share love when you honestly feel it in your heart, whether those around you are remaining aloof or not. You can also share love through recognizing the good within others and teaching those around you to feel that they are worthy of accepting love and strong enough not to lose their own identity. Or you can be very demonstrative, jealous, and possessive where love is concerned, thereby showing those drawn into your life exactly what it is they *don't* want. Yet this very process encourages the other person to look elsewhere for love that will allow them freedom.

Your ability to teach others to lighten up and not take things so seriously can bring happiness into the lives you touch, providing you don't take *yourself* too seriously. You have a tendency to come into the lives of persons who need cheering up, who feel the everyday duties of life are too mundane for them to handle. Through your ability to find pleasure you teach others to find it too. Those of you with this eclipse pattern who choose not to accept your natural ability can teach others the value of happiness through being overly devouring and jealous; this causes people to break from you and find happiness by going their own way.

When you don't understand what you are teaching, you can find yourself trapped in patterns of loneliness and self-pity. You can create a great deal of unhappiness and loneliness in your own life. You must learn to allow your glee and joyfulness to shine through, no matter how much negativity you draw to you. With your ability to spark creativity and love in others, you attract persons who are very down on themselves. It is extremely important that you remain centered and not allow those around you to knock you off-balance and change your way of looking at life. It is your duty to remain buoyant, teaching others to love the self.

If you should find yourself trapped in a pattern of loneliness, you need only to bring romance into your life to feel that spark of love inside. And if those around you refuse to accept your gift, it is important that you share in another area. If you have chosen to stay in a relationship with a person who is unwilling to love the self, you can share your love and creativity in many other areas. You can work with children or go into self-expressive fields such as teaching, creative arts, and acting. There are many areas of life where you can express this wealth of creativity and your ability to stimulate others into rejoicing about the self. You do not have to remain in morose patterns. If you do, it is self-inflicted, and you do not have the right to blame others since you have the strength and ability to climb out.

It is very important for you to save time for fun. Just as it is important for a Capricorn eclipse to be successful in business, the Leo eclipse must let the child shine through. Your example allows others to see that we are all children in life's eyes, and our lessons do not always have to be so serious.

As you allow the child energy to flow, you also allow the creative force from within to flow. You can be extremely creative yourself, and/or you have the ability to spark creativity in those around you just by validating the child in all. When we are children, our imaginations are not tarnished with the worries and anxieties of everyday life. And when your energy enters into another's life, your playfulness allows them to set aside their worries and to play. As you teach this to others you find those around you becoming more creative when their true inner spark begins to burn.

You are the true teachers of the zodiac, for in teaching those around you to lighten up and get in touch with their own creative source, you show them the goodness that lies within and afford them a means of bringing it forth. You have an innate ability to teach people to find their own self-worth and to motivate them to go forward in the world with their own natural abilities proudly shining.

As with the other eclipses, you can teach your lessons from a positive or negative standpoint. You can share love, sensitivity, and recognition with those around you, teaching them to become proud, creative, loving of self, and thereby able to share love with their fellow beings. Or you can go through life invalidating others, taking credit for their creativity, and devaluing those who are close to you. In this way you push others to the point of standing up for the self and recognizing: "Hey, I'm worth more than this." Either way, the lesson of loving yourself, being proud of yourself, and letting yourself shine is taught.

LUNAR ECLIPSE: You have come to learn how to accept love in this existence. In the previous lifetime you played a very strong role in the humanities and developed a humanitarian type of consciousness. You loved on a more universal level, not taking time to feel individual personal love, personal pride, or self-worth. In this existence you are learning to accept your own individuality, which includes developing the ego, learning to be proud of the spark of the collective consciousness that you carry within, and allowing your own individual spark to burn brightly to reflect the glory of the whole. You are beginning to realize that in performing your individual best you are truly honoring the oneness by shining your brightest. When connecting in a group consciousness, we honor one another by doing the best for each other that we possibly can.

What motivates us to do this "best" is to develop the ego. The idea is to develop the ego without selfishness and yet at the same time with self-love. You are learning to find things within that you can feel proud of. You are learning to be proud of the self and self-expression, but you must begin by learning to love the self.

You are beginning to recognize that the self is worthy of being loved and that it is not a negative thing to accept love and to feel self-pride. Many of you are coming from such a universal consciousness that you think it is negative to care about the self at all or to develop the ego. You may lose sight of the fact that although we are all part of the whole, we are also individuals. You realize that we are all connected and that we must all help one another. Your difficulty lies in recognizing that you have a responsibility to make your individual spark—your individual self—as valuable to your fellow beings as possible. In teaching one another personal pride and self-love, we spark the battery that encourages us all to perform at our highest.

Somehow you developed the spiritual misconception that your role is to be a doormat for society. You feel that if you think too highly of yourself, you will be singling yourself out as being more important than the group. What you need to learn in this lifetime is that you can only be of use to the group when you feel good about yourself; we all perform best when we feel confident inside.

You are learning that to truly love all you must first love yourself. You are learning to honor those things in your life that cause your individual spark to grow stronger, shine more brightly, and become as vibrant as it can possibly be. By learning to recognize your own self-worth, the flow of your creative energy, and your own special essence, you are adding to this plane by allowing the self to shine through. Those around you can benefit from your ability to inspire others to be more creative and more loving. Once you have found this space for yourself, you can be one of the most inspirational of teachers.

When you finally recognize that it is all right to love the self, you have reached the point where you can accept love from others. Your lesson is to accept love into the self as well as learn to love the self. You have a tendency to detach from loving situations, fearing that the involvement will be limiting. You need to realize that it is all right for love to remain a constant within your life. It is all right to allow yourself to be loved, and you do not have to be perfect first! You fear that if you are not perfect, you will hold back yourself or the other person, so you may drive yourself to a state of perfection before you allow yourself or another to truly commit.

During this lifetime this thought process needs to be reevaluated and changed. You need to recognize that we are here to give support to one another by accepting love and support from each other. This support makes our journeys easier, more loving, and more conscious; we are in our most comfortable, productive states when we allow ourselves to feel loved and be supported by those around us. You need to allow yourself to benefit from this love and support, and not isolate yourself with an unrealistic "reality."

There are three basic steps in allowing this love to enter your life. The first is for you to recognize that we are all separate entities within a whole. The separate divine spark within each of us needs to have support and love from other members of the whole. No one is an island—we all need love.

The second step is for you to realize that sharing and being loved are all right. They are not signs of weakness but natural, healthy human traits.

The third step leads directly to the other major lesson you have come to learn: the lesson of procreation, or individual creativity. You are learning that if you are to create anything worthwhile in this life, you must take in the love and support of those around you. Until your being is in total balance and harmony, you cannot connect with your truest creative forces—the forces of procreation. These have the power to create another entity, whether it be another human being, a painting, a book, a garden. To allow the "child" of your creativity to develop properly, you must reach this level of awareness and accept love.

Within this element of procreation and creativity you are learning to let your own creative spark flow so that you can give back to life the beauty that you see. You can express this spark in art, in writing, in choosing to teach a child how to learn and grow, or perhaps on the stage, sharing love, happiness, laughter, and drama with others.

Because Leo rules the factor of procreation, you are in touch with the creative energies, the Christ consciousness, the God consciousness. You are also in touch with the possibility of losing your identity to those you serve, just as actors and actresses often lose the privacy of their own lives by playing roles for the masses.

In the past you have dispersed your individuality into the whole so that now you have no recognition of individuality. Thus, you need to develop a conscious awareness that there is an individual spark so that this divine particle becomes validated. There is a fear of coming into the body and developing an ego within the body. The thought is: "Now I'll get caught up in the stream of life and really lose my identity." This is the phobia that unconsciously prevents you from coming into your own space. In actuality once you begin to manifest your individuality, freedom, not entrapment, is the result.

You may have a fear of becoming an individual because more is expected of individuals, and you don't know whether or not you can live up to it. You fear getting caught up in the responsibility of living up to your capabilities. And this is another lesson: not to concern yourself so much with the future outcome of the projection of ego but to live in the integrity of the moment, doing what brings uplifting feelings and happiness to the spark within the individual self. In giving happiness to your own spark—your self —your inner joy and sense of fulfillment will flood out and increase the quality of life for all those around you.

In this lifetime you are allowed to have happiness and love; you deserve it, and it is an individual duty for you to achieve this time. It is the factor that is missing in your soul growth. You have repaid your debt to society many times over, and what is owed to your soul growth pattern in this existence is individual, separate, personal love and development. You want to become a creative force within the self because in honoring the One, you must procreate. And your job is to create through sharing the joy within yourself.

This correlates directly to the lesson of learning to love the self. The creative energy is so strong within the Leo that if you don't develop your own individuality before your creativeness starts flowing, then others may recognize the spark before you do. This can lead to others ruling your life, which is exactly what you fear.

UNCONSCIOUS EXPRESSION: Operating unconsciously, you have a great deal of difficulty keeping any consistency in relationships. You are coming from a past life awareness of relationships holding you down. You fear that becoming involved in the feelings of others means being responsible for their feelings. What you fail to realize is that learning to interrelate, share feelings, and accept love is an essential part of humanness. You have an awareness of group consciousness and a recognition that the whole must be taken into consideration, not just the individual. That side of you is very well defined. But when it comes to personal self-worth and value, loving the self or allowing others to love you, you have a tendency to run from those experiences.

In order to turn this pattern around, you need to become aware that when you deny yourself the affection and support of another, you are only functioning at half steam, and sooner or later there will be no steam. Science has proven that a being cannot live without love. A simple technique that you can use to get in touch with the interchange of personal love with your fellow beings is to begin what is known as "hug therapy," allowing yourself to hug and be hugged.

Another area where you may have some difficulty because of a lack of self-esteem and self-love is in a tendency to give away your power. You do not recognize the value of your own creativity. You have the ability to create a winning situation for everyone concerned, yet when you give away your power you block your creativity from being used constructively. Sometimes you allow others to take credit for what you have created and often it isn't as constructive and successful as it would have been if you had stayed involved. As you become more in touch with the self and learn to value the self, you can reap the rewards of your own creativity without giving it away. Then you will afford yourself and others the joy of sharing a very special part of yourself.

On the unconscious level, through low self-esteem and being overly serious about the concept of universal consciousness, you can forget that it is all right to enjoy living on this planet. There is a subconscious fear that if you allow pleasures, this will trap you into a returning cycle. It seems that every part of the process you are going through boils down to allowing love into your life, bringing about a natural healing and balance within the entire personality.

But if you opt for continuing the process of *not* allowing yourself to feel love, you will destroy the very essence of your life. And in this destruction there is great sadness. You can find yourself wallowing in periods of depression created by your reticence to accept love. These self-inflicted depressions need to be understood so they can be removed.

It is not necessary, healthy, or even part of your lesson to go without love. The idea is for you to open your eyes to the beauty you have within and understand that because of this beauty you are valuable and worthwhile. Then you can remove the veil of self-inflicted depression and allow your creative juices to flow. As you create, spreading the happiness you feel to others, you are soon able to see what is within you that is worthy of being loved. The Leo eclipse truly is a humanitarian who has lost sight of individual value, and you must now open your heart to accept individual love. Through an overabundance of service you forgot to take time to regenerate the self.

If you get caught in the negative aspect of learning your lessons, you can be very detached, cold, and castrating to those around you. You may also be high-strung, unemotional, defensive, and double-dealing. You may not trust your own creativity but may steal the creative works of others, suffering a lonely, deprived existence. Until you can climb out of this negative state, you will feel a void around you. When you learn to turn your energies around, you will find an unquenchable desire to assist those who are less fortunate, as if you were paying back the years you deprived yourself of being around anyone. You become a crusader in the humanities and bring forth new and innovative ways to assist, entertain, and give pleasure to all.

Should the pattern of not honoring the love within the self continue, you will find yourself becoming nasty with those around you, rebellious, sarcastic, pushy, and domineering. The reason these patterns begin to surface is that you are not recognizing any self-worth and therefore not recognizing when someone else cares or wants to support you. You come on very strong and arrogant to get your needs met, but actually, if you opened your heart to those around you, they would be more than willing to assist and even find pleasure in supporting the extremely loving, vibrant, joyful Leo (eclipse) that you are capable of being when you don't block off your own creative energy.

To help reconnect with the flow of your creative energy, it would be useful for you to stop and say: "Does this feel right?" Learn to trust your body: If it feels right and is for the highest good of all concerned, do it; if it doesn't feel right, don't do it, no matter what anyone says. Establish this bond of trust with the self; your inner voice has the clarity to raise your self-esteem and self-confidence. Then you begin to follow your inner guidance and satisfy the child's longing within your own heart.

CONSCIOUS EXPRESSION: You recognize that the idea is to create, not from a basis of what others expect but rather from that sense of love and joy within. You are here to share love and to share yourself. Indeed, sharing yourself is a form of creation. You understand that the universe created us out of love, and we can't create at our finest until we can function from that base of love. And we cannot accept this universal love going forth to others in an effort to reunite the whole until we can really *feel* it. In order to feel it we must experience it in conscious awareness.

When you begin your journey into creativity, you find pleasure in sharing your expressions of love, whether in painting, acting, raising children, writing, or just finding creative ways to allow others to feel uplifted and sense the love that is flowing from you.

Once you allow yourself to tap that internal source, that spark of the collective consciousness that burns within, there is no end to your ability to create and to manifest exciting experiences in this lifetime.

You develop a way with children that is remarkable to behold. As your enthusiasm for life begins to accelerate, being in your presence can be like riding a roller coaster. Sometimes your expression of creativity exceeds what another would consider human endurance, yet to the driven Leo eclipse the boredom of noncreativity would be more than you could endure.

You do recognize some obstacles in learning how to accept the responsibility of love into your life. For both the unconscious and conscious eclipse, you are still learning how to accept love. The conscious eclipse, being aware that this is an obstacle to growth, has a driving need to answer the question, "Why am I doing this?" And you may experience many different relationships, constantly searching for this answer. You may be involved in self-evaluation techniques, whether it be meditation, yoga, or any other technique that can bring you out of the self. You are more comfortable in detaching and find that if you can remove yourself from the problem, you can see it more clearly. Once you understand it you are very capable of healing it.

You are gaining awareness of the self and the issues that block you from loving. In your mind if you allow anyone to love you, it means that there must be something special about you. And after all, "How could any of us be any more special than the next" if we are to have the universal consciousness of which you are so proud?

This would seem to invalidate your belief system, but what you must come to realize is that through the universal consciousness developed in previous existences, you forgot to recognize that you are also an individual embodiment of the spark of the collective whole, and that spark needs recognition. You are beginning to realize that you need to allow others to give you love in order to open yourself to the mental and emotional flow of life. Then you are cooperating with the heartfelt factor within you as well as the tide of events that is going on externally. By expressing the inner in combination with the events of the outer, a truly vital alchemical combination comes forth that is healing for all concerned.

On the conscious level you are learning to trust that others truly love you and to be open to accepting their love. As you expose the spark within to others, you can discover whether or not those with whom you are surrounding yourself truly appreciate you. You may find that there is no need to dominate the situation so you can allow yourself to trust those around you and interrelate with more harmony. Through bringing more harmony into your life you allow yourself to develop the true creativity that you have come to express.

TRANSPERSONAL EXPRESSION: You are learning to honor the divinity of the whole by doing those things that strengthen, honor, and allow for the preferences of the individual spark of divinity within yourself (Christ consciousness). By respecting the spark of the collective consciousness that burns in all, you are teaching others the energy of procreation. You have an intuitive understanding and awareness that this divine spark can be found within every living thing. It is up to us as individuals to respect and pay homage to that spark by fulfilling our personal life experiences to the utmost, by allowing the joy and pleasures of loving and being loved, and by sharing our creative energies with our fellow beings.

You are extremely creative and have an ability to inspire others to bring forth their creative essence. You desire to see all those around you become the best they can be, for if we are all achieving our highest potential, we are simultaneously aiding the whole. You are acutely aware of your place in the collective consciousness and the fact that you have been created in love. The energy of love is what gives life to everything: a child, an idea, or an action. Nothing in the universe can exist without love since the universal scheme of life is the essence of love. In the transpersonal expression you express this pure essence of love.

PHYSICAL INTEGRATION: When you choose not to allow yourself to feel love and affection in your life, whether it be by not loving yourself or by not allowing others to love you, the body has a tendency to weaken the heart muscle. The heart muscle seems to correlate directly to your ability to love and be loved. The essence of love is the very essence of survival for you or any other being. It seems to be the most important factor in human existence. Without love, as time passes, you lose the desire to live, thereby creating disorders within the body that directly correlate to the vitality of life.

The spinal column can also become affected. It seems that when the vibrancy of love is shut off from the heart center, the heart center isolates itself from the rest of the body. Then it does not allow the spinal column to carry the messages from the brain, thereby cutting off communication and vitality.

By breaking through these obstacles you can regain your vitality and restore health to the entire body. But it takes love to give you the desire to do so. Once you are determined, there is no holding you back from any achievement, including restoring health to the body.

Virgo

VIRGO

SOLAR ECLIPSE: (In order to fully activate the solar eclipse energy in Virgo, you first must integrate the lessons of the Virgo *lunar* eclipse with your emotional body. For a full explanation, see "How to Use Part II," page 166.)

You have incarnated this lifetime in order to teach people how to use their analytical faculties. Thus, you have a tendency to draw gullible people who need to learn how to put things in proper perspective. You attract people who live in illusionary states and need someone to teach them to take more responsibility for their actions. Through your ability to correctly assess most situations and bring reason to the problem-solving process, you can be of great help to those who have lost their direction.

When you accept your gifts, you are a natural-born counselor because you can sense what is needed to help people regain an objective focus. Through bypassing the emotions and gaining direct access to reason, your insights can guide people around emotional responses that might have been blocking them from seeing things more clearly. You can discern, by attending to people's usage of words and their body language, where they have weaknesses that need to be addressed. You can see where the emotional responses are, and you know how to get around these responses to allow people "in the back door" so they can get to what they really need to deal with. When necessary you can even help them to reprogram their thought processes.

You also teach others about assimilation, showing them how to stay more grounded while they integrate New Age concepts and expand their awareness. By teaching people how to organize their lives, you make sure that everyone is doing his or her part so that the planet can continue to evolve. You are the one who puts your "shoulder to the grindstone" to get the job done and takes care of all the details. You are a positive example of a hardworking person, showing your best effort by being very precise and analytical. Just by the way you live your life you teach those around you how to put things in proper perspective and do the work that needs to be done. You help them to learn not to feel sorry for themselves, not to get lost in a daydream world, and not to be overly sensitive. Your philosophy is: "Hey, we all have to work. Don't feel sorry for yourself. We need to do this, and we can't function unless everyone does his or her part."

Sometimes you are misunderstood because of your ability to see flaws. If you don't present your insight tactfully, you may not be appreciated by those you help.

Your contract with the universe is to point out flaws so that things can be put back in proper alignment. Since your motivation is the desire that everything and everyone function at the highest level, you will always call attention to something that isn't "right." It sometimes seems to others as though you are constantly putting your finger on a sore spot. Those you help may not appreciate you at the time, but later they do appreciate the correction that has been made.

In this process you do not get much validation for your work, and sometimes you wonder if it's all worth it. Yet it is almost a compulsion for you to continue pointing out people's flaws because your contract with the universe is to help put the planet back into alignment. Professionally, as a counselor, you may help to put people's consciousness back into focus. Or as a friend you may try to point out things in a tactful way. You have the ability to see the whole picture, and thus you know how to align the parts properly. Wherever you are, you find yourself adjusting the individual parts into harmony with the universal whole. You deal most with this aspect of "adjustment" since this is the main purpose of your sharing. You go through life creating responses in people that cause them to adjust. There is always a temporary irritation in the adjustment until they feel comfortable in the new groove, and then they appreciate what you have done. You need to know that people do come to appreciate the observations you have shared with them.

If you find that you are being misunderstood and that people are having difficulty getting along with you, it is time for you to analyze some of your own behavior. You may have reached a point where you have become so analytical that you have forgotten to be tactful and discerning. A pill is always easier to swallow when there is a little sugar on it. Remembering this will enable you to maximize your ability to be accepted by others, which in turn allows you to be of more assistance.

Timing is of the utmost importance. You need to remember that there is a proper time and place for criticism—tact alone is not enough. Even if you point out a flaw to someone very sensitively, if you do it at the wrong time and the wrong place, it can still be extremely hurtful. For example, you don't tell someone, "You have bad breath," just before the person gives a presentation and there is nothing he or she can do about it. Don't tell a person about something that can't be corrected at the time if it is going to make him or her self-conscious. You need to afford others their space and respect their ability to be comfortable with themselves so that they are able to function at their highest level. By criticizing people at the wrong time you can knock them off their stride at a time when they most need your support. You need to wait until their feet are planted firmly on the ground. Your observations will have the most impact when others can translate them into action immediately.

On the nonpersonal level you have the capacity to work in the field of systems analysis. You can work within large corporate structures, and you have the ability to work with important projects that call for someone who is really attuned to detail. You are also good at putting people and projects together. Because you can understand different processes you are able to recognize the people and information that belong in those areas. Thus, you would function quite comfortably as a systems analyst or director of human resources.

Work is very important to you, and when your career is stabilized, other areas of your life automatically become stabilized. You don't have a need to be a nitpicker at home if your work environment affords you an opportunity to use your discerning eye. This allows your critical ability to be used for its maximum benefit while keeping it out of the home where it can cause stress. It is recommended that you do not apply your analytical process with those close to you unless you have mastered using a great deal of tact. Being critical toward those in your home environment can cause detachment within the family unit. However, this energy can be used positively in the home in the area of the family's diet —selecting what the family should eat for proper nutrition and maximum health benefits. You also have a talent for keeping the mental stimulation and communication flowing through the family unit by not allowing blockages to form from emotional responses that have been misunderstood. For this alone you are a very valuable asset to any family, social, or work environment.

LUNAR ECLIPSE: In this incarnation you need to learn not to be so gullible and ready to believe what others tell you. In past lives you were overly involved in the spiritual realm, and this time you must adjust and get your feet back on the ground. You need to find out that you can function in the physical world and still retain a spiritual consciousness. And one of your major lessons is to find a balance between the spiritual and the physical worlds. You need to learn that while we are in physical bodies we have physical desires. Your gullibility lies in the fact that you don't take the desires and motives of others into account when you make decisions. You already recognize the God essence in everyone, but you also need to realize that being in the flesh and working on certain lessons adds a different flavor to the spiritual character of every person. This is why you must learn to put things in proper perspective and take the desires and motives of others into account.

You are psychic at birth and have very strong sensitivities, but because of your one-sided approach, many of the signals you receive seem mixed and clouded to you. In understanding and using your psychic awareness you need to remember that if an insight is useful to you, it is from the universe and you can trust it. It if isn't useful, discard it. In this way you can learn and assimilate what works in the physical universe through a process of personal discrimination.

As far as your problem with gullibility is concerned, it is not necessary for you to worry about who is telling you the truth and who isn't. You didn't incarnate with the ability to tell who is honest and who is dishonest—you just see everyone's spiritual essence. It is difficult, therefore, for you to sort out fact from fiction when dealing with their *physical* forms. Again, just concern yourself with whether what you are perceiving, being told, hearing, or reading is useful to you *personally*. If it is, then you can integrate it into your life and use it. If it isn't, no matter how useful it is to someone else or how truthful the information might be, you must discard it so that something else you need can come in. You are teaching yourself to assimilate and integrate information instead of functioning solely from your "inner perception" as you have in previous lifetimes.

By incorporating analytical thinking into your behavior patterns, you are able to take control over your life, be more decisive, and take charge of the direction in which your life is going. You are combatting an inner tendency to be wish-washy and easily victimized by others through your readiness to trust without first checking out pertinent information. Once you establish an analytical frame of mind, you are no longer plagued by manipulative parasites. You are taking responsibility for your own life instead of waiting around for others to lead you, and you are learning to discern where your associates are headed before agreeing to participate in unrealistic pursuits.

You are learning physical integration on a multitude of levels. It is when you incorporate your reasoning ability into your behavior patterns that you solidify a sense of adulthood and become an effective focus in the world. It is also important for you to learn to respect your physical body, especially your digestive system, since it correlates most directly to this eclipse pattern. You need to take responsibility for the foods you put into your body, just as you need to take responsibility for the thoughts you accept into your consciousness. You need to take responsibility for the cleanliness of your physical body and the organization that you bring into your environmentt. Paying attention to these physical processes gives you confidence in your ability to operate effectively in the world.

Through learning to pay attention to details, you learn to put things in proper perspective—placing them where they belong in your life. The digestive system does the same thing when it sends nutrients to the different areas of the body—where they belong.

So both internally and externally you need to ask: What is this? What value is it? Where does it belong? And as you practice keeping your physical environment in order, on a psychological level you are incorporating a sense of order, clarity, and definition that helps you to develop a strong reasoning ability.

You were born with psychic abilities and are working to develop reasoning abilities. You have been overly sensitized to the spiritual realms in prior incarnations, which has resulted in a tendency to be "spacey" and nonobservant in the present. Details in your environment are often overlooked so that you can continue your spiritual quest. But you must retain a sense of discipline, refinement, and responsibility to your fellow beings. You can truly be a spiritual herald for the planet through offering your services, once your gifts have been incorporated on the physical level. You are responsible for helping others to harvest what they have planted on the psychological level. The idea is not to make reality fit into the dream vision but rather to infuse the dream vision into the present lifetime. To do this you must learn the "nuts and bolts" of society's rules and be able to operate effectively within that framework.

UNCONSCIOUS EXPRESSION: If you choose to resist the flow of your lessons, you may become trapped in patterns of self-pity, martyrdom, self-indulgence, and other forms of escapism. You can have problems with overindulgence in alcohol, drugs, and/or food. You are drawn to these escape patterns because you feel that the physical world is too harsh. In severe cases you may allow the body to deteriorate and even entertain thoughts of leaving this plane to escape from your lessons. You need to realize that the *proper* way for you to escape from the unpleasant aspects of life on the physical plane is to learn the disciplines that enable you to establish your spiritual visions of happiness on a tangible level in your everyday existence.

Serving others enables you to get in touch with the sense of spirituality inside you because with a loving heart you can help your fellow beings raise their consciousness. Watching others establish positive behavior patterns helps you find proper connection with the physical plane. You need to realize that you are here to "serve or suffer"—there is no middle path.

When operating unconsciously you have a tendency to be overly critical due to a lack of balance in your life. If you don't hone your analytical abilities and develop your sense of tact, you will be constantly disappointed by the behavior of others. Learning not to take the actions of others so personally would greatly enhance your ability to interact with others harmoniously. Sometimes you are born into a family environment in which there is much harshness and criticism. To survive you may shut down your sensitive nature and function in the critical manner that you were exposed to in your own youth. In these cases you can become very cold and crude in your speech and mannerisms, finding fault with everything and everyone. Your intolerance is so great that you walk through life constantly pointing out the flaws and weaknesses in those around you, without tact or regard for their feelings.

Once you recognize this pattern it becomes possible for you to train yourself to be aware of others' feelings. Through this awareness you can learn to get in touch with your own feelings and chip away the crusts with which you have protected your fragile sensitivities. When you learn to recognize and take into account your own sensitivity and that of others, you are able to communicate your discerning observations in ways that strengthen the character and improve the life circumstances of those around you. And this is what you have come to learn and to integrate into your personality.

There can sometimes be a "hollow cylinder" aspect to this unconscious eclipse pattern, for there are times when you totally turn off to life experiences. Then you walk through life assimilating nothing and sensing nothing, caught in a void between the spiritual and physical worlds and not functioning in either. At times you may not have any sense of direction or see any reason to be on this planet at all. So strong is this fog that you can't even sense the spiritual realms. You are yearning to feel at home someplace —anyplace—and yet you don't know where "home" is.

The imbalance you find on this planet—and the challenge to readjust your consciousness to the needs of the physical plane so that you can be of use here—is sometimes so overwhelming that you totally detach, and this is when you seem to be a hollow cylinder. But you are learning to recognize that the Earth plane is where home is in this incarnation. As you accept being on the Earth and allow yourself to become grounded through effective participation here, you find a true sense of spiritual worth that anchors you in both worlds simultaneously.

CONSCIOUS EXPRESSION: Operating consciously, you intuitively gravitate to the lessons you came to learn in this lifetime, and you willingly take responsibility for how you interact with others. You find yourself constantly dealing with situations where you have to integrate your analytical abilities within your family unit, work environment, and social life. You are called upon to use your abilities to discern and discriminate, and you feel a strong sense of urgency to hone these skills so you can be of service.

You intuitively recognize the needs of others and are receptivie to fulfilling them. You have a strong sense of loyalty and the desire to be of service, although you often need to be taught how this service can be performed. You are very willing to help others if they will tell you what it is they need. You are a very growth-oriented being who recognizes the need for putting things in proper perspective, and you have come to learn to do this in your own life as well. You have walked a very loving spiritual path in previous existences and are putting that love to work in the here and now. You have a warm space in your heart for your fellow beings; thus, you want to be of service to humankind, and you need to learn how to do this effectively. It is for this purpose that you have come to the physical realm.

In this lifetime you experience a great deal of hard work, and when operating consciously you have very few problems accepting your role as a worker. You recognize that you are integrating the ability to work and function on the physical plane as a productive human being. You feel a sense of being in tune with the universe, and you recognize that everything in the universe has a physical counterpart.

Often you experience some situation in which you require counseling, for there are times when you need assistance in understanding how the mental faculties assimilate information. Normally, you seek this counseling yourself, recognizing when you are personally out of alignment, and this is one of your strengths. You are overcoming a need to handle everything by yourself and are voluntarily seeking aid to understand better what it is you are not perceiving accurately. By allowing someone else to assist in your growth process you are able to rise above any emotional disturbances or interferences that may block you from functioning at your highest level. Once back on track you rarely need this type of help again. The process that you learn through counseling is how to integrate your reasoning ability into the rest of your being. When you have mastered this you are ready to help others.

From a very early age you have been curious about the workings of the human mind. You are very inquisitive, and sometimes you are told by others that you are troublesome and nosy. But this is a necessary process, and you should not feel guilty since you need to have as many facts as possible. You require abundant information because you are learning to process things and put them in their proper place. This is an important part of your personal structure, for your greatest freedom lies in mastering your reasoning ability. You can relinquish the burden of requiring each detail when the assimilation process through which you learn to become more aware begins to operate automatically. You can simultaneously assimilate what you need as you pass through an experience, leading to your greatest and most joyful awareness: enjoying the vividness of life through the ability to *be totally here now.*

As a child born with this eclipse pattern you need to be allowed to satisfy your curiosity. Others should not have imposed their own behavior patterns on you (that is, children should be seen and not heard). It was necessary for you to learn how to integrate socially at a very early age in order to prevent blockages that could cause you difficulty in communicating with others and put you into an unconscious mode. Once in an unconscious mode it is difficult for you to become conscious again. If this should happen to you, others who make you feel useful and appreciated and who give you responsibility can "kick start" you back into the conscious mode. To help you remain conscious you should form habits of defining your goals and purposes and be careful to follow your chosen path.

TRANSPERSONAL EXPRESSION: On the transpersonal level you are teaching your fellow beings about the digestive process, whether it be spiritual, physical, or mental digestion. You are here to teach us to put things in their proper perspective and to put the proper foods into our bodies. You are the "Ralph Naders" of the planet, making sure that our foods are free of pollutants, our water is fit to drink, and our air is clean enough to breathe. You fight against anything that endangers the survival of the physical body so that the spirit will continue to have a vehicle through which to learn its lessons and evolve. You are helping to restore balance and harmony on the planet itself by teaching your fellow beings to take responsibility for what they put on the planet, into the atmosphere, and into their bodies and minds. You are here to teach the planet what to eat and what not to eat on all levels.

You make us aware of those things that will cause problems in the future. If we overeat and put food into our bodies that our bodies cannot use, it will show up later on the hips or someplace where we don't want it. The Earth, which is part of the universal body, can have the same experience. You are responsible for teaching us what *not* to put into our bodies and also what *not* to put on the Earth or into the atmosphere because you intuitively understand what can and cannot be assimilated. What cannot be assimilated is going to lie around and cause us problems in the future.

Like bees or ants, you work hard physically and keep things together so that, as spiritual beings, we have a safe and healthy environment in which to manifest. You bring spiritual energy onto the planet by physically working and doing the labors of love that make the planet a comfortable place for all beings to function. You are charged with the responsibility of manifesting spirituality in a practical, helpful way on Earth. You teach that we can have true spirituality if we are all willing to work together and for one another. We need to acknowledge that we are interdependent—just as the bees and the ants are interdependent—for our survival. When we are on the physical plane, *we are our brother's keeper*. You show us that we must learn to accept and incorporate this interdependency and work hand in hand for the greatest success.

PHYSICAL INTEGRATION: There is a direct correlation between the digestive system and what you need to learn. Thus, the digestive system in the body will communicate—through its own imbalances—when proper psychological integration has not taken place. The entire digestive tract can be affected. The large intenstine and even the spleen can develop knots and restrictions when you are not functioning properly on an analytical level. You need to recognize that when you are working to assimilate information on a mental and emotional level, at the same time you are programming your body to integrate nutrients appropriately.

If you teach your body negative patterns for integrating the substances you put into it, the body will rebel through the digestive track. This can show up in problems with elimination. When food is not properly digested, the consequences may be constipation (a result of ignoring problems and not processing them) or diarrhea (the result of overanalyzing a situation).

A severe reaction to ignoring the necessary process of thoughtful assimilation can be intestinal cramps and severe forms of gastritis. A bloated abdomen can indicate the need to reevaluate what is going on in the external world in terms of proper adjustment and assimilation. Inflammatory problems with the appendix can be another way the body communicates an immediate need for you to pay attention to integrating and assimilating what is going on in your life.

If you are too distracted to understand that the body is reflecting what you are experiencing on a psychological level, the lymphatic system may also be affected. This can lower the body's resistance, leaving you open to hidden infections and a breakdown of the immune system. It is important to recognize that the areas of the body ruled by the eclipse pattern can also be the strongest areas if you choose to pay attention at an early stage to what the body is trying to tell you.

Libra

LIBRA

SOLAR ECLIPSE: (In order to fully activate the solar eclipse energy in Libra, you first must integrate the lessons of the Libra *lunar* eclipse with your emotional body. For a full explanation, see "How to Use Part II," page 166.)

You have an ability to teach your fellow beings the subtleties of developing balance and harmony in their lives. You have an intuitive sense of what is fair in all areas of life, especially in the area of relationships, and you have come into this existence to teach others how to share. Thus, you will draw to you people who are either selfish, overly independent, or extremely childlike. You can meet with great resistance as you teach these people the give and take of life. The balance in any one-on-one relationship is a very fine line between giving and receiving, and the majority of those with whom you come in contact are excessively attached to one or the other. Because of your innate need never to settle for less than half or to give more than half, you may find yourself moving from one relationship to the next.

You are conscious of having two separate needs: to share half of yourself in a relationship and to keep half of yourself wholly to yourself. You are not comfortable with the other person giving more than half in a relationship because you fear that you may then be required to give more than half at another time. Essentially, you are teaching others how to keep their own identity in the context of a relationship.

As you teach this lesson you must keep your sense of fairness in balance, for if you become unbalanced, you can end up teaching the lesson through your own misuse of the sharing energies. Those who are in balance and teaching in a positive mode make excellent lawyers, counselors, and advisors of all kinds, for with your ability to sit on the fence you can truly see both sides and aid both parties in finding an amiable solution.

At times you can appear very stubborn and selfish in relationships because once you have reached that halfway mark in giving or receiving, a herd of elephants could not push you further. In relationships once you feel that your partner is not coming up with his or her fair share of giving, you begin to lose interest. You will give generously in a primary relationship, but once you feel the other person is asking you to cross the line of fairness, your attentions leave the relationship. You always have an ongoing relationship, and if your partner does not share fairly with you, you simply begin sharing with someone else. In this situation you teach the value of sharing through removing yourself (physically or emotionally) from the relationship.

Through sensitive communication others may be able to coax you into explaining the reasons for any of your decisions in life, even after you have reached the point of anger. When angered, however, you can be almost warlike, as if you were a general plotting a strategy. Before you will walk away from any relationship, you will use whatever means possible to show others just how unfair they have been. This can include treating them as unfairly as they have treated you.

Sharing every part of your life with one other person is your ideal, but when that is not possible, you will not compromise your need for fair play. You are capable of segmenting the different areas of your life. For instance, you are capable of staying within a marriage relationship for financial reasons only, partaking and sharing in the financial end of it so that things will remain fair for both parties. Simultaneously, you are capable of taking the loving side of yourself and sharing it outside of that relationship. Monogamy is your ideal, but it is not your motivation. Fair play, sharing, balance, and harmony are your priorities as well as what you are teaching others by the way you live your life.

This also holds true in business relationships. If you have made a commitment to a business deal that is not meeting your financial needs, you will follow through with this commitment but make future investments somewhere else.

You have the ability to teach fairness to those around you in any manner in which those who need this lesson are capable of accepting it. If people who give too much draw you into their lives, you will take until they realize that "hey, this is not fair." If they are the type of people who take too much, you will say, "Hey, this is not fair." Whichever role you feel you must play, the lesson is taught.

If you choose to ignore your innate ability to interrelate with others from a standpoint of balance, fair play, and harmony, your behavior patterns can become extremely selfish, insensitive, and self-destructive. You can give off an energy that repels people from becoming involved with you due to your unwillingness to share any part of yourself. If you choose not to deal with the energy of fairness from a standpoint of personal integrity, you can be very arrogant and self-righteous, thereby teaching the necessity of fairness through your own self-centered behavior.

You teach the value of sharing on a multitude of levels. You teach that when we give up our need for self-containment and come out of ourselves, we double our capacities. In sharing our thought processes with others we gain additional resources and learn to value their input. In sharing our finances we double our financial strength. You have an innate understanding of the need to band together and do more sharing, and you have the ability to bring people together who are of value in one another's lives. You help to show those around you the value of teaming up. Being extremely adept at recognizing when a merger is advantageous to both parties in business, friendship, and romance, you make an excellent marriage counselor, business consultant, or matchmaker.

Those who accept the energy of the Libra eclipse have learned to master the fine art of communication. You understand the importance of communication and the value of negotiation, and you teach this through your own communicative skills. Whether in business deals, intimate relationships, or the give and take of friendship, you teach others the most valuable part of communication: getting another perspective on their problems. By bringing issues of concern out of the self, people can be detached from their emotional influences, and this is very helpful in making intelligent decisions. You also have the ability to teach others the mirroring technique of seeing themselves through another's eyes.

By teaching the interdependency of relationships you show others the value of relating and the value of keeping their own identity. Thus, we learn and grow as individuals and always have something to share with others. If we become overly dependent on a relationship and do not involve ourselves in learning and growing on our own, we have nothing to bring to the relationship and thereby have ended the sharing process. You incarnated with this awareness and are sharing it with others. This is also why, in teaching the lesson of relationships, you find it so necessary to keep your individuality, for you intuitively understand that without that you can teach nothing. Basically, you teach us how to take the other person into account witout losing track of ourselves.

LUNAR ECLIPSE: You are learning how to be fair in all areas of life. You are learning to share your mind and recognize the value of bringing your thought processes out of the self to communicate with others. This allows you to see how the opinions and insights of others can help you make intelligent decisions.

In relationships you are learning the proper balance between giving and taking—not to take from another more than you are willing to give or give to another more than you are willing to take. Through this process comes the realization that taking from another human being when you are not willing to give is a theft of emotion, and this is very unfair to do to another. If you choose to live your life taking the affection of others when you are not willing to return it, you end up filling your life with "bodies" but no feelings.

On the other hand, if you are constantly giving to people who are not willing to take—people who are fearful of accepting love —it will be easy for you to fall into past patterns of holding on just to have a body there. You may be fearful that if you give up someone you care about, that place in your life may remain unfilled. But if you continue giving, you can totally drain your vitality and capacity to love. So whether you find selfishness in others and learn about fairness in that way or are selfish yourself until others demand fairness from you, the lesson of fairness in areas of relationships will be learned.

Some of you are learning about balance and harmony in areas of business. You are learning how to merge forces in order to work with others. Sometimes you may feel that everything in the business world must be accomplished by yourself and that if you join forces with another you will lose recognition and become lost in the crowd. Once you have learned to share and work with others you will realize that there is even more success for you in joining forces.

Those of you who come to this lesson from the opposite perspective will have a tendency to give all the credit to your partner in business or your mate in the home. You need to learn the value of taking your share of the credit. Whether in a business project or in a relationship, you tend to give all your time and energy and not save any to do what you need to do with your life. If you refuse to learn the lesson of fairness, life may take away whatever is "unfair" in your life. And life has no regard for whether *you* are being unfair or another person or situation is being unfair to you. The universe does not care what you have or do not have, only that you learn to share.

You incarnated with great difficulty in learning how to share because you are coming from past lifetimes of being extremely independent. The majority of you want to share, but you are so accustomed to doing it by yourself that it's difficult to learn how to depend on another. It feels awkward for you to slow down enough to allow someone to assist you, but accepting help from another validates that person's reasons for being involved in your life. If you continue to go through life being so self-contained, those around you will feel no need to be with you. It is important for you to slow down and allow others to participate in your life, or you will walk through life feeling lonely and keeping yourself from the very thing you promised to learn in this lifetime: relating with others and finding harmony within relationships. Reaching this point of balance within yourself and recognizing value in your partner are prerequisites for you to be able to have a partner in any area of your life.

Your "Daniel Boone-type" attitude comes from a previous existence of just going after what you wanted, walking through other people's territories, with no regard for others. You need to learn the social graces, including tact, sensitivity, and consideration because yours is a raw, emotional gut instinct. If you ignore your need for relationships, one of two things can happen in your old age: You can be lonely and feel a sense of incompletion, or you can become totally dependent as a last chance to learn the lesson of allowing others to assist you.

In all areas of your life you must learn to develop a balanced sense of commitment. You can be so insistent on moving forward that you forget about previous commitments, or you can be so tied into commitment that you are unable to function without one. Here again balance and fairness are the operative words. Commitment, whether it be by spoken word or legal contract, can be a sore spot until the concept of responsibility is accepted and demanded. You need to keep the commitments you have made and to demand that others keep their commitments to you. By being aware of the need for all involved to keep their promises, you are freed to interrelate in a positive way.

UNCONSCIOUS EXPRESSION: Operating unconsciously can bring you a great many relationship problems. You have a tendency to go from relationship to relationship, never understanding why they don't work out. You can be extremely unfair to your fellow human beings without even recognizing it, and you can be so self-centered that you take from life and relationships whatever you want with no regard or consideration for the other people involved. This can affect your business affairs if you become unconscious of how you are interacting with people on a financial level. This tendency can cause a great many financial as well as relationship problems in your life, causing you to go from job to job wondering: Why is everyone being unfair to me? Why is everyone picking on me? Why is no one thinking of *my* interests? Why is everyone being so demanding of me and holding me down?

If your are operating unconsciously, you need to stand still for five minutes and take a look around. Take a look *behind* you and see the expressions on the faces of people whom you have just raced past without even saying, "Excuse me" or "How are you?" or "How was your day?" Some basic considerations need to be incorporated into your makeup, and one of those considerations is slowing down long enough to allow other people to catch up to you.

On the other side of the scale, you can set yourself up as the martyr in relationships, not recognizing that you are always giving without asking for anything in return. You do not recognize that it is a form of selfishness not to give others an opportunity to aid you or feel they are an intricate part of your life. This is just as negative as going through life taking everything you want without regard for others. You tend to take over in relationships, providing everything *you* think your partner needs without even asking, "Is this what you want?" You feel you are doing a fabulous job aiding the relationship, bettering your partner and doing nothing for yourself, when in reality you are taking over without regard for the other. The only difference is that you're leading from behind, with a big push from the back.

What needs to be learned in both cases is to take other people into account in forming relationships. You need to stop, look, and listen as you become involved in any relationship. In this way you can take others into consideration without either ruling their lives or taking off in your own direction.

A technique that can be useful for you is sitting down with a pencil and paper and figuring out what you are willing to give to a relationship and what you expect from a relationship *before* you become involved. Through this process you can learn what inter-relating is all about. Taking time to think about it and saying, "These are my personality traits; this is why I expect; this is what I will not accept," enables you to relate with more clarity and to be truly yourself.

CONSCIOUS EXPRESSION: Operating consciously, you are aware that you have difficulties relating and are trying to overcome these problems by asking questions and getting feedback on what others think of you. In this existence you have reached the realization of what you want and where you are going. You are coming from previous existences of being in constant motion, and in this existence you must learn to appreciate relationships. Life is a journey, and in order to enjoy it you need to take others along with you. Otherwise you find yourself on a lonely path that has no end.

On a conscious level you realize that you want a mate, another person to make this journey with you. But you also realize that you have never learned how to relate. In the beginning phases of learning how to open yourself to another, there may be periods of opening, shutting down, going inside to evaluate what has been learned, and then coming out again. These periods of "inward shutdowns" are very necessary, for you are just beginning to learn how to interact. It is important for you not to become discouraged by this process since it is very easy for you to pull back into your strong sense of self-containment and self-sufficiency. Try to stay in touch with your yearning to share.

It is also important that you always seek honesty in your communications with others, for there can be a tendency toward rationalizing what is going on around you so that you remain in a past pattern of not taking others into account. You are learning to meet in the middle and to be willing to adjust yourself to the needs of those around you. Even the most conscious of you find it a challenge to adjust to another. Yet if you remain true to your inner desire to share, this process does eventually take place.

While learning how to relate you come to understand that communication is the key. You ask questions, get feedback, and find out who you are through others' eyes. You come into this existence finding it difficult to see yourself until another reflects your image. Through this need for reflection you are prodded on your path of learning to relate and communicate.

You are also learning to share and relate with your coworkers and business partners. You are learning to afford yourself an avenue of added success by incorporating the lessons that others have learned into the lessons that you are learning, thereby doubling your resources. As this process becomes a more integral part of your business, social, and romantic life, you become adept at relating to others and an avid spokesperson for teaching those around you the value of being conscious of their fellow beings.

TRANSPERSONAL EXPRESSION: On the transpersonal level you are aware of the needs and the delicate balances of those around you. You no longer relate only on a personal level but seek to find those modes of mutual expression that create a higher balance and harmony in each of your relationships.

On the level of group consciousness you are teaching those of the physical realm to connect and communicate with all realms. You intuitively understand the need to watch, respect, and nurture nature itself and our interdependency with the Earth while we are on this planet. You are aware of the interdependency we have with one another and the necessity of communicating clearly to aid one another's process on this plane. You understand our spiritual connection with the universe and the need to remain true to our spiritual self, staying clear on our journey into consciousness.

You are here to teach those of the physical realm to understand the interrelationship of the physical annd spiritual realms, as well as the role the Earth plays in the universal plan. When you assist those on this plane to gain a higher understanding of the value that all things have to one another, you are truly a valued spiritual worker.

PHYSICAL INTEGRATION: When you learn to pay attention to the subtleties of the body, you begin to understand the essence of sharing and communication. The body is an intricate communication system, and through listening to it you can learn when something is out of balance.

The body will draw attention to the kidneys and adrenal glands, and also the ovaries for women and the prostate for men. When there is an imbalance in the external world, the physical world will reflect this imbalance in these areas. Just as we live our everyday lives integrating our external relationships, deciding which are positive and which are not, our kidneys and adrenal glands do a similar job with our internal relationships. The kidneys filter the impurities of deception, whether self-deception or the deception of others. You can learn a very valuable lesson by listening to the body because it doesn't lie. By lying to yourself you do as much damage as if you are being unfair with another person, and your body will teach you this lesson. If you refuse to learn your lessons in the external world, your internal universe will impose them on you.

With the eclipse pattern of Libra it is wise to remember that the essence of this pattern is honesty. When your energies are out of balance with the self and those around you, and when you are not looking with clearness of vision and being true to yourself and those around you, you disturb the delicate balance of your body. This can cause your physical equilibrium to become unbalanced, and you can be subject to swaying from side to side, an inability to walk securely, and various other balance problems. This is because the balance the equilibrium represents within the internal physical world is an exact reflection of how you are dealing with your external worlds.

Scorpio

SCORPIO

SOLAR ECLIPSE: (In order to fully activate the solar eclipse energy in Scorpio, you first must integrate the lessons of the Scorpio *lunar* eclipse with your emotional body. For a full explanation, see "How to Use Part II," page 166.)

In this incarnation you have come to teach your fellow beings about the responsibility we all have to one another on this planet. We also have a responsibility to create our own destiny and manifest our desires on the physical plane, but we must do this without interfering with the destinies of others. You teach those around you to take total charge of themselves, to be accountable for their actions, and to understand that whatever is given out comes back to the self. The concept that every energy expelled from the physical being, the spiritual being, or the emotional being comes full circle to the source is very important, and the Scorpio eclipse rules this energy of "what goes around comes around." You teach that we are all held accountable for our actions, our desires, and even our creations, for we are responsible for whatever we manifest. You have the unnerving ability to see into the essence of a person and recognize what is in need of repair, and thus you are able to teach moral, financial, and spiritual responsibility. You draw people to you who need to know if there are any cracks in their foundations, for in bringing the Scorpio energy into their lives they become aware of any personal weaknesses. It is important for you to remember that you are responsbile for shedding light in areas where you expose ills. You do not have the right to inflict pain without cause. You are the eclipse pattern of the surgeon, and it would be just as great a karmic debt for a surgeon to open a living body and walk away as it is for you to expose a wound without shedding insight and using your energy for transformation and regeneration.

If you are functioning from negativity, you are capable of using the resources of others with little regard for how it may weaken them. On the negative plane you can be highly manipulative, forfeiting your free will to a cycle out of which it seems to be almost impossible to climb. If you yield to the temptation of altering your own behavior in order to elicit a certain response from others, you can find yourself trapped in a vicious cycle because when you use your ability to understand the psychological mechanisms of another for the purpose of manipulation, mutual entrapment is the result. You may continue this pattern until you recognize what it really does: The energy of manipulation in actuality limits your own life experience.

You must remain true to your own desires, whether or not those around you have the same desires. Others need the freedom to have separate goals, and you must avoid the temptation to sway them from their path. Your power comes from keeping the purest of personal integrity.

Keeping your personal integrity intact allows you to come from a positive place in sharing your knowledge of the workings of the universe, the depth of your spiritual awareness, your understanding of the cycles of life and death, and the motivation for the behavior patterns of those around you. In this way you can add insight and clarity to the lives you touch without giving in to the temptation of using your power to bend the will of others. When you are in a state of high integrity, you have the ability to help those around you locate what needs healing in themselves, which enables them to become clearer as to their own personal motives. Once they become clear about their motives, they are able to take responsibility for their actions and rise to a new level of personal power.

You have a tendency to draw to you people who have an improper prosperity consciousness, and you teach them to rise above the financial muck that they have imposed upon themselves. You can recognize when they have taken a wrong turn in terms of their values and need help to reestablish their own pathways in alignment with moral principles that will serve them. You are willing to lead people out of places that others would fear to enter, for you have the capacity to see future consequences from present actions. You can see where others are on the wrong track, and you have the integrity and courage to point out to them how they can realign themselves with their own best interests. You are teaching that it is more important to help others remove blocks to personal empowerment than it is to be tactful or to ignore the obstructions.

Because of your ability to help people who are out of alignment, you tend to attract all sorts of "lost sheep." If you are coming from negativity, you can incur a great deal of negative karma from misusing people in their moments of weakness. You are teaching the correct use of power and must take care not to misuse it yourself since you will be held accountable at a later date.

You possess a tremendous energy for healing in this lifetime. You heal peoples' value systems—moral, financial, and spiritual. During this process you empower others to tap their own creative resources and thus become successful. Many of you work within financial, counseling, and rehabilitative institutions of all kinds, whether physical, spiritual, or financial in nature. These could include mortgage companies, metaphysical counseling, the medical profession, collection agencies, the Internal Revenue Service or other investigative agencies.

People are drawn to you whose values are contrary to those of society. This is because they need contact with healing energy to come back into alignment with themselves and their own constructive use of power. These people sense that their energy is harmful to society, and yet their spiritual essence does not want to harm society, so they are looking for help. The universe wants to heal all its children, and therefore it empowers you with the energy to confront people with weaknesses in their values and to help them see how their actions affect other people.

You are teaching people that until their values are in alignment with correct universal principles, all of their actions will be self-defeating, fruitless, or disappointing in some way. You can show them where their internal base for relating with others is out of alignment with what would help them to establish their own personal power.

The proper use of sexual energy is another lesson you are teaching since you have a natural understanding of why people blend on a physical level. You know on an unconscious level that when we are not in the flesh, we are androgynous—not male or female but a completion of both energies. Upon entering the flesh one of those energies lies dormant within us unless we become aware enough to claim it and stop projecting it onto the opposite sex. But until this transformation takes place there is the need for the joining of bodies to attain a sense of spiritual completion. Sexual energy is such a powerful energy because it creates a vehicle for another soul to enter this plane. You understand that when two bodies are blending, it is more than the bodies that are blending, it is the actual souls. This is why the male energy blending with the female energy allows both a sense of completion.

A great deal of responsibility is incurred by sexual union because there is also a blending of the actual juices of life. The fluids of the male enter the female, and on a much more subtle level, the fluids of the female enter the male. Through this blending there is a completion of body, mind, and soul—an interweaving of energies on all three levels. If the couple is compatible, there is truly a feeling of stisfaction for both. If there is no compatibility, a disharmony is created within them both. You are aware of the magnitude of sexual interchange on the spiritual as well as the physical level and have the capacity to share this knowledge with others. You intuitively understand that the act of sex is a form of spiritual completion.

LUNAR ECLIPSE: You need to learn lessons relating to your value system. These lessons include not being swayed in your values, learning how to share your values, overcoming negative manipulative traits, and taking responsibility for your sexual behavior. You need to learn appropriate spiritual values and gain the understanding that, as part of an intricate whole, these values affect all those around you. As the energies you emit come back to you, you are learning that what goes around comes around. Learning to plant positive seeds is important since negative seeds grow like weeds and need no nurturing.

Realigning and readjusting your principles is sometimes difficult, for you are coming from previous existences of being concerned with setting proper foundations for the self and family. In this incarnation, however, you need to learn that society is interdependent and you are responsible for more than just yourself. We must all aid one another; the strong must help the weak, and the weak must learn how to be strong.

You also need to discover what the boundaries are for yourself and for other people. You have a strong desire to push others to their limit because you want to know the boundaries: How far can I push you? At what point will you give in? Will you stand up to me? If they give in, you have no use for them and will move on to someone—or something—new. You do this because, without a sense of your own boundaries, you are afraid of misusing your power unless someone else sets limits for you. Your energy is like raw power—like a rushing flood of water—and until you find something or someone to contain it, it just creates havoc in its path. When you do find containment, you become totally content. Once you know your limits you can direct your power from within them. Only then do you feel safe enough to claim your power fully.

Children born with this eclipse pattern need special attention and guidance to assist them in discovering their boundaries. Whatever limits are set must always be enforced, and when boundaries are expanded as children mature, these children must be told that the boundaries are being expanded and why. With this assistance they are able to learn their proper place in their family, play, and school environments, and in society.

Once the boundaries are set, however, these children will still try to test the strength of the walls. Others will continually have to say: "You can only go this far. I say it and I mean it, and you cannot cross that line." And if they are allowed to cross that line even once, there's no turning back. If these children denote weakness, they will push twice as hard the next time, even if you stand up to them. They will not stop pushing those close to them until you tell them, "That's *enough!*"

Even when you become an adult, your parents, lovers, and bosses must never back down to your power. If they can stand their ground and teach you the value of your place within their reality, you will trust them. Then they will find you are an invaluable ally, for you will do anything for those you trust; your loyalty is immeasurable, and you would trust them with your life. If they are careless enough to make a fool of you in any situation, they will find out that you only remained within the boundaries they set because you respected them.

One of your lessons is learning to respect others. You are looking for something within the human race that is deserving of respect. Yours is the energy of destruction, and you incarnated thinking that everything here is bad and needs to be rebuilt. Now you want to know who and what is of value here. The purpose of these thoughts is to purge and restructure yourself, keeping what is good and destroying what is not. You are looking for something or someone worthy of your respect. When you find it, you honor it, but when you find that you can't respect something, you try to destroy it.

You need to define those qualities in others that are valuable to you and begin building them in yourself. The way you do this is by testing others to discover the limits of their integrity, strength, values, and moral fiber. You are seeking to find if there is something really good and worthwhile in those around you and if they have the integrity to live their principles as well as preach them. You are seeking to find what values give other people the strength and self-confidence to work for the good of the planet so that you can emulate them and find peace.

In this lifetime you are becoming aware that in other incarnations you have allowed your values to slip. You have a misuse of power from past lives on your conscience. You feel that either you, or those you have been exposed to, deal in negative manipulative energy, and you want to transform the essence of your soul totally. You are desperately looking for something of value—something good—because this is the energy of transformation and regeneration. You want to get rid of what isn't good within you so that you can rebuild yourself and be of value to others and to society.

If you lose your way and don't meet with any limitations and don't find anyone with a strong enough value system to guide you in your youth, your life can become very difficult. You may even become imprisoned or institutionalized in places that will take responsibility for providing a structure for you and for giving you a substantial set of values. But with luck you will find something "good" in people and society that is worthy of your allegiance and support. Once your energy is aligned with something you believe in, something you have tested and know in your heart to be worthwhile and beyond reproach in its integrity, you pledge yourself to it with your whole heart. That principle, person, or cause then becomes your value: It can contain your energy and make use of your tremendous strength, and you can find peace within it.

When Scorpio energy is silent and reserved, it is because you are angry inside. You realize the extent of your power and know that if you let loose, society will lock you up. When you are resentful, it is because your energy has no outlet you can believe in.

Your energy desperately needs a focus and a cause that you can pledge your power to, and in the process of building this cause, your energy finds its own radiant expression. This is why the Scorpio energy is often the "power behind the throne"; your power is strong enough to lift anyone to success if you believe in him or her strongly enough. You have no need to be in the limelight yourself, but you have a tremendous need to find someone or something to believe in.

You have come to learn that there *is* good in the world. You are aware of the bad, and you have an intuitive ability to see anything that is in need of being repaired or destroyed. What you need to learn is that there are things around you that have strong, solid bases you can believe in. You feel such a need to share your tremendous energy because the Scorpio energy is that of joint values. You want to find someone to believe in so that you can share your values and build a strong power base.

Being in the limelight is not important to you, but you do want to operate from a strong base of power; you therefore tend to go through life gathering people around you whom you trust. If you give people your trust, there is something very special inside of them because you don't trust easily. You may trust certain people with one area of your life and not trust them with another. If that is the relationship you have with them, you will always have one eye on them. You won't be the "power behind the throne" for these people, but if you see value in them, you will let them be part of your "army." Every member of your support group is someone who is indebted to you. You have an exaggerated fear of failing in money matters, reputation, career—so you always have "markers" in your pocket as backup (people who owe you favors).

You need to develop more trust in the universe so that you are not constantly running scared. Then you can relax and allow the universe to help you build what you feel is truly good and worthwhile so you can find peace and enjoyment in life. Another lesson you are learning is that you cannot depend on other people to set your boundaries and contain your energy. You need to get in touch with what is good for you and begin to act within your own boundaries and be responsible for your own energy.

Human frailty frustrates you. You are driven to self-perfection, and you think that weaknesses in the physical body limit your power. You are seeking a sense of mastery over yourself and your environment, and you strive to master the physical body and learn its limits. You also push others to their limits but never beyond where you yourself have gone. Learning to feel your body and listen to it is important so that you won't push yourself to the point of breaking down your body. There can be a tendency to push your body past its limits to exhaustion, and then you have to rebuild your strength from scratch. You feel that you have to know how far your body will take you in a pinch. In your search for limits, therefore, the first place you tend to look is your physical body.

You are often a late bloomer financially. This is because you spend so much time doing favors for others and securing your power base that you don't spend time building your own success through your own merit. You expend time and energy on people you hope will support you because you are so fearful of having the rug pulled out from under you. But in actuality what you are doing is giving away your power a little bit here and a little bit there. As you learn to trust yourself you will know that you are strong enough to get back up again if you fall. You are beginning to realize that you don't need the support of all those around you because you are a mountain of power within yourself. When you connect with the power within you and learn to go with your natural inborn flow, you will find that the universe *does* support you and there *is* good in the world—and in you. That is what you are here to learn: discovery and belief in your own goodness.

You are also learning to stop projecting your goodness outward by looking for someone else to believe in. As you learn to support and trust yourself by being true to your own sense of goodness, you can begin to construct your own boundaries and contain your own energy. This gives you the freedom to be more trusting of those around you since it eliminates the need to give away your power. This will also lead to the realization that it is all right for you to be successful and to be in the limelight. Then you can be the power behind your *own* throne and rise to success. From this position you can support those around you—but from a purer motive since you no longer feel you need them to ensure your own strength. Now when you support others it will be from a place of true caring, and you will no longer be involved in a process that gives your power away.

The caliber of the people around you will also change. As long as you thought you needed others to support you, you unknowingly held yourself down by having leeches around you, feeding

off your energy. And this is why so often you have been disappointed in human nature. When you feel you are buying favors
from others rather than simply giving freely, without strings attached, you deprive those around you of giving of their own voli-
tion and love when you need their help. By not giving freely you
have robbed yourself of the opportunity to experience "what goes
around comes around" in a positive way.

Whatever you give to another has to come back to you—if not
through the person you gave it to, then through someone else
when you need it. As you learn to unblock the flow within yourself by giving freely, then you will see the goodness in others as
you experience them giving freely back to you. This feels very
different from begrudging indebtedness and obligation! You need
to learn that if you look for the worst in people, you will agitate
them until you bring out the quality you fear (at least in your own
mind). But if you expect the best, you are powerful enough to
evoke that quality in others.

By learning to give freely and without ulterior motives, you are
letting go of the energy of manipulation. You can have a tendency
to spend so much time manipulating the lives of those around you
that you become caught in this mode of expression, thereby stunt-
ing your own growth. As you release this negative energy you
begin to realize that just because people travel their own separate
paths doesn't mean they can't care about and support one another.
You start to understand that if others truly care about you, they
will be there when you need them, and if they're not, then maybe
they don't care as much as they say. This helps you to sort out the
people who really care about you from those who don't, and also
broadens your awareness of the many different ways people show
they care.

When you reach this awareness, you will operate from a sense
of your full power, and there will be no holding you back. You
also are learning about the proper use of power in this incarnation.
You are learning that it is negative to use your power over those
who are weaker, and positive to share your power to assist others
in coming into their own strength. In the process of empowering
others, you gain a sense of your own strength in a way that breeds
self-esteem.

UNCONSCIOUS EXPRESSION: Operating unconsciously,
you may have a negative behavior pattern of building your success

on the misfortune of others. If you are not aware of the lessons you have come to learn, you may find yourself surrounded with very negative people or being a very negative person. You may be someone who uses others in their weakest moments, such as a loan shark (legal or not), pimp, drug dealer, rip-off artist, or ambulance chaser. Another manifestation of this eclipse could be various forms of psychic manipulation, such as voodoo, the casting of spells or hexes, and so forth.

Coming from negativity, using others would be an unconscious method for learning the lessons you are here to learn. We must all learn our life's lessons, but how we choose to learn them is up to us. Through this pattern you would learn the lesson of "what goes around comes around." You can find yourself being forced into rehabilitation by society or suffering tremendous losses through your own schemes.

Many of you are coming directly from a previous incarnation in which your value system had a cracked foundation. Your moral, financial, and spiritual values have been shattered through abuse of your ethics, and you are here to strengthen them in this lifetime. If you don't go about this in a positive way, however, you may find yourself becoming something that you despise. If you choose to operate in a negative fashion, there is a tendency for your body to deteriorate as you set out to prove that there is no one you can depend on, not even yourself. You try to prove to yourself that there is nothing good on this plane and that everything must be destroyed.

When you finally reach bottom, you have an amazing ability (more so than any other eclipse pattern) to pull yourself out of the muck. Unfortunately, you may need to create a crisis in your life in order to do it unless you seek some sort of counseling or run into someone you respect enough to allow him or her to show you the light. Once you accept that there *is* good in the world—or once you have fallen as far as you can physically, emotionally, or financially—then you begin to make upward progress. The idea is for you to do this before you ruin your life.

One way to facilitate your growth is to begin to value yourself because once you feel you are worth saving, you are more than capable of pulling yourself up. You know your faults all too well. What you need to understand is what is *right* about yourself and to get in touch with the goodness inside you. You are gentle, you have an understanding of the workings of the universe, you are sensitive (even if you try to hide it), you care about others (even if you pretend not to), and you have a basic goodness of intent. If someone can tell you one positive thing every time you do something negative, it gives you the recognition of your goodness of intent without validating your antisocial behavior. Once you can see this spark of good you will have enough faith in yourself to climb out of the worst situations. You are capable of overcoming circumstances that would bury the average person.

When operating unconsciously you have difficulty handling other people's jealousy. This is because you are also working on issues of jealousy and know only too well that feeling of hatred for someone who is more successful than you. You are trying hard to overcome this and be sensitive to it because you don't like that part of yourself, but you tend to judge yourself too harshly.

Often when you get angry it is because someone got hurt and you want to protect or be loyal to that person. Negative reactions may come from not knowing socially acceptable responses to these situations. You care so much about your fellow beings that when you see a misuse of power, you feel compelled to assault it physically or to confront it and root it out. You want to destroy anything that is not positive.

It is important for you to recognize the good within yourself because this eclipse rules the energy of destruction, and until you see the spark of good within you, you will continue on a self-destructive path. You don't see your own value until someone else reflects it. You are here to learn your value to society, your value as a human being, and your worth to others.

CONSCIOUS EXPRESSION: You know instinctively that you are here to learn how to use the energy of transformation and regeneration in a positive mode. The energy of transformation is also the energy of destruction, and you intuitively understand that something must die for something else to be reborn. You recognize from a previous existence of dealing with your internal values that an integral part of your soul growth pattern was left out—the ability to incorporate your values with those of others. In this existence you have come to learn how to recognize what is valuable to all, not just what is valuable to the self. You tend to deal with this lesson by rooting out of your consciousness what is no longer useful and replacing it with something more positive.

The Scorpio energy is a very powerful energy. It is the energy of surging water, which knows no limits until it is contained. Thus, you can come on too strong within society and must learn how to control your energy. Until society or someone you respect tells you that you have reached the set limits, you will not stop pushing. Others must deal openly and honestly with you and not be afraid to stand up to you because you can learn your boundaries only through other people setting limits and holding their ground. It does you no good when people let you run over them since this teaches you nothing.

Operating consciously, you know that you must treat others the way you want to be treated. You recognize that just because other people do not alway stand up to you or are not always able to contain your energy does not mean you must destroy them. If you do try to destroy them, at another time there will be someone else more powerful who will try to destroy you. You understand that everything in the universe works as a cycle, and everything you give out comes home to roost. This also holds true for positive actions, thought, and emotions—whatever leaves the body on a mental, physical, or spiritual level comes back. Through this recognition you are learning the proper use of power.

In addition you are learning the lessons of joint manifestation. By intertwining your energies with another you are learning how to trust and be trusted. You are learning how to overcome past patterns of possessiveness that lead to jealousy. This is very important because if you do not learn to let go, it can pull you into a pattern of jealousy that prevents growth and holds you down. If instead you learn to develop trust, including self-trust, it allows you to overcome these negative possessive traits. This will give you the strength of personal integrity to deal very successfully with people on a joint level, for you know that truly trusting another means trusting the self.

If you do not trust others, unconsciously you are telling yourself that they have the power to affect your life, and you give them power over you. When you learn to trust others, you gain your strongest power. Then you recognize that you can relate with those around you without letting their actions affect you to the point where you become incapable of handling any situation. Through this process you learn to trust your own personal integrity and internal strength enough to know that you can rise above any depth and to any height you choose. You are the energy of the Scorpion transforming itself to the Eagle and then to the Phoenix.

TRANSPERSONAL EXPRESSION: On the transpersonal level you have the capacity to teach people to recognize and honor the good that lies in their own individuality. You teach that by honoring the good in oneself, each of us honors the whole. You help others to remove whatever is invalidating the self so that their spiritual essence can shine through; by validating what is right in themselves, they validate the whole. You teach that we are all part of a collective whole and have a spark of the collective consciousness within us. In keeping our own sparks kindled, we add power to the whole. You are using your power to transform the consciousness of humankind by rooting out old subconscious patterns that hold down the evolution of the individual soul as well as the evolution of planetary consciousness. Your ability to see through to the core of any situation can expose the diseases that prohibit a healthy body, mind, or spirit, and the result is purifying and healing. On the highest levels you are the psychic healers and spiritual regenerators, reconnecting the minds of your fellow beings to a magnetic relationship with the whole.

PHYSICAL INTEGRATION: You need to be aware constantly of your spiritual responsibility to the universal plan. If you put this responsibility aside, there can be a tendency toward deterioration of the reproductive organs since these correlate with the universal energy of creation and expansion. You must incorporate this principle into your everyday life—if not on a spiritual level, at least in your interactions with others. Thus, it is important that you learn to let go of your creations, whether trusting those around you with what you value or sharing your spiritual concepts. If you choose to ignore the responsibility of sharing these vital parts of yourself, your body will communicate to you by drawing attention to its reproductive areas.

If you are not dealing with the energy of transformation and regeneration—the energy of purging the old to make way for the energy of birth and rebirth—you may have problems with your rectum, colon, small intestine, or bowel. If on a spiritual level you are allowing yourself to create blockages, the body will reflect what you are doing. In order to let go of the obstruction and not experience physical problems from holding back what needs to be released, you must learn that you cannot control everything around you.

Sagittarius

SAGITTARIUS

SOLAR ECLIPSE: (In order to fully activate the solar eclipse energy in Sagittarius, you first must integrate the lessons of the Sagittarius *lunar* eclipse with your emotional body. For a full explanation, see "How to Use Part II," page 166.)

You have accepted the responsibility for teaching your fellow beings how to understand the common thread that runs through all the philosophies and various belief systems of humankind. You are spreading the awareness that we are all one, we are all heading in the same direction, and at the same time we have all come to learn something on our own unique paths. You are teaching that a spark of the collective consciousness burns strongly within all of us. We need to learn to respect one another, without prejudices, and to recognize that no matter which path a person has chosen, we are all traveling to the same destination. All the ways up the mountain lead to the same summit.

The lives that you touch in this existence are automatically stimulated to a higher consciousness. You have incarnated without any prejudices, and you need to be careful not to develop prejudices and to recognize that you already have the proper philosophy. In this existence, because of your philosophical nature and your personal belief system, you will have a tendency to attract very glib people. You will draw those who are socially oriented and overly conscious of their status. It is natural for you to try to change them because the various eclipse patterns always attract people who need to learn the lesson they are teaching. It is important that you do not compromise your belief system, for yours is the philosophy that actually reflects the higher consciousness. It is your duty to raise those around you to *your* level of spiritual awareness and not allow yourself to be influenced by others.

During your spiritual travels it is important for you to stay aware and not become stuck in thinking that "this way is the only way."

You truly understand that all souls are driven by the desire for perfection of self—to be one with the Father—reunited with the God of their consciousness. It is important for those of you who have chosen to be spiritual teachers in this lifetime to remain clear and unprejudiced. Thus, you may help your fellow beings to clarify their own awareness and guide them on their own journeys with the freedom to travel the path they have chosen. You have the strength and the understanding to assist people on their chosen paths without the ego involvement that might tempt you to bring them to *your* path.

It is not uncommon for you to experience the restrictions of religious overindoctrination in your youth. The rigidity of this approach provides the stimulus for you to break free later and begin your search for the common thread that underlies all belief systems and religions. In your resistance to the idea that ''one way is the only way,'' you serve humanity by heralding the spirit of tolerance for—and understanding of—religious philosophies.

You can be interested in taking care of the physical body but usually only because you understand the need to keep it moving. You recognize that all things on Earth must continually be in motion, for through your spiritual development you have learned that nothing is static within the universe. To be of the utmost usefulness to the soul and to the spark of God within it, the physical body must be fluid and move with the least restriction possible. In movement there is freedom, and through freedom comes the awareness to conceptualize many different ideas. Through allowing others in your environment true freedom of expression you receive the reward of bringing out the highest and the best in those around you.

Professionally, you make excellent philosophers, counselors, professors, spiritual teachers, and gurus. You are not at all desirous of people following you, however, even though you exude the type of energy that draws people to you. Your purpose is not to be a spiritual leader but to bring spiritual awareness and to give people back their spiritual freedom, but you do wish not to personify their consciousness and replace what or who they followed before. You want to set people free to find their own paths, believing that instead of having any individual gurus on this plane, humankind needs to find a greater sense of awareness from within. You are therefore comfortable in any profession that affords you the opportunity to help people develop a greater sense of reality and actualize their beliefs. You can help others deal with being different and support their needs to expand in unfamiliar areas. Because you do not feel guilty about being different, you give others permission to truly be themselves.

Through your innate ability to see the underlying truth in everything around you, you can teach others to remove the veils of illusion that obstruct clear thinking. Using logical deduction you are able to see a more exact reality, and you teach these techniques to others. This enables them to perceive truthful and precise information, and thus to make intelligent decisions. You have the ability to see the truth and to distill information, and you can help those around you to reach their goals by tuning in to the wider perspective that you can show them.

You have tremendous decision-making abilities since you can see the truth at a great distance. The adept person can learn a great deal about fundamental logic, and you get great pleasure in sharing this ability with all who are willing to learn from you. You have a tendency, however, to "expound" your beliefs and must be mindful that sometimes you express your ideas too strongly. This can frighten the more timid souls away from the very freedom and awareness you are trying so hard to offer them. You have a great love for your fellow beings and a strong sense of responsibility for helping them to develop their conscious awareness.

You often need to break the everyday structure of your environment since you fear being trapped in it. Because of this ability to exist within—yet separate from—the normal concepts of society, you remain a curiosity to those around you. This stimulates others to ask the questions that they need to have answered. You are truly happy in this role because you do not seek students, they seek you. This way, no dependency is formed, for students are often not aware that they have met a teacher until the teacher has moved on.

Should you choose to walk through this life "asleep" and unwilling to assist others in achieving more advanced states of awareness, you will be known for your shallowness of perception. In this way you *still* teach the same lesson, only you do it by being a repulsive example of how those around you do *not* want to live their lives.

LUNAR ECLIPSE: You have come into this life to break all prejudices and to learn to understand the common thread that runs through all forms of philosophy, religion, and spirituality. You have an unquenchable thirst for knowledge, higher insights, and information regarding conscious awareness.

In this incarnation you need to unlearn the prejudices that you absorbed in previous existences. In the past your perceptions were limited and narrow-minded; your ideas were based only on information from your own immediate environment. Due to this limited framework you became judgmental about how others should live and how things should be done. In this existence you will be exposed to many things outside your own belief systems. Once this happens it greatly accelerates your process, and your tendency to be inquisitive comes to the fore. It is as if you begin a crash course of study to expand your horizons and your consciousness. The way you go about this process can be different at different times of your life, yet the thrust is the same: to acquire the knowledge and information that can set you free from limiting past belief systems that kept you from connecting with a universal sense of wholeness.

Some of you acquire the information you need by traveling to foreign countries and exposing yourself to different cultures, philosophies, and theologies. As you explore these different cultures you investigate their belief systems, seeking the history of the various religions to find the common thread behind the different rules and regulations of their doctrines. For example, you may ask: "Why did Catholicism say not to eat meat on Fridays?" When you think about it from a practical point of view, you realize that at the time the rule was made, human consciousness was not aware that the human body needs a rest and that it takes a long time to digest a piece of meat. In this way you can break down the practicalities behind organized religion and understand that they were formulated to teach humankind how to be sociable, how to be civilized, and how to take care of the physical body so that the soul within could thrive.

You want to experience foreign countries firsthand so that you can better understand the individual cultures, background, and motivations of the people. This helps you to put your philosophy, ideas, and attitudes in alignment. For you, book knowledge is not enough. You want to see how people are living, if the culture works, and whether you respect the moral fiber of the people. You want to be aware of how the philosophy is integrated into the culture: Does what I have read and studied really fit with the people that have this philosophy and practice this religion? What type of personal consciousness does this belief system manifest? You are accustomed to functioning within different social groups and understanding social behavior patterns on a surface level. Now you are taking your understanding to a deeper level and gaining an awareness of the larger pattern. You are attracted to foreign countries so that you can find the common thread that runs through each of the different societies and cultures. This gives you a sense of belonging to an abstract consciousness that is inclusive of all social cultures.

The more cultures you are exposed to, the better, because you are distilling all the different belief systems and integrating what works for you. You are actually looking for your own direction and your own philosophy because you have lost your way. You became so accustomed to living on a superficial social level that you lost your drive to find your own path. And the only way you seem to be able to find your path in this lifetime is to distill what you need from many different philosophies. When you have a compilation of the things that you like, you experiment with what works for you spiritually, philosophically, and practically—what perceptions make you feel happy and confident. When you experience other religions and philosophies—without being judgmental, it is hoped—you learn that some things work and some things don't on an individual, personal level. You are developing your own religion, your own inner connection with truth.

Learning to overcome a tendency to prejudices, narrow-mindedness, and superficiality is very important to you in this lifetime. You want to know the "whys" behind the different philosophies and religions in order to gain a greater understanding. In a previous existence you had exposure to only tidbits of everything but no depth of information, so in this incarnation you have an unquenchable thirst for more information on a philosophical level. You are seeking the common denominator of truth beneath the social interactions and the pieces of information that you already have. You came to the planet with your mind set in a precise social structure, believing that things should be a certain way. You look at your own family environment and say: "Okay, this philosophy seems to work for my family. But I notice that my friends' families have different philosophies that seem to work for them. How can that be? How come they're not doing things the same way I am?" This exposure in your youth to different people with different belief systems really started you thinking.

You are seeking the common denominator, the common thread, so you can find peace. You feel a strong sense of separation from the "Father" or from the universe while in the body. You want to be back on a spiritual plane but are not totally sure how to get there. You are looking for answers, wanting to identify with something larger than the inconsistency of social interactions. You are looking for truth, and you feel the only way to find truth is to investigate everything personally. This is not investigation for its own sake but to gain the information you feel you need in order to make educated decisions.

As a spiritual teacher you have an innate undertanding that you are here to awaken the consciousness of your fellow beings, yet you don't automatically understand what it is you are supposed to awaken or exactly how you are to do it. Your quest for knowledge will eventually guide you to an understanding of how best to teach your lesson. You need to be very careful, however, not to become so strongly attached to any one path that you lead those around you down only that path. You have a great deal of persuasiveness because you mastered the lesson of salesmanship in previous existences and now you are concentrating on mastering the abilities of the mind.

You can best aid your fellow beings by helping them to find their own paths. You need to recognize that each individual has his or her own path: No two can travel exactly the same path because each path supports only an individual consciousness. To become whole, each of us must come from our own direction and find our way back to the initial existence. Part of the developmental process that you have come to learn and to share with those around you is that there are a multitude of paths and directions but only one center. Thus, it is most important for you to avoid using your "silver tongue" to try to persuade people to share your path. You need to be aware and responsible regarding what you say to others because you could be pulling them from their chosen paths onto yours. In this way you can be detrimental rather than helpful to those around you.

As you learn to listen more carefully to the needs of others, their motives and where they are coming from, you begin to understand why each person needs to travel his or her path in an individual way. By allowing those around you the freedom to choose their own paths you relieve yourself of the karmic burden of being the self-appointed pied piper of the planet. In this way you allow yourself to have exactly what you came to obtain: personal freedom. You are learning how to be free without carrying the burden of decision for your fellow beings.

Your job in this lifetime is not to steer others down any particular path but to share your philosophy of freedom and expansion. In this way you help to set others free to find their own chosen paths. You accumulate information and throw it all into one large melting pot, and when it is all melted down, you find a lump of gold. You are learning to distill information into truth. Through your investigations into different religions and philosophies, you have learned to accept what truly serves humankind and to discard what is too limiting. You are learning to break through man-made religious and philosophical structures to a more universal consciousness. In this way you find your own individual path.

Although you hope to find those of like consciousness along your path, you tend to be a lonely soul, for your journey into consciousness seems to be traveled by few. As you learn to set aside your prejudices and open yourself to new experiences, you are allowed to see the light of others around you. Then your feelings of loneliness are alleviated.

UNCONSCIOUS EXPRESSION: You have come to learn how to break down your prejudices and expand your narrow-mindedness. If you choose to learn these lessons the hard way, you can go through life being exposed to a great many narrow-minded people. You seem to run headlong into difficulties with others over their belief systems, often arguing with those who are just as limited in their views as you are. This helps you to recognize the narrow scope of your own beliefs.

If you resist your lesson, you may have to deal with the consequences of your prejudices against people from foreign countries or other religions. You have a tendency to think that anyone who speaks with a dialect that sounds different from yours is below you on an intellectual level. For example, you may think that slow speech patterns indicate a lack of mental alertness. Another example of this type of prejudice would be a reticence to hire someone who speaks with a foreign accent, fearing that the person would not do the job properly or could not communicate clearly with others. This attitude may lead to your missing out on the best person for the job. If the pattern is deeply ingrained from previous incarnations, you may be of a minority group yourself in this lifetime and have the experience of being on the receiving end of prejudice.

You need to accept that you have incarnated to change belief systems that leave no room for expansion of diversity. Your job is to stop being judgmental and self-righteous, and recognize that your way is not the only way. Just because you have chosen a particular path does not mean you cannot benefit from illumination or added insight from others who are on a different path. You are learning to accept the awareness that every human being is one of God's beings, and we all have the spark of the collective consciousness within us. We are all evolving and have the right to grow on our own set path: Not all the flowers of the earth can flourish in the same pot.

Your social consciousness is similar to those who belong to an elite group or an established country club that does not allow members who do not meet certain social criteria. With this type of consciousness you cannot respect the essence of your fellow beings or appreciate their contributions, which can be new, different, and exciting. For you, everything must remain the same and be within the "social graces." It is important for you to outgrow this tendency so you will no longer be limited to a path of narrow-mindedness and isolation. Once you begin to integrate a more expanded awareness, it becomes important for you to share your new insights with others on a human level and not to speak in an overly clinical way. You need to avoid technical terminology, which puts everything on such a lofty level that those around you cannot benefit from your newfound knowledge.

Another potential self-defeating mechanism is your tendency to stop listening to your fellow beings. You can become so attached to your chosen path that you end up with a form of tunnel vision —seeing only what you want to see and going straight ahead. You forget that you learn through interacting with other people and being exposed to their cultural beliefs. You can get so wrapped up in expanding your consciousness that you forget to enjoy and benefit from the essential human element. Also, information that originally increased your awareness can become a limitation if you do not remain receptive to new levels of awareness. It is through interacting with others that you gain what you need to continue in your own personal growth.

Because of habitual past life limitations to your immediate social environment, you can experience some fear when expanding your horizons beyond what is familiar. Going to parties with different types of people and eating new types of foods can cause you anxiety. You limit yourself if you fail to appreciate other dimensions of life and what those outside of your familiar circle have to offer. It is in journeying past your immediate environment that you gain some of your most pleasant and expansive insights.

CONSCIOUS EXPRESSION: Operating consciously, you go looking for intellectual fulfillment, and you are constantly learning and progressing on your path. You can be found in various institutions of learning, studying philosophy, theology, and the customs and cultures of different lands. You are learning to be more open and aware, and you find that interactions with others and exposure to their philosophies expand your mental capabilities.

You have a natural curiosity about spiritual matters, but you are most interested in understanding what motivates humankind to feel such a link to the spiritual realms while in the flesh. You need to align the principles of the body, mind, and soul in this lifetime. Thus, you actively point yourself in the direction of this alignment and do what is necessary in order to attain it. You enjoy physical activities and understand the body and its functions. You know that the body must be physically agile so that the mind can perform at its highest level. You acknowledge your respect for the God consciousness and realize that you are part of the collective whole. You are aware that there are lessons the soul wants to incorporate in this existence, and thus you allow yourself to be prodded to learn more about these three aspects of yourself and to organize them into an integrated whole. Yours is a quest for understanding body, mind, and soul—what their connections are and how they interact.

Operating at a conscious level you incorporate the philosophy that individuals travel the only road they are capable of conceptualizing at any given point in time. You realize that if you cannot see it or dream it, you cannot aspire to it. To satisfy your need to achieve higher levels of enlightenment you experience as much as you possibly can in the span of your lifetime. In this way you broaden your ability to conceptualize, thereby increasing your options.

You are highly motivated to attain the degree of consciousness that will free you from having to return to this plane. Thus, you spend a great deal of time and energy investigating all the options that lead to total freedom and liberation. The desire to be one with the whole and not to be a separate entity is intense, matching the intensity of the sorrow stemming from your feelings of separation.

You are seeking the path that will led you to the truth within yourself and thus to the feeling of connectedness with the whole. You want to understand the paths of all those around you so that you can ascertain whether you have chosen the right path.

TRANSPERSONAL EXPRESSION: You have actively aligned yourself with discovering the truth in this incarnation. You operate from the position of understanding that all paths are the right paths, and you make yourself available to others who need help in gaining this same core awareness. You realize that our state of consciousness is limited only by our concepts, so you work to expand other people's concepts. This increases the "win potential" for everyone, and you recognize that unless we all win, no one wins. You also encourage others through your own natural state of joy, which adds a lightness and sense of adventure to the road you travel. By doing what you can to lift the mood of those around you, you share the joy and lightheartedness you have found through your own connection with truth. It is not your philosophy that uplifts others so much as your freedom from rigid belief systems and prejudices.

You intuitively understand that your role in the New Age is to live and let live. You recognize that you are working off karma by breaking old, prejudicial patterns and establishing a more progressive mental attitude while on the physical plane. You constantly keep things in motion by helping to release humanity from its past so we can move into the future. You support the trend to bring more freedom and personal accountability into religion and philosophy. In fact, freedom with personal responsibility is the key word of the transpersonal eclipse pattern in Sagittarius.

PHYSICAL INTEGRATION: Your body communicates to you through irritations in the areas of the hips, thighs, and liver. If you choose not to release your prejudices, the liver, which filters impurities from the blood, will cease to function in a way that is supportive to the entire being. This is a reflection of the way that prejudice is not supportive to your psychological or philosophical well-being.

Problems with mobility and the hip joints can result if you allow yourself to slip into past patterns of being unaware, supporting the status quo, and remaining stagnant on a social level. To alert your consciousness to the fact that there has been immobility in your mental and spiritual processes, there can be problems with movement in the hip and thigh areas. These can cause restrictions and irritations varying from a slight degree of discomfort to an extreme amount of deterioration. The tendency toward mental stagnation can be remedied by expanding your consciousness and releasing prejudices and rigid beliefs.

On another level you can be prone to skin eruptions on different parts of the body. Acne, boils, and other impurities may surface if you are reluctant to get old concepts out of your system. The body is given to us by our parents, but the cell memory within the body has a certain level of awareness on its own. If you seem to have prejudices other than those imparted from your early family environment, this may be why. The body will begin to have skin eruptions because it recognizes that these patterns are detrimental to the overall health of the being, and it works to reject them from the body. Consequently, on the physical level you may develop boils, acne, and skin eruptions of all kinds as the body eliminates what it does not want to carry. This is necessary if you have taken an overabundance of prejudices on a cellular level through your family heredity.

Capricorn

CAPRICORN

SOLAR ECLIPSE: (In order to fully activate the solar eclipse energy in Capricorn you first must integrate the lessons of the Capricorn *lunar* eclipse with your emotional body. For a full explanation, see "How to Use Part II," page 166.)

You have the ability to teach your fellow beings the value of having a good reputation. You have an intuitive sense that if you don't present yourself properly in public, your behavior can come back to haunt you at the most inopportune times.

Operating negatively, you teach this lesson through suffering the consequences instead of reaping the rewards. Others can learn the value of a good reputation by seeing yours demeaned as a consequence of your own improper public behavior.

Operating positively, you teach by presenting yourself with dignity and reserve while you are in the company of others, even within your own family unit. Every action is well thought out. You are so self-disciplined that you can bring a good friend to the airport and refrain from kissing him or her goodbye just so it cannot possibly be misconstrued. Heaven forbid that anyone should say to the wrong person, "I saw John and Mary Lou kissing at the airport." You make sure that others have no opportunity to weaken your reputation in any way. You are always aware of your reputation, and that is why you are so reserved in public. Yet you are very demonstrative behind closed doors; you really let the tiger out of the cage when the bedroom door is closed and the shades are pulled.

You are teaching the true definition and necessity of protocol through your intuitive understanding that, when climbing the ladder of success, certain acknowledgments need to be made along the way. Recognizing that anyone above you on the ladder has a fear of looking down, you understand this fear comes from not wanting to be on a lower rung.

Whether striving for spiritual, material, or emotional success, everyone is comfortable in his or her chosen upward path. When someone else is encountered moving upward, it can either remind the person of where he or she was or cause the fear of not being recognized for accomplishments. Those who are not secure in their current status can be very dangerous adversaries because those who have fears are capable of pulling others down with them, just as a man who is drowning sometimes drowns the person who has come to save him.

In recognizing this need to respect another's achievements, you secure the ground for those with whom you work. This allows others to be more comfortable and gives them a clear vision to their own path, with no unnecessary obstacles in their way. Through this intuitive awareness of recognizing that all must be respected and acknowledged, your path to to the top can be an easier, if sometimes slower, journey. But the path you have chosen to the top is clear to you because you understand the necessity of protocol and teach the lesson of respecting those who have gone before and their accomplishments.

You also understand and teach that if you want to succeed in this lifetime, you must always conduct yourself as if someone were watching. Whatever examples you are setting, you find yourself living a very visible lifetime—or at least your behavior would indicate that this is so. You understand that it is in your best interests to act as if everything you do will be uncovered. Those around you learn that if they choose to go to the top, they must always conduct themselves as if every aspect of their lives were broadcast on television. Because you are teaching the value of maintaining a good reputation, your energy automatically draws attention to you so that others can learn. It's up to you to choose whether you depict yourself positively or negatively, but either way people learn about the importance of reputation through watching you.

Others can learn from you how to climb the ladder of success in all areas of life. You recognize that no forward motion can be taken until current ground is secured, whether it be in affairs of the heart or in business. You teach others that before the next step is taken in a business venture or in a relationship they must always be secure where they are. This is similar to the actions of a mountain goat who sometimes goes sideways or takes a few steps backward but gets to the top without falling because it does not step on insecure ground.

You are here to lead an exemplary lifetime and model in your own behavior the principles for which you stand. Through your ability to commit to an ideal and uphold it by virtue of the way you live your life, you teach others that it is possible to stand for a principle which is larger than their personal lives while still going about their day-to-day activities. You teach them the value of commitment since you have the capacity to materialize your goals through the power of your commitment and the ability to keep your goal solidly in mind. This level of awareness allows you to use everything that comes across your path to assist you in reaching your goal. In this way you teach those around you the value of adversity.

People drawn to you have the tendency to be overly emotional and overly sensitive, and they need to learn to function in the real world. Through your natural ability to teach responsibility and protocol you show them how to succeed in areas where previously they floundered. You aid others in not taking the external world so personally that they allow its harshness to cause them emotional upsets.

You teach those around you to be responsible for their actions because you know that whatever you do in life will be judged by others. You understand that society tends to be judgmental, and you are teaching others to get along with society, to interrelate, and to be successful. Through you they learn that by living within the limits society sets, they will be judged by those around them. It is very important to you to teach others to be useful and act in a manner that serves society since by doing this you feel you are living a responsible life.

For you, usefulness is of the utmost importance. Everything in your life must be useful, and you do not believe in waste, especially the waste of character. If people are not using their potential, not putting their best foot forward, or are losing their good reputation, it is a waste. You do not want to waste your time around people of poor character, for you recognize that society judges you not only by who you are but also by those with whom you associate.

Basically, you teach people the value of being responsible for the way they achieve their goals through a correct relationship with the society in which they live.

LUNAR ECLIPSE: You have come to learn the value of having a good reputation in this lifetime. Your lessons are how to fit in with society, how to be responsible for your actions, and how to be useful and keep the integrity in the external world. In previous existences you were very comfortable and secure within the home environment. In this existence you need to overcome a dependency on home and mother, and go out into the world to become a valuable member of society.

If you choose to learn these lessons in a negative way, it will be through society's restricting you, perhaps even through periods of incarceration. There may be times when you are constantly demeaned by those around you or when your reputation is ruined or when others find you of no value whatsoever and have no qualms about letting you know. Through these experiences you learn that it is very important to give and not just take. If you go through life taking and not giving, you encourage resentments and restrictions. These restrictions are really self-imposed when you choose to give nothing back to the society that can give you an avenue, a direction, and a place to claim a name for yourself.

If you learn your lessons positively, in the beginning it may be through trial and error in how you relate to other people. By persevering on the positive path establishing a proper reputation, giving, sharing, and making a useful contribution to your environment, you will earn a valued place in society. You learn not to take your reputation personally but to allow its rise and fall to teach you where you are "off the track" in your behavior. When others begin to lose respect for you, it is your signal to step back, pay attention, and note the areas in your life where you need to make some adjustments.

Learning how to climb the ladder of success is an important lesson for you in this lifetime. Though you are eager to meet this challenge, you need to learn patience and responsibility in order to make progress. There is a tendency for those of you who are rushing your success to forget to acknowledge those who have gone before you; through this acknowledgment you can gain assistance and support. If you try to climb the success ladder *without* recognizing these people, you will learn that they are stronger than you are and can make your journey very difficult. As you learn the proper use of recognition, respect, and protocol, you learn to take your time on a more deliberate upward path.

You are learning how to control your environment positively, for by taking responsibility for your actions you control the outcome of your own reality. Control is an important issue for you since in past incarnations you allowed your environment to control you. In this existence you must learn how to control yourself without trying to control those around you. If you try to control others, life becomes a very heavy experience. You get dragged down and become bitter and resentful of all your burdens, recognizing that those around you have become dependent on you but not recognizing that you have imposed this dependency. If you use your energy to take control of your life, you will have the strength and perseverance to climb to the top in any field of endeavor.

When you realize that this is a very visible lifetime, you learn how truly important it is to put your best foot forward always. You discover that because you have chosen to learn about the value of reputation and success in this existence, society holds you responsible for all your actions, personal and business. Society doesn't care whether its view of your personal life affects your ability to become successful in business or if your business reputation interferes with your personal life. Experience quickly teaches you always to protect your good name. Because yours is such a visible life, people may have a tendency to be judgmental, and you are unconsciously asking to be judged. You feel that the only way to know how you are doing is to be judged by the members of your own community, and measure your success by how much people respect you. It is important for you to recognize that not everyone is searching for the community approval that you feel is so necessary and for you to learn to live and let live.

Part of your need to become successful in this lifetime will be clear to you only after you recognize that it is not success alone you are striving for; it is recognition, respect, and a need to be useful. When you incorporate this awareness, you become a very important person who is held in high esteem in your community. You are learning to develop character along the way to achieving your goals.

UNCONSCIOUS EXPRESSION: You can suffer a great deal if you invalidate yourself to society by not being concerned with your reputation. It is important for you to recognize that this is a very visible lifetime for you and that you are going to be held accountable for your actions. Since your lesson is to learn the value of a good reputation, you have set yourself up to be judged; this is the only way you can find the meaning of your reputation within society. You must be willing to grow personally from these social judgments rather than to keep striving forward blindly.

When you choose to remain unconscious and not become useful within society, you can become a drain on society. You may decide not to take care of yourself financially and be on the welfare line —not for legitimate reasons but by refusing to take responsibility for yourself. You can be the person society belittles for not pulling your fair share or the person society incarcerates for unacceptable behavior (stealing, embezzlement, and so forth). Some of you may hide within the home, refusing to go out into the world and make a way for yourself. In these and other ways you may never learn to be independent and may be a burden to those within your family unit. Whether you choose to function in the home or out in the world, you must learn to become useful. If you are not taught to be useful within your home environment as a child, it makes it more difficult for you to learn to be useful within the community. To teach you to break unconscious dependency patterns, the use of a *gradual* process is best.

You may have difficulty dealing with anyone in a position of authority because you are learning the purpose and need for self-authority in this lifetime. Coming from a previous existence where others were always your authority, you are accustomed to giving your power too easily to others. In this existence there is a natural rebellion against authority until your own sense of personal authority has been incorporated into the soul growth pattern. It is very important for you to become respected and useful within the community so that you can incorporate that sense of authority into your own being.

By operating unconsciously in the business world you may have a tendency to manipulate as many business affairs as you possibly can. This is most likely to occur if you begin making your own way before you are confident of your ability to become a respected asset in the community. You can manipulate situations so that you are the only one with access to key bits of information that would complete the puzzle for others. Because you need to control your environment you may hold back at least one piece of this vital information, thinking this makes you indispensable. If you could learn to rise above this tendency and have enough faith in yourself to share completely, you would gain the respect and dignity you so strongly desire.

Under stress you can have such an exaggerated need for success that you feel you must win at all costs. In this mode you sometimes engage in extremely unscrupulous behavior. Just as you can achieve the height of success, when functioning negatively you can become the very lowest kind of person. In this negative consciousness you are capable of creating financial scams that can devastate the lives of other people. Playing a simple game of cards with you when you are in this pattern can be like being involved in a game of treachery, for this energy can drive you to cheat in even the friendliest of games. Sooner or later you must accept responsibility for your actions. When you become conscious, you willingly pay back your debt to society and are capable of being of great aid to humankind.

Even when not taken to this extreme, your need to be in control is so great that even when not operating in a proper consciousness you often try to control the lives of others. You have an inward fear that if anyone around you was allowed to stand on his or her own two feet for any length of time, that person would surpass you. You gain your greatest prestige by overcoming this need to control the direction of other people's lives. One way to work toward this goal is by volunteering your time to such service organizations as the Small Business Administration, your local chamber of commerce, or any type of association that assists others in business growth potentials; this puts your positive energy and experience back into the community.

CONSCIOUS EXPRESSION: Knowing that you must incorporate the lessons of responsibility into your personality, you begin by accepting responsibility for your actions and relationships on a social level. Those that are conscious from childhood first become responsible at an early age within the family unit. These are the children who have paper routes and lemonade stands or who are very aware of the home and are willing to help whenever needed. Children with this pattern can be aided by giving them additional responsibilities within the home, along with appropriate respect and recognition. This is a wonderful way to help them begin on the positive path.

You are industrious by nature and recognize the value of having a good reputation. Business success is extremely important to you, and you understand that to succeed in the outside world you must always be cognizant of your behavior in public. But even the most responsible may have to learn this lesson the hard way. You also learn that in order to achieve, each foot must be secure on its path before the other one leaves the ground. In this way you discover how to build your own security, and this includes the area of personal relationships. In previous incarnations there was an over-emphasis on emotions; this has left you with a fear of emotions. Although the most conscious of you can appear rigid and uncaring to the untrained eye, you actually have a wealth of emotion and sensitivity.

As you begin your upward journey to success, one of the most valuable lessons for you to take on your path is an understanding of the roles of respect and acknowledgment because you can have a fear of authority. It is important for you to respect persons of lesser, equal, and greater authority and not become an elitist, which is a very lonely pattern. If you remain conscious of the personal dignity of those around you while you are on your way to the top, when you get there you will have the esteem of the community behind you and the goodwill of all who look up to your accomplishments.

In affairs of the heart you are learning to find a balance between your natural reserve, the respect that you need, and the feelings and sensitivity that you are trying to incorporate. You are learning that your love life does not have to be set aside in order to achieve success, and you may find yourself attracting very dignified, respectable, sensitive, nurturing, supportive mates. You feel at your strongest with someone by your side, and you recognize that your home base must be secure in order for you to achieve your greatest success in the outside world.

Once success has been reached you have a tendency to want to play the "father role" in the community or within your business. Thus, you give others a chance to gain personal success by supplying jobs or scholarships, or just by sharing your personal resources in the community.

By honestly giving respect and admiration where it is due, you find that you can gain a great deal of insight and information from those to whom you pay attention. In recognizing and acknowledging the success of others you tap into a more universal support system where you can access what you need for your own personal growth. Thus, the lessons that teach you to become a more responsible, useful, respected member of the community will become assimilated in a much gentler way.

You are learning to view social judgments not as set and rigid conclusions but as indicators of how useful your current behavior actually is to others. To this end you need to accept criticism or disapproval as a temporary gauge of your effectiveness and to be open to modifying your behavior accordingly.

TRANSPERSONAL EXPRESSION: Operating at the highest level, your destiny is to be a pioneer on new spiritual paths. You are a natural-born guide and teacher, and can bring the heights of spirituality into the practical form necessary to show others the value of spirituality in their lives and to teach them how to walk the path on a useful daily level.

You understand the need for the group consciousness of this planet to teach its inhabitants to accept responsibility for one another. You teach others to become individually responsible for their consciousness and growth, to understand the necessity of learning their lessons and doing whatever is needed to achieve a sense of oneness with the whole. Through your expanded awareness of universal concepts you can help those on this plane accept that all are responsible for one another—that if just one is left out, we are still not whole.

Through your consciousness of perseverance and determination you teach that we must be responsible for our thoughts, actions, and deeds so that we will not think of ourselves as being more important than the next person. Then we can all stand shoulder to shoulder with arms and hearts extended, completing the circle of love within the universal consciousness.

PHYSICAL INTEGRATION: You stand for stability and responsibility just like the bone structure in the physical body. Without the stability of the bones, the body could not move or be responsible for itself; it would be nothing but a limp pile. You intuitively understand the need for taking responsibilty when you are in alignment with yourself. But stay aware of your physical structure, for if you are not accepting or teaching responsibility in a proper way, you are not teaching the body to be responsible for itself. If the structure malfunctions, it can weaken the knees, or you may become susceptible to problems with the bones, teeth, or anything that has to do with calcium in the body. You can also be prone to bruises, rashes, skin cancer, dry skin, eczema, spleen disorders, and rheumatism.

Such symptoms are the body's way of drawing attention to the need to reevaluate how you have claimed and maintained a sense of authority in your life. Has it been a rigid, closed, and fearful authority, or a sense of authority based on flexibility and openess to the input of others? When you are not functioning on a positive level, you may become resentful. The energy of resentment can dissipate calcium and cause difficulty with arthritis, bone marrow disorders, and general disfigurement of the bones, including the teeth and jawline. When functioning positively you can experience a great deal of physical strength and stamina, and remain in extremely good physical condition until very late in life.

If resentments in the body begin to build up there is an automatic warning mechanism so that you have time to reverse the process before it does any permanent damage. This warning system is in the stomach. When you are having problems with your stomach, you need to reevaluate your life, making some decisions for change, and correct patterns. If you do this, there should be no further negative manifestations in the body.

Aquarius

AQUARIUS

SOLAR ECLIPSE: (In order to fully activate the solar eclipse energy in Aquarius, you first must integrate the lessons of the Aquarius *lunar* eclipse with your emotional body. For a full explanation, see "How to Use Part II," page 166.)

You are teaching the lesson of detachment. You intuitively understand that your greatest awareness comes through motion and movement, and interaction with many people from all walks of life, with your "rolling stone," cavelier attitude. You teach those around you to break their inflexible patterns and appreciate the beauties of life. This lesson can be taught through different modes of personal behavior. You may stifle those close to you to the point that you become unbearable; this teaches them the lesson of detaching from those influences that bring them pain or retard their growth. You may also teach others to be objective by constantly detaching and moving forward yourself. Thus, your personal example helps people gain awareness of the ebb and flow of the universe, either through your own freedom or lack of it.

The lesson to be learned from exposure to an Aquarian eclipse is that of moving forward and not becoming fixated in unproductive experiences, even though letting go can be painful. To those who are unaware of your process you may appear to be very ungrounded as you move from one experience to the next. Actually, your process has the potential to revitalize every life you touch. You share what you have learned from your last experience in the present one, and you accumulate new information in the present to bring into the next situation.

Sometimes being with a person who has an Aquarian solar eclipse can feel like an explosion or a shattering of old perceptions of reality that have stopped the other person from experiencing the fullness of life. At other times you may teach this lesson through explosive behavior patterns that leave those around you feeling devastated until the smoke clears and they realize they have been set free.

You tend to draw very possessive, jealous people who need to learn detachment from their overinflated egos. Your nature can help them to incorporate a more universal approach to sharing love in relationships. Through loyalty to a universal sense of brotherhood that precludes any unhealthy attachment to individual form, you understand how to love freely and fully without possessiveness. You have an open channel to universal awareness and are able to see the highest good for the most people. You are able to introduce new ideas and concepts, thereby helping to usher in the Aquarian age.

By teaching detachment you help people to understand that we may not hold on to anything on the physical plane. Whatever we have accumulated must be passed on; all we can actually take with us is experience, and all we really have is time. You intuitively understand that we must make the best use of our time by not holding on to the past and choosing the most positive experiences in the present. Aquarius is the sign that represents the inventor, and you are innovative in your thinking, recognizing that we do not need to be held down by old thought patterns. Through your need for new experiences you teach others to break old, limited ways of thinking and open the doors to tomorrow.

Narrow-minded people who are not willing to believe that there can be a better way to do anything are attracted to you. When you come into the lives of these people, you help them open themselves to new ideas. You are so persistent and persevering in your enthusiastic approach to newness that you wear down those around you until they accept the prospect of change.

You also have a very strong sense of fair play, which is why you get so upset at the unfairness you see in the world. You have the ability to teach your fellow beings to be fair with one another by showing fairness in your dealings and by trusting those around you to be fair with you. However, you are not shy about speaking up when you feel that the other person has not been fair with you. People always start with a "clean page" as far as you are concerned, and it is up to them what they want to write on it. But once they have "soiled" their page, you hold them accountable. Through their behavior they have established their character in your eyes.

In your mind all of us begin as equals, with no one having more rights than another. As we live our lives, it is our behavior that allows us to keep—or causes us to lose—our rights. What you are teaching your fellow beings through this philosophy is that we can only hold ourselves accountable for our life situations. If we build a good character by being honest, trustworthy, and honorable, we will create a good situation for ourselves in this lifetime. If we want to change our life situation, our character is something that we are capable of refining through changing our behavior.

LUNAR ECLIPSE: Your lesson in this lifetime is detachment, and the challenge is to release your tendencies toward possessiveness and jealousy. The pace at which you learn your lessons is quite accelerated, so it essential that you allow things and people to flow through your life because you need to experience a great deal in this one incarnation. Nothing is allowed to crystallize in this life experience. Also, it is not permissible for you to consider only yourself when making decisions. The good of the whole is to be your main consideration, and the universe will take care of your personal needs when you are fulfiulling this role. If you can learn this detachment during this lifetime, it is not necessary for you to return to the Earth plane.

Part of the lesson is learning to detach from old set patterns of thinking. You are coming from a past consciousness of royal heritage—not necessarily of being a king or queen but set family patterns of "you must do this because it is what your ancestors have always done." You are learning to detach from belief systems that have held you down in the past, whether they were imposed by religion, family, or society. You realize that you do not need to conform to the beliefs of others. As long as you keep the good of the whole in mind and do not hurt others, you have the right to explore and enjoy your natural desire to experiment with life.

While learning your lessons you also have to satisfy a strong sense of curiosity. You have a need to understand the "why" behind everything. You feel that if you understand the "why," you can improve it, and you have an innate desire to improve the quality of life for all. You are the true humanitarian of the world.

In learning to become a humanitarian, you must learn how to adjust your consciousness to that of the masses. You are learning to detach from the ego enough to be able to think of what is for the good of all and at the same time retain a strong enough sense of ego to prod yourself to achieve what you have set out to accomplish.

One of the things you are here to achieve is the transition from thinking of yourself and your family alone to thinking of humanity. You are learning to take responsibility for directing your fellow beings into more positive areas of exploration on a planetary level as well as considering the expansion of your own family unit. This is an important lesson that must be learned with great respect and love for humankind.

You are also learning to develop a more universal consciousness regarding love. You must break past patterns of how you believed love should be. Previously, you were very jealous and possessive where love was concerned. You felt that things had to remain the way they always had been, which left no room for growth. Now you are learning that you do not need to hold on so tightly in affairs of the heart. To truly become a New Age thinker and be able to help expand the consciousness of others, you must always give freedom to those around you. If you want the freedom to expand and explore the world around you, you have to be open to others doing the same. By trying to hold on too tightly to anyone you care for, you will meet with such resistance that it can lead to a separation.

Giving love without attachment to whether or not it makes the other person love you more is a difficult lesson. You are seeking to separate yourself from an unconscious, self-defeating need for approval. Yours is the lesson of doing what is best for the most concerned and not for the individual gratification of personal love. You are in the process of accepting your humanitarian role on the planet, and as you practice giving love freely because you feel love for the other person, you learn to act without self-interest. You need to learn to share love for the sheer joy of the experience and not with the expectation of attachment or adoration.

In previous existences you were adored and put on a pedestal, and you have become attached to that kind of attention. Without this adoration you tend to confuse attachment with loyalty. You sometimes attach yourself to the wrong path because you feel the need of loyalty from others so strongly and think that if you are not loyal to their path, they won't be loyal to you. Because of this misconception you have a tendency to attach yourself to paths that are old and that you have already finished. It will help you to remember that, above all, everyone needs to follow his or her own path—"to thine own self be true." Self-loyalty is a very important lesson for you in this lifetime. You can keep yourself stuck in a rut for a long time because of this fixation on being loyal. You demand loyalty from others and from yourself, but you forget to be loyal to yourself!

An example of attachment to special attention and adoration would be a young harem girl who relished the special attention her exuberant youth brought her. Later, when it was time for her to shift into the role of teacher to the young girls who came after her (and to let go of the spotlight), she had to make a choice. She could either be a useful, vital part of the harem or a bitter, detached, isolated being. You are in the position of choosing what your response will be to the role of supporting others rather than being the spotlighted player on the stage.

When handling this on a positive level, you gain an understanding of the timing and cycles of life. There is a time for the spotlight, a time for stepping back, a time for teaching, a time for sharing, a time for loving—a time for every need. The idea is to be able to let go of attachment and proceed to the next level.

In this lifetime the need to love for the sake of love is very strong. You must learn to detach from the habit of dictating the behavior of those who fall in love with you. In previous lifetimes you were either loved because of your position in society or for what you could give in return. This time, in learning to be loved just for your own self, you need to let go of your attachment to certain behavior patterns that came with these previous expressions of love. This also frees you to love without pressure and to open yourself to being loved for yourself and not for a role you play. A king is loved because of his position and prestige; a leader because of his or her role of strength. In this lifetime you can finally experience the joy of being loved just for yourself.

Part of your lesson is to let go of needing those who are close to you to behave in a certain way. In learning to love without attachment to the behavior patterns of those you love, you are beginning to understand what it means to live and let live. In doing this you are fulfilling your own destiny and becoming a very loving, beautiful free spirit. Your process is truly embodied in the caterpillar becoming the butterfly; you are learning that love is like a butterfly: If you hold on to it too tightly, you kill it. On the other hand, if you allow those you love the freedom you demand for yourself, you find that both energies are satisfied. This is the way to attract a lifelong, loyal mate—both of you able to expand, explore, and grow separately while sharing love together.

UNCONSCIOUS EXPRESSION: If you choose to resist the flow of these lessons, you may find yourself experiencing a series of losses—things and people being unexpectedly removed from your life—until you learn to detach and let go. In tenaciously holding on to familiar experiences and people, you block new and vitalizing situations from coming into your life because there is no room for them.

You are learning that the next lesson is not always so terrible and that when you start something new, you don't always have to know how to do it perfectly from the very beginning. You have to learn how to ease into things and now base your judgment on your first impression. Aquarius is a fixed sign, giving you a tendency to attachment and difficulty in letting go. It is all right to allow yourself to get used to new things, people, and places. But you must learn to detach from one experience and move on to the next.

In past incarnations your creative tendencies were so extreme that you had to put all your attention into that one area of your life. You had to focus your energy on one narrow path and learn how to "block out" everything else. In this existence you bring with you that tendency to focus on only one area at a time, along with your intense creativity. Due to your fear of letting go you may not recognize that this creativity is a talent the soul has developed—you can't lose it, and you can bring it to any area or project that you choose. The trick is to use your talents not just for your own personal gratification but for humanity. Once you make the betterment of humankind your own life's goal, you will be able to flow easily with what is for the greater good. In this process you will discover that your own life begins to flow with more clarity of vision and a stronger sense of stability; you will no longer feel that things are being wrenched from you.

You can find yourself stuck in old patterns of ego gratification, however. You can become obsessed with the idea that others should pay homage to you. This attitude causes you to become stubborn, ego centered, and very unpleasant to be around. In this negative state you are fighting the very lesson you came to learn, which is giving up personal desires for the good of all concerned. You must learn to be less selfish and to detach from a need for glory before you can find happiness in this lifetime. Once you learn to consider others you find a renewed sense of happiness. Instead of feeling like an outsider begging to be noticed, you find the confidence and sense of belonging that comes from acting for the good of the whole.

If you choose not to learn the lesson of releasing old mind-sets and making way for new, innovative thinking, you may find yourself caught in a pattern of constantly conforming your behavior and thinking to those around you. Unconsciously, you can be enslaved by performing the role that is expected of you and not understand why you are constantly nervous and irritable. This is because inside you feel as if everything in your life is just a waste of time.

Basically, Aquarius is a very time-oriented sign. You have a strong sense of needing to accomplish certain things in certain periods of time. When you can let go of situations in which you have learned your lessons and allow yourself to move on to the next, you will begin to waste less and less time. The wasted time is the time spent in holding on, not the lesson itself. Time is wasted by not moving forward, and ultimately it is this recognition that frees you to operate on a conscious level and helps you to gain mastery over your life.

You have come to use your creativity and inventiveness in areas that better the quality of life for all. You cannot even begin to do this, however, until you learn to think with more open-mindeness. The first step is to overcome your habit of not wanting to listen to anyone else's ideals and then to give up the stubborn attachment to old, worn-out thought processes. You refuse to listen to the ideas of others because you feel that if someone has a concept different from yours, he or she is attacking the very basis of your thinking process. You are learning that when minds come together there is more strength, more reasoning ability, and more intellect. You need to recognize that "two minds are better than one" because each can show the other the weaknesses and strengths that each possesses. This gives you double the brain power.

Once you are willing to open up and listen you can process what you have heard and begin to utilize information from others.

With each old thought that you let go, with each new concept that you accept, you learn how to integrate new awarenesses, concepts, and insights from outside of the self. As you learn to make room for these new concepts, you realize that you never let go of anything that truly belonged to you. Every thought belongs to the universe. You never have to lose a thought to gain a new one—you just make room for more. At this point you become free to tap into the universal consciousness that can teach and guide you from a higher level, and your future growth can become easier and easier.

Operating unconsciously, you can be very judgmental and untrusting, fearing that everyone is out to take advantage of you. You can be class oriented and feel that others will never be any better or worse than the family they were born into. This class consciousness stems from your sense of royalty, which comes from a past lifetime when you *were* royalty or a person of high prestige in your community. These feelings are left over from a time when, in fact, it was not possible for people to rise above the social station dictated by their birth. This is possible in our society—the time of monarchy and keeping the people down is over. Now you need to release this consciousness; in doing so you help release this negative energy from the planet.

Upholding the old consciousness can result in holding down your own growth. Your lesson is to break a pattern of thinking that is oriented to the status quo and to develop a freer way of thinking that allows change and growth for everyone. You will realize eventually that we are all created equal.

CONSCIOUS EXPRESSION: Operating consciously, you understand the process of letting go and allow people and things to flow through your life. This enables you to incorporate a great number of experiences in this lifetime. You understand this process must take place if you are to get past the point of allowing physical and emotional desires to stop your personal growth. Once you have committed yourself to your growth process, the universe finds you to be a receptacle open to receiving your true heart's desire.

You are constantly striving to improve your ability to relate to life on a more universal level. You intuitively sense that humankind has spent too much time in selfish pursuits, and you feel that you must find a way to correct the world. You find yourself involved in humanitarian causes such as the Peace Corps, studying diseases that plague humanity, working to save the seals, or being the case worker for an underprivileged family. You have a strong desire to find out what you can do to help, and may act on this desire.

It is very important for you to save time for personal love. You want so much to help others that quite often you forget to spend time building a personal life. You love your fellow beings and are motivated to get your ego under control so you can be of service to humankind as a whole. You may feel that it is selfish to allow yourself time for love, and you have a tendency to become detached and aloof where affairs of the heart are concerned. You may fear that if you do allow yourself to attach and feel personal love, you will not be able to accomplish all that you want to do. What you really need is to acquire a balance between the two because everyone needs love. You have such a strong need to be loved that you spend all your time doing things for your fellow beings so that they will love you. But you forget to spend time on personal love and don't allow anyone to get close enough to give it.

From a conscious position you understand that humankind is just as delicate as love. You have a strong altruistic connection to humanity and understand that we should all do whatever is necessary to facilitate each other's process. You have "group consciousness" orientation, and it is important to you that all your fellow beings become more aware of their responsibility to the planet as a whole. You can be a very active environmentalist, working to change the way we treat the Earth, or you may put your energies into your local school system. The aware Aquarian eclipse has an ability to recognize where change is needed, the courage to bring this awareness into the open, and the energy to make it happen. You will not settle for stagnation or unfairness.

Many of you find it easier to relate to humankind by finding some abstract study or tool to use in fulfilling your urge to be of assistance. While you desire to help, you still need to remain detached enough not to fall into past patterns of allowing your will to take over, thereby not really being of any help to those you work with. Thus, especially while you are in the early stages of your own personal growth process, it is recommended that you find an objective tool through which you can see yourself as well as assist others (that is, astrology, psychology, tarot, a research foundation, and so forth). You need an external structure that allows you to see yourself objectively while you are developing your universal consciousness. You find great joy and satisfaction in helping others along the path, and when you can be learning and assisting others at the same time, you feel you are truly on the path yourself.

You have come into this lifetime feeling as if there is something inside that you must set straight. You recognize that on some level you still see humanity as segregated into different classes and that this is why you feel such a separateness from your fellow beings. Once you recognize that all of us are created equal and have the spark of the collective consciousness within, you can function more comfortably as an interdependent, beneficial part of the society within which you have chosen to incarnate. In past incarnations you had an overdeveloped ego that caused you to feel you were better than those around you. But in this existence you must learn to incorporate your own worth with the worth of all and detach from the need to feel that your accomplishments and/or needs are more important than those of others. It's as if you are stepping down from the past lifetimes of "royalty" to understand the lesson of being one of the many.

Part of this lesson is to recognize that all of us were born naked and dependent on others to sustain our lives. Some begin in affluence and end in poverty; some begin in poverty and end in affluence; still others maintain the status quo. Through this realization you can gain the awareness that we can make of our lives whatever we choose. You begin to notice that a person's class does not necessarily determine his or her happiness and that the only consistent factor in those who remain happy is that they have built a strong character. Thus, through observation you learn that the development of individual character is much more important that social status. A strong character frees a person to achieve his or her heart's desire, and that is your most important lesson.

TRANSPERSONAL EXPRESSION: You intuitively understand that the universe has a great deal for you to learn, and so you willingly accept the experiences and the lessons. You realize that if you are to evolve past the physical plane and the need to live on Earth and go through the experiences of Earth, you must detach from every phase of the physical body. Those who allow this detaching process to manifest may work as "channels," bringing in "outside" news for the Aquarian age.

At the most evolved level you serve as receptacles of information, which you pass on as though you were a receiving station from the universe and a transmitting station to the planet. When you have freed yourself enough to allow this process to materialize within the body, the information from the universe flows through you so that you can pass it on directly to your fellow beings. In this way you help to bring the energies of the Aquarian age into the world.

PHYSICAL INTEGRATION: Resistance to your lessons can lead to health warnings designed to alert you to the necessity of learning to "let go and let God." Such health warnings may include nervous tension, hypoglycemia, diabetes, swelling of the ankles, problems with circulation, and a craving for sugar. It is important for you take walks in order to keep your circulation flowing and balanced. This also assists in aligning yourself with your own spiritual lesson of learning that everything in the universe must circulate and that you can't keep anything confined in one location. The universe cannot exist in a static environment, and neither can the individual with an Aquarian eclipse. This eclipse is particularly subject to misdiagnosis as being "mentally unbalanced" due to the fluctuating sugar level in the body.

Pisces

PISCES

SOLAR ECLIPSE: (In order to fully activate the solar eclipse energy in Pisces, you first must integrate the lessons of the Pisces *lunar* eclipse with your emotional body. For a full explanation, see "How to Use Part II," page 166.)

You are here to help your fellow beings to develop their sensitivities. You have a tendency to draw to you very critical, overly analytical people, and you can teach these individuals to develop deeper levels of empathy. This also allows them to develop new ways of expressing their analytical abilities that will be more acceptable to others so they won't set themselves up for rejection as often. You are very sensitive to the energies around you and "pick up vibes" because you are so psychically developed. Thus, you need to be careful not to absorb the negativity of others.

With this natural gift of inborn intuition you can teach others the value of following their hunches and the usefulness of this awareness. Your hunches are accurate although often you are not even aware of why you are saying things and where the information is coming from. But you *are* enough in tune with your energies to know you should follow your hunches. For example, if an upcoming investment was mentioned and you said, "Don't purchase this one, purchase that one instead," it would be a good bet to follow this advice. This is true when you are following your *hunches*, not your mind. When such advice comes from a hunch, you have no idea why you said it. It's an intuitive instinct, and following it is extremely beneficial to the life processes of those you touch.

You are adept in sensing when someone is in a state of distress. You would be an excellent counselor or advisor because of your deep level of sensitivity. What you give your fellow beings is the freedom to be in distress without being judged. As you walk through life you draw to you people who are very self-judgmental and in need of seeing the larger whole. Through your natural compassion you can help others to regain their sense of self-worth.

Occasionally, even those born with this eclipse pattern lose their way and seem to be caught in a pattern of self-delusion. When this occurs you may tend to indulge in self-pity and destructive patterns of escapism. Unfortunately, you still draw critical people to you, so you will not be as lucky as those who find their way to you for help. If you lose your way, you need to seek professional assistance to get back to reality and to form more positive behavior patterns.

Because your innate nature is so sensitive, assistance not given in a loving, supportive manner can drive you deeper inside yourself. This can lead to a self-imposed state of martyrdom. You may feel it is only right that someone take the burden, and you set yourself up to be the victim. Ironically, even when negatively expressed in "victimhood," you model the principles of sensitivity and concern for your fellow beings and often evoke qualities of concern and compassion in others. It is your choice whether to teach this lesson through your negative or your positive behavior.

You are teaching these lessons on many levels: We are all "God's" children and to dishonor one is to dishonor Him; all human beings are part of the collective whole and contain within themselves the spark of the divine consciousness; we must have regard for all who are lost, even ourselves; we must have respect, love, and compassion for one another. Even if you feel lost you are teaching that we are all waifs along our earthly path. Since we have traveled away from the less confining spiritual realms into the denser physical worlds, we are constantly struggling to regain the feeling of connectedness with one another.

Like a magnet you absorb the negativity of those around you, then send back love, support, understanding, and whatever words of insight you think will ease the other person's pain. Your gift is that of healing through compassion, and people feel better simply by being in your presence. You allow people the freedom to be themselves because you recognize that everyone is in the state of being they need to be in to work on their lessons in this lifetime.

In the area of relationships you teach people not to analyze everything to death, remembering that too much separateness leads to unnecessary strains in relationships. You teach that un-connected categories can be self-isolating structures, and you help people to let go of feeling that they have to define themselves in order to relate.

You also help others to accept the subtleties of life. Through your own psychic receptivity, intuitive insights, and sensitive con-nectedness to others and to the whole, you validate that there are realms of perception beyond the norm of day-to-day living.

You teach others to sense and to feel and to get in touch with the spirit inside themselves and become one with the universe. You can do this through many different modes of expression: as a spiritual teacher and leader; as a living example of compassion and sensitivity; and as a person who is supportive and validating to the processes of those around you. Regardless of the mode, you teach others to relate with one another from an awareness of their inner divinity.

Basically, yours is the gift of modeling the principle of surrender in its highest, most loving form. Others are inspired by you to allow the principle of "let go and let God" to operate in their lives. You teach others to accept divine inspiration, either through a negative or a positive response flow. On the negative level you may play the devil's advocate by totally ignoring divine inspiration, not accepting any universal help and ignoring the spiritual gifts with which you incarnated. You may push away the compassion that others offer and remain a separate, detached entity. On the positive response level you allow spiritual assistance and human compassion to aid you and truly "let go and let God".

You teach your fellow beings how to remain in spiritual consciousness while incarnated. When you get into escapism patterns (drugs, alcohol, and so forth), you are actually seeking to regain an altered state of consciousness that you know you are capable of reaching. At some time during your life you have felt that gift of being connected with a kind of "bliss consciousness," and when it gets lost, you can fall into patterns of escapism because you are seeking so desperately to regain it. It is not the drugs or the alcohol that you want to experience, but you want to reconnect with the spiritual state that the drugs and alcohol artificially simulate.

This won't give you the sense of spiritual fulfillment you are seeking, however. It only takes the edge off the reality of the physical realm that is so difficult for you to deal with when you feel disconnected from your spiritual center. What you are really seeking is the altered state of consciousness that is the deep inner serenity and security of feeling the spiritual realm while in the flesh.

You help people learn to go with the flow. Yours is the philosophy that everything in the universe is working out exactly as it should and that if we will only let go, the flow will take each of us to our proper destination. You teach that by trusting the universal guidance and letting go of attachment to the ego, we can go with the flow of life and thereby receive the positive rewards we truly deserve.

LUNAR ECLIPSE: In this incarnation you have come to learn to deal with sensitivities. In past lifetimes you have been overly critical and have spent too much time putting everything in its proper perspective. Now it is time to recognize that everything blends together and is in reality an interacting part of everything else. When you realize this, you will be able to activate the "let go and let God" principle in your life.

In the lessons of this eclipse pattern you must learn to allow sensitivity to flow within your being—to listen to the inner voice and discern truth from fiction. During the process of these lessons it is important to retain your analytical abilities in order to ascertain whether each piece of information is useful; if it is not useful, it is from the imagination. This guiding principle frees you to let these thoughts or spiritual inspirations flow into your mind and allows you to decide if you will act on them. Through this process you can release the fear of becoming too sensitive and losing your grip on reality. You are allowed to develop these sensitivities and keep your feet on the ground at the same time.

Another lesson is not to be afraid to look at what the universe is trying to show you when you have premonitions, intuitions, and so forth. Once you learn to "let go and let God" and trust the intuitive information that comes through, you will recognize that the purpose is not to make you suffer because of what you "see" (if it's something painful) but to allow you to correct your direction or the direction of others before unnecessarily painful repercussions take place.

The idea is that life, or the God-consciousness, would prefer each of us to learn our lessons as gently as possible. You are learning to be a type of seer, either later on in this existence or in the next, who can warn us or allow us to see that we are headed down the wrong path. When you allow yourself to let go and be guided, others who don't have this gift of psychic foresight can be aided through your guidance.

It is important to realize that as you become more open to what is around you, you may in some ways become *overly* sensitive. Some of your feelings may not belong within your environment, and so it is important to exercise your ability to discern and discriminate, which you spent so much time developing in the past. This discerning attitude must be brought along on your journey into sensitivity, for without it you can get lost in the muddle and confusion.

By becoming more aware of your sensitivities you will tend to attract the emotional debris of those with whom you will come into contact. Your living environment may be too close to another's home or apartment that has conflict. If you forget to be discerning, you can absorb the negativity of those around you and claim it as your own. You need to stop and think, not just feel the energy pattern. When you become distracted and disoriented and sense anger within, ask yourself: Where is this anger coming from? Is it mine? Do I own it? Is it something that I need to handle? Or am I picking up something from someone around me?

Remember that as you develop psychically and become a very

sensitized being, you will need to take your strongest ally with you on this journey. This ally is your analytical ability, which will assist you in understanding what is going on around you. The universe would never have allowed you to enter onto the path of developing such acute sensitivity if you had not already developed your analytical abilities. The sensitivity that you are learning to develop is best supported by remembering to keep your feet on the ground.

Learning to trust your fellow beings is another challenge. In previous existences you overcategorized others, which has led to a tendency to need those around you to have set behavior patterns that allow you to keep things in order. In developing new patterns of trust you will come to grips with the fact that the universe unfolds differently for each person. Realizing this will enable you to increase your faith in the universal plan, which in turn allows you greater access to universal awareness. You can use this guidance for yourself and for those around you.

Provided that you overcome your tendency to be too critical and set aside your judgments of human behavior patterns, you can be among the fine psychics and mystics of the planet. You can also become an excellent diagnostician by using the best of your abilities to categorize, analyze, synthesize, and feel the energies of others.

If you wish to get on the path to learning these lessons, you may begin by trusting your own intuition and practicing in the context of your daily activities. For example, if you are accustomed to traveling a certain road from one location to the next and have an intuition to take a different route on a certain day for no apparent logical reason, the experiment would be to trust your instincts and follow that different route. Perhaps the Infinite has a reason for you not to travel your usual route. In following this inner guidance you validate your feelings and assure your higher self that you want this guidance and are able to accept it. This is important because it strengthens the connection. It is on these mundane levels that you train yourself to trust.

Another effective way to begin this training is to physically manifest your intuitions; for example, if your inner voice says that someone needs to hear from you, pick up the phone and call that person. The idea is to physically act on what the inner voice is telling you to do, as long as it is not harmful to anyone. In this way you let your higher consciousness know directly that you are willing for it to take a more active part in your life.

A different way to get in touch with inner guidance is to listen to your dream patterns. It is recommended that you become more aware of what you are learning, sensing, and perceiving from the dream state. Keeping a journal of your dreams will help you to combine your intuitive facilities with the practicalities of your daily life in a powerful way. And this is an easy place to begin this lesson!

When you learn to get in touch with these energies and to make sense of the continuity of the dream state, you may begin a course of meditation that will help you become aware of these energies while awake. Then, during the normal course of the day, you can take control of the energy and receive guidance and inspiration whenever you feel the need.

This will help you in overcoming a tendency to be overly self-critical, which can result in too much time being spent in finding flaws with the self. You need to understand that you are also a physical being working on this planet to evolve. You must let go of the need for perfection so that you can accept the spiritual guidance you came to learn. This will make your whole existence much easier and more gentle. Once you accept your imperfect state without guilt, you are ready to accept spiritual guidance, which can facilitate your growth process into a higher level of perfection.

UNCONSCIOUS EXPRESSION: With your unconscious eclipse in the sign of Pisces, you can resist the flow of your lesson by remaining overly critical and overly analytical, and refraining from any form of participation in the spiritual realms. There is a temptation to negate everything that comes through from spiritual consciousness by analyzing it to the point where it is impossible to perceive the true message. This keeps you from having the vision you need to realign your behavior in a way that would enable you to join with others as part of the whole.

You may not recognize the aid and the assistance you are given from the spiritual realms, and therefore you may not allow a sensitive nature to develop within your own being. This can lead to your being harsh and insensitive, and you may reject all assistance from those around you, including those who are trying to receive aid from the spiritual realms. When this happens there is a repetition of old errors because you have disallowed the new insight that would break the self-defeating patterns.

On the other hand, you may have come into this existence so

aware of the need to become sensitive that you open yourself too quickly from the very beginning. Opening and expanding too widely without prior physical, emotional, or spiritual training can "blow your circuits" and frighten you off your path. You may feel you have been "knocked off the path" through too intense an encounter with the spiritual realms because of your lack of education and inability to understand what is happening. In this case a reevaluation is necessary and a step-by-step, grounded process of psychic opening needs to take place. If handled in a way that honors both the spiritual and physical realms, this process can be rewarding and illuminating, and add a great deal of satisfaction to your life.

It is equally as important not to develop too rapidly as it is not to stay in old mind-sets of rigid separation. The idea is to gently become aware of wholeness. To leave behind your discerning abilities could lead to forms of escapism and overindulgence, whether it be food, alcohol, drugs, television, or prolonged sleeping patterns that are inappropriate to your life-style.

If you resist the lesson of learning to add sensitivity to your interactions with others, you may tend to alienate others through your harsh manner and rough behavior. One of the lessons you are learning is that through sensitivity you will be able to communicate with your fellow beings and to achieve what you have always wanted: to aid others in reaching their own individual states of perfection or at least to help others in regaining their direction so that they may become more secure beings.

When you first open to your sensitivity and compassion, unless you do it very consciously you can at times feel overwhelmed with the need to take on the burdens of others. Not understanding where this feeling is coming from, you may accept too much emotional debris from those around you, thereby making your burden heavier than it needs to be. You can recognize when this is happening because you will resent those coming to you for assistance. When you feel this sense of resentment, it's important to get in touch: Am I accepting more than I really want to? Have I made myself a self-appointed martyr? Am I shifting resentment and anger to those who are coming to me for help?

If the answer is "yes," then it is an important lesson because you begin to deal with the problems of friends, family, and co-workers *only* at times that you truly wish to help and to give *only* the assistance that you truly wish to give. When you give more than you have, you deplete your own energy and resent those who are "taking" from you, failing to realize that no one is taking, you are giving, and at all times we must be responsible for what we give. You are learning to be sensitive to the self as well as to others by learning when to say "no."

You have an innate ability to recognize when something is in need of strengthening or readjusting. From previous existences spent being harsh and overly critical, however, you can develop a pattern of finding flaws in everything and everyone. When you overdo this type of analysis, you repulse those around you because insensitive criticism is one of the most difficult things to accept.

You are learning in this lifetime to present your awarenesses in a different manner so that those you are trying to aid will not reject your advice solely because of the way it has been presented. If you confront someone with a weakness in a harsh or cold manner, it forces that person to put up a protective shell. You need to take care not to present your insights in a manner that is either humiliating or emotionally damaging. Otherwise, you will have placed such a barrier between yourself and the other person that no matter how beneficial your insights are, you will never be able to penetrate the wall the other person has erected for emotional self-protection. An essential part of your lesson is to develop tact and sensitivity in your mannerisms.

CONSCIOUS EXPRESSION: Operating consciously, you recognize that you need to incorporate sensitivity into your mannerisms. You are aware of the inspirational and intuitive side of your nature, and if you allow yourself an intelligent avenue to explore this intuition and sensitivity, these traits can be properly incorporated into your being. Only then can these gifts be used to aid and assist your fellow beings.

By recognizing where corrections need to be made, you can couple your previous exposure to the analytical mind and your awareness to detail with your ability to distill facts into a useful perspective. Once the intuitive faculty has been added you are able to be of great service to others. As your life progresses, sensitivity, spirituality, and psychic awareness become more and more a part of your being, and you become of even greater assistance to those around you.

Some of your abilities are similar to those who have premonitions since you can perceive what will be happening "down the road" and can then share your insights with those to be affected.

Then they have the opportunity to make a more educated decision about the direction they would like their lives to take.

Once your sensitivity and tact are developed you would make a good counselor since you are able to discern information, analyze it intelligently, and guide others into a proper perspective. When operating at a conscious level, you are developing the ability to take the element of human frailty into account as you critique those around you. When you do this, the information is accepted and used by others, and you are deeply appreciated by those who are in need of direction.

When expressing this eclipse pattern consciously, you are aware of subtleties that are transpiring within your being. You notice that you are becoming more intuitive as the days pass, having learned to listen to this intuitive guidance through trial and error. With awareness of this guidance, as you watch and critique what is transpiring, you can learn to feel and sense the difference between imagination and intuition.

Those of you who are more evolved appreciate the spiritual values and are curious to develop them. Many take courses in spiritual awareness, psychic abilities, dream analysis, Bible study, and meditation. All of these are excellent for opening up your consciousness, broadening your perspective and awareness, and enabling you to receive more information through your psychic faculties. As your psychic abilities grow, there are deeper insights into how you can most benefit your fellow beings as well as your-self with these awarenesses. You perceive that you are developing these gifts so that you can be of aid to others, and as you continue your work you may find many of your dreams to be precognitive in nature.

You are a sensitive, responsible being, and when operating at a conscious level, you may be drawn to occupations or situations where you can use this special sensitivity. You are aspiring to truly emanate love and compassion from your being.

TRANSPERSONAL EXPRESSION: On the level of group consciousness you are bringing great amounts of spiritual awareness to this planet by your ability to share love, peace, and harmony with those you come in contact and through the very way you think and live your life. You are born open and psychically aware of universal concepts that the average person is not even capable of imagining. You perceive the wholeness in everything and everyone. You truly understand and are able to conceptualize this awareness of this wholeness: that everything is whole within itself yet an integral part of another whole that encompasses yet another.

This awareness endows you with the ability to appreciate today, for tomorrow will always be part of a cycle yet to happen, and today is all we need to concern ourselves with when we have established enough faith in the universal plan and in our own integrity as a whole being.

You have a natural ability to walk through this lifetime without losing the sense of belonging to a greater whole; you remain assured that you are a loved and honored part of this universal whole. Thus, you are able to impart to others a sense of belonging to something greater than the self. This allows them to feel more confidence and freedom in exploring their chosen lessons, knowing they are always really "home."

PHYSICAL INTEGRATION: When you are resisting the developmental process you chose to acquire in this existence, your body will communicate to you that you are on the wrong track by drawing attention to the feet and the lymphatic system. Prior to these areas of the body becoming activated and oversensitized, you will have warning signals or symptoms in the digestive system. This is to let you know that you are overanalyzing and not allowing your psychic sensibilities to enter the picture. Through becoming more aware of your "overdigestive" process beginning on the psychological and then the physical level, you can form more sensitive habit pattterns and thereby free the digestive process to assimilate properly. You can do this by allowing spiritual energy to flow through you.

If this awareness is resisted or ignored, the result may be problems with the feet (including the arches and the instep) in the form of corns, calluses, swelling, sweatiness, and general irritations. Next, the lymphatic system of the body would become symptomatic. Pisces, being the last sign of the zodiac, is equivalent on the physical level to the last line of resistance within the body itself—the lymphatic system, which controls the immune system. If you choose to ignore your decision to develop spiritually in this lifetime, you may break down your lymphatic system. If you allow yourself to lose touch with your inner guidance, you may bring on these problems.

CHAPTER EIGHT

Houses

1ST

For additional insight into the 1st house eclipse, read the eclipse in Aries (page 175).

For further explanation of houses, see "How to Use Part II," page 166.

SOLAR ECLIPSE: You share what you have come to teach through direct one-to-one interactions, and you personally act out these life lessons through your physical mannerisms. When asked a direct question, you respond with full honesty—regardless of the repercussions—and you carry a childlike enthusiasm for accomplishing the tasks you have accepted.

In this lifetime you want to teach others how to expand their self-identity. Your natural understanding of how important it is for people to follow their own sense of independence and set their own goals gives you the ability to enhance that awareness in others. In this way you encourage those who are in need of expanding to reach a point of self-realization and self-direction.

You can teach those around you how to be successfully assertive and express themselves in a way that serves to attain their goals. You also motivate others to develop a stronger and more effective self-identity, which frees them to take assertive action in their lives.

LUNAR ECLIPSE: You are learning your lessons by noticing how people respond to your personality. Those you come in contact with will force you to take responsibility for your actions and will hold you accountable for your behavior and interactions with others. You are learning to integrate the qualities described by the sign of your lunar eclipse. Once this is accomplished your personality will become well rounded, and you will feel much more comfortable with other people.

You may find yourself going through life searching for who you really are, but by studying the sign of your lunar eclipse, your search for identity and self-sufficiency can be shortened.

2ND

For additional insight into the 2nd house eclipse, read the eclipse in Taurus (page 184).

SOLAR ECLIPSE: You are here to help those around you get in touch with their own deepest values. Through either a positive or negative experience with you, others can learn the importance of building a strong foundation in whatever area is weak in their personality structure. You teach them *how* to build a strong foundation by laying the blocks one at a time.

You can be especially helpful to others in the areas of the emotions and in building feelings of self-worth. They can learn from you how to determine what needs to be incorporated into their personalities to strengthen and broaden their emotional makeup. Through you, people can get in touch with what their emotional needs actually are, for you intuitively understand that in order to manifest anything you must know what it is you want.

You have a natural understanding of moral, financial, and spiritual values, and a knack for helping people recognize ways to strengthen their values and feel better about themselves. Being able to look at life with clear logic and an understanding of what is and what is not reality, you can quickly calculate the assets and liabilities of those with whom you come in contact. And you can teach others how to use their assets and eliminate their weaknesses.

LUNAR ECLIPSE: There is some basic flaw in your internal value system that you have come to restructure. You have to strengthen your foundation in whatever area is weak. It's like a missing brick that needs to be filled in so that at some stressful time in your life your internal structure doesn't topple over. What you are looking for is that missing brick in the basic foundation of your life—your values. Studying the sign of your lunar eclipse will help you, and when you have found and fixed this missing link, you will also be restored to balance and harmony within your being.

3RD

For additional insight into the 3rd house eclipse, read the eclipse in Gemini (page 195).

SOLAR ECLIPSE: You have the ability to teach people the necessity of sharing the experiences, ideas, and feelings in their everyday lives. In your environment you are usually the one counted on to keep the conversation flowing, and you teach those around you the necessity of keeping information and knowledge circulating. You keep everyone informed about what is going on, and the type of information you focus on is determined by the sign of your solar eclipse.

You teach that there are no limits. We can have as much as we want in any area of life—money, love, knowledge, and so forth—as long as we don't plug up our own flow by holding on to what we believe in or have now. You show us that as long as we keep it circulating, something new and better will always take its place.

LUNAR ECLIPSE: You are here to learn to allow things to flow through you in this lifetime. You have come to remove blockages, to communicate, to socialize and interact with your environment, especially in areas ruled by the sign of your lunar eclipse. Yours is the lesson of letting go and trusting the universe to provide what you need and replenish what you release. This is a lifetime for breaking stagnated energy patterns such as not sharing your resources, feeling you were the only one privy to certain information, being unable to communicate your feelings, or fearing that the energy flowing from you would not be reciprocated. In this existence you came to find the bounty available from the energy of circulation.

4TH

For additional insight into the 4th house eclipse, read the eclipse in Cancer (page 205).

SOLAR ECLIPSE: You are teaching people how to become comfortable within their home base, how to recognize their security needs and take responsibility for fulfilling these needs for their inner peace. Through you, others can get in touch with their inner nature and lay strong foundations to grow from so they will not be easily swept off-balance by their external surroundings. You teach people to develop a deeper understanding of themselves, which gives them security in relating to the world. You have the ability to teach those around you to feel comfortable with themselves, whether they need to learn lessons of detachment, attainment, or sharing. You help them to see that their souls are at exactly the right point in their evolution, regardless of their circumstances.

Your innate ability to be comfortable in the areas related to the sign of your solar eclipse allows you to teach people to be comfortable with that energy within themselves. You are a nurturer and can teach others to nurture their own self-esteem. You make people feel at ease and good about themselves, and secure about the foundations from which they are emerging. You bring out their capacity to feel and validate their sensitivities.

LUNAR ECLIPSE: You came into this incarnation with low self-esteem, and you are learning self-worth and self-identity in this lifetime. Learning to be comfortable within your family unit will help you to be comfortable within the essence of your soul. If you are an overachiever, it may be because you feel there is so much to improve. You may spend too much time judging yourself when what you really need to learn is how to build your self-esteem. You must spend as much time building self-esteem as you spend building in the external world. Remember to do those things that make you feel good about yourself and to validate your successes internally along the way. Learning to enjoy the process as much as reaching the goal is important for you.

As you begin to recognize your own self-worth you become less defensive, especially within the family unit. Allowing others to nurture you helps you to feel better about yourself. You are extremely good at seeing flaws within the self, and you need to learn to nurture your own identity and accept your soul's reason for being part of the universe. There is goodness in your essence, and you have much to share as you learn to express yourself from your own center.

5TH

For additional insight into the 5th house eclipse, read the eclipse in Leo (page 214).

SOLAR ECLIPSE: You have the responsibility of teaching others how to play in life. By following your heart you teach those around you how to approach life in a more carefree way. You are an extremely creative being, and you help other people to bring forth their own creativity. You have good organizational abilities, work well with children, and are comfortable with affairs of the heart. Generally an easygoing person, you do possess depth and intensity, and are success-oriented. Perhaps the most important lesson you teach others is to accept the pleasures that life offers and to stay out of self-denial.

You can dramatize your own life in a way that sparks others into taking chances and risks in their own lives. You demonstrate the lesson of "nothing ventured, nothing gained" and have the ability to break people out of old stagnant patterns. Yours is the energy of the child who knows better than to neglect the pleasure and enjoyment of life. By enjoying your life you help others to remove the crusts from around their hearts and accept love into their lives.

LUNAR ECLIPSE: You are learning how to take life less seriously and to play. You are also learning to accept good fortune and love. You tend to want to know the motive behind everything that comes to you and to doubt whether you are really worthy of receiving it. By learning to release old emotional insecurities, you are more willing to take chances, stepping out into life for the sheer enjoyment of pursuing a new pathway.

The lesson of accepting is a difficult one for you, and yet it is essential that it be learned. If you are going to love the universe, you must first learn to love yourself. To begin to love yourself you must get over your hesitancy about accepting love, gifts, and praise from others. When you are able to live in a state of acceptance, you are truly able to give love not only on an individual level but on a universal level. At that time you will come into your own true power and have the ability to teach universal concepts.

This lifetime you are learning how to deal with affairs of the heart, children, and your own creativity. Through procreation you learn how to incorporate the joy of your creativity into this existence. As you begin to allow yourself to be proud and accept love from what you create in this existence, you also allow yourself to develop an ego and self-identity through what you create. This helps you get more in touch with your creator and other universal energies.

Learning to recognize that you have the ability to create puts you in touch with your power to manifest your own positive destiny. Through consciously creating what makes your life happy, vital, and alive, you learn to accept responsibility for creating your own reality.

6TH

For additional insight into the 6th house eclipse, read the eclipse in Virgo (page 224).

SOLAR ECLIPSE: You are teaching others how to organize their lives by having clearly defined goals, putting things in proper perspective, and disciplining their visions to a practical application. You have the capacity to observe details *and* to see the larger picture involved. Your teaching those around you how to learn from their own lives, find their own flaws, and find their own remedies. This gives them the power to put things back in order for themselves.

Your concern with finding a healthy balance between the needs of mind and body teaches others to do the same. You also teach the value of self-improvement since you are willing to learn and grow from your various life experiences. Especially in the areas of work, service, and health, you share with others the gifts shown by the sign of your solar eclipse.

LUNAR ECLIPSE: You need to learn to make adjustments to your life-style that will allow you to have a healthy body, sensible work habits, and a positive attitude toward this service-oriented lifetime. In the process you will open to learning the lessons you seek through the signs of your lunar eclipse. In previous lifetimes you have neglected certain things concerning health, work, and service, and you need to reevaluate your ideals and intentions in these areas. You may need to learn about the body (what you can and cannot put into it) or break laziness patterns from previous incarnations.

Instead of wishing your life away you are learning to physically manifest what you want in this lifetime. You are putting your mind back into productive focus toward a direction or goal, and in the process you will learn the lessons dictated by the sign of your lunar eclipse.

7TH

For additional insight into the 7th house eclipse, read the eclipse in Libra (page 234).

SOLAR ECLIPSE: You are here to teach others how to relate. Yours is the gift of interaction and teaching others how to have successful partnerships and relationships. You are teaching the benefits of promises and contracts, and how necessary it is to honor commitments.

Through your ability to relate with others in the spirit of harmony, goodwill, and consideration of the other person, you can share your solar eclipse gift. You teach people that to see the self, or at least how the self is viewed by others, they must learn how to relate. Thus, you are teaching humankind how to use the mirror of "the other" to help reevaluate the self.

LUNAR ECLIPSE: You are learning how to master the lesson of your eclipse through your close relationships with others. You can experience the energy of relating by being aware of the effect you have on the lives and attitudes of those around you, and by learning to understand the roles that others play in your life. The meaning of commitment and the value of follow-through are becoming clearer to you as you learn to take the needs of others into consideration.

8TH

For additional insight into the 8th house eclipse, read the eclipse in Scorpio (page 243).

SOLAR ECLIPSE: In this lifetime you are teaching the energies of transformation. When you enter into powerful psychological interactions with others (whether business or sexual), you give them access to your gifts.

The financial, moral, and spiritual responsibility we have for one another is the lesson you teach. You make others aware of how their values affect those with whom they come in contact, and you help them to understand the importance of finding common values on all three levels. You can also use your powerful energy as a healer or metaphysician. By your example you can teach those around you the value of investing time, money, and awareness in humankind as a whole.

You have a natural intuitive awareness of the values and needs of those around you and understand their importance on a moral, financial, and spiritual level.

LUNAR ECLIPSE: You are learning to take responsibility for how your values affect the other people in your life. You need to learn why it is important for the strong to be responsible for the weak. As you enter into areas of joint responsibility and mutual empowerment, you gain access to what you need in order to learn the lessons determined by the sign of your lunar eclipse. You are also learning to take responsibility for how you express yourself sexually in this lifetime.

9TH

For additional insight into the 9th house eclipse, read the eclipse in Sagittarius (page 256).

SOLAR ECLIPSE: You are teaching others to have adventures in life, to take chances, and to be free. By encouraging others to pursue their sense of individual adventure and not to become fixed on one ideal or one location, you teach them how much can be learned by allowing their consciousness to expand and their body to travel while they are on the planet.

You encourage others to incorporate as many different lessons and experiences as possible into one existence by circulating in different cultures and environments. They follow your example of sharing what you have learned from other environments, showing that each type of culture has its own positive awareness and value. In the process of living an adventurous life-style you open yourself to share the gifts shown by the sign of your solar eclipse.

LUNAR ECLIPSE: You have incarnated with the responsibility to expand your awareness of both conditioned ideals and other cultures and social environments. You are here to realize that there is more to life than what you already know. Thus, you will feel a desire for freedom and movement and a curiosity for new experiences in this lifetime. You are reaching for idealistic goals, and in the process of pursuing your sense of adventure you will encounter lessons you need to learn as indicated by the sign of your lunar eclipse.

10TH

For additional insight into the 10th house eclipse, read the eclipse in Capricorn (page 266).

SOLAR ECLIPSE: You teach others about professional ethics and community responsibility. You are a leader in the community, teaching your peers to be aware of the interdependency that members of the community have with one another. You have the ability to be a politician, religious leader, or the parent who runs the P.T.A. You are capable of achieving goals easily in this lifetime, and through the process of your achievement you teach the qualities of your solar eclipse sign to others.

LUNAR ECLIPSE: You need to learn about community responsibility. You are learning to communicate your thoughts and feelings with a high level of integrity within your chosen fields of endeavor. The sign of your lunar eclipse shows the areas where you need the most work. You are learning to set and achieve career goals and to pursue these goals with a single-mindedness that enables you to develop character and learn your lessons along the way.

It is important not to allow your insecurities to get in the way. You may sometimes find yourself feeling sidetracked or having to take a few steps backward. Understand that this is natural in the process of learning how to use everything in your path to attain your goal.

11TH

For additional insight into the 11th house eclipse, read the eclipse in Aquarius (page 276).

SOLAR ECLIPSE: You are teaching your fellow beings to develop a group consciousness and to be more aware of the needs of others. You teach many of your lessons in group situations, helping others to develop group-oriented awareness. Much of your work is in humanitarian endeavors that are for the highest good of the most people. You can help bring about the realization that when the masses are taken care of, individual lives will also be fulfilled. One example of this is the family unit. If decisions are made that make the family happy, the individuals within the family are happy too.

In pursuing your own high ideals and aspirations you help others to become goal-oriented. You make them aware that nothing can be achieved in this life unless you strive for it. Through your own zest for life and accomplishment you teach other people to reach for the stars, and you show them that nothing is beyond their reach if they really focus their energy on it.

You encourage others to pursue their dreams, aspirations, and ideals, and are extremely supportive of your friends and acquaintances. You often put a great deal of time and energy into the efforts of those you feel have worthy goals or those with whom you feel a kinship. You encourage others to fulfill their dreams in ways explained in the sign of your solar eclipse.

LUNAR ECLIPSE: Besides learning to dream you are also learning that is is all right to improve the life you were born to and to acquire more than you have. Dreaming is a very healthy pastime for you because it helps to build your soul growth pattern. Regardless of the sign of your eclipse, when it is in the 11th house you must learn how to dream in order to aspire to new heights in this lifetime.

You are also learning about group consciousness and how to incorporate the good of all into your aspirations. You are learning to recognize that in fulfilling the group need, your own individual needs are automatically satisfied. As you begin to take into consideration the desires, goals, and aspirations of those around you (the group, not just individuals), you will discover your need to find your relatedness to the whole—either by giving to or receiving from them. You are learning to be aware of the group as a mutually supportive emotional system in terms of your dreams and aspirations.

You are beginning to allow your life to merge with the flow of the universe. If you follow your own inner guidance and intuition, you will be directed to the precise path you are to follow to reach your own personal goals.

12TH

For additional insight into the 12th house eclipse, read the eclipse in Pisces (page 286).

SOLAR ECLIPSE: Through the principle of "let go and let God" you are teaching others to have trust and confidence in the universal unfolding of events. You help other people learn how to cope with unexpected changes and the ups and downs of life, how to deal with limitations, how to listen to the inner world within, and how to appreciate the inspiration that can be received only when we are willing to listen to the inner voice. You teach others to accept and even to appreciate the confines of their own mind.

People can learn from you how to contact peace and inner serenity through meditation and how to gain the awareness that the universe can unfold to those who are willing to slow down and listen by going within. You also have the ability to deal with institutions of all kinds. You are excellent at counseling others because you are aware of their self-defeating patterns and can offer emotional encourgement according to the nature of the sign in which your solar eclipse is found.

LUNAR ECLIPSE: You are learning how to get in touch with the self by quieting the psyche long enough to go within and listen for inspiration and guidance. It is important for you to experience the serenity of meditation, to make time to be alone and go within. This process will enable you to discover your own self-defeating mechanisms so you can learn the lessons in the sign of your lunar eclipse.

Rooting out anything from a previous incarnation that is still buried within your psyche will help you to get rid of self-limiting habit patterns. You are learning to free yourself from internal mechansims that lead to unconscious withdrawl from situations rather than active participation. By going inward you are able to remove these blockages so you can participate in life with a free flow of energy.

If you don't learn to contact your inner self on your own, you may find it necessary to have the imposed structure of an institution. It's important for you to find healthy modes of going within instead of developing escapism patterns such as drugs, alcohol, television, sleeping too much, or self-pity. Through learning to make the corrections within yourself, you find that your external circumstances cease to pose any kind of a block to your own expression. As an added benefit you will develop at a rapid pace spiritually and psychically, and find yourself aiding others in areas that were once weaknesses for you.

CHAPTER NINE

Aspect Patterns

THERE are four major aspects possible between the lunar eclipse and the solar eclipse in your individual chart: opposition, quincunx (or inconjunct), semi-sextile, and conjunction. For the purpose of this book these aspects are to be calculated by sign only.

The aspects indicate the nature of the psychological relationship between your solar and lunar eclipses and are calculated by the distance the signs are from one another. To determine the aspect between your prenatal solar and lunar eclipses, use the following diagram wheel:

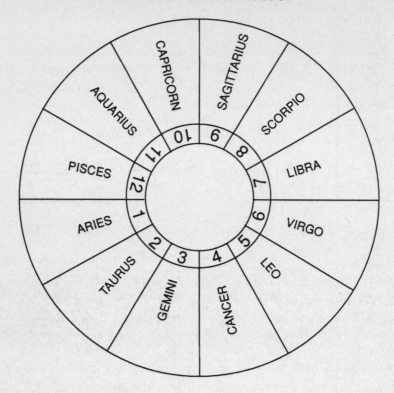

Counting your prenatal solar eclipse as "1," count each sign until you reach your prenatal lunar eclipse (it will be counted also), going in a counterclockwise direction. Then refer to the list below to find the aspect between your prenatal solar and lunar eclipses. (Please note that orbs—the degrees involved in mathematical aspecting—are not used in this particular system of aspecting. The aspecting referred to in this material is by sign quality alone.)

LIST OF ASPECTS

1 = conjunction
2 = semi-sextile
6 = inconjunct
7 = opposition
8 = inconjunct
12 = semi-sextile

Example No. 1: If your solar eclipse is in Leo and your lunar eclipse is in Aquarius, you would count Leo as 1 and, proceeding in a counterclockwise direction, Aquarius would be 7. On the list 7 is an "opposition"; therefore, the aspect between your solar and lunar eclipses is that of an opposition.

Example No. 2: If your solar eclipse is in Capricorn and your lunar eclipse is in Sagittarius, counting Capricorn as 1 and going in a counterclockwise direction, Sagittarius would be 12. On the list, 12 is a "semi-sextile"; therefore, the aspect between your solar and lunar eclipses is that of a semi-sextile.

OPPOSITION

You are learning from the people you teach. Your major avenue for personal growth evolves from the intensity of your relationship with those around you. As you work with others on a one-to-one basis, the people you support also provide the support you are seeking in your own life. Mutual growth occurs through this process of reciprocity.

The abstract goals of humankind are not your concern. Your challenge is in finding out how to relate to those around you in a way that produces harmony and justice for both parties. Extending your identity to include others gives you a greater sense of self-completion. The self, as developed in prior incarnations, is now ready for another major growth step, and input from the energy of other people is necessary. You are learning to accept the support and assistance of others in gaining awareness of what you need to complete your own development. This requires humility and grace because you must change personal patterns that separate you from those around you and allow—even invite—them to facilitate your growth process. As you become more open to this assistance, you find that the other person also gains self-awareness.

You are seeking to balance a feeling of self-importance in this lifetime by recognizing that all things are of equal importance. You learn this by accepting responsibility for making yourself as complete as you possibly can while remembering that others are doing the same thing and are just as important as you are.

As you work on ego development and relate with others, you find that those around you remind you of your lesson by saying, "Hey, I'm important too." This brings you back to Earth and helps you become more aware of your flaws, for without this awareness you cannot grow. By relating with others you can become the best you can possibly be. At the same time you gain awareness of the needs of others, which facilitates the social balance you are seeking.

You are also learning the value of diplomacy when expressing yourself to others, which leads to more mutually pleasant experiences. This is an equal-time issue; you are learning to share. In the process you gain a sense of ease about life and an ability to enjoy others while pursuing your own goals.

QUINCUNX (INCONJUNCT)

This is a karmic aspect. You have accepted the responsibility of teaching your fellow beings to become more aware. You are among those bringing in the New Age—the agitators, the healers, the new thinkers. It is a lifetime of "pearl and oyster": Through constant adjustments to the irritations of life you are able to create much beauty and awareness for yourself and other people. Because you are so sensitive to irritations you learn to adjust so that you can heal them quickly; this creates a great deal of growth in one lifetime, which is what you wanted. Your realization that through aiding others your own growth pattern is speeded up is the reason you can be one of the light workers and help to lay the foundation for the New Age.

This is a "serve or suffer" lifetime. The most growth and awareness comes to you when you are providing a service and helping others to grow and understand. When you are not, you can be deteriorating in one of three areas: your physical health, your mental and emotional health, or your financial situation. More than any other aspect pattern you are subject to these types of instabilities if you neglect your responsibilities to your own growth.

Your own insights do not come directly through the people that you are aiding and teaching in this lifetime, however, but in other ways. Your duty is to assist where you can, and the universe will reward you with another source to provide the knowledge you need, either directly through your own spirit or through some other person. As you help others to gain the awareness they need to grow and adjust to their personal life circumstances, you open yourself to receiving the awareness you need. You recognize that your rewards do not come from those you assist.

You are happiest when you are involved in some sort of service, and you are best suited for a profession that involves healing on some level. This could encompass many areas: working in a health-food store or being a dietitian, farmer, or doctor; assisting with psychological healing as a psychiatrist, psychologist, or astrologer; working with spiritual or emotional healing as a minister; or healing other people's financial, moral, or spiritual values.

You are one of the "worker bees" on the planet. You are preparing the way for the New Age in the same way a farmer clears the ground and makes it ready for the new seeds. You are learning a sense of humility in your role on the planet. You are also learning to appreciate the honor of being able to play a part in the evolution of the race and the access this gives you to higher sources of information.

In this lifetime you are gaining a larger perspective of the interrelatedness of all things. You are incorporating the feelings of equality and appreciation that come from realizing that everything on the Earth is part of the same life force. Just as the plants are food for us now, we will someday become food for them. Understanding this kind of relatedness keeps you humble, free, and happy in your life role.

SEMI-SEXTILE

The healing of your own identity is your primary concern during this lifetime since you need to gain a sense of wholeness within yourself. To this end you are continually putting your energies into building the things that are important to you, either financially, morally, or spiritually. When what you are striving for is out of alignment with your own true needs and values, you fall into self-defeating patterns that result in the dissolution of everything you have worked so hard to build. You are learning to build carefully and in more conscious alignment with your own personal identity.

Your work needs to be focused primarily on yourself. It is fine for you to work with others in partnership as long as you don't come to rely on them. You must learn that your destiny is an outgrowth of the strength of your inner character.

Your job is to clear out self-defeating patterns from past lifetimes. You encounter these patterns when building those things that you want for a sense of stability in the material world. If a project begins to fail, it is your job to identify the specific self-defeating pattern that has caused this turn of fortune, correct it, and eliminate it from your unconscious behavior.

On one level you are making new beginnings during this lifetime, and on another you are experiencing how to make effective completions. When the direction of your life is in alignment with your purpose, you go through a succession of tedious new beginnings that, when the proper energy is applied, culminate in successful endings. You have many similarities with the entrepreneur who is continually starting a new business and selling or dissolving the old in order to enter into the next new venture.

You have a need to build without attachment to the physical plane—including whatever it is you are building—and you find that you have the internal motivation and energy needed to propel you to new projects. When you attain completion of a project, you immediately start looking at ways to dissolve it, for you do not want to become attached to anything in this lifetime. You feel that attachment will hold you down since you realize that the process of dissolving things is at least half of what you came here to learn.

It is important that you do not judge yourself by what you have attained in the physical world. Instead, you should integrate the personal growth that has emerged from the combination of what you have acquired and what you have released in terms of material attachment. It is also important for you to understand that it is all right for you to have material possessions. Your purpose in this life is not to renounce the material plane but to understand and develop a proper value system by constantly letting go of what is not congruent with the deeper values you have incorporated into this lifetime. When this process is complete, you can acquire great wealth and also be very spiritually aware, taking responsibility for assisting those who are less fortunate. You can be truly charitable with both heart and pocketbook.

Learn to rely on yourself to move into new stages of personal growth. You cannot rely on others to prod you along but must prod yourself into action by physically taking that first step in the new direction.

CONJUNCTION

You have the responsibility of assimilating past life experiences into the personal identity of this lifetime. You are integrating separate facets of your personality into a wholeness and centeredness within yourself. It is as though the self was so involved with other projects and identities in prior incarnations that it lost its focus. Thus, in the present incarnation the urge is toward unity, self-sufficiency, and a sense of completion within the self.

After having been dispersed, the identity is now ready to integrate itself at a higher level than was available in past lifetimes. Your greatest growth comes not through objective awareness but through subjective experiences of your life situations. Your job is to allow the circumstances of your life to aid you in building a separate identity that will give you a true sense of individuality. When you reunite with that spark of identity within yourself, you find an inner strength emerging. This self-reliance will heal the nagging sense of incompletion you feel when you allow yourself to become dependent on others for your personal growth.

It is important for you to practice being real with the self because this is a lifetime for you to become fully conscious of reaping what you sow. You will get out of life only what you arc willing to put into it, in the sense of expressing what is really going on inside you. The degree of realness that you are willing to share with others reflects the realness that the universe will be willing to unfold to you.

If you can become capable of total honesty, your ability to perceive and share advanced spiritual concepts will be unlimited since the universe will unfold itself to you without reserve. If you choose to separate yourself from your own truth and reality, you can find yourself living a life of confusion and delusion, and possibly needing counseling to remove the veils you have placed over your own identity.

CHAPTER TEN

Conclusion: Eavesdropping on the Signs

Upon entering the Earth plane, these are the remarks heard from the various solar eclipse and Sun signs:

Aries: "Everybody out of my way!"
Taurus: "What's mine?"
Gemini: "Listen to me . . ."
Cancer: "Does anybody really care?"
Leo: "Who wants to play?"
Virgo: "We're not doing it right!"
Libra: "Is this the right direction?"
Scorpio: "Let's get to the bottom of it."
Sagittarius: "I know where you're coming from."
Capricorn: "I deserve better."
Aquarius: "I'm just curious."
Pisces: "What am I doing here?"

PART
III

MATHEMATICAL TABLES:
Finding the Signs in Which Your
PLANETS AND ECLIPSES
Are Located

CHAPTER ELEVEN

Introduction

THE purpose of Part III is to supply mathematical tables that will enable you to find the signs in which your planets and eclipses are located. In providing these tables it is our intention to allow you to gain a maximum of self-sufficiency and freedom in being able to read birthcharts. This in no way invalidates the furthering of your education through a reading with a qualified professional astrologer or through additional classes and studies. The purpose is to offer a beginning place for self-awareness and an astrological key that will assist you on your path of soul awareness.

CHAPTER TWELVE

How to Use Part III

THE mathematical tables for looking up the sign positions of all
your planets and prenatal solar and lunar eclipses are accurate
within twenty-four hours of the cut-off dates indicated, depending
on your exact time and place of birth. If you have a planet located
on a cut-off date—either the first date of a new period or the last
date of the old—read both sign descriptions. For total accuracy in
determining your sign positions as well as finding the houses in
which your planets and eclipses are located, you can utilize the
computer service listed on page 451.

It is easy to use Part III. Using your birthdate, simply find the
sign location for each of your planets and eclipses. Then look up
the corresponding *meaning* of each of your planets in Part I and of
each of your eclipses in Part II.

CHAPTER THIRTEEN

The Planets

THE SUN

Where was the Sun when you were born?

Date	Sun Sign
1/01 to 1/20	Capricorn
1/21 to 2/19	Aquarius
2/20 to 3/20	Pisces
3/21 to 4/19	Aries
4/20 to 5/20	Taurus
5/21 to 6/21	Gemini
6/22 to 7/21	Cancer
7/22 to 8/21	Leo
8/22 to 9/22	Virgo
9/23 to 10/22	Libra
10/23 to 11/21	Scorpio
11/22 to 12/21	Sagittarius
12/22 to 12/31	Capricorn

THE MOON

The Moon moves rapidly through the zodiac, spending only two and one-half days in each sign. Due to its rapid motion your time of birth could make a difference in accurately using the Moon tables listed here.

The Moon positions listed are calculated for 12 noon, Greenwich time (GMT), which is equivalent to 7 A.M. eastern standard time (EST), and 4 A.M. pacific standard time (PST).

The Moon moves one degree every two hours. Thus, if you were born in Los Angeles, California, at 4 A.M. (PST), on January 1, 1942, your Moon would be at 28° Gemini.

If instead of 4 A.M. you were born at 8 A.M., your Moon would be at 30° Gemini:

> 28° Gemini at 4 A.M.
> + 2° (8 A.M. − 4 A.M. = 4 hours;
> _____   4 hours ÷ 2 = 2°)
> 30° Gemini

There are thirty degrees in a sign. Thirty degrees of one sign is equivalent to zero degrees of the following sign. For example, thirty degrees Gemini is equivalent to zero degrees Cancer. So if, for example, on January 1, 1942, in Los Angeles, California, you were born at 2 P.M., your Moon would be at 3° of Cancer:

> 28° Gemini at 4 A.M. (PST)
> + 5° (2 P.M. − 4 A.M. = 10 hours;
> _____   10 hours ÷ 2 = 5°
> 33° Gemini
> −30° in a sign
> 3° Cancer

Due to space limitations, the symbols (or "glyphs") for the astrology signs have been used, following the degrees on the Moon tables. For your convenience the glyph equivalents are listed below:

> ♈ = Aries
> ♉ = Taurus
> ♊ = Gemini
> ♋ = Cancer
> ♌ = Leo
> ♍ = Virgo
> ♎ = Libra
> ♏ = Scorpio

♐ = Sagittarius
♑ = Capricorn
♒ = Aquarius
♓ = Pisces

With the Moon, the signs always progress in order. After Pisces, the cycle returns to Aries and begins again. Should you have any difficulty in reading the symbol for the sign on your date of birth, you can check one symbol backward or forward to make certain of your own.

MOON POSITIONS

JANUARY

	1	2	3	4	5	6	7	8	9	10	11	12	13	14	15
1900	10♑	24♑	9♒	24♒	8♓	23♓	7♈	21♈	5♉	18♉	1♊	14♊	27♊	9♋	22♋
01	25♌	9♍	23♍	7♎	21♎	4♏	17♏	29♏	12♐	24♐	6♑	18♑	0♒	11♒	24♒
02	8♎	20♎	2♏	14♏	26♏	8♐	20♐	2♑	14♑	26♑	9♒	22♒	5♓	18♓	2♈
03	8♒	20♒	2♓	15♓	27♓	10♈	23♈	7♉	21♉	5♊	20♊	5♋	21♋	6♌	21♌
04	16♊	0♋	15♋	0♌	15♌	0♍	15♍	29♍	13♎	27♎	10♏	23♏	5♐	18♐	0♑
05	17♏	1♐	15♐	28♐	11♑	24♑	7♒	19♒	2♓	13♓	25♓	7♈	19♈	1♉	13♉
06	28♓	10♈	22♈	4♉	16♉	28♉	10♊	22♊	4♋	17♋	29♋	13♌	27♌	10♍	24♍
07	29♋	11♌	23♌	6♍	18♍	1♎	15♎	28♎	12♏	27♏	12♐	27♐	12♑	27♑	11♒
08	6♐	21♐	6♑	21♑	6♒	21♒	6♓	20♓	4♈	18♈	1♉	14♉	26♉	9♊	21♊
09	9♉	23♉	6♊	19♊	2♋	15♋	27♋	9♌	21♌	3♍	15♍	27♍	9♎	21♎	3♏
1910	18♍	0♎	12♎	23♎	5♏	17♏	29♏	12♐	24♐	7♑	21♑	4♒	18♒	2♓	16♓
11	19♑	2♒	14♒	27♒	10♓	23♓	6♈	20♈	4♉	18♉	3♊	18♊	2♋	17♋	2♌
12	27♉	11♊	27♊	12♋	27♋	12♌	27♌	12♍	26♍	9♎	22♎	5♏	17♏	29♏	11♐
13	1♏	14♏	27♏	10♐	23♐	5♑	17♑	29♑	11♒	23♒	5♓	17♓	29♓	11♈	23♈
14	7♓	19♓	1♈	13♈	25♈	7♉	19♉	1♊	14♊	24♊	5♋	17♋	29♋	12♋	23♋
15	10♋	22♋	5♌	18♌	1♍	15♍	28♍	12♎	26♎	10♏	25♏	9♐	24♐	9♑	23♑
16	18♏	3♐	18♐	3♑	18♑	3♒	18♒	2♓	16♓	29♓	12♈	25♈	7♉	19♉	2♊
17	23♈	6♉	19♉	1♊	14♊	26♊	9♋	20♋	1♌	13♌	25♌	7♍	19♍	1♎	13♎
18	27♌	9♍	21♍	3♎	14♎	27♎	9♏	21♏	4♐	18♐	1♑	16♑	0♒	15♒	29♒
19	0♑	13♑	26♑	9♒	23♒	7♓	21♓	5♈	19♈	3♉	17♉	1♊	15♊	29♊	13♋
1920	9♉	24♉	9♊	24♊	9♋	24♋	8♌	23♌	6♍	20♍	3♎	15♎	28♎	9♏	21♏
21	14♎	27♎	10♏	22♏	4♐	16♐	28♐	10♑	22♑	4♒	15♒	27♒	9♓	22♓	4♈
22	17♒	29♒	10♓	22♓	4♈	16♈	28♈	11♉	24♉	8♊	22♊	6♋	21♋	6♌	21♌
23	20♊	4♋	17♋	1♌	15♌	29♌	13♍	27♍	11♎	25♎	9♏	23♏	7♐	21♐	5♑
24	1♏	15♏	0♐	15♐	0♑	14♑	29♑	13♒	27♒	10♓	23♓	5♈	17♈	29♈	11♉
25	5♈	18♈	0♉	12♉	25♉	7♊	18♊	0♋	12♋	24♋	6♌	18♌	0♍	12♍	25♍
26	7♌	18♌	0♍	12♍	24♍	6♎	19♎	1♏	15♏	28♏	12♐	27♐	12♑	27♑	12♒
27	10♐	24♐	8♑	22♑	6♒	20♒	5♓	19♓	4♈	18♈	2♉	16♉	29♉	13♊	26♊
28	23♈	8♉	22♉	6♊	21♊	5♋	19♋	3♌	16♌	0♍	12♍	25♍	7♎	19♎	1♏
29	26♍	8♎	21♎	3♏	15♏	27♏	8♐	20♐	2♑	14♑	26♑	8♒	21♒	4♓	16♓

MOON POSITIONS

JANUARY

	16	17	18	19	20	21	22	23	24	25	26	27	28	29	30
1900	4♌	16♌	28♌	10♍	22♍	3♎	15♎	28♎	10♏	23♏	6♐	19♐	3♑	18♑	2♒
01	6♐	18♐	1♑	15♑	28♑	12♒	27♒	11♓	25♓	10♈	24♈	8♉	22♉	6♊	19♊
02	16♈	29♈	13♉	28♉	12♊	27♊	11♋	26♋	10♌	24♌	8♍	21♍	4♎	16♎	28♎
03	6♍	20♍	3♎	17♎	29♎	12♏	24♏	6♐	18♐	0♑	11♑	23♑	5♒	17♒	0♓
04	12♑	24♑	6♒	18♒	0♓	12♓	23♓	5♈	18♈	0♉	13♉	26♉	9♊	24♊	8♋
05	26♉	8♊	22♊	5♋	19♋	3♌	18♌	3♍	18♍	2♎	16♎	0♏	14♏	28♏	11♐
06	8♎	22♎	6♏	20♏	4♐	19♐	3♑	17♑	1♒	14♒	28♒	11♓	23♓	6♈	18♈
07	26♒	10♓	24♓	7♈	19♈	2♉	14♉	26♉	8♊	20♊	2♋	13♋	25♋	8♌	20♌
08	3♋	14♋	26♋	8♌	20♌	2♍	14♍	26♍	8♎	21♎	4♏	17♏	0♐	15♐	29♐
09	16♏	28♏	12♐	25♐	9♑	24♑	9♒	24♒	9♓	23♓	8♈	22♈	6♉	20♉	3♊
1910	0♈	14♈	28♈	13♉	27♉	10♊	24♊	8♋	21♋	5♌	18♌	1♍	13♍	25♍	7♎
11	16♌	0♍	14♍	27♍	10♎	22♎	4♏	16♏	28♏	9♐	21♐	3♑	15♑	28♑	11♒
12	23♐	5♑	17♑	28♑	10♒	22♒	5♓	17♓	29♓	12♈	25♈	8♉	21♉	6♊	20♊
13	5♉	18♉	2♊	16♊	0♋	15♋	0♌	15♌	0♍	15♍	0♎	14♎	28♎	11♏	24♏
14	22♍	7♎	21♎	5♏	19♏	2♐	16♐	29♐	13♑	26♑	8♒	21♒	3♓	15♓	27♓
15	7♑	20♑	4♒	17♒	29♒	11♓	23♓	5♈	17♈	29♈	11♉	23♉	6♊	18♊	1♋
16	13♊	25♊	7♋	19♋	1♌	13♌	25♌	8♍	20♍	3♎	16♎	0♏	13♏	27♏	12♐
17	26♎	9♏	22♏	6♐	21♐	5♑	20♑	6♒	21♒	6♓	21♓	5♈	19♈	2♉	16♉
18	14♓	29♓	13♈	27♈	11♉	25♉	8♊	21♊	4♋	16♋	29♋	11♌	23♌	5♍	17♍
19	27♋	10♌	24♌	6♍	19♍	1♎	13♎	25♎	7♏	19♏	1♐	13♐	25♐	8♑	21♑
1920	3♐	15♐	27♐	9♑	21♑	3♒	16♒	29♒	12♓	25♓	8♈	22♈	5♉	19♉	4♊
21	17♈	0♉	13♉	27♉	11♊	26♊	11♋	26♋	12♌	27♌	12♍	26♍	10♎	23♎	6♏
22	6♏	21♏	5♐	19♐	3♑	16♑	29♑	12♒	25♒	7♓	19♓	1♈	13♈	25♈	7♉
23	18♑	1♒	14♒	26♒	9♓	21♓	3♈	14♈	26♈	8♉	20♉	3♊	15♊	28♊	12♋
24	23♉	5♊	17♊	29♊	11♋	24♋	7♌	20♌	3♍	16♍	0♎	14♎	28♎	12♏	26♏
25	8♎	21♎	4♏	18♏	3♐	17♐	2♑	17♑	2♒	17♒	2♓	16♓	0♈	13♈	26♈
26	27♒	12♓	26♓	11♈	24♈	8♉	21♉	4♊	16♊	28♊	10♋	22♋	4♌	15♌	27♌
27	9♋	21♋	4♌	16♌	28♌	10♍	22♍	4♎	16♎	28♎	10♏	22♏	5♐	18♐	2♑
28	13♏	24♏	6♐	19♐	1♑	14♑	27♑	10♒	24♒	8♓	22♓	6♈	20♈	4♉	18♉
29	29♓	13♈	26♈	10♉	24♉	9♊	23♊	8♋	23♋	8♌	22♌	7♍	20♍	4♎	17♎

MOON POSITIONS

JANUARY/FEBRUARY

	31	1	2	3	4	5	6	7	8	9	10	11	12	13	14
1900	17♒	3♓	18♓	3♈	17♈	1♉	15♉	28♉	11♊	24♊	6♋	18♋	1♌	13♌	25♌
01	3♋	16♋	29♋	12♌	25♌	8♍	20♍	2♎	14♎	26♎	7♏	19♏	1♐	14♐	26♐
02	10♏	22♏	4♐	16♐	28♐	10♑	22♑	5♒	18♒	1♓	15♓	29♓	12♈	26♈	10♉
03	12♓	24♓	7♈	20♈	3♉	16♉	0♊	15♊	29♊	14♋	29♋	14♌	29♌	14♍	28♍
04	23♋	9♌	24♌	9♍	24♍	8♎	22♎	6♏	19♏	2♐	15♐	27♐	9♑	21♑	3♒
05	25♐	8♑	20♑	3♒	15♒	28♒	10♓	22♓	3♈	15♈	27♈	9♉	21♉	3♊	16♊
06	0♉	12♉	23♉	5♊	17♊	0♋	12♋	25♋	9♌	22♌	6♍	20♍	4♎	18♎	3♏
07	3♍	15♍	28♍	11♎	25♎	9♏	23♏	7♐	21♐	6♑	20♑	5♒	19♒	4♓	18♓
08	14♑	29♑	14♒	29♒	14♓	29♓	13♈	27♈	10♉	23♉	5♊	18♊	0♋	11♋	23♋
09	16♊	29♊	11♋	23♋	6♌	18♌	0♍	12♍	24♍	5♎	17♎	29♎	11♏	24♏	6♐
1910	19♎	1♏	13♏	25♏	7♐	19♐	2♑	15♑	29♑	13♒	27♒	11♓	26♓	11♈	25♈
11	24♒	7♓	20♓	3♈	17♈	1♉	15♉	29♉	13♊	27♊	12♋	26♋	10♌	24♌	8♍
12	5♋	20♋	5♌	20♌	5♍	20♍	4♎	18♎	1♏	13♏	26♏	8♐	20♐	2♑	13♑
13	7♐	20♐	2♑	14♑	26♑	8♒	20♒	2♓	14♓	26♓	7♈	19♈	2♉	14♉	27♉
14	9♈	21♈	3♉	15♉	27♉	9♊	22♊	5♋	19♋	3♌	18♌	2♍	17♍	2♎	17♎
15	14♌	28♌	11♍	25♍	9♎	23♎	7♏	21♏	6♐	20♐	4♑	18♑	2♒	15♒	29♒
16	27♐	11♑	26♑	11♒	26♒	10♓	24♓	7♈	21♈	3♉	16♉	28♉	10♊	22♊	3♋
17	28♉	11♊	23♊	5♋	17♋	29♋	10♌	22♌	4♍	16♍	28♍	10♎	23♎	5♏	18♏
18	29♍	11♎	23♎	5♏	17♏	29♏	12♐	25♐	9♑	23♑	8♒	23♒	8♓	23♓	8♈
19	5♒	19♒	3♓	17♓	1♈	16♈	0♉	14♉	28♉	12♊	26♊	9♋	23♋	6♌	19♌
1920	18♊	3♋	17♋	2♌	16♌	0♍	14♍	28♍	11♎	23♎	5♏	17♏	29♏	11♐	23♐
21	19♏	1♐	13♐	25♐	7♑	19♑	1♒	12♒	24♒	7♓	19♓	1♈	14♈	26♈	9♉
22	19♓	1♈	13♈	25♈	7♉	19♉	2♊	16♊	0♋	14♋	29♋	14♌	29♌	15♍	0♎
23	25♋	9♌	24♌	8♍	23♍	7♎	22♎	6♏	20♏	4♐	18♐	1♑	14♑	27♑	10♒
24	10♐	25♐	9♑	23♑	7♒	21♒	4♓	17♓	0♈	13♈	25♈	7♉	19♉	1♊	13♊
25	9♉	21♉	3♊	15♊	27♊	9♋	21♋	3♌	15♌	27♌	9♍	22♍	5♎	18♎	1♏
26	9♍	21♍	3♎	15♎	28♎	10♏	23♏	7♐	21♐	5♑	20♑	5♒	20♒	5♓	20♓
27	15♑	0♒	14♒	29♒	14♓	29♓	14♈	28♈	12♉	26♉	10♊	23♊	5♋	18♋	0♌
28	2♏	16♏	0♐	14♐	28♐	11♑	24♑	7♒	20♒	3♓	15♓	27♓	9♈	20♈	2♉
29	29♎	11♏	23♏	5♐	17♐	29♐	10♑	23♑	5♒	17♒	0♓	13♓	26♓	10♈	23♈

MOON POSITIONS

FEBRUARY

	15	16	17	18	19	20	21	22	23	24	25	26	27	28	29
1900	6♍	18♍	0♎	12♎	24♎	6♏	19♏	1♐	14♐	27♐	11♑	26♑	10♒	26♒	
01	9♑	23♑	7♒	21♒	5♓	20♓	5♈	20♈	4♉	19♉	3♊	16♊	0♋	13♋	
02	24♉	8♊	23♊	7♋	21♋	5♌	19♌	2♍	16♍	29♍	11♎	24♎	6♏	18♏	
03	11♎	25♎	8♏	20♏	2♐	14♐	26♐	8♑	20♑	2♒	14♒	26♒	9♓	21♓	
04	15♒	27♒	9♓	20♓	2♈	14♈	27♈	9♉	22♉	5♊	18♊	2♋	17♋	2♌	17♌
05	29♊	13♋	27♋	11♌	26♌	11♍	26♍	11♎	26♎	10♏	25♏	8♐	22♐	5♑	
06	17♏	1♐	15♐	29♐	13♑	26♑	10♒	23♒	6♓	19♓	1♈	13♈	26♈	7♉	
07	1♈	15♈	27♈	10♉	22♉	4♊	16♊	28♊	10♋	22♋	4♌	16♌	29♌	12♍	
08	5♌	17♌	29♌	11♍	23♍	5♎	18♎	0♏	13♏	27♏	10♐	24♐	8♑	23♑	7♒
09	20♐	3♑	17♑	2♒	17♒	2♓	17♓	2♈	17♈	2♉	16♉	0♊	13♊	26♊	
1910	9♊	23♊	7♋	21♋	4♌	18♌	1♍	14♍	27♍	9♎	21♎	4♏	16♏	27♏	
11	22♍	5♎	17♎	0♏	12♏	24♏	5♐	17♐	29♐	11♑	24♑	6♒	19♒	2♓	
12	25♑	7♒	19♒	1♓	14♓	26♓	9♈	22♈	5♉	18♉	2♊	15♊	0♋	14♋	29♋
13	10♊	24♊	8♋	23♋	8♌	23♌	8♍	23♍	8♎	23♎	7♏	21♏	4♐	17♐	
14	1♏	15♏	29♏	13♐	26♐	9♑	22♑	5♒	17♒	29♒	12♓	23♓	5♈	17♈	
15	12♓	24♓	7♈	19♈	1♉	13♉	25♉	7♊	19♊	1♋	13♋	26♋	9♌	23♌	
16	15♋	27♋	9♌	22♌	4♍	17♍	0♎	13♎	27♎	10♏	24♏	8♐	22♐	6♑	21♑
17	1♐	15♐	29♐	14♑	28♑	13♒	27♒	11♓	25♓	9♈	23♈	7♉	20♉	3♊	
18	23♐	6♑	20♑	3♒	16♒	29♒	12♓	25♓	8♈	21♈	4♉	17♉	0♊	13♊	
19	2♍	14♍	27♍	9♎	21♎	3♏	15♏	27♏	9♐	21♐	3♑	16♑	29♑	13♒	
1920	5♑	17♑	29♑	12♒	25♒	8♓	21♓	5♈	18♈	2♉	16♉	0♊	14♊	28♊	13♋
21	23♉	6♊	20♊	5♋	20♋	5♌	20♌	5♍	20♍	4♎	18♎	1♏	14♏	27♏	
22	14♎	29♎	12♏	26♏	9♐	22♐	4♑	16♑	28♑	10♒	22♒	4♓	16♓	28♓	
23	22♒	5♓	17♓	29♓	11♈	23♈	4♉	16♉	28♉	10♊	23♊	6♋	19♋	3♌	
24	25♊	9♋	23♋	8♌	23♌	7♍	22♍	6♎	20♎	3♏	16♏	28♏	11♐	23♐	5♑
25	15♊	29♊	13♋	27♋	11♌	25♌	8♍	21♍	4♎	17♎	29♎	12♏	24♏	6♐	
26	5♈	19♈	3♉	17♉	1♊	15♊	29♊	12♋	24♋	6♌	18♌	0♍	12♍	24♍	
27	13♌	25♌	7♍	19♍	1♎	13♎	25♎	7♏	19♏	1♐	13♐	26♐	8♑	21♑	
28	14♐	28♐	12♑	25♑	9♒	23♒	7♓	21♓	4♈	18♈	2♉	16♉	0♊	13♊	27♊
29	7♉	21♉	5♊	19♊	3♋	18♋	2♌	16♌	1♍	15♍	28♍	11♎	24♎	7♏	

MOON POSITIONS

MARCH

	1	2	3	4	5	6	7	8	9	10	11	12	13	14	15
1900	11♓	26♓	11♈	26♈	10♉	24♉	8♊	21♊	3♋	16♋	28♋	10♌	22♌	3♍	15♍
01	26♋	9♌	21♌	4♍	16♍	28♍	10♎	22♎	4♏	16♏	28♏	9♐	22♐	4♑	17♑
02	0♐	12♐	23♐	6♑	18♑	0♒	13♒	26♒	10♓	24♓	8♈	22♈	7♉	21♉	5♊
03	4♈	17♈	0♉	13♉	27♉	11♊	25♊	9♋	24♋	8♌	23♌	7♍	22♍	6♎	19♎
04	2♍	17♍	2♎	17♎	1♏	15♏	28♏	11♐	24♐	6♑	18♑	0♒	12♒	24♒	6♓
05	17♑	0♒	12♒	24♒	6♓	18♓	0♈	12♈	24♈	6♉	18♉	0♊	12♊	25♊	8♋
06	19♉	1♊	13♊	25♊	8♋	20♋	3♌	16♌	0♍	14♍	29♍	14♎	28♎	13♏	28♏
07	25♍	8♎	22♎	6♏	19♏	3♐	18♐	2♑	16♑	0♒	14♒	28♒	12♓	26♓	9♈
08	22♒	7♓	22♓	7♈	21♈	5♉	19♉	2♊	14♊	26♊	8♋	20♋	2♌	14♌	25♌
09	8♋	21♋	3♌	15♌	27♌	9♍	20♍	2♎	14♎	26♎	8♏	20♏	3♐	15♐	28♐
1910	9♏	21♏	3♐	15♐	27♐	10♑	23♑	7♒	21♒	5♓	20♓	5♈	20♈	5♉	19♉
11	16♓	0♈	13♈	27♈	12♉	26♉	10♊	24♊	8♋	22♋	6♌	20♌	3♍	17♍	0♎
12	14♌	29♌	13♍	28♍	12♎	25♎	9♏	21♏	4♐	16♐	28♐	10♑	22♑	4♒	16♒
13	29♐	11♑	23♑	5♒	17♒	29♒	11♓	23♓	4♈	17♈	29♈	11♉	24♉	6♊	20♊
14	29♈	11♉	23♉	5♊	17♊	0♋	13♋	27♋	11♌	26♌	11♍	26♍	11♎	26♎	11♏
15	6♍	20♍	5♎	19♎	4♏	18♏	2♐	17♐	1♑	14♑	28♑	11♒	24♒	7♓	20♓
16	5♒	20♒	4♓	18♓	2♈	15♈	28♈	11♉	23♉	6♊	18♊	29♊	11♋	23♋	5♌
17	19♊	1♋	13♋	25♋	7♌	19♌	1♍	13♍	25♍	7♎	20♎	2♏	15♏	28♏	11♐
18	19♎	1♏	13♏	25♏	8♐	21♐	4♑	17♑	0♒	14♒	27♒	11♓	24♓	8♈	21♈
19	27♒	11♓	26♓	11♈	26♈	10♉	25♉	9♊	23♊	6♋	19♋	3♌	15♌	28♌	11♍
1920	27♋	11♌	25♌	9♍	22♍	6♎	18♎	1♏	13♏	25♏	7♐	19♐	1♑	13♑	25♑
21	9♐	22♐	3♑	15♑	27♑	9♒	21♒	3♓	15♓	28♓	11♈	23♈	6♉	20♉	3♊
22	10♈	22♈	4♉	16♉	28♉	11♊	25♊	8♋	23♋	7♌	22♌	7♍	23♍	8♎	23♎
23	17♍	2♎	17♎	2♏	17♏	1♐	16♐	0♑	14♑	28♑	11♒	24♒	7♓	19♓	1♈
24	19♒	3♓	16♓	0♈	13♈	26♈	8♉	21♉	3♊	15♊	27♊	9♋	20♋	2♌	15♌
25	29♊	11♋	23♋	5♌	17♌	29♌	11♍	23♍	6♎	18♎	1♏	14♏	28♏	12♐	25♐
26	0♎	12♎	25♎	7♏	20♏	3♐	16♐	0♑	14♑	28♑	11♒	26♒	10♓	24♓	8♈
27	8♓	20♓	2♈	13♈	25♈	7♉	18♉	0♊	12♊	23♊	5♋	17♋	28♋	10♌	22♌
28	11♌	23♌	5♍	17♍	29♍	12♎	24♎	7♏	19♏	1♐	14♐	26♐	9♑	21♑	4♒
29	19♏	2♐	14♐	27♐	10♑	22♑	5♒	18♒	0♓	13♓	26♓	8♈	21♈	4♉	17♉

MOON POSITIONS

MARCH	16	17	18	19	20	21	22	23	24	25	26	27	28	29	30
1900	27♍	9♎	21♎	3♏	15♏	28♏	11♐	23♐	7♑	20♑	4♒	19♒	4♓	19♓	4♈
01	1♒	14♒	29♒	14♓	29♓	14♈	29♈	14♉	28♉	13♊	26♊	10♋	23♋	6♌	18♌
02	19♊	3♋	17♋	1♌	15♌	28♌	11♍	24♍	7♎	20♎	2♏	14♏	26♏	8♐	20♐
03	2♏	15♏	28♏	10♐	22♐	4♑	16♑	28♑	10♒	22♒	4♓	17♓	0♈	13♈	26♈
04	17♓	29♓	11♈	24♈	6♉	19♉	2♊	15♊	28♊	12♋	26♋	11♌	25♌	10♍	25♍
05	21♋	5♌	19♌	4♍	18♍	2♎	16♎	29♎	13♏	25♏	8♐	20♐	2♑	14♑	25♑
06	12♐	26♐	10♑	23♑	7♒	20♒	2♓	15♓	27♓	10♈	22♈	4♉	16♉	28♉	9♊
07	22♈	5♉	18♉	0♊	12♊	24♊	6♋	17♋	29♋	12♌	24♌	7♍	20♍	4♎	17♎
08	7♍	20♍	2♎	15♎	27♎	10♏	24♏	7♐	20♐	4♑	18♑	2♒	17♒	1♓	16♓
09	12♑	26♑	10♒	25♒	10♓	25♓	11♈	26♈	11♉	25♉	9♊	22♊	5♋	17♋	0♌
1910	4♊	18♊	1♋	15♋	28♋	11♌	23♌	6♍	18♍	0♎	12♎	24♎	6♏	18♏	29♏
11	13♎	25♎	7♏	20♏	2♐	13♐	25♐	7♑	19♑	1♒	14♒	27♒	11♓	24♓	8♈
12	28♒	10♓	23♓	5♈	18♈	2♉	15♉	29♉	12♊	26♊	10♋	25♋	9♌	23♌	8♍
13	3♍	17♍	2♎	16♎	1♏	16♏	1♐	15♐	29♐	12♑	25♑	7♒	20♒	2♓	10♓
14	25♏	9♐	23♐	6♑	19♑	2♒	14♒	26♒	8♓	20♓	2♈	14♈	26♈	8♉	20♉
15	3♈	15♈	27♈	9♉	21♉	3♊	15♊	27♊	9♋	21♋	4♌	16♌	0♍	14♍	29♍
16	17♏	0♐	13♐	26♐	9♑	22♑	5♒	18♒	1♓	14♓	27♓	10♈	23♈	6♉	20♉
17	25♐	9♑	23♑	7♒	21♒	5♓	18♓	2♈	15♈	28♈	11♉	24♉	7♊	20♊	5♋
18	17♉	29♉	11♊	23♊	5♋	17♋	29♋	11♌	23♌	5♍	18♍	1♎	14♎	27♎	10♏
19	23♍	5♎	17♎	29♎	11♏	23♏	5♐	17♐	29♐	12♑	25♑	8♒	21♒	5♓	19♓
1920	7♒	20♒	3♓	16♓	0♈	14♈	28♈	12♉	26♉	10♊	25♊	9♋	23♋	7♌	21♌
21	17♊	1♋	15♋	29♋	14♌	29♌	13♍	28♍	12♎	26♎	9♏	22♏	5♐	17♐	0♑
22	7♏	21♏	5♐	18♐	1♑	13♑	25♑	7♒	19♒	1♓	13♓	25♓	11♈	23♈	5♉
23	14♓	25♓	7♈	19♈	1♉	13♉	25♉	7♊	19♊	2♋	15♋	28♋	11♌	25♌	10♍
24	27♋	10♌	23♌	6♍	19♍	2♎	15♎	28♎	11♏	25♏	8♐	22♐	6♑	20♑	13♒
25	9♐	23♐	7♑	21♑	5♒	19♒	3♓	17♓	1♈	15♈	29♈	13♉	26♉	9♊	19♊
26	28♈	10♉	22♉	4♊	16♊	28♊	10♋	23♋	5♌	18♌	1♍	14♍	27♍	9♎	21♎
27	4♍	16♍	28♍	10♎	22♎	5♏	18♏	1♐	14♐	27♐	10♑	22♑	5♒	18♒	1♓
28	17♑	0♒	14♒	28♒	12♓	26♓	10♈	25♈	9♉	23♉	7♊	21♊	5♋	19♋	4♌
29	2♊	15♊	29♊	12♋	25♋	9♌	22♌	5♍	19♍	2♎	16♎	29♎	12♏	26♏	9♐

MOON POSITIONS

MARCH/APRIL	31	1	2	3	4	5	6	7	8	9	10	11	12	13	14
1900	19♈	4♉	19♉	3♊	16♊	29♊	12♋	24♋	6♌	18♌	0♍	12♍	24♍	6♎	18♎
01	1♍	13♍	25♍	7♎	19♎	1♏	12♏	24♏	6♐	18♐	1♑	13♑	26♑	9♒	23♒
02	1♑	13♑	26♑	8♒	21♒	4♓	18♓	2♈	17♈	1♉	16♉	1♊	16♊	0♋	14♋
03	10♉	24♉	8♊	22♊	6♋	20♋	4♌	19♌	3♍	17♍	0♎	14♎	27♎	10♏	23♏
04	10♎	25♎	9♏	23♏	6♐	19♐	2♑	14♑	27♑	9♒	20♒	2♓	14♓	26♓	8♈
05	21♒	3♓	15♓	27♓	9♈	21♈	3♉	15♉	27♉	9♊	21♊	4♋	17♋	0♌	14♌
06	21♊	3♋	16♋	28♋	11♌	24♌	8♍	22♍	7♎	22♎	7♏	22♏	7♐	22♐	6♑
07	1♏	16♏	0♐	14♐	29♐	13♑	27♑	11♒	24♒	8♓	22♓	5♈	18♈	1♉	13♉
08	1♈	15♈	29♈	13♉	26♉	9♊	22♊	4♋	16♋	28♋	10♌	22♌	4♍	16♍	28♍
09	12♌	24♌	6♍	17♍	29♍	11♎	23♎	5♏	18♏	0♐	12♐	25♐	8♑	22♑	5♒
1910	11♐	23♐	6♑	18♑	1♒	15♒	29♒	13♓	28♓	13♈	28♈	14♉	29♉	13♊	27♊
11	23♈	7♉	22♉	6♊	21♊	5♋	19♋	3♌	16♌	0♍	13♍	26♍	9♎	21♎	4♏
12	22♍	6♎	20♎	3♏	16♏	29♏	12♐	24♐	6♑	18♑	0♒	12♒	24♒	6♓	18♓
13	2♒	14♒	26♒	8♓	19♓	1♈	13♈	26♈	8♉	21♉	4♊	17♊	29♊	14♋	27♋
14	2♊	14♊	26♊	9♋	21♋	6♌	20♌	4♍	19♍	4♎	19♎	4♏	19♏	4♐	18♐
15	13♎	28♎	13♏	28♏	13♐	27♐	11♑	25♑	8♒	21♒	4♓	17♓	29♓	12♈	24♈
16	13♓	27♓	10♈	23♈	6♉	19♉	1♊	13♊	25♊	7♋	19♋	1♌	13♌	25♌	8♍
17	24♋	7♌	19♌	2♍	14♍	27♍	9♎	21♎	3♏	15♏	27♏	9♐	21♐	4♑	18♑
18	24♏	8♐	22♐	6♑	20♑	4♒	18♒	2♓	16♓	0♈	14♈	28♈	12♉	25♉	9♊
19	4♈	18♈	3♉	17♉	1♊	15♊	28♊	11♋	23♋	6♌	18♌	0♍	12♍	24♍	6♎
1920	4♍	16♍	28♍	10♎	22♎	4♏	16♏	28♏	11♐	24♐	7♑	20♑	4♒	18♒	2♓
21	15♑	28♑	11♒	24♒	8♓	22♓	6♈	20♈	5♉	19♉	4♊	18♊	2♋	16♋	29♋
22	14♉	28♉	12♊	26♊	10♋	23♋	6♌	19♌	1♍	13♍	25♍	7♎	19♎	1♏	13♏
23	26♍	8♎	20♎	2♏	14♏	26♏	8♐	20♐	2♑	15♑	27♑	10♒	23♒	6♓	20♓
24	25♒	9♓	23♓	7♈	21♈	5♉	20♉	4♊	18♊	2♋	16♋	29♋	12♌	24♌	6♍
25	5♋	18♋	1♌	13♌	25♌	7♍	19♍	1♎	13♎	25♎	7♏	19♏	1♐	13♐	26♐
26	5♏	17♏	29♏	11♐	23♐	5♑	18♑	0♒	13♒	26♒	10♓	24♓	8♈	23♈	8♉
27	16♓	0♈	14♈	28♈	12♉	26♉	10♊	24♊	7♋	20♋	2♌	14♌	26♌	8♍	20♍
28	16♌	0♍	13♍	25♍	7♎	19♎	1♏	13♏	25♏	7♐	19♐	1♑	13♑	25♑	8♒
29	21♐	2♑	14♑	26♑	9♒	21♒	4♓	17♓	1♈	14♈	29♈	13♉	27♉	12♊	26♊

MOON POSITIONS

APRIL

	15	16	17	18	19	20	21	22	23	24	25	26	27	28	29
1900	0♏	12♏	25♏	8♐	20♐	4♑	17♑	1♒	14♒	29♒	13♓	28♓	13♈	28♈	12♉
01	7♓	22♓	7♈	22♈	7♉	22♉	7♊	22♊	6♋	19♋	2♌	15♌	28♌	10♍	22♍
02	28♋	12♌	25♌	8♍	21♍	4♎	16♎	28♎	10♏	22♏	4♐	16♐	28♐	10♑	22♑
03	6♐	18♐	0♑	12♑	24♑	6♒	18♒	0♓	12♓	25♓	8♈	22♈	5♉	19♉	4♊
04	20♈	3♉	16♉	29♉	12♊	25♊	9♋	23♋	7♌	21♌	5♍	20♍	4♎	19♎	3♏
05	28♉	13♊	27♊	13♋	28♋	13♌	28♌	12♍	27♍	10♎	23♎	6♏	18♏	0♐	12♐
06	20♉	4♊	17♊	29♊	12♋	24♋	6♌	19♌	1♍	12♍	24♍	6♎	18♎	0♏	12♏
07	20♉	8♊	20♊	2♋	13♋	25♋	7♌	19♌	1♍	15♍	28♍	12♎	26♎	10♏	25♏
08	11♎	24♎	7♏	20♏	2♐	17♐	1♑	15♑	29♑	13♒	27♒	12♓	26♓	10♈	25♈
09	19♒	4♓	19♓	4♈	19♈	4♉	19♉	3♊	17♊	0♋	13♋	26♋	8♌	20♌	2♍
1910	11♋	25♋	8♌	20♌	3♍	15♍	27♍	9♎	21♎	3♏	15♏	26♏	8♐	20♐	2♑
11	16♏	28♏	10♐	21♐	3♑	15♑	27♑	9♒	22♒	5♓	18♓	2♈	17♈	1♉	16♉
12	1♈	14♈	27♈	11♉	25♉	9♊	23♊	7♋	21♋	3♌	15♌	27♌	9♍	21♍	2♎
13	12♍	26♍	10♎	25♎	10♏	24♏	8♐	23♐	7♑	20♑	3♒	16♒	28♒	11♓	23♓
14	2♑	16♑	29♑	13♒	27♒	11♓	25♓	9♈	23♈	7♉	20♉	3♊	16♊	29♊	11♋
15	6♉	20♉	3♊	17♊	0♋	13♋	26♋	9♌	21♌	3♍	15♍	27♍	9♎	21♎	3♏
16	21♍	4♎	18♎	1♏	14♏	26♏	8♐	20♐	2♑	14♑	26♑	8♒	20♒	3♓	16♓
17	4♒	18♒	2♓	17♓	1♈	15♈	0♉	14♉	27♉	10♊	23♊	6♋	18♋	0♌	12♌
18	23♊	6♋	19♋	1♌	14♌	26♌	8♍	19♍	1♎	13♎	25♎	7♏	19♏	1♐	14♐
19	26♎	8♏	20♏	2♐	13♐	25♐	8♑	20♑	3♒	16♒	29♒	13♓	28♓	13♈	28♈
1920	11♓	25♓	8♈	23♈	7♉	22♉	7♊	21♊	6♋	20♋	4♌	18♌	1♍	15♍	28♍
21	26♋	10♌	24♌	9♍	23♍	7♎	20♎	4♏	17♏	0♐	13♐	25♐	7♑	19♑	1♒
22	13♐	26♐	9♑	22♑	4♒	16♒	28♒	9♓	21♓	3♈	15♈	27♈	10♉	22♉	5♊
23	16♈	28♈	10♉	22♉	4♊	16♊	28♊	11♋	24♋	7♌	20♌	4♍	18♍	3♎	18♎
24	1♍	14♍	29♍	13♎	28♎	13♏	28♏	13♐	28♐	12♑	26♑	10♒	23♒	6♓	19♓
25	19♑	3♒	17♒	1♓	14♓	28♓	11♈	25♈	8♉	20♉	3♊	15♊	27♊	9♋	21♋
26	3♊	16♊	29♊	11♋	23♋	5♌	18♌	29♌	11♍	23♍	5♎	18♎	0♏	13♏	27♏
27	6♎	18♎	0♏	12♏	25♏	7♐	19♐	2♑	15♑	28♑	11♒	25♒	10♓	25♓	10♈
28	21♒	5♓	19♓	4♈	19♈	4♉	19♉	4♊	18♊	3♋	17♋	1♌	14♌	27♌	10♍
29	11♋	25♋	9♌	23♌	6♍	19♍	1♎	15♎	28♎	11♏	23♏	5♐	17♐	29♐	11♑

MOON POSITIONS

APRIL/MAY

	30	1	2	3	4	5	6	7	8	9	10	11	12	13	14
1900	27♉	11♊	24♊	7♋	20♋	3♌	15♌	27♌	9♍	20♍	2♎	14♎	27♎	9♏	21♏
01	4♎	16♎	28♎	9♏	21♏	3♐	15♐	27♐	10♑	23♑	5♒	19♒	2♓	16♓	1♈
02	4♒	16♒	29♒	13♓	26♓	10♈	25♈	10♉	25♉	10♊	25♊	10♋	24♋	8♌	22♌
03	18♊	2♋	17♋	1♌	15♌	29♌	13♍	27♍	10♎	23♎	6♏	19♏	2♐	14♐	26♐
04	17♏	1♐	14♐	27♐	10♑	22♑	5♒	17♒	28♒	10♓	22♓	4♈	16♈	29♈	12♉
05	24♓	6♈	18♈	0♉	12♉	24♉	6♊	18♊	1♋	14♋	27♋	10♌	24♌	8♍	22♍
06	24♋	7♌	20♌	3♍	16♍	1♎	15♎	0♏	16♏	1♐	16♐	1♑	16♑	0♒	13♒
07	10♐	25♐	9♑	23♑	8♒	21♒	5♓	18♓	1♈	14♈	27♈	10♉	22♉	4♊	16♊
08	8♉	21♉	4♊	17♊	0♋	12♋	24♋	6♌	18♌	0♍	12♍	24♍	6♎	19♎	2♏
09	14♍	26♍	8♎	20♎	2♏	14♏	27♏	9♐	22♐	5♑	19♑	2♒	16♒	0♓	14♓
1910	15♑	27♑	10♒	24♒	8♓	22♓	7♈	21♈	7♉	22♉	7♊	22♊	6♋	20♋	4♌
11	1♊	16♊	1♋	15♋	29♋	13♌	27♌	10♍	23♍	6♎	18♎	0♏	12♏	24♏	6♐
12	28♎	12♏	24♏	7♐	19♐	2♑	14♑	26♑	8♒	19♒	1♓	14♓	26♓	9♈	22♈
13	25♒	7♓	19♓	1♈	13♈	25♈	7♉	20♉	2♊	15♊	28♊	11♋	24♋	8♌	21♌
14	3♈	15♈	27♈	10♉	22♉	5♊	18♊	1♋	14♋	27♋	10♌	23♌	6♍	19♍	2♎
15	23♎	5♏	18♏	0♐	13♐	25♐	8♑	20♑	2♒	14♒	26♒	9♓	22♓	5♈	19♈
16	19♈	1♉	13♉	25♉	7♊	19♊	2♋	15♋	27♋	10♌	23♌	6♍	19♍	2♎	15♎
17	23♌	5♍	17♍	0♎	12♎	25♎	8♏	21♏	4♐	18♐	2♑	16♑	0♒	15♒	29♒
18	27♐	10♑	23♑	7♒	21♒	5♓	19♓	4♈	19♈	4♉	18♉	3♊	17♊	1♋	14♋
19	13♉	28♉	13♊	28♊	12♋	26♋	9♌	22♌	5♍	17♍	29♍	11♎	23♎	5♏	17♏
1920	10♎	23♎	5♏	17♏	0♐	11♐	23♐	5♑	17♑	29♑	11♒	23♒	6♓	19♓	3♈
21	13♒	25♒	7♓	19♓	2♈	15♈	28♈	12♉	25♉	10♊	24♊	8♋	23♋	7♌	21♌
22	18♊	1♋	15♋	29♋	13♌	27♌	11♍	26♍	10♎	25♎	9♏	23♏	7♐	21♐	4♑
23	3♏	16♐	1♑	18♐	3♑	17♑	0♒	13♒	25♒	8♓	20♓	3♈	15♈	27♈	9♉
24	1♈	14♈	26♈	8♉	20♉	2♊	13♊	25♊	7♋	19♋	1♌	14♌	26♌	9♍	23♍
25	3♌	15♌	27♌	9♍	22♍	5♎	18♎	2♏	16♏	1♐	16♐	0♑	15♑	29♑	14♒
26	10♐	23♐	7♑	21♑	5♒	19♒	3♓	18♓	2♈	16♈	0♉	14♉	28♉	11♊	24♊
27	25♈	10♉	25♉	9♊	23♊	7♋	21♋	4♌	17♌	0♍	12♍	24♍	6♎	18♎	0♎
28	22♍	4♎	16♎	28♎	10♏	22♏	4♐	16♐	27♐	9♑	22♑	4♒	17♒	0♓	14♓
29	22♑	4♒	17♒	29♒	12♓	25♓	9♈	23♈	7♉	22♉	7♊	22♊	6♋	21♋	5♌

MOON POSITIONS

MAY

	15	16	17	18	19	20	21	22	23	24	25	26	27	28	29
1900	4♐	17♐	0♑	14♑	27♑	11♒	25♒	9♓	24♓	8♈	23♈	7♉	21♉	5♊	19♊
01	15♈	0♉	16♉	1♊	15♊	0♋	14♋	28♋	11♌	24♌	7♍	19♍	1♎	13♎	25♎
02	5♍	18♍	1♎	13♎	25♎	7♏	19♏	1♐	13♐	25♐	7♑	19♑	1♒	13♒	25♒
03	8♑	20♑	2♒	14♒	26♒	8♓	20♓	3♈	16♈	0♉	14♉	28♉	13♊	27♊	12♋
04	25♉	8♊	22♊	6♋	20♋	4♌	18♌	2♍	16♍	0♎	14♎	28♎	12♏	26♏	9♐
05	7♎	21♎	6♏	21♏	6♐	21♐	5♑	18♑	2♒	14♒	27♒	9♓	21♓	3♈	14♈
06	26♒	9♓	21♓	4♈	16♈	28♈	10♉	21♉	3♊	15♊	27♊	9♋	21♋	4♌	16♌
07	28♊	10♋	22♋	4♌	15♌	28♌	10♍	23♍	6♎	20♎	4♏	19♏	4♐	19♐	4♑
08	15♏	29♏	13♐	27♐	11♑	26♑	10♒	24♒	8♓	22♓	6♈	20♈	4♉	19♉	4♊
09	29♓	13♈	28♈	13♉	27♉	11♊	25♊	8♋	21♋	4♌	16♌	28♌	10♍	22♍	4♎
1910	17♌	29♌	12♍	24♍	6♎	18♎	0♏	12♏	23♏	5♐	17♐	0♑	12♑	24♑	7♒
11	18♐	0♑	12♑	24♑	6♒	18♒	1♓	13♓	27♓	10♈	25♈	9♉	24♉	9♊	25♊
12	6♉	20♉	4♊	18♊	3♋	18♋	2♌	17♌	1♍	15♍	28♍	11♎	25♎	8♏	21♏
13	21♍	5♎	19♎	3♏	17♏	1♐	15♐	28♐	11♑	24♑	6♒	18♒	0♓	12♓	24♓
14	7♒	20♒	2♓	14♓	26♓	8♈	20♈	2♉	14♉	26♉	8♊	20♊	3♋	16♋	29♋
15	8♊	20♊	2♋	14♋	26♋	8♌	21♌	4♍	17♍	1♎	15♎	0♏	15♏	0♐	16♐
16	26♎	10♏	25♏	10♐	25♐	10♑	24♑	9♒	23♒	7♓	20♓	3♈	16♈	29♈	12♉
17	13♓	27♓	11♈	25♈	9♉	22♉	6♊	18♊	1♋	13♋	26♋	8♌	19♌	1♍	13♍
18	27♋	10♌	22♌	4♍	16♍	28♍	10♎	22♎	4♏	16♏	28♏	11♐	24♐	7♑	20♑
19	29♏	10♐	22♐	5♑	17♑	29♑	12♒	25♒	9♓	22♓	7♈	21♈	6♉	21♉	6♊
1920	17♈	1♉	16♉	0♊	16♊	1♋	16♋	0♌	14♌	28♌	12♍	25♍	8♎	20♎	2♏
21	5♍	19♍	3♎	16♎	0♏	13♏	26♏	9♐	21♐	3♑	15♑	27♑	9♒	21♒	3♓
22	17♑	0♒	12♒	24♒	6♓	18♓	29♓	11♈	23♈	6♉	18♉	1♊	15♊	28♊	12♋
23	19♉	1♊	13♊	25♊	8♋	21♋	3♌	17♌	0♍	14♍	28♍	12♎	27♎	12♏	27♏
24	7♎	21♎	6♏	21♏	7♐	22♐	7♑	22♑	6♒	20♒	3♓	16♓	28♓	11♈	23♈
25	27♈	11♉	25♉	8♊	21♊	4♋	17♋	29♋	11♌	23♌	5♍	17♍	29♍	11♎	23♎
26	7♋	19♋	1♌	13♌	25♌	7♍	19♍	1♎	13♎	26♎	9♏	22♏	6♐	19♐	3♑
27	9♏	21♏	4♐	16♐	29♐	12♑	25♑	8♒	22♒	6♓	20♓	4♈	19♈	4♉	18♉
28	28♓	12♈	27♈	12♉	28♉	13♊	28♊	12♋	26♋	9♌	23♌	6♍	19♍	1♎	13♎
29	19♌	3♍	16♍	0♎	12♎	25♎	7♏	19♏	1♐	13♐	25♐	7♑	19♑	1♒	13♒

MOON POSITIONS

Year	MAY 30	31	JUNE 1	2	3	4	5	6	7	8	9	10	11	12	13
1900	2♋	15♋	28♋	10♌	23♌	5♍	17♍	29♍	10♎	22♎	5♏	17♏	0♐	13♐	26♐
01	6♏	18♏	0♐	12♐	24♐	7♑	20♑	2♒	16♒	29♒	13♓	26♓	11♈	25♈	10♉
02	8♓	21♓	5♈	19♈	3♉	18♉	3♊	18♊	4♋	19♋	3♌	18♌	1♍	15♍	27♍
03	27♋	12♌	26♌	10♍	24♍	7♎	20♎	3♏	16♏	28♏	10♐	23♐	5♑	17♑	28♑
04	22♐	5♑	18♑	0♒	13♒	24♒	6♓	18♓	0♈	12♈	24♈	7♉	20♉	3♊	17♊
05	26♈	8♉	20♉	3♊	15♊	28♊	11♋	24♋	7♌	21♌	4♍	18♍	2♎	17♎	1♏
06	29♌	12♍	26♍	10♎	24♎	9♏	24♏	9♐	25♐	10♑	24♑	8♒	22♒	5♓	18♓
07	19♑	3♒	18♒	2♓	15♓	28♓	11♈	24♈	7♉	19♉	1♊	13♊	25♊	7♋	19♋
08	13♊	26♊	8♋	20♋	2♌	14♌	26♌	8♍	20♍	2♎	14♎	27♎	10♏	24♏	8♐
09	16♎	28♎	10♏	23♏	6♐	19♐	2♑	15♑	29♑	13♒	27♒	11♓	25♓	9♈	24♈
1910	20♒	4♓	17♓	1♈	16♈	0♉	15♉	0♊	15♊	0♋	14♋	28♋	12♌	25♌	8♍
11	10♋	25♋	9♌	23♌	7♍	20♍	3♎	15♎	27♎	9♏	21♏	3♐	15♐	27♐	9♑
12	3♐	16♐	28♐	10♑	22♑	4♒	16♒	28♒	10♓	22♓	4♈	17♈	0♉	14♉	28♉
13	6♈	18♈	0♉	13♉	26♉	9♊	23♊	7♋	21♋	5♌	19♌	3♍	17♍	1♎	16♎
14	12♌	25♌	7♍	20♍	2♎	14♎	26♎	8♏	20♏	2♐	14♐	26♐	9♑	22♑	5♒
15	1♑	16♑	0♒	14♒	28♒	11♓	24♓	6♈	18♈	0♉	12♉	24♉	6♊	18♊	0♋
16	24♉	6♊	18♊	0♋	12♋	24♋	6♌	17♌	29♌	11♍	24♍	7♎	20♎	4♏	17♏
17	25♎	8♏	20♏	3♐	16♐	28♐	11♑	24♑	7♒	20♒	2♓	15♓	28♓	11♈	24♈
18	4♒	17♒	0♓	13♓	26♓	10♈	24♈	8♉	22♉	6♊	20♊	2♋	15♋	27♋	9♌
19	21♊	3♋	15♋	27♋	9♌	21♌	2♍	14♍	26♍	8♎	20♎	2♏	15♏	28♏	11♐
1920	14♏	26♏	8♐	20♐	2♑	14♑	26♑	8♒	20♒	2♓	15♓	28♓	11♈	25♈	9♉
21	15♓	27♓	10♈	23♈	6♉	20♉	3♊	18♊	2♋	16♋	0♌	13♌	27♌	10♍	23♍
22	26♋	10♌	24♌	8♍	22♍	6♎	20♎	4♏	16♏	28♏	11♐	23♐	5♑	16♑	28♑
23	12♐	27♐	11♑	25♑	8♒	21♒	4♓	16♓	28♓	10♈	22♈	4♉	16♉	28♉	10♊
24	5♉	17♉	29♉	11♊	23♊	4♋	16♋	28♋	10♌	23♌	5♍	18♍	2♎	16♎	0♏
25	5♍	17♍	0♎	13♎	25♎	7♏	19♏	1♐	13♐	25♐	7♑	20♑	3♒	16♒	0♓
26	17♑	2♒	16♒	0♓	14♓	28♓	12♈	26♈	10♉	24♉	7♊	20♊	3♋	15♋	27♋
27	3♊	15♊	27♊	9♋	21♋	3♌	15♌	27♌	9♍	21♍	3♎	15♎	27♎	9♏	21♏
28	25♎	7♏	19♏	1♐	13♐	25♐	7♑	19♑	1♒	14♒	26♒	9♓	22♓	5♈	18♈
29	25♒	7♓	20♓	3♈	17♈	1♉	15♉	0♊	15♊	0♋	15♋	29♋	13♌	29♌	13♍

MOON POSITIONS

JUNE

	14	15	16	17	18	19	20	21	22	23	24	25	26	27	28
1900	10♑	24♑	8♒	22♒	6♓	21♓	5♈	19♈	3♉	17♉	1♊	14♊	28♊	11♋	23♋
01	24♉	9♊	24♊	8♋	22♋	6♌	19♌	2♍	15♍	27♍	9♎	21♎	3♏	15♏	27♏
02	10♎	22♎	4♏	16♏	28♏	10♐	22♐	4♑	16♑	28♑	10♒	22♒	5♓	18♓	1♈
03	10♒	22♒	4♓	16♓	29♓	11♈	24♈	8♉	22♉	6♊	21♊	6♋	21♋	7♌	21♌
04	1♋	15♋	0♌	14♌	29♌	13♍	27♍	11♎	25♎	8♏	22♏	5♐	18♐	1♑	14♑
05	16♏	0♐	15♐	29♐	13♑	26♑	9♒	22♒	5♓	17♓	29♓	11♈	22♈	4♉	16♉
06	0♈	13♈	25♈	6♉	18♉	0♊	12♊	24♊	6♋	18♋	1♌	13♌	26♌	9♍	22♍
07	0♌	12♌	24♌	6♍	19♍	1♎	15♎	28♎	13♏	27♏	12♐	27♐	12♑	27♑	12♒
08	22♐	6♑	21♑	6♒	20♒	5♓	19♓	3♈	17♈	0♉	14♉	27♉	9♊	22♊	4♋
09	8♉	22♉	6♊	20♊	3♋	16♋	29♋	12♌	24♌	6♍	18♍	0♎	12♎	24♎	6♏
1910	20♍	3♎	15♎	26♎	8♏	20♏	2♐	14♐	26♐	9♑	21♑	4♒	17♒	1♓	14♓
11	21♑	3♒	15♒	27♒	10♓	23♓	6♈	19♈	3♉	18♉	3♊	18♊	3♋	18♋	3♌
12	12♊	27♊	12♋	27♋	12♌	27♌	11♍	25♍	9♎	22♎	5♏	18♏	0♐	12♐	25♐
13	29♎	13♏	27♏	10♐	24♐	7♑	19♑	2♒	14♒	26♒	8♓	20♓	2♈	14♈	26♈
14	10♓	22♓	4♈	16♈	28♈	10♉	22♉	4♊	17♊	29♊	12♋	25♋	9♌	22♌	6♍
15	11♋	23♋	6♌	18♌	1♍	14♍	27♍	10♎	25♎	9♏	24♏	9♐	24♐	9♑	24♑
16	3♐	18♐	3♑	19♑	4♒	18♒	3♓	17♓	0♈	13♈	26♈	9♉	21♉	3♊	15♊
17	22♈	5♉	19♉	2♊	14♊	27♊	12♋	24♋	0♌	13♌	26♌	9♍	21♍	3♎	16♎
18	0♑	12♑	24♑	6♒	18♒	0♓	12♓	24♓	7♈	20♈	3♉	16♉	0♊	14♊	28♊
19	1♑	14♑	26♑	9♒	22♒	5♓	19♓	3♈	17♈	1♉	15♉	0♊	15♊	0♋	14♋
1920	24♉	9♊	24♊	9♋	24♋	9♌	24♌	8♍	21♍	4♎	17♎	29♎	11♏	23♏	5♐
21	13♎	27♎	10♏	22♏	5♐	17♐	0♑	12♑	24♑	6♒	18♒	29♒	11♓	23♓	6♈
22	20♒	2♓	14♓	25♓	7♈	19♈	1♉	14♉	27♉	10♊	23♊	7♋	21♋	6♌	20♌
23	22♊	5♋	17♋	0♌	14♌	27♌	11♍	24♍	8♎	23♎	7♏	22♏	6♐	21♐	5♑
24	15♏	0♐	15♐	0♑	15♑	0♒	15♒	28♒	12♓	25♓	7♈	20♈	2♉	14♉	26♉
25	5♈	18♈	1♉	14♉	26♉	8♊	20♊	2♋	14♋	26♋	8♌	19♌	1♍	13♍	26♍
26	9♌	21♌	3♍	15♍	27♍	9♎	21♎	4♏	17♏	0♐	14♐	28♐	12♑	27♑	12♒
27	12♐	25♐	8♑	22♑	5♒	19♒	3♓	17♓	1♈	15♈	29♈	14♉	28♉	12♊	26♊
28	6♉	21♉	6♊	21♊	6♋	20♋	5♌	19♌	2♍	15♍	28♍	10♎	22♎	4♏	16♏
29	26♍	9♎	22♎	4♏	16♏	29♏	10♐	22♐	4♑	16♑	28♑	10♒	22♒	4♓	17♓

MOON POSITIONS

	JUNE 29	30	JULY 1	2	3	4	5	6	7	8	9	10	11	12	13
1900	6♌	18♌	1♍	13♍	25♍	6♎	18♎	0♏	13♏	25♏	8♐	21♐	5♑	19♑	3♒
01	9♐	21♐	3♑	16♑	29♑	12♒	26♒	9♓	23♓	7♈	21♈	5♉	20♉	4♊	18♊
02	14♈	28♈	12♉	27♉	12♊	27♊	12♋	27♋	12♌	26♌	10♍	23♍	6♎	19♎	1♏
03	6♍	20♍	4♎	17♎	0♏	13♏	25♏	7♐	20♐	2♑	13♑	25♑	7♒	19♒	1♓
04	26♑	9♒	21♒	2♓	14♓	26♓	8♈	20♈	2♉	15♉	28♉	12♊	25♊	10♋	24♋
05	29♉	11♊	24♊	7♋	20♋	4♌	17♌	1♍	15♍	29♍	13♎	28♎	12♏	26♏	10♐
06	6♎	20♎	4♏	18♏	2♐	16♐	0♑	14♑	28♑	12♒	26♒	10♓	24♓	9♈	21♈
07	27♏	11♐	24♐	8♑	22♑	6♒	20♒	3♓	16♓	0♈	13♈	25♈	8♉	20♉	2♊
08	16♋	29♋	12♌	25♌	7♍	20♍	3♎	16♎	29♎	11♏	24♏	7♐	20♐	2♑	15♑
09	18♏	2♐	16♐	0♑	14♑	28♑	12♒	26♒	10♓	23♓	7♈	21♈	5♉	18♉	2♊
1910	28♓	14♈	0♉	16♉	2♊	18♊	4♋	20♋	6♌	22♌	8♍	24♍	10♎	26♎	11♏
11	18♐	1♑	14♑	27♑	10♒	23♒	6♓	19♓	2♈	15♈	28♈	11♉	24♉	7♊	20♊
12	7♑	20♑	3♒	16♒	29♒	12♓	25♓	8♈	21♈	4♉	17♉	0♊	13♊	26♊	9♋
13	8♉	22♉	6♊	20♊	4♋	18♋	2♌	16♌	0♍	14♍	28♍	12♎	26♎	10♏	24♏
14	20♍	4♎	17♎	1♏	14♏	28♏	11♐	25♐	8♑	22♑	5♒	19♒	2♓	16♓	0♈
15	8♒	20♒	3♓	15♓	28♓	10♈	23♈	5♉	18♉	0♊	13♊	25♊	8♋	20♋	3♌
16	27♊	10♋	23♋	6♌	19♌	2♍	15♍	28♍	11♎	24♎	7♏	20♏	3♐	16♐	29♐
17	28♎	12♏	26♏	10♐	24♐	8♑	22♑	6♒	20♒	4♓	18♓	2♈	16♈	0♉	14♉
18	12♓	25♓	8♈	21♈	4♉	17♉	0♊	13♊	26♊	9♋	22♋	5♌	18♌	1♍	14♍
19	29♋	13♌	27♌	10♍	23♍	6♎	19♎	2♏	15♏	28♏	11♐	24♐	7♑	20♑	2♒
1920	17♐	0♑	13♑	26♑	9♒	22♒	5♓	18♓	1♈	14♈	27♈	10♉	23♉	6♊	19♊
21	18♈	1♉	14♉	27♉	10♊	24♊	8♋	21♋	5♌	18♌	2♍	15♍	28♍	11♎	24♎
22	4♍	19♍	3♎	17♎	1♏	15♏	28♏	12♐	25♐	8♑	21♑	3♒	16♒	28♒	10♓
23	19♑	3♒	16♒	29♒	12♓	24♓	6♈	18♈	0♉	12♉	24♉	6♊	18♊	1♋	14♋
24	7♊	20♊	3♋	16♋	29♋	12♌	25♌	8♍	21♍	4♎	17♎	0♏	13♏	26♏	9♐
25	8♎	21♎	4♏	17♏	0♐	13♐	26♐	9♑	22♑	5♒	18♒	1♓	14♓	27♓	10♈
26	26♒	9♓	22♓	4♈	17♈	29♈	11♉	24♉	6♊	19♊	2♋	15♋	28♋	13♌	29♌
27	10♋	22♋	5♌	18♌	0♍	12♍	25♍	7♎	20♎	2♏	15♏	28♏	10♐	22♐	4♑
28	27♏	11♐	25♐	9♑	23♑	7♒	20♒	3♓	16♓	29♓	12♈	25♈	8♉	20♉	1♊
29	29♓	13♈	27♈	12♉	26♉	10♊	24♊	8♋	23♋	7♌	22♌	6♍	21♍	5♎	19♎

MOON POSITIONS

JULY	14	15	16	17	18	19	20	21	22	23	24	25	26	27	28
1900	18♒	2♓	17♓	1♈	16♈	0♉	14♉	27♉	11♊	24♊	7♋	20♋	2♌	15♌	27♌
01	3♋	17♋	1♌	14♌	27♌	10♍	23♍	5♎	17♎	29♎	11♏	23♏	5♐	17♐	29♐
02	13♏	25♏	7♐	19♐	0♑	12♑	25♑	7♒	19♒	2♓	15♓	28♓	11♈	24♈	8♉
03	13♓	25♓	7♈	20♈	3♉	16♉	0♊	15♊	0♋	15♋	0♌	15♌	0♍	15♍	29♍
04	9♌	24♌	9♍	23♍	8♎	22♎	5♏	19♏	2♐	15♐	28♐	10♑	23♑	5♒	17♒
05	24♐	8♑	21♑	5♒	18♒	0♓	13♓	25♓	7♈	19♈	0♉	12♉	24♉	7♊	19♊
06	3♉	15♉	27♉	9♊	21♊	3♋	15♋	27♋	10♌	23♌	6♍	19♍	2♎	16♎	0♏
07	3♍	16♍	28♍	11♎	24♎	8♏	22♏	6♐	21♐	6♑	21♑	6♒	21♒	5♓	20♓
08	0♒	15♒	0♓	15♓	29♓	14♈	27♈	11♉	24♉	8♊	19♊	2♋	13♋	25♋	7♌
09	16♊	29♊	12♋	25♋	8♌	20♌	2♍	14♍	26♍	8♎	20♎	2♏	14♏	26♏	9♐
1910	23♎	5♏	16♏	28♏	10♐	22♐	5♑	18♑	0♒	14♒	27♒	11♓	25♓	9♈	23♈
11	24♒	7♓	19♓	2♈	16♈	29♈	13♉	27♉	12♊	27♊	12♋	27♋	12♌	26♌	10♍
12	21♋	6♌	21♌	6♍	21♍	5♎	19♎	2♏	15♏	27♏	9♐	22♐	4♑	16♑	28♑
13	7♐	20♐	3♑	16♑	28♑	10♒	22♒	4♓	16♓	28♓	10♈	22♈	4♉	16♉	29♉
14	12♈	24♈	6♉	18♉	0♊	12♊	25♊	8♋	21♋	5♌	18♌	2♍	16♍	1♎	15♎
15	15♉	28♉	11♊	24♊	7♋	20♋	3♌	16♌	29♌	12♍	25♍	8♎	21♎	4♏	17♏
16	12♍	25♍	8♎	21♎	4♏	17♏	0♐	13♐	26♐	9♑	22♑	5♒	18♒	1♓	14♓
17	29♉	12♊	25♊	8♋	21♋	4♌	17♌	0♍	13♍	26♍	9♎	22♎	5♏	18♏	1♐
18	2♒	15♒	28♒	11♓	24♓	7♈	20♈	3♉	16♉	29♉	12♊	25♊	8♋	21♋	4♌
19	6♒	19♒	2♓	15♓	28♓	11♈	24♈	7♉	20♉	3♊	16♊	29♊	12♋	25♋	8♌
1920	2♋	15♋	28♋	11♌	24♌	7♍	20♍	3♎	16♎	29♎	12♏	25♏	8♐	21♐	4♑
21	19♏	2♐	15♐	28♐	11♑	24♑	7♒	20♒	3♓	16♓	29♓	12♈	25♈	8♉	21♉
22	22♓	5♈	18♈	1♉	14♉	27♉	10♊	23♊	6♋	19♋	2♌	15♌	28♌	11♍	24♍
23	27♋	10♌	23♌	6♍	19♍	2♎	15♎	28♎	11♏	24♏	7♐	20♐	3♑	16♑	29♑
24	24♐	7♑	20♑	3♒	16♒	29♒	12♓	25♓	8♈	21♈	4♉	17♉	0♊	13♊	26♊
25	11♉	24♉	7♊	20♊	3♋	16♋	29♋	12♌	25♌	8♍	21♍	4♎	17♎	0♏	13♏
26	11♍	24♍	7♎	20♎	3♏	16♏	29♏	12♐	25♐	8♑	21♑	4♒	17♒	0♓	13♓
27	17♑	0♒	13♒	26♒	9♓	22♓	5♈	18♈	1♉	14♉	27♉	10♊	23♊	6♋	19♋
28	15♊	28♊	11♋	24♋	7♌	20♌	3♍	16♍	29♍	12♎	25♎	8♏	21♏	4♐	17♐
29	1♏	14♏	27♏	10♐	23♐	6♑	19♑	2♒	15♒	28♒	11♓	24♓	7♈	20♈	3♉

MOON POSITIONS

	JULY 29	30	31	AUG 1	2	3	4	5	6	7	8	9	10	11	12
1900	9♍	21♍	3♎	15♎	26♎	8♏	21♏	3♐	16♐	29♐	13♑	27♑	12♒	27♒	12♓
01	12♑	25♑	8♒	22♒	6♓	20♓	4♈	18♈	2♉	16♉	0♊	15♊	28♊	12♋	26♋
02	22♉	6♊	21♊	6♋	21♋	5♌	20♌	4♍	18♍	2♎	14♎	27♎	9♏	21♏	3♐
03	13♎	27♎	9♏	22♏	4♐	17♐	29♐	11♑	22♑	4♒	16♒	28♒	10♓	22♓	4♈
04	29♒	11♓	23♓	4♈	16♈	28♈	11♉	23♉	6♊	20♊	4♋	18♋	3♌	18♌	3♍
05	14♏	27♏	11♐	25♐	9♑	23♑	7♒	21♒	5♓	19♓	3♈	17♈	1♉	15♉	29♉
06	4♈	17♈	0♉	13♉	25♉	7♊	19♊	1♋	13♋	24♋	6♌	18♌	0♍	13♍	25♍
07	19♌	1♍	13♍	25♍	7♎	19♎	1♏	13♏	26♏	8♐	20♐	3♑	16♑	29♑	13♒
08	22♐	6♑	19♑	2♒	16♒	0♓	14♓	28♓	12♈	26♈	10♉	24♉	8♊	22♊	6♋
09	7♉	20♉	2♊	15♊	27♊	9♋	21♋	3♌	15♌	27♌	9♍	21♍	4♎	16♎	29♎
1910	24♍	7♎	20♎	2♏	14♏	26♏	8♐	20♐	2♑	14♑	26♑	9♒	21♒	4♓	17♓
11	9♒	21♒	3♓	15♓	27♓	9♈	22♈	4♉	18♉	1♊	15♊	29♊	14♋	28♋	13♌
12	12♊	26♊	9♋	22♋	4♌	16♌	28♌	10♍	22♍	4♎	16♎	29♎	11♏	23♏	6♐
13	29♎	11♏	23♏	5♐	17♐	29♐	11♑	23♑	6♒	18♒	1♓	14♓	28♓	12♈	26♈
14	14♓	27♓	10♈	23♈	6♉	19♉	3♊	17♊	1♋	15♋	29♋	13♌	27♌	11♍	24♍
15	0♌	13♌	25♌	7♍	18♍	0♎	13♎	26♎	9♏	23♏	7♐	21♐	5♑	20♑	5♒
16	2♐	16♐	0♑	14♑	27♑	11♒	24♒	6♓	19♓	2♈	15♈	28♈	11♉	24♉	7♊
17	22♈	6♉	20♉	5♊	18♊	2♋	15♋	28♋	10♌	22♌	4♍	16♍	28♍	10♎	22♎
18	4♍	17♍	29♍	11♎	24♎	6♏	18♏	0♐	13♐	24♐	6♑	19♑	2♒	15♒	28♒
19	20♑	4♒	18♒	2♓	15♓	29♓	12♈	26♈	9♉	22♉	6♊	19♊	2♋	15♋	28♋
1920	23♉	7♊	21♊	5♋	18♋	1♌	13♌	26♌	8♍	20♍	2♎	14♎	26♎	8♏	20♏
21	14♎	26♎	8♏	20♏	2♐	14♐	26♐	8♑	20♑	2♒	15♒	28♒	11♓	24♓	7♈
22	24♍	7♎	19♎	1♏	13♏	25♏	7♐	19♐	1♑	13♑	25♑	8♒	21♒	4♓	17♓
23	10♋	22♋	4♌	16♌	28♌	10♍	22♍	4♎	16♎	28♎	11♏	24♏	7♐	20♐	4♑
24	14♏	26♏	8♐	20♐	2♑	14♑	26♑	8♒	20♒	3♓	16♓	29♓	13♈	27♈	11♉
25	5♈	18♈	2♉	15♉	29♉	12♊	26♊	10♋	24♋	8♌	22♌	6♍	20♍	3♎	16♎
26	14♌	26♌	8♍	20♍	2♎	14♎	26♎	8♏	20♏	3♐	15♐	28♐	11♑	24♑	8♒
27	0♑	12♑	24♑	7♒	20♒	2♓	15♓	29♓	12♈	26♈	10♉	25♉	9♊	23♊	7♋
28	5♉	19♉	3♊	17♊	1♋	15♋	29♋	13♌	27♌	11♍	25♍	8♎	22♎	5♏	18♏
29	18♉	2♊	16♊	0♋	13♋	26♋	9♌	22♌	4♍	16♍	28♍	10♎	22♎	5♏	17♏

MOON POSITIONS

AUGUST

	13	14	15	16	17	18	19	20	21	22	23	24	25	26	27
1900	27♓	12♈	26♈	10♉	24♉	8♊	21♊	4♋	16♋	29♋	11♌	23♌	6♍	18♍	29♍
01	10♌	23♌	6♍	18♍	1♎	13♎	25♎	7♏	19♏	1♐	13♐	25♐	7♑	20♑	3♒
02	15♐	27♐	9♑	21♑	3♒	16♒	28♒	11♓	25♓	8♈	21♈	5♉	19♉	3♊	17♊
03	17♈	0♉	13♉	26♉	10♊	24♊	8♋	23♋	8♌	24♌	9♍	23♍	8♎	22♎	5♏
04	18♍	3♎	17♎	2♏	16♏	29♏	12♐	25♐	7♑	20♑	2♒	14♒	26♒	8♓	20♓
05	1♒	13♒	26♒	8♓	21♓	3♈	15♈	27♈	8♉	20♉	2♊	15♊	27♊	10♋	23♋
06	5♊	17♊	29♊	11♋	23♋	6♌	19♌	2♍	15♍	29♍	13♎	27♎	11♏	25♏	10♐
07	8♎	21♎	4♏	18♏	1♐	16♐	0♑	15♑	29♑	14♒	29♒	14♓	28♓	12♈	25♈
08	9♓	24♓	9♈	23♈	7♉	20♉	3♊	16♊	28♊	10♋	22♋	4♌	16♌	28♌	10♍
09	21♋	4♌	16♌	29♌	11♍	23♍	5♎	16♎	28♎	10♏	22♏	4♐	17♐	0♑	13♑
1910	24♏	6♐	18♐	0♑	13♑	26♑	9♒	23♒	7♓	21♓	5♈	19♈	4♉	18♉	2♊
11	29♓	13♈	26♈	10♉	23♉	7♊	22♊	6♋	21♋	6♌	20♌	5♍	19♍	2♎	15♎
12	0♍	15♍	0♎	14♎	28♎	11♏	24♏	6♐	19♐	1♑	13♑	25♑	6♒	18♒	0♓
13	12♑	25♑	7♒	19♒	1♓	13♓	25♓	6♈	18♈	0♉	12♉	25♉	7♊	21♊	4♋
14	14♉	26♉	8♊	20♊	3♋	16♋	0♌	13♌	27♌	12♍	26♍	11♎	25♎	10♏	24♏
15	21♍	4♎	18♎	2♏	16♏	0♐	14♐	28♐	13♑	27♑	11♒	25♒	9♓	22♓	5♈
16	20♒	5♓	20♓	4♈	18♈	1♉	15♉	27♉	9♊	20♊	3♋	15♋	26♋	8♌	20♌
17	3♋	15♋	27♋	9♌	21♌	3♍	15♍	27♍	9♎	21♎	3♏	15♏	28♏	11♐	25♐
18	4♏	16♏	28♏	10♐	23♐	6♑	19♑	3♒	18♒	3♓	18♓	3♈	17♈	2♉	16♉
19	12♓	26♓	10♈	24♈	8♉	22♉	6♊	20♊	5♋	18♋	2♌	16♌	29♌	13♍	25♍
1920	11♌	26♌	11♍	25♍	8♎	21♎	4♏	16♏	29♏	11♐	22♐	4♑	16♑	28♑	10♒
21	24♐	6♑	18♑	0♒	12♒	23♒	5♓	17♓	29♓	11♈	24♈	6♉	19♉	2♊	16♊
22	24♈	6♉	18♉	0♊	13♊	26♊	10♋	24♋	9♌	24♌	9♍	24♍	9♎	23♎	8♏
23	3♍	17♍	2♎	16♎	0♏	15♏	29♏	13♐	27♐	10♑	24♑	7♒	20♒	3♓	16♓
24	2♒	17♒	1♓	15♓	28♓	11♈	24♈	6♉	18♉	0♊	12♊	24♊	6♋	18♋	0♌
25	14♊	26♊	8♋	20♋	2♌	13♌	25♌	7♍	20♍	2♎	15♎	27♎	11♏	24♏	8♐
26	14♎	26♎	8♏	21♏	3♐	17♐	0♑	14♑	29♑	14♒	29♒	14♓	0♈	15♈	29♈
27	24♏	9♐	23♐	8♑	23♑	7♒	21♒	5♓	19♓	2♈	15♈	28♈	11♉	23♉	6♊
28	24♋	8♌	21♌	5♍	18♍	1♎	14♎	26♎	8♏	20♏	2♐	14♐	25♐	8♑	20♑
29	4♐	16♐	28♐	10♑	22♑	4♒	16♒	28♒	11♓	23♓	6♈	19♈	2♉	16♉	29♉

MOON POSITIONS

	AUGUST				SEPTEMBER										
	28	29	30	31	1	2	3	4	5	6	7	8	9	10	11
1900	11♎	23♎	5♏	17♏	29♏	12♐	24♐	8♑	21♑	5♒	20♒	5♓	20♓	6♈	21♈
01	17♒	1♓	15♓	0♈	14♈	29♈	13♉	27♉	11♊	25♊	9♋	23♋	6♌	19♌	2♍
02	1♋	16♋	0♌	15♌	29♌	13♍	26♍	10♎	22♎	5♏	17♏	29♏	11♐	23♐	5♑
03	18♏	1♐	13♐	25♐	7♑	19♑	1♒	13♒	25♒	7♓	19♓	1♈	14♈	27♈	10♉
04	1♈	13♈	25♈	7♉	19♉	1♊	13♊	25♊	7♋	19♋	1♌	14♌	27♌	11♍	25♍
05	7♌	21♌	6♍	20♍	5♎	19♎	3♏	16♏	29♏	12♐	24♐	6♑	18♑	0♒	12♒
06	24♐	8♑	22♑	6♒	20♒	3♓	16♓	29♓	12♈	25♈	7♉	20♉	2♊	14♊	26♊
07	8♉	21♉	3♊	15♊	27♊	9♋	21♋	3♌	15♌	27♌	9♍	21♍	3♎	15♎	27♎
08	22♍	4♎	16♎	28♎	10♏	23♏	5♐	17♐	29♐	11♑	24♑	6♒	19♒	2♓	15♓
09	27♑	12♒	26♒	11♓	27♓	12♈	27♈	12♉	25♉	9♊	23♊	6♋	18♋	1♌	13♌
1910	16♊	0♋	14♋	27♋	11♌	24♌	7♍	20♍	2♎	15♎	27♎	9♏	20♏	2♐	14♐
11	28♎	11♏	23♏	5♐	17♐	29♐	11♑	23♑	5♒	17♒	0♓	13♓	26♓	9♈	23♈
12	12♓	24♓	6♈	19♈	1♉	14♉	27♉	11♊	25♊	9♋	23♋	8♌	23♌	8♍	23♍
13	18♋	2♌	17♌	2♍	18♍	3♎	18♎	2♏	16♏	0♐	14♐	27♐	10♑	22♑	4♒
14	8♐	22♐	6♑	19♑	2♒	15♒	28♒	10♓	22♓	5♈	17♈	28♈	10♉	22♉	4♊
15	18♈	0♉	13♉	25♉	7♊	18♊	0♋	12♋	25♋	7♌	20♌	3♍	16♍	0♎	14♎
16	2♍	15♍	27♍	10♎	23♎	6♏	19♏	3♐	17♐	0♑	14♑	0♒	14♒	29♒	14♓
17	9♑	23♑	8♒	21♒	5♓	18♓	1♈	14♈	27♈	9♉	21♉	3♊	15♊	27♊	9♋
18	0♊	14♊	27♊	10♋	23♋	6♌	19♌	1♍	13♍	25♍	7♎	19♎	0♏	12♏	24♏
19	8♎	20♎	2♏	14♏	26♏	8♐	20♐	2♑	14♑	27♑	10♒	23♒	7♓	21♓	6♈
1920	23♒	5♓	18♓	1♈	14♈	28♈	11♉	25♉	9♊	23♊	7♋	22♋	6♌	20♌	5♍
21	0♌	14♌	29♌	14♍	29♍	14♎	29♎	14♏	28♏	12♐	25♐	8♑	20♑	3♒	15♒
22	22♏	5♐	19♐	2♑	14♑	27♑	9♒	21♒	3♓	15♓	27♓	9♈	20♈	2♉	14♉
23	28♓	10♈	22♈	4♉	16♉	28♉	10♊	22♊	4♋	17♋	0♌	14♌	28♌	12♍	26♍
24	13♌	26♌	9♍	22♍	5♎	18♎	1♏	14♏	27♏	10♐	23♐	5♑	17♑	29♑	11♒
25	22♐	6♑	20♑	4♒	18♒	1♓	15♓	29♓	12♈	26♈	10♉	23♉	6♊	19♊	2♋
26	13♉	27♉	10♊	23♊	6♋	18♋	0♌	12♌	23♌	5♍	17♍	29♍	11♎	23♎	5♏
27	18♍	0♎	12♎	24♎	6♏	18♏	1♐	13♐	25♐	8♑	20♑	4♒	18♒	2♓	17♓
28	3♒	16♒	29♒	13♓	27♓	11♈	25♈	9♉	24♉	8♊	22♊	6♋	20♋	4♌	17♌
29	13♊	28♊	12♋	27♋	11♌	26♌	11♍	25♍	9♎	22♎	5♏	18♏	0♐	12♐	24♐

MOON POSITIONS

SEPTEMBER

	12	13	14	15	16	17	18	19	20	21	22	23	24	25	26
1900	6♉	20♉	4♊	18♊	1♋	14♋	26♋	8♌	21♌	3♍	15♍	26♍	8♎	20♎	2♏
01	15♍	27♍	9♎	21♎	3♏	15♏	27♏	9♐	21♐	3♑	15♑	28♑	11♒	25♒	9♓
02	17♑	29♑	12♒	24♒	7♓	20♓	4♈	18♈	1♉	15♉	0♊	14♊	28♊	12♋	26♋
03	23♉	6♊	20♊	4♋	18♋	3♌	17♌	2♍	17♍	2♎	16♎	0♏	13♏	26♏	9♐
04	26♎	11♏	25♏	8♐	22♐	4♑	17♑	29♑	11♒	23♒	5♓	17♓	28♓	10♈	22♈
05	5♓	17♓	29♓	11♈	23♈	5♉	17♉	29♉	11♊	23♊	5♋	18♋	2♌	15♌	29♌
06	15♓	27♓	9♈	22♈	5♉	18♉	1♊	13♊	26♊	9♋	22♋	6♌	21♌	5♍	19♍
07	17♈	0♉	13♉	26♉	10♊	23♊	7♋	21♋	5♌	19♌	2♍	16♍	29♍	12♎	25♎
08	15♈	28♈	12♉	26♉	10♊	24♊	9♋	23♋	6♌	18♌	0♍	12♍	24♍	6♎	18♎
09	26♍	8♎	20♎	1♏	13♏	25♏	7♐	19♐	1♑	13♑	26♑	9♒	22♒	6♓	20♓
1910	26♐	8♑	21♑	4♒	17♒	29♒	14♓	27♓	11♈	25♈	9♉	23♉	13♊	27♊	11♋
11	6♉	20♉	4♊	18♊	2♋	15♋	29♋	13♌	27♌	11♍	25♍	9♎	23♎	6♏	19♏
12	8♎	22♎	6♏	19♏	2♐	15♐	27♐	9♑	21♑	3♒	15♒	27♒	9♓	21♓	3♈
13	16♒	28♒	10♓	22♓	3♈	15♈	27♈	9♉	21♉	4♊	17♊	0♋	13♋	27♋	11♌
14	16♊	28♊	11♋	25♋	9♌	23♌	6♍	20♍	3♎	16♎	29♎	11♏	23♏	6♐	18♐
15	28♊	12♋	26♋	11♌	25♌	9♍	23♍	7♎	20♎	4♏	17♏	0♐	13♐	26♐	8♑
16	28♓	12♈	25♈	9♉	22♉	5♊	18♊	1♋	14♋	25♋	8♌	21♌	4♍	16♍	29♍
17	28♌	10♎	22♎	5♏	17♏	0♐	12♐	24♐	6♑	18♑	0♒	12♒	24♒	6♓	18♓
18	6♋	18♑	1♒	14♒	27♒	10♓	23♓	7♈	21♈	5♉	20♉	4♊	19♊	3♋	17♋
19	20♈	4♉	19♉	3♊	17♊	1♋	15♋	29♋	12♌	25♌	9♍	21♍	4♎	16♎	29♎
1920	19♍	3♎	16♎	29♎	12♏	24♏	7♐	19♐	0♑	12♑	24♑	6♒	19♒	1♓	14♓
21	27♑	8♒	20♒	2♓	14♓	26♓	8♈	21♈	3♉	16♉	29♉	12♊	26♊	10♋	24♋
22	26♉	9♊	22♊	5♋	18♋	2♌	17♌	2♍	17♍	2♎	17♎	2♏	17♏	1♐	15♐
23	11♓	26♓	11♈	25♈	9♉	24♉	7♊	21♊	4♋	17♋	29♋	12♌	24♌	6♍	18♍
24	10♓	23♓	6♈	19♈	2♉	14♉	26♉	8♊	20♊	2♋	14♋	26♋	8♌	21♌	4♍
25	17♍	28♍	10♎	22♎	4♏	16♏	29♏	11♐	24♐	8♑	21♑	4♒	18♒	2♓	16♓
26	17♈	0♉	13♉	26♉	9♊	23♊	8♋	22♋	8♌	23♌	8♍	23♍	8♎	22♎	6♏
27	2♈	17♈	2♉	17♉	2♊	16♊	0♋	13♋	25♋	8♌	20♌	3♍	15♍	27♍	9♎
28	1♍	14♍	27♍	9♎	22♎	4♏	16♏	28♏	10♐	21♐	3♑	15♑	28♑	11♒	24♒
29	6♑	18♑	0♒	12♒	24♒	7♓	19♓	2♈	16♈	29♈	13♉	26♉	10♊	24♊	8♋

MOON POSITIONS

	SEPTEMBER				OCTOBER										
	27	28	29	30	1	2	3	4	5	6	7	8	9	10	11
1900	14♏	26♏	8♐	21♐	3♑	16♑	0♒	14♒	29♒	13♓	29♓	14♈	29♈	14♉	29♉
01	24♓	8♈	23♈	8♉	23♉	8♊	22♊	6♋	19♋	3♌	16♌	29♌	11♍	24♍	6♎
02	10♌	24♌	8♍	22♍	5♎	18♎	0♏	13♏	25♏	7♐	19♐	1♑	13♑	25♑	7♒
03	21♐	4♑	16♑	28♑	9♒	21♒	3♓	15♓	28♓	10♈	23♈	6♉	20♉	3♊	17♊
04	4♉	17♉	29♉	12♊	25♊	8♋	22♋	6♌	20♌	5♍	19♍	5♎	20♎	4♏	19♏
05	14♍	29♍	14♎	29♎	14♏	29♏	14♐	28♐	11♑	24♑	7♒	20♒	2♓	14♓	26♓
06	2♒	16♒	29♒	12♓	25♓	8♈	21♈	3♉	15♉	27♉	9♊	21♊	3♋	15♋	27♋
07	11♊	23♊	5♋	17♋	29♋	11♌	23♌	5♍	18♍	1♎	14♎	27♎	11♏	25♏	9♐
08	25♎	8♏	20♏	3♐	16♐	29♐	13♑	27♑	11♒	26♒	11♓	26♓	11♈	25♈	10♉
09	5♓	20♓	5♈	20♈	5♉	20♉	5♊	19♊	2♋	15♋	28♋	10♌	23♌	5♍	17♍
1910	24♋	8♌	21♌	4♍	16♍	29♍	11♎	23♎	5♏	17♏	29♏	10♐	22♐	4♐	17♐
11	1♐	13♐	25♐	7♑	19♑	1♒	13♒	25♒	8♓	21♓	5♈	18♈	2♉	16♉	1♊
12	16♈	28♈	11♉	24♉	8♊	21♊	5♋	19♋	3♌	18♌	2♍	17♍	2♎	16♎	0♏
13	26♌	11♍	26♍	11♎	26♎	11♏	25♏	9♐	23♐	6♑	19♑	1♒	13♒	25♒	7♓
14	16♑	29♑	12♒	25♒	7♓	19♓	1♈	13♈	25♈	7♉	19♉	1♊	13♊	25♊	7♋
15	21♉	3♊	15♊	26♊	8♋	20♋	2♌	15♌	28♌	11♍	25♍	9♎	23♎	8♏	22♏
16	6♎	19♎	3♏	16♏	0♐	14♐	27♐	11♑	26♑	10♒	24♒	9♓	23♓	7♈	20♈
17	17♒	1♓	17♓	2♈	17♈	2♉	16♉	0♊	13♊	26♊	9♋	21♋	3♌	15♌	27♌
18	7♋	20♋	3♌	15♌	28♌	10♍	22♍	4♎	15♎	27♎	9♏	21♏	3♐	15♐	27♐
19	10♏	22♏	4♐	16♐	28♐	10♑	22♑	5♒	18♒	1♓	15♓	0♈	14♈	29♈	14♉
1920	27♓	10♈	24♈	8♉	22♉	6♊	20♊	4♋	18♋	2♌	16♌	0♍	14♍	28♍	11♎
21	9♌	23♌	8♍	23♍	8♎	22♎	6♏	20♏	3♐	16♐	29♐	11♑	23♑	5♒	17♒
22	28♐	11♑	24♑	6♒	18♒	0♓	12♓	24♓	6♈	17♈	29♈	11♉	23♉	6♊	18♊
23	0♉	12♉	24♉	6♊	18♊	0♋	12♋	25♋	8♌	22♌	5♍	20♍	5♎	20♎	5♏
24	17♍	1♎	15♎	29♎	13♏	28♏	12♐	26♐	11♑	25♑	8♒	22♒	6♓	20♓	5♈
25	0♒	15♒	29♒	14♓	28♓	12♈	26♈	10♉	23♉	6♊	19♊	1♋	13♋	25♋	6♌
26	19♊	2♋	14♋	26♋	8♌	20♌	2♍	14♍	26♍	8♎	20♎	2♏	14♏	27♏	10♐
27	21♎	2♏	14♏	26♏	8♐	20♐	2♑	15♑	28♑	12♒	26♒	10♓	25♓	11♈	26♈
28	7♓	21♓	6♈	20♈	5♉	20♉	4♊	19♊	3♋	17♋	0♌	14♌	27♌	10♍	23♍
29	23♋	7♌	21♌	5♍	19♍	3♎	17♎	0♏	13♏	26♏	8♐	20♐	2♑	14♑	26♑

MOON POSITIONS

OCTOBER

Year	12	13	14	15	16	17	18	19	20	21	22	23	24	25	26
1900	13♊	27♊	10♋	23♋	5♌	17♌	0♍	12♍	23♍	5♎	17♎	29♎	11♏	23♏	5♐
01	18♎	0♏	12♏	23♏	5♐	17♐	29♐	11♑	24♑	6♒	19♒	3♓	17♓	2♈	16♈
02	19♒	2♓	15♓	29♓	12♈	26♈	11♉	25♉	10♊	24♊	9♋	23♋	7♌	21♌	5♍
03	1♋	15♋	29♋	13♌	27♌	12♍	26♍	10♎	24♎	8♏	21♏	4♐	17♐	29♐	12♑
04	3♈	17♈	0♉	13♉	26♉	8♊	20♊	2♋	13♋	25♋	7♌	19♌	1♍	13♍	26♍
05	8♉	20♉	2♊	14♊	26♊	8♋	20♋	2♌	14♌	26♌	8♍	20♍	2♎	14♎	26♎
06	9♌	22♌	5♍	18♍	1♎	14♎	27♎	10♏	24♏	7♐	21♐	5♑	18♑	3♒	17♒
07	23♐	7♑	21♑	4♒	18♒	1♓	15♓	28♓	11♈	24♈	8♉	20♉	3♊	15♊	27♊
08	24♉	7♊	20♊	2♋	14♋	26♋	8♌	20♌	1♍	13♍	25♍	7♎	19♎	1♏	13♏
09	29♍	10♎	22♎	4♏	16♏	28♏	10♐	22♐	4♑	16♑	28♑	10♒	23♒	5♓	18♓
1910	29♑	12♒	25♒	8♓	21♓	4♈	17♈	0♉	13♉	26♉	8♊	20♊	2♋	14♋	26♋
11	15♒	29♒	12♓	25♓	9♈	22♈	5♉	18♉	0♊	13♊	25♊	7♋	19♋	1♌	13♌
12	14♏	27♏	10♐	23♐	6♑	18♑	1♒	13♒	26♒	8♓	21♓	4♈	17♈	0♉	13♉
13	19♓	0♈	12♈	25♈	7♉	19♉	1♊	13♊	25♊	7♋	19♋	1♌	13♌	25♌	8♍
14	20♋	2♌	14♌	26♌	8♍	20♍	2♎	14♎	26♎	9♏	21♏	4♐	17♐	0♑	13♑
15	7♐	22♐	5♑	19♑	3♒	17♒	1♓	15♓	29♓	13♈	27♈	11♉	24♉	8♊	21♊
16	4♉	17♉	0♊	12♊	24♊	6♋	18♋	0♌	12♌	24♌	6♍	18♍	1♎	14♎	27♎
17	9♍	22♍	5♎	18♎	1♏	14♏	27♏	10♐	23♐	6♑	19♑	2♒	15♒	28♒	11♓
18	10♑	21♑	4♒	16♒	29♒	11♓	24♓	7♈	20♈	3♉	16♉	29♉	12♊	24♊	6♋
19	29♉	13♊	26♊	9♋	21♋	4♌	16♌	28♌	10♍	22♍	5♎	17♎	0♏	13♏	25♏
1920	24♎	7♏	20♏	2♐	14♐	26♐	9♑	21♑	3♒	16♒	29♒	12♓	25♓	9♈	22♈
21	29♒	11♓	23♓	6♈	18♈	1♉	14♉	27♉	10♊	23♊	5♋	18♋	1♌	13♌	25♌
22	1♋	14♋	26♋	8♌	20♌	2♍	14♍	26♍	8♎	20♎	2♏	14♏	26♏	9♐	21♐
23	20♍	2♎	15♎	27♎	10♏	22♏	5♐	18♐	0♑	13♑	25♑	7♒	20♒	3♓	15♓
24	15♈	27♈	10♉	22♉	5♊	17♊	29♊	11♋	23♋	5♌	17♌	29♌	11♍	24♍	6♎
25	18♌	0♍	13♍	25♍	7♎	20♎	2♏	14♏	26♏	8♐	21♐	3♑	15♑	27♑	10♒
26	23♐	6♑	19♑	1♒	14♒	27♒	10♓	23♓	6♈	18♈	1♉	14♉	27♉	10♊	23♊
27	11♉	23♉	5♊	17♊	29♊	11♋	23♋	5♌	16♌	28♌	10♍	22♍	4♎	16♎	29♎
28	6♎	18♎	0♏	12♏	24♏	6♐	18♐	1♑	13♑	25♑	7♒	20♒	3♓	16♓	29♓
29	8♒	22♒	5♓	19♓	2♈	16♈	29♈	13♉	26♉	10♊	23♊	7♋	20♋	4♌	18♌

MOON POSITIONS

Year	OCTOBER					NOVEMBER									
	27	28	29	30	31	1	2	3	4	5	6	7	8	9	10
1900	18♐	0♑	13♑	26♑	10♒	23♒	8♓	22♓	7♈	22♈	7♉	22♉	7♊	21♊	5♋
01	2♉	17♉	2♊	17♊	1♋	16♋	29♋	13♌	26♌	8♍	21♍	3♎	15♎	27♎	9♏
02	18♍	1♎	14♎	26♎	9♏	21♏	3♐	15♐	27♐	9♑	21♑	3♒	15♒	27♒	10♓
03	24♑	5♒	17♒	29♒	11♓	23♓	6♈	19♈	2♉	15♉	29♉	13♊	27♊	11♋	26♋
04	9♊	22♊	5♋	18♋	2♌	16♌	0♍	14♍	29♍	13♎	28♎	13♏	27♏	11♐	25♐
05	22♎	7♏	23♏	8♐	22♐	7♑	20♑	4♒	16♒	29♒	11♓	23♓	5♈	17♈	29♈
06	9♓	22♓	5♈	17♈	29♈	12♉	24♉	5♊	17♊	29♊	11♋	23♋	5♌	17♌	0♍
07	13♋	25♋	7♌	19♌	1♍	13♍	26♍	9♎	22♎	6♏	20♏	5♐	19♐	3♑	18♑
08	0♐	13♐	26♐	10♑	24♑	7♒	22♒	6♓	20♓	5♈	19♈	4♉	18♉	2♊	15♊
09	13♈	28♈	14♉	28♉	13♊	27♊	11♋	24♋	7♌	19♌	1♍	14♍	25♍	7♎	19♎
1910	1♍	13♍	26♍	8♎	20♎	2♏	14♏	26♏	7♐	19♐	1♑	13♑	25♑	8♒	20♒
11	3♑	15♑	26♑	8♒	21♒	3♓	16♓	29♓	13♈	27♈	11♉	25♉	10♊	25♊	10♋
12	21♉	4♊	18♊	1♋	16♋	0♌	14♌	28♌	13♍	27♍	11♎	25♎	8♏	22♏	5♐
13	4♎	19♎	4♏	19♏	3♐	17♐	1♑	14♑	27♑	9♒	22♒	3♓	15♓	27♓	9♈
14	22♒	4♓	16♓	28♓	10♈	22♈	4♉	16♉	28♉	10♊	22♊	4♋	16♋	28♋	10♌
15	23♊	5♋	17♋	29♋	11♌	23♌	5♍	17♍	29♍	11♎	23♎	5♏	17♏	29♏	11♐
16	11♏	23♏	5♐	17♐	29♐	11♑	23♑	5♒	17♒	29♒	11♓	23♓	5♈	17♈	29♈
17	26♓	8♈	20♈	2♉	14♉	26♉	8♊	20♊	2♋	14♋	26♋	8♌	20♌	2♍	14♍
18	8♌	20♌	2♍	14♍	26♍	8♎	20♎	2♏	14♏	26♏	8♐	20♐	2♑	14♑	26♑
19	18♐	0♑	12♑	24♑	6♒	18♒	0♓	12♓	24♓	6♈	18♈	0♉	12♉	24♉	6♊
1920	3♉	15♉	27♉	9♊	21♊	3♋	15♋	27♋	9♌	21♌	3♍	15♍	27♍	9♎	21♎
21	18♍	0♎	12♎	24♎	6♏	18♏	0♐	12♐	24♐	6♑	18♑	0♒	12♒	24♒	6♓
22	3♒	15♒	27♒	9♓	21♓	3♈	15♈	27♈	9♉	21♉	3♊	15♊	27♊	9♋	21♋
23	3♊	15♊	27♊	9♋	21♋	3♌	15♌	27♌	9♍	21♍	3♎	15♎	27♎	9♏	21♏
24	23♎	5♏	17♏	29♏	11♐	23♐	5♑	17♑	29♑	11♒	23♒	5♓	17♓	29♓	14♐
25	9♓	21♓	3♈	15♈	27♈	9♉	21♉	3♊	15♊	27♊	9♋	21♋	3♌	15♌	6♉
26	23♋	5♌	17♌	29♌	11♍	23♍	5♎	17♎	29♎	11♏	23♏	5♐	17♐	29♐	8♍
27	23♏	5♐	17♐	29♐	11♑	23♑	5♒	17♒	29♒	11♓	23♓	5♈	17♈	29♈	16♑
28	14♈	26♈	8♉	20♉	2♊	14♊	26♊	8♋	20♋	2♌	14♌	26♌	8♍	20♍	4♊
29	2♍	14♍	26♍	8♎	20♎	2♏	14♏	26♏	8♐	20♐	2♑	14♑	26♑	8♒	28♒

MOON POSITIONS

NOVEMBER

	11	12	13	14	15	16	17	18	19	20	21	22	23	24	25
1900	18♋	1♌	14♌	26♌	8♍	20♍	2♎	14♎	26♎	8♏	20♏	2♐	14♐	27♐	10♑
01	20♏	2♐	14♐	26♐	8♑	20♑	3♒	15♒	28♒	12♓	26♓	10♈	24♈	9♉	25♉
02	23♓	6♈	20♈	5♉	19♉	4♊	19♊	4♋	19♋	4♌	18♌	1♍	15♍	28♍	11♎
03	10♌	24♌	8♍	22♍	6♎	19♎	3♏	16♏	29♏	12♐	25♐	7♑	19♑	1♒	13♒
04	8♑	21♑	4♒	16♒	28♒	10♓	22♓	3♈	15♈	27♈	10♉	22♉	5♊	18♊	2♋
05	11♉	23♉	5♊	17♊	29♊	11♋	24♋	7♌	20♌	3♍	17♍	1♎	16♎	0♏	16♏
06	13♍	27♍	11♎	25♎	10♏	25♏	10♐	26♐	11♑	25♑	9♒	23♒	6♓	19♓	2♈
07	2♒	16♒	0♓	14♓	28♓	11♈	24♈	7♉	20♉	3♊	15♊	27♊	9♋	21♋	3♌
08	28♊	11♋	23♋	5♌	17♌	29♌	11♍	23♍	5♎	17♎	0♏	13♏	26♏	9♐	23♐
09	1♏	13♏	25♏	7♐	19♐	2♑	15♑	28♑	11♒	25♒	9♓	23♓	7♈	22♈	7♉
1910	4♈	17♈	1♉	16♉	1♊	16♊	1♋	16♋	0♌	14♌	27♌	10♍	23♍	5♎	17♎
11	24♋	9♌	23♌	6♍	20♍	3♎	16♎	28♎	11♏	23♏	5♐	17♐	29♐	11♑	23♑
12	18♐	1♑	13♑	25♑	7♒	19♒	1♓	13♓	25♓	7♈	20♈	3♉	16♉	0♊	14♊
13	21♈	4♉	17♉	0♊	13♊	26♊	9♋	22♋	5♌	17♌	0♍	12♍	24♍	6♎	18♎
14	25♌	8♍	20♍	3♎	15♎	28♎	10♏	22♏	5♐	17♐	29♐	11♑	23♑	6♒	18♒
15	16♑	28♑	10♒	22♒	4♓	16♓	29♓	11♈	24♈	7♉	20♉	4♊	18♊	2♋	16♋
16	8♊	21♊	4♋	17♋	0♌	13♌	25♌	8♍	20♍	2♎	14♎	26♎	8♏	20♏	2♐
17	11♎	23♎	5♏	17♏	29♏	11♐	23♐	5♑	17♑	29♑	12♒	24♒	7♓	20♓	3♈
18	16♒	28♒	11♓	23♓	6♈	19♈	2♉	16♉	0♊	14♊	28♊	12♋	26♋	11♌	25♌
19	7♋	20♋	2♌	14♌	26♌	8♍	20♍	2♎	14♎	26♎	8♏	20♏	3♐	15♐	27♐
1920	28♏	10♐	22♐	4♑	16♑	28♑	10♒	22♒	4♓	17♓	0♈	13♈	26♈	10♉	25♉
21	1♈	13♈	26♈	8♉	22♉	5♊	19♊	3♋	17♋	1♌	16♌	0♍	14♍	28♍	12♎
22	8♌	22♌	6♍	20♍	4♎	19♎	4♏	18♏	3♐	15♐	28♐	8♑	20♑	11♒	23♒
23	28♐	13♑	27♑	11♒	25♒	6♓	18♓	0♈	12♈	24♈	6♉	18♉	0♊	12♊	24♊
24	19♉	1♊	13♊	25♊	6♋	18♋	0♌	12♌	24♌	7♍	20♍	3♎	17♎	1♏	16♏
25	20♍	3♎	16♎	29♎	12♏	26♏	9♐	22♐	5♑	18♑	1♒	14♒	27♒	10♓	22♓
26	0♒	13♒	27♒	10♓	23♓	6♈	19♈	2♉	15♉	28♉	12♊	25♊	8♋	21♋	5♌
27	19♊	3♋	16♋	29♋	12♌	25♌	7♍	19♍	2♎	14♎	26♎	8♏	20♏	2♐	14♐
28	9♏	21♏	3♐	15♐	26♐	8♑	20♑	2♒	15♒	27♒	10♓	23♓	7♈	22♈	6♉
29	10♓	23♓	6♈	19♈	3♉	17♉	1♊	16♊	1♋	16♋	0♌	14♌	29♌	12♍	26♍

MOON POSITIONS

	NOVEMBER					DECEMBER									
	26	27	28	29	30	1	2	3	4	5	6	7	8	9	10
1900	23♑	6♒	20♒	4♓	18♓	2♈	17♈	1♉	16♉	0♊	15♊	29♊	13♋	26♋	9♌
01	10♊	25♊	10♋	24♋	8♌	22♌	5♍	17♍	0♎	12♎	24♎	6♏	17♏	29♏	11♐
02	23♎	6♏	18♏	0♐	12♐	24♐	6♑	17♑	29♑	11♒	23♒	6♓	18♓	1♈	14♈
03	25♒	7♓	19♓	1♈	14♈	27♈	10♉	24♉	8♊	22♊	7♋	21♋	6♌	21♌	5♍
04	15♋	29♋	12♌	26♌	10♍	24♍	9♎	23♎	7♏	20♏	4♐	17♐	29♐	11♑	23♑
05	1♐	16♐	0♑	13♑	26♑	9♒	22♒	5♓	18♓	0♈	13♈	26♈	8♉	20♉	2♊
06	14♈	26♈	8♉	20♉	2♊	14♊	26♊	8♋	20♋	2♌	14♌	26♌	7♍	19♍	1♎
07	15♌	27♌	9♍	21♍	3♎	15♎	27♎	9♏	21♏	3♐	16♐	28♐	11♑	24♑	7♒
08	6♑	20♑	4♒	18♒	2♓	16♓	0♈	14♈	29♈	13♉	27♉	11♊	25♊	9♋	21♋
09	22♉	6♊	21♊	5♋	19♋	2♌	15♌	28♌	10♍	22♍	4♎	16♎	27♎	9♏	21♏
1910	5♎	17♎	29♎	11♏	23♏	4♐	16♐	28♐	10♑	22♑	5♒	17♒	0♓	13♓	26♓
11	5♒	17♒	29♒	11♓	24♓	7♈	20♈	4♉	19♉	4♊	19♊	4♋	19♋	4♌	18♌
12	28♊	12♋	27♋	11♌	25♌	9♍	23♍	7♎	21♎	4♏	18♏	1♐	14♐	26♐	9♑
13	13♏	27♏	11♐	25♐	9♑	22♑	5♒	17♒	29♒	11♓	23♓	5♈	17♈	29♈	11♉
14	25♓	7♈	19♈	1♉	13♉	25♉	7♊	19♊	1♋	13♋	26♋	8♌	21♌	4♍	18♍
15	25♋	7♌	19♌	1♍	13♍	25♍	7♎	19♎	1♏	13♏	26♏	8♐	21♐	4♑	18♑
16	19♐	4♑	18♑	3♒	17♒	1♓	15♓	29♓	13♈	26♈	9♉	22♉	4♊	17♊	29♊
17	4♉	18♉	2♊	16♊	29♊	12♋	25♋	7♌	19♌	1♍	13♍	25♍	7♎	19♎	1♏
18	15♏	27♏	9♐	21♐	3♑	15♑	27♑	9♒	21♒	4♓	17♓	0♈	13♈	26♈	10♉
19	15♑	27♑	9♒	22♒	5♓	18♓	2♈	16♈	0♉	15♉	0♊	15♊	0♋	16♋	0♌
1920	10♊	25♊	10♋	25♋	9♌	24♌	8♍	21♍	4♎	17♎	0♏	13♏	25♏	7♐	19♐
21	26♎	9♏	23♏	6♐	19♐	2♑	14♑	27♑	9♒	21♒	2♓	14♓	26♓	7♈	19♈
22	5♓	17♓	29♓	11♈	23♈	5♉	17♉	0♊	12♊	25♊	8♋	21♋	5♌	18♌	2♍
23	6♋	18♋	1♌	13♌	26♌	9♍	23♍	7♎	21♎	6♏	21♏	6♐	22♐	6♑	21♑
24	1♐	16♐	1♑	16♑	1♒	15♒	29♒	13♓	26♓	8♈	21♈	3♉	15♉	28♉	10♊
25	17♈	1♉	14♉	27♉	10♊	22♊	4♋	17♋	29♋	10♌	22♌	4♍	16♍	28♍	11♎
26	25♌	7♍	19♍	0♎	12♎	25♎	7♏	20♏	2♐	16♐	29♐	13♑	26♑	10♒	24♒
27	26♐	9♑	21♑	4♒	17♒	1♓	15♓	29♓	13♈	28♈	13♉	27♉	12♊	27♊	11♋
28	22♉	7♊	22♊	7♋	22♋	6♌	20♌	4♍	17♍	0♎	12♎	24♎	6♏	18♏	0♐
29	9♎	22♎	5♏	18♏	0♐	12♐	24♐	6♑	18♑	0♒	12♒	24♒	6♓	18♓	1♈

MOON POSITIONS

DECEMBER

Year	11	12	13	14	15	16	17	18	19	20	21	22	23	24	25
1900	22♌	4♍	16♍	28♍	10♎	22♎	4♏	16♏	28♏	10♐	23♐	6♑	20♑	3♒	17♒
01	23♐	5♑	17♑	0♒	12♒	25♒	8♓	21♓	5♈	19♈	3♉	18♉	3♊	18♊	3♋
02	28♈	12♉	27♉	12♊	27♊	13♋	28♋	13♌	27♌	11♍	25♍	8♎	20♎	3♏	15♏
03	19♍	3♎	16♎	29♎	13♏	26♏	8♐	21♐	3♑	15♑	28♑	10♒	22♒	3♓	15♓
04	12♎	24♎	7♏	19♏	2♐	14♐	27♐	9♑	22♑	5♒	17♒	29♒	12♓	24♓	7♈
05	13♋	25♋	8♌	20♌	3♍	15♍	28♍	10♎	23♎	5♏	18♏	0♐	13♐	25♐	8♑
06	19♎	1♏	14♏	26♏	9♐	21♐	4♑	16♑	29♑	11♒	24♒	6♓	19♓	2♈	14♈
07	11♓	23♓	6♈	18♈	1♉	13♉	26♉	8♊	21♊	3♋	16♋	28♋	11♌	23♌	6♍
08	1♌	13♌	26♌	8♍	21♍	3♎	16♎	28♎	11♏	23♏	6♐	18♐	1♑	13♑	26♑
09	4♐	16♐	29♐	11♑	24♑	6♒	19♒	1♓	14♓	26♓	9♈	21♈	4♉	16♉	29♉
1910	10♈	22♈	5♉	17♉	0♊	12♊	25♊	7♋	20♋	2♌	15♌	27♌	10♍	22♍	5♎
11	3♍	15♍	28♍	10♎	23♎	5♏	18♏	0♐	13♐	25♐	8♑	20♑	3♒	15♒	28♒
12	21♑	3♒	16♒	28♒	11♓	23♓	6♈	18♈	1♉	13♉	26♉	8♊	21♊	3♋	16♋
13	24♉	6♊	19♊	1♋	14♋	26♋	9♌	21♌	4♍	16♍	29♍	11♎	24♎	6♏	19♏
14	2♎	14♎	27♎	9♏	22♏	4♐	17♐	29♐	12♑	24♑	7♒	19♒	2♓	14♓	27♓
15	24♒	6♓	19♓	1♈	14♈	26♈	9♉	21♉	4♊	16♊	29♊	11♋	24♋	6♌	19♌
16	11♋	23♋	6♌	18♌	1♍	13♍	26♍	8♎	21♎	3♏	16♏	28♏	11♐	23♐	6♑
17	14♏	26♏	9♐	21♐	4♑	16♑	29♑	11♒	24♒	6♓	19♓	1♈	14♈	26♈	9♉
18	24♓	6♈	19♈	1♉	14♉	26♉	9♊	21♊	4♋	16♋	29♋	11♌	24♌	6♍	19♍
19	15♌	27♌	10♍	22♍	5♎	17♎	0♏	12♏	25♏	7♐	20♐	2♑	15♑	27♑	10♒
1920	1♑	13♑	26♑	8♒	21♒	3♓	16♓	28♓	11♈	23♈	6♉	18♉	1♊	13♊	26♊
21	3♉	15♉	28♉	10♊	23♊	5♋	18♋	0♌	13♌	25♌	8♍	20♍	3♎	15♎	28♎
22	16♍	28♍	11♎	23♎	6♏	18♏	1♐	13♐	26♐	8♑	21♑	3♒	16♒	28♒	11♓
23	5♒	17♒	0♓	12♓	25♓	7♈	20♈	2♉	15♉	27♉	10♊	22♊	5♋	17♋	0♌
24	21♊	3♋	16♋	28♋	11♌	23♌	6♍	18♍	1♎	13♎	26♎	8♏	21♏	3♐	16♐
25	23♎	5♏	18♏	0♐	13♐	25♐	8♑	20♑	3♒	15♒	28♒	10♓	23♓	5♈	18♈
26	8♓	20♓	3♈	15♈	28♈	10♉	23♉	5♊	18♊	0♋	13♋	25♋	8♌	20♌	3♍
27	25♋	7♌	20♌	2♍	15♍	27♍	10♎	22♎	5♏	17♏	0♐	12♐	25♐	7♑	20♑
28	12♐	24♐	7♑	19♑	2♒	14♒	27♒	9♓	22♓	4♈	17♈	29♈	12♉	24♉	7♊
29	13♈	25♈	8♉	20♉	3♊	15♊	28♊	10♋	23♋	5♌	18♌	0♍	13♍	25♍	8♎

MOON POSITIONS

DECEMBER

	26	27	28	29	30	31
1900	1♓	15♓	29♓	13♈	27♈	11♉
01	18♋	2♌	16♌	0♍	13♍	26♍
02	27♏	9♐	21♐	3♑	14♑	26♑
03	27♓	9♈	22♈	4♉	18♉	1♊
04	23♌	7♍	21♍	5♎	19♎	3♏
05	9♑	23♑	7♒	20♒	3♓	16♓
06	17♉	29♉	11♊	23♊	5♋	17♋
07	17♍	29♍	12♎	25♎	8♏	22♏
08	14♒	29♒	13♓	28♓	12♈	26♈
09	29♊	13♋	26♋	10♌	23♌	5♍
1910	8♏	19♏	1♐	13♐	25♐	7♑
11	7♓	20♓	2♈	15♈	29♈	12♉
12	6♌	21♌	6♍	20♍	4♎	18♎
13	20♐	4♑	17♑	0♒	13♒	25♒
14	27♈	9♉	21♉	3♊	15♊	27♊
15	28♌	10♍	23♍	6♎	20♎	4♏
16	27♑	12♒	27♒	12♓	26♓	9♈
17	11♊	24♊	7♋	20♋	2♌	15♌
18	17♎	29♎	11♏	23♏	5♐	17♐
19	19♒	2♓	15♓	28♓	11♈	25♈
1920	18♋	4♌	19♌	3♍	17♍	1♎
21	2♐	15♐	28♐	10♑	23♑	5♒
22	7♈	18♈	0♉	12♉	25♉	7♊
23	10♌	23♌	6♍	19♍	3♎	17♎
24	9♑	25♑	9♒	24♒	8♓	22♓
25	24♉	6♊	19♊	1♋	13♋	25♋
26	26♍	8♎	20♎	2♏	15♏	27♏
27	1♒	14♒	28♒	11♓	25♓	9♈
28	0♋	15♋	0♌	15♌	29♌	12♍
29	15♏	27♏	9♐	21♐	3♑	15♑

MOON POSITIONS

JANUARY

	1	2	3	4	5	6	7	8	9	10	11	12	13	14	15
1930	27♑	9♒	21♒	2♓	14♓	27♓	9♈	22♈	5♉	19♉	3♊	17♊	2♋	17♋	3♌
31	0♊	14♊	28♊	12♋	27♋	12♌	27♌	12♍	26♍	10♎	24♎	7♏	21♏	4♐	17♐
32	16♎	0♏	14♏	28♏	12♐	26♐	10♑	23♑	7♒	20♒	2♓	14♓	26♓	8♈	20♈
33	16♓	28♓	11♈	23♈	5♉	16♉	28♉	10♊	22♊	4♋	17♋	29♋	12♌	25♌	8♍
34	17♋	29♋	11♌	23♌	5♍	17♍	0♎	13♎	26♎	10♏	24♏	8♐	23♐	8♑	24♑
35	21♏	4♐	19♐	3♑	18♑	3♒	18♒	3♓	17♓	2♈	16♈	29♈	12♉	25♉	8♊
36	8♈	22♈	6♉	20♉	4♊	17♊	1♋	14♋	27♋	9♌	22♌	4♍	16♍	28♍	10♎
37	6♍	18♍	1♎	13♎	25♎	6♏	18♏	0♐	12♐	24♐	7♑	20♑	2♒	16♒	29♒
38	7♑	19♑	1♒	13♒	26♒	8♓	21♓	4♈	17♈	1♉	15♉	0♊	14♊	29♊	14♋
39	11♉	24♉	9♊	24♊	9♋	24♋	9♌	24♌	9♍	23♍	7♎	21♎	4♏	16♏	29♏
1940	1♎	15♎	29♎	12♏	25♏	9♐	22♐	5♑	17♑	0♒	12♒	24♒	6♓	18♓	0♈
41	25♒	8♓	20♓	2♈	14♈	26♈	8♉	20♉	2♊	14♊	27♊	10♋	23♋	7♌	21♌
42	28♒	10♓	22♓	4♈	17♈	0♉	13♉	26♉	9♊	23♊	7♋	21♋	6♌	21♌	6♍
43	1♏	15♏	0♐	15♐	0♑	15♑	0♒	15♒	0♓	14♓	28♓	12♈	25♈	7♉	20♉
44	23♓	7♈	20♈	4♉	17♉	0♊	13♊	25♊	8♋	20♋	2♌	14♌	26♌	8♍	19♍
45	15♌	28♌	10♍	22♍	4♎	15♎	27♎	9♏	22♏	4♐	17♐	0♑	14♑	28♑	12♒
46	18♐	0♑	12♑	25♑	8♒	21♒	4♓	17♓	1♈	15♈	29♈	13♉	28♉	12♊	27♊
47	22♈	6♉	21♉	5♊	20♊	5♋	21♋	6♌	20♌	5♍	19♍	2♎	15♎	28♎	10♏
48	15♍	29♍	12♎	26♎	9♏	21♏	4♐	16♐	28♐	10♑	22♑	4♒	16♒	28♒	10♓
49	5♏	17♏	0♐	11♐	23♐	5♑	17♑	29♑	11♒	24♒	7♓	20♓	4♈	18♈	3♉
1950	8♊	20♊	3♋	16♋	29♋	12♌	26♌	10♍	24♍	7♎	22♎	6♏	20♏	4♐	18♐
51	14♐	28♐	12♑	27♑	11♒	27♒	12♓	27♓	11♈	25♈	9♉	22♉	5♊	18♊	0♋
52	6♓	20♓	4♈	17♈	0♉	12♉	25♉	7♊	19♊	1♋	13♋	24♋	6♌	18♌	0♍
53	25♋	7♌	19♌	1♍	13♍	25♍	7♎	19♎	1♏	14♏	27♏	11♐	25♐	9♑	24♑
54	28♏	10♐	23♐	6♑	20♑	3♒	17♒	1♓	15♓	0♈	14♈	28♈	12♉	26♉	10♊
55	6♈	20♈	4♉	18♉	3♊	18♊	2♋	17♋	1♌	15♌	29♌	12♍	25♍	8♎	20♎
56	27♌	11♍	25♍	8♎	21♎	3♏	15♏	27♏	9♐	21♐	3♑	14♑	26♑	8♒	20♒
57	15♑	27♑	9♒	21♒	3♓	15♓	27♓	9♈	21♈	4♉	17♉	1♊	15♊	29♊	14♋
58	17♉	0♊	13♊	26♊	10♋	24♋	9♌	23♌	8♍	22♍	7♎	21♎	5♏	18♏	2♐
59	28♍	12♎	26♎	10♏	25♏	9♐	24♐	8♑	22♑	6♒	19♒	2♓	15♓	27♓	9♈

MOON POSITIONS

JANUARY

Year	16	17	18	19	20	21	22	23	24	25	26	27	28	29	30
1930	18♌	3♍	18♍	2♎	16♎	29♎	11♏	24♏	6♐	18♐	0♑	12♑	24♑	6♒	18♒
31	29♐	12♑	24♑	7♒	19♒	1♓	12♓	24♓	6♈	18♈	0♉	12♉	25♉	8♊	22♊
32	2♉	14♉	26♉	8♊	21♊	4♋	18♋	1♌	15♌	0♍	14♍	28♍	12♎	27♎	11♏
33	21♍	4♎	18♎	2♏	16♏	1♐	15♐	0♑	14♑	29♑	13♒	27♒	10♓	23♓	6♈
34	9♒	24♒	8♓	22♓	6♈	19♈	2♉	14♉	27♉	9♊	20♊	2♋	14♋	26♋	8♌
35	20♊	3♋	15♋	27♋	9♌	21♌	2♍	14♍	26♍	8♎	20♎	3♏	16♏	29♏	12♐
36	22♎	4♏	16♏	28♏	11♐	24♐	8♑	22♑	6♒	20♒	5♓	20♓	4♈	19♈	3♉
37	13♓	27♓	11♈	25♈	9♉	23♉	7♊	21♊	6♋	20♋	3♌	17♌	0♍	13♍	26♍
38	29♋	14♌	29♌	13♍	26♍	10♎	22♎	5♏	17♏	29♏	10♐	22♐	4♑	16♑	28♑
39	11♐	23♐	5♑	17♑	29♑	11♒	23♒	5♓	17♓	29♓	11♈	23♈	6♉	19♉	3♊
1940	11♈	23♈	5♉	18♉	1♊	14♊	28♊	12♋	27♋	12♌	27♌	12♍	27♍	11♎	25♎
41	5♍	19♍	3♎	17♎	1♏	15♏	29♏	13♐	27♐	11♑	24♑	8♒	21♒	3♓	16♓
42	20♑	5♒	19♒	3♓	16♓	29♓	12♈	24♈	6♉	18♉	0♊	12♊	24♊	6♋	18♋
43	2♊	14♊	26♊	7♋	19♋	1♌	13♌	25♌	7♍	19♍	2♎	14♎	27♎	11♏	24♏
44	1♎	13♎	26♎	8♏	21♏	5♐	18♐	3♑	17♑	2♒	18♒	3♓	18♓	2♈	17♈
45	26♒	11♓	25♓	9♈	24♈	8♉	22♉	5♊	19♊	2♋	15♋	28♋	11♌	23♌	6♍
46	11♋	25♋	9♌	23♌	6♍	19♍	2♎	14♎	26♎	8♏	20♏	2♐	14♐	26♐	8♑
47	22♏	4♐	16♐	27♐	9♑	21♑	3♒	15♒	28♒	10♓	23♓	6♈	19♈	2♉	16♉
48	22♌	4♍	16♍	29♍	11♎	25♎	9♏	23♏	8♐	23♐	8♑	24♑	9♒	24♒	8♓
49	18♌	3♍	17♍	2♎	16♎	0♏	14♏	27♏	10♐	23♐	6♑	19♑	1♒	14♒	26♒
1950	2♑	16♑	0♒	13♒	26♒	9♓	22♓	4♈	16♈	27♈	9♉	21♉	3♊	15♊	28♊
51	12♉	24♉	6♊	17♊	29♊	12♋	24♋	6♌	19♌	1♍	14♍	27♍	11♎	24♎	8♏
52	12♍	24♍	7♎	19♎	2♏	16♏	0♐	14♐	29♐	14♑	29♑	15♒	0♓	14♓	29♓
53	9♒	24♒	9♓	23♓	8♈	22♈	5♉	19♉	2♊	15♊	27♊	10♋	22♋	4♌	16♌
54	24♊	7♋	21♋	4♌	16♌	29♌	11♍	23♍	5♎	17♎	29♎	11♏	23♏	5♐	18♐
55	2♏	14♏	26♏	7♐	19♐	1♑	14♑	26♑	9♒	22♒	5♓	19♓	3♈	17♈	1♉
56	3♓	15♓	28♓	11♈	24♈	7♉	21♉	5♊	19♊	6♋	20♋	5♌	20♌	5♍	19♍
57	29♋	15♌	0♍	15♍	29♍	14♎	27♎	10♏	23♏	6♐	18♐	0♑	12♑	24♑	6♒
58	15♐	28♐	11♑	24♑	7♒	19♒	1♓	13♓	25♓	7♈	19♈	1♉	13♉	25♉	8♊
59	21♈	3♉	15♉	27♉	9♊	21♊	4♋	17♋	0♌	13♌	27♌	11♍	25♍	9♎	23♎

MOON POSITIONS

JANUARY/FEBRUARY

	31	1	2	3	4	5	6	7	8	9	10	11	12	13	14
1930	0♓	12♓	24♓	6♈	18♈	1♉	14♉	28♉	11♊	26♊	11♋	26♋	11♌	26♌	11♍
31	6♋	20♋	5♌	21♌	6♍	21♍	6♎	20♎	4♏	18♏	1♐	14♐	27♐	9♑	21♑
32	25♏	9♐	22♐	6♑	19♑	2♒	15♒	28♒	10♓	22♓	4♈	16♈	28♈	10♉	22♉
33	19♈	1♉	13♉	25♉	6♊	18♊	0♋	13♋	25♋	8♌	21♌	4♍	18♍	1♎	15♎
34	20♌	2♍	14♍	27♍	10♎	23♎	6♏	19♏	3♐	18♐	2♑	17♑	2♒	17♒	2♓
35	27♐	11♑	26♑	11♒	26♒	11♓	26♓	11♈	25♈	9♉	22♉	5♊	18♊	0♋	12♋
36	17♉	1♊	14♊	27♊	10♋	23♋	6♌	18♌	0♍	12♍	24♍	6♎	18♎	0♏	12♏
37	8♎	20♎	2♏	14♏	26♏	8♐	20♐	2♑	15♑	28♑	11♒	25♒	9♓	23♓	7♈
38	10♒	23♒	5♓	18♓	1♈	14♈	26♈	11♉	25♉	9♊	24♊	8♋	23♋	8♌	22♌
39	17♊	2♋	17♋	2♌	17♌	3♍	18♍	2♎	16♎	0♏	13♏	26♏	8♐	20♐	2♑
1940	9♏	22♏	6♐	19♐	1♑	14♑	26♑	8♒	21♒	2♓	14♓	26♓	8♈	20♈	2♉
41	28♓	10♈	22♈	4♉	15♉	27♉	10♊	22♊	5♋	18♋	2♌	16♌	0♍	14♍	29♍
42	1♌	13♌	26♌	9♍	23♍	6♎	20♎	4♏	18♏	2♐	16♐	0♑	15♑	29♑	13♒
43	9♐	23♐	8♑	23♑	8♒	23♒	8♓	22♓	6♈	20♈	3♉	16♉	28♉	10♊	22♊
44	1♉	14♉	27♉	10♊	22♊	5♋	17♋	29♋	11♌	23♌	4♍	16♍	28♍	10♎	22♎
45	18♍	0♎	12♎	23♎	5♏	17♏	0♐	12♐	25♐	8♑	22♑	6♒	20♒	5♓	20♓
46	21♑	4♒	17♒	0♓	14♓	26♓	11♈	26♈	10♉	24♉	8♊	22♊	6♋	20♋	4♌
47	0♊	14♊	29♊	14♋	29♋	14♌	28♌	13♍	27♍	10♎	23♎	6♏	18♏	0♐	12♐
48	22♎	5♏	18♏	1♐	13♐	25♐	7♑	19♑	1♒	13♒	25♒	7♓	19♓	1♈	13♈
49	8♓	20♓	1♈	13♈	25♈	7♉	19♉	2♊	15♊	28♊	12♋	26♋	11♌	26♌	11♍
1950	11♋	24♋	8♌	21♌	6♍	20♍	4♎	18♎	2♏	17♏	1♐	15♐	28♐	12♑	26♑
51	22♏	6♐	21♐	6♑	20♑	5♒	19♒	3♓	17♓	0♈	13♈	26♈	8♉	20♉	2♊
52	12♈	26♈	9♉	21♉	4♊	16♊	28♊	10♋	21♋	3♌	15♌	27♌	9♍	21♍	4♎
53	28♌	10♍	21♍	3♎	15♎	27♎	10♏	22♏	5♐	19♐	2♑	17♑	2♒	17♒	2♓
54	1♑	14♑	28♑	12♒	26♒	11♓	26♓	10♈	25♈	9♉	23♉	7♊	20♊	4♋	17♋
55	15♉	29♉	13♊	27♊	11♋	26♋	10♌	23♌	7♍	20♍	3♎	15♎	28♎	10♏	22♏
56	3♎	16♎	29♎	12♏	24♏	6♐	18♐	29♐	11♑	23♑	5♒	17♒	0♓	12♓	25♓
57	18♒	0♓	12♓	24♓	6♈	18♈	0♉	13♉	26♉	9♊	23♊	7♋	22♋	7♌	23♌
58	21♊	4♋	18♋	3♌	17♌	2♍	17♍	2♎	17♎	1♏	15♏	29♏	12♐	25♐	8♑
59	7♏	21♏	5♐	19♐	3♑	17♑	1♒	14♒	27♒	10♓	23♓	5♈	17♈	29♈	11♉

MOON POSITIONS

FEBRUARY

Year	15	16	17	18	19	20	21	22	23	24	25	26	27	28	29
1930	26♏	10♎	24♎	7♏	20♏	3♐	15♐	27♐	9♑	21♑	3♒	14♒	26♒	8♓	
31	3♒	15♒	27♒	9♓	21♓	3♈	15♈	27♈	9♊	21♉	4♊	17♊	0♋	14♋	
32	4♊	16♊	29♊	12♋	26♋	9♌	24♌	8♍	23♍	8♎	22♎	7♏	21♏	5♐	19♐
33	29♎	13♏	27♏	11♐	26♐	10♑	24♑	8♒	22♒	5♓	18♓	1♈	14♈	26♈	
34	16♓	0♈	14♈	27♈	10♉	23♉	5♊	17♊	29♊	11♋	22♋	4♌	16♌	29♌	
35	24♋	6♌	17♌	29♌	11♍	23♍	5♎	17♎	29♎	12♏	25♏	8♐	21♐	5♑	
36	24♏	6♐	19♐	2♑	16♑	0♒	14♒	29♒	14♓	29♓	14♈	29♈	13♉	27♉	11♊
37	21♈	6♉	20♉	4♊	18♊	2♋	15♋	29♋	12♌	26♌	9♍	21♍	4♎	16♎	
38	7♏	21♏	4♎	17♎	0♏	13♏	25♏	7♐	18♐	0♑	12♑	24♑	6♒	19♒	
39	14♑	26♑	8♒	20♒	2♓	14♓	26♓	8♈	20♈	3♉	16♉	29♉	12♊	26♊	
1940	14♉	26♉	9♊	22♊	6♋	20♋	5♌	20♌	5♍	20♍	5♎	20♎	5♏	19♏	2♐
41	13♎	28♎	12♏	26♏	10♐	24♐	7♑	21♑	4♒	17♒	29♒	12♓	24♓	6♈	
42	27♒	11♓	24♓	7♈	20♈	2♉	14♉	26♉	8♊	20♊	2♋	14♋	26♋	9♌	
43	4♋	16♋	28♋	10♌	22♌	4♍	16♍	29♍	11♎	24♎	7♏	21♏	5♐	19♐	
44	4♏	17♏	0♐	13♐	27♐	11♑	25♑	10♒	25♒	11♓	26♓	11♈	25♈	10♉	23♉
45	5♈	20♈	4♉	18♉	2♊	16♊	29♊	12♋	25♋	7♌	20♌	2♍	14♍	26♍	
46	18♌	1♍	14♍	27♍	10♎	22♎	4♏	16♏	28♏	10♐	21♐	4♑	16♑	29♑	
47	24♐	6♑	18♑	0♒	12♒	24♒	7♓	20♓	3♈	16♈	29♈	13♉	27♉	11♊	
48	25♈	8♉	21♉	4♊	18♊	1♋	16♋	1♌	16♌	2♍	17♍	2♎	16♎	0♏	14♏
49	26♍	11♎	26♎	10♏	24♏	7♐	20♐	3♑	16♑	28♑	10♒	23♒	5♓	16♓	
1950	9♒	22♒	5♓	17♓	29♓	12♈	23♈	5♉	17♉	29♉	11♊	23♊	6♋	19♋	
51	14♊	26♊	8♋	20♋	2♌	15♌	27♌	11♍	24♍	7♎	21♎	5♏	19♏	3♐	
52	16♎	29♎	12♏	26♏	9♐	24♐	8♑	23♑	8♒	23♒	7♓	22♓	6♈	20♈	4♉
53	17♓	2♈	17♈	1♉	15♉	29♉	12♊	24♊	7♋	19♋	1♌	13♌	25♌	6♍	
54	0♌	12♌	25♌	7♍	19♍	1♎	13♎	25♎	7♏	19♏	1♐	13♐	26♐	9♑	
55	3♐	15♐	27♐	9♑	22♑	5♒	18♒	1♓	15♓	29♓	13♈	27♈	11♉	26♉	
56	8♈	21♈	4♉	17♉	1♊	15♊	29♊	14♋	29♋	13♌	28♌	13♍	27♍	11♎	24♎
57	8♍	23♍	8♎	22♎	6♏	20♏	2♐	15♐	27♐	9♑	21♑	3♒	15♒	27♒	
58	21♑	3♒	15♒	28♒	10♓	22♓	3♈	15♈	27♈	9♉	21♉	3♊	16♊	29♊	
59	23♉	5♊	17♊	29♊	12♋	25♋	8♌	22♌	6♍	20♍	5♎	19♎	3♏	18♏	

MOON POSITIONS

MARCH

Year	1	2	3	4	5	6	7	8	9	10	11	12	13	14	15
1930	21♓	3♈	16♈	28♈	11♉	24♉	8♊	21♊	6♋	20♋	5♌	20♌	4♍	19♍	4♎
1931	29♋	13♌	29♌	14♍	29♍	14♎	29♎	13♏	27♏	10♐	23♐	6♑	18♑	0♒	12♒
1932	3♑	16♑	29♑	12♒	24♒	7♓	19♓	1♈	13♈	24♈	6♉	18♉	0♊	12♊	24♊
1933	8♉	20♉	2♊	14♊	26♊	8♋	20♋	3♌	16♌	29♌	13♍	26♍	11♎	25♎	9♏
1934	11♍	24♍	6♎	20♎	3♏	16♏	0♐	14♐	28♐	12♑	27♑	11♒	26♒	10♓	24♓
1935	19♑	4♒	19♒	4♓	20♓	5♈	19♈	4♉	18♉	1♊	14♊	26♊	9♋	21♋	3♌
1936	24♊	7♋	20♋	2♌	15♌	27♌	9♍	21♍	3♎	15♎	27♎	8♏	20♏	3♐	15♐
1937	28♎	10♏	22♏	4♐	16♐	28♐	10♑	23♑	6♒	19♒	3♓	17♓	2♈	17♈	1♉
1938	1♓	14♓	28♓	11♈	25♈	8♉	22♉	6♊	20♊	4♋	18♋	3♌	17♌	1♍	15♍
1939	11♋	25♋	10♌	25♌	11♍	25♍	10♎	24♎	8♏	21♏	4♐	17♐	29♐	11♑	23♑
1940	16♐	28♐	11♑	23♑	6♒	18♒	29♒	11♓	23♓	5♈	17♈	29♈	11♉	23♉	5♊
1941	18♈	0♉	12♉	23♉	5♊	18♊	0♋	13♋	26♋	9♌	24♌	8♍	23♍	8♎	23♎
1942	22♌	5♍	18♍	2♎	16♎	0♏	14♏	29♏	13♐	27♐	11♑	25♑	9♒	23♒	6♓
1943	3♑	17♑	2♒	17♒	1♓	16♓	0♈	14♈	28♈	11♉	24♉	6♊	19♊	1♋	12♋
1944	7♊	19♊	2♋	14♋	26♋	8♌	20♌	1♍	13♍	25♍	7♎	19♎	1♏	14♏	27♏
1945	8♎	20♎	2♏	14♏	26♏	8♐	20♐	3♑	16♑	0♒	14♒	28♒	13♓	28♓	14♈
1946	12♌	26♌	10♍	24♍	8♎	22♎	6♏	20♏	4♐	18♐	2♑	16♑	0♒	14♒	27♒
1947	25♊	8♋	22♋	5♌	18♌	2♍	15♍	29♍	12♎	25♎	8♏	22♏	5♐	18♐	2♑
1948	27♏	9♐	22♐	4♑	17♑	29♑	11♒	23♒	5♓	17♓	29♓	11♈	23♈	5♉	18♉
1949	28♓	11♈	25♈	8♉	21♉	5♊	18♊	1♋	15♋	28♋	11♌	25♌	8♍	21♍	5♎
1950	2♌	25♌	9♍	22♍	6♎	19♎	3♏	16♏	0♐	13♐	27♐	10♑	24♑	7♒	18♒
1951	17♐	0♑	13♑	27♑	10♒	23♒	6♓	20♓	3♈	16♈	29♈	13♉	26♉	9♊	22♊
1952	17♉	29♉	11♊	24♊	6♋	18♋	0♌	13♌	25♌	7♍	20♍	2♎	14♎	27♎	9♏
1953	18♓	1♈	15♈	28♈	11♉	25♉	8♊	21♊	5♋	18♋	1♌	15♌	28♌	11♍	25♍
1954	22♑	6♒	20♒	4♓	18♓	2♈	16♈	0♉	14♉	28♉	12♊	26♊	10♋	24♋	8♌
1955	10♊	23♊	6♋	19♋	2♌	15♌	28♌	11♍	24♍	7♎	20♎	3♏	16♏	29♏	11♐
1956	7♏	19♏	2♐	14♐	27♐	9♑	21♑	4♒	16♒	28♒	11♓	23♓	6♈	18♈	1♉
1957	9♓	22♓	6♈	19♈	3♉	16♉	0♊	13♊	27♊	10♋	23♋	7♌	20♌	3♍	16♍
1958	12♋	26♋	10♌	24♌	8♍	23♍	7♎	21♎	5♏	20♏	4♐	18♐	2♑	16♑	0♒
1959	2♐	15♐	28♐	11♑	23♑	6♒	19♒	2♓	15♓	27♓	10♈	23♈	6♉	18♉	1♊

MOON POSITIONS

MARCH	16	17	18	19	20	21	22	23	24	25	26	27	28	29	30
1930	18♎	2♏	15♏	28♏	11♐	23♐	5♑	17♑	29♑	11♒	23♒	5♓	17♓	29♓	12♈
31	24♒	6♓	18♓	0♈	12♈	24♈	6♉	18♉	0♊	13♊	26♊	9♋	23♋	7♌	22♌
32	7♋	20♋	3♌	17♌	2♍	16♍	1♎	16♎	2♏	16♏	1♐	15♐	29♐	13♑	26♑
33	24♏	8♐	22♐	7♑	20♑	4♒	18♒	1♓	14♓	27♓	10♈	22♈	4♉	16♉	28♉
34	8♈	22♈	5♉	18♉	1♊	13♊	25♊	7♋	19♋	0♌	12♌	25♌	7♍	19♍	2♎
35	14♌	26♌	8♍	20♍	2♎	14♎	27♎	9♏	22♏	5♐	18♐	1♑	15♑	29♑	13♒
36	27♐	10♑	24♑	8♒	22♒	7♓	22♓	7♈	23♈	8♉	22♉	7♊	21♊	4♋	17♋
37	16♉	0♊	15♊	29♊	12♋	26♋	9♌	22♌	5♍	18♍	0♎	12♎	25♎	7♏	18♏
38	29♍	12♎	25♎	8♏	20♏	3♐	14♐	26♐	8♑	20♑	2♒	14♒	27♒	10♓	23♓
39	4♒	16♒	28♒	10♓	22♓	5♈	17♈	0♉	13♉	26♉	9♊	23♊	7♋	21♋	5♌
1940	18♊	1♋	15♋	29♋	13♌	28♌	13♍	28♍	13♎	28♎	13♏	27♏	11♐	25♐	8♑
41	7♏	22♏	6♐	21♐	4♑	18♑	1♒	14♒	26♒	8♓	21♓	3♈	15♈	26♈	8♉
42	19♓	2♈	15♈	28♈	10♉	22♉	4♊	16♊	28♊	10♋	22♋	4♌	17♌	0♍	13♍
43	24♋	6♌	18♌	0♍	12♍	25♍	8♎	21♎	4♏	18♏	2♐	15♐	29♐	13♑	28♑
44	9♐	23♐	6♑	20♑	4♒	19♒	4♓	19♓	4♈	19♈	4♉	18♉	2♊	15♊	28♊
45	29♈	14♉	28♉	12♊	26♊	9♋	22♋	4♌	17♌	29♌	11♍	23♍	5♎	17♎	29♎
46	10♍	23♍	5♎	18♎	0♏	12♏	24♏	6♐	17♐	29♐	11♑	24♑	6♒	20♒	3♓
47	14♑	26♑	8♒	20♒	3♓	16♓	29♓	12♈	26♈	10♉	23♉	7♊	22♊	6♋	20♋
48	1♊	14♊	28♊	12♋	26♋	10♌	25♌	10♍	25♍	10♎	24♎	8♏	22♏	5♐	18♐
49	20♎	5♏	19♏	3♐	17♐	0♑	13♑	25♑	8♒	20♒	2♓	13♓	25♓	7♈	19♈
1950	1♓	14♓	26♓	8♈	20♈	2♉	14♉	25♉	7♊	19♊	1♋	14♋	27♋	10♌	24♌
51	3♋	15♋	28♋	10♌	23♌	6♍	19♍	3♎	17♎	1♏	15♏	0♐	14♐	28♐	12♑
52	23♏	6♐	20♐	4♑	18♑	2♒	17♒	1♓	16♓	0♈	14♈	28♈	12♉	25♉	8♊
53	10♈	25♈	10♉	24♉	8♊	21♊	3♋	16♋	28♋	10♌	22♌	3♍	15♍	27♍	9♎
54	22♌	4♍	16♍	28♍	10♎	22♎	4♏	16♏	28♏	10♐	22♐	4♑	17♑	0♒	14♒
55	23♐	5♑	17♑	0♒	12♒	26♒	9♓	23♓	8♈	22♈	7♉	22♉	6♊	21♊	5♋
56	14♉	28♉	12♊	26♊	10♋	24♋	9♌	23♌	7♍	21♍	5♎	19♎	2♏	15♏	27♏
57	1♎	16♎	0♏	14♏	28♏	11♐	24♐	6♑	18♑	0♒	12♒	24♒	5♓	17♓	0♈
58	13♒	25♒	7♓	19♓	0♈	12♈	24♈	6♉	18♉	0♊	12♊	25♊	8♋	21♋	5♌
59	13♊	25♊	7♋	20♋	3♌	16♌	0♍	14♍	28♍	13♎	28♎	13♏	28♏	12♐	27♐

MOON POSITIONS

MARCH/APRIL	31	1	2	3	4	5	6	7	8	9	10	11	12	13	14
1930	25♈	8♉	21♉	5♊	18♊	2♋	16♋	1♌	15♌	29♌	14♍	28♍	12♎	26♎	10♏
31	7♍	22♍	7♎	22♎	7♏	21♏	5♐	19♐	2♑	15♑	27♑	9♒	21♒	3♓	15♓
32	9♒	21♒	4♓	16♓	28♓	9♈	21♈	3♉	15♉	27♉	9♊	21♊	3♋	16♋	29♋
33	10♊	22♊	4♋	16♋	28♋	11♌	24♌	7♍	21♍	5♎	19♎	4♏	19♏	4♐	19♐
34	16♎	29♎	13♏	27♏	11♐	25♐	9♑	23♑	7♒	21♒	5♓	19♓	3♈	17♈	0♉
35	28♒	13♓	28♓	13♈	27♈	12♉	26♉	9♊	22♊	5♋	17♋	29♋	11♌	23♌	5♍
36	29♋	12♌	24♌	6♍	18♍	0♎	12♎	24♎	5♏	17♏	29♏	12♐	24♐	7♑	20♑
37	0♐	12♐	24♐	6♑	18♑	1♒	14♒	27♒	11♓	25♓	10♈	25♈	10♉	25♉	10♊
38	6♈	20♈	4♉	18♉	3♊	17♊	1♋	15♋	29♋	13♌	27♌	11♍	24♍	8♎	21♎
39	20♌	5♍	19♍	4♎	18♎	2♏	16♏	29♏	12♐	24♐	7♑	19♑	1♒	13♒	24♒
1940	20♑	2♒	15♒	26♒	8♓	20♓	2♈	14♈	26♈	8♉	20♉	2♊	15♊	28♊	11♋
41	20♉	2♊	14♊	26♊	8♋	21♋	4♌	18♌	2♍	16♍	1♎	16♎	1♏	16♏	1♐
42	27♍	11♎	25♎	10♏	24♏	9♐	24♐	8♑	22♑	6♒	19♒	3♓	16♓	28♓	11♈
43	12♒	26♒	10♓	25♓	9♈	22♈	6♉	19♉	2♊	14♊	26♊	8♋	20♋	2♌	14♌
44	10♋	23♋	5♌	17♌	29♌	10♍	22♍	4♎	16♎	28♎	11♏	24♏	6♐	20♐	3♑
45	11♏	22♏	4♐	17♐	29♐	11♑	25♑	8♒	22♒	7♓	21♓	7♈	22♈	7♉	22♉
46	17♓	2♈	16♈	1♉	16♉	1♊	16♊	0♋	14♋	27♋	11♌	24♌	7♍	20♍	2♎
47	4♌	18♌	2♍	16♍	0♎	13♎	26♎	9♏	22♏	4♐	16♐	28♐	10♑	22♑	4♒
48	0♐	12♐	24♐	6♑	18♑	0♒	12♒	24♒	6♓	19♓	2♈	15♈	28♈	11♉	24♉
49	1♉	13♉	25♉	7♊	20♊	3♋	16♋	29♋	13♌	28♌	13♍	28♍	13♎	28♎	13♏
1950	8♍	22♍	7♎	22♎	7♏	22♏	7♐	21♐	6♑	19♑	3♒	15♒	28♒	11♓	23♓
51	26♑	10♒	24♒	7♓	21♓	4♈	16♈	29♈	11♉	24♉	6♊	18♊	29♊	11♋	23♋
52	20♊	2♋	14♋	26♋	8♌	20♌	2♍	14♍	26♍	9♎	22♎	5♏	19♏	3♐	17♐
53	21♎	3♏	16♏	28♏	11♐	24♐	7♑	21♑	5♒	19♒	4♓	19♓	4♈	19♈	3♉
54	28♒	13♓	28♓	13♈	28♈	13♉	28♉	13♊	27♊	10♋	24♋	6♌	19♌	1♍	13♍
55	18♋	2♌	15♌	29♌	12♍	24♍	7♎	19♎	2♏	14♏	26♏	8♐	19♐	1♑	13♑
56	10♐	22♐	4♑	15♑	27♑	9♒	21♒	4♓	17♓	0♈	13♈	27♈	10♉	24♉	9♊
57	12♈	24♈	7♉	19♉	2♊	16♊	29♊	13♋	27♋	11♌	26♌	10♍	25♍	10♎	24♎
58	19♌	4♍	19♍	4♎	19♎	4♏	19♏	4♐	18♐	1♑	14♑	27♑	9♒	22♒	4♓
59	10♑	24♑	7♒	20♒	3♓	15♓	28♓	10♈	22♈	4♉	16♉	27♉	9♊	21♊	3♋

MOON POSITIONS

APRIL

	15	16	17	18	19	20	21	22	23	24	25	26	27	28	29
1930	23♏	6♐	19♐	1♑	13♑	25♑	7♒	19♒	1♓	13♓	25♓	8♈	21♈	4♉	17♉
31	27♓	9♈	20♈	3♉	15♉	27♉	10♊	23♊	6♋	20♋	3♌	17♌	2♍	16♍	1♎
32	12♎	26♎	10♏	24♏	9♐	25♐	10♑	25♑	10♒	25♒	9♓	22♓	5♈	18♈	1♉
33	3♑	17♑	1♒	15♒	28♒	11♓	24♓	6♈	19♈	1♉	13♉	25♉	7♊	19♊	1♋
34	13♉	26♉	8♊	21♊	3♋	15♋	26♋	8♌	20♌	2♍	15♍	28♍	11♎	24♎	8♏
35	16♍	28♍	11♎	23♎	6♏	19♏	2♐	15♐	28♐	12♑	26♑	9♒	24♒	8♓	22♓
36	3♒	17♒	1♓	15♓	0♈	16♈	1♉	16♉	1♊	15♊	29♊	13♋	26♋	8♌	21♌
37	25♊	9♋	23♋	6♌	19♌	2♍	15♍	27♍	9♎	21♎	3♏	15♏	27♏	9♐	21♐
38	4♏	16♏	28♏	10♐	22♐	4♑	16♑	28♑	10♒	22♒	5♓	18♓	1♈	15♈	29♈
39	6♓	19♓	1♈	13♈	26♈	9♉	23♉	6♊	20♊	4♋	18♋	2♌	16♌	0♍	15♍
1940	24♋	8♌	22♌	7♍	22♍	7♎	22♎	6♏	21♏	5♐	19♐	3♑	16♑	29♑	11♒
41	16♐	0♑	14♑	28♑	11♒	23♒	6♓	18♓	0♈	12♈	23♈	5♉	17♉	29♉	11♊
42	24♈	6♉	18♉	0♊	12♊	24♊	6♋	18♋	0♌	12♌	25♌	8♍	21♍	5♎	19♎
43	26♌	8♍	21♍	3♎	17♎	0♏	14♏	28♏	12♐	26♐	10♑	24♑	9♒	23♒	7♓
44	16♑	0♒	14♒	28♒	13♓	28♓	13♈	27♈	12♉	26♉	10♊	23♊	6♋	19♋	1♌
45	7♊	21♊	5♋	18♋	1♌	14♌	26♌	8♍	20♍	2♎	14♎	26♎	8♏	20♏	2♐
46	14♎	26♎	8♏	20♏	2♐	14♐	26♐	8♑	20♑	2♒	15♒	28♒	11♓	25♓	9♈
47	16♒	28♒	11♓	24♓	7♈	21♈	5♉	19♉	3♊	18♊	2♋	16♋	1♌	15♌	29♌
48	8♌	22♌	6♍	19♍	2♎	15♎	28♎	11♏	24♏	6♐	19♐	1♑	13♑	26♑	8♒
49	27♏	9♐	21♐	3♑	16♑	28♑	10♒	22♒	4♓	17♓	0♈	14♈	28♈	10♉	22♉
1950	5♈	17♈	29♈	10♉	22♉	4♊	16♊	28♊	10♋	23♋	5♌	18♌	2♍	16♍	0♎
51	5♌	18♌	0♍	14♍	27♍	11♎	25♎	10♏	25♏	9♐	24♐	9♑	23♑	7♒	21♒
52	1♑	15♑	29♑	13♒	27♒	11♓	25♓	9♈	23♈	7♉	20♉	3♊	16♊	28♊	10♋
53	18♉	2♊	16♊	29♊	12♋	24♋	6♌	18♌	0♍	12♍	24♍	6♎	18♎	0♏	13♏
54	25♍	7♎	19♎	1♏	13♏	25♏	7♐	19♐	1♑	14♑	26♑	9♒	23♒	7♓	21♓
55	25♑	8♒	20♒	5♓	19♓	3♈	17♈	1♉	16♉	1♊	16♊	1♋	15♋	29♋	12♌
56	23♊	5♋	18♋	0♌	12♌	24♌	6♍	18♍	0♎	12♎	24♎	6♏	18♏	0♐	13♐
57	8♏	19♏	1♐	13♐	25♐	7♑	20♑	2♒	14♒	27♒	10♓	23♓	7♈	20♈	3♉
58	16♓	29♓	11♈	24♈	6♉	19♉	1♊	14♊	26♊	9♋	21♋	4♌	17♌	0♍	13♍
59	15♋	29♋	13♌	28♌	12♍	26♍	10♎	25♎	9♏	23♏	7♐	22♐	6♑	20♑	4♒

MOON POSITIONS

APRIL/MAY	30	1	2	3	4	5	6	7	8	9	10	11	12	13	14
1930	1♊	15♊	29♊	13♋	27♋	12♌	26♌	10♍	24♍	8♎	21♎	5♏	18♏	1♐	14♐
31	16♎	0♏	15♏	29♏	13♐	27♐	10♑	23♑	5♒	18♒	29♒	11♓	23♓	5♈	17♈
32	13♓	25♓	7♈	18♈	0♉	12♉	24♉	6♊	18♊	0♋	13♋	25♋	8♌	21♌	5♍
33	12♋	24♋	7♌	19♌	2♍	15♍	29♍	13♎	27♎	12♏	28♏	13♐	28♐	13♑	27♑
34	22♏	7♐	21♐	5♑	20♑	4♒	18♒	2♓	16♓	29♓	13♈	26♈	9♉	22♉	4♊
35	7♈	21♈	6♉	20♉	4♊	17♊	0♋	13♋	25♋	7♌	19♌	1♍	13♍	25♍	7♎
36	3♍	15♍	27♍	9♎	20♎	2♏	14♏	26♏	9♐	21♐	4♑	17♑	0♒	13♒	27♒
37	3♑	15♑	27♑	9♒	22♒	6♓	19♓	4♈	18♈	3♉	19♉	4♊	19♊	4♋	18♋
38	13♉	28♉	12♊	27♊	12♋	26♋	10♌	24♌	8♍	21♍	4♎	17♎	0♏	12♏	25♏
39	29♍	13♎	27♎	10♏	24♏	7♐	20♐	2♑	15♑	27♑	9♒	21♒	2♓	14♓	27♓
1940	23♒	5♓	17♓	29♓	10♈	22♈	4♉	17♉	29♉	12♊	25♊	8♋	21♋	5♌	19♌
41	23♊	5♋	18♋	0♌	13♌	27♌	10♍	24♍	9♎	24♎	9♏	24♏	10♐	24♐	9♑
42	4♏	19♏	4♐	19♐	4♑	18♑	2♒	16♒	0♓	13♓	25♓	8♈	20♈	3♉	15♉
43	20♓	4♈	18♈	1♉	14♉	27♉	10♊	22♊	4♋	16♋	28♋	10♌	22♌	4♍	16♍
44	13♌	25♌	6♍	18♍	0♎	12♎	25♎	7♏	20♏	3♐	16♐	0♑	13♑	27♑	11♒
45	14♐	26♐	9♑	21♑	4♒	18♒	2♓	16♓	0♈	15♈	0♉	15♉	0♊	15♊	29♊
46	25♈	10♉	25♉	10♊	25♊	9♋	24♋	7♌	21♌	4♍	17♍	29♍	11♎	23♎	5♏
47	12♍	26♍	9♎	22♎	5♏	18♏	0♐	12♐	24♐	6♑	18♑	0♒	12♒	24♒	6♓
48	2♒	14♒	26♒	8♓	20♓	2♈	15♈	27♈	10♉	24♉	7♊	21♊	5♋	19♋	3♌
49	4♊	17♊	0♋	13♋	26♋	10♌	23♌	8♍	22♍	7♎	21♎	6♏	21♏	5♐	20♐
1950	15♎	0♏	15♏	1♐	16♐	1♑	15♑	29♑	12♒	25♒	8♓	20♓	2♈	14♈	26♈
51	4♓	17♓	0♈	13♈	25♈	8♉	20♉	2♊	14♊	26♊	8♋	20♋	2♌	14♌	26♌
52	22♋	4♌	16♌	28♌	10♍	22♍	4♎	17♎	1♏	14♏	28♏	13♐	27♐	11♑	26♑
53	25♏	8♐	21♐	4♑	18♑	2♒	15♒	0♓	14♓	28♓	13♈	27♈	12♉	26♉	10♊
54	6♈	21♈	7♉	22♉	7♊	21♊	6♋	19♋	2♌	15♌	28♌	10♍	22♍	4♎	16♎
55	26♌	9♍	21♍	4♎	16♎	28♎	11♏	22♏	4♐	16♐	28♐	10♑	22♑	4♒	16♒
56	12♑	23♑	5♒	17♒	29♒	12♓	25♓	8♈	21♈	5♉	19♉	4♊	18♊	3♋	17♋
57	16♉	29♉	12♊	26♊	10♋	24♋	8♌	22♌	6♍	20♍	5♎	19♎	3♏	17♏	0♐
58	27♍	12♎	27♎	12♏	27♏	12♐	26♐	9♑	23♑	6♒	18♒	0♓	12♓	24♓	6♈
59	17♒	0♓	13♓	25♓	7♈	19♈	1♉	12♉	24♉	6♊	18♊	0♋	12♋	24♋	7♌

MOON POSITIONS

MAY

	15	16	17	18	19	20	21	22	23	24	25	26	27	28	29
1930	27♐	9♑	21♑	3♒	15♒	27♒	9♓	21♓	3♈	16♈	29♈	12♉	26♉	10♊	24♊
31	29♈	11♉	24♉	7♊	20♊	3♋	17♋	0♌	14♌	28♌	12♍	27♍	11♎	25♎	9♏
32	19♍	3♎	18♎	3♏	18♏	3♐	18♐	3♑	17♑	1♒	14♒	27♒	9♓	21♓	3♈
33	11♒	25♒	8♓	21♓	3♈	16♈	28♈	10♉	22♉	4♊	16♊	27♊	9♋	21♋	3♌
34	17♊	29♊	11♋	23♋	4♌	16♌	28♌	10♍	23♍	6♎	19♎	2♏	16♏	1♐	16♐
35	19♎	2♏	15♏	28♏	11♐	25♐	8♑	22♑	6♒	20♒	5♓	19♓	3♈	17♈	1♉
36	11♓	25♓	10♈	25♈	9♉	24♉	8♊	23♊	7♋	21♋	4♌	17♌	29♌	11♍	23♍
37	2♌	16♌	29♌	12♍	24♍	6♎	18♎	0♏	12♏	24♏	6♐	18♐	0♑	12♑	24♑
38	7♐	19♐	1♑	12♑	24♑	6♒	18♒	0♓	13♓	26♓	9♈	23♈	7♉	21♉	6♊
39	9♈	22♈	5♉	18♉	2♊	16♊	0♋	14♋	28♋	13♌	27♌	11♍	25♍	9♎	23♎
1940	3♍	17♍	1♎	16♎	0♏	15♏	29♏	14♐	27♐	11♑	24♑	7♒	19♒	1♓	13♓
41	23♑	7♒	20♒	2♓	15♓	27♓	9♈	20♈	2♉	14♉	26♉	8♊	20♊	2♋	15♋
42	27♉	9♊	21♊	3♋	14♋	26♋	8♌	21♌	3♍	16♍	29♍	13♎	27♎	12♏	27♏
43	29♍	11♎	25♎	8♏	23♏	7♐	21♐	6♑	21♑	5♒	19♒	4♓	17♓	1♈	14♈
44	25♒	9♓	23♓	8♈	22♈	7♉	20♉	4♊	18♊	1♋	14♋	26♋	9♌	21♌	2♍
45	13♋	27♋	10♌	22♌	5♍	17♍	29♍	11♎	22♎	4♏	16♏	28♏	11♐	23♐	6♑
46	17♍	29♍	11♎	23♎	5♏	17♏	29♏	11♐	24♐	7♑	20♑	4♒	18♒	3♓	18♓
47	19♓	2♈	15♈	29♈	13♉	28♉	12♊	27♊	12♋	27♋	11♌	25♌	9♍	23♍	6♎
48	17♉	2♊	16♊	0♋	14♋	28♋	11♌	25♌	8♍	21♍	4♎	16♎	28♎	10♏	22♏
49	3♑	17♑	0♒	12♒	25♒	7♓	19♓	0♈	12♈	24♈	6♉	18♉	1♊	13♊	26♊
1950	7♉	19♉	1♊	13♊	25♊	7♋	20♋	2♌	15♌	28♌	11♍	25♍	9♎	24♎	9♏
51	9♍	22♍	5♎	19♎	3♏	18♏	3♐	19♐	4♑	19♑	3♒	17♒	1♓	14♓	27♓
52	10♒	24♒	8♓	22♓	6♈	19♈	2♉	16♉	29♉	11♊	24♊	6♋	18♋	0♌	12♌
53	24♊	7♋	20♋	2♌	14♌	26♌	8♍	20♍	2♎	14♎	26♎	9♏	21♏	4♐	17♐
54	28♎	10♏	22♏	4♐	16♐	28♐	10♑	23♑	6♒	19♒	3♓	17♓	1♈	15♈	0♉
55	29♒	12♓	26♓	10♈	24♈	9♉	24♉	10♊	25♊	10♋	24♋	8♌	22♌	5♍	18♍
56	2♌	16♌	0♍	14♍	28♍	11♎	24♎	7♏	19♏	2♐	14♐	26♐	8♑	20♑	2♒
57	14♐	27♐	9♑	22♑	4♒	16♒	28♒	10♓	22♓	4♈	16♈	29♈	11♉	25♉	8♊
58	18♈	0♉	12♉	24♉	6♊	19♊	1♋	14♋	28♋	11♌	25♌	9♍	23♍	7♎	22♎
59	20♌	3♍	17♍	0♎	15♎	0♏	15♏	0♐	15♐	0♑	15♑	29♑	13♒	26♒	9♓

MOON POSITIONS

	MAY 30	MAY 31	JUNE 1	2	3	4	5	6	7	8	9	10	11	12	13
1930	9♋	23♋	8♌	22♌	7♍	21♍	5♎	18♎	1♏	14♏	27♏	10♐	23♐	5♑	17♑
31	24♏	8♐	21♐	5♑	18♑	1♒	13♒	25♒	7♓	19♓	1♈	13♈	25♈	7♉	20♉
32	15♈	27♈	9♉	21♉	3♊	15♊	27♊	10♋	22♋	5♌	18♌	2♍	15♍	29♍	13♎
33	15♌	28♌	11♍	24♍	7♎	21♎	6♏	21♏	6♐	21♐	7♑	22♑	6♒	20♒	4♓
34	0♑	15♑	0♒	15♒	29♒	13♓	26♓	10♈	23♈	6♉	18♉	1♊	13♊	25♊	7♋
35	15♉	29♉	12♊	25♊	8♋	21♋	3♌	15♌	27♌	9♍	21♍	3♎	15♎	27♎	10♏
36	5♎	17♎	29♎	11♏	23♏	5♐	18♐	0♑	13♑	27♑	10♒	23♒	7♓	21♓	5♈
37	6♒	19♒	2♓	15♓	29♓	13♈	27♈	12♉	27♉	12♊	27♊	12♋	27♋	11♌	24♌
38	21♋	6♌	21♌	6♍	20♍	4♎	18♎	1♏	14♏	27♏	9♐	21♐	4♑	15♑	27♑
39	6♏	20♏	3♐	15♐	28♐	10♑	23♑	5♒	17♒	28♒	10♓	22♓	5♈	17♈	0♉
1940	25♓	7♈	19♈	1♉	13♉	25♉	8♊	21♊	4♋	18♋	2♌	16♌	0♍	14♍	28♍
41	27♋	10♌	23♌	6♍	20♍	4♎	18♎	3♏	18♏	3♐	18♐	3♑	17♑	1♒	15♒
42	12♐	28♐	13♑	28♑	12♒	26♒	9♓	22♓	5♈	18♈	0♉	12♉	24♉	6♊	18♊
43	28♈	11♉	23♉	6♊	18♊	1♋	13♋	25♋	6♌	18♌	0♍	12♍	24♍	7♎	20♎
44	14♍	26♍	8♎	20♎	3♏	16♏	29♏	12♐	26♐	9♑	23♑	8♒	22♒	6♓	20♓
45	18♑	1♒	15♒	28♒	12♓	26♓	10♈	25♈	10♉	24♉	9♊	23♊	8♋	21♋	5♌
46	3♊	18♊	3♋	18♋	3♌	17♌	0♍	13♍	26♍	8♎	20♎	2♏	14♏	26♏	8♐
47	19♎	2♏	14♏	27♏	9♐	21♐	3♑	14♑	26♑	8♒	20♒	2♓	14♓	27♓	10♈
48	4♓	16♓	28♓	10♈	23♈	6♉	19♉	2♊	16♊	0♋	15♋	29♋	14♌	28♌	13♍
49	10♋	23♋	6♌	20♌	4♍	18♍	2♎	17♎	1♏	15♏	0♐	14♐	28♐	12♑	25♑
1950	24♏	9♐	24♐	9♑	23♑	7♒	21♒	4♓	16♓	29♓	11♈	23♈	4♉	16♉	28♉
51	10♈	23♈	5♉	17♉	29♉	11♊	23♊	5♋	17♋	28♋	10♌	22♌	5♍	17♍	0♎
52	24♌	5♍	18♍	0♎	12♎	25♎	9♏	23♏	7♐	22♐	6♑	21♑	6♒	20♒	5♓
53	1♑	15♑	28♑	12♒	26♒	10♓	25♓	9♈	23♈	7♉	21♉	5♊	19♊	2♋	15♋
54	15♉	0♊	15♊	0♋	14♋	27♋	11♌	24♌	6♍	18♍	0♎	12♎	24♎	6♏	18♏
55	1♎	13♎	26♎	8♏	19♏	1♐	13♐	25♐	7♑	19♑	1♒	13♒	25♒	8♓	21♓
56	13♒	25♒	8♓	20♓	3♈	16♈	29♈	13♉	27♉	12♊	27♊	12♋	27♋	12♌	26♌
57	6♋	20♋	4♌	18♌	2♍	16♍	29♍	13♎	26♎	9♏	22♏	5♐	9♐	22♐	5♑
58	21♏	6♐	20♐	4♑	18♑	1♒	14♒	26♒	8♓	20♓	2♈	14♈	26♈	8♉	21♉
59	22♓	4♈	16♈	28♈	10♉	21♉	3♊	15♊	27♊	9♋	22♋	4♌	17♌	0♍	13♍

MOON POSITIONS

JUNE	14	15	16	17	18	19	20	21	22	23	24	25	26	27	28
1930	29♑	11♒	23♒	5♓	17♓	29♓	11♈	24♈	7♉	20♉	4♊	18♊	3♋	18♋	3♌
31	3♊	16♊	29♊	13♋	27♋	11♌	25♌	9♍	23♍	7♎	22♎	5♏	19♏	3♐	17♐
32	28♎	12♏	27♏	12♐	27♐	11♑	25♑	9♒	22♒	5♓	18♓	0♈	12♈	24♈	5♉
33	17♓	0♈	13♈	25♈	7♉	19♉	1♊	13♊	24♊	6♋	18♋	0♌	13♌	25♌	7♍
34	19♍	1♎	13♎	25♎	7♏	19♏	1♐	14♐	27♐	11♑	25♑	9♒	24♒	9♓	24♓
35	23♏	6♐	20♐	4♑	18♑	2♒	17♒	1♓	16♓	0♈	14♈	28♈	11♉	25♉	8♊
36	20♈	4♉	19♉	3♊	18♊	2♋	15♋	29♋	12♌	25♌	7♍	19♍	1♎	13♎	25♎
37	8♍	21♍	3♎	15♎	27♎	9♏	21♏	3♐	15♐	27♐	9♑	21♑	3♒	16♒	29♒
38	9♑	21♑	3♒	15♒	27♒	9♓	22♓	4♈	18♈	1♉	15♉	0♊	15♊	0♋	15♋
39	13♉	26♉	10♊	24♊	9♋	24♋	9♌	23♌	8♍	22♍	6♎	20♎	3♏	16♏	29♏
1940	12♎	26♎	10♏	24♏	8♐	22♐	6♑	19♑	2♒	15♒	27♒	9♓	21♓	3♈	15♈
41	28♒	11♓	23♓	5♈	17♈	29♈	11♉	23♉	5♊	17♊	29♊	12♋	24♋	7♌	20♌
42	0♋	11♋	23♋	5♌	17♌	0♍	12♍	25♍	8♎	22♎	6♏	21♏	6♐	21♐	6♑
43	3♏	17♏	1♐	15♐	0♑	15♑	0♒	15♒	0♓	14♓	28♓	11♈	25♈	8♉	20♉
44	4♈	18♈	2♉	16♉	0♊	13♊	26♊	9♋	22♋	4♌	17♌	29♌	10♍	22♍	4♎
45	18♌	0♍	13♍	25♍	7♎	19♎	1♏	13♏	25♏	7♐	19♐	2♑	15♑	28♑	11♒
46	20♐	2♑	14♑	26♑	8♒	21♒	3♓	16♓	0♈	14♈	28♈	12♉	27♉	12♊	27♊
47	23♈	7♉	21♉	6♊	21♊	6♋	21♋	6♌	21♌	5♍	19♍	3♎	16♎	29♎	11♏
48	27♍	11♎	24♎	8♏	21♏	4♐	17♐	0♑	12♑	24♑	6♒	18♒	0♓	12♓	24♓
49	8♒	20♒	3♓	15♓	27♓	9♈	20♈	2♉	14♉	27♉	9♊	22♊	6♋	19♋	3♌
1950	10♊	22♊	4♋	17♋	29♋	12♌	25♌	8♍	21♍	5♎	19♎	3♏	18♏	3♐	18♐
51	14♎	27♎	12♏	27♏	12♐	27♐	12♑	27♑	12♒	27♒	10♓	24♓	7♈	20♈	2♉
52	19♓	3♈	16♈	29♈	12♉	25♉	8♊	20♊	3♋	15♋	27♋	8♌	20♌	2♍	14♍
53	28♋	10♌	22♌	4♍	16♍	28♍	10♎	22♎	4♏	17♏	0♐	13♐	26♐	10♑	24♑
54	0♐	12♐	25♐	7♑	20♑	3♒	16♒	0♓	13♓	27♓	11♈	26♈	10♉	25♉	9♊
55	5♈	19♈	3♉	18♉	3♊	18♊	3♋	18♋	3♌	17♌	1♍	14♍	27♍	10♎	22♎
56	11♍	24♍	8♎	21♎	4♏	16♏	29♏	11♐	23♐	5♑	16♑	28♑	10♒	22♒	4♓
57	17♑	0♒	12♒	24♒	6♓	18♓	0♈	12♈	24♈	7♉	19♉	3♊	16♊	0♋	15♋
58	20♉	2♊	15♊	28♊	11♋	24♋	8♌	22♌	6♍	20♍	4♎	18♎	2♏	16♏	0♐
59	26♍	10♎	24♎	9♏	24♏	9♐	24♐	9♑	23♑	8♒	21♒	5♓	18♓	0♈	12♈

MOON POSITIONS

	JUNE 29	30	JULY 1	2	3	4	5	6	7	8	9	10	11	12	13
1930	18♌	3♍	17♍	1♎	15♎	28♎	11♏	24♏	7♐	19♐	2♑	14♑	26♑	8♒	20♒
1931	0♑	13♑	26♑	9♒	21♒	3♓	15♓	27♓	9♈	21♈	3♉	15♉	28♉	11♊	24♊
1932	17♉	29♉	11♊	24♊	6♋	19♋	2♌	15♌	29♌	12♍	26♍	10♎	24♎	8♏	22♏
1933	20♍	3♎	17♎	1♏	15♏	0♐	15♐	0♑	15♑	29♑	13♒	27♒	13♓	26♓	9♈
1934	9♒	24♒	9♓	23♓	6♈	20♈	3♉	16♉	28♉	10♊	22♊	4♋	16♋	28♋	10♌
1935	21♊	4♋	17♋	29♋	11♌	23♌	5♍	17♍	29♍	11♎	23♎	5♏	18♏	1♐	14♐
1936	7♏	19♏	1♐	14♐	26♐	9♑	22♑	5♒	19♒	3♓	17♓	0♈	15♈	29♈	15♉
1937	12♓	25♓	9♈	23♈	6♉	20♉	3♊	16♊	29♊	11♋	23♋	5♌	18♌	1♍	15♍
1938	0♌	15♌	0♍	14♍	28♍	11♎	24♎	6♏	19♏	1♐	13♐	25♐	7♑	18♑	0♒
1939	12♐	24♐	7♑	19♑	1♒	13♒	25♒	7♓	19♓	1♈	13♈	25♈	8♉	21♉	4♊
1940	27♈	9♉	21♉	4♊	17♊	0♋	14♋	28♋	12♌	26♌	10♍	25♍	9♎	23♎	7♏
1941	3♍	17♍	0♎	14♎	28♎	13♏	27♏	12♐	27♐	11♑	26♑	9♒	23♒	6♓	19♓
1942	21♑	6♒	21♒	5♓	18♓	2♈	14♈	27♈	9♉	21♉	3♊	15♊	27♊	8♋	20♋
1943	3♊	15♊	27♊	9♋	21♋	3♌	15♌	27♌	9♍	21♍	3♎	15♎	28♎	11♏	25♏
1944	16♎	28♎	11♏	24♏	7♐	10♐	24♐	6♑	1♒	9♒	23♒	11♓	25♓	16♈	29♈
1945	25♒	9♓	23♓	7♈	27♈	10♉	20♉	4♊	18♊	2♋	16♋	18♋	13♌	26♌	8♌
1946	12♋	26♋	11♌	25♌	9♍	22♍	6♎	17♎	29♎	11♏	23♏	5♐	17♐	28♐	10♑
1947	24♏	6♐	18♐	29♐	11♑	23♑	5♒	17♒	29♒	11♓	23♓	6♈	19♈	2♉	16♉
1948	6♈	18♈	1♉	14♉	27♉	10♊	25♊	9♋	23♋	9♌	23♌	9♍	23♍	2♎	21♎
1949	17♌	1♍	15♍	29♍	13♎	27♎	12♏	25♏	9♐	23♐	7♑	20♑	3♒	16♒	28♒
1950	3♑	17♑	2♒	15♒	29♒	12♓	25♓	7♈	19♈	1♉	13♉	25♉	6♊	19♊	1♋
1951	14♉	26♉	8♊	20♊	2♋	14♋	26♋	7♌	20♌	2♍	14♍	27♍	10♎	23♎	7♏
1952	26♍	8♎	21♎	4♏	17♏	1♐	15♐	0♑	0♑	15♑	0♒	0♒	15♒	29♒	13♈
1953	8♒	23♒	7♓	21♓	6♈	20♈	4♉	18♉	1♊	15♊	28♊	11♋	24♋	6♌	18♌
1954	24♊	8♋	22♋	5♌	19♌	2♍	14♍	26♍	10♎	23♎	5♏	17♏	0♐	12♐	21♐
1955	4♏	16♏	28♏	10♐	22♐	4♑	16♑	28♑	10♒	23♒	6♓	18♓	1♈	15♈	29♈
1956	16♓	29♓	11♈	24♈	8♉	21♉	6♊	20♊	5♋	19♋	6♌	21♌	6♍	20♍	4♎
1957	0♌	14♌	29♌	14♍	28♍	12♎	26♎	9♏	23♏	6♐	19♐	1♑	14♑	26♑	8♒
1958	15♐	29♐	12♑	26♑	9♒	22♒	4♓	16♓	28♓	10♈	22♈	4♉	16♉	28♉	11♊
1959	24♈	6♉	18♉	0♊	12♊	24♊	6♋	18♋	1♌	14♌	27♌	10♍	23♍	7♎	20♎

MOON POSITIONS

JULY

	14	15	16	17	18	19	20	21	22	23	24	25	26	27	28
1930	2♓	13♓	25♓	7♈	20♈	2♉	15♉	28♉	12♊	27♊	12♋	27♋	12♌	27♌	12♍
31	8♋	22♋	6♌	21♌	5♍	20♍	4♎	18♎	2♏	16♏	0♐	13♐	27♐	10♑	22♑
32	7♐	21♐	6♑	20♑	4♒	17♒	0♓	13♓	25♓	8♈	20♈	2♉	13♉	25♉	7♊
33	21♈	4♉	16♉	28♉	10♊	21♊	3♋	15♋	27♋	10♌	22♌	4♍	17♍	0♎	13♎
34	22♌	3♍	15♍	28♍	10♎	23♎	6♏	19♏	3♐	18♐	2♑	18♑	3♒	18♒	3♓
35	28♐	12♑	27♑	12♒	27♒	11♓	26♓	10♈	25♈	8♉	22♉	5♊	18♊	1♋	13♋
36	29♉	13♊	27♊	11♋	24♋	7♌	20♌	3♍	15♍	27♍	9♎	21♎	3♏	15♏	27♏
37	11♎	24♎	6♏	18♏	29♏	11♐	23♐	5♑	17♑	0♒	13♒	25♒	9♓	22♓	6♈
38	12♒	24♒	6♓	18♓	1♈	14♈	27♈	10♉	24♉	9♊	23♊	8♋	23♋	9♌	24♌
39	18♊	3♋	18♋	3♌	18♌	3♍	18♍	2♎	16♎	0♏	13♏	26♏	9♐	21♐	4♑
1940	21♏	5♐	18♐	2♑	15♑	28♑	10♒	23♒	5♓	17♓	29♓	11♈	23♈	5♉	17♉
41	1♈	13♈	25♈	7♉	19♉	1♊	13♊	25♊	8♋	20♋	3♌	17♌	0♍	14♍	27♍
42	2♌	15♌	27♌	9♍	22♍	5♎	18♎	2♏	16♏	0♐	15♐	0♑	15♑	0♒	14♒
43	9♐	24♐	9♑	24♑	9♒	24♒	9♓	23♓	8♈	21♈	4♉	17♉	0♊	12♊	24♊
44	13♉	27♉	10♊	23♊	6♋	18♋	1♌	13♌	25♌	7♍	19♍	0♎	12♎	24♎	6♏
45	21♏	3♐	15♐	27♐	9♑	21♑	3♒	15♒	28♒	11♓	24♓	7♈	20♈	5♉	19♉
46	23♑	5♒	18♒	0♓	13♓	26♓	11♈	25♈	8♉	22♉	6♊	21♊	6♋	20♋	5♌
47	0♊	14♊	29♊	14♋	29♋	15♌	0♍	14♍	29♍	12♎	25♎	8♏	21♏	3♐	15♐
48	5♏	18♏	1♐	14♐	26♐	9♑	21♑	3♒	15♒	27♒	9♓	21♓	3♈	14♈	27♈
49	11♓	23♓	5♈	16♈	28♈	10♉	22♉	5♊	17♊	1♋	14♋	28♋	12♌	27♌	11♍
1950	13♋	26♋	9♌	22♌	5♍	18♍	2♎	16♎	0♏	14♏	28♏	13♐	27♐	12♑	26♑
51	21♏	5♐	20♐	6♑	21♑	6♒	21♒	5♓	19♓	3♈	16♈	28♈	11♉	23♉	5♊
52	26♈	9♉	22♉	5♊	17♊	29♊	12♋	23♋	5♌	17♌	29♌	11♍	23♍	5♎	17♎
53	0♍	12♍	24♍	6♎	18♎	0♏	12♏	25♏	8♐	21♐	5♑	19♑	3♒	18♒	2♓
54	3♑	16♑	29♑	13♒	26♒	10♓	24♓	8♈	22♈	7♉	21♉	5♊	19♊	3♋	17♋
55	13♉	27♉	12♊	27♊	11♋	26♋	11♌	25♌	9♍	23♍	6♎	18♎	1♏	13♏	25♏
56	18♎	1♏	13♏	26♏	8♐	20♐	2♑	13♑	25♑	7♒	19♒	1♓	13♓	25♓	8♈
57	20♒	2♓	14♓	26♓	8♈	20♈	2♉	15♉	27♉	11♊	25♊	9♋	24♋	9♌	24♌
58	23♊	6♋	20♋	4♌	18♌	2♍	16♍	0♎	15♎	29♎	13♏	27♏	11♐	24♐	8♑
59	4♏	19♏	3♐	18♐	3♑	17♑	2♒	16♒	0♓	13♓	26♓	8♈	21♈	3♉	14♉

MOON POSITIONS

Year	Jul 29	Jul 30	Jul 31	Aug 1	Aug 2	Aug 3	Aug 4	Aug 5	Aug 6	Aug 7	Aug 8	Aug 9	Aug 10	Aug 11	Aug 12
1930	27♍	11♎	25♎	8♏	21♏	4♐	16♐	29♐	11♑	23♑	5♒	17♒	28♒	10♓	22♓
31	5♒	17♒	0♓	12♓	24♓	5♈	17♈	29♈	11♉	23♉	6♊	19♊	2♋	16♋	0♌
32	20♊	2♋	15♋	28♋	11♌	25♌	9♍	22♍	7♎	21♎	5♏	19♏	3♐	17♐	1♑
33	27♎	11♏	25♏	9♐	24♐	9♑	24♑	8♒	23♒	7♓	21♓	4♈	17♈	0♉	12♉
34	18♓	2♈	16♈	29♈	12♉	25♉	7♊	19♊	1♋	13♋	25♋	7♌	19♌	0♍	12♍
35	25♋	8♌	20♌	1♍	13♍	25♍	7♎	19♎	1♏	13♏	26♏	9♐	22♐	6♑	21♑
36	9♐	22♐	5♑	18♑	1♒	15♒	0♓	14♓	29♓	13♈	27♈	12♉	26♉	10♊	23♊
37	19♈	3♉	17♉	1♊	16♊	0♋	15♋	29♋	13♌	27♌	11♍	24♍	7♎	19♎	2♏
38	8♍	23♍	7♎	20♎	3♏	15♏	27♏	9♐	21♐	3♑	15♑	27♑	9♒	21♒	3♓
39	16♑	28♑	10♒	22♒	4♓	15♓	27♓	9♈	21♈	4♉	16♉	29♉	13♊	27♊	11♋
1940	29♉	12♊	25♊	8♋	22♋	6♌	21♌	6♍	20♍	5♎	19♎	4♏	18♏	1♐	15♐
41	11♎	25♎	9♏	24♏	8♐	22♐	6♑	20♑	4♒	18♒	1♓	14♓	27♓	9♈	21♈
42	29♒	13♓	27♓	10♈	23♈	5♉	18♉	0♊	11♊	23♊	5♋	17♋	29♋	11♌	24♌
43	6♍	18♍	1♎	13♎	26♎	8♏	21♏	3♐	16♐	28♐	11♑	23♑	6♒	18♒	1♓
44	19♏	3♐	17♐	1♑	15♑	0♒	14♒	28♒	12♓	26♓	10♈	25♈	9♉	23♉	7♊
45	3♈	16♈	0♉	13♉	27♉	10♊	23♊	7♋	20♋	4♌	17♌	0♍	14♍	27♍	11♎
46	19♌	1♍	14♍	26♍	9♎	21♎	4♏	16♏	29♏	11♐	24♐	6♑	19♑	1♒	14♒
47	27♐	10♑	22♑	5♒	17♒	0♓	12♓	25♓	7♈	20♈	2♉	15♉	27♉	10♊	23♊
48	26♍	9♎	22♎	6♏	19♏	2♐	15♐	28♐	12♑	25♑	8♒	21♒	4♓	17♓	0♈
49	26♉	9♊	22♊	5♋	19♋	2♌	15♌	28♌	12♍	25♍	8♎	21♎	5♏	18♏	1♐
1950	10♒	23♒	5♓	18♓	0♈	13♈	25♈	8♉	20♉	3♊	15♊	28♊	10♋	22♋	5♌
51	17♊	0♋	13♋	25♋	8♌	21♌	4♍	16♍	29♍	12♎	24♎	7♏	20♏	2♐	15♐
52	29♎	12♏	26♏	9♐	22♐	5♑	18♑	2♒	15♒	28♒	11♓	24♓	8♈	21♈	4♉
53	17♓	0♈	13♈	26♈	9♉	22♉	5♊	18♊	1♋	14♋	27♋	10♌	23♌	6♍	19♍
54	0♌	12♌	25♌	7♍	20♍	2♎	15♎	27♎	10♏	22♏	5♐	17♐	0♑	12♑	25♑
55	7♐	20♐	3♑	16♑	28♑	11♒	24♒	7♓	20♓	3♈	16♈	28♈	11♉	24♉	7♊
56	20♈	4♉	19♉	3♊	17♊	2♋	16♋	0♌	15♌	29♌	13♍	28♍	12♎	26♎	10♏
57	9♍	22♍	5♎	18♎	1♏	14♏	27♏	10♐	23♐	6♑	19♑	2♒	16♒	29♒	12♓
58	21♑	3♒	16♒	28♒	10♓	23♓	5♈	18♈	0♉	12♉	25♉	7♊	20♊	2♋	15♋
59	26♉	9♊	22♊	5♋	18♋	2♌	15♌	28♌	11♍	24♍	7♎	20♎	3♏	16♏	29♏

MOON POSITIONS

AUGUST

	13	14	15	16	17	18	19	20	21	22	23	24	25	26	27
1930	4♈	16♈	29♈	11♉	24♉	7♊	21♊	5♋	20♋	5♌	20♌	6♍	21♍	6♎	20♎
31	15♌	0♍	15♍	0♎	14♎	29♎	13♏	27♏	10♐	23♐	6♑	19♑	2♒	14♒	26♒
32	15♑	29♑	12♒	26♒	8♓	21♓	3♈	16♈	28♈	9♉	21♉	3♊	15♊	28♊	10♋
33	24♉	6♊	18♊	0♋	12♋	24♋	6♌	18♌	1♍	14♍	27♍	10♎	24♎	8♏	22♏
34	25♏	7♐	19♐	2♑	15♑	29♑	13♒	27♒	11♓	26♓	11♈	26♈	11♉	26♉	10♊
35	5♒	20♒	5♓	21♓	6♈	20♈	5♉	19♉	3♊	15♊	28♊	10♋	22♋	5♌	16♌
36	7♋	20♋	3♌	16♌	29♌	11♍	23♍	5♎	17♎	29♎	11♏	23♏	5♐	17♐	0♑
37	14♏	26♏	7♐	19♐	1♑	13♑	26♑	8♒	21♒	5♓	18♓	2♈	16♈	0♉	14♉
38	16♓	28♓	11♈	24♈	7♉	20♉	4♊	18♊	3♋	17♋	2♌	17♌	2♍	17♍	1♎
39	26♋	11♌	27♌	12♍	27♍	12♎	26♎	10♏	23♏	6♐	18♐	1♑	13♑	25♑	7♒
1940	28♐	11♑	24♑	7♒	19♒	1♓	14♓	25♓	7♈	19♈	1♉	13♉	25♉	7♊	20♊
41	0♉	15♉	27♉	9♊	21♊	3♋	16♋	29♋	12♌	26♌	9♍	23♍	8♎	22♎	6♏
42	6♍	19♍	2♎	15♎	29♎	12♏	26♏	10♐	25♐	9♑	24♑	8♒	23♒	7♓	21♓
43	17♑	2♒	17♒	2♓	17♓	2♈	16♈	0♉	14♉	27♉	9♊	21♊	3♋	15♋	27♋
44	20♊	3♋	15♋	27♋	10♌	22♌	3♍	15♍	27♍	9♎	21♎	3♏	15♏	27♏	10♐
45	23♎	5♏	17♏	29♏	11♐	23♐	6♑	19♑	2♒	16♒	0♓	14♓	29♓	14♈	28♈
46	27♈	10♉	23♉	7♊	21♊	5♋	19♋	3♌	17♌	1♍	15♍	0♎	14♎	28♎	11♏
47	8♋	23♋	8♌	23♌	8♍	23♍	7♎	21♎	4♏	17♏	29♏	11♐	23♐	5♑	17♑
48	11♈	23♈	6♉	18♉	0♊	12♊	24♊	6♋	18♋	29♋	11♌	23♌	6♍	18♍	1♎
49	13♈	24♈	6♉	18♉	0♊	13♊	26♊	9♋	22♋	6♌	21♌	6♍	20♍	5♎	20♎
1950	18♌	1♍	15♍	29♍	13♎	27♎	11♏	25♏	9♐	23♐	7♑	21♑	5♒	19♒	2♓
51	0♑	15♑	29♑	14♒	29♒	13♓	27♓	11♈	24♈	7♉	19♉	1♊	13♊	25♊	7♋
52	2♊	14♊	27♊	9♋	20♋	2♌	14♌	26♌	8♍	20♍	2♎	14♎	26♎	9♏	22♏
53	2♎	14♎	26♎	8♏	20♏	3♐	16♐	29♐	13♑	27♑	11♒	26♒	11♓	26♓	11♈
54	8♒	22♒	6♓	20♓	4♈	19♈	3♉	18♉	2♊	16♊	0♋	13♋	26♋	10♌	23♌
55	22♊	6♋	21♋	5♌	19♌	4♍	17♍	1♎	14♎	27♎	9♏	21♏	3♐	15♐	27♐
56	22♏	5♐	17♐	29♐	11♑	23♑	5♒	17♒	29♒	11♓	23♓	6♈	18♈	0♉	13♉
57	23♓	5♈	16♈	28♈	10♉	23♉	6♊	19♊	2♋	16♋	0♌	14♌	28♌	18♍	3♎
58	14♐	28♐	12♑	26♑	10♒	24♒	8♓	21♓	5♈	18♈	1♉	14♉	26♉	8♊	14♊
59	14♐	28♐	12♑	27♑	11♒	24♒	8♓	21♓	4♈	16♈	28♈	11♉	22♉	4♊	16♊

MOON POSITIONS

Year	Aug 28	Aug 29	Aug 30	Aug 31	Sep 1	Sep 2	Sep 3	Sep 4	Sep 5	Sep 6	Sep 7	Sep 8	Sep 9	Sep 10	Sep 11
1930	4♏	17♏	1♐	13♐	26♐	8♑	20♑	2♒	14♒	25♒	7♓	19♓	1♈	13♈	26♈
31	8♓	20♓	2♈	14♈	26♈	7♉	19♉	2♊	14♊	27♊	10♋	24♋	8♌	23♌	8♍
32	23♋	6♌	20♌	4♍	18♍	2♎	17♎	1♏	16♏	0♐	14♐	28♐	12♑	25♑	9♒
33	6♐	20♐	4♑	19♑	3♒	17♒	1♓	15♓	29♓	12♈	25♈	8♉	20♉	2♊	14♊
34	24♈	8♉	21♉	4♊	16♊	28♊	10♋	22♋	4♌	15♌	27♌	9♍	22♍	4♎	17♎
35	28♌	10♍	22♍	4♎	16♎	28♎	10♏	22♏	5♐	18♐	1♑	15♑	29♑	14♒	29♒
36	13♑	26♑	10♒	24♒	8♓	23♓	8♈	23♈	8♉	22♉	6♊	20♊	4♋	17♋	0♌
37	28♉	12♊	26♊	11♋	25♋	8♌	22♌	6♍	19♍	2♎	15♎	27♎	10♏	22♏	3♐
38	15♎	28♎	11♏	24♏	6♐	18♐	0♑	12♑	23♑	5♒	17♒	0♓	12♓	25♓	8♈
39	19♒	1♓	12♓	24♓	6♈	18♈	1♉	13♉	26♉	9♊	22♊	6♋	20♋	5♌	20♌
1940	3♋	16♋	0♌	15♌	29♌	14♍	29♍	14♎	29♎	14♏	28♏	12♐	25♐	8♑	21♑
41	20♏	5♐	19♐	3♑	17♑	0♒	14♒	27♒	10♓	22♓	5♈	17♈	29♈	11♉	23♉
42	5♈	18♈	1♉	13♉	26♉	8♊	20♊	1♋	13♋	25♋	7♌	20♌	2♍	15♍	28♍
43	9♌	21♌	3♍	15♍	27♍	9♎	21♎	4♏	17♏	0♐	14♐	28♐	12♑	26♑	11♒
44	23♐	7♑	21♑	5♒	20♒	5♓	20♓	5♈	20♈	5♉	19♉	3♊	17♊	0♋	12♋
45	13♉	27♉	11♊	25♊	8♋	22♋	5♌	18♌	0♍	13♍	25♍	7♎	19♎	1♏	13♏
46	25♍	8♎	21♎	3♏	15♏	27♏	9♐	21♐	3♑	15♑	27♑	10♒	22♒	6♓	19♓
47	29♑	11♒	23♒	5♓	17♓	0♈	13♈	26♈	9♉	22♉	5♊	19♊	3♋	18♋	2♌
48	14♊	27♊	11♋	26♋	11♌	26♌	11♍	26♍	11♎	26♎	10♏	24♏	7♐	20♐	3♑
49	5♏	19♏	3♐	17♐	0♑	13♑	26♑	9♒	21♒	3♓	15♓	27♓	9♈	21♈	3♉
1950	15♓	28♓	11♈	23♈	5♉	17♉	29♉	11♊	22♊	5♋	17♋	0♌	13♌	26♌	10♍
51	19♋	1♌	13♌	25♌	8♍	21♍	4♎	17♎	0♏	14♏	28♏	12♐	26♐	10♑	24♑
52	5♐	19♐	3♑	17♑	2♒	17♒	2♓	17♓	2♈	16♈	1♉	14♉	28♉	11♊	23♊
53	26♈	11♉	25♉	8♊	22♊	5♋	17♋	29♋	12♌	24♌	6♍	17♍	29♍	11♎	23♎
54	5♍	18♍	0♎	13♎	25♎	7♏	18♏	0♐	12♐	24♐	7♑	19♑	2♒	16♒	0♓
55	8♑	21♑	3♒	15♒	28♒	11♓	25♓	8♈	22♈	6♉	20♉	4♊	18♊	2♋	16♋
56	27♉	10♊	24♊	8♋	23♋	8♌	23♌	8♍	23♍	7♎	21♎	5♏	18♏	1♐	13♐
57	18♎	2♏	16♏	29♏	12♐	25♐	8♑	20♑	2♒	14♒	26♒	8♓	20♓	2♈	13♈
58	26♏	9♐	21♐	3♑	15♑	26♑	8♒	20♒	2♓	14♓	27♓	9♈	23♈	7♉	21♉
59	28♊	10♋	23♋	6♌	19♌	2♍	16♍	29♍	14♎	28♎	12♏	26♏	10♐	25♐	9♑

MOON POSITIONS

SEPTEMBER

	12	13	14	15	16	17	18	19	20	21	22	23	24	25	26
1930	8♉	21♉	4♊	17♊	1♋	15♋	29♋	14♌	29♌	14♍	29♍	14♎	28♎	12♏	26♏
31	23♍	8♎	23♎	8♏	23♏	7♐	20♐	3♑	16♑	29♑	11♒	23♒	5♓	17♓	29♓
32	22♒	5♓	17♓	29♓	12♈	24♈	6♉	18♉	29♉	11♊	23♊	6♋	18♋	1♌	14♌
33	26♊	8♋	20♋	2♌	14♌	27♌	10♍	23♍	6♎	20♎	4♏	18♏	2♐	17♐	1♑
34	29♎	12♏	26♏	9♐	23♐	7♑	21♑	5♒	20♒	5♓	20♓	4♈	18♈	2♉	16♉
35	14♓	29♓	14♈	29♈	14♉	28♉	11♊	24♊	7♋	19♋	2♌	14♌	25♌	7♍	19♍
36	13♌	25♌	8♍	20♍	2♎	14♎	26♎	8♏	19♏	1♐	13♐	25♐	8♑	21♑	4♒
37	15♐	27♐	9♑	21♑	4♒	17♒	0♓	13♓	27♓	12♈	26♈	10♉	25♉	9♊	23♊
38	21♈	4♉	17♉	1♊	15♊	29♊	13♋	27♋	12♌	26♌	11♍	25♍	9♎	23♎	6♏
39	5♍	20♍	5♎	20♎	4♏	18♏	2♐	15♐	27♐	10♑	22♑	4♒	16♒	28♒	9♓
1940	4♒	16♒	28♒	10♓	22♓	4♈	16♈	28♈	9♉	21♉	4♊	16♊	28♊	11♋	25♋
41	5♊	17♊	29♊	11♋	24♋	7♌	20♌	4♍	18♍	2♎	17♎	2♏	16♏	1♐	15♐
42	12♎	25♎	9♏	23♏	7♐	21♐	5♑	20♑	4♒	18♒	2♓	16♓	29♓	13♈	26♈
43	26♒	11♓	26♓	10♈	25♈	9♉	22♉	5♊	18♊	0♋	12♋	24♋	6♌	17♌	29♌
44	25♋	7♌	19♌	1♍	12♍	24♍	6♎	18♎	0♏	12♏	24♏	7♐	19♐	2♑	16♑
45	25♏	7♐	19♐	1♑	14♑	27♑	10♒	24♒	8♓	23♓	8♈	23♈	8♉	23♉	7♊
46	3♈	17♈	1♉	15♉	0♊	14♊	28♊	12♋	26♋	10♌	23♌	7♍	20♍	3♎	16♎
47	17♌	2♍	17♍	1♎	15♎	29♎	12♏	25♏	7♐	20♐	2♑	13♑	25♑	7♒	19♒
48	15♑	27♑	9♒	21♒	3♓	15♓	26♓	8♈	20♈	3♉	15♉	28♉	10♊	23♊	7♋
49	15♉	27♉	9♊	21♊	4♋	17♋	1♌	15♌	29♌	14♍	29♍	14♎	29♎	14♏	29♏
1950	24♍	8♎	22♎	7♏	21♏	6♐	20♐	4♑	18♑	2♒	15♒	28♒	11♓	24♓	6♈
51	9♒	23♒	7♓	21♓	5♈	19♈	2♉	15♉	27♉	9♊	21♊	3♋	15♋	27♋	9♌
52	5♋	17♋	29♋	11♌	23♌	5♍	17♍	29♍	11♎	23♎	6♏	19♏	2♐	15♐	29♐
53	5♏	17♏	29♏	12♐	24♐	5♑	21♑	5♒	19♒	4♓	19♓	5♈	20♈	5♉	20♉
54	14♓	29♓	14♈	29♈	14♉	28♉	12♊	26♊	10♋	23♋	6♌	19♌	2♍	15♍	27♍
55	1♌	15♌	29♌	12♍	26♍	9♎	22♎	5♏	17♏	29♏	11♐	23♐	4♑	16♑	28♑
56	25♐	7♑	19♑	1♒	13♒	25♒	7♓	19♓	2♈	14♈	27♈	10♉	24♉	7♊	21♊
57	25♈	8♉	20♉	2♊	15♊	28♊	12♋	26♋	11♌	25♌	11♍	26♍	11♎	26♎	10♏
58	5♍	20♍	5♎	20♎	5♏	20♏	4♐	18♐	2♑	15♑	28♑	11♒	23♒	5♓	17♓
59	23♑	6♒	20♒	3♓	16♓	29♓	12♈	24♈	6♉	18♉	0♊	12♊	24♊	6♋	18♋

MOON POSITIONS

	SEPTEMBER				OCTOBER										
	27	28	29	30	1	2	3	4	5	6	7	8	9	10	11
1930	9♐	22♐	4♑	16♑	28♑	10♒	22♒	4♓	16♓	28♓	10♈	23♈	5♉	18♉	1♊
31	11♈	23♈	5♉	17♉	28♉	11♊	23♊	6♋	19♋	3♌	17♌	1♍	16♍	1♎	17♎
32	28♌	12♍	26♍	11♎	26♎	11♏	26♏	10♐	25♐	9♑	22♑	6♒	19♒	1♓	14♓
33	15♑	29♑	13♒	27♒	11♓	24♓	7♈	20♈	3♉	16♉	28♉	10♊	22♊	4♋	16♋
34	29♊	9♋	20♋	0♌	10♌	21♌	1♍	11♍	21♍	2♎	12♎	22♎	2♏	12♏	22♏
35	1♎	14♎	27♎	10♏	24♏	7♐	20♐	4♑	17♑	0♒	14♒	27♒	10♓	24♓	7♈
36	18♒	2♓	16♓	0♈	14♈	28♈	12♉	26♉	10♊	24♊	8♋	22♋	7♌	21♌	5♍
37	7♋	20♋	2♌	15♌	28♌	10♍	23♍	6♎	18♎	1♏	14♏	27♏	9♐	22♐	5♑
38	19♏	2♐	14♐	27♐	9♑	22♑	4♒	17♒	29♒	12♓	24♓	7♈	19♈	1♉	14♉
39	21♓	5♈	18♈	1♉	15♉	28♉	12♊	25♊	8♋	22♋	5♌	18♌	2♍	15♍	29♍
1940	9♌	23♌	7♍	21♍	5♎	19♎	3♏	17♏	1♐	15♐	29♐	13♑	27♑	11♒	25♒
41	0♑	13♑	25♑	8♒	20♒	3♓	15♓	28♓	10♈	23♈	5♉	18♉	0♊	13♊	25♊
42	9♉	22♉	4♊	17♊	0♋	12♋	25♋	7♌	20♌	2♍	15♍	27♍	10♎	23♎	5♏
43	11♍	25♍	8♎	22♎	5♏	19♏	2♐	16♐	29♐	13♑	26♑	10♒	23♒	7♓	20♓
44	29♒	11♓	23♓	5♈	17♈	29♈	10♉	22♉	4♊	16♊	28♊	10♋	22♋	4♌	16♌
45	22♊	4♋	17♋	29♋	11♌	24♌	6♍	18♍	1♎	13♎	25♎	8♏	20♏	3♐	15♐
46	29♎	12♏	24♏	7♐	20♐	2♑	15♑	28♑	10♒	23♒	5♓	18♓	0♈	13♈	26♈
47	1♓	15♓	28♓	12♈	26♈	9♉	23♉	6♊	20♊	3♋	17♋	0♌	14♌	27♌	11♍
48	21♋	5♌	19♌	3♍	17♍	1♎	15♎	29♎	12♏	26♏	10♐	24♐	8♑	22♑	6♒
49	13♐	25♐	8♑	20♑	2♒	14♒	26♒	9♓	21♓	3♈	16♈	28♈	10♉	22♉	5♊
1950	19♈	2♉	14♉	27♉	10♊	22♊	5♋	18♋	0♌	13♌	26♌	8♍	21♍	4♎	17♎
51	21♌	5♍	19♍	2♎	16♎	0♏	13♏	27♏	11♐	24♐	8♑	22♑	5♒	19♒	3♓
52	13♑	27♑	10♒	24♒	8♓	21♓	5♈	19♈	3♉	16♉	0♊	14♊	28♊	12♋	26♋
53	4♊	16♊	28♊	11♋	23♋	5♌	18♌	0♍	12♍	24♍	7♎	19♎	1♏	14♏	26♏
54	9♎	22♎	4♏	17♏	0♐	12♐	25♐	8♑	20♑	3♒	15♒	28♒	11♓	24♓	7♈
55	11♒	25♒	9♓	23♓	7♈	20♈	4♉	18♉	2♊	16♊	0♋	13♋	27♋	11♌	25♌
56	5♋	19♋	2♌	16♌	29♌	13♍	26♍	10♎	23♎	7♏	20♏	4♐	18♐	1♑	15♑
57	25♏	7♐	19♐	2♑	14♑	26♑	8♒	21♒	3♓	15♓	28♓	10♈	22♈	5♉	17♉
58	29♓	12♈	24♈	7♉	20♉	3♊	15♊	28♊	11♋	24♋	7♌	19♌	2♍	15♍	28♍
59	1♌	15♌	29♌	13♍	27♍	11♎	25♎	9♏	23♏	7♐	21♐	5♑	19♑	3♒	17♒

MOON POSITIONS

OCTOBER

	12	13	14	15	16	17	18	19	20	21	22	23	24	25	26
1930	14♊	27♊	11♋	25♋	9♌	24♌	8♍	23♍	7♎	22♎	6♏	20♏	4♐	17♐	0♑
31	2♏	17♏	1♐	16♐	29♐	13♑	25♑	8♒	20♒	2♓	14♓	26♓	8♈	19♈	1♉
32	26♓	8♈	20♈	2♉	14♉	26♉	8♊	20♊	2♋	14♋	26♋	9♌	22♌	6♍	20♍
33	27♋	10♌	22♌	5♍	18♍	1♎	15♎	29♎	14♏	28♏	13♐	27♐	12♑	26♑	10♒
34	6♐	20♐	3♑	17♑	1♒	16♒	0♓	14♓	29♓	13♈	27♈	11♉	24♉	7♊	20♊
35	23♈	7♉	22♉	6♊	20♊	3♋	16♋	28♋	10♌	22♌	4♍	16♍	28♍	10♎	22♎
36	17♍	29♍	11♎	23♎	5♏	16♏	28♏	10♐	22♐	4♑	17♑	29♑	13♒	26♒	10♓
37	17♑	29♑	12♒	24♒	8♓	21♓	6♈	20♈	4♉	20♉	5♊	19♊	4♋	18♋	2♌
38	28♉	12♊	26♊	10♋	24♋	8♌	22♌	6♍	20♍	4♎	18♎	1♏	14♏	27♏	9♐
39	13♎	28♎	12♏	26♏	10♐	23♐	6♑	18♑	0♒	12♒	24♒	6♓	18♓	0♈	12♈
1940	7♓	19♓	1♈	13♈	25♈	7♉	18♉	1♊	13♊	25♊	8♋	21♋	4♌	18♌	2♍
41	7♌	19♌	2♍	15♍	28♍	12♎	26♎	10♏	25♏	10♐	26♐	11♑	25♑	10♒	24♒
42	19♍	3♎	18♎	2♏	16♏	1♐	14♐	28♐	12♑	25♑	8♒	21♒	4♓	17♓	29♓
43	4♈	19♈	3♉	17♉	0♊	13♊	26♊	8♋	20♋	2♌	14♌	25♌	7♍	19♍	0♎
44	27♌	9♍	21♍	3♎	15♎	27♎	9♏	21♏	4♐	16♐	29♐	12♑	25♑	9♒	23♒
45	27♐	9♑	22♑	5♒	18♒	2♓	16♓	1♈	16♈	2♉	17♉	2♊	17♊	1♋	15♋
46	11♉	25♉	10♊	24♊	9♋	23♋	7♌	20♌	4♍	17♍	0♎	12♎	25♎	7♏	19♏
47	26♏	10♐	23♐	7♑	20♑	3♒	15♒	27♒	9♓	21♓	3♈	15♈	27♈	9♉	22♉
48	18♒	29♒	11♓	23♓	5♈	17♈	29♈	12♉	25♉	7♊	20♊	4♋	17♋	1♌	15♌
49	18♊	0♋	13♋	26♋	9♌	23♌	7♍	22♍	7♎	22♎	7♏	22♏	7♐	22♐	6♑
1950	2♏	16♏	1♐	16♐	1♑	15♑	29♑	12♒	25♒	8♓	21♓	3♈	15♈	27♈	9♉
51	17♓	0♈	14♈	27♈	10♉	23♉	5♊	17♊	29♊	11♋	23♋	5♌	17♌	29♌	11♍
52	7♌	19♌	1♍	13♍	25♍	7♎	20♎	3♏	16♏	29♏	12♐	26♐	9♑	23♑	7♒
53	9♐	21♐	4♑	17♑	0♒	14♒	28♒	13♓	28♓	13♈	28♈	13♉	28♉	12♊	26♊
54	23♈	8♉	23♉	8♊	22♊	6♋	20♋	3♌	16♌	29♌	12♍	24♍	6♎	18♎	0♏
55	8♍	22♍	5♎	18♎	0♏	13♏	25♏	7♐	19♐	1♑	12♑	24♑	6♒	18♒	0♓
56	27♑	9♒	21♒	3♓	15♓	28♓	10♈	23♈	7♉	20♉	4♊	18♊	2♋	16♋	0♌
57	29♉	12♊	25♊	8♋	22♋	6♌	20♌	5♍	20♍	4♎	19♎	4♏	18♏	3♐	16♐
58	13♎	29♎	14♏	29♏	13♐	27♐	11♑	25♑	7♒	20♒	2♓	14♓	26♓	8♈	20♈
59	0♓	13♓	26♓	8♈	21♈	3♉	15♉	27♉	9♊	20♊	2♋	14♋	26♋	9♌	21♌

MOON POSITIONS

	OCTOBER 27	28	29	30	31	NOVEMBER 1	2	3	4	5	6	7	8	9	10
1930	12♑	25♑	7♒	18♒	0♓	12♓	24♓	6♈	19♈	1♉	14♉	27♉	11♊	24♊	8♋
31	13♉	26♉	8♊	20♊	3♋	16♋	29♋	13♌	26♌	11♍	25♍	10♎	25♎	10♏	25♏
32	4♎	19♎	4♏	19♏	5♐	20♐	4♑	18♑	2♒	15♒	28♒	11♓	23♓	5♈	17♈
33	24♈	7♉	20♉	3♊	16♊	29♊	12♋	24♋	6♌	18♌	0♍	12♍	24♍	5♎	18♎
34	2♋	14♋	26♋	8♌	20♌	2♍	14♍	26♍	9♎	21♎	5♏	18♏	2♐	16♐	0♑
35	4♍	16♍	29♍	11♎	24♎	7♏	21♏	5♐	18♐	2♑	17♑	1♒	16♒	1♓	16♓
36	25♓	8♈	21♈	4♉	16♉	29♉	12♊	25♊	8♋	21♋	4♌	16♌	29♌	12♍	25♍
37	16♌	29♌	12♍	25♍	7♎	20♎	3♏	16♏	29♏	12♐	25♐	7♑	20♑	3♒	16♒
38	22♐	5♑	18♑	1♒	13♒	26♒	9♓	22♓	5♈	18♈	1♉	13♉	26♉	9♊	22♊
39	24♈	7♉	20♉	3♊	15♊	28♊	11♋	24♋	7♌	20♌	3♍	15♍	28♍	11♎	24♎
1940	16♍	29♍	12♎	25♎	7♏	20♏	3♐	16♐	29♐	12♑	25♑	7♒	20♒	3♓	16♓
41	7♒	20♒	3♓	16♓	28♓	11♈	24♈	7♉	20♉	3♊	16♊	28♊	11♋	24♋	7♌
42	12♊	25♊	8♋	21♋	3♌	16♌	29♌	12♍	25♍	8♎	21♎	3♏	16♏	29♏	12♐
43	14♎	27♎	10♏	23♏	5♐	18♐	1♑	14♑	27♑	10♒	23♒	5♓	18♓	1♈	14♈
44	7♓	20♓	3♈	16♈	28♈	11♉	24♉	7♊	20♊	3♋	16♋	28♋	11♌	24♌	7♍
45	28♋	11♌	24♌	7♍	19♍	2♎	15♎	28♎	11♏	24♏	7♐	19♐	2♑	15♑	28♑
46	1♈	14♈	27♈	10♉	22♉	5♊	18♊	1♋	14♋	27♋	10♌	22♌	5♍	18♍	1♎
47	5♈	18♈	1♉	13♉	26♉	9♊	22♊	5♋	18♋	1♌	14♌	26♌	9♍	22♍	5♎
48	29♍	12♎	25♎	7♏	20♏	3♐	16♐	29♐	12♑	25♑	8♒	20♒	3♓	16♓	29♓
49	19♑	2♒	15♒	28♒	10♓	23♓	6♈	19♈	2♉	15♉	28♉	10♊	23♊	6♋	19♋
1950	21♉	4♊	17♊	29♊	12♋	25♋	8♌	21♌	4♍	16♍	29♍	12♎	25♎	8♏	21♏
51	24♍	7♎	20♎	3♏	15♏	28♏	11♐	24♐	7♑	19♑	2♒	15♒	28♒	11♓	24♓
52	21♒	4♓	17♓	29♓	12♈	25♈	8♉	21♉	4♊	17♊	29♊	12♋	25♋	8♌	21♌
53	10♋	23♋	6♌	19♌	1♍	14♍	27♍	10♎	23♎	6♏	19♏	1♐	14♐	27♐	10♑
54	12♏	25♏	8♐	20♐	3♑	16♑	29♑	12♒	25♒	8♓	20♓	3♈	16♈	29♈	12♉
55	14♓	27♓	10♈	23♈	5♉	18♉	1♊	14♊	27♊	10♋	23♋	5♌	18♌	1♍	14♍
56	14♌	27♌	10♍	22♍	5♎	18♎	1♏	14♏	27♏	10♐	22♐	5♑	18♑	1♒	14♒
57	0♑	13♑	26♑	9♒	21♒	4♓	17♓	0♈	13♈	26♈	9♉	21♉	4♊	17♊	0♋
58	2♉	15♉	28♉	11♊	23♊	6♋	19♋	2♌	15♌	28♌	11♍	23♍	6♎	19♎	2♏
59	4♍	17♍	29♍	12♎	25♎	8♏	21♏	4♐	17♐	29♐	12♑	25♑	8♒	21♒	4♓

MOON POSITIONS

NOVEMBER

	11	12	13	14	15	16	17	18	19	20	21	22	23	24	25
1930	22♋	6♌	20♌	4♍	19♍	3♎	17♎	1♏	15♏	28♏	12♐	25♐	8♑	20♑	2♒
1931	9♐	24♐	8♑	21♑	4♒	16♒	29♒	11♓	23♓	4♈	16♈	28♈	10♉	22♉	5♊
1932	29♈	11♉	23♉	5♊	17♊	29♊	11♋	23♋	5♌	18♌	1♍	14♍	28♍	12♎	27♎
1933	0♍	12♍	25♍	9♎	23♎	7♏	22♏	7♐	22♐	7♑	22♑	6♒	20♒	4♓	17♓
1934	14♑	28♑	12♒	27♒	11♓	25♓	8♈	22♈	6♉	19♉	2♊	15♊	28♊	10♋	22♋
1935	0♊	14♊	28♊	11♋	24♋	6♌	18♌	0♍	12♍	24♍	6♎	18♎	0♏	13♏	25♏
1936	20♎	2♏	13♏	25♏	7♐	19♐	1♑	14♑	26♑	9♒	22♒	6♓	20♓	4♈	19♈
1937	20♒	3♓	16♓	29♓	14♈	28♈	13♉	28♉	13♊	28♊	13♋	28♋	12♌	26♌	9♍
1938	6♋	19♋	2♌	16♌	29♌	12♍	26♍	9♎	22♎	6♏	19♏	2♐	16♐	29♐	12♑
1939	19♏	2♐	15♐	28♐	12♑	25♑	8♒	22♒	5♓	18♓	1♈	15♈	28♈	11♉	25♉
1940	10♈	23♈	6♉	19♉	3♊	16♊	29♊	13♋	26♋	9♌	22♌	6♍	19♍	2♎	16♎
1941	10♌	23♌	7♍	20♍	4♎	18♎	1♏	15♏	29♏	12♐	26♐	10♑	23♑	7♒	21♒
1942	28♐	11♑	24♑	7♒	21♒	4♓	17♓	1♈	14♈	27♈	10♉	24♉	7♊	20♊	4♋
1943	11♉	24♉	7♊	20♊	4♋	17♋	0♌	14♌	27♌	10♍	23♍	7♎	20♎	3♏	17♏
1944	0♎	13♎	26♎	9♏	23♏	6♐	19♐	3♑	16♑	29♑	12♒	26♒	9♓	22♓	6♈
1945	7♒	20♒	3♓	16♓	0♈	13♈	26♈	10♉	23♉	6♊	19♊	3♋	16♋	29♋	13♌
1946	19♊	2♋	15♋	29♋	12♌	25♌	9♍	22♍	5♎	19♎	2♏	15♏	29♏	12♐	26♐
1947	2♏	15♏	28♏	12♐	25♐	8♑	22♑	5♒	18♒	2♓	15♓	28♓	12♈	25♈	9♉
1948	19♓	2♈	15♈	28♈	11♉	24♉	7♊	20♊	3♋	16♋	29♋	12♌	25♌	8♍	22♍
1949	22♋	5♌	19♌	3♍	17♍	0♎	14♎	28♎	12♏	26♏	9♐	23♐	7♑	21♑	5♒
1950	10♐	23♐	6♑	20♑	3♒	17♒	0♓	14♓	27♓	10♈	24♈	7♉	21♉	4♊	18♊
1951	23♈	6♉	19♉	3♊	16♊	29♊	13♋	26♋	9♌	22♌	6♍	19♍	2♎	15♎	29♎
1952	9♍	22♍	5♎	18♎	2♏	15♏	28♏	12♐	25♐	8♑	21♑	5♒	18♒	1♓	15♓
1953	21♑	4♒	17♒	0♓	14♓	27♓	10♈	24♈	7♉	20♉	3♊	17♊	0♋	13♋	27♋
1954	1♊	14♊	27♊	10♋	24♋	7♌	20♌	4♍	17♍	0♎	13♎	27♎	10♏	23♏	7♐
1955	14♎	27♎	10♏	23♏	7♐	20♐	3♑	17♑	0♒	13♒	26♒	10♓	23♓	6♈	20♈
1956	29♒	12♓	25♓	8♈	22♈	5♉	18♉	2♊	15♊	28♊	11♋	25♋	8♌	21♌	5♍
1957	5♋	18♋	1♌	14♌	28♌	11♍	24♍	8♎	21♎	4♏	17♏	1♐	14♐	27♐	11♑
1958	22♏	5♐	18♐	1♑	15♑	28♑	11♒	25♒	8♓	21♓	4♈	18♈	1♉	14♉	28♉
1959	5♈	18♈	1♉	14♉	28♉	11♊	24♊	8♋	21♋	4♌	17♌	1♍	14♍	27♍	11♎

MOON POSITIONS

	NOVEMBER					DECEMBER									
	26	27	28	29	30	1	2	3	4	5	6	7	8	9	10
1930	14≈	26≈	8♓	20♓	2♈	14♈	27♈	9♉	22♉	6♊	20♊	4♋	18♋	2♌	17♌
31	17♊	0♋	13♋	26♋	9♌	23♌	7♍	21♍	5♎	19♎	4♏	18♏	3♐	17♐	2♑
32	12♏	27♏	13♐	28♐	13♑	27♑	11≈	25≈	7♓	20♓	2♈	14♈	26♈	8♉	20♉
33	0♈	13♈	26♈	8♉	21♉	3♊	15♊	27♊	8♋	20♋	2♌	14♌	26♌	8♍	21♍
34	4♌	16♌	28♌	9♍	22♍	4♎	16♎	29♎	12♏	26♏	10♐	25♐	10♑	24♑	9≈
35	8♐	21♐	4♑	18♑	2≈	15≈	29≈	13♓	27♓	11♈	26♈	10♉	24♉	8♊	22♊
36	3♉	19♉	4♊	19♊	3♋	17♋	1♌	15♌	28♌	10♍	22♍	5♎	16♎	28♎	10♏
37	22♍	5♎	17♎	29♎	11♏	23♏	5♐	17♐	28♐	10♑	22♑	4≈	16≈	29≈	11♓
38	24♑	5≈	17≈	29≈	11♓	24♓	6♈	19♈	3♉	17♉	1♊	16♊	1♋	15♋	0♌
39	28♉	12♊	25♊	9♋	23♋	7♌	22♌	6♍	20♍	4♎	18♎	2♏	16♏	29♏	13♐
1940	25♎	9♏	24♏	9♐	24♐	8♑	22♑	5≈	18≈	0♓	12♓	24♓	6♈	18♈	0♉
41	13♓	25♓	7♈	19♈	1♉	13♉	25♉	7♊	19♊	1♋	13♋	25♋	7♌	20♌	3♍
42	14♋	26♋	7♌	19♌	1♍	14♍	26♍	9♎	23♎	7♏	22♏	7♐	22♐	7♑	22♑
43	19♏	3♐	17♐	1♑	15♑	29♑	14≈	28≈	12♓	26♓	10♈	23♈	5♉	24♉	11♈
44	16♈	1♉	16♉	0♊	14♊	28♊	12♋	25♋	7♌	20♌	2♍	14♍	26♍	8♎	20♎
45	3♍	16♍	28♍	10♎	22♎	4♏	15♏	27♏	9♐	21♐	3♑	16♑	28♑	11≈	24≈
46	4♑	15♑	27♑	9≈	21≈	4♓	17♓	0♈	14♈	28♈	12♉	27♉	12♊	28♊	13♋
47	9♎	23♎	7♏	22♏	5♐	18♐	1♑	14♑	27♑	9≈	22≈	4♓	16♓	28♓	10♈
48	9♐	23♐	7♑	21♑	5≈	18≈	1♓	14♓	27♓	9♈	24♈	7♉	20♉	3♊	16♊
49	23≈	6♓	18♓	0♈	12♈	23♈	5♉	17♉	29♉	11♊	24♊	7♋	19♋	2♌	16♌
1950	24♊	6♋	18♋	0♌	12♌	25♌	8♍	21♍	4♎	18♎	3♏	18♏	3♐	18♐	4♑
51	29♎	13♏	28♏	13♐	28♐	13♑	28♑	12≈	26≈	10♓	24♓	7♈	20♈	3♉	15♉
52	0♈	14♈	28♈	12♉	26♉	9♊	22♊	5♋	17♋	29♋	11♌	23♌	5♍	17♍	29♍
53	13♌	26♌	8♍	20♍	3♎	16♎	29♎	12♏	20♏	2♐	15♐	28♐	11♑	24♑	7≈
54	14♐	26♐	8♑	21♑	3≈	16≈	29≈	12♓	26♓	10♈	24♈	9♉	24♉	9♊	24♊
55	20♈	4♉	19♉	4♊	19♊	4♋	19♋	4♌	18♌	2♍	15♍	28♍	11♎	24♎	6♏
56	23♍	7♎	20♎	4♏	17♏	29♏	12♐	25♐	7♑	19♑	1≈	13≈	25≈	6♓	18♓
57	3≈	15≈	27≈	9♓	21♓	3♈	15♈	27♈	9♉	22♉	5♊	18♊	1♋	15♋	29♋
58	5♊	17♊	29♊	12♋	24♋	7♌	20♌	4♍	17♍	1♎	16♎	0♏	15♏	0♐	15♐
59	10♎	24♎	9♏	24♏	9♐	25♐	10♑	25♑	9≈	23≈	7♓	19♓	2♈	14♈	27♈

MOON POSITIONS

DECEMBER

	11	12	13	14	15	16	17	18	19	20	21	22	23	24	25
1930	1♍	15♍	29♎	13♎	27♎	11♏	24♏	7♐	20♐	3♑	16♑	28♑	10♒	22♒	4♓
31	15♑	29♑	12♒	24♒	7♓	19♓	1♈	12♈	24♈	6♉	18♉	1♊	13♊	26♊	9♋
32	2♊	14♊	26♊	8♋	20♋	2♌	15♌	28♌	11♍	24♍	8♎	22♎	6♏	21♏	6♐
33	4♎	17♎	1♏	15♏	0♐	15♐	1♑	16♑	1♒	16♒	0♓	14♓	27♓	10♈	23♈
34	23♒	7♓	21♓	5♈	19♈	2♉	15♉	28♉	11♊	24♊	6♋	18♋	0♌	12♌	24♌
35	6♋	19♋	2♌	14♌	26♌	8♍	20♍	2♎	14♎	26♎	8♏	21♏	3♐	16♐	0♑
36	22♏	4♐	16♐	28♐	11♑	23♑	6♒	19♒	2♓	16♓	0♈	14♈	28♈	13♉	27♉
37	24♓	8♈	22♈	6♉	21♉	6♊	21♊	6♋	21♋	6♌	21♌	5♍	18♍	1♎	14♎
38	15♌	0♍	14♍	27♍	11♎	24♎	7♏	19♏	2♐	14♐	26♐	8♑	20♑	2♒	14♒
39	26♐	9♑	21♑	4♒	16♒	28♒	10♓	22♓	3♈	15♈	28♈	10♉	23♉	6♊	20♊
1940	12♉	24♉	6♊	19♊	1♋	14♋	28♋	11♌	25♌	8♍	22♍	6♎	20♎	4♏	19♏
41	16♐	29♐	13♑	27♑	12♒	27♒	12♓	27♓	12♈	27♈	11♉	25♉	9♊	21♊	4♋
42	7♒	21♒	5♓	19♓	2♈	15♈	28♈	10♉	23♉	5♊	17♊	29♊	11♋	22♋	4♌
43	16♊	29♊	11♋	24♋	6♌	18♌	29♌	11♍	23♍	5♎	17♎	0♏	13♏	27♏	11♐
44	2♍	14♍	26♍	9♎	22♎	5♏	19♏	2♐	16♐	0♑	14♑	28♑	13♒	27♒	11♓
45	7♓	21♓	5♈	19♈	3♉	18♉	3♊	18♊	3♋	17♋	1♌	15♌	29♌	11♍	24♍
46	28♋	12♌	26♌	10♍	23♍	6♎	19♎	1♏	13♏	25♏	7♐	19♐	1♑	12♑	24♑
47	7♐	19♐	1♑	13♑	25♑	7♒	19♒	1♓	13♓	25♓	7♈	20♈	3♉	17♉	1♊
48	21♈	4♉	16♉	29♉	12♊	26♊	10♋	24♋	8♌	23♌	7♍	21♍	5♎	19♎	3♏
49	29♌	13♍	27♍	11♎	25♎	10♏	24♏	9♐	23♐	8♑	22♑	5♒	19♒	1♓	14♓
1950	19♑	3♒	17♒	1♓	14♓	27♓	9♈	21♈	3♉	15♉	27♉	9♊	21♊	3♋	15♋
51	27♉	10♊	22♊	4♋	16♋	27♋	9♌	21♌	3♍	15♍	28♍	10♎	23♎	7♏	21♏
52	11♎	23♎	6♏	19♏	3♐	17♐	1♑	15♑	0♒	14♒	29♒	13♓	27♓	11♈	25♈
53	21♒	5♓	19♓	3♈	17♈	2♉	16♉	0♊	15♊	28♊	12♋	25♋	8♌	21♌	3♍
54	9♋	24♋	8♌	21♌	4♍	17♍	0♎	12♎	24♎	6♏	17♏	29♏	11♐	23♐	5♑
55	18♏	0♐	12♐	24♐	6♑	17♑	29♑	11♒	23♒	6♓	18♓	1♈	14♈	28♈	12♉
56	1♈	13♈	26♈	9♉	23♉	7♊	21♊	6♋	21♋	6♌	21♌	5♍	20♍	4♎	17♎
57	13♌	27♌	12♍	26♍	10♎	24♎	8♏	22♏	5♐	19♐	2♑	15♑	28♑	11♒	23♒
58	0♑	14♑	28♑	11♒	25♒	7♓	20♓	2♈	13♈	25♈	7♉	19♉	1♊	13♊	26♊
59	8♉	20♉	2♊	14♊	26♊	8♋	20♋	2♌	14♌	27♌	9♍	22♍	5♎	19♎	3♏

MOON POSITIONS

DECEMBER

	26	27	28	29	30	31
1930	16♓	28♓	10♈	22♈	4♉	17♉
31	23♋	6♌	20♌	4♍	18♍	2♎
32	21♐	6♑	21♑	5♒	19♒	3♓
33	5♉	18♉	0♊	12♊	24♊	5♋
34	6♍	18♍	0♎	12♎	24♎	7♏
35	13♑	27♑	11♒	25♒	10♓	24♓
36	12♊	27♊	11♋	25♋	9♌	22♌
37	26♎	8♏	20♏	2♐	14♐	25♐
38	26♒	8♓	20♓	2♈	14♈	27♈
39	4♋	18♋	3♌	18♌	2♍	17♍
1940	3♐	18♐	2♑	16♑	29♑	13♒
41	16♈	28♈	10♉	22♉	4♊	16♊
42	16♌	28♌	10♍	22♍	5♎	18♎
43	25♐	9♑	24♑	9♒	24♒	8♓
44	25♉	9♊	23♊	6♋	20♋	3♌
45	6♎	18♎	0♏	12♏	24♏	6♐
46	6♒	18♒	1♓	13♓	26♓	9♈
47	15♊	0♋	15♋	0♌	15♌	0♍
48	17♏	0♐	14♐	27♐	10♑	23♑
49	26♓	8♈	20♈	1♉	13♉	25♉
1950	27♋	9♌	22♌	4♍	17♍	0♎
51	6♐	21♐	6♑	21♑	7♒	21♒
52	9♉	22♉	5♊	18♊	1♋	13♋
53	15♍	27♍	9♎	21♎	3♏	15♏
54	18♑	0♒	13♒	26♒	9♓	22♓
55	27♉	11♊	27♊	12♋	27♋	12♌
56	0♏	13♏	26♏	9♐	21♐	3♑
57	5♓	17♓	29♓	11♈	23♈	5♉
58	8♋	21♋	4♌	17♌	1♍	14♍
59	17♏	2♐	18♐	3♑	18♑	3♒

MOON POSITIONS

JANUARY

Year	1	2	3	4	5	6	7	8	9	10	11	12	13	14	15
1960	17♒	2♓	15♓	28♓	11♈	23♈	5♉	17♉	29♉	11♊	23♊	5♋	17♋	29♋	11♌
1961	6♋	18♋	0♌	11♌	23♌	5♍	17♍	29♍	12♎	24♎	8♏	21♏	6♐	20♐	5♑
1962	7♏	20♏	3♐	17♐	1♑	15♑	0♒	15♒	29♒	14♓	28♓	13♈	27♈	10♉	24♉
1963	20♓	4♈	18♈	3♉	17♉	1♊	15♊	29♊	13♋	26♋	9♌	22♌	5♍	17♍	29♍
1964	8♌	22♌	5♍	18♍	1♎	13♎	25♎	7♏	19♏	1♐	13♐	25♐	7♑	19♑	2♒
1965	26♐	8♑	20♑	1♒	13♒	25♒	8♓	20♓	3♈	15♈	29♈	12♉	27♉	11♊	26♊
1966	27♈	10♉	23♉	7♊	21♊	6♋	21♋	6♌	21♌	6♍	20♍	5♎	19♎	2♏	15♏
1967	13♍	27♍	11♎	25♎	9♏	23♏	7♐	20♐	3♑	16♑	29♑	12♒	24♒	7♓	19♓
1968	28♑	12♒	25♒	8♓	21♓	3♈	15♈	27♈	9♉	21♉	3♊	15♊	27♊	9♋	22♋
1969	16♊	28♊	10♋	22♋	4♌	16♌	29♌	11♍	24♍	7♎	20♎	4♏	18♏	2♐	17♐
1970	17♎	0♏	13♏	27♏	12♐	27♐	12♑	27♑	12♒	27♒	12♓	26♓	10♈	23♈	6♉
1971	5♓	19♓	3♈	17♈	1♉	15♉	28♉	11♊	25♊	7♋	20♋	2♌	15♌	27♌	8♍
1972	18♋	2♌	15♌	28♌	10♍	23♍	5♎	17♎	28♎	10♏	22♏	5♐	17♐	0♑	13♑
1973	6♐	18♐	0♑	12♑	24♑	7♒	19♒	2♓	15♓	28♓	12♈	26♈	10♉	24♉	9♊
1974	8♈	21♈	4♉	18♉	2♊	17♊	2♋	15♋	29♋	12♌	25♌	7♍	20♍	2♎	14♎
1975	27♌	11♍	26♍	10♎	23♎	7♏	20♏	3♐	15♐	28♐	10♑	22♑	4♒	16♒	28♒
1976	9♑	21♑	4♒	16♒	29♒	11♓	24♓	6♈	19♈	1♉	14♉	26♉	9♊	21♊	4♋
1977	6♉	19♉	2♊	15♊	28♊	11♋	24♋	8♌	21♌	4♍	17♍	0♎	13♎	27♎	10♏
1978	12♍	25♍	8♎	21♎	5♏	18♏	1♐	14♐	27♐	11♑	24♑	7♒	20♒	3♓	17♓
1979	0♒	13♒	26♒	10♓	23♓	6♈	19♈	2♉	15♉	28♉	11♊	25♊	8♋	21♋	4♌
1980	0♋	13♋	26♋	10♌	23♌	6♍	19♍	2♎	15♎	28♎	11♏	24♏	7♐	20♐	3♑
1981	16♏	28♏	12♐	25♐	8♑	21♑	4♒	17♒	0♓	13♓	26♓	9♈	22♈	5♉	18♉
1982	20♓	3♈	16♈	29♈	12♉	25♉	8♊	21♊	4♋	17♋	0♌	13♌	26♌	9♍	22♍
1983	9♌	24♌	5♍	18♍	1♎	14♎	27♎	10♏	23♏	6♐	19♐	2♑	15♑	28♑	11♒
1984	20♐	3♑	16♑	29♑	12♒	25♒	8♓	21♓	4♈	17♈	0♉	13♉	26♉	9♊	22♊
1985	6♉	19♉	2♊	15♊	28♊	11♋	24♋	7♌	20♌	3♍	16♍	29♍	12♎	25♎	8♏
1986	12♍	25♍	8♎	21♎	5♏	18♏	1♐	14♐	27♐	11♑	24♑	7♒	20♒	3♓	17♓
1987	0♒	13♒	26♒	10♓	23♓	6♈	19♈	2♉	15♉	28♉	11♊	25♊	8♋	21♋	4♌
1988	11♊	24♊	7♋	20♋	3♌	16♌	29♌	12♍	25♍	8♎	21♎	4♏	17♏	0♐	13♐
1989	25♎	7♏	20♏	4♐	17♐	0♑	13♑	26♑	9♒	22♒	5♓	18♓	1♈	14♈	27♈

MOON POSITIONS

JANUARY

	16	17	18	19	20	21	22	23	24	25	26	27	28	29	30
1960	24♌	6♍	19♍	2♎	15♎	29♎	13♏	27♏	12♐	26♐	11♑	26♑	11♒	25♒	9♓
61	20♑	6♒	21♒	6♓	20♓	4♈	18♈	1♉	14♉	26♉	9♊	21♊	3♋	15♋	27♋
62	7♊	20♊	2♋	15♋	27♋	9♌	21♌	3♍	15♍	27♍	8♎	20♎	3♏	15♏	28♏
63	11♎	23♎	5♏	17♏	29♏	11♐	24♐	7♑	20♑	4♒	18♒	2♓	16♓	1♈	15♈
64	14♒	27♒	10♓	24♓	7♈	21♈	5♉	19♉	4♊	18♊	3♋	17♋	1♌	15♌	29♌
65	11♋	26♋	11♌	26♌	11♍	25♍	9♎	22♎	5♏	17♏	29♏	11♐	23♐	5♑	17♑
66	28♏	11♐	23♐	6♑	17♑	29♑	11♒	23♒	5♓	17♓	29♓	11♈	23♈	5♉	18♉
67	1♈	12♈	24♈	6♉	18♉	1♊	13♊	27♊	10♋	24♋	9♌	23♌	8♍	23♍	8♎
68	5♌	19♌	2♍	16♍	0♎	13♎	27♎	11♏	26♏	10♐	24♐	8♑	22♑	6♒	20♒
69	2♑	17♑	2♒	17♒	2♓	16♓	29♓	12♈	25♈	7♉	19♉	1♊	13♊	25♊	7♋
1970	19♉	1♊	14♊	26♊	8♋	20♋	2♌	13♌	25♌	7♍	19♍	1♎	13♎	26♎	9♏
71	20♍	2♎	14♎	26♎	8♏	21♏	4♐	17♐	1♑	15♑	0♒	14♒	29♒	14♓	29♓
72	26♑	10♒	23♒	7♓	21♓	6♈	20♈	4♉	18♉	2♊	16♊	0♋	14♋	27♋	10♌
73	23♊	8♋	23♋	7♌	22♌	5♍	19♍	2♎	15♎	27♎	9♏	22♏	3♐	15♐	27♐
74	10♏	22♏	4♐	16♐	28♐	10♑	22♑	4♒	15♒	27♒	10♓	22♓	4♈	17♈	0♉
75	10♓	22♓	4♈	16♈	28♈	11♉	24♉	7♊	21♊	5♋	20♋	5♌	20♌	6♍	21♍
76	16♋	0♌	15♌	29♌	14♍	28♍	12♎	27♎	11♏	24♏	8♐	21♐	5♑	18♑	1♒
77	15♐	29♐	14♑	28♑	12♒	26♒	9♓	22♓	4♈	17♈	29♈	10♉	22♉	4♊	16♊
78	0♉	12♉	24♉	6♊	18♊	0♋	12♋	24♋	6♌	18♌	1♍	13♍	26♍	9♎	22♎
79	0♍	12♍	24♍	6♎	18♎	1♏	14♏	28♏	12♐	26♐	11♑	26♑	11♒	27♒	12♓
1980	7♑	21♑	6♒	20♒	5♓	20♓	4♈	19♈	3♉	16♉	0♊	13♊	26♊	9♋	22♋
81	7♊	21♊	5♋	19♋	3♌	16♌	29♌	12♍	24♍	6♎	18♎	0♏	12♏	24♏	6♐
82	20♎	3♏	15♏	27♏	8♐	20♐	2♑	14♑	26♑	9♒	21♒	4♓	17♓	0♈	13♈
83	20♒	2♓	15♓	27♓	9♈	22♈	5♉	19♉	2♊	17♊	2♋	17♋	2♌	17♌	2♍
84	27♊	12♋	26♋	11♌	26♌	11♍	26♍	11♎	25♎	8♏	22♏	5♐	17♐	0♑	12♑
85	29♍	13♎	26♎	10♏	23♏	6♐	19♐	1♑	14♑	26♑	8♒	20♒	1♓	13♓	25♓
86	10♈	22♈	4♉	16♉	28♉	10♊	22♊	4♋	16♋	29♋	12♌	25♌	8♍	22♍	6♎
87	11♌	23♌	5♍	18♍	0♎	13♎	26♎	10♏	24♏	8♐	23♐	8♑	23♑	8♒	23♒
88	18♐	2♑	17♑	2♒	18♒	3♓	18♓	2♈	16♈	0♉	13♉	26♉	8♊	21♊	3♋
89	21♉	4♊	18♊	1♋	14♋	27♋	9♌	22♌	4♍	16♍	27♍	9♎	21♎	3♏	15♏

MOON POSITIONS

JANUARY/FEBRUARY

	31	1	2	3	4	5	6	7	8	9	10	11	12	13	14
1960	23♓	6♈	19♈	1♉	14♉	26♉	7♊	19♊	1♋	13♋	25♋	8♌	20♌	3♍	16♍
61	8♌	20♌	2♍	14♍	26♍	9♎	21♎	4♏	17♏	1♐	15♐	29♐	14♑	29♑	14♒
62	11♐	25♐	9♑	23♑	8♒	23♒	8♓	23♓	8♈	23♈	7♉	20♉	4♊	17♊	29♊
63	29♈	14♉	28♉	11♊	25♊	9♋	22♋	5♌	18♌	0♍	13♍	25♍	7♎	19♎	1♏
64	13♏	26♏	9♐	21♐	3♑	15♑	27♑	9♒	21♒	3♓	15♓	28♓	10♈	23♈	7♉
65	28♑	10♒	22♒	5♓	17♓	0♈	12♈	25♈	9♉	22♉	6♊	20♊	5♋	19♋	4♌
66	1♊	15♊	29♊	14♋	29♋	14♌	29♌	14♍	29♍	14♎	28♎	12♏	25♏	8♐	20♐
67	22♎	6♏	20♏	3♐	17♐	0♑	13♑	26♑	8♒	21♒	3♓	15♓	27♓	9♈	20♈
68	3♓	16♓	29♓	11♈	23♈	5♉	17♉	28♉	10♊	22♊	5♋	18♋	1♌	14♌	28♌
69	19♍	1♎	13♎	25♎	8♏	21♏	4♐	17♐	0♑	14♑	28♑	12♒	27♒	11♓	26♓
1970	22♏	6♐	20♐	5♑	20♑	5♒	20♒	5♓	20♓	5♈	19♈	2♉	15♉	28♉	11♊
71	14♈	28♈	12♉	25♉	8♊	21♊	4♋	17♋	29♋	11♌	23♌	5♍	17♍	29♍	10♎
72	23♌	6♍	18♍	0♎	12♎	24♎	6♏	18♏	0♐	12♐	25♐	8♑	21♑	4♒	18♒
73	9♑	21♑	3♒	16♒	29♒	12♓	25♓	9♈	23♈	6♉	20♉	5♊	19♊	3♋	17♋
74	13♉	27♉	11♊	26♊	10♋	25♋	11♌	26♌	11♍	25♍	9♎	23♎	6♏	19♏	1♐
75	5♎	20♎	3♏	17♏	0♐	13♐	25♐	7♑	19♑	1♒	13♒	25♒	7♓	19♓	1♈
76	13♒	26♒	8♓	20♓	2♈	14♈	26♈	8♉	20♉	2♊	14♊	27♊	11♋	24♋	9♌
77	28♊	11♋	24♋	6♌	20♌	3♍	17♍	1♎	15♎	29♎	13♏	27♏	11♐	25♐	9♑
78	5♏	19♏	3♐	17♐	2♑	17♑	2♒	17♒	1♓	16♓	29♓	13♈	26♈	9♉	21♉
79	26♓	11♈	24♈	8♉	21♉	3♊	16♊	28♊	10♋	22♋	4♌	16♌	27♌	9♍	21♍
1980	4♌	16♌	28♌	10♍	22♍	4♎	16♎	28♎	10♏	22♏	5♐	18♐	1♑	15♑	29♑
81	18♐	1♑	14♑	27♑	10♒	24♒	8♓	22♓	7♈	21♈	5♉	19♉	4♊	18♊	1♋
82	27♈	11♉	25♉	9♊	24♊	8♋	23♋	7♌	22♌	6♍	19♍	3♎	16♎	28♎	11♏
83	17♍	1♎	15♎	29♎	12♏	24♏	6♐	18♐	0♑	12♑	24♑	6♒	17♒	29♒	12♓
84	24♑	6♒	18♒	0♓	12♓	24♓	6♈	18♈	0♉	12♉	25♉	8♊	21♊	5♋	19♋
85	8♊	20♊	3♋	17♋	1♌	15♌	29♌	14♍	29♍	13♎	28♎	12♏	26♏	10♐	23♐
86	19♎	3♏	17♏	1♐	16♐	0♑	14♑	28♑	12♒	26♒	10♓	23♓	6♈	18♈	0♉
87	8♓	22♓	6♈	19♈	2♉	14♉	26♉	8♊	20♊	2♋	14♋	26♋	8♌	20♌	2♍
88	15♋	27♋	9♌	21♌	2♍	14♍	26♍	8♎	20♎	3♏	15♏	28♏	12♐	26♐	10♑
89	28♏	10♐	23♐	7♑	21♑	5♒	20♒	5♓	20♓	5♈	19♈	4♉	18♉	1♊	15♊

MOON POSITIONS

FEBRUARY

	15	16	17	18	19	20	21	22	23	24	25	26	27	28	29
1960	29♍	12♎	26♎	10♏	23♏	8♐	22♐	6♑	21♑	5♒	19♒	3♓	17♓	1♈	14♈
61	29♒	14♓	28♓	13♈	26♈	10♉	23♉	5♊	18♊	0♋	11♋	23♋	5♌	17♌	
62	12♋	24♋	6♌	18♌	0♍	12♍	23♍	5♎	17♎	29♎	11♏	24♏	6♐	20♐	
63	13♏	25♏	7♐	19♐	2♑	15♑	28♑	12♒	26♒	11♓	26♓	10♈	25♈	10♉	
64	20♓	4♈	18♈	2♉	16♉	0♊	14♊	28♊	12♋	26♋	10♌	24♌	8♍	21♍	4♎
65	19♈	4♉	19♉	3♊	17♊	0♋	13♋	25♋	8♌	20♌	1♍	13♍	25♍	7♎	
66	2♌	14♌	26♌	8♍	20♍	2♎	14♎	26♎	8♏	20♏	2♐	15♐	27♐	10♑	
67	2♉	14♉	26♉	9♊	21♊	5♋	18♋	2♌	17♌	2♍	17♍	2♎	17♎	2♏	
68	12♍	26♍	10♎	24♎	8♏	22♏	7♐	21♐	4♑	18♑	2♒	15♒	28♒	11♓	24♓
69	11♒	25♒	9♓	23♓	7♈	20♈	3♉	15♉	27♉	9♊	21♊	3♋	15♋	27♋	
1970	23♊	5♋	17♋	29♋	10♌	22♌	4♍	16♍	28♍	10♎	23♎	6♏	19♏	2♐	
71	22♎	4♏	17♏	29♏	12♐	25♐	9♑	23♑	7♒	22♒	8♓	23♓	8♈	23♈	
72	2♓	17♓	1♈	16♈	0♉	15♉	29♉	13♊	27♊	10♋	23♋	6♌	19♌	2♍	14♍
73	2♌	16♌	0♍	13♍	27♍	10♎	22♎	5♏	17♏	29♏	11♐	23♐	4♑	16♑	
74	13♐	25♐	7♑	18♑	0♒	12♒	24♒	6♓	19♓	1♈	14♈	27♈	10♉	24♉	
75	13♈	25♈	7♉	20♉	2♊	16♊	29♊	13♋	28♋	13♌	28♌	14♍	29♍	14♎	
76	23♌	8♍	23♍	8♎	23♎	7♏	21♏	5♐	18♐	2♑	15♑	27♑	10♒	22♒	5♓
77	23♐	7♑	21♑	4♒	17♒	0♓	12♓	24♓	6♈	18♈	0♉	12♉	24♉	6♊	
78	3♊	15♊	27♊	8♋	20♋	2♌	15♌	27♌	10♍	22♍	5♎	19♎	2♏	16♏	
79	3♎	15♎	28♎	10♏	23♏	7♐	21♐	5♑	19♑	4♒	19♒	4♓	20♓	4♈	
1980	14♒	29♒	14♓	29♓	14♈	28♈	13♉	27♉	10♊	23♊	6♋	19♋	1♌	13♌	25♌
81	15♋	28♋	11♌	24♌	7♍	20♍	2♎	14♎	26♎	8♏	20♏	2♐	14♐	26♐	
82	23♏	5♐	16♐	28♐	10♑	22♑	4♒	17♒	0♓	13♓	26♓	10♈	24♈	8♉	
83	24♓	6♈	19♈	2♉	15♉	28♉	12♊	26♊	10♋	25♋	10♌	25♌	10♍	25♍	
84	4♌	19♌	5♍	20♍	5♎	20♎	4♏	18♏	1♐	14♐	27♐	9♑	21♑	3♒	15♒
85	6♑	19♑	2♒	15♒	28♒	10♓	22♓	4♈	16♈	28♈	10♉	21♉	3♊	16♊	
86	12♉	24♉	6♊	18♊	0♋	12♋	24♋	7♌	20♌	4♍	18♍	2♎	16♎	0♏	
87	15♍	27♍	10♎	23♎	7♏	20♏	4♐	18♐	2♑	17♑	2♒	16♒	1♓	16♓	
88	25♑	10♒	26♒	11♓	26♓	11♈	25♈	9♉	22♉	5♊	18♊	0♋	12♋	24♋	6♌
89	28♊	11♋	23♋	6♌	18♌	0♍	12♍	24♍	6♎	18♎	0♏	11♏	24♏	6♐	

MOON POSITIONS

MARCH	1	2	3	4	5	6	7	8	9	10	11	12	13	14	15
1960	27♈	9♉	21♉	3♊	15♊	27♊	9♋	21♋	3♌	16♌	28♌	11♍	25♍	8♎	22♎
61	29♌	11♍	23♍	6♎	18♎	1♏	14♏	27♏	11♐	25♐	9♑	23♑	8♒	22♒	7♓
62	3♑	17♑	1♒	16♒	1♓	16♓	2♈	17♈	1♉	16♉	0♊	13♊	26♊	9♋	21♋
63	24♉	8♊	22♊	5♋	19♋	1♌	14♌	27♌	9♍	21♍	3♎	15♎	27♎	9♏	21♏
64	17♎	29♎	14♏	26♏	8♐	20♐	3♑	15♑	28♑	10♒	23♒	5♓	18♓	29♓	13♈
65	19♒	1♓	14♓	26♓	9♈	22♈	6♉	19♉	3♊	17♊	1♋	15♋	29♋	13♌	28♌
66	24♊	8♋	22♋	7♌	22♌	7♍	23♍	8♎	23♎	8♏	22♏	6♐	20♐	3♑	16♑
67	16♏	0♐	14♐	27♐	10♑	23♑	5♒	17♒	0♓	12♓	24♓	6♈	17♈	29♈	11♉
68	7♈	19♈	1♉	13♉	24♉	6♊	18♊	0♋	13♋	25♋	8♌	22♌	6♍	20♍	5♎
69	9♌	21♌	4♍	17♍	0♎	14♎	27♎	11♏	25♏	9♐	23♐	7♑	22♑	6♒	20♒
1970	15♐	29♐	13♑	27♑	11♒	25♒	9♓	23♓	7♈	21♈	5♉	19♉	3♊	17♊	1♋
71	7♉	21♉	5♊	18♊	1♋	14♋	27♋	9♌	21♌	3♍	15♍	27♍	9♎	21♎	3♏
72	26♍	9♎	21♎	4♏	17♏	0♐	13♐	26♐	9♑	22♑	5♒	18♒	1♓	13♓	25♓
73	29♌	11♍	24♍	7♎	20♎	3♏	16♏	0♐	13♐	26♐	10♑	24♑	8♒	22♒	6♓
74	7♊	20♊	3♋	17♋	0♌	14♌	28♌	12♍	26♍	10♎	24♎	8♏	22♏	6♐	21♐
75	28♎	11♏	24♏	6♐	19♐	1♑	14♑	26♑	9♒	21♒	4♓	16♓	29♓	11♈	22♈
76	17♓	0♈	13♈	26♈	9♉	22♉	5♊	18♊	1♋	14♋	27♋	10♌	23♌	6♍	19♍
77	19♋	3♌	17♌	1♍	15♍	29♍	13♎	27♎	11♏	25♏	9♐	22♐	6♑	20♑	3♒
78	29♏	13♐	26♐	10♑	24♑	7♒	21♒	4♓	18♓	2♈	15♈	29♈	12♉	26♉	10♊
79	19♈	1♉	14♉	26♉	8♊	21♊	3♋	15♋	28♋	10♌	22♌	5♍	17♍	29♍	12♎
1980	7♍	20♍	3♎	16♎	29♎	12♏	25♏	8♐	20♐	3♑	16♑	29♑	11♒	24♒	7♓
81	8♑	22♑	6♒	20♒	4♓	18♓	2♈	16♈	0♉	14♉	28♉	12♊	26♊	10♋	24♋
82	22♉	5♊	19♊	2♋	16♋	29♋	13♌	26♌	10♍	23♍	7♎	20♎	4♏	17♏	0♐
83	9♎	21♎	4♏	16♏	29♏	11♐	24♐	6♑	19♑	1♒	14♒	26♒	8♓	21♓	3♈
84	27♒	10♓	23♓	6♈	19♈	2♉	15♉	28♉	11♊	23♊	6♋	19♋	2♌	15♌	28♌
85	28♊	10♋	22♋	4♌	16♌	28♌	10♍	22♍	4♎	16♎	28♎	10♏	22♏	4♐	16♐
86	14♏	27♏	11♐	24♐	7♑	20♑	4♒	17♒	0♓	14♓	27♓	10♈	24♈	7♉	20♉
87	0♈	12♈	25♈	7♉	20♉	2♊	15♊	27♊	9♋	22♋	4♌	17♌	29♌	12♍	24♍
88	18♌	1♍	14♍	27♍	10♎	23♎	6♏	19♏	2♐	15♐	28♐	11♑	24♑	7♒	19♒
89	19♐	3♑	17♑	1♒	15♒	29♒	13♓	27♓	11♈	26♈	10♉	24♉	8♊	22♊	6♋

MOON POSITIONS

MARCH	16	17	18	19	20	21	22	23	24	25	26	27	28	29	30
1960	6♏	20♏	4♐	19♐	3♑	17♑	1♒	15♒	29♒	12♓	26♓	9♈	22♈	5♉	17♉
61	22♓	6♈	20♈	4♉	18♉	1♊	13♊	26♊	8♋	20♋	2♌	13♌	25♌	7♍	19♍
62	3♌	15♌	27♌	9♍	20♍	2♎	14♎	26♎	8♏	21♏	3♐	16♐	29♐	12♑	26♑
63	3♐	15♐	27♐	10♑	23♑	6♒	20♒	4♓	19♓	4♈	19♈	4♉	19♉	4♊	18♊
64	28♈	12♉	27♉	11♊	25♊	9♋	23♋	7♌	20♌	3♍	17♍	0♎	12♎	25♎	7♏
65	13♍	27♍	11♎	25♎	8♏	21♏	3♐	15♐	27♐	9♑	21♑	3♒	15♒	27♒	10♓
66	23♑	5♒	17♒	0♓	11♓	23♓	5♈	17♈	29♈	12♉	24♉	7♊	20♊	4♋	18♋
67	23♉	5♊	17♊	0♋	13♋	26♋	10♌	25♌	10♍	25♍	10♎	25♎	10♏	25♏	9♐
68	19♎	4♏	19♏	3♐	17♐	1♑	15♑	29♑	12♒	25♒	8♓	20♓	3♈	15♈	27♈
69	4♓	18♓	1♈	15♈	28♈	10♉	23♉	5♊	17♊	29♊	11♋	23♋	5♌	17♌	0♍
1970	13♋	25♋	7♌	19♌	1♍	13♍	25♍	7♎	20♎	3♏	16♏	29♏	12♐	26♐	10♑
71	13♌	26♌	8♍	21♍	4♎	18♎	1♏	16♏	1♐	16♐	1♑	16♑	1♒	16♒	0♓
72	10♈	25♈	10♉	25♉	9♊	23♊	7♋	20♋	3♌	16♌	29♌	11♍	23♍	5♎	17♎
73	25♌	9♍	22♍	5♎	18♎	0♏	13♏	25♏	7♐	19♐	0♑	12♑	24♑	7♒	19♒
74	3♑	15♑	27♑	9♒	21♒	3♓	15♓	28♓	11♈	24♈	7♉	21♉	4♊	18♊	2♋
75	4♑	16♑	29♑	12♒	25♒	9♓	23♓	7♈	22♈	7♉	22♉	7♊	22♊	7♋	21♋
76	1♎	17♎	2♏	16♏	1♐	15♐	28♐	12♑	25♑	7♒	20♒	2♓	14♓	26♓	8♈
77	17♒	0♓	13♓	26♓	8♈	20♈	2♉	14♉	26♉	8♊	20♊	2♋	14♋	26♋	9♌
78	23♊	5♋	16♋	28♋	10♌	23♌	5♍	18♍	1♎	15♎	28♎	12♏	26♏	10♐	24♐
79	25♎	7♏	20♏	3♐	17♐	1♑	15♑	29♑	13♒	28♒	13♓	28♓	12♈	27♈	11♉
1980	22♓	7♈	22♈	7♉	22♉	6♊	20♊	3♋	15♋	28♋	10♌	22♌	4♍	16♍	28♍
81	8♌	21♌	3♍	16♍	28♍	10♎	22♎	4♏	16♏	28♏	10♐	22♐	4♑	17♑	29♑
82	12♐	24♐	6♑	18♑	0♒	12♒	25♒	8♓	22♓	5♈	19♈	4♉	18♉	3♊	17♊
83	16♈	29♈	13♉	25♉	13♊	27♊	10♋	23♋	6♌	19♌	4♍	19♍	3♎	17♎	1♏
84	13♍	28♍	13♎	28♎	13♏	27♏	10♐	23♐	6♑	18♑	0♒	12♒	24♒	6♓	18♓
85	29♑	12♒	24♒	7♓	19♓	1♈	13♈	25♈	6♉	18♉	0♊	12♊	24♊	7♋	20♋
86	2♊	14♊	25♊	7♋	20♋	2♌	15♌	28♌	12♍	26♍	11♎	25♎	10♏	24♏	9♐
87	7♎	20♎	3♏	17♏	1♐	15♐	29♐	13♑	27♑	12♒	26♒	10♓	24♓	8♈	21♈
88	4♓	19♓	4♈	19♈	3♉	17♉	0♊	13♊	26♊	8♋	21♋	2♌	14♌	26♌	8♍
89	21♋	3♌	15♌	27♌	9♍	21♍	3♎	15♎	26♎	8♏	20♏	3♐	15♐	28♐	11♑

MOON POSITIONS

MARCH/APRIL

	31	1	2	3	4	5	6	7	8	9	10	11	12	13	14
1960	29♉	11♊	23♊	5♋	17♋	29♋	11♌	24♌	6♍	20♍	3♎	17♎	1♏	16♏	0♐
1961	2♎	15♎	27♎	11♏	24♏	8♐	21♐	5♑	19♑	3♒	18♒	2♓	16♓	1♈	15♈
1962	10♒	25♒	9♓	25♓	10♈	25♈	10♉	24♉	8♊	22♊	5♋	17♋	0♌	12♌	24♌
1963	2♋	16♋	29♋	11♌	24♌	6♍	18♍	0♎	12♎	24♎	6♏	18♏	0♐	12♐	24♐
1964	19♏	1♐	13♐	25♐	7♑	19♑	1♒	13♒	26♒	10♓	23♓	8♈	22♈	7♉	22♉
1965	22♓	5♈	18♈	2♉	16♉	29♉	13♊	27♊	11♋	26♋	10♌	24♌	8♍	22♍	6♎
1966	2♌	16♌	1♍	16♍	1♎	16♎	0♏	15♏	28♏	12♐	25♐	7♑	20♑	2♒	14♒
1967	23♐	7♑	20♑	2♒	15♒	27♒	9♓	21♓	2♈	14♈	26♈	8♉	20♉	2♊	14♊
1968	9♑	21♑	3♒	14♒	26♒	8♓	21♓	3♈	16♈	0♉	14♉	28♉	13♊	28♊	13♋
1969	12♍	25♍	9♎	23♎	7♏	21♏	5♐	20♐	4♑	18♑	2♒	16♒	0♓	14♓	27♓
1970	24♑	8♒	23♒	7♓	22♓	6♈	21♈	5♉	18♉	2♊	15♊	27♊	9♋	21♋	3♌
1971	14♊	27♊	10♋	23♋	5♌	17♌	29♌	11♍	22♍	4♎	16♎	28♎	10♏	23♏	5♐
1972	29♎	11♏	23♏	5♐	17♐	29♐	11♑	24♑	7♒	20♒	4♓	19♓	3♈	19♈	4♉
1973	2♓	16♓	0♈	14♈	28♈	13♉	27♉	12♊	26♊	10♋	24♋	8♌	22♌	5♍	18♍
1974	4♐	18♐	0♑	13♑	25♑	7♒	19♒	1♓	13♓	25♓	8♈	20♈	4♉	17♉	0♊
1975	16♋	0♌	14♌	29♌	13♍	27♍	11♎	25♎	8♏	22♏	4♐	17♐	29♐	11♑	23♑
1976	19♈	1♉	13♉	25♉	7♊	19♊	2♋	15♋	27♋	10♌	24♌	8♍	22♍	6♎	21♎
1977	22♌	6♍	20♍	4♎	19♎	3♏	18♏	2♐	16♐	0♑	13♑	26♑	9♒	21♒	3♓
1978	9♑	23♑	7♒	21♒	5♓	19♓	3♈	16♈	29♈	11♉	24♉	6♊	18♊	0♋	12♋
1979	24♉	8♊	20♊	3♋	15♋	27♋	9♌	21♌	3♍	14♍	27♍	9♎	21♎	4♏	17♏
1980	9♎	21♎	3♏	15♏	28♏	10♐	23♐	6♑	19♑	2♒	16♒	0♓	15♓	0♈	15♈
1981	12♒	26♒	10♓	25♓	10♈	25♈	10♉	25♉	10♊	24♊	8♋	22♋	5♌	18♌	1♍
1982	1♋	15♋	29♋	13♌	26♌	10♍	23♍	6♎	19♎	2♏	14♏	26♏	8♐	20♐	2♑
1983	15♏	28♏	10♐	23♐	5♑	17♑	28♑	10♒	22♒	4♓	17♓	29♓	12♈	25♈	8♉
1984	0♈	12♈	24♈	6♉	18♉	1♊	14♊	27♊	10♋	24♋	8♌	22♌	7♍	22♍	7♎
1985	3♌	17♌	1♍	16♍	1♎	16♎	1♏	16♏	1♐	15♐	29♐	13♑	26♑	9♒	21♒
1986	23♐	7♑	21♑	5♒	18♒	2♓	15♓	27♓	10♈	22♈	4♉	16♉	28♉	10♊	22♊
1987	4♉	17♉	0♊	12♊	24♊	6♋	18♋	0♌	12♌	24♌	6♍	19♍	2♎	15♎	29♎
1988	20♍	2♎	14♎	27♎	9♏	22♏	5♐	18♐	2♑	16♑	0♒	14♒	28♒	13♓	28♓
1989	24♑	8♒	22♒	6♓	21♓	6♈	22♈	7♉	22♉	6♊	20♊	4♋	17♋	0♌	12♌

MOON POSITIONS

APRIL

	15	16	17	18	19	20	21	22	23	24	25	26	27	28	29
1960	15♐	29♐	14♑	28♑	12♒	26♒	9♓	22♓	5♈	18♈	1♉	13♉	25♉	7♊	19♊
61	29♈	12♉	26♉	9♊	21♊	4♋	16♋	28♋	9♌	21♌	3♍	15♍	28♍	10♎	23♎
62	5♍	17♍	29♍	11♎	23♎	5♏	18♏	0♐	13♐	26♐	9♑	23♑	6♒	20♒	4♓
63	6♑	18♑	1♒	15♒	28♒	12♓	27♓	12♈	28♈	13♉	28♉	13♊	27♊	11♋	25♋
64	7♊	21♊	6♋	20♋	4♌	17♌	0♍	13♍	26♍	9♎	21♎	4♏	16♏	28♏	9♐
65	20♎	3♏	16♏	29♏	11♐	23♐	5♑	17♑	29♑	11♒	23♒	5♓	18♓	0♈	14♈
66	25♒	7♓	19♓	1♈	13♈	26♈	8♉	21♉	4♊	17♊	1♋	14♋	28♋	12♌	27♌
67	27♊	9♋	22♋	6♌	20♌	4♍	18♍	3♎	18♎	4♏	19♏	3♐	18♐	2♑	15♑
68	28♏	13♐	27♐	12♑	25♑	9♒	22♒	5♓	17♓	0♈	12♈	24♈	6♉	18♉	29♉
69	10♈	23♈	6♉	18♉	1♊	13♊	25♊	7♋	19♋	1♌	13♌	25♌	7♍	20♍	3♎
1970	15♌	27♌	9♍	21♍	3♎	16♎	29♎	12♏	25♏	9♐	23♐	7♑	21♑	5♒	19♒
71	18♐	1♑	14♑	27♑	11♒	25♒	10♓	24♓	9♈	24♈	9♉	24♉	8♊	22♊	6♋
72	19♉	4♊	19♊	3♋	17♋	0♌	13♌	26♌	8♍	20♍	2♎	14♎	26♎	8♏	20♏
73	1♎	14♎	26♎	9♏	21♏	3♐	15♐	27♐	8♑	20♑	2♒	15♒	27♒	10♓	24♓
74	5♒	17♒	29♒	11♓	23♓	6♈	19♈	3♉	17♉	0♊	14♊	29♊	13♋	27♋	11♌
75	9♊	22♊	5♋	19♋	3♌	17♌	1♍	16♍	1♎	16♎	0♏	15♏	29♏	12♐	26♐
76	10♏	25♏	10♐	24♐	8♑	21♑	4♒	16♒	28♒	11♓	23♓	5♈	16♈	28♈	10♉
77	22♓	5♈	17♈	29♈	11♉	23♉	5♊	16♊	28♊	10♋	22♋	5♌	17♌	1♍	14♍
78	24♋	6♌	18♌	1♍	13♍	26♍	10♎	23♎	7♏	22♏	6♐	21♐	5♑	20♑	4♒
79	0♐	14♐	27♐	11♑	25♑	9♒	24♒	8♓	22♓	7♈	21♈	5♉	19♉	2♊	15♊
1980	0♉	15♉	0♊	14♊	28♊	11♋	24♋	7♌	19♌	1♍	13♍	24♍	6♎	18♎	0♏
81	13♍	25♍	7♎	19♎	1♏	13♏	25♏	7♐	19♐	1♑	13♑	25♑	8♒	21♒	5♓
82	14♑	26♑	8♒	20♒	3♓	16♓	0♈	14♈	28♈	13♉	28♉	12♊	27♊	12♋	26♋
83	22♉	6♊	19♊	3♋	16♋	1♌	16♌	0♍	14♍	28♍	12♎	26♎	9♏	23♏	6♐
84	4♓	16♓	28♓	10♈	22♈	5♉	18♉	2♊	16♊	0♋	14♋	27♋	11♌	24♌	8♍
85	24♒	6♓	19♓	2♈	15♈	28♈	11♉	24♉	7♊	20♊	3♋	16♋	29♋	12♌	26♌
86	4♍	16♍	28♍	10♎	22♎	5♏	18♏	1♐	14♐	27♐	10♑	23♑	6♒	20♒	3♓
87	13♏	26♏	8♐	21♐	4♑	16♑	29♑	12♒	25♒	8♓	22♓	5♈	19♈	3♉	17♉
88	12♈	25♈	8♉	21♉	4♊	17♊	0♋	13♋	26♋	8♌	20♌	2♍	14♍	26♍	8♎
89	24♌	6♍	18♍	0♎	12♎	24♎	6♏	18♏	1♐	13♐	25♐	7♑	20♑	3♒	17♒

MOON POSITIONS

APRIL/MAY	30	1	2	3	4	5	6	7	8	9	10	11	12	13	14
1960	1♋	13♋	25♋	7♌	19♌	2♍	14♍	27♍	11♎	25♎	10♏	24♏	9♐	24♐	9♑
1961	6♏	20♏	4♐	18♐	2♑	16♑	0♒	14♒	29♒	13♓	27♓	10♈	24♈	8♉	21♉
1962	19♓	4♈	18♈	3♉	18♉	2♊	16♊	0♋	13♋	26♋	8♌	20♌	2♍	14♍	26♍
1963	8♌	21♌	3♍	15♍	27♍	9♎	21♎	3♏	15♏	27♏	9♐	21♐	3♑	15♑	28♑
1964	21♐	3♑	15♑	27♑	9♒	22♒	4♓	18♓	2♈	16♈	1♉	15♉	1♊	16♊	1♋
1965	27♈	11♉	25♉	9♊	24♊	8♋	22♋	7♌	21♌	5♍	19♍	2♎	16♎	29♎	12♏
1966	11♍	25♍	10♎	24♎	9♏	23♏	6♐	20♐	3♑	15♑	28♑	10♒	22♒	4♓	15♓
1967	28♉	12♊	27♊	11♋	24♋	8♌	21♌	5♍	18♍	1♎	14♎	27♎	9♏	21♏	4♐
1968	11♊	25♊	9♋	21♋	4♌	16♌	28♌	10♍	22♍	4♎	16♎	28♎	11♏	24♏	6♐
1969	17♎	1♏	16♏	0♐	15♐	29♐	13♑	27♑	11♒	24♒	7♓	20♓	3♈	16♈	28♈
1970	3♓	17♓	1♈	15♈	29♈	13♉	26♉	10♊	23♊	5♋	17♋	29♋	11♌	23♌	5♍
1971	19♋	1♌	13♌	25♌	7♍	19♍	1♎	13♎	25♎	8♏	21♏	3♐?	15♐	28♐	11♑
1972	2♐	14♐	26♐	8♑	20♑	3♒	16♒	29♒	13♓	27♓	12♈	27♈	12♊	27♊	13♊
1973	8♈	22♈	7♉	22♉	7♊	22♊	6♋	20♋	4♌	17♌	0♍	13♍	25♍	11♎	23♎
1974	25♌	9♏	23♏	6♐	19♐	2♑	15♑	27♑	10♒	22♒	4♓	17♓	29♓	12♈	24♈
1975	8♉	21♉	4♊	17♊	0♋	12♋	25♋	7♌	19♌	1♍	13♍	25♍	7♎	19♎	2♏
1976	22♉	4♊	16♊	28♊	11♋	23♋	5♌	18♌	0♍	13♍	26♍	9♎	22♎	5♏	18♏
1977	28♍	12♎	27♎	11♏	26♏	11♐	25♐	9♑	23♑	7♒	20♒	3♓	16♓	29♓	11♈
1978	18♒	2♓	15♓	29♓	12♈	26♈	9♉	23♉	6♊	19♊	2♋	14♋	27♋	9♌	21♌
1979	28♊	11♋	23♋	6♌	18♌	0♍	12♍	24♍	6♎	18♎	0♏	12♏	24♏	7♐	19♐
1980	12♏	25♏	9♐	23♐	7♑	21♑	5♒	18♒	2♓	15♓	28♓	11♈	24♈	7♉	20♉
1981	19♓	3♈	16♈	0♉	14♉	27♉	11♊	24♊	7♋	19♋	2♌	14♌	26♌	8♍	20♍
1982	10♌	23♌	5♍	17♍	29♍	11♎	23♎	5♏	17♏	29♏	11♐	23♐	5♑	18♑	0♒
1983	18♐	0♑	12♑	24♑	6♒	18♒	0♓	12♓	25♓	7♈	20♈	3♉	17♉	1♊	15♊
1984	3♉	15♉	28♉	11♊	24♊	7♋	20♋	4♌	18♌	2♍	17♍	1♎	16♎	0♏	15♏
1985	10♍	24♍	7♎	20♎	2♏	14♏	26♏	8♐	20♐	2♑	14♑	26♑	8♒	13♓	25♓
1986	2♒	15♒	29♒	12♓	26♓	9♈	19♈	2♉	13♉	25♉	7♊	18♊	0♋	12♋	24♋
1987	8♏	20♏	2♐	14♐	26♐	8♑	20♑	2♒	14♒	27♒	10♓	23♓	7♈	22♈	6♉
1988	23♎	5♐	18♏	2♐	15♐	29♐	13♑	27♑	11♒	25♒	9♓	23♓	7♈	22♈	6♉
1989	1♓	15♓	29♓	15♈	0♉	15♉	0♊	14♊	27♊	9♋	25♋	8♌	21♌	3♍	15♍

MOON POSITIONS

MAY

Year	15	16	17	18	19	20	21	22	23	24	25	26	27	28	29
1960	24♑	8♒	22♒	6♓	19♓	2♈	15♈	27♈	10♉	22♉	4♊	16♊	28♊	10♋	22♋
61	4♊	17♊	29♊	12♋	24♋	6♌	17♌	29♌	11♍	23♍	6♎	18♎	1♏	15♏	29♏
62	7♎	19♎	2♏	14♏	27♏	10♐	23♐	6♑	19♑	3♒	17♒	1♓	15♓	29♓	14♈
63	11♒	24♒	8♓	22♓	6♈	21♈	6♉	21♉	6♊	21♊	6♋	20♋	3♌	17♌	29♌
64	15♋	0♌	14♌	27♌	10♍	23♍	6♎	18♎	1♏	13♏	25♏	6♐	18♐	0♑	12♑
65	24♏	7♐	19♐	1♑	13♑	25♑	7♒	19♒	1♓	13♓	26♓	8♈	22♈	5♉	19♉
66	27♓	9♈	22♈	4♉	17♉	0♊	14♊	27♊	11♋	25♋	9♌	23♌	7♍	22♍	6♎
67	2♌	16♌	29♌	14♍	28♍	12♎	27♎	12♏	27♏	11♐	26♐	10♑	23♑	7♒	19♒
68	6♑	21♑	5♒	19♒	2♓	14♓	27♓	9♈	21♈	3♉	15♉	26♉	8♊	20♊	2♋
69	15♉	27♉	9♊	21♊	3♋	15♋	27♋	9♌	21♌	3♍	15♍	28♍	12♎	25♎	9♏
1970	17♍	29♍	11♎	24♎	7♏	21♏	4♐	19♐	3♑	17♑	2♒	16♒	0♓	14♓	28♓
71	24♑	8♒	21♒	5♓	20♓	4♈	19♈	3♉	18♉	2♊	16♊	0♋	14♋	27♋	9♌
72	27♊	12♋	26♋	9♌	22♌	5♍	17♍	29♍	11♎	23♎	5♏	17♏	29♏	11♐	23♐
73	6♓	18♓	0♈	12♈	23♈	5♉	17♉	29♉	11♊	23♊	6♋	19♋	2♌	17♌	0♍
74	7♓	19♓	1♈	14♈	28♈	11♉	25♉	10♊	24♊	9♋	23♋	8♌	22♌	6♍	20♍
75	16♋	0♌	14♌	28♌	12♍	26♍	11♎	25♎	9♏	23♏	7♐	20♐	3♑	16♑	29♑
76	18♐	2♑	16♑	29♑	12♒	25♒	7♓	19♓	1♈	13♈	25♈	7♉	19♉	1♊	13♊
77	26♉	8♊	20♊	2♋	13♋	25♋	7♌	19♌	1♍	14♍	26♍	9♎	23♎	7♏	21♏
78	26♑	9♒	21♒	4♓	17♓	1♈	16♈	0♉	15♉	0♊	15♊	0♋	14♋	28♋	12♌
79	8♉	22♉	6♊	20♊	4♋	19♋	3♌	17♌	0♍	14♍	27♍	11♎	24♎	6♏	19♏
1980	8♊	23♊	6♋	20♋	2♌	15♌	27♌	9♍	21♍	3♎	15♎	27♎	9♏	21♏	4♐
81	16♎	28♎	10♏	22♏	4♐	16♐	28♐	10♑	22♑	5♒	17♒	0♓	14♓	28♓	12♈
82	16♒	29♒	11♓	24♓	8♈	22♈	6♉	21♉	6♊	21♊	6♋	21♋	6♌	20♌	4♍
83	29♊	14♋	28♋	12♌	27♌	11♍	25♍	9♎	22♎	5♏	18♏	1♐	14♐	26♐	9♑
84	29♍	13♎	26♎	9♏	22♏	5♐	17♐	29♐	11♑	23♑	5♒	17♒	29♒	11♓	24♓
85	7♈	18♈	0♉	12♉	24♉	6♊	18♊	0♋	13♋	26♋	9♌	22♌	6♍	20♍	4♎
86	6♌	19♌	2♍	15♍	28♍	12♎	27♎	12♏	27♏	12♐	27♐	12♑	27♑	11♒	25♒
87	21♏	6♐	20♐	5♑	19♑	3♒	17♒	0♓	13♓	26♓	9♈	22♈	4♉	16♉	28♉
88	19♉	3♊	16♊	29♊	11♋	24♋	6♌	19♌	1♍	13♍	25♍	7♎	19♎	1♏	14♏
89	26♍	8♎	20♎	3♏	16♏	29♏	12♐	25♐	9♑	22♑	5♒	18♒	1♓	11♓	26♓

MOON POSITIONS

MAY: 30–31 JUNE: 1–13

Year	30	31	1	2	3	4	5	6	7	8	9	10	11	12	13
1960	4♌	16♌	28♌	10♍	23♍	6♎	19♎	3♏	18♏	3♐	18♐	3♑	18♑	3♒	18♒
61	13♐	27♐	12♑	26♑	11♒	25♒	9♓	23♓	7♈	21♈	4♉	17♉	0♊	13♊	25♊
62	28♈	12♉	27♉	11♊	24♊	8♋	21♋	3♌	16♌	28♌	10♍	22♍	4♎	15♎	28♎
63	12♍	24♍	6♎	18♎	0♏	12♏	23♏	5♐	18♐	0♑	12♑	25♑	8♒	21♒	4♓
64	24♑	6♒	18♒	0♓	13♓	27♓	10♈	24♈	9♉	24♉	9♊	24♊	9♋	24♋	9♌
65	4♊	18♊	3♋	18♋	3♌	17♌	1♍	15♍	29♍	13♎	26♎	8♏	21♏	4♐	16♐
66	20♎	4♏	18♏	1♐	15♐	28♐	11♑	23♑	5♒	18♒	0♓	11♓	23♓	5♈	17♈
67	2♓	14♓	26♓	8♈	20♈	1♉	13♉	25♉	8♊	20♊	3♋	16♋	29♋	13♌	26♌
68	14♋	26♋	9♌	21♌	4♍	18♍	1♎	15♎	0♏	14♏	0♐	15♐	0♑	15♑	0♒
69	24♏	9♐	24♐	9♑	24♑	9♒	23♒	7♓	21♓	4♈	17♈	29♈	12♉	24♉	6♊
1970	12♈	25♈	9♉	22♉	5♊	18♊	1♋	13♋	25♋	7♌	19♌	1♍	13♍	25♍	7♎
71	22♌	4♍	15♍	27♍	9♎	21♎	3♏	16♏	28♏	11♐	24♐	7♑	21♑	5♒	18♒
72	5♑	17♑	0♒	13♒	26♒	9♓	23♓	7♈	21♈	6♉	21♉	6♊	21♊	6♋	20♋
73	15♉	0♊	15♊	0♋	15♋	0♌	14♌	28♌	12♍	25♍	8♎	20♎	3♏	15♏	27♏
74	4♎	17♎	0♏	13♏	26♏	9♐	21♐	3♑	15♑	27♑	9♒	21♒	3♓	15♓	27♓
75	11♒	23♒	5♓	17♓	29♓	11♈	23♈	6♉	18♉	1♊	14♊	28♊	12♋	26♋	10♌
76	25♊	8♋	21♋	4♌	17♌	29♌	14♍	29♍	13♎	28♎	12♏	27♏	11♐	26♐	10♑
77	6♏	21♏	6♐	21♐	6♑	21♑	5♒	19♒	3♓	16♓	29♓	11♈	23♈	5♉	17♉
78	26♓	9♈	22♈	4♉	17♉	29♉	11♊	23♊	5♋	17♋	29♋	11♌	23♌	5♍	17♍
79	1♌	13♌	25♌	7♍	18♍	0♎	13♎	25♎	8♏	21♏	5♐	19♐	3♑	18♑	2♒
1980	16♐	29♐	12♑	26♑	9♒	23♒	7♓	21♓	5♈	19♈	4♉	18♉	3♊	17♊	1♋
81	27♈	12♉	27♉	12♊	27♊	12♋	26♋	10♌	23♌	6♍	19♍	1♎	13♎	25♎	7♏
82	17♍	0♎	13♎	25♎	8♏	20♏	2♐	14♐	25♐	7♑	19♑	1♒	13♒	25♒	7♓
83	21♑	2♒	14♒	26♒	8♓	20♓	3♈	15♈	28♈	12♉	25♉	10♊	24♊	9♋	24♋
84	7♊	20♊	3♋	17♋	1♌	15♌	29♌	13♍	28♍	12♎	26♎	10♏	24♏	8♐	21♐
85	18♎	1♏	14♏	27♏	10♐	23♐	6♑	19♑	2♒	14♒	27♒	9♓	21♓	3♈	15♈
86	8♓	21♓	4♈	16♈	28♈	10♉	22♉	4♊	16♊	28♊	10♋	22♋	5♌	18♌	0♍
87	10♋	22♋	4♌	16♌	28♌	10♍	22♍	5♎	18♎	1♏	15♏	0♐	15♐	0♑	15♑
88	27♏	11♐	25♐	9♑	23♑	7♒	22♒	6♓	20♓	4♈	18♈	2♉	15♉	29♉	12♊
89	10♈	24♈	9♉	24♉	8♊	23♊	7♋	20♋	3♌	16♌	29♌	11♍	23♍	5♎	16♎

MOON POSITIONS

JUNE	14	15	16	17	18	19	20	21	22	23	24	25	26	27	28
1960	2♓	16♓	29♓	12♈	25♈	7♉	19♉	1♊	13♊	25♊	7♋	19♋	1♌	12♌	25♌
61	8♋	20♋	2♌	14♌	25♌	7♍	19♍	1♎	14♎	26♎	9♏	23♏	7♐	21♐	6♑
62	10♏	22♏	5♐	19♐	2♑	16♑	0♒	14♒	28♒	12♓	26♓	10♈	24♈	8♉	22♉
63	18♓	2♈	16♈	1♉	15♉	0♊	15♊	0♋	14♋	28♋	11♌	25♌	7♍	20♍	2♎
64	23♌	7♍	20♍	3♎	15♎	28♎	10♏	22♏	3♐	15♐	27♐	9♑	21♑	3♒	15♒
65	28♐	10♑	22♑	4♒	15♒	27♒	9♓	21♓	4♈	17♈	0♉	13♉	27♉	12♊	27♊
66	0♉	12♉	25♉	9♊	22♊	6♋	21♋	5♌	20♌	4♍	19♍	3♎	17♎	1♏	14♏
67	10♍	24♍	8♎	23♎	7♏	21♏	6♐	20♐	4♑	18♑	2♒	15♒	27♒	10♓	22♓
68	14♒	27♒	11♓	23♓	6♈	18♈	0♉	12♉	23♉	5♊	17♊	29♊	11♋	24♋	6♌
69	18♊	0♋	12♋	24♋	6♌	18♌	0♍	12♍	24♍	7♎	20♎	4♏	18♏	2♐	17♐
1970	19♎	2♏	15♏	29♏	13♐	27♐	12♑	27♑	12♒	26♒	11♓	25♓	9♈	22♈	6♉
71	2♓	16♓	0♈	15♈	29♈	13♉	27♉	11♊	25♊	9♋	22♋	5♌	17♌	29♌	11♍
72	4♌	17♌	0♍	13♍	26♍	8♎	20♎	2♏	13♏	25♏	7♐	19♐	2♑	14♑	27♑
73	9♐	20♐	2♑	14♑	26♑	8♒	20♒	2♓	15♓	28♓	11♈	25♈	9♉	24♉	8♊
74	9♈	22♈	6♉	19♉	4♊	18♊	3♋	18♋	3♌	18♌	2♍	17♍	1♎	14♎	27♎
75	24♋	9♌	23♌	7♍	21♍	5♎	19♎	2♏	16♏	29♏	12♐	24♐	7♑	19♑	1♒
76	24♑	7♒	21♒	4♓	16♓	28♓	10♈	21♈	3♉	15♉	27♉	9♊	22♊	5♋	17♋
77	29♊	10♋	22♋	4♌	16♌	28♌	11♍	23♍	6♎	19♎	2♏	16♏	0♐	15♐	29♐
78	29♍	12♎	26♎	10♏	24♏	9♐	24♐	9♑	24♑	9♒	24♒	8♓	22♓	6♈	19♈
79	17♒	1♓	15♓	29♓	13♈	27♈	10♉	24♉	7♊	20♊	2♋	15♋	27♋	9♌	21♌
1980	14♋	28♋	10♌	23♌	5♍	17♍	29♍	11♎	23♎	5♏	17♏	29♏	12♐	25♐	8♑
81	19♏	1♐	13♐	25♐	7♑	19♑	2♒	14♒	27♒	11♓	24♓	8♈	22♈	6♉	21♉
82	20♓	3♈	17♈	0♉	15♉	0♊	15♊	0♋	15♋	0♌	15♌	29♌	13♍	26♍	9♎
83	8♌	23♌	7♍	21♍	5♎	19♎	2♏	15♏	28♏	10♐	23♐	5♑	17♑	29♑	11♒
84	4♍	17♍	0♎	13♎	25♎	7♏	19♏	1♐	13♐	25♐	7♑	19♑	2♒	15♒	29♒
85	9♐	21♐	3♑	15♑	27♑	10♒	23♒	6♓	19♓	2♈	16♈	0♉	14♉	29♉	13♊
86	11♍	24♍	7♎	21♎	6♏	20♏	5♐	20♐	6♑	21♑	6♒	20♒	4♓	17♓	0♈
87	0♒	15♒	29♒	13♓	27♓	10♈	23♈	6♉	19♉	1♊	13♊	25♊	7♋	19♋	1♌
88	25♊	8♋	20♋	3♌	15♌	26♌	8♍	20♍	2♎	14♎	26♎	9♏	22♏	5♐	19♐
89	28♎	10♏	23♏	5♐	18♐	1♑	14♑	27♑	11♒	24♒	8♓	22♓	6♈	21♈	5♉

MOON POSITIONS

Year	June 29	30	July 1	2	3	4	5	6	7	8	9	10	11	12	13
1960	7♍	19♍	2♎	15♎	28♎	12♏	27♏	11♐	26♐	12♑	27♑	12♒	27♒	11♓	25♓
61	21♑	6♒	21♒	6♓	20♓	4♈	18♈	1♉	14♉	27♉	10♊	22♊	4♋	17♋	29♋
62	6♊	20♊	3♋	16♋	29♋	11♌	24♌	6♍	18♍	0♎	11♎	23♎	6♏	18♏	1♐
63	14♎	26♎	8♏	20♏	2♐	14♐	26♐	9♑	22♑	5♒	18♒	1♓	15♓	29♓	13♈
64	27♒	10♓	23♓	6♈	20♈	4♉	18♉	3♊	17♊	3♋	18♋	2♌	17♌	1♍	15♍
65	12♋	27♋	12♌	27♌	11♍	26♍	9♎	23♎	6♏	18♏	1♐	13♐	25♐	7♑	19♑
66	27♏	11♐	24♐	6♑	19♑	1♒	14♒	26♒	8♓	19♓	1♈	13♈	25♈	8♉	20♉
67	4♈	16♈	28♈	11♉	24♉	7♊	20♊	3♋	16♋	29♋	12♌	25♌	8♍	21♍	5♎
68	19♏	2♐	15♐	28♐	11♑	24♑	7♒	20♒	3♓	16♓	29♓	12♈	25♈	8♉	21♉
69	3♑	16♑	29♑	12♒	26♒	9♓	22♓	6♈	19♈	2♉	15♉	29♉	12♊	25♊	9♋
1970	19♉	1♊	13♊	25♊	7♋	20♋	2♌	14♌	26♌	8♍	21♍	3♎	15♎	27♎	10♏
71	23♍	6♎	19♎	2♏	15♏	28♏	11♐	25♐	8♑	21♑	4♒	17♒	0♓	13♓	27♓
72	10♒	23♒	7♓	21♓	5♈	19♈	3♉	17♉	1♊	15♊	29♊	13♋	27♋	11♌	25♌
73	24♊	7♋	20♋	3♌	16♌	0♍	13♍	26♍	9♎	22♎	6♏	19♏	2♐	15♐	29♐
74	10♏	22♏	4♐	16♐	28♐	11♑	23♑	5♒	17♒	29♒	12♓	24♓	6♈	18♈	1♉
75	13♓	26♓	9♈	23♈	6♉	19♉	3♊	16♊	29♊	13♋	26♋	9♌	23♌	6♍	20♍
76	1♌	14♌	28♌	12♍	26♍	10♎	24♎	8♏	22♏	6♐	20♐	4♑	18♑	2♒	16♒
77	14♐	27♐	10♑	23♑	6♒	20♒	3♓	16♓	29♓	12♈	26♈	9♉	22♉	5♊	19♊
78	1♉	13♉	25♉	7♊	19♊	1♋	13♋	26♋	8♌	20♌	2♍	14♍	26♍	8♎	21♎
79	3♍	16♍	29♍	13♎	26♎	10♏	23♏	7♐	20♐	3♑	17♑	0♒	14♒	27♒	11♓
1980	22♑	5♒	19♒	3♓	17♓	1♈	15♈	29♈	12♉	26♉	10♊	24♊	8♋	22♋	6♌
81	6♊	19♊	2♋	15♋	28♋	11♌	24♌	7♍	20♍	3♎	16♎	29♎	12♏	25♏	9♐
82	22♎	4♏	16♏	28♏	10♐	23♐	5♑	17♑	29♑	11♒	24♒	6♓	18♓	0♈	13♈
83	23♒	6♓	20♓	3♈	17♈	0♉	14♉	28♉	11♊	25♊	8♋	22♋	5♌	19♌	3♍
84	13♋	26♋	10♌	24♌	8♍	21♍	5♎	19♎	3♏	17♏	0♐	14♐	28♐	12♑	26♑
85	27♏	10♐	23♐	6♑	19♑	2♒	15♒	28♒	11♓	24♓	7♈	20♈	3♉	16♉	29♉
86	13♈	25♈	7♉	19♉	1♊	14♊	26♊	8♋	20♋	2♌	15♌	27♌	9♍	21♍	4♎
87	22♌	5♍	18♍	1♎	14♎	27♎	10♏	23♏	6♐	19♐	2♑	15♑	28♑	11♒	24♒
88	4♑	17♑	1♒	15♒	29♒	12♓	26♓	10♈	24♈	8♉	21♉	5♊	19♊	3♋	17♋
89	19♉	1♊	14♊	27♊	10♋	22♋	5♌	18♌	1♍	14♍	26♍	9♎	22♎	5♏	18♏

MOON POSITIONS

JULY	14	15	16	17	18	19	20	21	22	23	24	25	26	27	28
1960	8♈	21♈	4♉	16♉	28♉	10♊	22♊	4♋	16♋	28♋	10♌	22♌	4♍	16♍	29♍
61	10♌	22♌	4♍	16♍	28♍	10♎	22♎	5♏	18♏	1♐	15♐	0♑	14♑	0♒	15♒
62	14♐	27♐	11♑	25♑	9♒	23♒	8♓	22♓	7♈	21♈	5♉	19♉	3♊	16♊	29♊
63	27♈	11♉	26♉	10♊	24♊	8♋	22♋	6♌	20♌	3♍	15♍	28♍	10♎	22♎	4♏
64	29♍	11♎	24♎	6♏	18♏	0♐	12♐	24♐	6♑	18♑	0♒	12♒	24♒	7♓	20♓
65	0♒	12♒	24♒	6♓	18♓	0♈	13♈	26♈	9♉	22♉	6♊	20♊	5♋	20♋	5♌
66	3♊	17♊	1♋	15♋	0♌	15♌	29♌	14♍	29♍	13♎	27♎	11♏	24♏	8♐	20♐
67	19♎	2♏	14♏	26♏	11♐	25♐	8♑	21♑	4♒	17♒	1♓	14♓	27♓	10♈	24♈
68	19♓	1♈	14♈	26♈	8♉	20♉	3♊	15♊	27♊	10♋	22♋	4♌	17♌	29♌	11♍
69	21♋	3♌	15♌	27♌	9♍	21♍	3♎	16♎	29♎	13♏	27♏	11♐	26♐	11♑	26♑
1970	24♏	8♐	22♐	6♑	20♑	4♒	18♒	3♓	17♓	1♈	15♈	29♈	13♉	29♉	12♊
71	12♈	26♈	10♉	24♉	8♊	21♊	4♋	18♋	0♌	13♌	25♌	7♍	19♍	1♎	13♎
72	9♍	21♍	4♎	16♎	28♎	10♏	22♏	4♐	16♐	28♐	10♑	23♑	6♒	19♒	3♓
73	11♑	23♑	5♒	17♒	29♒	12♓	25♓	8♈	21♈	5♉	19♉	3♊	18♊	2♋	17♋
74	14♉	28♉	12♊	26♊	10♋	25♋	9♌	23♌	7♍	21♍	5♎	19♎	3♏	18♏	3♐
75	4♎	18♎	2♏	16♏	29♏	12♐	25♐	8♑	21♑	3♒	15♒	27♒	9♓	21♓	3♈
76	29♈	11♉	24♉	6♊	29♊	12♋	25♋	8♌	21♌	18♌	0♍	13♍	26♍	10♎	24♌
77	1♋	13♋	25♋	8♌	20♌	3♍	16♍	29♍	13♎	26♎	10♏	25♏	9♐	24♐	8♑
78	5♏	18♏	2♐	17♐	2♑	3♒	3♒	18♒	3♓	17♓	1♈	15♈	28♈	11♉	23♏
79	26♓	10♈	24♈	7♉	21♉	4♊	17♊	29♊	11♋	24♋	6♌	18♌	29♌	11♍	23♍
1980	18♌	1♍	13♍	25♍	7♎	19♎	1♏	13♏	25♏	7♐	20♐	3♑	17♑	1♒	15♒
81	21♐	3♑	16♑	28♑	11♒	24♒	7♓	21♓	5♈	19♈	3♉	17♉	1♊	16♊	0♋
82	26♈	10♉	24♉	8♊	23♊	8♋	23♋	8♌	23♌	8♍	22♍	5♎	18♎	1♏	13♏
83	17♍	2♎	16♎	29♎	12♏	25♏	7♐	20♐	2♑	14♑	26♑	8♒	19♒	1♓	13♓
84	8♒	21♒	3♓	15♓	27♓	9♈	21♈	3♉	15♉	27♉	10♊	23♊	7♋	21♋	6♌
85	11♊	23♊	6♋	19♋	2♌	15♌	29♌	13♍	27♍	11♎	25♎	9♏	23♏	7♐	22♐
86	17♎	1♏	7♏	20♏	3♐	16♐	28♐	10♑	22♑	4♒	16♒	28♒	10♓	21♓	3♉
87	9♓	23♓	7♈	20♈	3♉	16♉	28♉	10♊	22♊	4♋	16♋	28♋	10♌	22♌	4♍
88	29♌	11♎	23♎	5♏	17♏	28♏	10♐	22♐	4♑	17♑	0♒	14♒	28♐	12♒	27♒
89	1♐	13♐	26♐	9♑	23♑	7♒	20♒	5♓	19♓	3♈	17♈	2♉	16♉	0♊	14♊

MOON POSITIONS

	JULY 29	30	31	AUGUST 1	2	3	4	5	6	7	8	9	10	11	12
1960	11♎	24♎	8♏	22♏	6♐	20♐	5♑	20♑	5♒	20♒	5♓	19♓	3♈	17♈	0♉
61	0♓	15♓	29♓	14♈	28♈	11♉	24♉	7♊	19♊	2♋	14♋	26♋	7♌	19♌	1♍
62	12♋	25♋	8♌	20♌	2♍	14♍	26♍	8♎	20♎	2♏	14♏	26♏	9♐	22♐	5♑
63	16♏	28♏	10♐	22♐	5♑	17♑	0♒	14♒	27♒	11♓	25♓	9♈	24♈	8♉	22♉
64	3♈	16♈	0♉	14♉	28♉	12♊	27♊	11♋	26♋	11♌	25♌	10♍	23♍	7♎	20♎
65	21♌	6♍	20♍	5♎	19♎	2♏	15♏	27♏	10♐	22♐	4♑	16♑	27♑	9♒	21♒
66	3♑	16♑	28♑	10♒	22♒	4♓	16♓	28♓	10♈	22♈	4♉	16♉	29♉	12♊	25♊
67	6♉	17♉	29♉	12♊	24♊	7♋	21♋	4♌	18♌	3♍	17♍	1♎	16♎	0♏	14♏
68	25♍	8♎	22♎	6♏	20♏	4♐	19♐	3♑	18♑	2♒	16♒	0♓	14♓	27♓	10♈
69	12♒	27♒	11♓	25♓	9♈	22♈	5♉	18♉	0♊	12♊	24♊	6♋	18♋	0♌	12♌
1970	24♊	7♋	19♋	1♌	12♌	24♌	6♍	18♍	0♎	12♎	24♎	6♏	19♏	2♐	16♐
71	25♎	7♏	19♏	2♐	14♐	27♐	11♑	25♑	9♒	24♒	8♓	23♓	8♈	22♈	7♉
72	16♓	0♈	14♈	28♈	12♉	27♉	11♊	25♊	9♋	23♋	7♌	20♌	4♍	17♍	29♍
73	2♌	17♌	1♍	16♍	29♍	13♎	25♎	8♏	20♏	2♐	14♐	26♐	8♑	20♑	2♒
74	15♐	27♐	9♑	21♑	3♒	14♒	26♒	8♓	20♓	2♈	14♈	26♈	8♉	20♉	2♊
75	15♈	27♈	9♉	22♉	5♊	19♊	1♋	15♋	0♌	14♌	29♌	14♍	29♍	14♎	29♎
76	8♏	22♏	6♐	21♐	5♑	19♑	3♒	17♒	1♓	14♓	28♓	11♈	24♈	7♉	19♉
77	23♑	8♒	22♒	6♓	20♓	3♈	15♈	28♈	10♉	22♉	4♊	16♊	27♊	10♋	22♋
78	5♎	18♎	1♏	14♏	27♏	10♐	22♐	5♑	17♑	29♑	11♒	24♒	7♓	20♓	4♈
79	5♏	17♏	29♏	11♐	23♐	5♑	17♑	29♑	11♒	24♒	6♓	20♓	3♈	17♈	1♉
1980	29♒	14♓	28♓	13♈	27♈	10♉	23♉	6♊	19♊	1♋	13♋	25♋	7♌	19♌	1♍
81	14♋	29♋	12♌	26♌	9♍	22♍	5♎	17♎	29♎	11♏	23♏	5♐	17♐	29♐	12♑
82	26♏	8♐	19♐	1♑	13♑	25♑	7♒	20♒	3♓	16♓	0♈	14♈	28♈	12♉	26♉
83	25♓	7♈	20♈	2♉	15♉	28♉	12♊	26♊	11♋	26♋	11♌	26♌	11♍	26♍	11♎
84	20♌	5♍	20♍	5♎	19♎	2♏	14♏	27♏	10♐	22♐	4♑	16♑	28♑	10♒	22♒
85	6♓	19♓	3♈	17♈	0♉	13♉	26♉	9♊	22♊	5♋	17♋	29♋	11♌	23♌	5♍
86	15♉	27♉	9♊	22♊	4♋	16♋	28♋	11♌	23♌	6♍	19♍	2♎	15♎	28♎	12♏
87	16♏	28♏	10♐	23♐	6♑	19♑	2♒	15♒	29♒	13♓	27♓	11♈	25♈	9♉	23♉
88	12♒	27♒	12♓	26♓	10♈	23♈	6♉	19♉	1♊	13♊	25♊	7♋	19♋	1♌	13♌
89	27♊	11♋	24♋	7♌	20♌	2♍	15♍	27♍	10♎	23♎	5♏	18♏	1♐	14♐	27♐

MOON POSITIONS

AUGUST

	13	14	15	16	17	18	19	20	21	22	23	24	25	26	27
1960	12♉	25♉	7♊	19♊	1♋	12♋	24♋	6♌	18♌	1♍	13♍	26♍	8♎	22♎	5♏
61	13♍	25♍	7♎	19♎	1♏	14♏	27♏	10♐	24♐	8♑	23♑	8♒	23♒	8♓	23♓
62	19♑	3♒	17♒	2♓	17♓	2♈	17♈	2♉	16♉	0♊	13♊	26♊	9♋	22♋	4♌
63	6♊	20♊	4♋	18♋	2♌	15♌	28♌	11♍	24♍	6♎	18♎	0♏	12♏	24♏	6♐
64	2♏	15♏	27♏	9♐	20♐	2♑	14♑	26♑	8♒	21♒	4♓	17♓	0♈	13♈	27♈
65	3♓	15♓	27♓	10♈	22♈	5♉	18♉	1♊	15♊	29♊	14♋	29♋	14♌	29♌	14♍
66	9♋	23♋	8♌	23♌	8♍	24♍	9♎	23♎	7♏	21♏	4♐	17♐	0♑	13♑	25♑
67	28♏	12♐	26♐	9♑	23♑	6♒	19♒	1♓	14♓	26♓	8♈	20♈	2♉	14♉	25♉
68	22♈	4♉	16♉	28♉	10♊	22♊	4♋	16♋	29♋	11♌	24♌	8♍	21♍	5♎	19♎
69	24♌	6♍	18♍	1♎	13♎	26♎	9♏	23♏	7♐	21♐	6♑	20♑	5♒	20♒	5♓
1970	0♑	14♑	29♑	14♒	29♒	14♓	29♓	14♈	28♈	12♉	26♉	9♊	21♊	4♋	16♋
71	21♉	4♊	18♊	1♋	14♋	27♋	9♌	22♌	4♍	16♍	28♍	10♎	22♎	3♏	15♏
72	12♎	24♎	6♏	18♏	0♐	11♐	24♐	6♑	18♑	1♒	14♒	28♒	12♓	26♓	10♈
73	25♎	9♏	22♏	4♐	17♐	29♐	11♑	23♑	5♒	17♒	0♓	10♓	22♓	4♈	17♈
74	11♓	23♓	5♈	17♈	29♈	11♉	23♉	5♊	18♊	1♋	15♋	29♋	14♌	29♌	14♍
75	14♌	27♌	11♍	25♍	9♎	23♎	7♏	22♏	6♐	20♐	4♑	18♑	2♒	16♒	29♒
76	26♏	10♐	24♐	7♑	20♑	2♒	13♒	26♒	9♓	21♓	3♈	10♈	22♈	4♉	16♉
77	2♈	14♈	25♈	7♉	19♉	1♊	13♊	25♊	8♋	21♋	5♌	19♌	3♍	17♍	2♎
78	12♐	26♐	11♑	26♑	11♒	26♒	11♓	26♓	10♈	23♈	6♉	19♉	2♊	14♊	26♊
79	4♉	17♉	1♊	14♊	26♊	9♋	21♋	3♌	15♌	26♌	8♍	20♍	2♎	14♎	26♎
1980	21♍	3♎	15♎	27♎	9♏	21♏	3♐	16♐	28♐	11♑	25♑	9♒	23♒	8♓	23♓
81	24♑	7♒	20♒	4♓	17♓	1♈	15♈	0♉	14♉	28♉	12♊	26♊	10♋	24♋	8♌
82	4♊	18♊	3♋	17♋	2♌	17♌	1♍	16♍	0♎	13♎	27♎	9♏	22♏	4♐	16♐
83	25♎	9♏	22♏	5♐	17♐	29♐	11♑	23♑	5♒	17♒	0♓	10♓	22♓	4♈	17♈
84	11♓	23♓	5♈	17♈	29♈	11♉	23♉	6♊	18♊	1♋	15♋	29♋	14♌	29♌	14♍
85	14♌	27♌	11♍	25♍	9♎	23♎	7♏	22♏	6♐	20♐	4♑	18♑	2♒	16♒	29♒
86	26♏	10♐	24♐	7♑	19♑	1♒	13♒	25♒	7♓	19♓	1♈	13♈	25♈	8♉	20♉
87	16♈	29♈	11♉	23♉	5♊	17♊	29♊	11♋	23♋	7♌	19♌	1♍	13♍	25♍	7♎
88	2♍	13♍	25♍	7♎	19♎	1♏	13♏	26♏	9♐	22♐	6♑	20♑	5♒	20♒	5♓
89	4♑	17♑	1♒	15♒	29♒	14♓	29♓	13♈	28♈	12♉	27♉	11♊	24♊	8♋	21♋

MOON POSITIONS

	AUGUST				SEPTEMBER										
	28	29	30	31	1	2	3	4	5	6	7	8	9	10	11
1960	18♏	2♐	16♐	1♑	15♑	0♒	14♒	29♒	13♓	27♓	11♈	25♈	8♉	20♉	3♊
61	8♈	23♈	7♉	20♉	3♊	16♊	28♊	11♋	23♋	4♌	16♌	28♌	10♍	22♍	4♎
62	17♌	29♌	11♍	23♍	4♎	16♎	28♎	10♏	22♏	4♐	17♐	0♑	13♑	27♑	11♒
63	18♐	0♑	12♑	25♑	9♒	22♒	6♓	20♓	5♈	20♈	4♉	19♉	3♊	17♊	1♋
64	11♉	25♉	9♊	23♊	7♋	21♋	6♌	20♌	4♍	18♍	1♎	15♎	28♎	10♏	23♏
65	29♍	13♎	27♎	11♏	24♏	6♐	19♐	1♑	12♑	24♑	6♒	18♒	0♓	12♓	24♓
66	7♒	19♒	1♓	13♓	25♓	7♈	19♈	1♉	13♉	25♉	7♊	20♊	4♋	17♋	2♌
67	7♊	20♊	2♋	15♋	29♋	13♌	27♌	11♍	26♍	11♎	26♎	10♏	25♏	9♐	23♐
68	3♏	17♏	1♐	15♐	29♐	13♑	27♑	11♒	25♒	9♓	22♓	5♈	18♈	0♉	12♉
69	19♓	4♈	17♈	1♉	14♉	26♉	8♊	21♊	2♋	14♋	26♋	8♌	20♌	2♍	15♍
1970	28♋	10♌	21♌	3♍	15♍	27♍	9♎	21♎	3♏	16♏	28♏	11♐	25♐	9♑	23♑
71	27♏	10♐	22♐	6♑	19♑	3♒	17♒	2♓	17♓	2♈	17♈	2♉	17♉	1♊	15♊
72	25♈	9♉	23♉	8♊	22♊	6♋	19♋	3♌	16♌	29♌	12♍	25♍	7♎	20♎	2♏
73	10♍	24♍	7♎	21♎	4♏	16♏	28♏	10♐	22♐	4♑	16♑	28♑	10♒	22♒	5♓
74	18♑	0♒	11♒	23♒	5♓	17♓	29♓	12♈	24♈	7♉	20♉	3♊	16♊	0♋	14♋
75	18♉	0♊	13♊	26♊	9♋	23♋	8♌	23♌	8♍	23♍	8♎	23♎	8♏	22♏	6♐
76	17♎	1♏	16♏	0♐	14♐	27♐	11♑	24♑	7♒	20♒	3♓	16♓	28♓	10♈	22♈
77	1♓	14♓	28♓	11♈	23♈	6♉	18♉	0♊	12♊	23♊	5♋	18♋	0♌	12♌	25♌
78	8♏	20♏	2♐	14♐	26♐	8♑	20♑	2♒	15♒	28♒	11♓	25♓	8♈	22♈	6♉
79	8♏	21♏	3♐	17♐	0♑	14♑	29♑	14♒	29♒	14♓	29♓	14♈	29♈	13♉	27♉
1980	8♈	23♈	7♉	22♉	6♊	20♊	3♋	16♋	29♋	11♌	24♌	6♍	18♍	0♎	12♎
81	21♌	5♍	18♍	0♎	13♎	25♎	7♏	19♏	1♐	13♐	25♐	7♑	19♑	2♒	15♒
82	28♐	9♑	21♑	3♒	15♒	28♒	10♓	23♓	6♈	20♈	3♉	17♉	1♊	15♊	29♊
83	29♈	12♉	25♉	8♊	21♊	5♋	20♋	4♌	19♌	5♍	20♍	5♎	19♎	4♏	17♏
84	29♍	14♎	29♎	13♏	27♏	11♐	24♐	7♑	20♑	2♒	14♒	26♒	8♓	20♓	2♈
85	12♐	25♐	8♑	21♑	3♒	15♒	27♒	9♓	21♓	3♈	15♈	27♈	9♉	22♉	5♊
86	17♏	29♏	11♐	23♐	6♑	18♑	1♒	14♒	27♒	11♓	25♓	9♈	23♈	7♉	22♉
87	20♈	3♉	16♉	29♉	13♊	27♊	11♋	26♋	11♌	26♌	11♍	25♍	10♎	24♎	7♏
88	20♉	5♊	20♊	5♋	19♋	2♌	15♌	28♌	11♍	23♍	5♎	17♎	29♎	10♏	22♏
89	4♌	16♌	29♌	11♍	23♍	5♎	17♎	29♎	11♏	23♏	5♐	17♐	29♐	12♑	25♑

MOON POSITIONS

SEPTEMBER

	12	13	14	15	16	17	18	19	20	21	22	23	24	25	26
1960	15♊	27♊	9♋	21♋	3♌	15♌	27♌	9♍	22♍	5♎	18♎	2♏	15♏	29♏	13♐
61	16♎	28♎	11♏	24♏	7♐	20♐	4♑	18♑	2♒	17♒	1♓	16♓	1♈	16♈	1♉
62	26♒	11♓	26♓	11♈	26♈	11♉	26♉	10♊	23♊	6♋	19♋	1♌	14♌	26♌	8♍
63	15♋	28♋	11♌	24♌	7♍	20♍	2♎	14♎	26♎	8♏	20♏	2♐	14♐	26♐	8♑
64	5♐	16♐	28♐	10♑	22♑	4♒	17♒	29♒	12♓	26♓	9♈	23♈	7♉	21♉	5♊
65	7♈	19♈	2♉	15♉	28♉	12♊	25♊	9♋	24♋	8♌	23♌	8♍	22♍	7♎	21♎
66	17♌	2♍	17♍	2♎	17♎	2♏	16♏	0♐	14♐	27♐	10♑	22♑	4♒	16♒	28♒
67	6♑	20♑	3♒	15♒	28♒	10♓	23♓	5♈	17♈	28♈	10♉	22♉	4♊	16♊	28♊
68	24♉	6♊	18♊	0♋	12♋	24♋	7♌	19♌	2♍	15♍	28♍	11♎	24♎	6♏	20♏
69	27♍	10♎	23♎	6♏	20♏	4♐	18♐	2♑	16♑	0♒	15♒	29♒	13♓	28♓	12♈
1970	8♒	22♒	8♓	23♓	8♈	23♈	7♉	21♉	4♊	17♊	0♋	12♋	25♋	7♌	18♌
71	28♊	11♋	24♋	6♌	19♌	1♍	13♍	25♍	7♎	18♎	0♏	12♏	24♏	6♐	19♐
72	14♏	26♏	8♐	19♐	1♑	14♑	26♑	9♒	22♒	6♓	20♓	5♈	20♈	5♉	19♉
73	18♓	1♈	15♈	28♈	12♉	26♉	10♊	24♊	7♋	21♋	5♌	18♌	1♍	14♍	26♍
74	29♋	14♌	29♌	14♍	29♍	13♎	28♎	11♏	24♏	6♐	20♐	2♑	14♑	26♑	8♒
75	19♐	2♑	15♑	27♑	9♒	22♒	4♓	16♓	29♓	12♈	25♈	8♉	21♉	6♊	19♊
76	4♉	15♉	27♉	9♊	21♊	3♋	16♋	29♋	13♌	26♌	10♍	24♍	9♎	24♎	9♏
77	8♍	22♍	5♎	18♎	1♏	14♏	27♏	10♐	22♐	5♑	17♑	29♑	11♒	23♒	5♓
78	21♑	5♒	18♒	2♓	15♓	29♓	13♈	27♈	11♉	25♉	10♊	23♊	6♋	18♋	1♌
79	10♊	23♊	6♋	18♋	0♌	12♌	23♌	5♍	17♍	29♍	11♎	23♎	5♏	18♏	0♐
1980	24♎	5♏	17♏	29♏	11♐	24♐	6♑	20♑	3♒	17♒	0♓	16♓	1♈	17♈	2♉
81	29♒	12♓	26♓	11♈	25♈	10♉	25♉	9♊	23♊	7♋	21♋	4♌	18♌	1♍	14♍
82	13♋	27♋	11♌	26♌	10♍	24♍	8♎	21♎	5♏	17♏	0♐	12♐	24♐	6♑	17♑
83	0♐	13♐	26♐	8♑	20♑	2♒	14♒	25♒	7♓	19♓	0♈	12♈	24♈	6♉	17♉
84	14♈	26♈	8♉	20♉	2♊	14♊	27♊	10♋	22♋	5♌	18♌	1♍	14♍	27♍	10♎
85	19♌	3♍	17♍	2♎	16♎	1♏	15♏	29♏	13♐	27♐	11♑	24♑	7♒	20♒	3♓
86	5♑	19♑	3♒	16♒	29♒	12♓	25♓	8♈	21♈	4♉	17♉	0♊	13♊	25♊	7♋
87	20♉	3♊	16♊	28♊	10♋	22♋	4♌	16♌	28♌	9♍	21♍	4♎	17♎	0♏	13♏
88	4♎	16♎	28♎	10♏	23♏	5♐	18♐	1♑	15♑	29♑	13♒	28♒	13♓	28♓	13♈
89	9♒	23♒	8♓	23♓	8♈	23♈	8♉	21♉	5♊	18♊	0♋	13♋	25♋	7♌	18♌

MOON POSITIONS

	SEPTEMBER				OCTOBER										
	27	28	29	30	1	2	3	4	5	6	7	8	9	10	11
1960	27♐	11♑	26♑	10♒	24♒	8♓	22♓	6♈	19♈	3♉	16♉	28♉	11♊	23♊	5♋
61	15♉	29♉	12♊	25♊	7♋	19♋	1♌	13♌	25♌	7♍	18♍	0♎	13♎	25♎	8♏
62	20♍	1♎	13♎	25♎	7♏	19♏	1♐	13♐	26♐	9♑	22♑	5♒	19♒	4♓	19♓
63	20♑	3♒	16♒	0♓	14♓	29♓	14♈	29♈	14♉	29♉	13♊	28♊	12♋	25♋	8♌
64	20♊	4♋	18♋	2♌	16♌	0♍	13♍	27♍	10♎	23♎	6♏	18♏	0♐	12♐	24♐
65	5♏	19♏	2♐	14♐	27♐	9♑	21♑	3♒	14♒	26♒	8♓	21♓	3♈	16♈	29♈
66	10♓	22♓	4♈	16♈	28♈	10♉	22♉	4♊	17♊	0♋	13♋	27♋	11♌	25♌	10♍
67	11♋	24♋	7♌	21♌	5♍	20♍	5♎	20♎	5♏	20♏	5♐	19♐	3♑	16♑	0♒
68	12♐	26♐	10♑	24♑	8♒	21♒	5♓	18♓	1♈	13♈	26♈	8♉	20♉	2♊	14♊
69	25♈	9♉	21♉	4♊	16♊	29♊	10♋	22♋	4♌	16♌	28♌	11♍	23♍	6♎	19♎
1970	0♍	12♍	24♍	6♎	18♎	0♏	13♏	25♏	8♐	22♐	5♑	19♑	3♒	17♒	1♓
71	1♑	14♑	27♑	11♒	25♒	10♓	25♓	10♈	26♈	11♉	26♉	10♊	24♊	8♋	21♋
72	4♊	18♊	3♋	16♋	0♌	13♌	26♌	9♍	21♍	4♎	16♎	28♎	10♏	22♏	4♐
73	16♎	29♎	12♏	24♏	6♐	18♐	0♑	12♑	24♑	6♒	18♒	0♓	13♓	26♓	10♈
74	20♒	2♓	14♓	26♓	9♈	21♈	4♉	17♉	0♊	13♊	27♊	11♋	25♋	9♌	23♌
75	22♊	5♋	18♋	2♌	16♌	1♍	16♍	1♎	17♎	2♏	16♏	1♐	15♐	28♐	11♑
76	26♏	10♐	24♐	8♑	21♑	4♒	17♒	0♓	12♓	25♓	7♈	19♈	0♉	12♉	24♉
77	6♈	19♈	1♉	14♉	26♉	8♊	20♊	1♋	13♋	25♋	7♌	19♌	3♍	17♍	0♎
78	10♌	22♌	4♍	16♍	29♍	12♎	25♎	8♏	21♏	5♐	19♐	3♑	17♑	1♒	16♒
79	13♐	26♐	10♑	24♑	8♒	22♒	7♓	22♓	7♈	22♈	7♉	21♉	5♊	19♊	4♋
1980	17♉	2♊	16♊	0♋	13♋	26♋	8♌	21♌	3♍	15♍	27♍	9♎	20♎	2♏	14♏
81	26♍	9♎	21♎	4♏	16♏	28♏	9♐	21♐	3♑	15♑	27♑	10♒	23♒	6♓	20♓
82	29♑	11♒	24♒	6♓	19♓	2♈	16♈	29♈	13♉	27♉	11♊	25♊	10♋	24♋	8♌
83	5♊	18♊	1♋	15♋	29♋	14♌	29♌	13♍	28♍	13♎	28♎	12♏	25♏	9♐	21♐
84	8♏	23♏	7♐	20♐	4♑	16♑	29♑	11♒	23♒	5♓	17♓	29♓	11♈	23♈	5♉
85	17♓	0♈	12♈	24♈	6♉	17♉	29♉	11♊	23♊	5♋	17♋	0♌	13♌	27♌	11♍
86	19♋	1♌	14♌	26♌	9♍	23♍	6♎	20♎	5♏	19♏	3♐	17♐	2♑	16♑	0♒
87	26♏	10♐	23♐	7♑	22♑	6♒	20♒	5♓	19♓	4♈	18♈	2♉	15♉	28♉	11♊
88	28♈	13♉	27♉	11♊	24♊	7♋	20♋	2♌	14♌	26♌	7♍	19♍	1♎	13♎	25♎
89	8♍	20♍	2♎	14♎	26♎	7♏	19♏	1♐	13♐	25♐	8♑	21♑	4♒	17♒	1♓

MOON POSITIONS

OCTOBER

Year	12	13	14	15	16	17	18	19	20	21	22	23	24	25	26
1960	17♋	29♋	10♌	23♌	5♍	17♍	0♎	13♎	27♎	11♏	25♏	9♐	24♐	8♑	22♑
61	21♏	4♐	17♐	0♑	14♑	28♑	12♒	26♒	11♓	25♓	10♈	25♈	9♉	23♉	7♊
62	4♈	19♈	5♉	20♉	4♊	19♊	2♋	15♋	28♋	11♌	23♌	5♍	17♍	28♍	10♎
63	21♌	4♍	16♍	29♍	11♎	23♎	5♏	17♏	29♏	11♐	22♐	4♑	16♑	29♑	11♒
64	6♑	18♑	0♒	12♒	24♒	7♓	20♓	4♈	18♈	2♉	17♉	1♊	16♊	0♋	15♋
65	12♉	25♉	9♊	22♊	6♋	20♋	4♌	18♌	3♍	17♍	2♎	16♎	0♏	13♏	27♏
66	25♍	10♎	25♎	10♏	25♏	9♐	22♐	5♑	18♑	1♒	13♒	25♒	7♓	19♓	0♈
67	12♒	25♒	7♓	19♓	1♈	13♈	25♈	7♉	19♉	1♊	13♊	25♊	7♋	19♋	2♌
68	26♊	8♋	20♋	2♌	14♌	27♌	10♍	24♍	8♎	23♎	7♏	22♏	7♐	22♐	6♑
69	3♏	16♏	0♐	14♐	28♐	13♑	27♑	11♒	25♒	9♓	23♓	7♈	20♈	4♉	17♉
1970	16♓	1♈	16♈	1♉	15♉	29♉	13♊	26♊	8♋	21♋	3♌	15♌	27♌	8♍	20♍
71	3♌	16♌	28♌	10♍	22♍	4♎	15♎	27♎	9♏	21♏	3♐	15♐	28♐	10♑	23♑
72	16♐	28♐	10♑	22♑	4♒	17♒	0♓	14♓	29♓	13♈	28♈	13♉	29♉	14♊	28♊
73	24♈	8♉	22♉	6♊	21♊	5♋	19♋	3♌	17♌	1♍	15♍	28♍	11♎	24♎	7♏
74	8♍	23♍	7♎	21♎	6♏	19♏	3♐	15♐	28♐	10♑	22♑	4♒	16♒	28♒	10♓
75	24♑	6♒	18♒	0♓	12♓	24♓	6♈	18♈	0♉	12♉	24♉	6♊	19♊	2♋	15♋
76	6♊	18♊	0♋	12♋	25♋	8♌	21♌	5♍	19♍	4♎	19♎	4♏	19♏	4♐	19♐
77	14♎	29♎	13♏	28♏	12♐	27♐	11♑	26♑	9♒	23♒	6♓	19♓	2♈	15♈	27♈
78	0♓	14♓	28♓	12♈	26♈	9♉	22♉	5♊	18♊	0♋	12♋	24♋	6♌	18♌	0♍
79	14♋	26♋	8♌	20♌	2♍	15♍	27♍	9♎	21♎	4♏	16♏	29♏	11♐	24♐	7♑
1980	26♏	8♐	20♐	3♑	15♑	28♑	12♒	26♒	10♓	25♓	10♈	25♈	10♉	25♉	10♊
81	5♈	20♈	4♉	20♉	4♊	19♊	4♋	18♋	1♌	15♌	28♌	11♍	23♍	6♎	18♎
82	22♌	6♍	19♍	3♎	17♎	0♏	13♏	25♏	8♐	20♐	2♑	13♑	25♑	7♒	19♒
83	4♑	16♑	28♑	10♒	22♒	4♓	16♓	28♓	10♈	23♈	5♉	18♉	2♊	15♊	28♊
84	17♉	29♉	11♊	24♊	6♋	19♋	3♌	17♌	1♍	16♍	1♎	16♎	1♏	16♏	1♐
85	26♍	10♎	25♎	11♏	26♏	10♐	25♐	9♑	23♑	6♒	19♒	2♓	14♓	27♓	9♈
86	14♒	28♒	11♓	24♓	7♈	20♈	3♉	15♉	27♉	9♊	21♊	3♋	15♋	27♋	9♌
87	26♊	8♋	20♋	2♌	15♌	28♌	11♍	24♍	7♎	20♎	4♏	18♏	2♐	16♐	0♑
88	7♏	20♏	2♐	15♐	28♐	11♑	25♑	9♒	23♒	7♓	22♓	7♈	22♈	6♉	21♉
89	16♓	1♈	16♈	1♉	17♉	2♊	16♊	0♋	14♋	27♋	10♌	23♌	5♍	17♍	29♍

MOON POSITIONS

Year	Oct 27	Oct 28	Oct 29	Oct 30	Oct 31	Nov 1	Nov 2	Nov 3	Nov 4	Nov 5	Nov 6	Nov 7	Nov 8	Nov 9	Nov 10
1960	6♒	20♒	4♓	18♓	2♈	15♈	28♈	11♉	24♉	6♊	19♊	1♋	13♋	25♋	6♌
61	20♊	3♋	15♋	27♋	9♌	21♌	3♍	15♍	27♍	9♎	21♎	4♏	17♏	0♐	14♐
62	22♎	4♏	16♏	28♏	11♐	23♐	6♑	19♑	2♒	15♒	29♒	13♓	28♓	13♈	28♈
63	25♒	8♓	22♓	7♈	22♈	7♉	22♉	8♊	23♊	7♋	21♋	5♌	18♌	1♍	14♍
64	29♋	13♌	26♌	10♍	23♍	6♎	19♎	2♏	14♏	27♏	9♐	21♐	2♑	14♑	26♑
65	10♐	22♐	5♑	17♑	29♑	10♒	22♒	4♓	16♓	29♓	11♈	24♈	7♉	21♉	5♊
66	12♈	24♈	7♉	19♉	1♊	14♊	27♊	10♋	23♋	7♌	21♌	5♍	20♍	4♎	19♎
67	16♌	29♌	13♍	28♍	13♎	28♎	13♏	28♏	13♐	28♐	12♑	26♑	9♒	22♒	4♓
68	21♑	5♒	18♒	2♓	15♓	27♓	10♈	22♈	5♉	17♉	29♉	10♊	22♊	4♋	16♋
69	29♉	12♊	24♊	6♋	18♋	0♌	12♌	24♌	6♍	18♍	1♎	14♎	28♎	11♏	26♏
1970	2♎	14♎	27♎	9♏	22♏	5♐	18♐	2♑	16♑	29♑	13♒	27♒	12♓	26♓	10♈
71	7♒	20♒	4♓	19♓	3♈	19♈	4♉	19♉	4♊	19♊	3♋	16♋	29♋	12♌	25♌
72	13♋	26♋	10♌	23♌	6♍	18♍	1♎	13♎	25♎	7♏	19♏	1♐	13♐	24♐	6♑
73	20♏	2♐	14♐	26♐	8♑	20♑	1♒	13♒	26♒	8♓	21♓	4♈	18♈	2♉	17♉
74	22♓	5♈	17♈	0♉	13♉	26♉	10♊	24♊	7♋	21♋	6♌	20♌	4♍	18♍	2♎
75	28♋	12♌	26♌	10♍	25♍	10♎	25♎	10♏	24♏	9♐	23♐	6♑	19♑	2♒	14♒
76	4♐	18♐	1♑	14♑	27♑	9♒	22♒	4♓	15♓	27♓	9♈	21♈	3♉	15♉	27♉
77	10♉	22♉	4♊	16♊	28♊	9♋	21♋	3♌	16♌	28♌	11♍	24♍	8♎	22♎	7♏
78	12♍	24♍	7♎	20♎	3♏	17♏	1♐	15♐	0♑	14♑	28♑	12♒	26♒	10♓	24♓
79	20♑	4♒	18♒	2♓	16♓	1♈	16♈	0♉	15♉	29♉	13♊	26♊	9♋	22♋	4♌
1980	25♊	9♋	22♋	5♌	18♌	0♍	12♍	24♍	6♎	17♎	29♎	11♏	23♏	5♐	18♐
81	0♏	12♏	24♏	6♐	18♐	0♑	11♑	23♑	6♒	18♒	1♓	15♓	28♓	13♈	28♈
82	1♓	14♓	27♓	10♈	24♈	8♉	22♉	7♊	21♊	6♋	20♋	5♌	19♌	2♍	16♍
83	12♋	26♋	10♌	24♌	9♍	23♍	7♎	22♎	6♏	20♏	3♐	16♐	29♐	12♑	24♑
84	15♐	29♐	12♑	25♑	8♒	20♒	2♓	14♓	26♓	8♈	20♈	2♉	14♉	26♉	8♊
85	21♈	2♉	14♉	26♉	8♊	20♊	2♋	14♋	26♋	9♌	22♌	5♍	19♍	4♎	18♎
86	21♌	4♍	17♍	0♎	14♎	29♎	13♏	28♏	13♐	28♐	12♑	27♑	11♒	25♒	8♓
87	4♑	18♑	3♒	17♒	1♓	15♓	29♓	13♈	27♈	10♉	23♉	6♊	19♊	1♋	14♋
88	5♊	19♊	2♋	15♋	28♋	10♌	22♌	4♍	16♍	27♍	9♎	21♎	4♏	16♏	29♏
89	11♎	23♎	4♏	16♏	28♏	10♐	22♐	5♑	17♑	0♒	13♒	26♒	10♓	24♓	9♈

MOON POSITIONS

NOVEMBER

	11	12	13	14	15	16	17	18	19	20	21	22	23	24	25
1960	18♌	0♍	13♍	25♍	8♎	21♎	5♏	20♏	4♐	19♐	4♑	18♑	3♒	17♒	1♓
61	27♐	11♑	25♑	9♒	23♒	7♓	21♓	5♈	19♈	3♉	17♉	1♊	15♊	28♊	10♋
62	13♉	28♉	12♊	27♊	10♋	24♋	7♌	19♌	1♍	13♍	25♍	7♎	19♎	1♏	13♏
63	26♍	8♎	20♎	2♏	14♏	26♏	8♐	19♐	1♑	13♑	25♑	8♒	20♒	4♓	17♓
64	8♒	20♒	2♓	15♓	28♓	12♈	26♈	9♉	25♉	10♊	25♊	10♋	25♋	9♌	23♌
65	19♊	3♋	17♋	1♌	15♌	29♌	14♍	28♍	11♎	25♎	9♏	22♏	5♐	18♐	0♑
66	4♏	18♏	3♐	17♐	0♑	13♑	26♑	9♒	21♒	3♓	15♓	27♓	9♈	21♈	3♉
67	16♓	28♓	10♈	22♈	4♉	16♉	28♉	10♊	22♊	4♋	16♋	29♋	12♌	25♌	9♍
68	28♋	10♌	23♌	5♍	18♍	2♎	16♎	1♏	15♏	1♐	16♐	1♑	16♑	1♒	15♒
69	10♐	24♐	9♑	23♑	8♒	22♒	6♓	20♓	3♈	16♈	29♈	12♉	25♉	8♊	20♊
1970	25♈	9♉	23♉	7♊	20♊	4♋	16♋	29♋	11♌	23♌	4♍	16♍	28♍	10♎	22♎
71	7♍	19♍	0♎	12♎	24♎	6♏	18♏	0♐	13♐	25♐	8♑	20♑	3♒	17♒	0♓
72	18♑	0♒	13♒	26♒	9♓	23♓	7♈	21♈	6♉	22♉	7♊	22♊	7♋	22♋	6♌
73	1♊	16♊	0♋	14♋	27♋	10♌	23♌	6♍	18♍	0♎	12♎	24♎	6♏	18♏	0♐
74	16♎	0♏	14♏	27♏	11♐	23♐	6♑	18♑	0♒	12♒	24♒	6♓	18♓	0♈	12♈
75	27♈	9♉	20♉	2♊	14♊	26♊	8♋	21♋	3♌	16♌	29♌	12♍	25♍	9♎	22♎
76	27♊	9♋	21♋	4♌	14♌	26♌	8♍	21♍	3♎	16♎	29♎	12♏	25♏	9♐	22♐
77	22♏	7♐	22♐	7♑	22♑	6♒	20♒	3♓	16♓	29♓	12♈	24♈	6♉	19♉	1♊
78	22♈	7♉	22♉	7♊	22♊	6♋	20♋	3♌	16♌	29♌	12♍	24♍	7♎	20♎	2♏
79	16♌	28♌	10♍	22♍	4♎	16♎	28♎	11♏	24♏	7♐	20♐	3♑	17♑	1♒	15♒
1980	0♑	12♑	25♑	8♒	21♒	5♓	19♓	3♈	18♈	3♉	18♉	3♊	18♊	3♋	17♋
81	13♉	28♉	13♊	28♊	13♋	27♋	11♌	25♌	8♍	20♍	3♎	15♎	27♎	9♏	21♏
82	0♎	13♎	26♎	9♏	21♏	4♐	16♐	28♐	10♑	21♑	3♒	15♒	27♒	9♓	22♓
83	6♒	18♒	0♓	12♓	24♓	6♈	18♈	1♉	14♉	27♉	11♊	25♊	9♋	23♋	7♌
84	21♊	3♋	16♋	0♌	13♌	27♌	11♍	25♍	10♎	25♎	9♏	24♏	9♐	23♐	7♑
85	3♏	19♏	4♐	19♐	4♑	18♑	2♒	15♒	29♒	11♓	24♓	6♈	18♈	0♉	11♉
86	21♓	4♈	17♈	29♈	12♉	24♉	6♊	18♊	0♋	11♋	23♋	5♌	17♌	0♍	12♍
87	26♋	8♌	19♌	1♍	13♍	25♍	8♎	21♎	4♏	18♏	1♐	16♐	0♑	15♑	29♑
88	12♐	25♐	8♑	22♑	5♒	19♒	3♓	17♓	2♈	16♈	1♉	15♉	29♉	13♊	27♊
89	24♈	9♉	25♉	10♊	25♊	9♋	23♋	6♌	19♌	2♍	14♍	26♍	8♎	19♎	1♏

MOON POSITIONS

	NOVEMBER					DECEMBER									
	26	27	28	29	30	1	2	3	4	5	6	7	8	9	10
1960	15♓	28♓	12♈	25♈	7♉	20♉	3♊	15♊	27♊	9♋	21♋	3♌	15♌	26♌	8♍
61	23♋	5♌	17♌	29♌	11♍	22♍	4♎	17♎	29♎	12♏	25♏	9♐	23♐	7♑	21♑
62	25♏	7♐	20♐	3♑	16♑	29♑	12♒	25♒	9♓	23♓	8♈	22♈	7♉	21♉	6♊
63	1♈	15♈	0♉	15♉	0♊	16♊	1♋	15♋	0♌	14♌	27♌	10♍	23♍	5♎	17♎
64	7♍	20♍	3♎	16♎	29♎	11♏	23♏	5♐	17♐	29♐	11♑	23♑	4♒	16♒	28♒
65	12♑	24♑	6♒	18♒	0♓	12♓	24♓	6♈	19♈	2♉	15♉	29♉	13♊	28♊	12♋
66	15♉	28♉	10♊	23♊	7♋	20♋	4♌	18♌	2♍	16♍	0♎	14♎	29♎	13♏	27♏
67	22♍	7♎	21♎	6♏	21♏	6♐	21♐	6♑	20♑	4♒	17♒	0♓	13♓	25♓	7♈
68	28♒	12♓	24♓	7♈	19♈	2♉	14♉	25♉	7♊	19♊	1♋	13♋	25♋	7♌	19♌
69	2♋	14♋	26♋	8♌	20♌	2♍	14♍	26♍	9♎	22♎	5♏	19♏	4♐	19♐	3♑
1970	5♏	18♏	1♐	15♐	28♐	12♑	26♑	10♒	24♒	8♓	22♓	6♈	20♈	4♉	18♉
71	14♓	28♓	13♈	27♈	12♉	27♉	12♊	26♊	11♋	24♋	7♌	20♌	3♍	15♍	27♍
72	19♌	2♍	15♍	28♍	10♎	22♎	4♏	16♏	28♏	10♐	21♐	3♑	15♑	27♑	10♒
73	22♐	4♑	16♑	28♑	10♒	22♒	4♓	16♓	29♓	12♈	26♈	10♉	24♉	9♊	24♊
74	25♈	8♉	21♉	5♊	19♊	3♋	18♋	2♌	16♌	1♍	15♍	29♍	13♎	26♎	10♏
75	6♍	21♍	5♎	19♎	4♏	18♏	3♐	17♐	1♑	14♑	27♑	10♒	22♒	5♓	17♓
76	10♒	23♒	6♓	18♓	0♈	12♈	24♈	6♉	18♉	0♊	12♊	24♊	6♋	18♋	1♌
77	12♊	24♊	6♋	18♋	0♌	12♌	24♌	7♍	19♍	3♎	16♎	0♏	15♏	0♐	15♐
78	15♎	28♎	12♏	26♏	10♐	25♐	9♑	24♑	9♒	23♒	7♓	21♓	5♈	18♈	1♉
79	29♒	13♓	27♓	11♈	25♈	9♉	24♉	7♊	21♊	4♋	17♋	0♌	12♌	24♌	6♍
1980	0♌	13♌	26♌	8♍	20♍	2♎	14♎	26♎	8♏	20♏	2♐	14♐	27♐	9♑	22♑
81	3♐	15♐	27♐	8♑	20♑	2♒	15♒	27♒	10♓	23♓	7♈	21♈	6♉	21♉	6♊
82	5♈	18♈	2♉	16♉	1♊	16♊	1♋	16♋	0♌	15♌	29♌	13♍	27♍	10♎	23♎
83	21♌	5♍	19♍	4♎	17♎	1♏	15♏	28♏	12♐	24♐	7♑	19♑	2♒	14♒	26♒
84	20♑	3♒	16♒	28♒	10♓	22♓	4♈	16♈	28♈	10♉	22♉	4♊	17♊	0♋	13♋
85	23♉	5♊	17♊	29♊	11♋	23♋	6♌	18♌	1♍	15♍	28♍	13♎	27♎	12♏	27♏
86	25♍	8♎	22♎	6♏	21♏	6♐	21♐	7♑	22♑	6♒	21♒	5♓	18♓	1♈	14♈
87	14♒	28♒	12♓	26♓	9♈	23♈	6♉	19♉	2♊	15♊	27♊	10♋	22♋	4♌	15♌
88	10♋	23♋	6♌	18♌	0♍	12♍	24♍	5♎	17♎	0♏	12♏	25♏	8♐	21♐	4♑
89	13♏	25♏	7♐	19♐	2♑	14♑	27♑	10♒	23♒	6♓	20♓	4♈	18♈	3♉	18♉

MOON POSITIONS

DECEMBER

	11	12	13	14	15	16	17	18	19	20	21	22	23	24	25
1960	21♏	3♎	16♎	29♎	13♏	27♏	12♐	27♐	12♑	28♑	13♒	27♒	11♓	25♓	9♈
61	5♒	19♒	4♓	18♓	2♈	16♈	0♉	13♉	27♉	10♊	23♊	6♋	18♋	1♌	13♌
62	20♊	4♋	18♋	1♌	14♌	27♌	9♍	21♍	3♎	15♎	27♎	9♏	21♏	3♐	16♐
63	29♎	11♏	23♏	4♐	16♐	28♐	10♑	23♑	5♒	17♒	0♓	13♓	27♓	11♈	25♈
64	11♓	23♓	6♈	20♈	4♉	18♉	3♊	18♊	3♋	18♋	3♌	18♌	3♍	16♍	0♎
65	27♑	11♒	26♒	10♓	24♓	8♈	22♈	5♉	18♉	1♊	14♊	26♊	8♋	21♋	3♌
66	11♐	25♐	8♑	21♑	4♒	17♒	29♒	11♓	23♓	5♈	16♈	28♈	11♉	23♉	6♊
67	19♈	1♉	12♉	24♉	6♊	18♊	1♋	13♋	26♋	9♌	22♌	5♍	19♍	3♎	17♎
68	2♏	14♏	27♏	11♐	24♐	9♑	23♑	9♒	24♒	9♓	24♓	9♈	24♈	7♉	21♉
69	18♑	3♒	18♒	2♓	16♓	0♈	13♈	26♈	9♉	22♉	4♊	17♊	29♊	11♋	23♋
1970	2♊	15♊	29♊	12♋	24♋	6♌	19♌	0♍	12♍	24♍	6♎	18♎	0♏	13♏	26♏
71	9♎	21♎	2♏	14♏	27♏	9♐	21♐	4♑	17♑	0♒	14♒	27♒	11♓	25♓	9♈
72	22♒	5♓	18♓	2♈	16♈	0♉	15♉	0♊	15♊	0♋	15♋	0♌	14♌	28♌	11♍
73	9♋	25♋	9♌	24♌	8♍	22♍	5♎	18♎	1♏	13♏	25♏	7♐	19♐	1♑	13♑
74	23♏	6♐	19♐	1♑	14♑	26♑	8♒	20♒	2♓	14♓	26♓	8♈	20♈	3♉	16♉
75	28♓	10♈	22♈	4♉	16♉	29♉	12♊	25♊	8♋	21♋	5♌	19♌	3♍	17♍	1♎
76	14♌	27♌	10♍	24♍	7♎	22♎	6♏	21♏	6♐	21♐	5♑	20♑	4♒	18♒	1♓
77	0♑	16♑	1♒	15♒	29♒	13♓	26♓	9♈	21♈	4♉	16♉	28♉	9♊	21♊	3♋
78	14♉	27♉	9♊	22♊	4♋	16♋	28♋	10♌	22♌	4♍	16♍	28♍	10♎	23♎	6♏
79	18♍	0♎	12♎	24♎	6♏	19♏	2♐	15♐	29♐	13♑	27♑	11♒	25♒	10♓	24♓
1980	5♒	18♒	2♓	15♓	29♓	13♈	28♈	12♉	27♉	12♊	26♊	11♋	25♋	8♌	21♌
81	21♊	6♋	21♋	6♌	20♌	4♍	17♍	29♍	12♎	24♎	6♏	18♏	0♐	12♐	24♐
82	5♏	18♏	0♐	12♐	24♐	6♑	18♑	0♒	12♒	24♒	6♓	18♓	0♈	13♈	26♈
83	7♓	19♓	1♈	14♈	26♈	9♉	22♉	5♊	19♊	4♋	18♋	3♌	17♌	2♍	16♍
84	27♋	10♌	24♌	8♍	22♍	6♎	20♎	4♏	19♏	3♐	17♐	1♑	15♑	28♑	11♒
85	12♐	27♐	11♑	26♑	10♒	24♒	7♓	20♓	2♈	14♈	26♈	8♉	20♉	2♊	13♊
86	26♈	9♉	21♉	3♊	15♊	26♊	8♋	20♋	2♌	14♌	26♌	8♍	20♍	2♎	13♎
87	27♌	9♍	21♍	3♎	16♎	28♎	12♏	26♏	10♐	24♐	9♑	24♑	9♒	24♒	8♓
88	18♑	2♒	16♒	0♓	14♓	28♓	12♈	26♈	10♉	24♉	8♊	22♊	5♋	18♋	1♌
89	3♊	18♊	2♋	17♋	1♌	14♌	27♌	10♍	22♍	4♎	16♎	28♎	10♏	22♏	4♐

MOON POSITIONS

DECEMBER

	26	27	28	29	30	31
1960	22♈	4♉	17♉	29♉	12♊	24♊
61	25♌	7♍	18♍	0♎	12♎	24♎
62	29♐	12♑	25♑	9♒	22♒	6♓
63	9♉	24♉	9♊	24♊	9♋	23♋
64	13♎	26♎	8♏	20♏	2♐	14♐
65	15♒	26♒	8♓	20♓	2♈	14♈
66	19♊	2♋	16♋	0♌	14♌	28♌
67	1♏	15♏	0♐	15♐	29♐	14♑
68	4♈	16♈	28♈	11♉	22♉	4♊
69	5♌	17♌	28♌	10♍	22♍	4♎
1970	9♐	23♐	7♑	21♑	6♒	20♒
71	23♈	7♉	22♉	6♊	21♊	5♋
72	24♍	7♎	19♎	1♏	13♏	25♏
73	25♑	7♒	18♒	0♓	13♓	25♓
74	29♌	13♊	27♊	12♋	27♋	12♌
75	16♎	0♏	14♏	28♏	12♐	25♐
76	14♓	27♓	9♈	21♈	3♉	14♉
77	15♋	27♋	9♌	21♌	3♍	16♍
78	19♏	3♐	18♐	3♑	18♑	3♒
79	8♉	22♈	6♉	19♉	3♊	16♊
1980	4♍	16♍	28♍	10♎	22♎	4♏
81	5♑	17♑	0♒	12♒	24♒	7♓
82	10♉	24♉	9♊	24♊	9♋	24♋
83	0♎	14♎	28♎	11♏	25♏	8♐
84	24♒	6♓	18♓	0♈	12♈	24♈
85	26♊	8♋	20♋	3♌	16♌	28♌
86	0♏	15♏	29♏	14♐	29♐	15♑
87	22♓	6♈	20♈	4♉	16♉	29♉
88	14♌	26♌	8♍	20♍	1♎	13♎
89	16♐	28♐	11♑	24♑	7♒	20♒

MERCURY

Relative to the Earth, Mercury always travels in a constellation very near to the one occupied by the Sun. Consequently, on the date of your birth Mercury could only be in one of three signs: the sign your Sun is in, or one sign away, ahead or behind. The following table will tell you where Mercury was when you were born.

DATE		ZODIAC SIGN
1900		
1/01 to	1/08	Sagittarius
1/08 to	1/29	Capricorn
1/29 to	2/14	Aquarius
2/14 to	3/03	Pisces
3/03 to	3/29	Aries
3/29 to	4/16	Pisces
4/17 to	5/10	Aries
5/10 to	5/26	Taurus
5/26 to	6/09	Gemini
6/09 to	6/27	Cancer
6/27 to	9/02	Leo
9/02 to	9/18	Virgo
9/18 to	10/07	Libra
10/07 to	10/30	Scorpio
10/30 to	11/18	Sagittarius
11/19 to	12/12	Scorpio
12/12 to	12/31	Sagittarius

1901		
1/01 to	1/02	Sagittarius
1/02 to	1/20	Capricorn
1/21 to	2/07	Aquarius
2/07 to	4/15	Pisces
4/15 to	5/03	Aries
5/03 to	5/17	Taurus
5/17 to	6/01	Gemini
6/01 to	8/09	Cancer
8/10 to	8/25	Leo
8/25 to	9/10	Virgo

9/11 to	9/30	Libra
10/01 to	12/06	Scorpio
12/06 to	12/26	Sagittarius
12/26 to	12/31	Capricorn

1902		
1/01 to	1/13	Capricorn
1/13 to	2/01	Aquarius
2/01 to	2/17	Pisces
2/17 to	3/18	Aquarius
3/18 to	4/09	Pisces
4/09 to	4/25	Aries
4/25 to	5/09	Taurus
5/09 to	5/29	Gemini
5/29 to	6/25	Cancer
6/26 to	7/13	Gemini
7/13 to	8/02	Cancer
8/02 to	8/17	Leo
8/17 to	9/03	Virgo
9/03 to	9/28	Libra
9/28 to	10/15	Scorpio
10/15 to	11/10	Libra
11/10 to	11/29	Scorpio
11/29 to	12/18	Sagittarius
12/18 to	12/31	Capricorn

1903		
1/01 to	1/06	Capricorn
1/06 to	3/14	Aquarius
3/14 to	4/01	Pisces
4/01 to	4/16	Aries
4/16 to	5/02	Taurus

DATE	ZODIAC SIGN
5/02 to 7/10	Gemini
7/10 to 7/25	Cancer
7/25 to 8/09	Leo
8/09 to 8/28	Virgo
8/29 to 11/03	Libra
11/04 to 11/22	Scorpio
11/22 to 12/11	Sagittarius
12/11 to 12/31	Capricorn

1904

1/01 to 1/02	Capricorn
1/02 to 1/13	Aquarius
1/13 to 2/15	Capricorn
2/15 to 3/07	Aquarius
3/07 to 3/23	Pisces
3/23 to 4/07	Aries
4/07 to 6/13	Taurus
6/14 to 7/01	Gemini
7/01 to 7/15	Cancer
7/15 to 8/01	Leo
8/01 to 8/28	Virgo
8/28 to 9/07	Libra
9/07 to 10/08	Virgo
10/08 to 10/26	Libra
10/26 to 11/14	Scorpio
11/14 to 12/04	Sagittarius
12/04 to 12/31	Capricorn

1905

1/01 to 2/08	Capricorn
2/09 to 2/27	Aquarius
2/27 to 3/15	Pisces
3/15 to 4/01	Aries
4/01 to 4/28	Taurus
4/28 to 5/15	Aries
5/15 to 6/08	Taurus
6/08 to 6/23	Gemini
6/23 to 7/07	Cancer
7/07 to 7/27	Leo

7/27 to 10/01	Virgo
10/01 to 10/19	Libra
10/19 to 11/07	Scorpio
11/07 to 12/01	Sagittarius
12/02 to 12/09	Capricorn
12/09 to 12/31	Sagittarius

1906

1/01 to 1/12	Sagittarius
1/12 to 2/02	Capricorn
2/02 to 2/19	Aquarius
2/19 to 3/07	Pisces
3/07 to 5/14	Aries
5/14 to 5/31	Taurus
5/31 to 6/14	Gemini
6/14 to 6/30	Cancer
6/30 to 9/07	Leo
9/07 to 9/23	Virgo
9/23 to 10/11	Libra
10/11 to 11/01	Scorpio
11/01 to 12/06	Sagittarius
12/06 to 12/12	Scorpio
12/12 to 12/31	Sagittarius

1907

1/01 to 1/06	Sagittarius
1/06 to 1/25	Capricorn
1/25 to 2/12	Aquarius
2/12 to 3/03	Pisces
3/03 to 3/13	Aries
3/13 to 4/18	Pisces
4/18 to 5/08	Aries
5/08 to 5/23	Taurus
5/23 to 6/06	Gemini
6/06 to 6/27	Cancer
6/27 to 7/26	Leo
7/26 to 8/12	Cancer
8/12 to 8/30	Leo
8/31 to 9/15	Virgo
9/16 to 10/04	Libra
10/04 to 12/10	Scorpio

12/10 to 12/30	Sagittarius
12/30 to 12/31	Capricorn

1908

1/01 to	1/18	Capricorn
1/18 to	2/04	Aquarius
2/04 to	4/12	Pisces
4/12 to	4/29	Aries
4/29 to	5/13	Taurus
5/13 to	5/29	Gemini
5/29 to	8/06	Cancer
8/06 to	8/21	Leo
8/21 to	9/07	Virgo
9/07 to	9/28	Libra
9/28 to	11/01	Scorpio
11/01 to	11/11	Libra
11/11 to	12/03	Scorpio
12/03 to	12/22	Sagittarius
12/22 to	12/31	Capricorn

1909

1/01 to	1/10	Capricorn
1/10 to	3/17	Aquarius
3/17 to	4/05	Pisces
4/05 to	4/21	Aries
4/21 to	4/05	Taurus
5/05 to	7/12	Gemini
7/13 to	7/29	Cancer
7/29 to	8/13	Leo
8/13 to	8/31	Virgo
8/31 to	11/07	Libra
11/07 to	11/26	Scorpio
11/26 to	12/15	Sagittarius
12/15 to	12/31	Capricorn

1910

1/01 to	1/03	Capricorn
1/03 to	1/30	Aquarius
1/30 to	2/15	Capricorn
2/15 to	3/11	Aquarius
3/11 to	3/29	Pisces

3/29 to	4/12	Aries
4/12 to	4/30	Taurus
4/30 to	6/01	Gemini
6/01 to	6/11	Taurus
6/11 to	7/06	Gemini
7/06 to	7/21	Cancer
7/21 to	8/05	Leo
8/05 to	8/26	Virgo
8/27 to	9/28	Libra
9/28 to	10/11	Virgo
10/12 to	10/31	Libra
10/31 to	11/19	Scorpio
11/19 to	12/08	Sagittarius
12/08 to	12/31	Capricorn

1911

1/01 to	2/12	Capricorn
2/12 to	3/04	Aquarius
3/04 to	3/20	Pisces
3/20 to	4/05	Aries
4/05 to	6/12	Taurus
6/12 to	6/28	Gemini
6/28 to	7/12	Cancer
7/12 to	7/30	Leo
7/30 to	10/06	Virgo
10/06 to	10/23	Libra
10/23 to	11/11	Scorpio
11/11 to	12/02	Sagittarius
12/02 to	12/27	Capricorn
12/27 to	12/31	Sagittarius

1912

1/01 to	1/14	Sagittarius
1/14 to	2/06	Capricorn
2/06 to	2/24	Aquarius
2/25 to	3/11	Pisces
3/11 to	5/16	Aries
5/17 to	6/04	Taurus
6/05 to	6/19	Gemini
6/19 to	7/04	Cancer
7/04 to	7/26	Leo

DATE		ZODIAC SIGN
7/26 to	8/20	Virgo
8/21 to	9/10	Leo
9/10 to	9/27	Virgo
9/28 to	10/16	Libra
10/16 to	11/04	Scorpio
11/04 to	12/31	Sagittarius

1913

1/01 to	1/09	Sagittarius
1/09 to	1/29	Capricorn
1/29 to	2/16	Aquarius
2/16 to	3/04	Pisces
3/04 to	4/07	Aries
4/07 to	4/13	Pisces
4/13 to	5/11	Aries
5/12 to	5/27	Taurus
5/27 to	6/10	Gemini
6/10 to	6/27	Cancer
6/27 to	9/04	Leo
9/04 to	9/20	Virgo
9/20 to	10/08	Libra
10/08 to	10/30	Scorpio
10/30 to	11/23	Sagittarius
11/23 to	12/13	Scorpio
12/13 to	12/31	Sagittarius

1914

1/01 to	1/03	Sagittarius
1/03 to	1/22	Capricorn
1/22 to	2/08	Aquarius
2/08 to	4/16	Pisces
4/16 to	5/04	Aries
5/04 to	5/19	Taurus
5/19 to	6/02	Gemini
6/03 to	8/10	Cancer
8/11 to	8/27	Leo
8/27 to	9/12	Virgo
9/12 to	10/01	Libra
10/02 to	12/07	Scorpio

12/07 to	12/27	Sagittarius
12/27 to	12/31	Capricorn

1915

1/01 to	1/14	Capricorn
1/14 to	2/02	Aquarius
2/02 to	2/23	Pisces
2/23 to	3/19	Aquarius
3/19 to	4/10	Pisces
4/10 to	4/26	Aries
4/26 to	5/10	Taurus
5/10 to	5/29	Gemini
5/29 to	8/04	Cancer
8/04 to	8/18	Leo
8/19 to	9/05	Virgo
9/05 to	9/28	Libra
9/28 to	10/20	Scorpio
10/20 to	11/11	Libra
11/11 to	12/01	Scorpio
12/01 to	12/20	Sagittarius
12/20 to	12/31	Capricorn

1916

1/01 to	1/07	Capricorn
1/07 to	3/14	Aquarius
3/14 to	4/02	Pisces
4/02 to	4/17	Aries
4/17 to	5/02	Taurus
5/02 to	7/10	Gemini
7/10 to	7/25	Cancer
7/25 to	8/09	Leo
8/09 to	8/28	Virgo
8/28 to	11/04	Libra
11/04 to	11/22	Scorpio
11/22 to	12/11	Sagittarius
12/12 to	12/31	Capricorn

1917

1/01 to	1/17	Aquarius
1/17 to	2/14	Capricorn

2/14 to 3/08 Aquarius
3/08 to 3/25 Pisces
3/25 to 4/08 Aries
4/08 to 6/14 Taurus
6/14 to 7/03 Gemini
7/03 to 7/17 Cancer
7/17 to 8/02 Leo
8/02 to 8/26 Virgo
8/26 to 9/14 Libra
9/14 to 10/09 Virgo
10/09 to 10/27 Libra
10/27 to 11/15 Scorpio
11/15 to 12/05 Sagittarius
12/05 to 12/31 Capricorn

1918

1/01 to 2/10 Capricorn
2/10 to 2/28 Aquarius
3/01 to 3/16 Pisces
3/16 to 4/02 Aries
4/02 to 6/09 Taurus
6/09 to 6/24 Gemini
6/24 to 7/08 Cancer
7/08 to 7/27 Leo
7/27 to 10/02 Virgo
10/02 to 10/28 Libra
10/29 to 11/08 Scorpio
11/08 to 12/01 Sagittarius
12/01 to 12/15 Capricorn
12/15 to 12/31 Sagittarius

1919

1/01 to 1/13 Sagittarius
1/13 to 2/03 Capricorn
2/03 to 2/21 Aquarius
2/21 to 3/09 Pisces
3/09 to 5/15 Aries
5/15 to 6/02 Taurus
6/02 to 6/16 Gemini
6/16 to 7/01 Cancer
7/01 to 9/08 Lco

9/08 to 9/25 Virgo
9/25 to 10/13 Libra
10/13 to 11/02 Scorpio
11/02 to 12/31 Sagittarius

1920

1/01 to 1/07 Sagittarius
1/07 to 1/27 Capricorn
1/27 to 2/13 Aquarius
2/13 to 3/02 Pisces
3/02 to 3/19 Aries
3/19 to 4/17 Pisces
4/17 to 5/08 Aries
5/08 to 5/23 Taurus
5/23 to 6/06 Gemini
6/06 to 6/26 Cancer
6/26 to 8/02 Leo
8/02 to 8/10 Cancer
8/10 to 8/31 Leo
8/31 to 9/16 Virgo
9/16 to 10/05 Libra
10/05 to 10/30 Scorpio
10/30 to 11/10 Sagittarius
11/10 to 12/10 Scorpio
12/10 to 12/31 Sagittarius

1921

1/01 to 1/18 Capricorn
1/18 to 2/05 Aquarius
2/05 to 4/13 Pisces
4/13 to 4/30 Aries
5/01 to 5/15 Taurus
5/15 to 5/30 Gemini
5/30 to 8/07 Cancer
8/08 to 8/23 Leo
8/23 to 9/08 Virgo
9/08 to 9/29 Libra
9/29 to 12/04 Scorpio
12/04 to 12/23 Sagittarius
12/24 to 12/31 Capricorn

DATE   *ZODIAC SIGN*

1922

1/01 to	1/11	Capricorn
1/11 to	2/01	Aquarius
2/01 to	2/08	Pisces
2/08 to	3/17	Aquarius
3/18 to	4/07	Pisces
4/07 to	4/22	Aries
4/22 to	5/06	Taurus
5/07 to	5/31	Gemini
5/31 to	6/10	Cancer
6/10 to	7/13	Gemini
7/13 to	7/31	Cancer
7/31 to	8/15	Leo
8/15 to	9/01	Virgo
9/01 to	10/01	Libra
10/01 to	10/04	Scorpio
10/04 to	11/08	Libra
11/08 to	11/27	Scorpio
11/27 to	12/16	Sagittarius
12/16 to	12/31	Capricorn

1923

1/01 to	1/04	Capricorn
1/04 to	2/06	Aquarius
2/06 to	2/13	Capricorn
2/13 to	3/12	Aquarius
3/13 to	3/30	Pisces
3/30 to	4/14	Aries
4/14 to	4/30	Taurus
5/01 to	7/08	Gemini
7/08 to	7/22	Cancer
7/22 to	8/07	Leo
8/07 to	8/27	Virgo
8/27 to	10/04	Libra
10/04 to	10/11	Virgo
10/11 to	11/01	Libra
11/01 to	11/20	Scorpio
11/20 to	12/09	Sagittarius
12/09 to	12/31	Capricorn

1924

1/01 to	2/13	Capricorn
2/13 to	3/04	Aquarius
3/04 to	3/21	Pisces
3/21 to	4/05	Aries
4/05 to	6/12	Taurus
6/12 to	6/29	Gemini
6/29 to	7/13	Cancer
7/13 to	7/30	Leo
7/30 to	10/06	Virgo
10/06 to	10/24	Libra
10/24 to	11/12	Scorpio
11/12 to	12/02	Sagittarius
12/02 to	12/31	Capricorn

1925

1/01 to	1/13	Sagittarius
1/14 to	2/06	Capricorn
2/07 to	2/25	Aquarius
2/25 to	3/13	Pisces
3/13 to	4/01	Aries
4/01 to	4/15	Taurus
4/15 to	5/16	Aries
5/16 to	6/06	Taurus
6/06 to	6/20	Gemini
6/20 to	7/05	Cancer
7/05 to	7/26	Leo
7/26 to	8/26	Virgo
8/27 to	9/10	Leo
9/10 to	9/29	Virgo
9/29 to	10/16	Libra
10/16 to	11/05	Scorpio
11/05 to	12/31	Sagittarius

1926

1/01 to	1/10	Sagittarius
1/11 to	1/31	Capricorn
1/31 to	2/17	Aquarius
2/17 to	3/05	Pisces

3/05 to	5/13	Aries
5/13 to	5/29	Taurus
5/29 to	6/12	Gemini
6/12 to	6/28	Cancer
6/28 to	9/05	Leo
9/05 to	9/21	Virgo
9/21 to	10/09	Libra
10/09 to	10/31	Scorpio
10/31 to	11/27	Sagittarius
11/27 to	12/13	Scorpio
12/13 to	12/31	Sagittarius

1927

1/01 to	1/04	Sagittarius
1/04 to	1/23	Capricorn
1/23 to	2/09	Aquarius
2/10 to	4/17	Pisces
4/17 to	5/06	Aries
5/06 to	5/20	Taurus
5/20 to	6/04	Gemini
6/04 to	6/28	Cancer
6/28 to	7/13	Leo
7/13 to	8/11	Cancer
8/11 to	8/28	Leo
8/28 to	9/13	Virgo
9/13 to	10/03	Libra
10/03 to	12/09	Scorpio
12/09 to	12/29	Sagittarius
12/29 to	12/31	Capricorn

1928

1/01 to	1/16	Capricorn
1/16 to	2/03	Aquarius
2/03 to	2/28	Pisces
2/29 to	3/17	Aquarius
3/17 to	4/10	Pisces
4/10 to	4/27	Aries
4/27 to	5/11	Taurus
5/11 to	5/28	Gemini
5/28 to	8/04	Cancer
8/04 to	8/19	Leo

8/19 to	9/05	Virgo
9/05 to	9/27	Libra
9/27 to	10/24	Scorpio
10/24 to	11/11	Libra
11/11 to	12/01	Scorpio
12/01 to	12/20	Sagittarius
12/20 to	12/31	Capricorn

1929

1/01 to	1/08	Capricorn
1/08 to	3/15	Aquarius
3/15 to	4/03	Pisces
4/03 to	4/18	Aries
4/18 to	5/03	Taurus
5/03 to	7/11	Gemini
7/11 to	7/27	Cancer
7/27 to	8/11	Leo
8/11 to	8/29	Virgo
8/30 to	11/05	Libra
11/05 to	11/24	Scorpio
11/24 to	12/13	Sagittarius
12/13 to	12/31	Capricorn

1930

1/01 to	1/02	Capricorn
1/02 to	1/22	Aquarius
1/22 to	2/15	Capricorn
2/15 to	3/09	Aquarius
3/09 to	3/26	Pisces
3/26 to	4/10	Aries
4/10 to	4/30	Taurus
5/01 to	5/17	Gemini
5/17 to	6/14	Taurus
6/14 to	7/04	Gemini
7/04 to	7/18	Cancer
7/18 to	8/03	Leo
8/03 to	8/26	Virgo
8/26 to	9/19	Libra
9/19 to	10/10	Virgo
10/10 to	10/29	Libra
10/29 to	11/16	Scorpio

DATE	ZODIAC SIGN
11/16 to 12/06	Sagittarius
12/06 to 12/31	Capricorn

1931

1/01 to 2/11	Capricorn
2/11 to 3/02	Aquarius
3/02 to 3/18	Pisces
3/18 to 4/03	Aries
4/03 to 6/10	Taurus
6/11 to 6/26	Gemini
6/26 to 7/10	Cancer
7/10 to 7/28	Leo
7/28 to 10/04	Virgo
10/04 to 10/21	Libra
10/21 to 11/09	Scorpio
11/09 to 12/01	Sagittarius
12/01 to 12/19	Capricorn
12/20 to 12/31	Sagittarius

1932

1/01 to 1/14	Sagittarius
1/14 to 2/04	Capricorn
2/04 to 2/22	Aquarius
2/22 to 3/09	Pisces
3/09 to 5/15	Aries
5/15 to 6/02	Taurus
6/02 to 6/16	Gemini
6/16 to 7/02	Cancer
7/02 to 7/27	Leo
7/27 to 8/09	Virgo
8/10 to 9/08	Leo
9/09 to 9/25	Virgo
9/25 to 10/13	Libra
10/13 to 11/02	Scorpio
11/02 to 12/31	Sagittarius

1933

1/01 to 1/08	Sagittarius
1/08 to 1/27	Capricorn

1/27 to 2/13	Aquarius
2/13 to 3/03	Pisces
3/03 to 3/25	Aries
3/25 to 4/17	Pisces
4/17 to 5/10	Aries
5/10 to 5/25	Taurus
5/25 to 6/08	Gemini
6/08 to 6/26	Cancer
6/26 to 9/01	Leo
9/02 to 9/17	Virgo
9/17 to 10/06	Libra
10/06 to 10/30	Scorpio
10/30 to 11/15	Sagittarius
11/15 to 12/11	Scorpio
12/11 to 12/31	Sagittarius

1934

1/01 to 1/01	Sagittarius
1/02 to 1/20	Capricorn
1/20 to 2/06	Aquarius
2/06 to 4/14	Pisces
4/14 to 5/02	Aries
5/02 to 5/16	Taurus
5/16 to 6/01	Gemini
6/01 to 8/09	Cancer
8/09 to 8/24	Leo
8/24 to 9/10	Virgo
9/10 to 9/30	Libra
9/30 to 12/05	Scorpio
12/05 to 12/25	Sagittarius
12/25 to 12/31	Capricorn

1935

1/01 to 1/12	Capricorn
1/12 to 2/01	Aquarius
2/01 to 2/14	Pisces
2/14 to 3/18	Aquarius
3/18 to 4/08	Pisces
4/08 to 4/24	Aries

4/24 to	5/08	Taurus
5/08 to	5/29	Gemini
5/29 to	6/20	Cancer
6/20 to	7/13	Gemini
7/13 to	8/01	Cancer
8/01 to	8/16	Leo
8/16 to	9/03	Virgo
9/03 to	9/28	Libra
9/28 to	10/12	Scorpio
10/12 to	11/09	Libra
11/09 to	11/28	Scorpio
11/29 to	12/18	Sagittarius
12/18 to	12/31	Capricorn

1936

1/01 to	1/05	Capricorn
1/05 to	3/12	Aquarius
3/13 to	3/30	Pisces
3/30 to	4/14	Aries
4/14 to	4/30	Taurus
4/30 to	7/08	Gemini
7/08 to	7/23	Cancer
7/23 to	8/07	Leo
8/07 to	8/27	Virgo
8/27 to	11/02	Libra
11/02 to	11/20	Scorpio
11/20 to	12/09	Sagittarius
12/10 to	12/31	Capricorn

1937

1/01 to	1/01	Capricorn
1/02 to	1/09	Aquarius
1/09 to	2/13	Capricorn
2/13 to	3/06	Aquarius
3/06 to	3/22	Pisces
3/22 to	4/06	Aries
4/06 to	6/13	Taurus
6/13 to	6/30	Gemini
6/30 to	7/14	Cancer
7/14 to	7/31	Leo
7/31 to	10/08	Virgo

10/08 to	10/25	Libra
10/25 to	11/13	Scorpio
11/13 to	12/03	Sagittarius
12/03 to	12/31	Capricorn

1938

1/01 to	1/06	Capricorn
1/06 to	1/12	Sagittarius
1/12 to	2/08	Capricorn
2/08 to	2/26	Aquarius
2/26 to	3/14	Pisces
3/14 to	4/01	Aries
4/01 to	4/23	Taurus
4/23 to	5/16	Aries
5/16 to	6/07	Taurus
6/07 to	6/22	Gemini
6/22 to	7/06	Cancer
7/06 to	7/26	Leo
7/26 to	9/02	Virgo
9/02 to	9/10	Leo
9/10 to	9/30	Virgo
9/30 to	10/18	Libra
10/18 to	11/06	Scorpio
11/06 to	12/31	Sagittarius

1939

1/01 to	1/11	Sagittarius
1/12 to	2/01	Capricorn
2/01 to	2/19	Aquarius
2/19 to	3/07	Pisces
3/07 to	5/14	Aries
5/14 to	5/30	Taurus
5/30 to	6/13	Gemini
6/13 to	6/30	Cancer
6/30 to	9/06	Leo
9/06 to	9/22	Virgo
9/22 to	10/10	Libra
10/10 to	11/01	Scorpio
11/01 to	12/02	Sagittarius
12/02 to	12/13	Scorpio
12/13 to	12/31	Sagittarius

DATE   ZODIAC SIGN

1940

1/01 to	1/06	Sagittarius
1/06 to	1/25	Capricorn
1/25 to	2/11	Aquarius
2/11 to	3/04	Pisces
3/04 to	3/07	Aries
3/07 to	4/16	Pisces
4/16 to	5/06	Aries
5/06 to	5/21	Taurus
5/21 to	6/04	Gemini
6/04 to	6/26	Cancer
6/26 to	7/20	Leo
7/20 to	8/11	Cancer
8/11 to	8/29	Leo
8/29 to	9/14	Virgo
9/14 to	10/03	Libra
10/03 to	12/09	Scorpio
12/09 to	12/29	Sagittarius
12/29 to	12/31	Capricorn

1941

1/01 to	1/16	Capricorn
1/16 to	2/03	Aquarius
2/03 to	3/06	Pisces
3/07 to	3/16	Aquarius
3/16 to	4/12	Pisces
4/12 to	4/28	Aries
4/28 to	5/12	Taurus
5/12 to	5/29	Gemini
5/29 to	8/05	Cancer
8/05 to	8/20	Leo
8/20 to	9/06	Virgo
9/06 to	9/28	Libra
9/28 to	10/29	Scorpio
10/29 to	11/11	Libra
11/11 to	12/02	Scorpio
12/02 to	12/21	Sagittarius
12/21 to	12/31	Capricorn

1942

1/01 to	1/09	Capricorn
1/09 to	3/16	Aquarius
3/16 to	4/04	Pisces
4/05 to	4/20	Aries
4/20 to	5/04	Taurus
5/04 to	7/12	Gemini
7/12 to	7/28	Cancer
7/28 to	8/12	Leo
8/12 to	8/31	Virgo
8/31 to	11/06	Libra
11/06 to	11/25	Scorpio
11/25 to	12/14	Sagittarius
12/14 to	12/31	Capricorn

1943

1/01 to	1/03	Capricorn
1/03 to	1/27	Aquarius
1/27 to	2/15	Capricorn
2/15 to	3/10	Aquarius
3/10 to	3/28	Pisces
3/28 to	4/11	Aries
4/11 to	4/30	Taurus
4/30 to	5/26	Gemini
5/26 to	6/13	Taurus
6/13 to	7/06	Gemini
7/06 to	7/20	Cancer
7/20 to	8/05	Leo
8/05 to	8/26	Virgo
8/27 to	9/25	Libra
9/25 to	10/11	Virgo
10/11 to	10/30	Libra
10/30 to	11/18	Scorpio
11/18 to	12/07	Sagittarius
12/07 to	12/31	Capricorn

1944

1/01 to	2/12	Capricorn
2/12 to	3/02	Aquarius
3/02 to	3/19	Pisces

3/19 to 4/03 Aries
4/03 to 6/11 Taurus
6/11 to 6/26 Gemini
6/26 to 7/11 Cancer
7/11 to 7/28 Leo
7/28 to 10/04 Virgo
10/04 to 10/22 Libra
10/22 to 11/10 Scorpio
11/10 to 12/01 Sagittarius
12/01 to 12/23 Capricorn
12/23 to 12/31 Sagittarius

1945

1/01 to 1/13 Sagittarius
1/13 to 2/05 Capricorn
2/05 to 2/23 Aquarius
2/23 to 3/11 Pisces
3/11 to 5/16 Aries
5/16 to 6/04 Taurus
6/04 to 6/18 Gemini
6/18 to 7/03 Cancer
7/03 to 7/26 Leo
7/26 to 8/17 Virgo
8/17 to 9/10 Leo
9/10 to 9/27 Virgo
9/27 to 10/14 Libra
10/14 to 11/03 Scorpio
11/03 to 12/31 Sagittarius

1946

1/01 to 1/09 Sagittarius
1/09 to 1/29 Capricorn
1/29 to 2/15 Aquarius
2/15 to 3/04 Pisces
3/04 to 4/01 Aries
4/01 to 4/16 Pisces
4/16 to 5/11 Aries
5/11 to 5/26 Taurus
5/26 to 6/09 Gemini
6/09 to 6/27 Cancer

6/27 to 9/03 Leo
9/03 to 9/19 Virgo
9/19 to 10/07 Libra
10/07 to 10/30 Scorpio
10/30 to 11/20 Sagittarius
11/20 to 12/12 Scorpio
12/12 to 12/31 Sagittarius

1947

1/01 to 1/02 Sagittarius
1/02 to 1/21 Capricorn
1/21 to 2/07 Aquarius
2/07 to 4/15 Pisces
4/15 to 5/03 Aries
5/04 to 5/18 Taurus
5/18 to 6/02 Gemini
6/02 to 8/10 Cancer
8/10 to 8/26 Leo
8/26 to 9/11 Virgo
9/11 to 10/01 Libra
10/01 to 12/07 Scorpio
12/07 to 12/26 Sagittarius
12/26 to 12/31 Capricorn

1948

1/01 to 1/13 Capricorn
1/14 to 2/01 Aquarius
2/01 to 2/19 Pisces
2/19 to 3/18 Aquarius
3/18 to 4/08 Pisces
4/08 to 4/24 Aries
4/24 to 5/08 Taurus
5/09 to 5/28 Gemini
5/28 to 6/28 Cancer
6/28 to 7/11 Gemini
7/11 to 8/02 Cancer
8/02 to 8/17 Leo
8/17 to 9/03 Virgo
9/03 to 9/27 Libra
9/27 to 10/16 Scorpio

DATE	ZODIAC SIGN
10/16 to 11/09	Libra
11/09 to 11/29	Scorpio
11/29 to 12/18	Sagittarius
12/18 to 12/31	Capricorn

1949

1/01 to 1/06	Capricorn
1/06 to 3/14	Aquarius
3/14 to 4/01	Pisces
4/01 to 4/16	Aries
4/16 to 5/01	Taurus
5/01 to 7/09	Gemini
7/09 to 7/24	Cancer
7/24 to 8/09	Leo
8/09 to 8/28	Virgo
8/28 to 11/03	Libra
11/03 to 11/22	Scorpio
11/22 to 12/11	Sagittarius
12/11 to 12/31	Capricorn

1950

1/01 to 1/01	Capricorn
1/02 to 1/14	Aquarius
1/15 to 2/14	Capricorn
2/14 to 3/07	Aquarius
3/07 to 3/24	Pisces
3/24 to 4/08	Aries
4/08 to 6/14	Taurus
6/14 to 7/02	Gemini
7/02 to 7/16	Cancer
7/16 to 8/01	Leo
8/01 to 8/27	Virgo
8/27 to 9/10	Libra
9/10 to 10/09	Virgo
10/09 to 10/27	Libra
10/27 to 11/14	Scorpio
11/14 to 12/04	Sagittarius
12/04 to 12/31	Capricorn

1951

1/01 to 2/09	Capricorn
2/09 to 2/28	Aquarius
2/28 to 3/16	Pisces
3/16 to 4/01	Aries
4/01 to 5/14	Aries
5/15 to 6/09	Taurus
6/09 to 6/23	Gemini
6/23 to 7/08	Cancer
7/08 to 7/27	Leo
7/27 to 10/02	Virgo
10/02 to 10/19	Libra
10/19 to 11/07	Scorpio
11/07 to 12/01	Sagittarius
12/01 to 12/12	Capricorn
12/12 to 12/31	Sagittarius

1952

1/01 to 1/12	Sagittarius
1/13 to 2/03	Capricorn
2/03 to 2/20	Aquarius
2/20 to 3/07	Pisces
3/07 to 5/14	Aries
5/14 to 5/31	Taurus
5/31 to 6/14	Gemini
6/14 to 6/30	Cancer
6/30 to 9/07	Leo
9/07 to 9/23	Virgo
9/23 to 10/11	Libra
10/11 to 11/01	Scorpio
11/01 to 12/31	Sagittarius

1953

1/01 to 1/05	Sagittarius
1/06 to 1/24	Capricorn
1/25 to 2/10	Aquarius
2/11 to 3/01	Pisces
3/02 to 3/14	Aries

3/15 to	4/16	Pisces
4/17 to	5/07	Aries
5/08 to	5/22	Taurus
5/23 to	6/05	Gemini
6/06 to	6/25	Cancer
6/26 to	7/27	Leo
7/28 to	8/10	Cancer
8/11 to	8/29	Leo
8/30 to	9/14	Virgo
9/15 to	10/03	Libra
10/04 to	10/30	Scorpio
10/31 to	11/05	Sagittarius
11/06 to	12/09	Scorpio
12/10 to	12/29	Sagittarius
12/30 to	12/31	Capricorn

1954

1/01 to	1/17	Capricorn
1/18 to	2/03	Aquarius
2/04 to	4/12	Pisces
4/13 to	4/29	Aries
4/30 to	5/13	Taurus
5/14 to	5/29	Gemini
5/30 to	8/06	Cancer
8/07 to	8/21	Leo
8/22 to	9/07	Virgo
9/08 to	9/28	Libra
9/29 to	11/03	Scorpio
11/04 to	11/10	Libra
11/11 to	12/03	Scorpio
12/04 to	12/22	Sagittarius
12/23 to	12/31	Capricorn

1955

1/01 to	1/09	Capricorn
1/10 to	3/16	Aquarius
3/17 to	4/05	Pisces
4/06 to	4/21	Aries
4/22 to	5/05	Taurus
5/06 to	7/12	Gemini

7/13 to	7/29	Cancer
7/30 to	8/13	Virgo
8/14 to	8/31	Virgo
9/01 to	11/07	Libra
11/08 to	11/26	Scorpio
11/27 to	12/15	Sagittarius
12/16 to	12/31	Capricorn

1956

1/01 to	1/03	Capricorn
1/04 to	2/01	Aquarius
2/02 to	2/14	Capricorn
2/15 to	3/10	Aquarius
3/11 to	3/27	Pisces
3/28 to	4/11	Aries
4/12 to	4/28	Taurus
4/29 to	7/05	Gemini
7/06 to	7/20	Cancer
7/21 to	8/04	Leo
8/05 to	8/25	Virgo
8/26 to	9/28	Libra
9/29 to	10/10	Virgo
10/11 to	10/30	Libra
10/31 to	11/17	Scorpio
11/18 to	12/07	Sagittarius
12/08 to	12/31	Capricorn

1957

1/01 to	2/11	Capricorn
2/12 to	3/03	Aquarius
3/04 to	3/19	Pisces
3/20 to	4/03	Aries
4/04 to	6/11	Taurus
6/12 to	6/27	Gemini
6/28 to	7/11	Cancer
7/12 to	7/29	Leo
7/30 to	10/05	Virgo
10/06 to	10/22	Libra
10/23 to	11/10	Scorpio
11/11 to	12/01	Sagittarius

DATE		ZODIAC SIGN
12/02 to	12/27	Capricorn
12/28 to	12/31	Sagittarius

1958

1/01 to	1/13	Sagittarius
1/14 to	2/05	Capricorn
2/06 to	2/23	Aquarius
2/24 to	3/11	Pisces
3/12 to	4/01	Aries
4/02 to	4/09	Taurus
4/10 to	5/16	Aries
5/17 to	6/04	Taurus
6/05 to	6/19	Gemini
6/20 to	7/03	Cancer
7/04 to	7/25	Leo
7/26 to	8/22	Virgo
8/23 to	9/10	Leo
9/11 to	9/27	Virgo
9/28 to	10/15	Libra
10/16 to	11/04	Scorpio
11/05 to	12/31	Sagittarius

1959

1/01 to	1/09	Sagittarius
1/10 to	1/29	Capricorn
1/30 to	2/16	Aquarius
2/17 to	3/04	Pisces
3/05 to	5/11	Aries
5/12 to	5/27	Taurus
5/28 to	6/10	Gemini
6/11 to	6/27	Cancer
6/28 to	9/04	Leo
9/05 to	9/20	Virgo
9/21 to	10/08	Libra
10/09 to	10/30	Scorpio
10/31 to	11/24	Sagittarius

11/25 to	12/12	Scorpio
12/13 to	12/31	Sagittarius

1960

1/01 to	1/03	Sagittarius
1/04 to	1/22	Capricorn
1/23 to	2/08	Aquarius
2/09 to	4/15	Pisces
4/16 to	5/03	Aries
5/04 to	5/18	Taurus
5/19 to	6/01	Gemini
6/02 to	6/30	Cancer
7/01 to	7/05	Leo
7/06 to	8/09	Cancer
8/10 to	8/26	Leo
8/27 to	9/11	Virgo
9/12 to	9/30	Libra
10/01 to	12/06	Scorpio
12/07 to	12/26	Sagittarius
12/27 to	12/31	Capricorn

1961

1/04 to	1/13	Capricorn
1/14 to	1/31	Aquarius
2/01 to	2/23	Pisces
2/24 to	3/17	Aquarius
3/18 to	4/09	Pisces
4/10 to	4/25	Aries
4/26 to	5/09	Taurus
5/10 to	5/27	Gemini
5/28 to	8/03	Cancer
8/04 to	8/17	Leo
8/18 to	9/03	Virgo
9/04 to	9/26	Libra
9/27 to	10/21	Scorpio
10/22 to	11/09	Libra
11/10 to	11/29	Scorpio
11/30 to	12/19	Sagittarius
12/20 to	12/31	Capricorn

1962

1/01 to	1/06	Capricorn
1/07 to	3/14	Aquarius
3/15 to	4/02	Pisces
4/03 to	4/17	Aries
4/18 to	5/02	Taurus
5/03 to	7/10	Gemini
7/11 to	7/25	Cancer
7/26 to	8/09	Leo
8/10 to	8/28	Virgo
8/29 to	11/04	Libra
11/05 to	11/22	Scorpio
11/23 to	12/11	Sagittarius
12/12 to	12/31	Capricorn

1963

1/01 to	1/01	Capricorn
1/02 to	1/19	Aquarius
1/20 to	2/14	Capricorn
2/15 to	3/08	Aquarius
3/09 to	3/25	Pisces
3/26 to	4/08	Aries
4/09 to	5/02	Taurus
5/03 to	5/09	Gemini
5/10 to	6/13	Taurus
6/14 to	7/03	Gemini
7/04 to	7/17	Cancer
7/18 to	8/02	Leo
8/03 to	8/25	Virgo
8/26 to	9/15	Libra
9/16 to	10/09	Virgo
10/10 to	10/27	Libra
10/28 to	11/15	Scorpio
11/16 to	12/05	Sagittarius
12/06 to	12/31	Capricorn

1964

1/01 to	2/09	Capricorn
2/10 to	2/28	Aquarius
2/29 to	3/15	Pisces
3/16 to	4/01	Aries
4/02 to	6/08	Taurus
6/09 to	6/23	Gemini
6/24 to	7/08	Cancer
7/09 to	7/26	Leo
7/27 to	10/02	Virgo
10/03 to	10/19	Libra
10/20 to	11/07	Scorpio
11/08 to	11/29	Sagittarius
11/30 to	12/15	Capricorn
12/16 to	12/31	Sagittarius

1965

1/01 to	1/12	Sagittarius
1/13 to	2/02	Capricorn
2/03 to	2/20	Aquarius
2/21 to	3/08	Pisces
3/09 to	5/14	Aries
5/15 to	6/01	Taurus
6/02 to	6/15	Gemini
6/16 to	6/30	Cancer
7/01 to	7/30	Leo
7/31 to	8/02	Virgo
8/03 to	9/07	Leo
9/08 to	9/24	Virgo
9/25 to	10/11	Libra
10/12 to	11/01	Scorpio
11/02 to	12/31	Sagittarius

1966

1/01 to	1/06	Sagittarius
1/07 to	1/26	Capricorn
1/27 to	2/12	Aquarius
2/13 to	3/02	Pisces
3/03 to	3/21	Aries
3/22 to	4/16	Pisces
4/17 to	5/08	Aries
5/09 to	5/23	Taurus
5/24 to	6/06	Gemini
6/07 to	6/25	Cancer
6/26 to	8/31	Leo

DATE	ZODIAC SIGN
9/01 to 9/16	Virgo
9/17 to 10/04	Libra
10/05 to 10/29	Scorpio
10/30 to 11/12	Sagittarius
11/13 to 12/10	Scorpio
12/11 to 12/31	Sagittarius

1967

1/01 to 1/18	Capricorn
1/19 to 2/05	Aquarius
2/06 to 4/13	Pisces
4/14 to 4/30	Aries
5/01 to 5/15	Taurus
5/16 to 5/30	Gemini
5/31 to 8/07	Cancer
8/08 to 8/23	Leo
8/24 to 9/08	Virgo
9/09 to 9/29	Libra
9/30 to 12/04	Scorpio
12/05 to 12/23	Sagittarius
12/24 to 12/31	Capricorn

1968

1/01 to 1/11	Capricorn
1/12 to 1/31	Aquarius
2/01 to 2/10	Pisces
2/11 to 3/16	Aquarius
3/17 to 4/06	Pisces
4/07 to 4/21	Aries
4/22 to 5/05	Taurus
5/06 to 5/28	Gemini
5/29 to 6/12	Cancer
6/13 to 7/12	Gemini
7/13 to 7/30	Cancer
7/31 to 8/14	Leo
8/15 to 8/31	Virgo
9/01 to 9/27	Libra
9/28 to 10/06	Scorpio
10/07 to 11/07	Libra

11/08 to 11/26	Scorpio
11/27 to 12/15	Sagittarius
12/16 to 12/31	Capricorn

1969

1/01 to 1/03	Capricorn
1/04 to 3/11	Aquarius
3/12 to 3/29	Pisces
3/30 to 4/13	Aries
4/14 to 4/29	Taurus
4/30 to 7/07	Gemini
7/08 to 7/21	Cancer
7/22 to 8/06	Leo
8/07 to 8/26	Virgo
8/27 to 10/06	Libra
10/07 to 10/08	Virgo
10/09 to 10/31	Libra
11/01 to 11/19	Scorpio
11/20 to 12/08	Sagittarius
12/09 to 12/31	Capricorn

1970

1/01 to 2/12	Capricorn
2/13 to 3/04	Aquarius
3/05 to 3/21	Pisces
3/22 to 4/05	Aries
4/06 to 6/12	Taurus
6/13 to 6/29	Gemini
6/30 to 7/13	Cancer
7/14 to 7/30	Leo
7/31 to 10/06	Virgo
10/07 to 10/25	Libra
10/26 to 11/12	Scorpio
11/13 to 12/02	Sagittarius
12/03 to 12/31	Capricorn

1971

1/01 to 1/01	Capricorn
1/02 to 1/13	Sagittarius

1/14 to	2/06	Capricorn
2/07 to	2/25	Aquarius
2/26 to	3/13	Pisces
3/14 to	3/31	Aries
4/01 to	4/17	Taurus
4/18 to	5/16	Aries
5/17 to	6/06	Taurus
6/07 to	6/20	Gemini
6/21 to	7/05	Cancer
7/06 to	7/25	Leo
7/26 to	8/28	Virgo
8/29 to	9/10	Leo
9/11 to	9/29	Virgo
9/30 to	10/16	Libra
10/17 to	11/05	Scorpio
11/06 to	12/31	Sagittarius

1972

1/01 to	1/10	Sagittarius
1/11 to	1/30	Capricorn
1/31 to	2/17	Aquarius
2/18 to	3/04	Pisces
3/05 to	5/11	Aries
5/12 to	5/28	Taurus
5/29 to	6/11	Gemini
6/12 to	6/27	Cancer
6/28 to	9/04	Leo
9/05 to	9/20	Virgo
9/21 to	10/08	Libra
10/09 to	10/29	Scorpio
10/30 to	11/28	Sagittarius
11/29 to	12/11	Scorpio
12/12 to	12/31	Sagittarius

1973

1/01 to	1/03	Sagittarius
1/04 to	1/22	Capricorn
1/23 to	2/08	Aquarius
2/09 to	4/15	Pisces
4/16 to	5/05	Aries

5/06 to	5/19	Taurus
5/20 to	6/03	Gemini
6/04 to	6/26	Cancer
6/27 to	7/15	Leo
7/16 to	8/10	Cancer
8/11 to	8/27	Leo
8/28 to	9/12	Virgo
9/13 to	10/01	Libra
10/02 to	12/07	Scorpio
12/08 to	12/27	Sagittarius
12/28 to	12/31	Capricorn

1974

1/01 to	1/15	Capricorn
1/16 to	2/01	Aquarius
2/02 to	3/01	Pisces
3/02 to	3/16	Aquarius
3/17 to	4/10	Pisces
4/11 to	4/27	Aries
4/28 to	5/11	Taurus
5/12 to	5/28	Gemini
5/29 to	8/04	Cancer
8/05 to	8/19	Leo
8/20 to	9/05	Virgo
9/06 to	9/27	Libra
9/28 to	10/25	Scorpio
10/26 to	11/10	Libra
11/11 to	12/01	Scorpio
12/02 to	12/20	Sagittarius
12/21 to	12/31	Capricorn

1975

1/01 to	1/07	Capricorn
1/08 to	3/15	Aquarius
3/16 to	4/03	Pisces
4/04 to	4/18	Aries
4/19 to	5/03	Taurus
5/04 to	7/11	Gemini
7/12 to	7/27	Cancer
7/28 to	8/11	Leo

DATE	ZODIAC SIGN
8/12 to 8/29	Virgo
8/20 to 11/05	Libra
11/06 to 11/24	Scorpio
11/25 to 12/13	Sagittarius
12/14 to 12/31	Capricorn

1976

1/01 to	1/01	Capricorn
1/02 to	1/24	Aquarius
1/25 to	2/14	Capricorn
2/15 to	3/08	Aquarius
3/09 to	3/25	Pisces
3/26 to	4/09	Aries
4/10 to	4/28	Taurus
4/29 to	5/18	Gemini
5/19 to	6/12	Taurus
6/13 to	7/03	Gemini
7/04 to	7/17	Cancer
7/18 to	8/02	Leo
8/03 to	8/24	Virgo
8/25 to	9/20	Libra
9/21 to 10/09		Virgo
10/10 to 10/28		Libra
10/29 to 11/15		Scorpio
11/16 to 12/05		Sagittarius
12/06 to 12/31		Capricorn

1977

1/01 to	2/09	Capricorn
2/10 to	3/01	Aquarius
3/02 to	3/17	Pisces
3/18 to	4/02	Aries
4/03 to	6/09	Taurus
6/10 to	6/25	Gemini
6/26 to	7/09	Cancer
7/10 to	7/27	Leo
7/28 to 10/03		Virgo
10/04 to 10/20		Libra

10/21 to 11/08	Scorpio
11/09 to 11/30	Sagittarius
12/01 to 12/20	Capricorn
12/21 to 12/31	Sagittarius

1978

1/01 to	1/12	Sagittarius
1/13 to	2/03	Capricorn
2/04 to	2/21	Aquarius
2/22 to	3/09	Pisces
3/10 to	5/15	Aries
5/16 to	6/02	Taurus
6/03 to	6/16	Gemini
6/17 to	7/01	Cancer
7/02 to	7/26	Leo
7/27 to	8/12	Virgo
8/13 to	9/08	Leo
9/09 to	9/25	Virgo
9/26 to 10/13		Libra
10/14 to 11/02		Scorpio
11/03 to 12/31		Sagittarius

1979

1/01 to	1/07	Sagittarius
1/08 to	1/27	Capricorn
1/28 to	2/13	Aquarius
2/14 to	3/02	Pisces
3/03 to	3/27	Aries
3/28 to	4/16	Pisces
4/17 to	5/09	Aries
5/10 to	5/25	Taurus
5/26 to	6/08	Gemini
6/09 to	6/26	Cancer
6/27 to	9/01	Leo
9/02 to	9/17	Virgo
9/18 to 10/06		Libra
10/07 to 10/29		Scorpio
10/30 to 11/17		Sagittarius
11/18 to 12/11		Scorpio
12/12 to 12/31		Sagittarius

1980

1/01 to	1/01	Sagittarius
1/02 to	1/20	Capricorn
1/21 to	2/06	Aquarius
2/07 to	4/13	Pisces
4/14 to	5/01	Aries
5/02 to	5/15	Taurus

5/16 to	5/30	Gemini
5/31 to	8/08	Cancer
8/09 to	8/23	Leo
8/24 to	9/09	Virgo
9/10 to	9/29	Libra
9/30 to	12/04	Scorpio
12/05 to	12/24	Sagittarius
12/25 to	12/31	Capricorn

VENUS

Like Mercury, Venus stands between the Earth and the Sun, and consequently, relative to the Earth, is always located in a constellation near that currently occupied by the Sun. Venus is located either in the same sign as your Sun or as much as two signs away from your Sun, ahead or behind. Venus takes two hundred twenty-five days to pass once around the zodiac, spending approximately nineteen days in each sign.

Because the position of Venus nearly repeats itself on the same day of the year every eight years, the Venus table has been abbreviated. The position of Venus on January 1, 1910, will vary from its position on January 1, 1918, by less than a degree. Thus, the table covering 1890 through 1897 can be used for other years by carefully following instructions for the year involved. The following table will tell you where Venus was when you were born.

DATE   *ZODIAC SIGN*

1890

1/01 to	1/01	Sagittarius
1/02 to	1/25	Capricorn
1/26 to	2/18	Aquarius
2/19 to	3/14	Pisces
3/15 to	4/07	Aries
4/08 to	5/01	Taurus
5/02 to	5/26	Gemini
5/27 to	6/20	Cancer
6/21 to	7/15	Leo
7/16 to	8/10	Virgo
8/11 to	9/06	Libra

9/07 to	10/07	Scorpio
10/08 to	12/31	Sagittarius

1891

1/01 to	2/05	Sagittarius
2/06 to	3/05	Capricorn
3/06 to	4/01	Aquarius
4/02 to	4/26	Pisces
4/27 to	5/22	Aries
5/23 to	6/16	Taurus
6/17 to	7/10	Gemini
7/11 to	8/04	Cancer
8/05 to	8/28	Leo
8/29 to	9/21	Virgo

DATE	ZODIAC SIGN
9/22 to 10/15	Libra
10/16 to 11/08	Scorpio
11/09 to 12/02	Sagittarius
12/03 to 12/26	Capricorn
12/27 to 12/31	Aquarius

1892

1/01 to 1/20	Aquarius
1/21 to 2/13	Pisces
2/14 to 3/09	Aries
3/10 to 4/04	Taurus
4/05 to 5/04	Gemini
5/05 to 9/07	Cancer
9/08 to 10/07	Leo
10/08 to 11/02	Virgo
11/03 to 11/27	Libra
11/28 to 12/22	Scorpio
12/23 to 12/31	Sagittarius

1893

1/01 to 1/15	Sagittarius
1/16 to 2/08	Capricorn
2/09 to 3/04	Aquarius
3/05 to 3/28	Pisces
3/29 to 4/22	Aries
4/23 to 5/16	Taurus
5/17 to 6/09	Gemini
6/10 to 7/04	Cancer
7/05 to 7/28	Leo
7/29 to 8/22	Virgo
8/23 to 9/16	Libra
9/17 to 10/11	Scorpio
10/12 to 11/06	Sagittarius
11/07 to 12/04	Capricorn
12/05 to 12/31	Aquarius

1894

1/01 to 1/08	Aquarius
1/09 to 2/12	Pisces
2/13 to 4/02	Aquarius

4/03 to 5/05	Pisces
5/06 to 6/02	Aries
6/03 to 6/29	Taurus
6/30 to 7/24	Gemini
7/25 to 8/18	Cancer
8/19 to 9/12	Leo
9/13 to 10/06	Virgo
10/07 to 10/30	Libra
10/31 to 11/23	Scorpio
11/24 to 12/17	Sagittarius
12/18 to 12/31	Capricorn

1895

1/01 to 1/10	Capricorn
1/11 to 2/03	Aquarius
2/04 to 2/27	Pisces
2/28 to 3/23	Aries
3/24 to 4/17	Taurus
4/18 to 5/12	Gemini
5/13 to 6/07	Cancer
6/08 to 7/06	Leo
7/07 to 8/13	Virgo
8/14 to 9/12	Libra
9/13 to 11/06	Virgo
11/07 to 12/08	Libra
12/09 to 12/31	Scorpio

1896

1/01 to 1/03	Scorpio
1/04 to 1/29	Sagittarius
1/30 to 2/23	Capricorn
2/24 to 3/18	Aquarius
3/19 to 4/12	Pisces
4/13 to 5/06	Aries
5/07 to 5/31	Taurus
6/01 to 6/24	Gemini
6/25 to 7/19	Cancer
7/20 to 8/12	Leo
8/13 to 9/05	Virgo
9/06 to 9/29	Libra
9/30 to 10/24	Scorpio

10/25 to 11/17	Sagittarius		1920	1896	1 day
11/18 to 12/12	Capricorn		1921	1897	1 day
12/13 to 12/31	Aquarius		1922	1890	1 day
			1923	1891	1 day
1897			1924	1892	1 day
1/01 to 1/06	Aquarius		1925	1893	1 day
1/07 to 2/01	Pisces		1926	1894	1 day
2/02 to 3/04	Aries		1927	1895	1 day
3/05 to 7/07	Taurus		1928	1896	1 day
7/08 to 8/05	Gemini		1929	1897	1 day
8/06 to 8/31	Cancer		1930	1890	2 days
9/01 to 9/26	Leo		1931	1891	2 days
9/27 to 10/20	Virgo		1932	1892	2 days
10/21 to 11/13	Libra		1933	1893	2 days
11/14 to 12/07	Scorpio		1934	1894	2 days
12/08 to 12/31	Sagittarius		1935	1895	2 days
			1936	1896	2 days

YEAR	USE TABLE FOR YEAR	DEDUCTING	YEAR	USE TABLE FOR YEAR	DEDUCTING
			1937	1897	2 days
			1938	1890	3 days
1898	1890	1 day	1939	1891	3 days
1899	1891	1 day	1940	1892	3 days
1900	1892	1 day	1941	1893	3 days
1901	1893	1 day	1942	1894	3 days
1902	1894	1 day	1943	1895	3 days
1903	1895	1 day	1944	1896	3 days
1904	1896	1 day	1945	1897	3 days
1905	1897	1 day	1946	1890	3 days
1906	1890	—	1947	1891	3 days
1907	1891	—	1948	1892	3 days
1908	1892	—	1949	1893	3 days
1909	1893	—	1950	1894	3 days
1910	1894	—	1951	1895	3 days
1911	1895	—	1952	1896	3 days
1912	1896	—	1953	1897	3 days
1913	1897	—	1954	1890	4 days
1914	1890	1 day	1955	1891	4 days
1915	1891	1 day	1956	1892	4 days
1916	1892	1 day	1957	1893	4 days
1917	1893	1 day	1958	1894	4 days
1918	1894	1 day	1959	1895	4 days
1919	1895	1 day	1960	1896	4 days

YEAR	USE TABLE FOR YEAR	DEDUCTING	1970	1890	5 days
			1971	1891	5 days
1961	1897	4 days	1972	1892	5 days
1962	1890	4 days	1973	1893	5 days
1963	1891	4 days	1974	1894	5 days
1964	1892	4 days	1975	1895	5 days
1965	1893	4 days	1976	1896	5 days
1966	1894	4 days	1977	1897	5 days
1967	1895	4 days	1978	1890	6 days
1968	1896	4 days	1979	1891	6 days
1969	1897	4 days	1980	1892	6 days

MARS

The planet Mars spends close to two years in traveling one time through the zodiac, nearly two months in each sign. The following table will tell you in which sign Mars was located on the specific day and year when you were born.

DATE   ZODIAC SIGN   **1902**

1900

			1/01 to	1/01	Capricorn
1/01 to	2/28	Aquarius	1/02 to	2/08	Aquarius
3/01 to	4/07	Pisces	2/09 to	3/17	Pisces
4/08 to	5/16	Aries	3/18 to	4/26	Aries
5/17 to	6/26	Taurus	4/27 to	6/06	Taurus
6/27 to	8/09	Gemini	6/07 to	7/20	Gemini
8/10 to	9/26	Cancer	7/21 to	9/04	Cancer
9/27 to	11/22	Leo	9/05 to	10/23	Leo
11/23 to	12/31	Virgo	10/24 to	12/19	Virgo
			12/20 to	12/31	Libra

1901

			1903		
1/01 to	3/01	Virgo	1/01 to	4/19	Libra
3/02 to	5/10	Leo	4/20 to	5/30	Virgo
5/11 to	7/13	Virgo	5/31 to	8/06	Libra
7/14 to	8/31	Libra	8/07 to	9/22	Scorpio
9/01 to	10/14	Scorpio	9/23 to	11/02	Sagittarius
10/15 to	11/23	Sagittarius	11/03 to	12/11	Capricorn
11/24 to	12/31	Capricorn	12/12 to	12/31	Aquarius

1904

1/01 to	1/19	Aquarius
1/20 to	2/26	Pisces
2/27 to	4/06	Aries
4/07 to	5/17	Taurus
5/18 to	6/30	Gemini
7/01 to	8/14	Cancer
8/15 to	10/01	Leo
10/02 to	11/19	Virgo
11/20 to	12/31	Libra

1905

1/01 to	1/13	Libra
1/14 to	8/21	Scorpio
8/22 to	10/07	Sagittarius
10/08 to	11/17	Capricorn
11/18 to	12/27	Aquarius
12/28 to	12/31	Pisces

1906

1/01 to	2/04	Pisces
2/05 to	3/16	Aries
3/17 to	4/28	Taurus
4/29 to	6/11	Gemini
6/12 to	7/27	Cancer
7/28 to	9/12	Leo
9/13 to	10/29	Virgo
10/30 to	12/16	Libra
12/17 to	12/31	Scorpio

1907

1/01 to	2/04	Scorpio
2/05 to	4/01	Sagittarius
4/02 to	10/13	Capricorn
10/14 to	11/28	Aquarius
11/29 to	12/31	Pisces

1908

1/01 to	1/10	Pisces
1/01 to	2/22	Aries

2/23 to	4/06	Taurus
4/07 to	5/22	Gemini
5/23 to	7/07	Cancer
7/08 to	8/23	Leo
8/23 to	10/09	Virgo
10/10 to	11/25	Libra
11/26 to	12/31	Scorpio

1909

1/01 to	1/09	Scorpio
1/10 to	2/23	Sagittarius
2/24 to	4/09	Capricorn
4/10 to	5/25	Aquarius
5/26 to	7/20	Pisces
7/21 to	9/26	Aries
9/27 to	11/20	Pisces
11/21 to	12/31	Aries

1910

1/01 to	2/22	Aries
2/23 to	3/13	Taurus
3/14 to	5/01	Gemini
5/02 to	6/18	Cancer
6/19 to	8/05	Leo
8/06 to	9/21	Virgo
9/22 to	11/06	Libra
11/07 to	12/19	Scorpio
12/20 to	12/31	Sagittarius

1911

1/01 to	1/31	Sagittarius
2/01 to	3/13	Capricorn
3/14 to	4/22	Aquarius
4/23 to	6/02	Pisces
6/03 to	7/15	Aries
7/16 to	9/05	Taurus
9/06 to	11/29	Gemini
11/30 to	12/31	Taurus

DATE   ZODIAC SIGN

1912

1/01 to	1/30	Taurus
1/31 to	4/04	Gemini
4/05 to	5/27	Cancer
5/28 to	7/16	Leo
7/17 to	9/02	Virgo
9/03 to	10/17	Libra
10/18 to	11/29	Scorpio
11/30 to	12/31	Sagittarius

1913

1/01 to	1/10	Sagittarius
1/11 to	2/18	Capricorn
2/19 to	3/29	Aquarius
3/30 to	5/07	Pisces
5/08 to	6/16	Aries
6/17 to	7/28	Taurus
7/29 to	9/15	Gemini
9/16 to	12/31	Cancer

1914

1/01 to	5/01	Cancer
5/02 to	6/25	Leo
6/26 to	8/14	Virgo
8/15 to	9/28	Libra
9/29 to	11/10	Scorpio
11/11 to	12/21	Sagittarius
12/22 to	12/31	Capricorn

1915

1/01 to	1/29	Capricorn
1/30 to	3/09	Aquarius
3/10 to	4/16	Pisces
4/17 to	5/25	Aries
5/26 to	7/05	Taurus
7/06 to	8/18	Gemini
8/19 to	10/07	Cancer
10/08 to	12/31	Leo

1916

1/01 to	5/28	Leo
5/29 to	7/22	Virgo
7/23 to	9/08	Libra
9/09 to	10/21	Scorpio
10/22 to	12/01	Sagittarius
12/02 to	12/31	Capricorn

1917

1/01 to	1/09	Capricorn
1/10 to	2/16	Aquarius
2/17 to	3/26	Pisces
3/27 to	5/04	Aries
5/05 to	6/14	Taurus
6/15 to	7/27	Gemini
7/28 to	9/11	Cancer
9/12 to	11/01	Leo
11/02 to	12/31	Virgo

1918

1/01 to	1/10	Virgo
1/11 to	2/25	Libra
2/26 to	6/23	Virgo
6/24 to	8/16	Libra
8/17 to	9/30	Scorpio
9/31 to	11/10	Sagittarius
11/11 to	12/19	Capricorn
12/20 to	12/31	Aquarius

1919

1/01 to	1/26	Aquarius
1/27 to	3/06	Pisces
3/07 to	4/14	Aries
4/15 to	5/25	Taurus
5/26 to	7/08	Gemini
7/09 to	8/22	Cancer
8/23 to	10/09	Leo
10/10 to	11/29	Virgo
11/30 to	12/31	Libra

1920

1/01 to	1/31	Libra
2/01 to	4/23	Scorpio
4/24 to	7/10	Libra
7/11 to	9/04	Scorpio
9/05 to	10/18	Sagittarius
10/18 to	11/27	Capricorn
11/28 to	12/31	Aquarius

1921

1/01 to	1/04	Aquarius
1/05 to	2/12	Pisces
2/13 to	3/24	Aries
3/25 to	5/05	Taurus
5/06 to	6/19	Gemini
6/20 to	8/02	Cancer
8/03 to	9/18	Leo
9/19 to	11/06	Virgo
11/07 to	12/25	Libra
12/26 to	12/31	Scorpio

1922

1/01 to	2/18	Scorpio
2/19 to	9/13	Sagittarius
9/14 to	10/30	Capricorn
10/31 to	12/11	Aquarius
12/12 to	12/31	Pisces

1923

1/01 to	1/20	Pisces
1/21 to	3/03	Aries
3/04 to	4/15	Taurus
4/16 to	5/30	Gemiini
5/31 to	7/15	Cancer
7/16 to	8/31	Leo
9/01 to	10/17	Virgo
10/18 to	12/03	Libra
12/04 to	12/31	Scorpio

1924

1/01 to	2/19	Scorpio
2/20 to	3/06	Sagittarius
3/07 to	4/24	Capricorn
4/25 to	6/24	Aquarius
6/25 to	8/24	Pisces
8/25 to	10/19	Aquarius
10/20 to	12/18	Pisces
12/19 to	12/31	Aries

1925

1/01 to	2/04	Aries
2/05 to	3/23	Taurus
3/24 to	5/09	Gemini
5/10 to	6/25	Cancer
6/26 to	8/12	Leo
8/13 to	9/28	Virgo
9/29 to	11/13	Libra
11/14 to	12/27	Scorpio
12/28 to	12/31	Sagittarius

1926

1/01 to	2/08	Sagittarius
2/09 to	3/22	Capricorn
3/23 to	5/03	Aquarius
5/04 to	6/14	Pisces
6/15 to	7/31	Aries
8/01 to	12/31	Taurus

1927

1/01 to	2/21	Taurus
2/22 to	4/16	Gemini
4/17 to	6/05	Cancer
6/06 to	7/24	Leo
7/25 to	9/10	Virgo
9/11 to	10/25	Libra
10/26 to	12/07	Scorpio
12/08 to	12/31	Sagittarius

DATE	ZODIAC SIGN

1928

1/01 to	1/18	Sagittarius
1/19 to	2/27	Capricorn
2/28 to	4/07	Aquarius
4/08 to	5/16	Pisces
5/17 to	6/25	Aries
6/26 to	8/08	Taurus
8/09 to	10/02	Gemini
10/03 to	12/19	Cancer
12/20 to	12/31	Gemini

1929

1/01 to	3/10	Gemini
3/11 to	5/12	Cancer
5/13 to	7/03	Leo
7/04 to	8/21	Virgo
8/22 to	10/05	Libra
10/06 to	11/18	Scorpio
11/19 to	12/26	Sagittarius
12/27 to	12/31	Capricorn

1930

1/01 to	2/06	Capricorn
2/07 to	3/16	Aquarius
3/17 to	4/24	Pisces
4/25 to	6/02	Aries
6/03 to	7/14	Taurus
7/15 to	8/27	Gemini
8/28 to	10/20	Cancer
10/21 to	12/31	Leo

1931

1/01 to	2/15	Leo
2/16 to	3/29	Cancer
3/30 to	6/09	Leo
6/10 to	7/31	Virgo
8/01 to	9/16	Libra
9/17 to	10/29	Scorpio
10/30 to	12/09	Sagittarius
12/10 to	12/31	Capricorn

1932

1/01 to	1/17	Capricorn
1/18 to	2/24	Aquarius
2/25 to	4/02	Pisces
4/03 to	5/11	Aries
5/12 to	6/21	Taurus
6/22 to	8/03	Gemini
8/04 to	9/19	Cancer
9/20 to	11/12	Leo
11/13 to	12/31	Virgo

1933

1/01 to	7/05	Virgo
7/06 to	8/25	Libra
8/26 to	10/08	Scorpio
10/09 to	11/18	Sagittarius
11/19 to	12/27	Capricorn
12/28 to	12/31	Aquarius

1934

1/01 to	2/03	Aquarius
2/04 to	3/13	Pisces
3/14 to	4/21	Aries
4/22 to	6/01	Taurus
6/02 to	7/14	Gemini
7/15 to	8/29	Cancer
8/30 to	10/17	Leo
10/18 to	12/10	Virgo
12/11 to	12/31	Libra

1935

1/01 to	7/28	Libra
7/29 to	9/15	Scorpio
9/16 to	10/27	Sagittarius
10/28 to	12/06	Capricorn
12/07 to	12/31	Aquarius

1936

| 1/01 to | 1/13 | Aquarius |
| 1/14 to | 2/21 | Pisces |

2/22 to	3/31	Aries
4/01 to	5/12	Taurus
5/13 to	6/24	Gemini
6/25 to	8/09	Cancer
8/10 to	9/25	Leo
9/26 to	11/13	Virgo
11/14 to	12/31	Libra

1937

1/01 to	3/12	Scorpio
3/13 to	5/13	Sagittarius
5/14 to	8/07	Scorpio
8/08 to	9/29	Sagittarius
9/30 to	10/11	Capricorn
10/12 to	12/20	Aquarius
12/21 to	12/31	Pisces

1938

1/01 to	1/29	Pisces
1/30 to	3/11	Aries
3/12 to	4/22	Taurus
4/23 to	6/06	Gemini
6/07 to	7/21	Cancer
7/22 to	9/06	Leo
9/07 to	10/24	Virgo
10/25 to	12/10	Libra
12/11 to	12/31	Scorpio

1939

1/01 to	1/28	Scorpio
1/29 to	3/20	Sagittarius
3/21 to	5/23	Capricorn
5/24 to	7/20	Aquarius
7/21 to	9/23	Capricorn
9/24 to	11/18	Aquarius
11/19 to	12/31	Pisces

1940

1/01 to	1/02	Pisces
1/03 to	2/16	Aries
2/17 to	3/31	Taurus

4/01 to	5/16	Gemini
5/17 to	7/02	Cancer
7/03 to	8/18	Leo
8/19 to	10/04	Virgo
10/05 to	11/19	Libra
11/20 to	12/31	Scorpio

1941

1/01 to	1/03	Scorpio
1/04 to	2/16	Sagittarius
2/17 to	4/01	Capricorn
4/02 to	5/15	Aquarius
5/16 to	7/01	Pisces
7/02 to	12/31	Aries

1942

1/01 to	1/10	Aries
1/11 to	3/06	Taurus
3/07 to	4/25	Gemini
4/26 to	6/13	Cancer
6/14 to	7/31	Leo
8/01 to	9/16	Virgo
9/17 to	10/31	Libra
11/01 to	12/14	Scorpio
12/15 to	12/31	Sagittarius

1943

1/01 to	1/25	Sagittarius
1/26 to	3/07	Capricorn
3/08 to	4/16	Aquarius
4/17 to	5/26	Pisces
5/27 to	6/06	Aries
6/07 to	8/22	Taurus
8/23 to	12/31	Gemini

1944

1/01 to	3/27	Gemini
3/28 to	5/21	Cancer
5/22 to	7/11	Leo
7/12 to	8/28	Virgo
8/29 to	10/12	Libra

DATE	ZODIAC SIGN
10/13 to 11/24	Scorpio
11/25 to 12/31	Sagittarius

1945

1/01 to 1/04	Sagittarius
1/05 to 2/13	Capricorn
2/14 to 3/24	Aquarius
3/25 to 5/01	Pisces
5/02 to 6/10	Aries
6/11 to 7/22	Taurus
7/23 to 9/06	Gemini
9/07 to 11/10	Cancer
11/11 to 12/25	Leo
12/26 to 12/31	Cancer

1946

1/01 to 4/21	Cancer
4/22 to 6/19	Leo
6/20 to 8/08	Virgo
8/09 to 9/23	Libra
9/24 to 11/05	Scorpio
11/06 to 12/16	Sagittarius
12/17 to 12/31	Capricorn

1947

1/01 to 1/24	Capricorn
1/25 to 3/03	Aquarius
3/04 to 4/10	Pisces
4/11 to 5/20	Aries
5/21 to 6/30	Taurus
6/31 to 8/12	Gemini
8/13 to 9/30	Cancer
10/01 to 11/30	Leo
12/01 to 12/31	Virgo

1948

1/01 to 2/11	Virgo
2/12 to 5/17	Leo
5/18 to 7/16	Virgo

7/17 to 9/02	Libra
9/03 to 10/16	Scorpio
10/17 to 11/25	Sagittarius
11/26 to 12/31	Capricorn

1949

1/01 to 1/03	Capricorn
1/04 to 2/10	Aquarius
2/11 to 3/20	Pisces
3/21 to 4/29	Aries
4/30 to 6/09	Taurus
6/10 to 7/22	Gemini
7/23 to 9/06	Cancer
9/07 to 10/26	Leo
10/27 to 12/25	Virgo
12/26 to 12/31	Libra

1950

1/01 to 3/27	Libra
3/28 to 6/10	Virgo
6/11 to 8/09	Libra
8/10 to 9/24	Scorpio
9/25 to 11/05	Sagittarius
11/06 to 12/14	Capricorn
12/15 to 12/31	Aquarius

1951

1/01 to 1/21	Aquarius
1/22 to 2/28	Pisces
3/01 to 4/09	Aries
4/10 to 5/20	Taurus
5/21 to 7/02	Gemini
7/03 to 8/17	Cancer
8/18 to 10/03	Leo
10/04 to 11/23	Virgo
11/24 to 12/31	Libra

1952

1/01 to 1/19	Libra
1/20 to 8/26	Scorpio
8/27 to 10/11	Sagittarius

10/12 to 11/20	Capricorn
11/21 to 12/29	Aquarius
12/30 to 12/31	Pisces

1953

1/01 to 2/07	Pisces
2/08 to 3/19	Aries
3/20 to 4/30	Taurus
5/01 to 6/13	Gemini
6/14 to 7/28	Cancer
7/29 to 9/13	Leo
9/14 to 10/31	Virgo
11/01 to 12/19	Libra
12/20 to 12/31	Scorpio

1954

1/01 to 2/08	Scorpio
2/09 to 4/11	Sagittarius
4/12 to 7/02	Capricorn
7/03 to 8/23	Sagittarius
8/24 to 10/20	Capricorn
10/21 to 12/03	Aquarius
12/04 to 12/31	Pisces

1955

1/01 to 1/14	Pisces
1/15 to 2/25	Aries
2/26 to 4/09	Taurus
4/10 to 5/25	Gemini
5/26 to 7/10	Cancer
7/11 to 8/26	Leo
8/27 to 10/12	Virgo
10/13 to 11/28	Libra
11/29 to 12/31	Scorpio

1956

1/01 to 1/13	Scorpio
1/14 to 2/27	Sagittarius
2/28 to 4/13	Capricorn
4/14 to 6/02	Aquarius

6/03 to 12/05	Pisces
12/06 to 12/31	Aries

1957

1/01 to 2/27	Aries
2/28 to 3/16	Taurus
3/17 to 5/03	Gemini
5/04 to 6/20	Cancer
6/21 to 8/07	Leo
8/08 to 9/23	Virgo
9/24 to 11/07	Libra
11/08 to 12/22	Scorpio
12/23 to 12/31	Sagittarius

1958

1/01 to 2/02	Sagittarius
2/03 to 3/16	Capricorn
3/17 to 4/26	Aquarius
4/27 to 6/06	Pisces
6/07 to 7/20	Aries
7/21 to 9/20	Taurus
9/21 to 10/28	Gemini
10/29 to 12/31	Taurus

1959

1/01 to 2/09	Taurus
2/10 to 4/09	Gemini
4/10 to 5/31	Cancer
6/01 to 7/19	Leo
7/20 to 9/04	Virgo
9/05 to 10/20	Libra
10/21 to 12/02	Scorpio
12/03 to 12/31	Sagittarius

1960

1/01 to 1/13	Sagittarius
1/14 to 2/22	Capricorn
2/23 to 4/01	Aquarius
4/02 to 5/10	Pisces
5/11 to 6/19	Aries
6/20 to 8/01	Taurus

DATE	ZODIAC SIGN
8/02 to 9/20	Gemini
9/21 to 12/31	Cancer

1961

1/01 to 5/05	Cancer
5/06 to 6/27	Leo
6/28 to 8/16	Virgo
8/17 to 9/30	Libra
10/01 to 11/12	Scorpio
11/13 to 12/23	Sagittarius
12/24 to 12/31	Capricorn

1962

1/01 to 1/31	Capricorn
2/01 to 3/11	Aquarius
3/12 to 4/18	Pices
4/19 to 5/27	Aries
5/28 to 7/08	Taurus
7/09 to 8/21	Gemini
8/22 to 10/10	Cancer
10/11 to 12/31	Leo

1963

1/01 to 6/02	Leo
6/03 to 7/26	Virgo
7/27 to 9/11	Libra
9/12 to 10/24	Scorpio
10/25 to 12/04	Sagittarius
12/05 to 12/31	Capricorn

1964

1/01 to 1/12	Capricorn
1/13 to 2/19	Aquarius
2/20 to 3/28	Pisces
3/29 to 5/06	Aries
5/07 to 6/16	Taurus
6/17 to 7/29	Gemini
7/30 to 9/14	Cancer

9/15 to 11/05	Leo
11/06 to 12/31	Virgo

1965

1/01 to 6/28	Virgo
6/29 to 8/19	Libra
8/20 to 10/03	Scorpio
10/04 to 11/13	Sagittarius
11/14 to 12/22	Capricorn
12/23 to 12/31	Aquarius

1966

1/01 to 1/29	Aquarius
1/30 to 3/08	Pisces
3/09 to 4/16	Aries
4/17 to 5/27	Taurus
5/28 to 7/10	Gemini
7/11 to 8/24	Cancer
8/25 to 10/11	Leo
10/12 to 12/03	Virgo
12/04 to 12/31	Libra

1967

1/01 to 2/11	Libra
2/12 to 3/31	Scorpio
4/01 to 7/18	Libra
7/19 to 9/09	Scorpio
9/10 to 10/22	Sagittarius
10/23 to 11/30	Capricorn
12/01 to 12/31	Aquarius

1968

1/01 to 1/08	Aquarius
1/09 to 2/16	Pisces
2/17 to 3/26	Aries
3/27 to 5/07	Taurus
5/08 to 6/20	Gemini
6/21 to 8/04	Cancer
8/05 to 9/20	Leo
9/21 to 10/08	Virgo

10/09 to 12/28   Libra
12/29 to 12/31   Scorpio

1969

1/01 to   1/24   Scorpio
1/25 to   9/20   Sagittarius
9/26 to 11/04   Capricorn
11/05 to 12/13   Aquarius
12/14 to 12/31   Pisces

1970

1/01 to   1/23   Pisces
1/24 to   3/06   Aries
3/07 to   4/17   Taurus
4/18 to   6/01   Gemini
6/02 to   7/17   Cancer
7/18 to   9/02   Leo
9/03 to 10/19   Virgo
10/20 to 12/05   Libra
12/06 to 12/31   Leo

1971

1/01 to   1/23   Scorpio
1/24 to   3/12   Sagittarius
3/13 to   5/03   Capricorn
5/04 to 11/06   Aquarius
11/07 to 12/26   Pisces
12/27 to 12/31   Aries

1972

1/01 to   2/10   Aries
2/11 to   3/27   Taurus
3/28 to   5/12   Gemini
5/13 to   6/28   Cancer
6/29 to   8/15   Leo
8/16 to   9/30   Virgo
10/01 to 11/15   Libra
11/16 to 12/30   Scorpio
12/30 to 12/31   Sagittarius

1973

1/01 to   2/12   Sagittarius
2/13 to   3/26   Capricorn
3/27 to   5/08   Aquarius
5/09 to   6/20   Pisces
6/21 to   8/12   Aries
8/13 to 10/29   Taurus
10/30 to 12/24   Aries
12/25 to 12/31   Taurus

1974

1/01 to   2/27   Taurus
2/28 to   4/20   Gemini
4/21 to   6/09   Cancer
6/10 to   7/27   Leo
7/28 to   9/12   Virgo
9/13 to 10/28   Libra
10/29 to 12/10   Scorpio
12/11 to 12/31   Sagittarius

1975

1/01 to   1/21   Sagittarius
1/22 to   3/03   Capricorn
3/04 to   4/11   Aquarius
4/12 to   5/21   Pisces
5/22 to   7/01   Aries
7/02 to   8/14   Taurus
8/15 to 10/17   Gemini
10/18 to 11/25   Cancer
11/26 to 12/31   Gemini

1976

1/01 to   3/18   Gemini
3/19 to   5/16   Cancer
5/17 to   7/06   Leo
7/07 to   8/24   Virgo
8/25 to 10/08   Libra
10/09 to 11/20   Scorpio
11/21 to 12/31   Sagittarius

DATE   ZODIAC SIGN

1977

1/01 to 2/09	Capricorn
2/10 to 3/20	Aquarius
3/21 to 4/27	Pisces
4/28 to 6/06	Aries
6/07 to 7/17	Taurus
7/18 to 9/01	Gemini
9/02 to 10/26	Cancer
10/27 to 12/31	Leo

1978

1/01 to 1/26	Leo
1/27 to 4/10	Cancer
4/11 to 6/14	Leo
6/15 to 8/04	Virgo
8/05 to 9/19	Libra
9/20 to 11/02	Scorpio
11/03 to 12/12	Sagittarius
12/13 to 12/31	Capricorn

1979

1/01 to 1/20	Capricorn
1/21 to 2/27	Aquarius
2/28 to 4/07	Pisces
4/08 to 5/16	Aries
5/17 to 6/26	Taurus
6/27 to 8/08	Gemini
8/09 to 9/24	Cancer
9/25 to 11/19	Leo
11/20 to 12/31	Virgo

1980

1/01 to 3/11	Virgo
3/12 to 5/04	Libra
5/05 to 7/10	Scorpio
7/11 to 8/29	Sagittarius
8/30 to 10/12	Capricorn
10/13 to 11/22	Aquarius
11/23 to 12/31	Pisces

JUPITER

Jupiter takes twelve years to travel once through the constellations of the zodiac, spending approximately eleven months in each sign. The following table will tell you where Jupiter was when you were born.

DATE   ZODIAC SIGN

1/01/1900 to 1/18/1901	Sagittarius
1/19/1901 to 2/06/1902	Capricorn
2/07/1902 to 2/19/1903	Aquarius
2/20/1903 to 2/29/1904	Pisces
3/01/1904 to 8/08/1904	Aries
8/09/1904 to 8/31/1904	Taurus
9/01/1904 to 3/07/1905	Aries
4/08/1905 to 7/20/1905	Taurus
7/21/1905 to 12/04/1905	Gemini

12/05/1905 to 3/09/1906	Taurus
3/10/1906 to 7/30/1906	Gemini
7/31/1906 to 8/18/1907	Cancer
8/19/1907 to 9/11/1907	Leo
9/12/1908 to 10/11/1909	Virgo
10/12/1909 to 11/11/1910	Libra
11/12/1910 to 12/09/1911	Scorpio
12/10/1911 to 1/02/1913	Sagittarius
1/03/1913 to 1/21/1914	Capricorn
1/22/1914 to 2/03/1915	Aquarius
2/04/1915 to 2/11/1916	Pisces
2/12/1916 to 6/25/1916	Aries
6/26/1916 to 10/26/1916	Taurus
10/27/1916 to 2/12/1917	Aries
2/13/1917 to 6/29/1917	Taurus
6/30/1917 to 7/12/1918	Gemini
7/13/1918 to 8/01/1919	Cancer
8/02/1919 to 8/26/1920	Leo
8/27/1920 to 9/25/1921	Virgo
9/26/1921 to 10/26/1922	Libra
10/27/1922 to 11/24/1923	Scorpio
11/25/1923 to 12/17/1924	Sagittarius
12/18/1924 to 1/05/1926	Capricorn
1/06/1926 to 1/17/1927	Aquarius
1/18/1927 to 6/05/1927	Pisces
6/06/1927 to 9/10/1927	Aries
9/11/1927 to 1/22/1928	Pisces
1/23/1928 to 6/03/1928	Aries
6/04/1928 to 6/11/1929	Taurus
6/12/1929 to 6/26/1930	Gemini
6/27/1930 to 7/16/1931	Cancer
7/17/1931 to 8/10/1932	Leo
8/11/1932 to 9/09/1933	Virgo
9/10/1933 to 10/10/1934	Libra
10/11/1934 to 11/08/1935	Scorpio
11/09/1935 to 12/01/1936	Sagittarius
12/02/1936 to 12/19/1937	Capricorn
12/20/1937 to 5/13/1938	Aquarius
5/14/1938 to 7/29/1938	Pisces
7/30/1938 to 12/28/1938	Aquarius
12/29/1938 to 5/10/1939	Pisces

5/11/1939 to 10/29/1939	Aries
10/30/1939 to 12/19/1939	Pisces
12/20/1939 to 5/15/1940	Aries
5/16/1940 to 5/25/1941	Taurus
5/26/1941 to 6/09/1942	Gemini
6/10/1942 to 6/29/1943	Cancer
6/30/1943 to 7/25/1944	Leo
7/26/1944 to 8/24/1945	Virgo
8/25/1945 to 9/24/1946	Libra
9/25/1946 to 10/23/1947	Scorpio
10/24/1947 to 11/14/1948	Sagittarius
11/15/1948 to 4/11/1949	Capricorn
4/12/1949 to 6/26/1949	Aquarius
6/27/1949 to 11/29/1949	Capricorn
11/30/1949 to 4/14/1950	Aquarius
4/15/1950 to 9/14/1950	Pisces
9/15/1950 to 12/01/1950	Aquarius
12/02/1950 to 4/20/1951	Pisces
4/21/1951 to 4/27/1952	Aries
4/28/1952 to 5/08/1953	Taurus
5/09/1953 to 5/23/1954	Gemini
5/24/1954 to 6/11/1955	Cancer
6/12/1955 to 11/16/1955	Leo
11/17/1955 to 1/17/1956	Virgo
1/18/1956 to 7/06/1956	Leo
7/07/1956 to 12/11/1956	Virgo
12/12/1956 to 2/18/1957	Libra
2/19/1957 to 8/05/1957	Virgo
8/06/1957 to 1/12/1958	Libra
1/13/1958 to 3/19/1958	Scorpio
3/20/1958 to 9/06/1958	Libra
9/07/1958 to 2/09/1959	Scorpio
2/10/1959 to 4/23/1959	Sagittarius
4/24/1959 to 10/04/1959	Scorpio
10/05/1959 to 2/29/1960	Sagittarius
3/01/1960 to 6/09/1960	Capricorn
6/10/1960 to 10/24/1960	Sagittarius
10/25/1960 to 3/14/1961	Capricorn
3/15/1961 to 8/11/1961	Aquarius
8/12/1961 to 11/03/1961	Capricorn
11/04/1961 to 3/24/1962	Aquarius

3/25/1962 to 4/03/1963	Pisces
4/04/1963 to 4/11/1964	Aries
4/12/1964 to 4/21/1965	Taurus
4/22/1965 to 9/20/1965	Gemini
9/21/1965 to 11/16/1965	Cancer
11/17/1965 to 5/04/1966	Gemini
5/05/1966 to 9/26/1966	Cancer
9/27/1966 to 1/15/1967	Leo
1/16/1967 to 5/22/1967	Cancer
5/23/1967 to 10/18/1967	Leo
10/19/1967 to 2/26/1968	Virgo
2/27/1968 to 6/14/1968	Leo
6/15/1968 to 11/14/1968	Virgo
11/15/1968 to 3/29/1969	Libra
3/30/1969 to 7/14/1969	Virgo
7/15/1969 to 12/15/1969	Libra
12/16/1969 to 4/29/1970	Scorpio
4/30/1970 to 8/14/1970	Libra
8/15/1970 to 1/14/1971	Scorpio
1/15/1971 to 6/05/1971	Sagittarius
6/06/1971 to 9/11/1971	Scorpio
9/12/1971 to 2/06/1972	Sagittarius
2/07/1972 to 7/24/1972	Capricorn
7/25/1972 to 9/25/1972	Sagittarius
9/26/1972 to 2/23/1973	Capricorn
2/24/1973 to 3/08/1973	Aquarius
3/09/1974 to 3/18/1975	Pisces
3/19/1975 to 3/26/1976	Aries
3/27/1976 to 8/23/1976	Taurus
8/24/1976 to 10/16/1976	Gemini
10/17/1976 to 4/03/1977	Taurus
4/04/1977 to 8/20/1977	Gemini
8/21/1977 to 12/31/1977	Cancer
1/01/1978 to 4/12/1978	Gemini
4/13/1978 to 9/05/1978	Cancer
9/06/1978 to 3/01/1979	Leo
3/02/1979 to 4/20/1979	Cancer
4/21/1979 to 9/29/1979	Leo
9/30/1979 to 10/27/1980	Virgo

SATURN

Saturn, a slower moving planet, requires about twenty-nine years to circle the zodiac, spending approximately two and one-half years in each of the signs. The following table will tell you where Saturn was when you were born.

DATE	ZODIAC SIGN
1/01/1900 to 1/20/1900	Sagittarius
1/21/1900 to 7/18/1900	Capricorn
7/19/1900 to 10/16/1900	Sagittarius
10/17/1900 to 1/19/1903	Capricorn
1/20/1903 to 4/12/1905	Aquarius
4/13/1905 to 8/16/1905	Pisces
8/17/1905 to 1/07/1906	Aquarius
1/08/1906 to 3/18/1908	Pisces
3/19/1908 to 5/16/1910	Aries
5/17/1910 to 12/14/1910	Taurus
12/15/1910 to 1/19/1911	Aries
1/20/1911 to 7/06/1912	Taurus
7/07/1912 to 11/30/1912	Gemini
12/01/1912 to 3/25/1913	Taurus
3/26/1913 to 8/24/1914	Gemini
8/25/1914 to 12/06/1914	Cancer
12/07/1914 to 5/11/1915	Gemini
5/12/1915 to 10/16/1916	Cancer
10/17/1916 to 12/07/1916	Leo
12/08/1916 to 6/23/1917	Cancer
6/24/1917 to 8/11/1919	Leo
8/12/1919 to 10/07/1921	Virgo
10/08/1921 to 12/19/1923	Libra
12/20/1923 to 4/05/1924	Scorpio
4/06/1924 to 9/13/1924	Libra
9/14/1924 to 12/02/1926	Scorpio
12/03/1926 to 3/29/1929	Sagittarius
3/30/1929 to 5/04/1929	Capricorn
5/05/1929 to 11/29/1929	Sagittarius
11/30/1929 to 2/22/1932	Capricorn
2/23/1932 to 8/12/1932	Aquarius
8/13/1932 to 11/18/1932	Capricorn
11/19/1932 to 2/13/1935	Aquarius

2/14/1935 to 4/24/1937	Pisces
4/25/1937 to 10/17/1937	Aries
10/18/1937 to 1/13/1938	Pisces
1/14/1938 to 7/05/1939	Aries
7/06/1939 to 9/21/1939	Taurus
9/22/1939 to 3/19/1940	Aries
3/20/1940 to 5/07/1942	Taurus
5/08/1942 to 6/19/1944	Gemini
6/20/1944 to 8/01/1946	Cancer
8/02/1946 to 9/18/1948	Leo
9/19/1948 to 4/02/1949	Virgo
4/03/1949 to 5/28/1949	Leo
5/29/1949 to 11/19/1950	Virgo
11/20/1950 to 3/06/1951	Libra
3/07/1951 to 8/12/1951	Virgo
8/13/1951 to 10/21/1953	Libra
10/22/1953 to 1/11/1956	Scorpio
1/12/1956 to 5/13/1956	Sagittarius
5/14/1956 to 10/09/1956	Scorpio
10/10/1956 to 1/04/1959	Sagittarius
1/05/1959 to 1/09/1962	Capricorn
1/10/1962 to 12/16/1964	Aquarius
12/17/1964 to 3/02/1967	Pisces
3/03/1967 to 4/28/1969	Aries
4/29/1969 to 6/18/1971	Taurus
6/19/1971 to 1/10/1972	Gemini
1/11/1972 to 2/21/1972	Taurus
2/22/1972 to 8/01/1973	Gemini
8/02/1973 to 1/07/1974	Cancer
1/08/1974 to 4/18/1974	Gemini
4/19/1974 to 9/17/1975	Cancer
9/18/1975 to 1/14/1976	Leo
1/15/1976 to 6/05/1976	Cancer
6/06/1976 to 11/17/1977	Leo
11/18/1977 to 1/05/1978	Virgo
1/06/1978 to 7/26/1978	Leo
7/27/1978 to 9/21/1980	Virgo

URANUS

Uranus, one of the slower moving planets, takes slightly more than eighty-four years to travel through all the constellations of the zodiac. Uranus spends approximately seven years in each sign. The following table will tell you in which sign Uranus was located at the time of your birth.

DATE	ZODIAC SIGN
1900	
1/01/00 to 12/19/04	Sagittarius
12/30/04 to 12/31/09	Capricorn
1910	
1/01/10 to 1/30/12	Capricorn
1/31/12 to 9/04/12	Aquarius
9/05/12 to 11/11/12	Capricorn
11/12/12 to 3/31/19	Aquarius
4/01/10 to 8/16/19	Pisces
8/17/19 to 12/31/19	Aquarius
1920	
1/01/20 to 1/21/20	Aquarius
1/22/20 to 3/30/27	Pisces
3/31/27 to 11/04/27	Aries
11/05/27 to 1/12/28	Pisces
1/13/28 to 12/31/29	Aries
1930	
1/01/30 to 6/06/34	Aries
6/07/34 to 10/09/34	Taurus
10/10/34 to 3/28/35	Aries
3/29/35 to 12/31/39	Taurus
1940	
1/01/40 to 8/06/41	Taurus
8/07/41 to 10/04/41	Gemini
10/05/41 to 5/13/42	Taurus
5/14/42 to 8/29/48	Gemini
8/30/48 to 11/11/48	Cancer
11/12/48 to 6/09/49	Gemini
6/10/49 to 12/31/49	Cancer
1950	
1/01/50 to 8/23/55	Cancer
8/24/55 to 1/27/56	Leo
1/28/56 to 6/08/56	Cancer
6/09/56 to 12/31/59	Leo
1960	
1/01/60 to 10/31/61	Leo
11/01/61 to 1/09/62	Virgo
1/10/62 to 8/08/62	Leo
8/09/62 to 9/27/68	Virgo
9/28/68 to 5/20/69	Libra
5/21/69 to 6/23/69	Virgo
6/24/69 to 12/31/69	Libra
1970	
1/01/70 to 11/21/74	Libra
11/22/74 to 5/02/75	Scorpio
5/03/75 to 9/07/75	Libra
9/08/75 to 2/16/81	Scorpio

NEPTUNE

Neptune, one of the slowest planets, takes nearly one hundred sixty-five years to travel once through the zodiac, or approximately fourteen-and-a-half years in each astrological sign. The following table will tell you in which sign Neptune was located when you were born.

DATE	ZODIAC SIGN

1900

7/20/01 to 12/25/01	Cancer
12/26/01 to 5/20/02	Gemini
5/21/02 to 12/31/09	Cancer

1910

1/01/10 to 9/22/14	Cancer
9/23/14 to 12/15/14	Leo
12/16/14 to 7/18/15	Cancer
7/19/15 to 3/20/16	Leo
3/21/16 to 5/01/16	Cancer
5/02/16 to 12/31/19	Leo

1920

1/01/20 to 9/20/28	Leo
9/21/28 to 2/18/29	Virgo
2/19/29 to 7/23/29	Leo
7/24/29 to 12/31/29	Virgo

1930

1/01/30 to 12/21/39	Virgo

1940

1/01/40 to 10/02/42	Virgo
10/03/42 to 4/18/43	Libra
4/19/43 to 8/02/43	Virgo
8/03/43 to 12/31/49	Libra

1950

1/01/50 to 12/23/55	Libra
12/24/55 to 3/11/56	Scorpio
3/12/56 to 10/18/56	Libra
10/19/56 to 6/16/57	Scorpio
6/17/57 to 8/04/57	Libra
8/05/57 to 12/31/59	Scorpio

1960

1/01/60 to 12/31/69	Scorpio

1970

1/01/70 to 1/04/70	Scorpio
1/05/70 to 5/02/70	Sagittarius
5/03/70 to 11/05/70	Scorpio
11/06/70 to 12/31/79	Sagittarius

1980

1/01/80 to 1/18/84	Sagittarius

PLUTO

Pluto, the slowest moving of all the planets, spends two hundred and forty-eight years in traveling just one time through all the constellations of the zodiac. Pluto stays an average of twenty years in each sign, although it moves through some of the signs much more rapidly than through others. Pluto's shortest time, in the sign of Scorpio, is twelve years, while spending the longest time, thirty years, traveling through the constellation of Taurus. The following table will tell you where Pluto was when you were born.

DATE	*ZODIAC SIGN*		
1/01/00 to 7/09/13	Gemini	8/19/57 to 4/11/58	Virgo
7/10/13 to 12/27/13	Cancer	4/12/58 to 6/10/58	Leo
12/28/13 to 5/26/14	Gemini	6/11/58 to 10/04/71	Virgo
5/27/14 to 8/03/38	Cancer	10/05/71 to 4/16/72	Libra
8/04/38 to 2/07/39	Leo	4/17/72 to 7/30/72	Virgo
2/08/39 to 6/13/39	Cancer	7/31/72 to 11/06/83	Libra
6/14/39 to 8/18/57	Leo		

CHAPTER FOURTEEN

The Prenatal Eclipses

SOLAR ECLIPSES

Find the date closest to your birthdate to locate your prenatal solar eclipse. Be sure that the date is prior to your birthdate because these eclipses are prenatal.

DATE	SIGN	DEGREE
May 28, 1900	Gemini	06'47"
December 22, 1900	Scorpio	29'33"
May 18, 1901	Taurus	26'34"
November 11, 1901	Scorpio	18'14"
April 08, 1902	Aries	17'48"
May 07, 1902	Taurus	16'25"
October 23, 1902	Scorpio	06'59"
March 29, 1903	Aries	07'11"
September 21, 1903	Virgo	27'01"
March 17, 1904	Pisces	26'13"
September 09, 1904	Virgo	16'42"
March 06, 1905	Pisces	14'59"
August 30, 1905	Virgo	06'28"
February 23, 1906	Pisces	03'48"
July 21, 1906	Cancer	27'50"
August 20, 1906	Leo	26'07"
January 14, 1907	Capricorn	22'56"
July 10, 1907	Cancer	17'12"

DATE	SIGN	DEGREE
January 03, 1908	Capricorn	12'08"
June 28, 1908	Cancer	06'32"
December 23, 1908	Capricorn	01'17"
June 17, 1909	Gemini	26'05"
December 12, 1909	Sagittarius	20'11"
May 09, 1910	Taurus	17'43"
November 02, 1910	Scorpio	08'46"
April 28, 1911	Taurus	07'30"
October 22, 1911	Libra	27'38"
April 17, 1912	Aries	27'05"
October 10, 1912	Libra	16'53"
April 06, 1913	Aries	16'19"
August 31, 1913	Virgo	07'48"
September 30, 1913	Libra	06'25"
February 25, 1914	Pisces	05'33"
August 21, 1914	Leo	27'35"
February 14, 1915	Aquarius	24'25"
August 10, 1915	Leo	17'12"
February 03, 1916	Aquarius	13'31"
July 30, 1916	Leo	06'34"
December 24, 1916	Capricorn	02'44"
January 23, 1917	Aquarius	02'45"
June 19, 1917	Gemini	27'39"
July 19, 1917	Cancer	25'51"
December 14, 1917	Sagittarius	21'50"
June 08, 1918	Gemini	17'16"
December 03, 1918	Sagittarius	10'40"
May 29, 1919	Gemini	07'06"
November 22, 1919	Scorpio	29'17"
May 18, 1920	Taurus	26'60"
November 10, 1920	Scorpio	17'58"
April 08, 1921	Aries	17'59"
October 01, 1921	Libra	07'47"
March 28, 1922	Aries	07'04"
September 21, 1922	Virgo	27'24"
March 17, 1923	Pisces	25'55"
September 10, 1923	Virgo	17'06"
March 05, 1924	Pisces	14'49"
July 31, 1924	Leo	08'16"
August 30, 1924	Virgo	06'40"

January 24, 1925	Aquarius	04'08"
July 20, 1925	Cancer	27'37"
January 14, 1926	Capricorn	23'21"
July 09, 1926	Cancer	16'57"
January 03, 1927	Capricorn	12'29"
June 29, 1927	Cancer	06'31"
December 24, 1927	Capricorn	01'21"
May 19, 1928	Taurus	28'17"
June 17, 1928	Gemini	26'22"
November 12, 1928	Scorpio	19'46"
May 09, 1929	Taurus	18'07"
November 01, 1929	Scorpio	08'35"
April 28, 1930	Taurus	07'45"
October 21, 1930	Libra	27'46"
April 18, 1931	Aries	27'03"
September 12, 1931	Virgo	18'27"
March 07, 1932	Pisces	16'32"
August 31, 1932	Virgo	08'10"
February 24, 1933	Pisces	05'29"
August 21, 1933	Leo	27'42"
February 14, 1934	Aquarius	24'39"
August 10, 1934	Leo	17'02"
January 05, 1934	Capricorn	13'57"
February 03, 1935	Aquarius	13'56"
June 30, 1935	Cancer	08'04"
July 30, 1935	Leo	06'18"
December 25, 1935	Capricorn	03'01"
June 19, 1936	Gemini	27'44"
December 13, 1936	Sagittarius	21'49"
June 08, 1937	Gemini	17'36"
December 02, 1937	Sagittarius	10'23"
May 29, 1938	Gemini	07'32"
November 22, 1938	Scorpio	29'02"
April 19, 1939	Aries	28'44"
October 12, 1939	Libra	18'37"
April 07, 1940	Aries	17'51"
October 01, 1940	Libra	08'11"
March 27, 1941	Aries	06'46"
September 21, 1941	Virgo	27'48"
March 16, 1942	Pisces	25'46"
August 12, 1942	Leo	18'45"

DATE	SIGN	DEGREE
September 12, 1942	Virgo	17'18"
February 04, 1943	Aquarius	15'17"
August 01, 1943	Leo	08'03"
January 25, 1944	Aquarius	04'33"
July 20, 1944	Cancer	27'22"
January 14, 1945	Capricorn	23'41"
July 09, 1945	Cancer	16'57"
January 12, 1946	Capricorn	12'33"
May 08, 1946	Gemini	08'49"
June 29, 1946	Cancer	06'49"
November 23, 1946	Sagittarius	00'50"
May 20, 1947	Taurus	28'42"
November 12, 1947	Scorpio	19'36"
May 09, 1948	Taurus	18'22"
November 08, 1948	Scorpio	08'44"
April 28, 1949	Taurus	07'42"
October 21, 1949	Libra	28'09"
March 18, 1950	Pisces	27'28"
September 12, 1950	Virgo	18'48"
March 07, 1951	Pisces	16'29"
September 01, 1951	Virgo	08'16"
February 25, 1952	Pisces	05'43"
August 20, 1952	Leo	27'31"
February 14, 1953	Aquarius	25'03"
July 11, 1953	Cancer	18'30"
August 09, 1953	Leo	16'45"
January 05, 1954	Capricorn	14'13"
June 30, 1954	Cancer	08'10"
December 25, 1954	Capricorn	02'59"
June 20, 1955	Gemini	28'05"
December 14, 1955	Sagittarius	21'31"
June 08, 1956	Gemini	18'02"
December 02, 1956	Sagittarius	10'09"
April 29, 1957	Taurus	09'23"
October 23, 1957	Libra	29'31"
April 19, 1958	Aries	28'34"
October 12, 1958	Libra	19'01"
April 08, 1959	Aries	17'34"
October 02, 1959	Libra	08'34"
March 27, 1960	Aries	06'39"

September 20, 1960	Virgo	27'58"
February 15, 1961	Aquarius	26'25"
August 11, 1961	Leo	18'31"
February 05, 1962	Aquarius	15'43"
July 31, 1962	Leo	07'49"
January 25, 1963	Aquarius	04'52"
July 20, 1963	Cancer	27'24"
January 14, 1964	Capricorn	23'43"
June 10, 1964	Gemini	19'19"
July 09, 1964	Cancer	17'16"
December 04, 1964	Sagittarius	11'56"
May 30, 1965	Gemini	09'13"
November 23, 1965	Sagittarius	00'40"
May 20, 1966	Taurus	28'55"
November 12, 1966	Scorpio	19'45"
May 09, 1967	Taurus	18'18"
November 02, 1967	Scorpio	09'07"
March 28, 1968	Aries	08'19"
September 22, 1968	Virgo	29'30"
March 18, 1969	Pisces	27'25"
September 11, 1969	Virgo	18'53"
March 07, 1970	Pisces	16'44"
August 31, 1970	Virgo	08'04"
February 25, 1971	Pisces	06'09"
July 22, 1971	Cancer	28'56"
August 20, 1971	Leo	27'15"
January 16, 1972	Capricorn	25'25"
July 10, 1972	Cancer	18'37"
January 04, 1973	Capricorn	14'10"
June 30, 1973	Cancer	08'32"
December 24, 1973	Capricorn	02'40"
June 20, 1974	Gemini	28'30"
December 13, 1974	Sagittarius	21'17"
May 11, 1975	Taurus	19'59"
November 03, 1975	Scorpio	10'29"
April 29, 1976	Taurus	09'13"
October 23, 1976	Libra	29'55"
April 18, 1977	Aries	28'17"
October 12, 1977	Libra	19'24"
April 07, 1978	Aries	17'27"
October 02, 1978	Libra	08'43"

DATE	SIGN	DEGREE
February 26, 1979	Pisces	07'29"
August 22, 1979	Leo	29'01"
February 16, 1980	Aquarius	26'50"
August 10, 1980	Leo	18'17"
February 04, 1981	Aquarius	16'02"
July 31, 1981	Leo	07'51"
January 25, 1982	Aquarius	04'54"
June 21, 1982	Gemini	29'47"
July 20, 1982	Cancer	27'43"
December 15, 1982	Sagittarius	23'04"
June 11, 1983	Gemini	19'43"
December 04, 1983	Sagittarius	11'47"
May 30, 1984	Gemini	09'26"
November 22, 1984	Sagittarius	00'50"
May 19, 1985	Taurus	28'50"
November 12, 1985	Scorpio	20'09"
April 09, 1986	Aries	19'06"
October 03, 1986	Libra	10'16"
March 29, 1987	Aries	08'18"
September 23, 1987	Virgo	29'34"
March 18, 1988	Pisces	27'42"
September 11, 1988	Virgo	18'40"
March 07, 1989	Pisces	17'10"
August 31, 1989	Virgo	07'48"
January 26, 1990	Aquarius	06'35"
July 22, 1990	Cancer	29'04"
January 15, 1991	Capricorn	25'20"
July 11, 1991	Cancer	18'59"
January 04, 1992	Capricorn	13'51"
June 30, 1992	Cancer	08'57"
December 24, 1992	Capricorn	02'28"
May 21, 1993	Gemini	00'31"
November 13, 1993	Scorpio	21'32"
May 10, 1994	Taurus	19'48"
November 03, 1994	Scorpio	10'54"
April 29, 1995	Taurus	08'56"
October 24, 1995	Scorpio	00'18"
April 17, 1996	Aries	28'12"
October 12, 1996	Libra	19'32"
March 09, 1997	Pisces	18'31"

September 01, 1997	Virgo	09'34"
February 26, 1998	Pisces	07'55"
August 22, 1998	Leo	28'48"
February 16, 1999	Aquarius	27'08"
August 11, 1999	Leo	18'21"
February 05, 2000	Aquarius	16'02"
July 31, 2000	Leo	08'11"
December 25, 2000	Capricorn	04'14"

LUNAR ECLIPSES

Find the date closest to your birthdate to locate your prenatal lunar eclipse. Be sure that the date is prior to your birthdate because these eclipses are prenatal.

DATE	SIGN	DEGREE
June 13, 1900	Sagittarius	21'39"
December 06, 1900	Gemini	13'53"
May 03, 1901	Scorpio	12'36"
October 27, 1901	Taurus	03'30"
April 22, 1902	Scorpio	01'42"
October 17, 1902	Aries	22'56"
April 12, 1903	Libra	20'56"
October 06, 1903	Aries	12'11"
March 02, 1904	Virgo	11'07"
March 31, 1904	Libra	10'23"
September 24, 1904	Aries	01'14"
February 19, 1905	Virgo	00'29"
August 15, 1905	Aquarius	21'37"
February 09, 1906	Leo	19'40"
August 04, 1906	Aquarius	11'13"
January 29, 1907	Leo	08'31"
July 25, 1907	Aquarius	24'25"
January 18, 1908	Aquarius	27'05"
June 14, 1908	Sagittarius	23'04"
July 13, 1908	Capricorn	21'02"
December 07, 1908	Gemini	15'25"
June 04, 1909	Sagittarius	12'46"
November 27, 1909	Gemini	04'29"

DATE	SIGN	DEGREE
May 24, 1910	Sagittarius	02'10"
November 17, 1910	Taurus	23'47"
May 13, 1911	Scorpio	21'22"
November 06, 1911	Taurus	13'07"
April 01, 1912	Libra	11'49"
September 26, 1912	Aries	02'60"
March 22, 1913	Libra	01'16"
September 15, 1913	Pisces	22'03"
March 12, 1914	Virgo	20'46"
September 04, 1914	Pisces	11'11"
January 31, 1915	Leo	10'14"
March 01, 1915	Virgo	10'06"
July 26, 1915	Aquarius	02'25"
August 24, 1915	Pisces	00'37"
January 20, 1916	Cancer	28'58"
July 15, 1916	Capricorn	22'20"
January 08, 1917	Cancer	17'29"
July 04, 1917	Capricorn	12'18"
December 28, 1917	Cancer	06'07"
June 24, 1918	Capricorn	02'05"
December 17, 1918	Gemini	25'04"
May 15, 1919	Scorpio	23'09"
November 07, 1919	Taurus	14'31"
May 03, 1920	Scorpio	12'19"
October 27, 1920	Taurus	03'52"
April 22, 1921	Scorpio	01'38"
October 16, 1921	Aries	23'02"
March 13, 1922	Virgo	22'06"
April 11, 1922	Libra	21'10"
October 06, 1922	Aries	11'59"
March 03, 1923	Virgo	11'32"
August 26, 1923	Pisces	02'09"
February 20, 1924	Virgo	00'46"
August 14, 1924	Aquarius	21'43"
February 08, 1924	Leo	19'39"
August 04, 1925	Aquarius	11'34"
January 28, 1926	Leo	08'14"
June 25, 1926	Capricorn	03'31"
July 25, 1926	Aquarius	01'30"
December 19, 1926	Gemini	26'35"

June 15, 1927	Sagittarius	23'14"
December 08, 1927	Gemini	15'38"
June 03, 1928	Sagittarius	12'39"
December 27, 1928	Gemini	04'54"
May 23, 1929	Sagittarius	01'53"
November 17, 1929	Taurus	24'10"
April 13, 1930	Libra	22'35"
October 07, 1930	Aries	13'47"
April 02, 1931	Libra	12'07"
September 26, 1931	Aries	02'45"
March 22, 1932	Libra	01'41"
September 14, 1932	Pisces	21'49"
February 10, 1933	Leo	21'22"
March 12, 1933	Virgo	21'05"
August 05, 1933	Aquarius	12'53"
September 04, 1933	Pisces	11'12"
January 30, 1934	Leo	10'07"
July 26, 1934	Aquarius	02'48"
January 19, 1935	Cancer	28'39"
July 16, 1935	Capricorn	22'45"
January 08, 1936	Cancer	17'19"
July 04, 1936	Capricorn	12'51"
December 28, 1936	Cancer	06'16"
May 25, 1937	Sagittarius	03'40"
November 18, 1937	Taurus	25'35"
May 14, 1938	Scorpio	22'54"
November 07, 1938	Taurus	14'51"
May 03, 1939	Scorpio	12'18"
October 28, 1939	Taurus	03'57"
March 23, 1940	Libra	03'01"
April 22, 1940	Scorpio	01'54"
October 16, 1940	Aries	22'49"
March 13, 1941	Virgo	22'31"
September 05, 1941	Pisces	12'45"
March 03, 1942	Virgo	11'48"
August 26, 1942	Pisces	02'17"
February 20, 1943	Virgo	00'43"
August 15, 1943	Aquarius	22'05"
February 09, 1944	Leo	19'21"
July 06, 1944	Capricorn	13'58"
August 04, 1944	Aquarius	11'59"

DATE	SIGN	DEGREE
December 29, 1944	Cancer	07'47"
June 25, 1945	Capricorn	03'40"
December 19, 1945	Gemini	26'50"
June 14, 1946	Sagittarius	23'05"
December 08, 1946	Gemini	16'03"
June 03, 1947	Sagittarius	12'22"
November 28, 1947	Gemini	05'16"
April 23, 1948	Scorpio	03'18"
October 18, 1948	Aries	24'37"
April 13, 1949	Libra	22'54"
October 07, 1949	Aries	13'30"
April 02, 1950	Libra	12'22"
September 26, 1950	Aries	02'31"
February 21, 1951	Virgo	02'26"
March 23, 1951	Libra	02'00"
August 17, 1951	Aquarius	23'25"
September 15, 1951	Pisces	21'52"
February 11, 1952	Leo	21'14"
August 05, 1952	Aquarius	13'17"
January 29, 1953	Leo	09'48"
July 26, 1953	Aquarius	03'12"
January 19, 1954	Cancer	28'30"
July 16, 1954	Capricorn	22'57"
January 08, 1955	Cancer	17'28"
June 05, 1955	Sagittarius	14'08"
November 29, 1955	Gemini	06'42"
May 24, 1956	Sagittarius	03'25"
November 18, 1956	Taurus	25'55"
May 13, 1957	Scorpio	22'52"
November 07, 1957	Taurus	14'55"
April 04, 1958	Libra	13'52"
May 03, 1958	Scorpio	12'34"
October 27, 1958	Taurus	03'43"
March 24, 1959	Libra	03'26"
September 17, 1959	Pisces	23'24"
March 13, 1960	Virgo	22'47"
September 05, 1960	Pisces	12'53"
March 02, 1961	Virgo	11'45"
August 26, 1961	Pisces	02'39"
February 19, 1962	Virgo	00'25"

July 17, 1962	Capricorn	24'25"
August 15, 1962	Aquarius	22'30"
January 09, 1963	Cancer	18'59"
July 06, 1963	Capricorn	14'06"
December 30, 1963	Cancer	08'01"
June 25, 1964	Capricorn	03'30"
December 19, 1964	Gemini	27'14"
June 14, 1965	Sagittarius	22'48"
December 08, 1965	Gemini	16'25"
May 04, 1966	Virgo	13'56"
October 29, 1966	Taurus	05'32"
April 24, 1967	Scorpio	03'57"
October 18, 1967	Aries	24'21"
April 13, 1968	Libra	23'20"
October 06, 1968	Aries	13'17"
April 02, 1969	Libra	12'51"
August 27, 1969	Pisces	03'58"
September 25, 1969	Aries	02'35"
February 21, 1970	Virgo	02'18"
August 17, 1970	Aquarius	23'49"
September 15, 1970	Pisces	22'12"
February 10, 1971	Leo	20'55"
August 06, 1971	Aquarius	13'41"
January 30, 1972	Leo	09'39"
August 26, 1972	Aquarius	03'24"
January 18, 1973	Cancer	28'40"
June 15, 1973	Sagittarius	24'35"
July 15, 1973	Capricorn	22'51"
December 10, 1973	Gemini	17'51"
June 04, 1974	Sagittarius	13'54"
November 29, 1974	Gemini	07'01"
May 25, 1975	Sagittarius	03'25"
November 18, 1975	Taurus	25'58"
May 13, 1976	Scorpio	23'10"
November 06, 1976	Taurus	14'41"
April 04, 1977	Libra	14'17"
September 27, 1977	Aries	04'07"
March 24, 1978	Libra	03'40"
September 16, 1978	Pisces	23'33"
March 13, 1979	Virgo	22'42"
September 22, 1979	Pisces	13'16"

DATE	SIGN	DEGREE
March 01, 1980	Virgo	11'26"
July 27, 1980	Aquarius	04'52"
August 26, 1980	Pisces	03'03"
January 20, 1981	Leo	00'10"
July 17, 1981	Capricorn	24'31"
January 09, 1982	Cancer	19'14"
July 06, 1982	Capricorn	13'55"
December 30, 1982	Cancer	08'27"
June 25, 1983	Capricorn	03'14"
December 20, 1983	Gemini	27'36"
May 15, 1984	Scorpio	24'31"
June 13, 1984	Sagittarius	22'45"
November 08, 1984	Taurus	16'30"
May 04, 1985	Scorpio	14'17"
October 28, 1985	Taurus	05'15"
April 24, 1986	Scorpio	04'03"
October 17, 1986	Aries	24'07"
April 14, 1987	Libra	23'38"
October 07, 1987	Aries	13'22"
March 08, 1988	Virgo	13'18"
August 27, 1988	Pisces	04'23"
February 20, 1989	Virgo	01'59"
August 17, 1989	Aquarius	24'12"
February 09, 1990	Leo	20'47"
August 06, 1990	Aquarius	13'52"
February 30, 1991	Leo	09'51"
June 27, 1991	Capricorn	04'60"
July 26, 1991	Aquarius	03'16"
December 31, 1991	Gemini	29'03"
June 15, 1992	Sagittarius	24'20"
December 09, 1992	Gemini	18'10"
June 04, 1993	Sagittarius	13'55"
November 29, 1993	Gemini	07'03"
May 25, 1994	Sagittarius	03'43"
November 18, 1994	Taurus	25'42"
April 15, 1995	Libra	25'04"
October 08, 1995	Aries	14'54"
April 04, 1995	Libra	14'31"
September 27, 1996	Aries	04'17'
March 24, 1997	Libra	03'35"

September 16, 1997	Pisces	23'56"
March 13, 1998	Virgo	23'24"
August 08, 1998	Leo	15'21"
September 06, 1998	Pisces	13'40"
January 31, 1999	Leo	11'20"
July 28, 1999	Aquarius	04'58"
January 21, 2000	Leo	00'26"
July 16, 2000	Capricorn	24'19"

FULL COMPUTER SERVICE

Although the planetary positions given in the preceding tables will prove accurate for the overwhelming majority of birthcharts, persons born on the cut-off dates given, depending upon their birth time, may find their planet in the next sign.

To provide the reader with maximum accuracy in the mathematical calculations of the planets, as well as to determine the houses your planets are located in, the computer chart is recommended.

To obtain a copy of your individual astrology chart, send the following:

· your date of birth
· your time of birth (if known)
· your place of birth
· $4 (check or money order) for first chart; $3 each additional chart, per order

(price is good as of September 1, 1988)
to this address:

> ORBIT ENTERPRISES
> P.O. Box 1567
> Soquel, CA 95073

The best sources for obtaining an accurate birth time are your birth certificate and written family records (baby book and so forth).

There are three copies of your birth certificate on file in the city in which you were born. Only one of these copies has your birth time on it. Therefore, in sending for your birth certificate it is important to emphasize that you want the copy that states your time of birth.

To obtain a copy write to:

> County Clerk
> Hall of Records
> County Court House
> (City and State in which you were born)

In requesting your birth certificate, include the following:

- your name (as it was recorded on the birth certificate) and birth date
- your mother's maiden name
- your father's name
- $5 (the fee for the service may be slightly more or less depending on the state. A money order receives a faster response than a personal check)
- self-addressed, stamped envelope